MODERNITY BRITAIN

A Shake of the Dice, 1959–62

BY THE SAME AUTHOR

King Labour: The British Working Class, 1850–1914
The Secretary of State
The Chancellor of the Exchequer

Bobby Abel, Professional Batsman
Archie's Last Stand: MCC in New Zealand, 1922–23
WG's Birthday Party

The Financial Times: A Centenary History
Cazenove & Co: A History
LIFFE: A Market and its Makers
Phillips & Drew: Professionals in the City (with W. J. Reader)
Siegmund Warburg: A Centenary Appreciation

The City of London, Volume I: A World of its Own, 1815–90
The City of London, Volume II: Golden Years, 1890–1914
The City of London, Volume III: Illusions of Gold, 1914–45
The City of London, Volume IV: A Club No More, 1945–2000
City State: How the Markets Came to Rule our World (with Richard Roberts)

Edited:
Henry James, London Stories and Other Writings
The Bank of England: Money, Power and Influence, 1694–1994 (with Richard Roberts)

Tales of a New Jerusalem
Austerity Britain, 1945–51
Family Britain, 1951–57
Modernity Britain: Opening the Box, 1957–59

MODERNITY BRITAIN

A Shake of the Dice, 1959–62

David Kynaston

B L O O M S B U R Y

LONDON • NEW DELHI • NEW YORK • SYDNEY

First published in Great Britain 2014

Bloomsbury Publishing Plc
50 Bedford Square
London
WC1B 3DP

www.bloomsbury.com

Bloomsbury Publishing, London, New Delhi, New York and Sydney

A CIP catalogue record for this book is available from the British Library

ISBN 978 1 4088 4439 7

10 9 8 7 6 5 4 3 2 1

Typeset by Hewer Text UK Ltd, Edinburgh
Printed and bound in Great Britain by CPI Group (UK) Ltd, Croydon CR0 4YY

Contents

Author's Note

Tales of a New Jerusalem is a projected sequence of books about Britain between 1945 and 1979. The first two books, *A World to Build* and *Smoke in the Valley*, are gathered together in the volume *Austerity Britain*; the next two books, *The Certainties of Place* and *A Thicker Cut*, in the volume *Family Britain*. The fifth book in the sequence is *Opening the Box*, now complemented by the sixth book, *A Shake of the Dice*, together comprising the volume *Modernity Britain* and between them covering the years 1957 to 1962.

A SHAKE OF THE DICE

This book is dedicated to the memory of Deborah Rogers

PART ONE

1

Sure as Progress Itself

'Met a most charming young married woman on underground,' recorded Judy Haines on Friday the 16th, just over a week after Harold Macmillan's October 1959 election triumph. 'We put her right for Marshall & Snelgrove's.' The Chingford diarist was on a shopping trip with her neighbour opposite, and after lunch at D. H. Evans (soup and tomato juice respectively, 'then heaps of steak and kidney pie and veg', followed by ice cream and coffee) they got down to business. 'I bought blue with white circles for Pam, red with white spots for Ione and yellow Viyella for me. Win bought black organza and blue blouse material (sort of Broderie Anglaise). She wanted a hat but hadn't the difficult-to-match winter coat on (it is very fine and warm still) so daren't chance it. I bought a sort of "lamp shade" and was thrilled.' That evening's television featured Tony Hancock in full rhetorical flight as foreman of the jury in 'Twelve Angry Men' ('Does Magna Carta mean nothing to you? Did she die in vain?'), clashing with *Any Questions?* on the Light Programme. 'What were the team's reactions,' asked Harold R. Marr from the audience at the Town Hall, Eastleigh, 'on hearing that the guardsman on sentry-go at Buckingham Palace had to retreat behind the railings?' Following an episode in August when a guardsman had been confined to barracks after a woman complained of being kicked, it had recently been announced that from the 17th the sentries would be mounted in the forecourt in front of the building. 'It is a bad show,' declared Enoch Powell. 'I hope it will be reversed and that they will be brought outside again. It seems to me to be one of those comparatively rare lapses from the British sense of humour.'

The British sense of humour struggled also, post-Suez, to embrace national decline. 'I have been struck as, of course, any observer must have been, by the efforts to build up British achievements and hail them as being in some way superior to those of the United States and Russia,' Michael Young privately reflected later in October. And referring to his sociological study (with Peter Willmott) of largely middle-class Woodford in suburban Essex, he added, 'These people were by no means leaders of the elite. They did not seem to register the decline in British power, and were defensively touchy at the suggestion that there had been any.' Soon afterwards, the Queen's Speech promised independence for Cyprus and Nigeria, but attitudes remained largely Podsnappian – not least in relation to the English football team, despite severe recent disappointments. 'Storm Dooms the Swedes' was the *Daily Mirror*'s confident headline on the 28th, ahead of that afternoon's match at Wembley, with Bill Holden explaining how 'the storm which lashed Britain has swept fear into the hearts of Sweden's Soccer stars,' whereas their English opponents 'couldn't care less if it snows – THEY'LL KEEP GOING'. No doubt they did, but Sweden won 3–2, as Middlesbrough's Brian Clough in his second (and last) England outing hit the woodwork twice but failed to score, leaving Holden to rue 'the blackest day' in England's 'once-proud Soccer history'. 'England,' he declared, 'didn't resemble an international team. They lacked method, fight and control. Name any attribute a team should have had – AND ENGLAND JUST HADN'T GOT IT.'[1]

The theatrical revolution continued. *Serjeant Musgrave's Dance* by John Arden would ultimately become an anti-colonial classic, but it opened on the 22nd at the Royal Court to largely negative notices, mainly on the grounds of incomprehensibility, followed by gapingly empty houses. Al Alvarez in the *New Statesman* had a particular gripe with Lindsay Anderson's direction. 'Having used Dudley Moore's music so effectively to create a background of emotion,' he noted, 'it is a pity he did not bring it in where most needed: to set off the bits of doggerel with which Mr Arden studs his text.' More immediately, the greater impact was made by Alun Owen's *No Trams to Lime Street*, shown four days earlier in ITV's pioneering *Armchair Theatre* slot on Sunday evenings. 'A strikingly successful piece of work,' acclaimed *The Times*, 'catching with unobtrusive skill the cadence of everyday speech but heightening, concentrating and shaping to make each line tell.' The plot concerned three sailors (played by Alfred Lynch, Jack Hedley and Tom Bell) going ashore in Liverpool one evening – 'never degenerating into the slapdash regional caricatures which often take the place of characterisation in television drama' – while 'Miss Billie Whitelaw's Liverpool widow was a brilliantly observed piece of acting'. Such plaudits did not stop a blizzard of angry letters and phone calls to the *Liverpool Echo*. 'I thought it was sordid, nasty, cheap,' complained one local woman. 'You get that sort of thing in any seaport, and to bring Liverpool into the picture with a public house of drunks was absolutely deplorable. I am proud of my city, and I thought the play was a definite aspersion.' Owen, himself Liverpool-Welsh, was unabashed. 'I have fought for two years now to get plays performed in the Liverpool accent,' he informed the paper. 'I was told the accent was ridiculous, comical, absurd and very ugly . . . I could quite easily have set this play in some never-never land of the north with everybody talking like Gracie Fields . . .'

The fiction title of the autumn was undoubtedly Vladimir Nabokov's *Lolita*, while for non-fiction the accolade went to *The Lore and Language of Schoolchildren* by Iona and Peter Opie, an astonishing exercise in retrieval that included, as one reviewer put it, 'rhymes, riddles, nicknames, catch-phrases, counting-out chants, and the whole *lingua franca* of the playground'. It made an immediate mark, including a lengthy review on the leader page of *The Times*, and was further evidence of an increasing appetite for 'ordinary' voices and faces. Contributions came from some 5,000 children attending over 70 schools, none of them private, and it included some of the names that those at secondary moderns directed at their neighbourhood peers: 'Grammar grubs', 'Grammar-bugs stinking slugs, dirty little humbugs', 'Grammar School Slops', 'Grammar School Spivs', 'Grammar School Sissies', 'Filthy twerps' and, naturally, 'Slaps'. The Prime Minister, however, still preferred the non-ordinary, noting at the start of November that he was reading Anthony Powell's 'The House of Acceptance' – ie, presumably *The Acceptance World* – and that he was finding it 'witty but pointless'.[2]

The election had come and gone, but the whirlwind of urban development remained relentless. During these weeks, the model was unveiled for the 'ultra modern' new Co-op building in the centre of

Basingstoke, replacing 'a whole string of small shops' and billed as 'the first major step towards a bright, modern shopping centre for the town'; the property developer Jack Cotton revealed his latest plans for transforming Piccadilly Circus's north-east corner (the Monico site) into a brightly illuminated 13-storey building with what the *Daily Mirror* admiringly called a 'space-age look'; Madge Martin in Oxford took a walk through 'the queer devastated slums of St Ebbe's', then in the process of being cleared; a single issue of the *East London Advertiser* reported on the housing scheme in Locton Street, Limehouse (to include a 16-storey block of flats), the rehousing in Poplar of more than 230 families in the Rowsell Street area under an LCC clearance plan, the compulsory purchase of several acres of rundown housing in Stepney's Cayley Street neighbourhood, and, in Canning Town, 'on the site of the famous Trinity Church, Barking Road', the erection of a large block of flats in West Ham Corporation's new Ascot estate; the *New Yorker* profiled 'Metamorphosis in the Gorbals', where the comprehensive redevelopment scheme then under way would 'result in the disappearance of the existing Gorbals, or most of it, and the creation of a new community, which promises to bear no resemblance to the old except in name'; and, some 7 miles away in Paisley, the locals contemplated not only the first of six 15-storey blocks of flats but also plans for the complete redevelopment of the town centre – plans which, according to the *Paisley Daily Express*, would turn that centre into 'a show-place and a cynosure for years to come' (though the paper conceded that 'so futuristic' were the models that 'people have had difficulty in grasping all that it means'). Frederic Osborn, a long-ago founder of Welwyn Garden City and still a passionate advocate of dispersal and New Towns, looked on with horror. 'The architects,' he wrote in late October to Lewis Mumford, 'want to go up into the air . . . They are supported by the lucky people in country houses and parks who don't want their Arcadia invaded. They have succeeded to some extent, owing to the structure of our democracy. But they are overriding the inarticulate yet vast majority . . .'[3]

Occasionally the voices of those most intimately affected did break through. When, around this time, A.W. Davey, housing manager for St Pancras Council, publicly contrasted the 'good-hearted fun, laughter and happiness' of the old slums with 'the atmosphere of worry, tension, slobbishness, and all that goes with these things which are immediately obvious on any modern housing estate', the *Evening Standard* took the pulse in the multi-storey flats of the big new Regent's Park estate behind Euston Station. Two young housewives were adamant that Davey was wrong, with 21-year-old Barbara Pike, married to a lorry driver and with three small children, praising the friendliness of her neighbours and saying that, after getting out of her leaking Kentish Town slum, she had never been so happy in her life; but 79-year-old George Phelps agreed with Davey and spoke of how 'the people are nosy, there are too many snobs and the children are badly behaved and rude.' Or take Liverpool soon afterwards, where Dr Ronald Bradbury, the City Architect, complained that 'the stay-putters are one of our biggest problems' – ie slum-dwellers refusing to move. Whereupon a local paper found in Toxteth some evidence backing Bradbury – 'When you have lived here this long you don't want to move just anywhere, do you?' said Teresa McVeigh, living at 241 Beaufort Street with her aged mother – while other slum-dwellers waited impatiently for a move to new housing: 'People like 30-year-old Mr Albert Lee, his wife and two children, Shirley (8) and Albert (3), who live in a damp, cramped cellar at 41 Park Street with only one living room. They wash in a converted air-raid shelter and sleep in the one room upstairs.' The paper also quoted Mr Lee, a motor driver suffering from congestion of the lung and frequent attacks of bronchitis: 'We have been living here for six years. They keep telling us it will only be another 18 months before we are re-housed but that 18 months is the longest I've ever come across.'

Feelings were mixed too in Sheffield, where the Park Hill development was still being built but was about to receive its first tenants. 'Some people, particularly the elderly, had no wish to move at all,' recalled Mrs J. F. Demers, who that October moved in as assistant estate manager and welfare officer. 'Inadequate, uneconomic and unhygienic as their old houses were, they were familiar and had spelled home to them for many years. Not only were they worried about the impending move, they were naturally concerned over increased costs, who their new neighbours might be, whether they would get used to "living in the sky" and so on.' Life in the sky indeed, but a local paper was meanwhile reassuring potential residents that 'THE PLANNERS HAVE GONE

TO GREAT LENGTHS TO MINIMISE THE NECESSARY ADJUSTMENTS', and that 'the deck system' (providing 'on every third floor a 10 feet wide "street"') would enable 'neighbours to chat' and 'small children to play'. Soon afterwards, on the 22nd, two well-attended public meetings included 'varied reactions' to the announcement that no dogs or cats would be allowed, with some prospective tenants 'obviously distressed at the prospect of having to part with loved pets when they move from clearance areas to the new flats'. However, Councillor George Cooper, chairman of the Housing Management Committee, took the larger view, insisting that Park Hill would become 'the finest modern housing estate in Europe', adding, 'The scheme has the finest contemporary features. Semi-detached houses are "square" in comparison and forward-looking people should look forward to living there. These are almost perfect dwellings. It is now up to you, the would-be tenants, to make this a really worthwhile community which is not just technically correct but also socially correct.' Just over a fortnight later, on 7 November, at a ceremony presided over by the Lord Mayor, a key was handed over to 61-year-old Helen Jackson, who with her husband Fred lived in a condemned house in nearby Duke Street and were due to move into Park Hill on the 11th. 'A historic occasion,' Councillor Harold Lambert, chairman of the Housing Development Committee, predictably called it, acclaiming Park Hill as 'a tribute to public enterprise in its best form'.[4]

There were two other notable beginnings that autumn. On 30 October, in a Soho basement at 39 Gerrard Street, Ronnie Scott's Club was born. 'Too many clubs seem to degenerate into "jiving palaces",' claimed Scott in advance, whereas 'here, there will be plenty of room to dance, but also plenty of room to sit and listen – to the musicians.' Opening night featured not only the Tubby Hayes Quartet but also (noted the *Melody Maker* ad written by Scott himself) 'a young Alto Saxophonist PETER KING, an old Tenor Saxophonist RONNIE SCOTT, plus first appearance in a Jazz Club since the Relief of Mafeking, of JACK PARNELL'. The other opening was three days later, on Monday, 2 November. 'Today is the beginning of a new era,' proclaimed a quarter-page ad for the Caterpillar Tractor Co in that morning's *Times*:

> But only the beginning. Our highways will reflect the Nation's prosperity, save the Nation more than they cost to build, benefit each and every one of us – and we need them NOW.
>
> Caterpillar has contributed much towards these new avenues of progress and opportunity – and will contribute more. For Caterpillar earth-moving equipment is as reliable and sure as progress itself.

The highway starting that day was the first completed stretch, some 55 miles, of what at this stage was usually referred to as the London–Birmingham Motorway, subsequently the M1. It had taken only 19 months (helped by 1959's glorious weather), and anticipation was particularly keen in Luton, close to the southern end (where the opening ceremony was to be) and itself a car-manufacturing town. 'The Police will have their work cut out patrolling the road – not for speedsters but for cars and other vehicles going too slow, and holding up the pace of the road,' predicted the *Luton News*. 'Every motorist will be calling it his Dream Road, for he will be king of his own little realm as he speeds down this vast Motorway.' And the front-page article ended with a roll of the drums: 'The whole world will be looking to this Motorway. And to Luton falls the honour of knowing it was in on the start of a revolution.'

The new Minister of Transport, the energetic, self-promoting Ernest Marples, duly did the business at nearby Pepperstock, from where he gave a radio signal to police along the route to open the motorway's approaches, before himself walking a few hundred yards to a bridge spanning the new road, from where he watched the pioneering traffic. 'I was frightened when I watched the first users of this road today,' he frankly told a celebratory luncheon in London a few hours later. 'I have never seen anybody going so fast and ignoring the rules and regulations. Of the first four cars, three were not in traffic lines and one broke down . . . People must learn to master these great roads. Otherwise there will be many grave accidents.' In fact, seven cars broke down in the first half-hour – overheating (two), out of petrol (two), punctures (two), out of oil (one) – while an AA patrolman also admitted to being unimpressed: 'There is a fair amount of motorists trying out the old bus to "see what she'll do" – and often hugging the outside lane at 60 mph, not thinking of the car behind doing 80 or 100.' But should the speedometers even be hitting three figures? 'We are keeping an open mind at the moment on the question of speed limits,' observed Marples. 'We will see what happens.'[5]

The decade was drawing to an end, including for four very fifties people. 'A real master in making comedy of everyday situations' was a typically enthusiastic viewer reaction to Tony Hancock's current television series, but Hancock himself spent a week in October at a nursing home. 'I was doing my nut,' he explained afterwards to a sympathetic journalist. 'Got a bit strained. Couldn't remember my lines.' Gilbert Harding at the same time was endorsing Macleans new double-action indigestion tablets. 'I could write a treatise on indigestion,' he told newspaper readers. 'I know. I get it. I get indigestion because I like good food; because I worry about totally unimportant things; because I rush around much more than I should.' These tablets, though, 'always do the trick'. Princess Margaret spent 28 October at the opening in Old Bethnal Green Road of St Jude's Church of England Secondary School, destroyed by enemy action in 1940 and now rebuilt in the shadow of a modern housing estate. 'In these days, a plethora of material pleasures are constantly being offered as ideal goals for prosperity and happiness, and we need the inspiration of our Christian faith to maintain our spiritual resources to help us over our problems,' the Princess, wearing a full-length sable coat, told her audience. 'It is no good,' she added with reference to the latest Soviet satellite, 'for man to seek escape in luniks and rocketry and to leave his soul morally earthbound among the television sets and espresso bars.'

A week or two later, an even more glamorous figure, accompanied by her tiny Pekinese dog Powder Puff, was also in East London. 'It's been so exciting,' announced Jayne Mansfield after a visit to The George in Glengall Grove, Millwall, where she pulled pints of bitter, sang and played the piano, as well as scoring 45 points with her first three darts. 'I love the pub, the drink and atmosphere.' As for the tough dockers crowded admiringly round the bar: 'They are so sweet.'[6]

2

A Real Love Match

Harold Macmillan may in the immediate flush of electoral victory have declared the class war dead, but it was class that fuelled a couple of episodes in November 1959. In one, Kingsley Amis, in the course of making an advertisement in the company of the photographer Antony Armstrong-Jones, happened to comment unfavourably on the intelligence of Princess Margaret, before being offered by him a lift to Staines. En route, they stopped at Slough for an apparently cordial drink, after which Armstrong-Jones abruptly left Amis and his wife standing on the pavement to make their own way to Staines. 'He's upper-*class*,' a friend helpfully explained afterwards. 'Which means he doesn't end up one down to the likes of fucking you.' The other episode featured sardonic treatment by the *Daily Express* society gossip columnist 'William Hickey' directed at an Old Etonian, Jeremy Sandford, and his heiress-wife, Nell Dunn. Their crime was daring to move from their 'fashionable, bow-windowed flat' in Cheyne Walk, Chelsea to 'a block of condemned houses' on the other side of the river – from where he was 'anxious to experience life "with real people", so he tells his friends', while she, 'carrying his philosophy to the extreme, has taken a job in a local chocolate factory'. The payoff came a week or so later when 79 Lavender Road, Battersea was burgled. 'The Sandfords get their first real taste of low life,' exalted Hickey, who, after giving details of what had been stolen, slipped in the killer touch: 'They are particularly upset because the new pink bath which they have had specially installed – theirs is the only bathroom in the street – has been badly scratched.'[1]

Largely unconcerned – at least on the surface – with questions of class, the musical flow continued. On 15 November the Light Programme launched Alan Keith's *The 100 Best Tunes in the World* (shortened before long to *Your Hundred Best Tunes*), a Sunday-night staple, especially with female listeners, for over four decades; five days later, at Bruce Forsyth's 'I'm in Charge' show at the Palace Theatre, Manchester, Sam and Kitty Lunn were summoned to the stage as that evening's longest-married couple (51 years), where they sang 'My Old Dutch' before she had a heart attack and died in the host's arms; late in November, mainly favourable reviews started appearing of the film version of Wolf Mankowitz's satire on Tin Pan Alley, *Expresso Bongo*, including a cameo role for Gilbert Harding (as himself) complaining about 'plastic palm trees' and 'teenage rebellion' – though the part of the teenage idol was played so straight that one critic, Isabel Quigly, was 'left with the disturbing feeling that here is Cliff Richard in person, as credulous and as nice as Bongo, as simple and as duped'; by early December, Adam Faith's unanswerably of-the-moment 'What Do You Want (If You Don't Want Money)', arranged by John Barry, was settling in at the top of the charts; and on the 11th, Bernard Manning's Embassy Club opened in Manchester, with his mother on the till and the 29-year-old Manning singing 'High Hopes'. 'A barely prettified working men's club, with harsh lighting, formica-topped tables and hard-working, white-jacketed waiters sweating under the weight of trays of brimming pint glasses' is how his biographer describes the Embassy, while a day or two later, across the Pennines in Huddersfield, the sociologist Dennis Marsden was at the bar of the Scape Goat Hill Band Club, taking notes:

> Talk about TV which they'd all been watching earlier in the evening. 'Ah like that Billy Cotton Show. He's a wonderful turn is that. He can make that band sound real good – just like a brass band.' 'Ah like that little fat chap,' said another. 'What's his name, Eric something or other. He gets some real good singers on his programme, opera singers' . . . Somebody else said, 'Vic Oliver's a good turn an' all tha knows. He allus conducts a bit on his show. Just at t'beginning he conducts t'full orchestra.'

'And,' to clinch the case, 'he never gets any o'these, what d'you call him, Bing Crosbies on his programme.'[2]

Most cinema-goers would surely have endorsed Anthony Heap's diary lament in November about the 'total disappearance of newsreels from cinema programmes' – because of television – and how 'in their place we usually get short "interest" films that, as often as not, are of no interest whatever.' For radio listeners, though, there was always the comfort of Ambridge. 'The Archers to me are completely real – I worry about them all, talk about them, and plan for them,' a typical addict told the BBC that autumn. 'I *never* miss an episode if I can help it,' affirmed another. 'I should be very sad indeed to see this programme ended, and would feel I had lost a lot of friends.' Even so, the accompanying audience-research report noted quite a widespread view that 'in recent months events have been altogether too sensational – escaped criminals, international gangs of thieves with Interpol on their tail, and the mysterious and sudden disappearance of Madam Garonne do not fit with Ambridge, while on the domestic scene we are "now reaching a point where a man can't climb a ladder without falling off or get on a horse without taking a toss."' To judge by Nella Last's diary comment a few months later ('The Archers – getting further from reality'), this melodramatic trend would continue, while a further vexation was the possibility – as yet unconfirmed – that Jill Archer was pregnant again:

> Several thought this showed Phil had no sympathy with or understanding of his wife, some considered it quite disgusting ('As an ex-nurse and a Mother I know it is never easy and sometimes fated to have babies. She should not have had intercourse at all yet, let alone conceived') and some thought Jill much too placid if it were true ('If I were having babies like a machine (one out – one in) I'd be very, very irritable'). All those who raised the matter were united in feeling that it should not be allowed to happen, and it was suggested that Phil and Jill should get in touch with the Family Planning Association immediately.

As always, Walter Gabriel provoked a 'very sharp division of opinion'. Some regarded him as a 'miserable old curmudgeon' with a 'stupid cackle', but almost twice as many enjoyed this 'loveable old rascal'.

In London, the run-up to Christmas featured as usual the Regent Street decorations – 'the best yet', reckoned Madge Martin, with 'glittering chandeliers' and 'festoons of lights', given the full Richard

Dimbleby treatment in a live outside broadcast on *Panorama*. 'I kept hoping he might be led in his solemn enthusiasm to refer to "this great street",' recorded *Punch*'s Henry Turton. 'When at last he did, my festive season was made.' And it was in Regent Street, at Burberry's on a dank December day, that a young Canadian writer, Leonard Cohen, now bought a not-yet-famous blue raincoat. Meanwhile, in theatreland, Cliff Richard found himself at the Globe in Stockton-on-Tees, performing in the panto *Babes in the Wood* in white trousers and a cropped jacket, but for the capital's small children nothing beat *Noddy in Toyland* at the Prince's Theatre. 'Can no one convince Miss Enid Blyton,' asked Alan Brien in vain, 'that in this day and age, before audiences which include coloured children, it is displaying the crassest insensitivity to portray the golliwogs as idiot victims of toyland *apartheid*, with the parallel made quite explicit by a nasty song and dance by three of them called "I'm Golly, I'm Woggy, I'm Nigger"?' On Christmas Day itself, almost the biggest Home Service audience was for the nostalgic *The Tommy Handley Story*, though it was an unmistakable sign of increasingly TV-oriented times that four days later marked the end of the sixth and final radio series of *Hancock's Half Hour*.[3]

At about the same time, Gallup's regular end-of-year poll had 60 per cent looking back on a good 1959 and only 6 per cent expecting 1960 to be a worse year. Probably neither David Blunkett nor Tony Garrett was in the majority. Blunkett's father was a highly respected foreman at a water gas plant, but in early December he fell, owing to the incompetence of a fellow-worker, into a giant vat of boiling water, dying an agonising death a month later. Blunkett's widowed mother in Sheffield was left in poverty after the East Midlands Gas Board behaved in a manner (in her son's unforgiving words) 'more reminiscent of the worst private employer than a publicly owned industry'. As for Garrett, he was living with the writer Angus Wilson in the Suffolk village of Felsham Woodside and working locally for the Probation Service. But malicious gossip spread, and a few weeks before Christmas he was informed by the Chief Probation Officer that he could continue in the Service only if he stopped living with Wilson and moved 40 miles away – a compromise that Garrett refused, resigning in January. 'The offer was distressing on many levels,' notes Wilson's biographer Margaret

Drabble, and Garrett himself, for whom his job had been a vocation, developed a stammer in consequence.[4]

A trio of reports this winter considered different aspects of the welfare of the young. The Crowther Report of December 1959, entitled *15–18*, argued cogently in favour of raising the school-leaving age from 15 to 16 and of making part-time attendance at county colleges compulsory, but, despite being well received, it failed to sway ministerial minds. The following month, a QC's report into the previous summer's disturbances at Carlton Approved School pinned much of the blame on what *The Times* in its summary called 'the emergence of a small but exceedingly difficult hard core of anti-authority young people'. Soon afterwards, in early February, a committee chaired by the 'youthful grandmother' Lady Albemarle issued a report on the Youth Service that found it failing to reach at least one person in three and urged a ten-year development plan. 'All this preoccupation with youth, with teenagers is so high-minded,' reflected John Vaizey in an overview of Crowther and Albemarle. 'Is there *really* a teenage problem? Do they want or need to be done good to?' These were pertinent questions, and indeed a survey of youth clubs in Cardiff in 1960 encountered 'considerable distrust of "missionary" activity in many of them', as well as more generally observing, on the part of that city's teenage population without contact with youth clubs, an entirely qualm-less preference for 'more individual and more passive uses of leisure, with a heavy emphasis on television viewing and cinema going'.

Certainly one teenager in 1960 – 14-year-old Jacqueline Aitken (later Wilson), living in Kingston-upon-Thames and going to school in New Malden – had plenty of her own fish to fry. 'We got some smashing bargains so I'm jolly glad I went,' she wrote in her new diary on 2 January after going to the Bentalls' sale with her mother, and over the coming weeks a succession of rather breathless entries followed:

> *9 January.* I did the shopping with Dad and you'll never guess what we bought! A RECORD PLAYER! ... It is an automatic kind and plays beautifully. We bought 'Travelling Light' by Cliff Richard and Dad chose a Mantovani long player ... I've been playing them, and all our old 78 records, all the afternoon.

18 January. In Latin we had 28 vocabs to learn! Not homework, mind you, but just to be done in our spare time! Honestly, isn't it ridiculous? I'm just dying to leave school.

22 January. In the evening I went to see 'Expresso Bongo' with Carol at the Regal. We saw tons of girls from school there, all dressed up pretending to be sixteen.

8 February. We had chips, corned beef and American salad and mince and apple tart for dinner today, not bad for school dinners.

9 February. Dinner was steak pie, greens and mashed potato, and semolina and jam for pud. Pretty awful, n'est-ce pas?

12 February. In the evening I went dancing. Sue didn't come or Judith, but Carol and Jill did. I wore my new nail varnish and new flatties which were lovely for dancing in. We did a lot of complicated Samba steps and I had Peter for a partner. After Ken I think he's terribly ordinary.

13 February. Mum said she wanted to see the film 'The Reluctant Debutante' so we went together. On the way we went into the Bentalls' record department. I saw P. Wilson and Y. McCarthy in turquoise duffle coats, extremely tight jeans and cha-cha shoes being cuddled by a group of horrible spotty teddy boys.

Just over a week later, she was at Kingston's Granada cinema for her first pop concert. 'I've never experienced anything like it, you don't feel at all self conscious, just madly *hep*,' she recorded. 'Of course Adam was wonderful. Honestly, I've never believed girls could scream so loud! Adam looked ever so handsome though!' And on another page of her diary she stuck in a photo of him with the words – in green biro – 'Adam for Always!' and 'Faith Forever'.[5]

The Goon Show in effect bowed out with 'The Last of the Smoking Seagoons', but there were plenty of beginnings during the early weeks of 1960. From New Year's Day, the BBC had a new director-general in Hugh Carleton Greene, who was determined (as he later put it) 'to dissipate the ivory tower stuffiness'; on 8 January, at Portishead in Somerset,

Margaret Thatcher made her *Any Questions?* debut, was asked in the first question about show-business personalities being used to advertise products, and replied that her usual reaction was 'Hmm, I wonder what they're being paid for this'; on the 21st a literary career was launched when the Wintersons adopted baby Jeanette and took her home to 200 Water Street, Accrington; two days later, a 17-year-old red-headed Scot, Billy Bremner, was blooded for Leeds United in a 3–1 win at Chelsea; next day in the *Observer*, Bridget Colgan (real name Lydia James) started a monthly 'Within the Family' column, probably the first in a British newspaper to give parenting and child-care advice; on the 25th, American-style ten-pin bowling reached Britain, as Sir John Hunt of Everest fame sent down the first bowl at an old ABC cinema in Stamford Hill, with boxing's Henry Cooper among those in attendance; two evenings later at London's Conway Hall, 'an audience of 70 sat transfixed with gloom' (according to someone present) as the young avant-garde composer Cornelius Cardew gave 'a concert of really stunning boredom'; on BBC TV on the 29th, up against *The Army Game*, Eric Sykes and Hattie Jacques were together for the first time in *Sykes And A. . .*; a week later, on 5 February, Thatcher delivered a well-organised maiden speech in the Commons, earning the compliment from a Labour MP that she had hardly needed to refer to her notes; next afternoon, 'a vaunted figure in school football', 17-year-old Terry Venables from Dagenham, made his league debut for Chelsea in a 4–2 defeat at West Ham; and the following week another early-vaunted figure, Dennis Potter, had his first book published, *The Glittering Coffin*, fairly described in the *Sunday Times* on the 14th as 'a wordy but eloquent plea for a Socialist Britain, for an end to what the author considers the inertia, mortmain and commercialisation that are cankering our society'. But beginnings could also be endings, and around this time there appeared on billboards and television a memorable advertisement for a new brand of cigarette: a man in a trench coat, standing on the Albert Bridge at night and lighting up, with the accompanying slogan 'You're never alone with a Strand'. The unfortunate assumption was widely made that to smoke a Strand was to be lonely and therefore a loser; the cigarette itself proved too hot for smokers' fingers; and the campaign, along with the brand itself, was rapidly pulled.[6]

It was almost fifteen years since the war, and the war-film boom was at last over. But on 11 February, the Duke of Edinburgh and Admiral of the Fleet the Earl Mountbatten of Burma were among those at the Odeon, Leicester Square attending the premier of *Sink the Bismarck!*, starring Kenneth More as the Director of Naval Operations. 'To my mind it seems stupid to have shown the Bismarck crew as oafs and simpletons, and their commander, the distinguished Admiral Lutyens, as nothing better than a bully and a Hitler toady,' commented the *Observer*'s Caroline Lejeune, while *Films and Filming* found it 'an incredibly old-fashioned film, almost as if one were watching a 1940 piece of flag-waving instead of a 1960 piece of drama'. But these and similar strictures failed to prevent *Sink the Bismarck!* becoming the year's top-grossing film in Britain. That same evening saw a rather different West End first night, of the Cockney musical *Fings Ain't Wot They Used T'Be*, which since its initial production a year earlier at the Theatre Royal in Stratford East had been given a major revamp and upgrade by Joan Littlewood. The result was considerable critical acclaim – predictably not shared that first night by the diarist Anthony Heap ('low life squalor on the stage') – and a two-year run at the Garrick. 'This tough and virile musical has been improved out of all recognition,' declared Harold Hobson, while Eric Keown praised the cast's 'enormous comic gusto', including particular mentions for Miriam Karlin as the gangster's moll ('a coarse brilliance') and Barbara Windsor as the prostitute ('asking in a baby voice where little birds go in the winter'). Who came to *Fings*? When a book version was published some months later, Littlewood asserted in her introduction that the Garrick had been 'packed night after night with Cockney people', a claim that one reviewer flatly denied. 'Chuck it, Miss Littlewood!' expostulated John Bowen in *Punch*. 'Even at Stratford East it wasn't Cockney people, on the night I saw *Fings*, who drove away in their posh cars or took the tube back to Chelsea.' The other *Fings* tailpiece came soon afterwards, in October 1960, when the 23-year-old Barbara Windsor – from Hackney Road, Bethnal Green, but now sitting in her dressing-room at the Garrick – was interviewed by the *East London Advertiser*. Would 'The Dish', as the article repeatedly called her, eventually be returning to the East End, to act again at the Theatre Royal? '"Are you kidding?" she shrieked. "I'm finished with all that ten quid a week lark. I'm not in this business for art's sake, you know – I'm in it for the money. Besides, I've got too many expenses to keep up. I've just bought a telly."'[7]

Fings was merely one example of a broader trend. *Clea*, the final part of Lawrence Durrell's *The Alexandria Quartet*, was published in February to a mixed reception, but the landmark novel that month, starting to mark out 1960 as 'The Year of the North', was David Storey's unsparingly realistic *This Sporting Life*, set in the world of rugby league. The reviews were largely positive, though tending to suggest a gulf between reviewer and subject matter. 'A piece of field work in darkest Yorkshire' was the *TLS*'s characterisation, while Karl Miller informed *Observer* readers that 'the whole team plays a very grim kind of Rugby and there is none of the complexity, none of the loveable dramatic appeal, which there is in soccer.' Just as Storey's novel was being published, the *TLS* sought to offer a larger perspective on the phenomenon in a leading article called 'Roots'. 'It is rather ironical,' reflected the paper, 'that, at a time when the British working classes seem to be growingly conservative in their political views and growingly middle-class in their tastes and habits, we should be enjoying for the first time in many years something like a renaissance of working-class literature.' Obvious examples were cited – including the work of Arnold Wesker, Shelagh Delaney, Alan Sillitoe and Keith Waterhouse – and the point made that 'what is called "the New Left" in politics is very much concerned with breaking down the dominance in our cultural life, in our literary monthlies and weeklies, for instance, of what is often called "the genteel tradition".' Yet inevitably the *TLS* entered a reservation: 'One has an uneasy feeling that any novel or play with a working-class setting and with a note of protest about it, is setting off, perhaps for the next five years or so, with a flying start' – in other words, irrespective of literary merit. Even so, not every working-class novelist was flying in 1960. *The Big Room* was Sid Chaplin's first novel in a decade, but in February it got the treatment from Keith Waterhouse in the *New Statesman*. 'Something has gone seriously wrong,' Waterhouse reckoned, before expressing the wish that the author had 'stuck to the ordinary, dreadful lives of this ordinary, dreadful family in this great room'. Chaplin himself, though, was stoical. 'It's been nice,' he wrote from Newcastle to a friend, 'to see another one launched after all these weary years', adding hopefully that the novel he was completing 'may be better for them to understand'.[8]

On far more people's lips in early 1960 were the titillating 'My Confessions' being peddled by Diana Dors each Sunday in the *News of the World*. Arguably the first authentic kiss-and-tell, and earning her some £35,000, they began on 24 January with an attempt on the front page to soften criticism: 'I know I've been a naughty girl. I know they call me the film star with a lurid past. But today I'm a happy wife. Soon I hope to become a devoted mother.' A week later, another message: 'Thank you, all of you, for writing. I'm delighted you are finding my story so exciting. Forgive me for not replying personally, but it's impossible just now as my baby is expected any moment.' And on 7 February: 'Well, he's arrived. He's in my arms now, my wonderful 7lb son Mark Richard. I'm so proud and so happy.' Nella Last, not a *News of the World* reader, tried to keep up. 'Dear me,' she noted that day, 'I am intrigued about the articles about Diana Dors life – Mrs Salisbury [her cleaner] was very censorious but vague, but for it to be mentioned in Parliament & John Gordon thought it of enough "news" value to include in his "jottings," make me wonder, what exactly she did write.' John Gordon was the habitually censorious *Sunday Express* columnist on 'Current Events', and Last had just read this: 'I would like to have congratulated Miss Diana Dors on achieving motherhood. Instead I extend my sympathy to an innocent baby born at a time when his mother is publicly degrading herself as few women have done before.' 'Poor Diana,' reflected the kindlier Last, 'she will perhaps welcome such publicity now – but knowing little boys pretty well, her "punishment" for such, is to come . . .'

That same evening, Tony Hancock was the subject of John Freeman's *Face to Face* – a compelling half-hour, with Hancock chain-smoking and deeply uneasy, that left many viewers at the time dissatisfied:

> I'd prefer to think of Mr Hancock as a character in 'H—ancock's Half-Hour'.
>
> Seemed unable to cope with the stringent demands of the programme. Lost without a script.
>
> Hancock's utterings seemed to be the outpourings of a confused mind. I failed to understand them all and wonder if he did himself, e.g. on religion.

> I thought John Freeman hit below the belt and was at times impertinent.
>
> Does it really matter whether Hancock wants children or how much the BBC pays him? These are the sort of questions one would expect from a Sunday newspaper reporter.

Punch soon afterwards noted that Freeman 'sometimes overdoes it and causes an uprush of sympathy for the victim, as in the Hancock programme', but for Hancock himself it was a fateful turning point. 'It was the biggest mistake he ever made,' his brother Roger would reflect. 'I think it all started from that, really. Self-analysis – that was his killer.' As for Freeman, barely a fortnight later on *Panorama* he conducted another controversial interview, in this case going a long way to demolish the credibility of Frank Foulkes, President of the Communist-run Electrical Trades Union, recently accused again of ballot-rigging. Whereupon, five prominent Labour figures (none remotely pro-Communist) wrote to *The Times* complaining about 'trial by television'; dissenting letters followed from Malcolm Muggeridge and Christopher Chataway, among others; but a future Tory MP, John Stokes, agreed with the Labour five. 'Indeed,' he declared, 'I would go further; why must the Prime Minister, the Foreign Secretary, and other important persons of the day be constantly badgered, e.g. when getting into or out of aeroplanes, &c., to give their views at a moment's notice on grave issues?'[9]

The other union in the news that February was the National Union of Railwaymen, threatening strike action from the 15th. 'There is undoubtedly much sympathy for the most cruelly underpaid railwaymen,' Mollie Panter-Downes on the 10th told her *New Yorker* readers, but next day the diarist Florence Turtle was probably more representative of opinion, certainly of middle-class opinion: 'The Rail Strike seems inevitable, a complete deadlock. Blackmail by the Unions it seems, they are the curse of this country. All they seem to want is more pay for less work & less efficient work. The First Class carriage I travelled in last week was filthy.' In the event, the government blinked first, conceding a 5-per-cent wage increase. 'Irresponsibility has been made respectable,' complained *The Times*, but as ever there was also a general sense of relief, prompting the *Sunday Times* to praise the new Minister of Labour, Edward Heath, for his 'diplomacy and powers of gentle persuasion'. Almost everyone knew, though, that the underlying issue was the industry itself. 'British Railways must be taken in hand,' insisted the *Daily Mail* in the immediate wake of the settlement. 'They must be rationalised and streamlined.' The *Economist* concurred: 'The only possible economic future for the railways of this country is to become much smaller in scale (and staff) and vastly more efficient in organisation and more specialised in operation.' It was an unsentimental prospect that dismayed the writer Sylvia Townsend Warner. 'We still have some very sweet little branch-lines,' she wrote to a friend on the 14th from her home in Dorset.

> There is one from Taunton to Castle Cary which ten years ago I used very often, coming back from visiting my poor witless mother in her nursing-home. I caught its last journey of the day; and at each little station the guard got out, locked up the ticket office, looked round like a mother to see that everything was as it should be, put out the lights, and no doubt said God Bless You to it. This idyllic artless journey ended at Castle Cary, the train took itself off to sleep in a siding, and I waited half an hour for the express to come dashing & flashing in like something of a different breed. There is also a God-fearing train from Yeovil to Taunton that doesn't run on Sundays, and our own local pet from Maiden Newton to Bridport that has the best blackthorn brakes I know, and trots like a horse under the neolithic fort of Eggardon, & crosses a quantity of narrow bridges with screams of apprehension.

'As for the primroses along the cuttings,' she added, 'you can lean out of the window and smell them.'[10]

The week after the railway strike was called off was dominated by one subject: the imminent prospect of the first child born to a reigning monarch for over a century. 'Kept listening yesterday & today to the hourly news on Light Programme about the Queen, & Doctors coming & going,' noted Marian Raynham in Surbiton on Thursday the 18th. That afternoon, the left-wing Janet Hase – 'fed to the teeth with all the sentimental crap and shoddy sentiment being spewed forth by the press and radio, but disguised for the occasion as a bland Australian journalist' – interviewed nearly 50 people out of the crowd of several hundred (mainly middle-aged, middle-class women) waiting outside the gates of Buckingham Palace. 'She's an example to us all – a wonderful wife and mother – such a happy family – I'm so interested because my daughter is her age and has a little girl almost the same age as Princess Anne,' said one woman. Hase was generally struck by the high degree of personal identification. 'I think she'd *like* to know that we're out here, wishing her well,' said another. 'I've got three children myself – boy, girl and another boy. That's why I hope her third's a boy.' Next day, Judy Haines in Chingford was also on the *qui vive*: 'After lunch heard that the Queen's doctors were in attendance on her. Listened to all news bulletins. Then just after 4 o'c John Snagge announced: "The Queen has had her baby. It's a boy."' Among other diarists, Mrs Raynham switched the radio back on just in time to hear the news, Madge Martin (on holiday in Brighton) saw the newspaper placards announcing 'The Queen's Baby – A PRINCE', and Nella Last missed the first announcement but after hearing the news wondered 'if the fact there's another "direct" heir will change Princess Margaret's life a little – make her choice a bit less "rigid"'. Most of the diarists, and presumably most people, were pleased by the news (the baby not yet named Andrew), while in the press next day the *Sketch* and the *Mirror* ('OH BOY!') devoted six pages each to the story, the *Mail* only five.

Constitutional continuity was further assured the following Wednesday when David Dimbleby (undergraduate) and Jonathan Dimbleby (schoolboy) made their TV debuts on Richard Dimbleby's *No Passport* holiday programme, with the pair going to the Lakes for a fortnight. 'They went by car, stayed in hotels costing up to £3 per day for each of them, and presented papa on return with a bill for between £70 and £80,' noted Hilary Corke in the *Listener*. 'Surely this was an appalling example? If this was intended as a sample holiday for young persons, then it should have been adjusted to a normal young persons's economy, with stays in youth-hostels and so on. If it was intended as a sample holiday for adults, then adults should have been sent on it.' But the week's big constitutional moment was still to come – a secret known only to a few, including the PM. 'I fear,' Macmillan had reflected on the 16th, 'it will not be very popular, but I think nevertheless that people will feel that the Princess has been very unlucky. So long as the young man is (as he appears to be) a gentleman, *not* divorced, & a Protestant,

I cannot see that the Queen or Ministers have any right (still less duty) to interfere under the Act of 1772.'[11]

It all went public on Friday the 26th, succinctly recorded by Jennie Hill, living near Winchester: 'T.V. Gardener's Club was interrupted to announce Princess Margaret engaged to be married to Tony Armstrong-Jones.' Judy Haines for her part was 'staggered' but 'thrilled' to hear the news, Madge Martin was 'delighted' for the Princess ('she had seemed so lost, somehow'), and Kingsley Amis in Swansea had a particular interest as he watched the television in his kitchen: 'There was the oleaginous Godfrey Talbot, always kept on hand for these do's, mouthing, "And everybody's so delighted because this is so obviously a real love match."' A love match perhaps, but Florence Turtle's immediate comment was 'not a particularly good match I would think', while next day Nella Last (herself 'glad') was 'pegging out some tea towels on the line' when her neighbour Mrs Atkinson called over: 'She was *shocked* at Princess Margaret's engagement to a common photographer – for once, not asking me what I thought before she began . . . She said "Why, she will be Mrs Armstrong-*Jones*." I said, "Oh no, she is a princess & will keep her title – perhaps they will give her husband a title." She said "I hope they *do*."' The press of course went to town: not just the fulsome guff from the usual suspects, but even the *Guardian*, extolling as it did 'a fairy-story romance of the young man working for his living, like countless other young men, who has won the hand of a princess', though managing to refrain from following the example of the *Mirror* and the *Herald* by calling the Old Etonian a 'working lad'. Altogether, it was, as Anthony Heap noted soon afterwards, an 'awful lot of gush and ballyhoo' about the whole thing. As for the Princess herself, Heap offered the thought that 'maybe marriage will help her to acquire a little more dignity and decorum.'[12]

'The building sites are damp,' John Berger wrote in November 1959 about Frank Auerbach's latest London paintings. 'The mud clings. The tarpaulins are heavy with moisture. The light in the sky is far less comforting than a cup of tea.' But the pace of urban change was insufficient for the influential, left-wing architectural-*cum*-design writer Reyner Banham. 'Our city centres, untouched by even piecemeal redevelopment since 1939, are now at least twenty years out of date, clogged with inefficient buildings in the wrong places,' he declared soon afterwards. 'Simply as physical equipment our urban hubs are intolerable and must be replaced . . .' Architecture was becoming an increasingly fashionable topic, and in March 1960 a three-part television series by Sir Kenneth Clark, *The Art of Architecture*, was the occasion for *TV Times* to commission a piece ('Building for Beauty') by the best-known architect of the day, Basil Spence, that offered an uncompromising defence of the modern idiom:

> Not all this newness will succeed. But it is far better that some of it should fail and people should *try* than we should continue copying past styles paradoxically called traditional. Modern architecture is as exciting as any adventure in history for it looks straight into the future, not backwards.
>
> We have new materials, new techniques to apply. Modern architecture is sweeping in like the tide. The future is bright.

It wasn't bright for all, though, as witnessed by the destruction of the solid, red-bricked Victorian barracks at Aldershot, where E. S. Turner had recently observed that 'today the demolishers are cutting a great swathe across the Camp', with for instance 'a new military housing estate' rising 'on the site of the old Waterloo Barracks'. Turner's sympathies were clear, and he found one source of consolation: 'In the town those curious shops which call themselves military stores have made few concessions to modern taste. In one window I saw an array of tea cosies, elaborately worked in bright regimental colours, like inflated Valentines.'[13]

London's rapidly evolving skyline remained on the front line of urban change and debate. In the *Spectator*'s last Christmas number of the 1950s, John Betjeman issued a blast devoid of festive cheer:

> A few solemn pundits, but very few Londoners, praise the new tall office blocks and regimented flats which are choking the city and mucking up the skyline in what once were countrified suburbs . . . In the office blocks of the City and West End, the idea is to make as much money as possible for their promoters out of the rents. In Council

> blocks of flats the idea is to pack in as many people as possible at a minimum cost to the rates and regardless of the fact that London is a horizontal city and that Londoners have always preferred living in streets with their own back gardens . . .

The march of the vertical was undeniable: Marylebone Road's Castrol House and St Martin's Lane's Thorn House ('London's townscape has been greatly enriched,' declared the town planner Walter Bor about them in March 1960); Berwick Street's 18-storey block of shops, offices and flats rising by this time in otherwise intimate Soho; London Wall's Moor House, the first of an intended cluster of tower blocks there, to be linked together by pedestrian walkways ('pedways') in the air; and, in Camberwell, the newly completed Sceaux Gardens estate, dominated by two 15-storey blocks and set amid the district's Georgian and Regency buildings (but, insisted the *Architects' Journal* in January 1960, 'the architects have succeeded admirably in continuing this tradition'). One of the more balanced architectural writers, Kenneth Robinson, wondered in April about the long-term consequences. 'Will discretion be used, or will we make as much of a mess with vertical slashes across the skyline as we have done with ribbons across the landscape?' he asked. 'I'm appalled to find that the LCC has no policy about the siting of high buildings: it considers each case on its merits.' The LCC itself had recently stated explicitly that it had 'no intention of turning London into New York', but Robinson was not satisfied: 'We wouldn't mind the invigorating skyline of a Manhattan. What we fear is the crudeness of a Shanghai waterfront.'[14]

The great *cause célèbre* of these months was Jack Cotton's proposed scheme for the Monico site at Piccadilly Circus, as opinion rapidly hardened after his naive if hubristic unveiling in late October 1959 of what the *Architects' Journal* dismissed as 'a clumsy office block on a crude podium of shops, using neon advertisements in the most obvious manner'. An effective campaign – including the dubbing of it as 'Chewing Gum House' – rapidly led to a public enquiry being announced for mid-December. The enquiry lasted several weeks, the bow-tied Cotton 'beamed on all and sundry as though he were playing host at an amusing party that could only end with the guests thanking him and going quietly' (Panter-Downes), the architectural profession stood almost four-square behind the Civic Trust in condemning the vulgar design, and Osbert Lancaster declared that 'the present level of advertising in the Circus was acceptable, but the unrestricted vertical space on the proposed tower would encourage the worst excesses of Times Square, New York.' The eventual upshot was the blocking of Cotton's scheme. But already a new *cause célèbre* was taking shape: the Great Arch at Euston, which British Railways proposed to demolish. The two best-known architectural critics (and rivals) now had their public say, with John Betjeman demanding the arch's reconstruction in the Euston Road itself, and Nikolaus Pevsner adamant that 'if the Euston Arch were destroyed, that would be the worst loss to the Georgian style in London architecture since most of Soane's Bank of England fell shortly before the war.'

That outcome remained uncertain, but one development definitely set to happen was the brutalist Barbican, narrowly endorsed in principle by the City authorities in December 1959. 'The intention underlying our design is to create a coherent residential precinct in which people can live both conveniently and with pleasure,' declared the architects Chamberlin, Powell and Bon. 'Despite its high density the layout is spacious; the buildings and the space between them are composed in such a way as to create a clear sense of order without monotony.' Denys Lasdun's Bethnal Green cluster blocks, meanwhile, were now complete, with the Claredale Street scheme (one 14-storey cluster block and two 6-storey blocks at right angles to each other) complementing the earlier Usk Street blocks. Accompanied by plenty of glamorous-looking photos, the *Architectural Review* (in May 1960) applauded the new scheme as more 'decisive' and 'authoritative', explained that the 14-storey block was 'intended to be read as a type of vertical street of stairs, lifts, services and public spaces', and generally perceived the best of all worlds: 'The cluster concept offers a viable alternative on the visual side by creating tower accents without visually destroying the existing grain; on the human side it shows promise in possessing domestic scale in the component parts of these towers and maintaining something like the pre-existing sociological groupings of the streets that gave the original urban grain to the district.'[15]

Outside the capital, Birmingham remained at the forefront of change. Early in 1960 the Corporation accepted a design (from the

London-based Laing Development Co) for the Bull Ring Centre, in effect to be a covered shopping centre operating on five levels – a scheme that, reckoned the *Architects' Journal*, had 'much to commend it'. Traffic was by now flowing on the first completed section of the Inner Ring Road, the 400-yard stretch known as Smallbrook Ringway (later Smallbrook Queensway) that was officially opened by Ernie Marples in March. Shortly before the opening, the *Liverpool Daily Post*'s admiring George Eglin was shown round the ring road – 'the equivalent of driving the M1 through the heart of the city' – and reflected ruefully how, while Liverpool had been 'sitting tight and thinking that nothing else mattered but building houses', Birmingham had been 'boldly and imaginatively planning for the future'. Eglin also had a word with Frank Price, 'a vital, bubbling volcano of a man', until recently chairman of Birmingham's Public Works Committee. 'The central fringes of all our older cities are ill-planned, overcrowded and insanitary,' asserted the vertically minded alderman. 'Birmingham is no exception. The street pattern is out of date, there is a shortage of open space, and land is used in a most uneconomic fashion.' Rather touchingly, Price added, 'When I see all that's going on in the city I feel frightened myself . . .'

There tended to be less Price-like drive among Edinburgh's staid city fathers, but at 6 Beaumont Place on a rainy night in late November 1959 the final collapse and evacuation of what became known as the 'Penny Tenement' dramatically highlighted the Scottish capital's festering slum problem. Questions were asked in the House, while when officials and councillors toured one of the city's worst slums, Greenside, tenants shouted angrily at them from windows. Two key Edinburgh developments, meanwhile, now got the green light. In December the city administration's 'big five' (town clerk, city chamberlain, town planning officer, city engineer, city assessor) all publicly agreed to the 'bold implementation' of a scheme to develop the St James Square slum area at the eastern end of Princes Street – a scheme having at its heart what would become the unloved 'sprawling grey concrete leviathan' of the St James Centre. Three months later, and after many years of controversy, the Secretary of State for Scotland endorsed Robert Matthew's plan (based in part on an earlier one by Basil Spence) to destroy George Square's south-east corner with a 15-storey Arts Tower for the university – a square full of eighteenth-century domestic architecture that was, according to the *Architects' Journal*, 'of great charm and historic interest but only modest architectural distinction'. As for Glasgow, the momentous decision of these months was the Corporation's to approve in principle, as the *Glasgow Herald* reported in February 1960, 'plans for the building of a multi-lane highway which will encircle the city for about four and a half miles', involving the demolition of 'thousands of houses' and to 'be built in conjunction with the comprehensive redevelopment of seven areas bordering the route'. The planning convenor, Bailie William Taylor, was adamant that such was the increasing traffic congestion in central Glasgow that only an inner ring road could prevent it dying 'of slow strangulation'. The *Herald* itself unambiguously backed both 'the timing and the logic', considered that 'redevelopment of the central areas provides the opportunity for road building on the boldest lines', and proudly praised the 'local initiative' that had led to Glasgow having 'produced a blueprint for the first urban motorway in Britain, probably in Europe', albeit for the moment forgetting Birmingham's already roaring lanes.[16]

Glasgow Corporation took its decision on the same day – the 18th – that Salford City Council approved by thirty-six votes to five the ambitious Broad Street Redevelopment Scheme. 'The scheme,' summarised the *Guardian*, 'entails the construction of 2,652 homes in multi-storey flats and maisonettes; the demolition of all the main road shops and their rebuilding as a shopping precinct; and major improvements to Broad Street, which is part of the A6 highway.' In the debate itself, Councillor Albert Jones, chairman of the Planning and Development Committee, inevitably referred to Walter Greenwood's famous Salford novel of the 1930s, *Love on the Dole*, and went on: 'We may be 30 years late but we are trying now to obliterate Hanky Park as it was known and propose to make the area something of which we can be proud . . .' Nearby, the demolition men were almost on the doorsteps of the 70 small shopkeepers in the Ellor Street Clearance Area. 'They are having to hang on and lose money while their customers are being moved out of the area,' noted the local paper in April, for 'if they move now they lose compensation rights.' And, the reporter added, 'the general impression one gets from the shopkeepers is of complete uncertainty.' 'The way in which the Council have gone about the whole thing,' complained Mr E. Clarke, a dyer and cleaner, 'has been dictatorial and they have not considered us in any way.' But Mr H. W. Hartley, general storekeeper, was reflective rather than bitter: 'Although we cannot stand in the way of progress I will be very sorry to leave, for I came to Ellor Street in 1912.'

Over in Sheffield, keys had been given by the end of 1959 for 400 of the new flats at Park Hill. 'At one time, there was a certain amount of prejudice against flats, but now, thanks to publicity in the local Press and the development of Park Hill and other schemes, people have begun to want them,' confidently asserted an official in the Housing Department at the start of 1960. 'They now realise the many advantages the flat-dweller has, particularly in a scheme such as Park Hill where tenants have shopping facilities on the doorstep, covered roadways, central heating, easy refuse disposal, and other benefits not available to people living in traditional houses.' All the more troubling, then, were the findings of 'a sociological report' for the City Council's Housing Management Committee that the *Sheffield Telegraph* revealed in March, as the streets in the sky continued to be filled as soon as they were ready. 'Life in Sheffield's new multi-storey Park Hill flats is becoming a nightmare for many tenants,' the paper began bluntly, and some details from the report followed: canvassers, selling everything from washing machines and electric razors to laundries and indoor photographs, 'clutter up hallways of dwellings with handbills of all descriptions – and worse, repeatedly ply their wares at house doors'; 'lifts have been a magnet for children of all ages and continue to be so', causing frequent breakdowns; 'a more dangerous and harmful "game" is that of throwing objects – milk bottles, saucepans, open knives, steel etc, off the decks and roof'; and 'there have been many instances of violence among teenage groups gathered round the coffee bar.' The report itself reached a sombre conclusion, far removed from all those feel-good sentiments that had so liberally – and understandably – been wafted around the previous autumn:

> If the central part of Park Hill is already unsafe for residents, this may prove to be a vital factor of the success or failure in building up an effective community. They need all possible support to help them achieve as high a standard of community pride as possible. The estate on its side must foresee and avert dangerous and socially disintegrating trends.

Or, as the *Telegraph* put it, preferring at this delicate stage to focus on the early troubles of one particular age group, 'the move to Park Hill seems to have been a great strain for many old people, even those fortunate enough to have the support of relatives and friends.'[17]

Generally, 1960 was the year when 'high-rise' became 'higher', with work starting (or authorised to start) on blocks of flats of 20 storeys or more in, among other places, Southampton, Edinburgh, Newcastle, Smethwick and Liverpool. Undoubtedly the concept had its glamour, or at the least a curiosity value: when in January the Scottish Special Housing Association opened its first high-rise block in Dundee, of a mere ten storeys, some 25,000 people inspected the flats. Harder evidence of attitudes, though, came that spring from Leeds and Merseyside. In the former, S. I. Benson, a senior figure in the Housing Department, frankly informed the Housing Committee in March that, in terms of placing families, 'our experience shows that it is far better to avoid larger dwellings in multi-storey development', not least given that the average family still wished to be rehoused 'in a semi-detached two-storey house, with a second choice of a terrace-type house'. The 'traditional objections' to flats, he went on, remained strong, including in relation to internal layout, noise, general appearance and lack of privacy, while 'many families from clearance areas wish for a private garden, especially where young children are concerned.' In short, he reiterated, for those 'thousands of families from the clearance areas' facing compulsory rehousing, their 'aspirations do not include rehousing in tall storey blocks or, indeed, in flats/maisonettes of any kind'. Instead, 'these people are looking for dwellings which will enable them to "spread" and enjoy open space – with privacy – immediately around their homes.' Benson's uncompromising message was anathema to Karl Cohen, dynamic chairman of the Housing Committee and wholly committed to the high-rise solution to Leeds's housing problems; a few weeks later, he read out to his fellow-councillors an unsolicited letter from a Mr Ryan, a new tenant in a recently opened multi-storey block, Beevers Court: 'I must admit that I never relished the idea of living in a flat until I saw this "Point" block. The Housing Department are to be congratulated on this design which gives ample privacy with all amenities. If you have any more "doubters" on your waiting list I can honestly say that they would be well advised to accept one of these flats.'[18]

About the same time in Bootle, where opinion was apparently divided by the sight of two 11-storey blocks of flats being built in Marsh Lane (involving the demolition of 'little Wales', a cluster of streets named after Welsh towns and counties), the *Liverpool Echo* obtained some representative-sounding vox pop from those living nearby:

> I like them. I like their appearance. I think it would take some time, however, to get used to living in them, but once you were accustomed, everything would be all right. (*Mrs Eleanor Tanner*)
>
> I think these flats are an eyesore. If there was more space surrounding them, it would not be so bad. This kind of development of large blocks of flats needs a lot of open space and we have not got that here. (*Mr Samuel Wood*)
>
> The main thing is that they will give homes to so many people. I like them because when they are finished, it will put an end to the no-man's land we have looked at for so long. They will at least look tidy and that is a big thing. (*Mrs Edna Traynor*)
>
> I am the mother of seven children and I need fresh accommodation badly. I like the flats and I would go anywhere if I could find accommodation for my family. (*Mrs Teresa Flynn*)

One should not exaggerate the high-rise phenomenon at this stage. Local authorities in England and Wales during 1960 gave tender approvals to 58,256 houses and 36,372 low-rise flats, compared to 15,685 high-rise flats (five or more storeys), and it would not be until the mid-1960s that the real spike came in high-rise, especially the taller blocks. Predictably, then, the new or newish low-rise estates still tended at the start of the decade to be the main focus of attention, as in a cluster of stories in the *Evening News* about London County Council's 'out-county' estates. At Borehamwood, the Rev. J. W. Larter claimed that young families were always 'looking back to London' instead of settling down, with too many parents 'guilty of putting personal pleasures above showing an interest in their children's hobbies'; at Sheerwater near Woking, the chairman of the Community Association complained that 'if the present apathy and lack of interest in our activities continues there is no point in continuing the association'; and at Belhus in Essex, a Hungarian refugee, Zoltan Glotter, who was an art teacher, likened the estate to 'the Wild West' and lamented how it was 'so segregated from culture'.[19]

A particularly authoritative – because from the inside – assessment of life on a mixed-development council estate came from J. L. Hayes, for nine years a tenant on the Churchill Gardens estate in Pimlico and now chairman of the fairly recently formed London Standing Conference of Housing Estate Community Groups. 'Very few housing managers, housing assistants, or even chairmen of housing committees are actually council tenants,' he pointedly observed at the outset in an address in January to the Society of Housing Managers. Arguing that 'it is basically a feeling of insecurity that wrecks the idea of community,' and adamant that 'the majority of council tenants are proud of their homes, feel fortunate, and are very grateful to have them,' he noted that the philanthropic days of Octavia Hill (a Victorian pioneer of social housing) had gone: 'Standards of living are higher, social aspirations are greater, and what is required today is good housing, with efficient and sympathetic management – not charity. The paternal approach is definitely out. The burning problem on many estates today is not to provide more wash-houses but to provide garages or car-parks.' Nothing, though, vexed Hayes more than what (according to him) were usually called 'Conditions of Occupation and General Rules for Housing Estates' – ie the tyrannical, often nit-picking lists of do's and don'ts. 'I often wonder just how many private tenants would stomach such a list of fifty to sixty regulations designed to cover every aspect of their home life,' he reflected. 'The council tenant, for example, agrees "not to keep any animal in the dwelling" or any bird "except as may be authorised in writing by the housing manager." "No singing, dancing or playing musical instruments is allowed after 11 pm," not even at Christmas, apparently!'

Of course, it all depended, and the variables were enormous – whether between person and person or between place and place. Nevertheless, there was a ring of authenticity about the findings of a study published in March on the early collective experience of the thousands of Londoners who in recent years had settled in Swindon's new housing estates:

> Many of them have lived in rooms in London and are longing for a home of their own. When they move into their new house the reaction is one of delight. They are building a nest, settling in.
>
> After the first few weeks have passed, the man finds he has to keep on overtime to cope with extra expenses, and his wife is left alone. The novelty begins to wear off and the wife feels lonely and a little homesick.
>
> Then she goes back and sees the place she has come from with new eyes. She sees the drab houses and the smoky street, and the reaction is, 'Oh, let me get back to my own home, quick.'

Certainly there were plenty of smoky streets on Liverpool's Everton Heights, where a local journalist, William Amos, listened in January to some of the women facing demolition of the houses that had been their homes for most of their lives:

> You can do and do and do, and it never gets clean. My sister's got a brand new house and she has half the work I've got in this place.
>
> The smog's terrible. You can't have the windows open – those, that is, that will open. Unless you have the back door open you don't get a breath of air in the house.
>
> Some walls are so damp you have to keep the wallpaper up with drawing pins.
>
> Four of my five married sons have modern homes. When I go to see them and then come back to this, I could scream.

'Each of the women I spoke to,' reckoned Amos, 'was looking forward to the move' – ie, out of the district, and 'their only regret was that they would lose their neighbours.'

Among the many thousands on the move were Tom Courtenay's parents, in December 1959 leaving their home in Harrow Street near the Fish Dock in Hull and going to what his mother Annie called a 'Corporation house', on the new Longhill estate on the city's outskirts, where the fresher air might improve her health. 'I went through the back door and into the kitchen,' recalled their son (poised for breakthrough as an actor) about going there for the first time on Christmas Eve. 'It was much bigger than its Harrow Street equivalent. Likewise the sitting room, which doubled as the front room. It had a small square hallway rather than a passage, and upstairs were three bedrooms and, glory of glories, a bathroom.' Even so:

> It wasn't so homely and it wasn't what Mother had been used to all her life. And two bus rides for Dad to get to work. He would sometimes come home at lunchtime in Harrow Street, but not any more. Nor Ann [Tom's sister]: Longhill was too far from her office in the city centre. Aunt Alice was there, true. But she was the only one. No kindly Mrs Hinchcliffe next door, or Annie Brooks' shop alongside us. No Mrs Hales' beer off shop for a natter. No Aunt Phyllis calling in for a sub till Friday, and no Grandma Quest to sit there and get on her nerves. Full though I was of my coming opportunity, I had the ominous feeling that she would be very lonely out at Longhill.

On Monday, 2 May, Tom spent the day with his mother: 'I tried to reassure her that they had been right to move, especially with summer coming. But I wasn't at all convinced. It just wasn't as homely as mucky, scruffy Harrow Street.' Next morning his eyes filled with tears as he left to get the bus to Paragon Station: 'She looked so lost and lonely waving from the front door of 20 Duddon Grove.'[20]

Saturday early evening was as usual *Dixon of Dock Green* time. 'Continues to be tremendously popular,' noted a BBC report on reaction to the episode on 27 February, the day after Princess Margaret's engagement. 'In fact, it might almost be said that *Dixon of Dock Green* is now an institution. Time and again viewers insisted that this was one programme they "*never* missed – for whatever reason."' Or, as an engineer put it, 'It's hard to think of old Dixon and company as actors now. They are all just perfect.' Distinctly imperfect in some viewers' eyes was *Living for Kicks*, an ITV documentary four days later investigating teenage life in London, Brighton and Northampton. 'The probe is gentle, sympathetic,' promised *TV Times*, but in the event the 'misrepresentation of modern youth' left three apprentices at Cranfield's College of Aeronautics unable to contain their indignation: 'We are fully aware that the sensation value of these programmes attracts a wide audience, but we feel moved to point out that there is also a considerable number of teenagers who possess a modicum of intelligence whose existence seems to be denied.' Jacqueline S. Wicks of Sevenoaks was similarly impelled to write to the magazine: 'I reassure those who are beginning to fear for the future of England that all over the country there are teenagers in thousands who, in spite of liking jazz, coffee-bars, and the society of the opposite sex, are both intelligent and well-mannered.' To which the editor appended a note that 'many other readers have written expressing similar views on this programme.'

Next morning, on Thursday, 3 March, a DC-7 on its way from Germany to New Jersey stopped briefly for refuelling at Prestwick Airport, and the 26-year-old Elvis Presley, about to be discharged from the US Army, set foot for probably the only time on British soil. *The Times* that day, attuned to the rather different preoccupations of its core readership, was in Trollopian mode. 'To be either Prime Minister of England or Chancellor of Oxford University is each sufficient for any one man without his being also the other,' it asserted on the first day of voting at Oxford in a head-to-head between Macmillan and the distinguished mandarin-*cum*-banker Sir Oliver Franks. Among those voting for the former was Isaiah Berlin, largely on the negative grounds that he considered Franks 'a planner, a puritan & over energetic'. With voting in abeyance on the Friday, the press looked elsewhere. 'There has been a revolution in the savings habits of Britain,' explained the *Daily Mirror* about its decision to launch a regular column on stocks and shares, adding that 'no longer is The City the exclusive domain of Big Money'; while at the strait-laced *FT*, a feature on the new oral contraceptive just announced by British Drug Houses led to agonised editorial discussion about what to call the piece, before eventually hitting upon 'Limiting the World's Population'. Saturday saw a second day of voting for the Oxford chancellorship, with in due course Haroldus Macmillanus declared the winner by 1,976 votes to Oliverus Frankus' 1,697. 'He got most of the *women* MAs & a lot of the Oxford dons,' reflected the victor that evening. 'But Trevor-Roper (Professor of Modern History) ran a brilliant campaign on my behalf, & lots of friends all over the country rallied to my support. It was quite a gamble for me. There was little to gain, & much to lose. But it came off.'[21]

Macmillan's day job, with the post-election honeymoon over, had its strains by that spring. 'Governor of Bank and Chancellor are suddenly very pessimistic about the future – inflation, too much imports, balance of payments difficulties, loss of gold and dollar reserves etc. etc. – the same old story,' he privately observed in late February. 'So they want violent disinflationary measures and a fierce Budget . . .' Over the next few weeks, he applied the full weight of his office and personality to ensure that his Chancellor, Derick Heathcoat Amory ('fundamentally, he lacks nerve'), presented an essentially neutral – as opposed to deflationary – Budget in early April. 'I have won this battle quite definitively,' recorded the expansion-minded PM on the 4th, hours after the dandyish Leo Abse had offended some fellow Welsh Labour MPs by attending his first Budget day in a grey top hat. Across the floor, a group of free-market, tax-cutting Tory MPs, headed by the almost equally flamboyant Gerald Nabarro, was even more dismayed. 'Whose side does he think he's on?' asked one after Amory had announced a higher profits tax and measures against dividend stripping, while the luxuriantly moustached Nabarro accused Amory of 'practising Socialism' and returning the country to 'the dreariest period of the post-war years characterised by Butskellism'. The Chancellor himself, unsurprisingly, soon cut an increasingly disenchanted figure. 'Nasty about the threatened resignation of Mr Amory!' noted Philip Larkin, in economics a man of the right, soon afterwards. 'But I fancy they have been getting at him to produce "popular" measures wch no doubt feeds him up.'

Notwithstanding growing consumer prosperity, the underlying relative health of economy was now an increasing cause of legitimate concern. 'In terms of economic expansion and production and so on,' declared Anthony Crosland on *Any Questions?* a few days after Amory's budget, in a vein that did not seem particularly outlandish to the Wiltshire audience in the village hall at Winsley, 'this country has recently been falling very badly behind, not merely Soviet Russia, which we're falling catastrophically behind, but also all the leading countries in Europe.' Ian Fleming's analysis of post-Suez decline was military and diplomatic rather than economic, but in one of the James Bond stories published later in April in *For Your Eyes Only* he had an American millionaire condescendingly describe England as a 'pleasant little country' (with 'old buildings and the Queen and so on') that had 'gone broke'. It was not difficult to find symbols of decline, but arguably the creaking railway system was as resonant as anything. 'The industry must be of a size and pattern suited to modern conditions and prospects,' Macmillan told the Commons in March, before Marples in early April announced the composition of an advisory body to examine its structure and finances. Two of the four chosen members were rising, middle-aged industrialists, Frank Kearton of Courtaulds and Dr Richard Beeching of ICI. 'I get "absolutely first-rate" from very reliable sources,' the Bank of England's Cameron (Kim) Cobbold subsequently reported on the latter to a Treasury mandarin. 'One of the few first-rate scientists who is also a first-rate administrator and business man: top-level quality.'[22]

Easter that year fell in mid-April – and the long weekend by now included a new ritual. 'Gathering strength all the way along its route through London,' reported the *Guardian* about the Easter Monday climax, 'the Aldermaston anti-nuclear march quickly developed into a column roughly six miles long and 40,000 strong':

> At three o'clock, after a stately progress up Whitehall, its only music the plod of this multitude of tired feet and the tattoo of a single drummer at the head, it began to overwhelm Trafalgar Square. A crowd of spectators – also estimated at 40,000 – awaited them in the square. At first it seemed there would be no room for the marchers, but, somehow, space was made as unit after unit, banners flying, came trooping up towards Nelson's Column.
>
> Within an hour the police had conceded that the Aldermaston pilgrims had staged the biggest demonstration ever held in Trafalgar Square . . . Supporters were jubilant and so were the many speakers from the plinth. One after another they stepped to the microphone to say, in so many words, 'Nobody can ignore us now.'

'Weirdies and beardies, colonels and conchies, Communists and Liberals, vegetarians and alcoholics, beauties and beasts' was Alan Brien's assessment of the heterogeneous composition of his fellow-marchers, while according to Sylvia Plath, proudly taking her recently born baby to watch the lengthy column enter Trafalgar Square, '40 per cent were London housewives.' 'The Aldermaston march,' already reckoned Anthony Wedgwood Benn on Easter Sunday, 'is a stupendous triumphant success and is getting massive and sympathetic publicity' – and to a large extent that indeed seems to have been the case. The *Daily Express*, though, declined to waver from outright hostility, with René MacColl depicting Trafalgar Square as full of 'the sort of hairy horrors who think it intellectual not to wash more than once every three weeks'. So too the crusty farmer-writer A. G. Street, still an *Any Questions?* fixture. 'I personally,' he informed a probably sympathetic audience the following Friday at the British Legion Hall in Middle Wallop, 'do not fear now annihilation, instant annihilation, half as much as I should fear to live the rest of my life under the rule of either the Communists or the Aldermaston Marchers.'[23]

Anti-apartheid was the other great cause in the air by spring 1960, but Larkin for one remained unmoved. 'Seven pounds ten if you don't mind,' he had written to Monica Jones in early February – the day after Macmillan's famous 'wind of change' speech in Cape Town had, among other things, unequivocally condemned apartheid – in the wake of applying for tickets for South Africa's Test at Lord's in June. 'Still,' he went on, 'we may not get the best seats, though we shall if people decide to boycott the tour!' March saw a month-long boycott (backed by the Labour Party, the TUC and Christian Action) of South African goods and produce, a boycott that, to the pleasure of Anthony Heap, was reported as a failure by the *Express* on the 14th. 'So much,' he observed, 'for the mischievous efforts of our nigger-supporting reds to undermine the white supremacy in South Africa.' Exactly a week later came the massacre at Sharpeville, leaving 67 dead, and soon afterwards Gallup found that, of countries from which the British people would prefer not to buy goods, South Africa ranked second only to Japan. How would this affect the impending South African cricket tour? 'Large numbers of British feel strongly that politics ought to be kept out of sport,' noted Mollie Panter-Downes on 12 April, a view not shared by the cricketing parson, the Rev David Sheppard, who about this time let it be known that he would refuse to play against the tourists so long as the colour bar operated in the selection of their team.

Among those who should on merit have arrived with the tourists on Easter Sunday was a 28-year-old 'Cape-coloured' cricketer, Basil D'Oliveira. Instead, the following Saturday, the 23rd, he made his first appearance on English soil for a Central Lancashire League club,

Middleton. The cricket writer and broadcaster John Arlott had played a key role in securing this berth for D'Oliveira as the club's new professional, and though he took a while to settle to English conditions, it was clear by the end of the summer that this was a gifted cricketer of high but hitherto thwarted potential. Arlott himself, Liberal in politics and liberal-minded in most aspects of life, pondered three days after D'Oliveira's debut on the rights and wrongs of the South African tour. 'Some of the many British people who have been roused to indignation by Sharpeville and all it represents are now – in the absence of anyone at hand more immediately culpable – prepared to make McGlew's cricketers the object and sounding board of their disapproval,' he reflected. 'It is to be hoped – but is by no means certain – that common sense will show the cricketers to be an inappropriate target.' Arlott added that 'if their tour were to collapse', then 'English cricket would find itself in a very awkward financial position.'[24]

'Another City Cinema Closing', announced the *Sheffield Telegraph* on 22 March, bringing the total there to 16 in the previous five years, while for one distinguished film director, Michael Powell, the spring was also more or less terminal. 'It's a long time since a film disgusted me as much as *Peeping Tom*,' declared Caroline Lejeune in the *Observer* about this study of a psychopathic photographer; 'stinks . . . muck . . . peculiarly nauseous . . . morbidity . . .' caught the tone of William Whitebait in the *New Statesman*; and in Bristol a young journalist, Tom Stoppard, writing in the *Evening World*, called it 'a loathsome, mawkish, barely excusable, out-and-out commercial and thoroughly sickening piece of horror for horror's sake', in short 'a nasty, unwholesome, catchpenny picture'. The distributors rapidly took fright, the film disappeared from sight, and Powell's reputation would take decades to recover. No such problems, though, for *Carry On Constable* – 'the successful mixture of rather blue jokes and not very subtle slapstick as before,' approvingly noted Heap – while on TV the great news was that, as one critic put it, 'Hancock is back and the streets lie deserted on Friday evenings.' Around this time, when the Labour politician Aneurin Bevan was reported as 'depressed and horrified' by the current low standard of TV programmes, he identified *Hancock's Half Hour* as almost the only exception.

The teenage pound, meanwhile, continued on the march. 'It is no secret,' wrote Katharine Whitehorn in April, 'that *Vogue*, by dropping to 2s 6d, coming out oftener and filling its pages with things like jazz, little-girl dresses and young male models, is aiming at the vast teenage spending potential for its advertising.' The same month saw the launch of *Honey*, with Jacqueline Aitken devoting an hour and a half to reading the first issue 'solidly'; and in Chingford, Judy Haines recorded Ione wearing 'Jeans' and Pamela a 'Top Ten sweater'. Number 1 in that Top Ten between late March and late April was Lonnie Donegan's 'My Old Man's a Dustman'. But the iconic moment occurred around midnight on Easter Saturday at Chippenham in Wiltshire, where a Ford Consul crashed, the American singer Eddie Cochran was killed, his fellow passenger Gene Vincent was seriously injured – and among the first to arrive on the scene was an 18-year-old police cadet, Dave 'Dee' Harman, who retrieved Cochran's guitar from the wreck and subsequently enjoyed 'a good strum' before returning it to the family.[25]

That spring one play sought to nail the zeitgeist by focusing on Coventry, boom city of the West Midlands. *Never Had It So Good*, by a young South African called John Wiles, opened at the Belgrade Theatre on 29 February and attracted national attention, with the *Daily Mail*'s reviewer recording how 'one long litany of protest sounds throughout the play – at false values bred by bursting wage packets, the creed of greed and "I'm all right, Jack", the scramble for bigger T.V. screens and glossier veneers, trade unions ("they are there to protect the worker from his own inefficiency"), failing churches, Coventry Corporation, and "the technicolour plastic boxes" of contemporary architecture with the emphasis on "temporary".' Local dignitaries were broadly unimpressed – 'a one-sided, cynical picture' (Bishop of Coventry); 'a very harsh caricature' (Councillor H. Richards); 'very exaggerated' (Alderman Mrs P. M. Hyde) – while the *Coventry Evening Telegraph* called it 'not a portrait of Coventry', but instead 'a collection of unflattering glimpses of some of us who live in Coventry, as seen by a visitor'. The following week, *Panorama* featured an item on the controversy surrounding the play, including some Coventrian vox pop from shoppers in the Precinct, a place that, according to the reporter, Ludovic Kennedy, was 'dedicated to household gods':

> I'm having a marvellous time. I like to buy clothes and go a lot to the pictures. (*Young married woman*)
>
> It has changed for the better. You have to move with the times. (*Older woman*)
>
> Yes, I've never had it so good. I spend money on everything I want. You can't spend the money when you are dead. (*Married woman*)

'The people of the city are largely indifferent to their critics,' summed up Kennedy. 'They can afford to be. They have never had it so good and they mean to have it better.'

Two rather more distinguished playwrights were experiencing contrasting fortunes. 'A work of far less clarity and dramatic energy than its two predecessors' was the verdict of *The Times* on Arnold Wesker's *I'm Talking About Jerusalem*, the last of his trilogy, after the first performance at Coventry in early April. A local paper agreed, calling it 'on the whole an anti-climax', being 'long and too drawn-out'. But for Harold Pinter, these were life-changing times. On Tuesday, 22 March, an ITV production of his once-scorned *The Birthday Party* attracted 11 million viewers, a figure no doubt helped by the fact that the counter-attraction on BBC was a performance of Mendelssohn's Violin Concerto in E Minor. Indeed, most of the letters subsequently published in *TV Times* were negative, as with Miss M. Taylor of Middle Lane, N8: 'The only reason I suffered until the end was in the hope that I might get some explanation. But, alas, no!' Then, a month later, on 24 April and again on ITV, almost immediately following *Sunday Night at the London Palladium*, Pinter's relatively realistic, conventional play *A Night Out* was showcased by *Armchair Theatre*, where it usefully clashed with the arts programme *Monitor*, preceded the western *Cheyenne* and attracted 14 million viewers. But Pinter's real breakthrough came three days later on the 27th, with the first night at the Arts Theatre of *The Caretaker*, starring Donald Pleasence as the tramp. Tumultuous cheers and 12 curtain calls preceded a round of mainly enthusiastic reviews, typified by Cuthbert Worsley's assertion in the *FT* that the play was not only 'immensely funny' and 'rich in observation', but 'below that level a disturbing and moving experience'. Al Alvarez in the *New Statesman* declined to join the chorus – 'it is bitty, haphazard, too long by about a third' – but Noël Coward went along on about the third night and, despite himself, was gripped ('squalor, repetition, lack of action, etc – but somehow it seizes hold of you'). Within a few weeks *The Caretaker* had transferred triumphantly to the Duchess in the West End. Although Anthony Heap was an unforgiving first-nighter there ('oh what a depressingly melancholy evening à la Godot it all amounts to'), a more typical reaction was probably that of the young Richard Eyre. 'It was the first really modern play that I'd seen in a theatre,' he recalled, 'and it seemed to me that the author had a way of looking at the world that was completely singular . . . partly that it was about working-class people, partly that the play didn't seek to explain itself . . . It was as original and striking as when I first saw a Francis Bacon.'[26]

On Saturday, 30 April, three days after the unveiling of Pinter's meditation on power, Yorkshire's season began at Lord's, with that proud county playing for the first time in the twentieth century under a professional captain, Vic Wilson. On the same day down at Arundel, the Duke of Norfolk's XI had to make do without their usual captain, David Sheppard, and lost to the South Africans by five wickets, while up at Deepdale the much-loved, ultimate one-club footballer, Tom Finney, made his final league appearance for Preston North End, at home to Luton Town. 'The band played "Keep Right On to the End of the Road," followed by "For He's a Jolly Good Fellow," in which the crowd joined,' reported the *Lancashire Evening Post* about the moving pre-match scene. 'After a pause for cheering to subside, this unique ceremony concluded with "Auld Lang Syne," in the singing of which match officials and the players of both sides joined hands in the traditional fashion, to the accompaniment of continued applause.' At nearby Burnley there was little room for sentiment, as that unfashionable club moved within reach of the league championship title – eventually attained on Monday, 2 May with a 2–1 win at Manchester City. Harry Potts was Burnley's understated manager, the beating heart of the team was the staunchly loyal hometown wing-half Brian Miller, and the unexpected outcome was a direct reflection of how the maximum wage of £20 a week continued to make the top division a not wholly unlevel playing field. The following evening, the still badly injured Gene Vincent reluctantly dragged himself on stage at Liverpool Stadium, top of a bill that also included Gerry and the Pacemakers (already singing 'You'll Never Walk Alone') and other Merseyside acts – but not the Beatals, as the former Quarry Men were now briefly known, John Lennon instead being photographed watching proceedings with, in his biographer's words, 'envy and longing in his eyes'. Next day, Wednesday the 4th, Larkin informed Monica Jones that he had given his niece 'My Old Man's a Dustman', adding that he hoped it was driving her parents 'insane, in their house they built to be so U in'; while 6.30 in the north-east saw the Tyne Tees TV debut of *Young at Heart*, billed as 'a teenage programme with Mum-and-Dad appeal'. The studio was set up to resemble a coffee bar, the guest artiste recorded a song live on a disc-cutting machine that became a competition prize, the compère was Jimmy Savile (each week his hair a different colour), and, in one of the turning-points of history that failed to turn, he very nearly got the sack for continually saying, 'How's about that, then?'[27]

This was also the week of Princess Margaret's wedding, with every serviceman having sixpence docked from his pay to contribute to a present (a marble-topped commode). The major hiccup between engagement and nuptials concerned the best man. Jeremy Fry of the chocolate family was originally chosen, before in early April he (as Mollie Panter-Downes nicely put it) 'cancelled for the highly unusual reason, as reported in the press, that he expected to be ill between now and May', reference being made to recurrent attacks of jaundice. The real backstory was that the press had become aware that, eight years earlier, Fry had been fined £2 for homosexual importuning, and it seemed too risky. The youngish Liberal politician Jeremy Thorpe was briefly in the frame as Fry's replacement, but in the end Armstrong-Jones settled on the impeccably heterosexual Roger Gilliatt, son of the Queen's gynaecologist and himself a consultant neurologist. Anticipation was rising by the start of May – and on Monday the 2nd, Kingsley Amis let himself go. 'Such a symbol of the age we live in,' he wrote to American friends, 'when a royal princess, famed for her devotion to all that is most vapid and mindless in the world of entertainment, her habit of reminding people of her status whenever they venture to disagree with her in conversation, and her appalling taste in clothes, is united with a dog-faced tight-jeaned fotog of fruitarian tastes such as can be found in dozens in any pseudo-arty drinking cellar in fashionable-unfashionable London. They're made for each other.' Two days later the Queen gave a huge ball for the couple at Buckingham Palace. Joe Loss and his band played tunes from *Fings Ain't Wot They Used T'Be*, but the evening ended unhappily when the Duchess of Buccleuch discovered she had lost a £2,700 brooch, inevitably with some of the photographer's loucher friends high on the list of suspects. Noël Coward, who was among those attending, found Armstrong-Jones 'a charmer . . . easy and unflurried and a sweet smile'.[28]

Friday, 6 May was a working day, but in glorious sunshine the streets of London were crowded, while across the country 54 per cent of the population aged five or over (schoolchildren had the day off) saw the wedding on BBC television. 'For one moment,' ran a typical part of Richard Dimbleby's commentary, 'we see the bride now as she looks about her at the Abbey in this lovely gown of white silk organza, with the glittering diadem on her head, the orchids in her hand, and the comforting, tall, friendly, alert figure of the Duke of Edinburgh on whose right arm she can rely . . .' Guests at the Abbey included Winston Churchill, John Betjeman and Antonia Fraser (wearing a white shepherdess's bonnet), while among diarists watching were Judy Haines ('Queen looked heavy, almost scowling'), a Derbyshire schoolteacher called May Marlor ('Queen looks a bit down in the dumps'), Madge Martin ('Princess Margaret looked enchanting') and Nella Last ('our first experience of seeing a "big" event on Television, & memory will never fade', but disappointed by 'the bridegroom's *awful* pants, like a pair of compressed flannel, emphasised by his queer "knock kneed" stance'). Another diarist, Florence Turtle, was appalled by the thought that Margaret's new father-in-law had 'two ex-wives & is now married to an Air Hostess! half his age!' Macmillan was altogether more relaxed, taking pleasure in 'the slightly "raffish" element' present at the ceremony. Later in the day, the couple inched their way through a packed City of London, en route to Tower Pier, the Royal Yacht and a Caribbean honeymoon:

> For all but the newly married it was fiesta gaiety [wrote Patrick Keatley in the *Guardian*], a marvellous change from the grinding sameness of a

> working day in the City. High overhead, while Princess Margaret fought back tears and exhaustion and managed a brave smile, a fur broker leaned out of his suite of third-floor offices, telephone in hand, gaily describing the scene of heat and paralysis below. A trunk call to New York (perhaps) or Leningrad? A thrill for those at the other end to hear the roar of the London crowds? This was glamour, perhaps, on the international scale, but for one small Englishwoman down below in Cannon Street it was sheer, plain agony.

'Yet,' concluded Keatley, 'the Princess fastened on still another brave Bowes-Lyon smile and saw it through to the end. Her mother would have been proud of her.'

In Barrow that evening, Nella Last 'made supper while my husband watched *The Army Game*. It makes him laugh & I appreciate it for that – but not to the extent of watching it.' If the reception had been better, they probably would have been watching the BBC, where Tony Hancock and Sid James made one last appearance together in what was the final *Hancock's Half Hour*, the end of Railway Cuttings – a decision to call time on their partnership (after 12 series on radio and television) that was entirely of Hancock's volition. The episode was 'The Poison Pen Letters', with Tony found to have been writing hate mail to himself in his sleep. 'You see, boy, you've been over-working,' kindly explains Sid. 'You're all strung up. Your nerves are like violin strings, and secretly, underneath it all, you don't like the life you've been living, so your subconscious mind has revolted. I mean, you're like everybody else, really. *You* don't like you either . . . all you need is a bit of rest, a long break.'[29]

3

To the Rear of the Column

'Never before has a party won three elections in succession with an increased majority each time,' reflected a triumphant Conservative supporter, Anthony Heap, on 9 October 1959, the day after polling. One predictable consequence was Labour's most profound existential crisis since the harrowing experience of 1931.[1] 'Hugh Cudlipp's *Daily Mirror* in the 1940s and 1950s was the voice of postwar popular socialism, of the factory workers in the factory age,' William Rees-Mogg would accurately recall; but that age now seemed to be passing. Within days of the election, the *Mirror* not only ruthlessly dropped both its celebrated masthead 'Forward With The People' and its even more celebrated strip-cartoon heroine Jane (indelibly associated with wartime solidarity) but it pointed the way to a different sort of future by starting a regular 'petticoat page' and explicitly putting the emphasis on 'youth', 'fun', 'gaiety' and 'finding the girl with the smartest autumn sparkle'. Politics were temporarily off the agenda, the Labour frontbencher Richard Crossman lost his column, and the *Observer* commented sourly that the tabloid's new slogan should be 'Forward With The Shareholders'.[2]

Within the Labour Party itself, the revisionist wing – whose key text was Anthony Crosland's *The Future of Socialism* (1956) – moved rapidly into action. 'Douglas Jay started off with a great oration on the moral of the election defeat,' noted the veteran Hugh Dalton about a gathering on the 11th at the Hampstead home (18 Frognal Gardens) of the Labour leader, Hugh Gaitskell. 'He wanted (1) to drop "nationalisation", (2) drop the trade unions, (3) drop the name "Labour Party" . . . Otherwise, he said, we should never win.' Others were 'more cautious', and Gaitskell himself 'said little', but later that day he repeated several times to Anthony Wedgwood Benn (then a fairly centrist figure in the party), 'I'm not prepared to lose another Election for the sake of nationalisation.' The next evening, one of Gaitskell's key allies, Roy Jenkins, warned on *Panorama* about the dangers of advocating further nationalisation, before dropping in on Benn on the way home. 'We had a flaming row,' recorded his host. 'As a matter of fact I was very calm and collected and he got into a semi-hysterical state. Usually it's the other way round. "We must use this shock to drop nationalisation entirely at this forthcoming Conference" he said, and I concentrated on the dangers to our integrity if we were to be so reckless.'

The post-election conference was in the event to be held at Blackpool during the last weekend of November, and – among those who cared about these matters – passions ran high during the weeks leading up to it, especially after Jay published an article insisting that Labour was condemned to further defeats unless it adopted a more socially up-market image and scaled back its commitment to public ownership. 'They got so heated that they yelled (and booed) at each other,' noted the 'Bloomsbury' diarist Frances Partridge in early November about two friends, both of them left-leaning public intellectuals. 'Philip [Toynbee] thought that if one believed one's principles were right one shouldn't scrap them just because of failure, but consider how to persuade one's adversary more forcefully; Robert [Kee] that we must beat the Conservatives, and use any means to that end.' 'The Labour Party,' reckoned the almost invariably shrewd Mollie Panter-Downes soon afterwards, 'has arrived at a critical moment of truth and choice, in which the arguing protagonists are its middle-class intellectuals – the clever chaps, the dons and journalists and economists of the Gaitskell stamp, who think they know what is wrong with the movement and often burst into print to say so – and the old trade union Party faithful, who act like pious widows reluctant to change a thing in the house that has been set up by some revered departed hand.'[3]

By this time it was clear that the crux of the argument concerned nationalisation – specifically, whether the leadership would dare to attempt to scrap or revise the commitment, as embodied in Clause 4 of the party's constitution, to achieving 'the common ownership of the means of production, distribution and exchange'. That cause had of course been significantly advanced by Clement Attlee's 1945–51 government, when the electricity, gas, coal and railway industries had all been nationalised, as had the steel industry before being denationalised in 1953 by the Conservative government. Even on the left, it was by the mid-to-late 1950s no longer a policy, or indeed a subject, that aroused huge enthusiasm. 'Of course we had to wait 3 days for the Elect. Board! Nationalisation!!!,' the moderate-minded writer Sid Chaplin, who himself worked for the National Coal Board, told a friend after moving house in 1957. That same year, from the other end of the left spectrum, the South Wales miners' leader Will Paynter declared that a decade of public ownership had 'shattered' the idea that nationalisation was 'a half-way step to socialism and an ally in the struggle to end private enterprise', given that in practice there had been only marginal improvement in wages and conditions, that the same people remained in charge, and that 'the relationship of master and servant still operates'. Those and other criticisms of the nationalised industries were cogently made, from a left-wing perspective, by the ambitious trade unionist Clive Jenkins in his book *Power at the Top*, published shortly before the 1959 election. 'Let's face it, comrades, nationalisation is a boring subject,' began the review by the socialist, definitely non-revisionist, intellectual Ralph Miliband, who fully conceded the difficulty of making the nationalised industries 'islands of socialist virtues' in 'a sea of capitalist impulses'. 'Ultimately,' he went on, 'there is only one way of giving the public corporations a different character, and that is by an extension of nationalisation to the point where the public sector [currently some 20 per cent of the economy] is overwhelmingly more important and powerful than the private one. Even then, a socialised base will not amount to socialism, or resolve all the problems attendant upon a socialist organisation of industry. But it will constitute the essential beginning, for this, and for much else. Without it, any talk of socialism must remain a poor joke.'

The whole question played a significant part in the election itself, not least through the much-publicised results of a survey – mainly funded by steel companies, anxious about Labour's renationalisation pledge – revealing 63 per cent of people 'favouring no more nationalisation' and only 18 per cent favouring more. 'As for public ownership, it has certainly proved a liability in the election,' admitted the strongly pro-nationalisation Barbara Castle in the immediate wake. 'So conditioned has the public mind become as a result of the Tory advertising campaign, that even the announcement right in the middle of the election campaign that the nationalised electricity industry had made a profit of £27 million last year made not the slightest impact on the general belief that all nationalised industries are losing money.' Soon afterwards, the replies to questionnaires sent to 600 Labour candidates and organisers confirmed that nationalisation had been the single most damaging issue. What, then, would Gaitskell say at Blackpool? 'Hugh feels that Nationalisation was a vote loser at the Polls,' noted the most prominent trade unionist of the day, the left-wing Frank Cousins of the Transport and General Workers' Union, after a pre-conference dinner at the Euston Hotel attended by several union leaders as well as Gaitskell and his famous deputy. 'Nye [Bevan] thinks it was a vote winner when tackled boldly.'[4]

The weather at Blackpool was suitably miserable for a fractious weekend by the sea. 'We regard public ownership,' Gaitskell told the conference on Saturday afternoon, 'not as an end in itself but as a means – and not necessarily the only or the most important one – to certain ends, such as full employment, greater equality and higher productivity. We do not aim to nationalise every private firm or to create an endless series of state monopolies.' The problem, he went on, was that the continued existence of Clause 4 laid Labour open to damaging misrepresentation: 'It implies that we propose to nationalise everything, but do we? Everything? – the whole of light industry, the whole of agriculture, all the shops – every little pub and garage? Of course not. We have long ago come to accept a mixed economy . . . Had we not better say so?' At this point there were hostile interruptions, and when Gaitskell's speech ended a few minutes later, one observer was struck by 'the thinness of the applause'. 'A ghastly failure,' reckoned Benn, who thought it had been too negative and added that 'he is quite incapable of inspiring people.'

There followed soon afterwards (in the words of the watching Bernard Levin) a 'violent attack on the leadership' by Michael Foot, showing 'nothing but contempt and hatred for those who would bring the Labour Party up to date, and a fine, mad arrogance for those who abated a jot of the ancient faith'. This produced 'hysterical cheers', and over the rest of the weekend most other speeches were highly critical of any attempt to revise or scrap Clause 4. Among those relatively few who made 'sensible and moderate speeches', Levin identified such rising figures as Denis Healey, Merlyn Rees, Dick Taverne and Shirley Williams, the last 'one of the brightest of all the bright hopes'. Given the scale of dissent from his initiative just weeks after a crushing election defeat, was Gaitskell's very leadership threatened? Much would depend on Bevan, who in what proved to be his final major speech disappointed some by going out of his way on Sunday afternoon to be a unifying figure and seeking to square the circle. On the one hand, he insisted on 'a planned economy' and described 'the so-called affluent society' as 'an ugly society' in which 'priorities have gone all wrong'; on the other, he explicitly accepted Gaitskell's argument that public ownership should not 'reach down into every piece of economic activity', because, as Bevan put it, 'that would be asking for a monolithic society'. 'In manner,' appraised Levin, 'one of the most splendid orations I have ever heard, and in matter a pitiful succession of threadbare attitudes and windy platitudes.' It only remained for the *Spectator*'s political correspondent to catch the train back to London. This took seven hours and twenty minutes to travel 226½ miles; much of the way 'seemed to be calling regularly, every hour on the hour, at Sheffield'. Finally, at journey's end, 'a trainload of tired, sick, filthy, bruised, late travellers were formed up on arrival at Marylebone into a huge, heaving mob and forced in single file through a narrow gate so that their tickets could be examined again.' Obviously, Levin reflected, the nationalised British Railways had been bribed by Gaitskell.[5]

Foot was unamused. 'Like it or not, one of the most spectacular events of our age is the comparative success of the Communist economic systems,' he wrote in Levin's magazine in early 1960. 'Khrushchev,' he went on,

> tells the Russians quite as plainly as Macmillan tells the English, that they never had it so good. Considering the tumultuous forty years through which the Russians have lived, the achievement by any reckoning is stupendous. Or does the *Spectator* dissent from that judgement? And

> does the *Spectator* really ask us to suppose that public ownership and the allocation of resources it makes possible are irrelevant to those achievements? Do not tell us, please, as the clinching, specious argument in reply to the challenge of nationalised sputniks and the Soviet industrial revolution, that British Railways do not always run on time or that they sometimes serve cold soup in the dining cars.

For the anti-revisionists – call them the fundamentalists – the apparent Soviet success story was the trump card in the rhetorical battle for the retention of Clause 4. 'In terms of military power, of industrial development, of technological advance, of mass literacy and, eventually, of mass consumption too, the planned Socialist economy, as exemplified in the Communist States, is proving its capacity to outpace and overtake the wealthy and comfortable Western economies,' declared Richard Crossman that spring in a Fabian pamphlet on *Labour in the Affluent Society*. He concluded (with truly Wykehamist confidence): 'We can predict with mathematical certainty that, as long as the public sector of industry remains the minority sector throughout the Western world, we are bound to be defeated in every kind of peaceful competition which we undertake with the Russians and the Eastern bloc.'

Among others in the fundamentalist camp was the *New Statesman*, which now had firmly in its sights the Labour MP whom it called 'the cup-bearer of the revisionist draught'. 'Though he has a general sympathy for equality,' noted its profile of the 42-year-old (and undeniably arrogant) Anthony Crosland, 'it rarely leads him to the tea-room of the House of Commons and the company of its trade union members . . . He specialises in insolence with a smile – a special charm in an only son which tends, however, to wear a little thin when the chin thickens.' Crosland himself had just sought to explain, in a lengthy *Encounter* article on 'The Future of the Left', that Gaitskell's Blackpool speech had essentially been about the pursuit of clarity, to end the 'series of very confused noises' that had bedevilled Labour through the 1950s. 'The leadership, both Left and Right, tended to speak with two voices – one for the electors and another for the Party militants,' he explained. 'The Left-wing leaders, especially, were schizophrenic on the subject of nationalisation; intellectually they accepted a mixed economy, emotionally they still clung to the dogma of wholesale public ownership.'

Damagingly, therefore, 'the extremist phraseology of the Party's formal aims bore no relation to the moderate, practical content of its short-term programme.' Ultimately, reckoned this champion of Keynesian managed capitalism with a liberal-*cum*-egalitarian twist, the great problem was psychological. 'Revisionism destroys the simplicity, the certainty, and the unquestioning conviction that come from having clear-cut crusading objectives to fight for,' Crosland reflected (condescendingly or sympathetically according to taste). 'It makes everything complicated and ambiguous; it is an explicit admission that many of the old dreams are either realised or dead. No wonder it is resented – especially in the moment of defeat.'[6]

The revisionists never stood a chance, especially once the trade union leaders – even the right-wing ones who usually supported Gaitskell – made a dead set against any attempt to tamper with Clause 4. The whole issue was, the *New Statesman* jubilantly proclaimed in March after a key meeting of Labour's National Executive Committee, 'now water under the bridge'. Three months later, after another party meeting, Benn noted how 'the trade unionists' were 'strongly critical of Gaitskell and particularly attacked his assault on Clause 4 and "his little coterie of friends"'. None more critical than Cousins, in whose private view the revisionists were 'reformists with a main purpose to secure political power for themselves, quite satisfied to maintain the existing structure of society with kindly alterations'. The foot soldiers seemingly agreed. On the day in early July that Bevan died of cancer, the National Union of Mineworkers agreed at their annual conference that there should be no modifying of Clause 4, let alone jettisoning of it, which out of the six major unions made it the fifth to adopt that adamantine stance. The trade union movement as a whole was by this time beginning its long march leftwards. Ralph Miliband observed with satisfaction, in his scathing indictment of *Parliamentary Socialism* (published in 1961 but written in 1960), that a Labour leadership 'whose purpose it is to reduce the Party's commitment to socialist policies' could 'no longer rely on the trade unions to help it in achieving its aims'.

The role of sentiment had been, as Crosland identified, undoubtedly crucial to the outcome. 'The present constitution and statement of objects, adopted so long ago [1918], has a place in our hearts and in our traditions that makes it quite impossible to delete or rewrite it,' George

Brown, a leading member of the Gaitskellite wing, told a meeting in his Belper constituency. There was also the question of Gaitskell's tactical wisdom in deciding at Blackpool to make so much of the Clause 4 issue. It would, Crosland had already told him, 'start a battle in the Party that will cause far more trouble than the thing is worth'. As post-Blackpool played out, the revisionists, as a result of these reservations, arguably lacked a certain collective fire in their bellies. The class element was a further negative aspect, with the gulf now painfully visible between the habits of mind and lifestyles of the Hampstead (or Frognal) set of intellectuals around Gaitskell on the one hand and the trade unionist backbone of the Labour movement on the other. Even trade unionists on Labour's right, including many members of the Parliamentary Labour Party, 'remained attached', to quote the labour historian David Howell, 'to the view that the party was fundamentally, if cautiously, committed to the ending of capitalism'. Or, as Cousins succinctly put it from Labour's left, 'We can have nationalisation without socialism – we cannot have socialism without nationalisation.' The most celebrated verdict on the episode came from the non-revisionist, broadly Bevanite Shadow Chancellor, Harold Wilson. 'We were being asked,' he told an interviewer a few years later, 'to take Genesis out of the Bible. You don't have to be a fundamentalist to say that Genesis is part of the Bible.' At the time, though, Wilson did have a typically astute view about how Gaitskell should have gone about the job of selling abolition of Clause 4 to an essentially tribalist party if as leader he really felt there was no alternative but to try. 'Comrades, in our deliberations on what this great party of ours must do next, let us never forget one undeniable fact: the Tories are a bunch of bastards,' began Wilson's mock speech (as delivered over dinner at the Athenaeum to a trio of *Guardian* journalists including John Cole). 'But as we consider the future of public ownership, let us not leave ourselves open to the slanders and lies our opponents will throw at us. For never forget, comrades, that the Tories are a bunch of bastards. But do we really want the state to take over every corner sweet-shop or petrol station? Of course we don't, but that's what the Tories will say about us, because the Tories are a bunch of bastards . . .'[7]

Yet that, of course, was hardly Gaitskell's style, and Labour by the second half of 1960 still remained 'spiritually enfeebled because of its continued refusal to resolve the issue once and for all', in the despairing words (the previous autumn) of the gifted left-of-centre economic commentator Andrew Shonfield. 'Until capitalism is explicitly accepted by the Labour Party as a permanent, proper, and indeed superior form of organisation for the overwhelming bulk of industry,' he had added, 'it will be hard to remove the doctrinal confusion which at present impoverishes the thinking of the British Left.' Yet during that very autumn of 1959, not only was an election resoundingly lost by the Labour Party, but a month later in West Germany, its counterpart, the Social Democrats, agreed at Bad Godesberg, following a run of election defeats, a Basic Programme that, as an understandably envious Crosland put it soon afterwards, 'accepts categorically the doctrine of the diminished importance of ownership' – in effect turning the SDP into a modern social democratic party, by the mid-1960s under the leadership of Willy Brandt. Elsewhere, the Dutch Labour Party, the Swedish Social Democratic Party and the Swiss Social Democratic Party were all by 1960 moving to an explicitly pragmatic, mixed-economy position over the issue of public ownership. 'No doubt it is usually pointless to urge the example of continental Europe on the insular British,' reflected Crosland in *Encounter* that spring. 'But at least to the internationalists on the British Left, the example may bring some comfort.' Was the Labour Party even trying to march in step with the others? Crosland diplomatically claimed it was, but, as he conceded with some understatement, it was doing so 'a bit to the rear of the column'.[8]

Labour's Clause 4 debate coincided with the launch of the *New Left Review*. The term 'New Left' seems to have become current in 1959, three years after the defining event of the Soviet invasion of Hungary. Shortly before Christmas, the new magazine – an amalgam of the *New Reasoner* and the *Universities and Left Review* – was launched on a chilly Monday evening at St Pancras Town Hall. 'Not everyone was young, amongst the 700 or so present at this public meeting,' noted W. John Morgan. 'Lawrence Daly, a Fife miner, made a very moving speech; Mrs Jeger [the left-wing Labour MP Lena Jeger] spoke very pertinently; Raymond Williams and Stuart Hall said the kind of things, sensible, imaginative and modest, which suggest that the enterprise may well succeed.' The 27-year-old Hall, who had come from Jamaica earlier in the decade and been one of the *ULR*'s founding editors, would be the *NLR*'s first editor. In a 'soft, compelling voice' he emphasised his hope that the *NLR* would help to break down the wariness between intellectual and industrial workers. The meeting lasted from 8.00 p.m. to 10.40 p.m., at which point many adjourned to The Partisan, the New Left's Soho coffee house, where Morgan observed 'grave faces considering grave events and the problems of post-capitalist society'.

'The humanist strengths of socialism – which are the foundations of a genuinely popular socialist movement – must be developed in cultural and social terms, as well as in economic and political,' insisted the editorial in issue number 1, dated January–February 1960. 'The task of socialism is to meet people where they *are*, where they are touched, bitten, moved, frustrated, nauseated – to develop discontent and, at the same time, to give the socialist movement some direct sense of the times and ways in which we live.' The bimonthly's first issue (circulation around 9,000) included Ralph Miliband on 'The Sickness of Labourism', concluding that it 'has now all but spent itself', but that 'the battle for socialism has barely begun'; a study of the working-class Tory voter by Ralph (later Raphael) Samuel, based on preliminary surveys in Clapham and Stevenage; an 'open letter to the British Comrades of the New Left, Victory for Socialism, Tribune etc' by the young London-based American writer Clancy Sigal, claiming that 'the launching of a genuine Youth and Student movement in Britain, owing allegiance to a socialist picture of life, can ensure not only the substance of the Labour Party but may provide a truly important touchstone for the whole country'; and 'Something Rotten in Denmark Street' by Brian Groombridge and Paddy Whannel, who, while trying to avoid 'the tyrannical asceticism' of the Communist states ('we read that keeping it groovy with Elvis Presley is an indictable offence in East Germany'), nevertheless argued that heavily commercialised pop music was offering up 'a surfeit of mediocrity' and that 'the teenage culture does not only consist of coffee bars and juke boxes.' The early issues were inevitably of mixed quality, but to an impressive degree the *NLR* at this stage fulfilled its original prospectus, with one youthful reader, Fred Inglis, warmly recalling two decades later 'the tabloid format, the grainy social realist photography, the instantly intelligent commentary on the world of the times' – in short, a seductive mixture of 'pace and immediacy' and 'large-hearted left eclecticism'. Not every item, admittedly, was large-hearted. The May–June issue featured a review by Colin Falck of Dennis Potter's hot-tempered tract *The Glittering Coffin*; Falck, clearly irked by the assumption in earlier, more mainstream reviews that 'here at last is the authentic voice of the New Left', did not refrain from putting the boot in. Potter's 'too liberal recourse to second-hand vision' meant that his rhetoric began 'to wear thin'; he had 'never really focussed and reflected for himself' on the problems of 'working-class culture and the new affluent society'; and, perhaps most damningly, 'the contradiction between his strictures on Labour politicians and his professed ambition to become one himself remains unresolved.'[9]

The dominant figure in the New Left of the late 1950s and early 1960s was the historian Edward (E. P.) Thompson – handsome, charismatic, difficult and, from his Halifax fastness, inherently suspicious of metropolitan modishness. The New Left's first book, *Out of Apathy*, was published in spring 1960, and although it included pieces by Samuel on '"Bastard" Capitalism', by Hall on 'The Supply of Demand' ('Has the Labour Movement come through the fire and brimstone of the last fifty years to lie down and die before the glossy magazines?') and by Alasdair MacIntyre on 'Breaking the Chains of Reason' (calling on philosophers to make 'a decisive break with utilitarianism'), the leading voice was Thompson's. 'How much longer,' he asked in his introduction 'At the Point of Decay', 'can the Labour Movement hold on to its defensive positions and still maintain morale? Is the aim of socialism to recede forever in the trivia of circumstances? Are we to remain forever as exploited, acquisitive men? It is because the majority of Labour politicians have ceased to hold any real belief in an alternative to capitalism that their kind of politics has become irrelevant.' A second essay, 'Outside the Whale', in large part a meditation on W. H. Auden and George Orwell, put the question, 'Can a new generation, East and West, break simultaneously with the pessimism of the old world and the authoritarianism of the new, and knit together human consciousness into a single socialist humanism?' A third piece, 'Revolution', ended the book and saw Thompson laying into Crosland's recent *Encounter* article on 'The Future of the Left'. He accused him and Gaitskell of bowing down before 'the permanent Cold War', and condemned both 'the permanent dependence of Labour upon "affluent" capitalism' and 'the permanent defensive ideology of defeatism and piecemeal reform'.

The essay's last section addressed the question of revolution itself. There, Thompson rejected the two usual models – on the one hand, 'the evolutionary model' of 'gradual piecemeal reform in an institutional continuum', and on the other, 'the cataclysmic model' with its 'aroma of barricades and naval mutinies in an age of flamethrowers' – before offering a third way. Essentially, this was non-violent and extra-parliamentary, involving in effect a rainbow coalition. 'Alongside the industrial workers, we should see the teachers who want better schools, scientists who wish to advance research, welfare workers who want hospitals, actors who want a National Theatre, technicians impatient to improve industrial organisation.' Together, deploying 'constructive skills within a conscious revolutionary strategy' and asserting 'the values of the common good', they would build 'the socialist community' and thereby progressively undermine capitalism's stranglehold. Finally, after noting how 'it is the greatest illusion of the ideology of apathy that politicians make events' ('Did *Lord Attlee* really free India? Did *Lord Morrison of Lambeth* wrest the pits from the coal owners?'), he ended with a passage about 'the long and tenacious revolutionary tradition of the British commoner' that was distilled essence of Thompson:

> It is a dogged, good-humoured, responsible, tradition: yet a revolutionary tradition all the same. From the Leveller corporals ridden down by Cromwell's men at Burford to the weavers massed behind their banners at Peterloo, the struggle for democratic and for social rights has always been intertwined. From the Chartist camp meeting to the dockers' picket line it has expressed itself most naturally in the language of moral revolt. Its weaknesses, its carelessness of theory, we know too well; its strengths, its resilience and steady humanity, we too easily forget.

'It is a tradition,' in short, 'which could leaven the socialist world.'

Reactions were mixed. David Caute in the *New Statesman* praised the collection's 'verve and confidence', but doubted whether 'the hope that the patient educational activity of left clubs and trade union groups will bring the people to socialist maturity' truly comprehended 'the lessons of twentieth-century history'; A. J. Ayer in the *Spectator* described as 'exaggerated' the authors' picture of a society 'dominated by a business outlook and by business values', found their solutions 'disappointingly vague', and concluded that 'moral indignation is not enough'. The *TLS* (which had given Thompson such a hard time over his Marxist biography of William Morris five years earlier) was surprisingly sympathetic in tone, but ultimately unconvinced:

> How can we know that a community of equals, rather than a world of I'm-all-right-Jacks and kept-up-with-Joneses, is what the average free man would choose? May he not prefer material goods to hospitals, lavish Hollywood epics to documentaries, television commercials to Shakespeare? And how much difference would more education and more communication make? It is quite possible that, if the capitalist system did not exist, the vast majority of people would want to invent it. At any rate, it is hardly possible to assume the opposite . . .
>
> The New Left put their faith in the community and the mutual interests it contains, demanding a standard of clear thinking and unselfishness that the ordinary man cannot bear. They overrate people in their social behaviour. And in doing so they run the risk of overrating themselves, both by demanding so high a standard of idealism that they reject even the most satisfactory compromise, and by imagining that their own recipe for the future is the only right one.

The most hostile critique of *Out of Apathy* came from the young politics lecturer (and Labour supporter) Bernard Crick. 'All is denunciation and sectarian polemic,' he wrote in the *Political Quarterly*. 'It is, brothers, the revolution or nothing; damn your mess of potage and God bless mine.' Orwell's future biographer was generally a controversialist who took few prisoners, and 'the ranting near-hysteria, the self-righteousness, the good old Marxist style of souped-up violence' was as little to his taste as its 'wind of rhetoric'.[10]

The New Left's relationship with the Labour Party, and indeed the broader labour movement, was of course fraught. 'What we need is a living movement of people, battering away at the problems of socialism in the mid-Twentieth century, pooling their experiences, yet, at every point, breaking back into the Labour Movement, thrusting forward like so many uninvited guests into Constituency Parties and Trade Union branches, pushing within CND, picking up the quick tissues in the society, sloughing off the dead,' proclaimed the *NLR*'s first editorial. The quite rapidly growing Left Clubs were seen as the vanguard of this broadening strategy, and in the next issue an open letter to readers in them spoke of how what was needed was 'the *consciousness* that the constituency worker, fighting to get the Conference floor, and the duffle-coated jazz fan on the Aldermaston March are both *running* in the same direction', thereby breaking down 'mutual hostility and suspicion'. Yet if these were conciliatory words, the editorial in the May–June issue had all guns blazing in its attack on Gaitskell ('incapable any longer of understanding what a popular, democratic movement of people would be like . . . a bourgeois politician') and the Labour right ('sheer dishonesty when facing the implications of the facts about our society'). 'I am convinced that in order to progress towards socialism the British labour movement must ultimately find a way of accommodating within itself the radical idealism and dynamic impulse to action characteristic of the New Left,' reflected Jay Blumler (a lecturer at Ruskin College, Oxford) soon afterwards in the revisionist-friendly *Socialist Commentary*. 'But the New Left must not make this accommodation impossible. From this point of view its addiction to Marxist tenets is unfortunate, and the increasing shrillness of its attack upon those in the labour movement who do not share its outlook is quite ominous.' Or, as an *SC* reader, Ronald Parker of Middlesbrough, put it in October 1960 (some six months after the purportedly anti-cataclysmic Thompson had privately invoked the memory of Russia in 1917 and foreseen 'a new kind of revolution lying around in Britain in 1969 or 1974'), although '*New Left Review* is an organ of dissident Marxism and would avoid the errors committed by Stalin, its authors have the same quite disconcerting sense that history is with them which characterised the Stalinists, the theological certainty of latter-day saints and a touching feeling that the second coming is at hand'.[11]

Only half the 1959 electorate old enough to have voted in a pre-war general election, one family in every six moving between 1948 and 1958 into a newly built house or flat, the industrial worker's average real earnings rising by over 20 per cent between 1951 and 1958, rapidly growing consumption (especially on durable 'white goods') and hire-purchase credit, the living room and the TV set displacing the pub and the cinema, family life increasingly focused on the newly acquired car, the number of white-collar workers up by over a million between 1951 and 1959, manual workers falling in the same period by half a million, the Butler Act of 1944 enabling working-class children to advance via grammar schools to become middle-class adults – one way and another, reflected David Butler and Richard Rose in their instant but authoritative account of the 1959 election, 'the last ten years have eroded some of the traditional foundations of Labour strength.' 'Social changes,' they went on, 'have been weakening traditional working-class political loyalties; simultaneously the middle classes have become more prosperous and more self-confident. Full employment and the welfare state have made the well-paid worker much less dependent on his trade union or on the Labour party than before the war. At the bench a man may still be plainly working-class, but in his new home, in his car, or out shopping, his social position may be more difficult to assess. He may well think of himself as a consumer first and only secondly as a worker.' Moreover, they added, 'television, women's weeklies, and the popular press have on the whole emphasised values which foster any inclinations people may have to identify their interests with the more prosperous part of the nation – which, in political terms, means voting Conservative.'

Unsurprisingly, Anthony Crosland and his fellow-revisionists tended to agree with this pessimistic (from a Labour standpoint) analysis. 'The scales today are weighted against the Labour Party,' he told a Fabian audience in April 1960, 'so long as it preserves its one-class image.' Further grist to the revisionist mill soon followed with the celebrated Abrams survey. This was conducted by the Labour-sympathising sociologist-*cum*-market-research expert Mark Abrams, published by *Socialist Commentary* between May and August, and, that autumn, turned into a Penguin Special, *Must Labour Lose?* On the basis of 724 in-depth interviews (including with 255 Labour supporters) in the first two months of 1960, Abrams sought 'to establish those attitudes and social values which have led the electorate to turn away steadily from the Labour Party over the past ten years and to reject it decisively at the latest General Election'.

Perhaps his most striking finding was that whereas an overwhelming majority agreed with the proposition that Labour 'stands mainly for the working class', 50 per cent of non-Labour supporters who were in fact working-class nevertheless perceived themselves as middle-class. Indeed, among the unskilled working-class respondents who did not vote Labour, 'three-quarters of them rejected their "objective" social status of "labouring working class".' Unsurprisingly, and whatever their self-selected social status, working-class non-Labour supporters agreed particularly strongly (67 per cent) with the statement that the Conservatives 'would make the country more prosperous', a criterion that only 7 per cent believed to be applicable to Labour. Abrams also turned to the much-publicised question of youth (defined as 18 to 24) and politics, at a time when 21 was still the minimum voting age. '35 per cent of all working-class young people are ready to identify themselves with the Conservative Party,' he found, 'and only 10 per cent of middle-class young people support the Labour Party.' He added that 'young people were much more emphatic than their elders in seeing Labour as overwhelmingly the party which stands mainly for the working class, as out to help the underdog and to abolish class differences.' Unfortunately for Labour, though, 'none of these traits seemed of much significance to young people when they indicated the most important features of a good political party', with five times more choosing 'out to raise standard of living' than 'out to help the underdog'. 'They are,' concluded Abrams about the nation's youth in the first year of the 1960s, 'highly optimistic about the future, and very satisfied with their jobs. They know very little about the Labour Party's programme, and where their own interests are concerned they are convinced – by an almost 2 to 1 majority – that Conservative policies would suit them best.'

Ralph Samuel was unimpressed. 'Dr Abrams and the End of Politics' was the title of his *New Left Review* piece in September, attacking Abrams for having succumbed to 'a species of status determinism, supported by a behaviourist psychology of opinions and informed by the assumptions of motivational and market research'. It was, according to Samuel,

> a gloomy characterisation of contemporary British man; one which allows him no core of conviction or steady centre, but only a moral

> vacuum in which the fast-flowing streams of status deposit their sediment. He sees people as *consumers* of politics, behaving in politics much as they would – in the motivational research imagination – when confronted with mass-market commodities: they 'buy' political labels and allegiances as they would any brand-image – because of the pleasurable associations it promises to afford . . . These associations may have an organic or only an accidental connection with people's desires; they may bear a real or only a fancied relation to people's genuine needs; but for this political philosophy, it does not matter at all.

There followed some detailed criticism of Abrams's methodology, not least his 'cavalier' treatment of young people – 'Teds and Mods, Beatniks and Ravers, Aldermaston Marchers and Nuclear Campaigners, they all disappear amidst the whirrings of his Hollerith machines, to re-emerge on his Punch Cards, an almost undifferentiated mass' – before the inevitable uplifting peroration in dark times: 'Behind the image scores, and the identity tables which here encapsulate them, there are real living, breathing, thinking, feeling people: Tredegar steel workers and Cannock miners, Blackheath teachers and Suffolk farmers, Kentish Town mothers and Wythenshawe clerks: the common people; not all of them with Labour, and not as many as in the past, but still, Radical England, *us* and not *them*.' And 'if the Labour Movement,' concluded Samuel, 'were finally to abandon its traditional way of thinking about people – and that alone is truly fundamental – to lose its faith in the power of the word to move people, and of the idea to change them, if it were to let go its conviction in the capacity of human beings rationally to choose between the alternatives which face them, and purposefully to re-shape the society in which they live, then it would be finished, and would find itself trapped in that limbo of the political imagination whose features Dr Abrams has so meticulously outlined.'[12]

Just for a moment in 1960 there appeared to be a chance of a whole new political flank opening – with little or nothing to do with the New Left – in the wake of the crushing election defeat for the two progressive parties, Labour and Liberal.

'Real tea is so welcome at Dover,' Michael Young had written back in January 1958 (soon after starting the instantly successful *Which?* magazine),

> you hardly notice the cracked cup it comes in. Corpses of ham sandwiches may arouse a kind of affection for the archaism of England. But what about the people? How polite we are compared to foreigners! How gentle the swearing of the porters! How sedate and how safe!
>
> Too sedate, too quiet, too safe – where has the vitality gone? We all seem such willing victims of oppression. Are we all terrified of authority? In restaurants, bars, shops we put up with cold food, warm beer and the icy look. We seem to be a nation that has ceased to protest. We accept housing estates, smoke, British Railways, external pipes, rockets, and shoddy shoes as though everything was so royally blessed as to be beyond criticism.

The consumer as king (or even queen)? It seemed a preposterous thought amidst such a deeply entrenched culture of passivity and uncomplaint. But by November 1959, weeks after the election, Mark Abrams was giving a talk on the Third Programme about 'The Home-centred Society' (a phrase that now entered the mainstream) which analysed changing habits of spending, especially the rapid rise of household goods, and noted not only how women's magazines were increasingly geared to appeal to 'the housewife as a consumer' but also how in industry it had become marketing directors, 'buttressed by sales managers and advertising experts', who had become 'today's innovators and risk-bearers', poised to 'earn the largest managerial salaries and dominate the boardrooms of the future'. In short, concluded Abrams about society at large, the unmistakable trend was towards 'the supremacy of the consumer'.

The politics were tantalising. 'Chris is really out of sympathy with the Party as it now exists and thinks we must gradually break loose of the trade unions and become a consumers' Party,' recorded Anthony Wedgwood Benn in June 1960 about Christopher Mayhew, the Labour politician and resolute opponent of commercial television. That same month, a Gallup poll revealed that 25 per cent would be willing to vote for a consumers' party, not in the pocket of either the unions or big business, at a new general election, with 37 per cent undecided. Four months later, Young published a pamphlet – turned down by the Fabian

Society as anti-Labour – with the title *The Chipped White Cups of Dover*, explicitly projected as 'a discussion of the possibility of a new progressive party'. At the heart of his case was the argument that henceforth 'politics will become less and less the politics of production and more and more the politics of consumption'. Accordingly, he envisaged a reforming party that, among many other things, would 'mount an attack on the monopolies and restrictive practices by which Britain is more ridden than any other country in the world', and he cited such major irritants as resale price maintenance, the absurdly restricted opening hours permitted by the Shops Act, and the lofty disregard of the user prevalent in the public services (whether health, education, housing or social security). He then specifically considered the reforming credentials of the Labour Party – whose manifesto he himself had written in 1945 – and found them wanting, largely because of that party's umbilical link with the trade unions, which 'to consumers seem too small-minded about their own sectional interest as producers'. Altogether, wrote Young near the end, after a nod to the television age as a political game-changer, 'I do not think a new party would find itself at a disadvantage if it was a much less elaborate affair than the old parties, with less ponderous headquarters than the one where I worked, with a less tight discipline, with less insistence on conformity, with less subordination of members to the national office, and above all with more plain speaking by MPs emancipated from the Whips.'

It was probably never a runner. 'It all sounds very reasonable,' reflected Benn after his conversation with Mayhew. 'But politics is about power and if we are not firmly linked to the working-class movement, then we shall never be anything at all except a lot of Liberals with bright ideas.'[13] Yet arguably the indissolubility of that link (in effect with the unions) was not just a question of power. To have accepted the new reality that many working-class people were starting to become, in their self-image and even their way of life, relatively classless consumers at least as much as they were class-conscious producers would have required for middle-class socialists like Benn a profound recasting of a heroic, moralistic mythology. In the event, it would take a full three decades before Labour had a leader who was not sentimental about the working class and who finally – more or less – persuaded his party to accept that chipped cups were no longer good enough.

4

Some Fearful Risks

On Saturday, 7 May the newly wed Princess Margaret was on her way to Mustique as Wolverhampton Wanderers comfortably beat Blackburn Rovers 3–0 in yet another no-substitutes Cup Final marred by injury, this time a broken leg for the Rovers defender Dave Whelan. 'Not a moment of beauty or of transcendent football to cherish,' regretted John Arlott, while in Blackburn itself the outcome merely compounded the sense of grievance already fuelled by an unfair system of ticket allocation that had prevented life-long supporters from going to Wembley. Next day saw *Bonanza*'s debut – the 'painfully familiar juvenile melodramas', according to *Punch*'s Henry Turton, of 'yet another Western series bought from American TV for our delight' – before on Monday a great moment in the Heap household. 'Glory be!' recorded a relieved diarist. 'Frainy has passed his 11 Plus exam!' There followed next evening the promised (if he passed) 'celebration dinner' at the Chicken Inn, Leicester Square: 'A wing of chicken with thin "French fried" chips each, plus a "knickerbocker glory" and orangeade for F, a sherry trifle and lager for me'.

A week later the Cold War took a chilly turn with the comprehensive failure of the Paris summit. Most people blamed the Russians – 'Kruschev a menace', bluntly noted the middle-aged Jennie Hill – but a younger diarist, Kate Paul, castigated 'pig-headed, proud individuals' across the board. 'I want to grip these maniacs by the shoulders and shout: "Don't you dare destroy me!" How can I live on probation like this? How can anyone? But we do.' Next day, the 18th, the first and last act of corporal punishment ('2 on seat') took place at Risinghill School, a newly opened co-educational comprehensive in Islington under the progressive leadership of Michael Duane; that evening, in the European Cup Final at Hampden Park, Real Madrid's sumptuous 7–3 thrashing of Eintracht Frankfurt lit the European flame for at least one of the 135,000 awed Glaswegians, the 18-year-old part-time professional Alex Ferguson; on Thursday, 14-year-old Jacqueline Aitken had dinner at a friend's house ('liver, baked beans, cauliflower and new potatoes', followed by 'rhubarb and evaporated milk', altogether '*very nice*!'); soon afterwards, Penelope Gilliatt, in her *Spectator* review of Doris Lessing's sociological *In Pursuit of the English*, argued that, 'with post-Orwellian insight, she knows in her heart that for a middle-class intellectual like herself the idea of the working class is essentially talismanic and unattainable'; simultaneously, an emerging giant among middle-class intellectuals, Eric Hobsbawm, deplored in the *New Statesman* (in his capacity as jazz critic 'Francis Newton') the 'present vogue' among the young for Miles Davis, describing him as not only 'of surprisingly narrow technical and emotional range' but also as unhealthily close to 'self-pity and the denial of love'; on the 25th the hitherto jazz-oriented Cavern in Liverpool had its first all-beat session; and, three days later, Gateshead were dropped from the Football League in favour of Peterborough United, a decision not implausibly attributed by the *Newcastle Evening Chronicle* to a conspiracy by 'a cosy clique of southern clubs'.[1]

There was hardly a youthquake yet in 1960 Britain, but older people that May continued to resent even the relatively early tremors. 'I was deeply shocked,' noted Nella Last on the 22nd after the first-ever televising of the Royal Variety Performance, 'when that queer neurotic youth Lonnie Donegan forgot his lines – wondered how he got on the bill . . .' About the same time, the *East London Advertiser*'s Tom Duncan interviewed the actor Jack Warner, 'a Bow boy for a great chunk of his life' and now of course best known as PC George Dixon. The interview took place as Warner drove the journalist round central London in his new car, starting off at Broadcasting House:

> We were just beginning to infiltrate into that part of the West End which is occupied by the weirdies, and Jack pulled my attention to a couple of misguided delinquents who were lounging in front of a café. 'Look at them,' he insisted, a tone of disgust ricocheting through his voice.

'They're beatniks,' I murmured.

'What do they do?' he replied.

'I can tell you what they don't do,' I answered. 'They don't wash and they comb their hair once every other month.'

'Bring back the birch,' Jack scowled, commandeering his car through a thin gap in the traffic.

Another local paper had been rather more tolerant, but was now half-regretting it. 'Our picture page last week, featuring impressionistic views of 'teen-age dancing in the Northern Meeting Rooms, aroused some controversy,' apologised the Inverness-based *Highland News* on the 20th about a vivid full-page photo feature that had been headed 'LET'S GO MAN GO!' and had included the caption 'A little relaxation is a good thing' for the photo of a couple in a tight clinch away from the dance floor. 'Certainly there was no intention to impute laxness of conduct on the part of the management ... The page was intended to be a study in *joie de vivre*, and if the, necessarily, contrasting tones had an element of sensationalism about them, the effect intended was to present an ensemble of youthful motion and emotion in a particular setting.'

Northern Border Dances held their nerve and, the following evening, Saturday the 21st, proudly presented something for everyone: downstairs, 'Old Thyme Dancing to Lindsay Ross and His Famous Broadcasting Band'; upstairs, 'Modern Dancing to THE BEAT BALLAD SHOW', starring 'T.V. and Decca Recording Star JOHNNY GENTLE and his Group'. Gentle's backing group were in fact the Silver Beetles, as they were now briefly known; and this date in Inverness was the second of seven on an ill-planned Scottish tour that also included St Thomas' Hall in Keith, the town hall in Forres and the Regal Ballroom in Nairn, eventually leading a hungry John Lennon to place a desperate reverse-charges phone call to the promoter, demanding, 'Where's the bloody money?' Everyday life along the north-east coast went on sweetly oblivious. Forres Junior Farmers' Club held a stock-judging competition, with three classes of pigs and two of sheep; the monthly meeting of the Altyre Women's Rural Institute featured 'an interesting demonstration of floral arrangements' as well as a talk on 'what one would do to protect one's home and family in the case of nuclear warfare'; Glen Urquhart, with seven of its 12 players either Mackintoshes or Macdonalds, won a junior shinty championship; and in Keith the greatest buzz was around the third-placed appearance of the Keith Townswomen's Guild team in the final at the Royal Albert Hall of a national quiz sponsored by the Electricity Development Association.[2]

Fame still lay some way ahead for Lennon et al, completing their tour at Peterhead on Saturday the 28th, but for the 25-year-old and very left-wing Dennis Potter a degree of celebrity was already becoming familiar. The following Friday, the BBC showed *Between Two Rivers*, about Potter returning to his native mining village in the increasingly affluent and consumerist Forest of Dean after three years at Oxford. 'Seemed bitter and full of rancour,' thought one viewer. 'He was the odd man out, refusing to recognise the signs of the times.' Certainly he was never likely to be one of the angels in marble – those working-class Conservatives (so cherished by Disraeli) whom the political scientists Robert McKenzie and Allan Silver were now trying to tease out, especially after the hat-trick of Tory election victories. Their interviewees in late May and early June lived in council flats off the Edgware Road in London W2:

> You've got to have people with money to run the country. That's my feeling. (*Housewife, 51*)
>
> I suppose there's only really two classes – the people with the real money . . . I don't think anyone is really in the poor class today . . . It's the middle class and as near to it as they could ever be. I don't think anyone is really bad off – in a poor class. (*Self-employed man delivering paraffin, 37*)
>
> You'll always find the upper dog and the under dog, no matter which party is there . . . (*Housewife, 45*)
>
> The Conservative Party I think are run by people that know a bit, and are more sensible and classy . . . They keep the country better than what a Labour man would . . . They keep the country decent, sort of thing . . . When we had these Labour in, things don't go so nice . . . They just want Dick, Tom and Harry to have the money all the time, and they forget that there's other people in the country to keep going . . . I do like it when the Conservatives are in . . . They always do their best and do

> things for both sides . . . They've done no end of buildings since they've been in, flats and things . . . I think Unions cause a lot of trouble in the country . . . I think they cause more strikes and everything . . . (*Housewife, 59*)[3]

'Some silly people on the right nowadays wish the sixties hadn't happened because that was when people discovered sex and pot-smoking,' observed Alan Bennett three decades later. 'I wish the sixties hadn't happened because that was when avarice and stupidity got to the wheel of the bulldozer. They called it enterprise and still do, but the real enterprise would have been if someone in 1960 had had the clout and the imagination to say, "Let us leave this city much as it is, convert it perhaps, replumb it, but nothing else."' 'If they had,' he added regretfully about the city he had grown up in, 'Leeds today would have been one of the architectural showpieces of the kingdom, a Victorian Genoa or Florence, on the buildings of which many of its banks and commercial properties were modelled. Instead it's now like anywhere else.' Many other British cities and towns, and indeed the built environment generally, also changed fundamentally during the 1960s. In this respect at least, the '1960s' were well under way by 1960 itself; for by that summer and autumn, the pace of change in the urban built environment – whether actual change or planned change for the future – was becoming as rapid as at any time since the Industrial Revolution.

In hitherto sleepy Basingstoke, for example, the town centre was turned into a cluster of one-way streets; in Birmingham, the construction of the Inner Ring Road continued to devour everything in its way (including Smallbrook's Scala cinema, bowing out with *Teenage Loves*), and work started on the landmark Rotunda, with the projected height of the circular tower now doubled from 12 storeys to 24; in Coventry, the City Arcade of 1932 began to be replaced by a concrete version; in Derby, the Coliseum cinema (previously a Congregational church) was demolished with the construction of Bradshaw Way; in the Great Parndon neighbourhood of Harlow New Town, a brutalist 'casbah' housing project won an architectural competition and would prove, in Lionel Esher's words, 'a fish out of water in the arcadian scene'; in Leeds itself, the completion of the Saville Green 10-storey flats, part of the Ebor Gardens scheme in York Road, was the latest addition to the city's skyline, now (as a local paper put it) 'quite dwarfing the gigantic mill chimneys of our youthful recollection'; and in Liverpool, the headline was 'City's soaring skyline' as the city council signed contracts for a range of multi-storey schemes, while the university's just completed physics building, on a site 'still surrounded by condemned slum property', was the latest tower block by the newly knighted Basil Spence. In London, meanwhile, amid much else, new buildings included the BBC's gleamingly modern Television Centre at White City and Sir Giles Gilbert Scott's 325-foot-high Bankside Power Station (the future Tate Modern); buildings under construction included the massive *Daily Mirror* headquarters in Holborn Circus and the London County Council's highest block of flats yet (19 storeys, in Stepney); demolition work was in hand, courtesy of the developer Charles Clore, on the site for Park Lane's London Hilton ('this long-awaited, much-discussed addition to London's roster of super-hotels'); Spence got the go-ahead to design a tower block at Knightsbridge Barracks; and the winning design for the Elephant and Castle Shopping Centre featured a cruciform glass-roofed arcade rising through two floors and laid out with planting, fountains and pavement cafés. In Newcastle, the Scandinavian-style Civic Centre began to be built, while nearby there was a green light for Northumberland County Council to redevelop Killingworth, in due course becoming (in Elain Harwood's words) 'the most comprehensive megastructure in Britain . . . a whole town centre and flanking housing conceived as a single unit with walkways over the main roads'; in Oxford, the demolition of rundown St Ebbe's continued apace, with the Gas Works no longer the first glimpse of the city from the train, while on the Blackbird Leys estate work started on a 15-storey block of flats, Windrush Tower; in Plymouth, the local paper's year-end progress report gave pride of place to the newly extending inner ring road ('progress should be as rapid as the rehousing of displaced families permits'); and in Sheffield the last of Park Hill's 995 dwellings was handed over to tenants shortly after the city's trams headed for the breaker's yard. It was much the same in Scotland, above all in the two biggest cities. In Edinburgh, demolition started in historic George Square, and the massive Leith Fort redevelopment began (including two 21-storey point blocks); while in Glasgow the latest Development

Plan envisaged the comprehensive demolition and rebuilding of 29 areas (more than a third of the city) over the next 20 years, and the Corporation – stimulated by Wimpey's rapid completion in Royston Road (amid a tangle of railway lines and a canal) of three 20-storey blocks, Scotland's tallest so far – moved decisively in favour of high-rise flats within the city boundaries.[4]

One way and another, 1960 was undoubtedly a 'moment', not just because it was the start of a decade. That autumn, the *Yorkshire Post*'s Harry Franz sought to capture it in a piece called 'New brick, concrete, steel and glass . . . AMONG THE ALIEN BLACK OF BRADFORD STONE':

> Bradford's £5,000,000 facelift continues at breakneck pace with old buildings in the former congested central area disappearing as swiftly as snow in a sudden thaw. Towering modern office and shopping blocks are creeping skyward in their place. This expensive and expansive building project is going hand in hand with the Corporation's new road plans, which will eventually open up the city centre with an inner ring road . . .
>
> Above the traffic's roar comes the distinctive note of the pneumatic drill, biting clearly and cleanly into some hard tough object. The rasping circular saw shrills out a higher pitch as its teeth tear into timber and plank. The lighter duller noise of hammer and chisel break through occasionally under the rhythmic movement of the master craftsman's hands . . .

'Bradford is indeed a progressive city these days,' declared Franz. And he added, with just possibly a nod to J. B. Priestley, who on television two years earlier had urged his home city to advance into the twentieth century: 'Exiles returning to it will hardly know it in its modern shape . . .'

'In the long run it is enlightened public opinion that matters most,' a government minister, Lord Craigton, told the Town and Country Planning summer school. How to make that public opinion sufficiently enlightened? Politicians themselves sometimes expressed views – 'with much greater vigour,' urged Labour's Patrick Gordon Walker, 'we must rebuild our whole environment of working and living in terms of the motor car' – while modernist architects (and not only Spence) were naturally not shy in coming forward. 'In 10 years London could be a beautiful skyscraper city,' Ernö Goldfinger explained to the *Sunday Times*, 'and the view from the river could be as it was in Wren's London, except that instead of churches you would have skyscrapers towering over the lower buildings.' But what strikes one about the state of play in 1960 is the key cheerleading role played by the still much-read local press. When in July, for instance, the winning design was unveiled for Dumbarton's fundamental redevelopment, including a new main road through the town to be raised on pillars, the *Lennox Herald*'s response was unambiguously positive, declaring that 'the whole scheme hangs together effortlessly'. Later that month it was the turn of south London, with the *Peckham & Dulwich Advertiser & News* trumpeting the news that 'the Elephant and Castle is to have the most fabulous, up-to-date shopping centre in Britain . . . perhaps in Europe.'

Ultimately, perhaps it all came down to zeitgeist, to a certain something in the air. 'There is about such buildings more than the excitement of unaccustomed height and variety of scale,' reflected the middle-aged landscape painter William Townsend in a radio talk inspired by the Golden Lane flats just north of the Barbican and by Denys Lasdun's cluster blocks in Bethnal Green. 'I cannot help feeling a sense of relief at seeing them there, as though they were something we should not be without, something one has to have these days, like nylon and neon signs and television; and this not to make sure we do not feel inferior to the United States or Brazil [a reference presumably to embryonic modernist Brasília], but because they stand in a special way, like abstract painting, good or bad, for where human societies have really got to.'[5]

One local figure, leader from early 1960 of the Labour group in Newcastle and in effect that city's boss, was poised to become emblematic of the new spirit of the age. 'A Practical VISIONARY' was the title in March of a local paper's profile of T. Dan Smith – the start of the mythologising of the sixties man who, as Martin Linton would aptly put it in the 1970s, 'came to sort out local government with a strong belief in business efficiency and a burning social purpose'. Describing him as 'more than six feet tall' with 'a powerful though sympathetic personality', the *Evening Chronicle* heralded Councillor Smith as 'the first man since the war with the dedicated enthusiasm, ability and perseverance to tackle the problem of re-building the city'. As Smith himself told the interviewer, 'So little has been done in the past, we are painting a new canvas as it were.' That spring, amid facing down the City Engineer and securing the appointment of Newcastle's first City Planning Officer (Wilfred Burns), Smith spoke at the annual meeting of the Town Planning Institute (held in Newcastle), and outlined in his usual fluent and expansive way what would become familiar themes. His city needed to be at the heart of a region (serviced by a regional planning authority) creating 'a compelling interest to forward-looking industrialists to come North'; the city's slums would be cleared within five years; in terms of what replaced them, 'increasing standards of amenity', including 'new parklands, adequate community buildings, modern shopping centres and children's playing centres', would be 'sought after all the time'; and as for the city centre itself, the aim was to make Newcastle 'the most outstanding provincial capital in the country'. In passing, Smith noted: 'I oppose the traffic "Canutes" – the modern city needs as much traffic as possible and it must deal with tomorrow's traffic problems today.' At this stage, the aspect of redevelopment closest to his heart was Cruddas Park, a cleared 5-acre site where work was under way on erecting a cluster of 15-storey point blocks. Cruddas Park, Smith told the conference, not only would be 'the focal point of the Scotswood Road Development Area' but also – through the quality of the modern, well-equipped blocks themselves, together with 'landscaping and other features' (including a sculpture to be unveiled on the centenary of the Blaydon Races in June 1962) – would 'contribute locally to the stimulation of the arts on Tyneside and nationally to a wider appreciation of the cultural and industrial potentialities of the Tyneside of tomorrow'.

Not everyone fell tamely into line. 'Our life is dominated by television programmes which we do not wish to hear,' wrote a malcontent flat-dweller, Norman Lingham, to the *Sunday Times* – a fortnight after Goldfinger's high-rise vision – from his 'cacophonous pigeon-hole' in London SE15. So too with Park Hill in Sheffield. 'THE VERDICT: It's "SMASHING" living right up IN THE SKY' was the *Star*'s headline in May. However, a few months later a letter to the paper from 'New Sheffield' disparaged 'the whole dismal, slablike mass' of 'the city's newest eyesore', while a local businessman, Anthony Greenfield, expressed himself 'certain' that 'within a quarter of a century' the flats would be 'regarded as slums'. Slum clearance also had its critics. 'All these houses were well cared for and I think they would still have been in good condition in 50 or a 100 years,' complained E. Macdonald, 'a Middletonian of the Fourth Generation', to his local paper in Lancashire about a recent spate of demolition, while in Bristol the newly elected, anti-socialist 'Citizen' councillors tried unsuccessfully to persuade the Conservative housing minister, Henry Brooke, to allow a more selective approach in that city. Or take one of the areas of most intense clearance. 'Living as the *City Reporter* does on the boundary of the Ellor Street slum clearance area,' noted Saul Reece in his column in August, 'we are visited almost daily by residents, indignant, angry, or just plain sarcastic, complaining about the chaotic progress (or lack of progress) of the demolition. One or two large areas have been cleared around Hankinson Street, but street after street of houses stand empty in various states of ruin . . .' Ellor Street, in short, 'now looks like the worst kind of blitzed area on the morning after the raid, a disgrace to Salford in its death as it has been for half a century in its life'.[6]

The juggernaut was rolling, albeit with varying speed and efficiency, and usually it seemed irresistible. In Glasgow, Councillor Derek Wood declared that 'what disturbed him most' about that city's radical Development Plan was that 'they were treating people like cattle' in the sense that 'the proposals were being imposed from the planner's point of view without regard to other considerations.' Almost certainly during this complicated process, what one might call a regretful fatalism was widely felt, if not always by the majority of people, who may well have been largely indifferent or perhaps even mildly positive. It was an indifference that might have puzzled the Vale of Leven's David Stevenson. 'Demolishing old buildings and erecting others in their place,' began his ponderously eloquent letter to the local paper about the early-Victorian settlement in Bonhill known as 'the Wee Field' and its almost complete destruction, 'is in these days always keeping up a steady pace in endeavouring to meet the demands of this age of progress and speed, wiping out with one fell blow, changing completely old familiar landscapes which have been in existence for many a long year, becoming part and parcel so to speak of succeeding generations as they lived and moved and had their being.'

One of the more contested cities – though only ever with one outcome

– was Birmingham, site of arguably the most rapid and fundamental change anywhere in urban Britain. 'Dramatic surgery – but it may well kill a city' was the *News Chronicle* headline in September for a powerful critique by the young and bearded architectural writer Peter Rawsthorne, who argued that Birmingham's officials were, in their understandable attempt to solve the traffic problem, 'tearing their city apart' and making it 'alarmingly impersonal'. The villain of the piece was of course the Inner Ring Road, 'slicing' its way 'across the cosy tangle of old streets and buildings'; soon afterwards, in an architectural magazine, Rawsthorne called this 'massively ambitious' project 'a menacingly misguided colossus that may well overpower the withering vestiges of informality altogether'. In October the *Birmingham Mail* helpfully published a large map showing the new central Birmingham (within the still-under-construction Inner Ring Road) that was taking, or planned to take, shape. The accompanying article by the chairman of the City Council's Public Works Committee was the usual stuff – 'outdated, overcrowded . . . being reborn . . . huge, clean, new concrete buildings . . . modern and comprehensive . . . tremendous redevelopment . . .' – while on another page the blurb for an artist's impression of the future Bull Ring expressed complete satisfaction with how 'clean, flowing lines and a 20th century symmetry' would be replacing 'the old untidy jumble and bustle of the city's traditional market place'. Two self-styled 'old Brummies' responded on the letters page. Although conceding that 'long acquaintance, and a measure of sentiment, may cause regret over the disappearance of familiar buildings and landmarks', T. Austin of Birmingham 24 reckoned that 'the Ring Road scheme, and vast rebuilding, considered as a whole, will give Birmingham a status it has lacked'; by contrast, 'I do not see anything of beauty in it – only some copy of Continental ideas,' was the view of Birmingham 23's 'Citizen', who, after adding that 'putting huge blocks of offices and skyscrapers – some call them houses – is not sufficient', declared himself 'utterly disgusted'.

Perhaps the most resonant charges came from a former Lord Mayor, Norman Tiptaft. 'Second Thoughts on the New Look in Birmingham' was the title in November of his trenchant *Daily Telegraph* piece, arguing that – far from it being the case of 'a few nostalgic old fogies' having qualms – in reality there had grown up 'a deep, underlying resentment'. Partly this was about 'handing over to developers more concerned with financial profits than with building the city beautiful of the future'; partly it was about 'the type of city being constructed'. Noting that high-rise flats had 'never been asked for by Birmingham citizens', Tiptaft went on:

> In the new city, we shall be housed in 16-storey flats, shop in brick or concrete boxes, and be segregated in zones – some for houses, some for shops, some for factories. The little shop on the corner or in the side street will disappear, along with the self-employed boot repairer or tobacconist or little grocer ... Never mind how convenient the odd building would be. The planners and the zoners and the believers in monotony and in everybody being exactly alike won't allow it.

Altogether, the new Birmingham was, concluded Tiptaft, 'the vision of "1984"'.[7]

They did things differently in Bury St Edmunds. 'COUNCIL HEARS REVOLUTIONARY PLAN TO DEVELOP THE TOWN CENTRE' announced the *Bury Free Press* back in November 1959, as the essence of an audacious deal emerged: a cluster of handsome old buildings (Corn Exchange, public library, School of Art) to be demolished, the site to be sold to developers, a large block of shops and offices to be built. 'It will make Bury St Edmunds one of the best shopping centres in East Anglia,' noted the paper, but over the following nine or so months opposition to the scheme steadily increased. 'Why the sudden craze to speed up the tempo of change, to make revolutionary developments which must tear the guts out of the old place?' asked Colonel Sidney Rogerson, who had lived near Bury for 25 years. When the councillors eventually came to vote in October 1960, the Corn Exchange was saved for posterity; altogether, the scheme had seemingly been, as the *Bury Free Press* put it, 'strangled to death by public opinion'. Yet what is striking is that, in the only systematic test of what Bury's residents actually wanted (a postal referendum in Northgate Ward shortly before the decisive meeting), the voting went 933 for the scheme, 922 against. Perhaps the last word should go to 'Winkle Picker', who in a letter to the local paper declared that the outcome had been 'a victory to a bunch of elderly barnacles on the backside of progress'.

The trenchant architectural critic Ian Nairn, who would presumably have been on the side of the angels, was in any case still travelling more or less hopefully during these months on a tour of some of the major provincial cities. In Birmingham he was nervous about the effect of the Inner Ring Road, though overall he reckoned that it would be 'all right' despite 'some fearful risks' having been taken; Newcastle had the potential to be 'one of the great cities of Europe', but all depended on the Corporation's quality of patronage; in Manchester the crux was whether 'public and private enterprise' could combine in the central area, currently dead after the working day, to achieve 'not only "urban renewal" (which so often means replacing lively old dirt by dead new cleanness) but urban awakening'; and in Glasgow, Nairn focused mainly on the Gorbals, where some parts were undeniably 'past repair' but others 'could easily be salvaged, not as a stop-gap or cut-rate measure, but because of the innate qualities of the buildings' (adding that 'all over Glasgow' there were 'similar terraces in a similar condition'). Yet over and above the individual fates of individual cities, there existed in Nairn's eyes a more fundamental problem:

> Very few people are really trying to find out what a city is like to be in, not only in terms of their own life but for every kind of person who uses it . . . Does any planner in Birmingham or Liverpool or Manchester know how the corporation dustmen live, what they enjoy in the city centre and what they abhor? The problem is at least as important as plot ratio, daylight angles and sight lines. To take one related example, most Cockney families like to live in the kitchen. The architect's job is not to ask why, nor to persuade Cockneys to live like young married architects, but to build big kitchens in the specific proportion that they are needed, as far as can be assessed. But do they? – not on your life . . .

'Choice, or multiple use, is one key to a happy city,' he concluded. 'Humanity, or care with the details, is perhaps the other.'[8]

But of course, for all the obvious importance of long-established cities, the fact was that a rapidly increasing number of people – probably at least several million – were now living in a wide variety of new (or newly expanded) towns and housing estates on the periphery of those cities, or even well outside them. One such fast-growing settlement, in effect a new town without the advantages of being an official new town, would come during the 1960s to embody that trend for better or (usually) worse: Kirkby.

'On the drearily flat, wet plain of South-West Lancashire, it repeats many of the less pleasing features of similar developments elsewhere,' observed the sociologist John Barron Mays in 1963 about a place, some 6 miles north-east of Liverpool, whose population had mushroomed from 3,000 in 1951 to 52,000 only ten years later. 'There are the usual long avenues of similar houses, some taller buildings and blocks, but little architectural elegance. An atmosphere of organised anonymity prevails throughout its length and breadth; a new raw, hardly-lived-in place, unsoftened by time and unrelieved by local colour.' A dip into the *Liverpool Echo* for the autumn of 1960 suggests that Kirkby had already become a byword for undesirability. 'Kirkby is still being troubled by gangs of young vandals who leave a weekly trail of havoc' ran a story about how the vicar of St Chad's could take it no longer and was moving to genteel Southport. Moreover, although Southdene (the oldest part of the Kirkby estate) had 'settled down', elsewhere there was 'no sign of improvement', and householders were 'alarmed by the gangs and hesitant of taking action'. The local MP was Harold Wilson, Labour's Shadow Chancellor; in September he officially opened Kirkby County Comprehensive School, the first comp in the county, declaring that 'only the best is good enough for Lancashire girls and boys.' The headmaster, Mr S. Bury, was more modestly optimistic. 'I think Kirkby is settling down,' he told the press. 'We attach great importance to training for citizenship and we are proud of the progress we have made. The children are loyal and keen to help every good cause.'[9]

The great majority of Kirkby's windswept residents had previously lived in Liverpool – usually in slum or rundown areas, one of which had been the subject of Liverpool University's 'Crown Street' survey in 1956. Four years later, during the summer of 1960, the Department of Social Science returned to the fray and investigated the process of social adjustment in Kirkby. There they found a young town in every sense (half the population under 15, only 3 per cent over 60); the inevitable chronic shortage of facilities; a marked dislike of living in blocks of flats (at this stage mainly four storeys or under); and, overall, though often with negative exceptions, a reluctant acceptance by residents of their new situation. 'For the majority of ex-inner city dwellers the new estate is desirable or at least adequate,' claimed the cautiously positive Mays. 'Certainly the residents interviewed did not seem to be unusually isolated. Only 29 per cent found their neighbours less friendly in Kirkby than they had found their neighbours in Crown Street.' 'In the end,' he hoped and even predicted, that 'long trek from the dingy, cramped back-streets of central Liverpool' would prove for Kirkby's newcomers 'a step towards a happier and fuller life'.[10]

The voices of the interviewees themselves come through in the surviving fieldwork. Perhaps inevitably the brickbats tended to outnumber the bouquets:

> The accommodation was no good [ie, in 'Crown Street'], but we were a sight happier there . . . Atmosphere not same – nowhere to go . . . I'd rather live among foreigners than live among this lot. (*26-year-old housewife with four children*)
>
> You can hear people eating celery next door. (*Married couple in thirties living in flat with seven-year-old daughter*)
>
> The only friend I have made is the neighbour next-door . . . I'm just a bit lost for somewhere to go – can't belong to the club because not an RC and I don't like to depend on people – I would like to get out . . . I've been to the Woolworths – and got lost. (*32-year-old wife of brewery driver, three children*)
>
> They should have put the roughs in flats and the respectable ones in houses to look after gardens. (*Machinist's wife, two daughters*)
>
> With having children it's very difficult in a flat, we're always worried in case the children make a noise. (*Married couple in twenties, husband a rigger, four children*)
>
> There's nothing for teenagers – they started a Youth Club. Then there was complaints from neighbours. They spoil it for themselves. (*29-year-old docker's wife, two children*)
>
> Don't get on with children – they smash windows. I deal with that! (*75-year-old retired handyman at trams depot*)

Did this first generation of Kirkby newcomers ever feel like guinea pigs? 'A clear example of failure to settle in K – and of psychological distress because of it', began the interviewer's rather clinical report on a

40-year-old housewife who was married to a butcher and had five children of 11 or under:

> Her doctor is reinforcing her application to the Housing Department for transfer back to the centre. She is not very bright – some of her 'don't know' responses may be the result of apathy but the I.Q. here may be no more than 80–85. The place is not particularly well kept but is 'passable'. She has very little to do with neighbours, suffers from depression including crying fits. She lost a baby (before birth?) recently . . . She has no contact with any church, nor have the children. She is rather vaguely 'Protestant'.[11]

'In a week's time I shall leave Cambridge for good,' recorded Margaret Drabble on Saturday, 4 June. 'Everything seems to be making a deliberate attack on my capacity for regret and nostalgia; the weather is perfect, exams are over forever, Pimm's is flowing, and people are surrounded by a halo of curious sunset charm.' So too in Oxford this first summer of the 1960s, where Peter Jay (son of the Labour politician Douglas Jay and already engaged to the daughter of James Callaghan) was going down with the treble of President of the Union, a First in PPE and passing first into the Civil Service. Golden lasses, golden lads . . . Not so in Yeovil, where, also on the 4th, a sensitive young diarist, Kate Paul, went into town with a friend. 'It was terrible,' she wrote. 'We slunk into Woolworth's the back way, masses of slowly shifting morons, passing rows of greasy faces, wafting smells. Great bunches of odious spotty youths chewing gum, staring at white pimply girls in sloppy thin dresses, exposing their pink spotted backs.' Jacqueline Aitken that same Saturday was dutifully shopping with her mother ('a pair of cream flatties' in Richmond, 'very soft and comfortable'), while on the other side of the park a week later, the carnival procession as usual marked the start of Malden's Youth Week. The theme that year was 'Scenes from Television': first and third prize went to 'Captain Pugwash' floats; second prize to Malden Methodist youth club for its 'Black and White Minstrel' float (including 'banjo-strumming black-faced "coons"'); and fourth prize to 4th Malden senior air scouts for their moralistic 'Emergency-Ward 10' ('the float was apparently the scene of a traffic accident and bore a large poster warning viewers to "Honour their (highway) code"'). The small dormitory borough of Malden and Coombe had as many as 56 different youth organisations, and one journalist lingered to take the pulse of this 'pleasant residential corner' of suburban Surrey. 'There are no cinemas and the only sign of life of an evening in the tree-lined main shopping street [in New Malden] is the solitary milk bar. It is a quiet place with a first-rate youth record.'[12]

Later in June, the singer Jimmy Young made a career-changing move by presenting *Housewives' Choice* for a fortnight; the publisher Rupert Hart-Davis spent a broiling day in Oxford among 'bearded youths naked to the waist, negresses and other exotics, all sweating and jostling'; the Queen Mother opened Hull University's new library and responded, 'Oh, what a lovely thing to be' when told, 'This is Mr Larkin, our poet-librarian'; the Conservative government, eight months after its Keynesian election triumph, felt compelled to raise the Bank Rate in response to inflationary pressures and was rebuked by the *Financial Times* for having 'allowed its own expenditure to rise this year in a reckless way'; Princess Margaret carried out her first post-wedding public engagement, with Judy Haines noting that 'Tony', so far titleless, 'doesn't fancy office life and wants something "arty"'; Evelyn Waugh appeared on John Freeman's *Face to Face* ('a magnificent interrogation', thought the Manchester doctor Hugh Selbourne), confessing to irritability as his major fault, the same Sunday evening that a short television film on *The Patience of Job* featured the comic actor Deryck Guyler as the voice of God; and Thomas Dibble, a letter-writer to the *Glasgow Herald*, dismissed any sentimentality about the impending disappearance of that city's trams, asserting that 'we have endured their inconvenience, clankings, and groaning for too long.' That was on Thursday the 28th, destined to be one of the sombre dates in the collective memory of South Wales, as an explosion at the Six Bells Colliery outside Abertillery killed 45 miners. 'There is hardly a house in the street which has not lost a relative,' Mrs Joyce Frampton of Arrael Street, just a hundred yards away from the colliery gate, told the *South Wales Echo*. 'We are so dazed that none of us is doing housework in the normal way. We just want to stand around and think for a while.' One of those killed, Danny Bancroft, had lived in nearby Griffin Street; his son-in-law mused, 'It's an awful price to pay for coal, and people don't realise it.'[13]

The following evening, the 29th, the House of Commons discussed for the second time the Wolfenden recommendation of 1957 to decriminalise homosexual conduct between consenting adults. 'I fully appreciate that this subject is one which is distasteful and even repulsive to many people,' began the Labour MP Kenneth Robinson, who was proposing early action. 'I have no wish to suggest that I regard homosexuality as a desirable way of life.' The ensuing debate followed broadly predictable lines. Some wholly unreconstructed speakers were typified by Godfrey Lagden, Conservative MP for Hornchurch, who described homosexuals as 'people with warped minds who have little self-control', adding that 'in the general run the homosexual is a dirty-minded danger to the virile manhood of this country'. The middle position, elegantly put forward by Rab Butler as Home Secretary, was that there was 'a very great deal of work still to be done', including in terms of educating public opinion, before it would be possible to decriminalise. For the reformers, Roy Jenkins urged MPs not to be 'too eager to stand out as an island against the general current of civilised world opinion'. Robinson's motion to decriminalise was defeated 213–99 on a free vote. The former camp included well over 150 Conservative MPs as well as 41 Labour MPs (including the robustly commonsensical Fred Peart and Ray Gunter); the latter camp included 75 Labour MPs, the handful of Liberal MPs (including Jeremy Thorpe) and 22 Conservatives (including Enoch Powell, Margaret Thatcher and a solitary minister, Richard Wood). Those not voting – of whom there were many – included Harold Macmillan, Harold Wilson, Jim Callaghan and Edward Heath.

'The battle was not yet conclusively won,' insisted the Sheffield *Star* next day, arguing that 'the strong pressure group which demands social recognition for homosexuals' would soon prepare 'a new attack', being determined 'to have the public believe that the real "queer" is he who is intolerant of moral laxity'; therefore, it all depended on 'the moral fibre of the nation' to resist them. What in truth motivated those who had voted in favour of early decriminalisation? 'The proponents of reform,' acutely notes the historian Richard Davenport-Hines about the larger debate, 'repudiated not only homosexuality, but also homosexuals.

They argued that the existing law degraded or corrupted the police charged with enforcing it, that it facilitated blackmail, that it was ineffective, that its severity compared with equivalent laws on the European mainland reflected poorly on Britain's reputation for tolerance or justice. Almost no one spoke positively of homosexuality.' And he quotes the society lady to her friend in Osbert Lancaster's *Daily Express* cartoon two days afterwards: 'What I particularly admired about the debate was the way that every speaker managed to give the impression that he personally had never met a homosexual in his life.' One Labour MP who had declined to vote was the redoubtable Bessie Braddock, and a Liverpool constituent wondered in the *Spectator* why not. 'Perhaps she prefers,' replied her agent on her behalf, 'to devote her considerable energies to helping the helpless rather than the self-pitying.'[14]

Twenty-four hours after the people's tribunes had done their worst, Anthony Heap was at the New Theatre for the first night of *Oliver!* – 'the overwhelming, rip-roaring success of which firmly establishes Lionel Bart as the foremost writer and composer of musicals in Britain today'. 'Small wonder,' Heap added, 'that the reception was the most rousing, ecstatic and prolonged since the memorable First Night of "Oklahoma" thirteen years ago. It could scarcely have been *better* deserved.' Bart, son of an East End tailor, was still in his twenties; the cast included Barry Humphries, who had arrived from Australia the previous summer; and most critics were similarly enthusiastic. 'This is the first time we have seen that it is possible to combine the *milieu* of Beckett and Pinter with the verve of *Oklahoma!*,' declared Harold Hobson in the *Sunday Times*; he was particularly struck by 'the fog, the gloom, the gin, the darkness and corruption of early industrial England evoked by Sean Kenny's settings'. Gusto amid grimness did not do it, though, for Alan Brien. 'This tasty strip-cartoon fillet of Dickens by the composer-lyricist of *Fings* is served with a thin, sugared gruel of words and music,' he wrote in the *Spectator*; it relied 'almost entirely on ingratiation and insinuation as techniques for courtship of its audience', and, altogether, the result was 'a safe, cosy, comfortable evening out'. Either way, it was an indisputable smash hit for a mercurial, self-taught talent justly remembered by an obituarist as 'one of the few composers' of the time 'to deal uncondescendingly with the working classes, transposing their life styles and vernacular to the stage'. That was also, in a somewhat different genre, the purpose of Arnold Wesker, whose recently completed trilogy (*Chicken Soup with Barley*, *Roots* and *I'm Talking About Jerusalem*) was performed that summer at the Royal Court. A key theme of the last of the three plays was a caustic reappraisal of the achievements of the post-war Attlee government, and this was also a moment for reappraisal of Wesker himself. Kenneth Tynan remained supportive – 'one of the few Western dramatists,' he asserted in the *Observer*, 'who can write about political idealists without mockery or condescension' – but for the most part there was now a marked degree of scepticism. Hobson found himself listening 'with growing impatience' to 'the tedious repetitions of the most ordinary forms of illiterate speech'; Al Alvarez in the *New Statesman* noted that whereas 'in *Roots* the characters were alive, in *Jerusalem* they merely talk endlessly about the *idea* of being alive'; and Brien dismissed the whole thing as 'a Forsyte Saga of the Left'. Bart and Wesker: one at his zenith, the other getting his first glimpse of the other side of the hill.

The latter anyway was now not just a playwright. 'Wesker wants to lead unions to culture' was the *Daily Mail* headline at the end of June, after he had called a press conference to explain how he was actively urging trade unions to build theatres in industrial cities without one and – in order no longer to be 'at the mercy of the cultural cheapjacks and easy entertainment boys' concocting 'travesties like *I'm All Right, Jack*' – to sponsor film productions. But, he emphasised, his campaign was not just about money; it was even more about getting the unions 'to accept the principle that the Arts are as important as bread and butter'. 'It will take a long time,' he concluded. 'There is union machinery to go through, but our first aim is to establish the principle that the Arts are not just for the nobs.' And, one novelist might have added, not just about the nobs. 'Working men and women who read do not have the privilege of seeing themselves honestly and realistically portrayed in novels,' declared the working-class Alan Sillitoe in a *cri de coeur*, 'Both Sides of the Street', that appeared in the *TLS* barely a week later. Then, after noting how 'novelists of the Right', if they did try to portray the working class, were able to 'delineate only stock characters', he called on novelists of the left to emerge capable of 'encouraging ordinary people to think of themselves not as a mass but as individuals and ridding themselves of narrow patriotic attitudes'. As it happened, a new and rather different working-class novelist was just appearing. The life of what he called 'a "lace-curtain" working-class family' – respectable to the core – was Stan Barstow's subject, and the result was *A Kind of Loving*, published in July to mainly warm reviews. Maurice Richardson in the *New Statesman*, for instance, found this story of 'white-collared subtopians' in a West Riding industrial town 'satisfyingly up to the minute without being overstrained'; altogether, Barstow was 'a scrupulous naturalist' who had produced something 'seductively readable'. The mandarin *TLS* dissented. 'Flatly realistic', regretted its brief review, with 'much repetitive dialogue of the semi-illiterate kind', while – still worse – 'the interesting material in this monotonously styled fiction is all but swamped by its dreary preoccupation with sex.'[15]

Kingsley Amis was by now shifting decisively to the mandarin side of the broader socio-cultural argument. Writing in *Encounter* that summer, the focus of his critique was what he called, from his vantage-point as a decade-long lecturer at Swansea University, 'the pit of ignorance and incapacity into which British education has sunk since the war'. The ever-more-nominal socialist went on:

> The trouble is not just illiteracy, even understanding this as including unsteady grasp of the fundamentals of the subject as well as unsteadiness with hard words like *goes* and *its*. But for the moment I want to drum the fact of that illiteracy into those who are playing what I have heard called the university numbers racket, those quantitative thinkers who believe that Britain is *falling behind* America and Russia by not producing as many university graduates per head, and that she must *catch up* by building *more* colleges which will turn out *more* graduates and so give us *more* technologists (especially them) and *more* school-teachers. I wish I could have a little tape-and-loudspeaker arrangement sewn into the binding of this magazine, to be triggered off by the light reflected from the reader's eyes on to this part of the page, and set to bawl out at several bels: MORE WILL MEAN WORSE.

More will mean worse . . . 'One of the most eloquent defences of a hierarchical society that I have ever read,' commented the right-wing columnist Henry Fairlie. 'I agree with all he says: but to find Mr Amis in 1960 protesting against democratic values is well worth noticing, and even thinking about in one's bath.'

A charismatic, egalitarian politician who sometimes despaired of the mediocrity of popular taste passed away on 6 July, twelve years and a day after his creation of the National Health Service. 'ANEURIN BEVAN DIED NO FRIEND OF MINE "STILL GOD REST HIS SOUL",' wrote Florence Turtle in her diary. What was striking over the next few days was 'a rush of deep national emotion', as Mollie Panter-Downes put it, 'that the departure of no other statesman, bar Winston Churchill, would evoke' – a 'sense of acute loss' not only 'among the admiring millions of Labour's rank and file' but also 'among large numbers of the far from adoring sections of the community that had suffered at one time or another from his reckless invective'. The Tory press led the way, with the *Daily Mail* calling Bevan's early death 'one of the biggest political tragedies of our times'; Churchill himself made a rare appearance in the Commons to listen to the tributes; and the memorial service in the Abbey later in the month was a suitably grand affair. 'I know that it was impossible to be with him without quarrelling, that he was a leader with feet of clay and that sometimes he was selfish and unrewarding,' mused his on-off ally Richard Crossman during it. 'Nevertheless, oh dear, oh dear, oh dear . . .'

Bevan's service on the 26th came shortly after Crossman had spent a thought-provoking weekend in Pembrokeshire at a Fabian summer school:

> In the discussion a comrade got up and complained, 'What's the good of your saying you're progressive in social problems? On capital punishment the Party doesn't have a line and concedes a free vote. The same with the Wolfenden Report. Anything really difficult you funk.' And then another one got up and said, 'And what about your attitude to fee-paying schools? How can we believe in the Party when its leaders send their children there?' I made the usual reply about admitting the democratic principle that one has the right to pay fees, and to this I got the annihilating reply, 'Of course that applies, Mr Crossman, to everyone, except to you. Other people, who don't set themselves up as Socialist leaders, can pay fees. You can't.'

The coda came a month later, when the diarist gave dinner at the Athenaeum to Harold Wilson. 'He talked a good deal, and I was pleased that he did,' noted Crossman, 'about the need to revive some kind of Puritanism in the Party, some self-dedication, and he was careful to remind me twice that he couldn't tell the difference between hock and burgundy.' Afterwards, as Wilson dropped him off at Vincent Square, Crossman told him about the problems he was having deciding what to do about his son's education. 'Suddenly Harold said, "It was the worst mistake of my life when I sent my boys to [the private] University College School. You're right that we can't afford to sacrifice our principles".'[16]

'Shocking Summer weather,' recorded May Marlor, in Swadlincote, on 16 July. 'Heavy showers, an odd gleam of sun, then a depressingly cool dull evening – not cold enough for a fire but not warm enough to settle down with a book indoors in comfort.' The following weekend, the *People* featured a double-page exposé ('THIS IS THE BEATNIK HORROR') of the squalid living conditions of a flat rented by Liverpool art students, one of them John Lennon; on Wednesday the 27th, the day that a young Australian, Carmen Callil, arrived in England and was struck by how low the skies were as well as by the immediately visible difference between rich and poor, a government reshuffle saw the dogged Selwyn Lloyd going to No. 11, amid hopes that he could restore optimism to economic policy; two days later, Madge Martin and her husband arrived in Scarborough for their annual holiday ('down to the Spa, and enjoyable Max Jaffa concert'), while elsewhere in Yorkshire the industrious East Riding smallholder, Dennis Dee, borrowed a friend's boar for the white sow, 'but he was tired out, a bit like me'; and on Saturday the 30th in Sussex, the Bluebell Line was re-opened by volunteers three years after being closed by British Railways, and in Dorset the sun mercifully shone on the church fete at Loders – with 'the thing that really made the husbands sit up', according to the Rev. Oliver Willmott in his Parish Notes, being 'the parade of the Women's Institute wearing home-made hats that had cost no more than a shilling'.[17]

In retrospect, the book of the moment, though not a bestseller until its Penguin edition five years later, was *The Divided Self* by a radically minded 32-year-old Glaswegian psychoanalyst, R. D. Laing. The *New*

Statesman's hard-working critic Maurice Richardson praised this 'study of schizophrenia from the existentialist point of view', in particular how some of Laing's case histories were 'remarkable for the way he is able to preserve an integrated view of the patient as a person'. But Edward Glover in the *Listener* was unimpressed by Laing's sprinkling of 'existential arcana' and concluded, loftily enough, that 'his theoretical presentation of "subject–object" relations does not provide sufficient recompense for the sacrifice of most of the laboriously acquired analytical insights of the past seventy years.' Richardson surely called it right. Demystifying madness, demonstrating a continuum between the sane and the insane, providing an understanding of 'mad' behaviour – 'It made,' recalled Anthony Clare after Laing's death, 'an immense impact on me', and Clare was far from alone.

Top of the charts at the end of July was Cliff Richard's 'Please Don't Tease', but with 'Tie Me Kangaroo Down Sport' by Rolf Harris and 'Apache' by Cliff's backing group The Shadows both on their way up. It was the start of the Shadows phenomenon, defined by Hank Marvin's echo-laden vibrato on his Fender Stratocaster with tremolo arm. 'As the evening drew to a close and the live band was playing a Shadows tune, we would form lines,' recalled Yvonne Wilson about teenage Saturday-night dances in small-town Kendal. 'There'd be row after row of us doing the Shadow walk. The atmosphere was electric!' A more male constituency attended the Beaulieu Jazz Festival on August Bank Holiday (still early in the month), when outright, bottle-throwing warfare broke out between the 'traddies' loyal to the New Orleans tradition and the modernists inspired by Charlie Parker's bebop. The traddies tended to be bearded and wear long sweaters (frequently under duffel-coats), were often members of CND, and saw the modernists as not only betraying jazz's roots but as unacceptably close to American consumer culture, while the modernists deplored the increasing commercial popularity of trad jazz. Acker Bilk, definitely on the trad side of the fence, played for over an hour in an attempt to calm what he called the 'phoney imitation beatniks'. Jazz wars in Hampshire were complemented by Prom wars in South Kensington. 'There is really no "old" or "new" music – only music, good or bad,' rather nervously noted the *Radio Times* about the 'New Look' for that year's Proms, as BBC's new Controller of Music, William Glock, put the emphasis on the modern. 'Many, though they thought the

BBC right to broadcast new music, had not listened to any of it themselves,' reported Audience Research after the Proms were over; a minority declared their outright hostility to '"psychopathic muck" masquerading as music'. Thea Musgrave's *Triptych* won an Appreciation Index rating of only 39 (out of 100), but the evening of Gilbert and Sullivan excerpts proved 'very popular'. 'The Proms,' complained an accountant after watching Glock defend his policy on *Monitor*, 'have been ruined by this compulsory listening to modern music. In fact one would rather not attend them now as the programmes are spoiled – the new music is not even placed that one can leave the hall conveniently.'[18]

Two diarists, neither of them Prom-goers, had rather different Augusts. 'It was very good in beautiful colour; moral: count your blessings,' recorded Judy Haines on Tuesday the 2nd after taking her daughters up to town to see Hayley Mills in *Pollyanna* at Studio One. 'I acceded to Ione's request to see it through again. Came away at 5.45 and what a rush hour! Queued in long line for tickets but we soon got seats in the train. Ione felt ill and Pamela had splitting head-ache. I was just weary.' Next week, Friday the 12th, a perhaps even wearier Prime Minister spent the day in bed at Chequers 'dozing, reading, & doing a little work'. The work involved regular updates on a threatened power strike, with a settlement reached late that night; the reading was Trollope's *Orley Farm*, 'a fine story'. Three days later it was an unofficial shipping strike that concerned Macmillan – 'doing a great deal of harm, & a great loss of money' – while the following day Judy Haines took the girls to Kew Gardens (by boat from Westminster Pier). 'Queue for Cafeteria, but pleasant people. However, we passed through to the tea pavilion and how we enjoyed that delightful 3/- set tea. So fresh and plentiful.' On Thursday the 18th, having heard the welcome news that the *Queen Elizabeth* had managed to sail, thus signalling the imminent end of the shipping strike, the PM set off to Yorkshire for some shooting. 'Outside Leeds there was anti-H Bomb demonstration of a dozen or so youths with placards. The only good one was "I'm not a Grouse. I want to live"!' A day later, and for one mother in Chingford, as presumably for many elsewhere by this time, the summer holidays suddenly seemed endless: 'It is a lovely morning and I was irritated that the children were frowsily indoors instead of out treasure-hunting or something.'[19]

5

An Act of Holy Communion

'Full of silly pseudo-intellectual jokes,' pencilled the Lord Chamberlain's Office – still the theatre's censor – on the original script. More or less unbutchered, but to a sparse and initially puzzled audience, *Beyond the Fringe* debuted on 22 August 1960 as part of the Edinburgh Festival. Earlier in the evening at the Lyceum, a young working-class actor from Hull, Tom Courtenay, had been making his name in *The Seagull*; now in the same theatre it was the turn of four Oxbridge graduates, two of them working-class.

A national newspaper critic who got it immediately was the *Daily Mail*'s Peter Lewis. Hailing 'the funniest, most intelligent, and most original revue to be staged in Britain for a very long time', he noted how *Beyond the Fringe* disregarded 'all the jaded trimmings of conventional sketches, production numbers, dancing, and girls', instead getting down to 'the real business of intimate revue, which is satire and parody'. So too *Punch*'s Eric Keown and, inevitably, the *Spectator*'s Alan Brien. Between them they described Peter Cook (writer of most of the material) as 'brilliant wearing Mr Macmillan's teeth' and 'a little man whose ambition to be a judge was thwarted by lack of Latin'; Jonathan Miller as 'a lanky, tow-haired, staring-eyed disciple of St Vitus with the face of an aggrieved unicorn'; 'gig-lamped, square-faced' Alan Bennett as not only a 'preternaturally old schoolboy giving an anti-intellectual pi-jaw' but a 'strangulated' Anglican clergyman ('Life's like a tin of sardines, we're all looking for the key . . .'); and Dudley Moore (providing the music) as 'a born jester' who was 'at his most hysterical as a pianist who couldn't finish'. Houses were packed from the second night onwards for these 'four young men in fluorescent shirts', a West End run was soon being planned, and in the convincing judgement almost half a century later of Michael Billington (present at the 'slightly shambolic opening performance'), this moment – even more than the first night of *Look Back in Anger* four years earlier – 'marked a genuine cultural turning point', launching as it did 'a whole era of snook-cocking disrespect'.[1]

Full houses too that August at the Queen's in Blackpool, where a rather different sort of revue, *The Time of Your Life*, starred George Formby, Jimmy Clitheroe and Yana – 'a busty, sultry-voiced chanteuse' famous, according to Formby's biographer, for her fish-tail dresses and 'huge gay following'. Elsewhere it was a less happy seaside picture. At Southend, the local paper complained about the absence of 'the Carnival spirit' at that town's 1960 Carnival. 'Where were the streamers, balloons and the wavers? Crowds on long stretches of the route watched the procession pass by with hardly a clap or a cheer. Far too many of Saturday's crowd were television-conditioned. They had seen just about all there was to see . . .' Apathy was not the problem at Porthcawl, where a European heavyweight championship fight between Newport's Dick Richardson and Blackpool's Brian London finished with a full-scale brawl in the ring, while at Whitby, an American visitor found her brief stay there 'depressingly mucky', all too typical of English seaside resorts. 'Of course,' explained Sylvia Plath in her letter home, 'the weather is hardly ever sheer fair, so most people are in woollen suits and coats and tinted plastic raincoats. The sand is muddy and dirty. The working class is also dirty, strewing candy papers, gum and cigarette wrappers.'[2]

The resort where the TUC gathered in early September was Douglas on the Isle of Man. In its preview, the *Daily Herald*, in effect the paper of the trade union movement, urged support for a resolution – put forward by the Association of Cine, TV and Allied Technicians, and inspired by Arnold Wesker – calling on unions to participate more actively in the arts. 'Perhaps it is an idea that takes a little getting used to,' conceded the *Herald*, before declaring that 'the heritage of music and plays and films and books and painting and fine buildings is the heritage of everyone.' 'We do not accept,' the ACTT's Ralph Bond told Congress on the 8th, 'that culture is the preserve of an enlightened intelligentsia and that any old rubbish is good enough for the masses.'

After noting that the only difference between tap water and TV was that 'tap water is purified before we get it', he argued that 'our spiritual heritage, its culture, its songs, its living drama, its poetry is dying away, distorted and vulgarised by the purveyors of mass-production entertainment.' Resolution 42 was carried – but, significantly, against the wishes of the General Council, for whom Wilfred Beard insisted that 'unions have enough difficulty in raising subscriptions high enough to pay for their industrial work, without the additional expense of encouraging culture.'

Next day, Macmillan had a fatherly chat at Balmoral with the 'very sensible' Antony Armstrong-Jones about his career ('he realises that the Stock Exchange, or an advertising firm, or even photography of fashion models will not do'); on Saturday the 10th, the civil servant Henry St John took a train to Dorset ('opposite me sat a girl in light blue trousers, no stockings, sandals, with lacquered toe nails and long straight straw-coloured hair'), while that evening's sequence on ITV included the short-lived experiment of the second half of a live league match (Blackpool v Bolton, no Stanley Matthews, one goal) and debuts for *77 Sunset Strip* (an American import) and *Candid Camera* ('nothing very clever', thought the *Daily Mail*'s Peter Black, about 'making fools of simple feelings'); over the next two days, an inexorable pull to the capital was suggested by the *Guardian* for the first time printing in London, though *Woman's Hour* ran a special East Anglian edition featuring 'Allan Smethurst, postman' singing 'one of his own Norfolk songs'; on the 14th, Florence Turtle visited the packed but 'horrible' Picasso exhibition at the Tate ('Talk about Whistler's Chucking a Paint pot at the Public. Picasso chucks a dust bin!'); and, the following Saturday, the even sterner Hugh Selbourne watched on his set the 'farrago of nonsense' that was the Last Night of the Proms, including 'a poor speech' by Sir Malcolm Sargent.[3]

But September's main cultural event was a first night – that of *Billy Liar*, adapted for the stage from the Keith Waterhouse novel, directed by Lindsay Anderson and starring an aspiring Salford actor. 'For all the commendable efforts of Albert Finney,' reckoned Anthony Heap on the 13th, 'young Billy remains an unamusing, uninteresting and unappetising clod throughout,' with indeed the whole piece 'trashy, tedious and totally unfunny', reducing the diarist to 'counting the number of "bloody's" uttered by the foul-mouthed father'. Other critics, though all praising Finney, were rather more nuanced. Keown likewise wanted 'to throttle the father', but admired how the 'unattractive delinquent' Billy became 'an extraordinarily complete character', by turn 'shambling, cunning, cowardly yet childishly eager'; Brien regretted that, despite its wonderfully convincing depiction of Billy's working-class northern family ('a milieu too often cartooned on the stage'), the play ultimately degenerated into 'over-stuffed emptiness like the aftermath of a cream bun feast', largely because of 'Billy's isolation from the complicated confusions of the world outside'. For Kenneth Tynan, an admirer of the 'exuberant' original, the shame was that its 'broader implications' had been 'skirted or ignored', with instead an emphasis on 'pure farce'. 'The present state of the English theatre is one of deadlock,' he more broadly argued in his *Observer* review of the 18th. 'Its audience is still predominantly conservative, wedded by age and habits to the old standards; its younger playwrights, meanwhile, are predominantly anti-conservative, irretrievably divorced from the ideological *status quo.*' And, he concluded, 'the only general assumption in which Mr Wesker, his colleagues and their audiences seem to be substantially agreed is that the lower strata of English society deserve a more central place on the English stage.'[4]

The cover of the current *Radio Times* featured the 53-year-old Gilbert Harding, thus accurately reflecting his broadcasting ubiquity: on the panel of television's *What's My Line?*, chairman of radio's *Twenty Questions* and *Round Britain Quiz*, and – that particular Sunday evening – subject of John Freeman's *Face to Face*. The programme would always be remembered for Harding coming close to breaking down as he referred to watching his mother die, though at the time there seems to have been as much controversy about his confession that he would prefer to be dead himself. 'A brilliant piece of interviewing, but painful to watch' was the general consensus among the Viewers' Panel, with many agreeing with the opinion that 'unexpected exposure of grief is not for public exhibition'. Older viewers were especially disconcerted, one describing 'publicly prying into personal private lives' as 'not viewers' business', another feeling 'terribly uneasy when John Freeman probes into a man's soul'. As for the subject, famously the rudest man on television, there was considerable sympathy. 'The personality of

"Old Grumpy" certainly came over well,' thought the wife of an armature winder, 'and proved him to be a most kind and gentle man for whom we now have much feeling', while a teacher's wife found herself 'terribly sorry for Harding – not because of the interview itself, but because of what it revealed of the man'.

'These changes do not mark the end of an old era; in a sense they are the beginning of a new one,' unconvincingly explained the same issue of the *Radio Times*. 'They are the extension and adaptation of the past to provide a service which is suited to the needs of listeners today and adjusted to the tempo of modern life.' The key change, announced a few months earlier and about to take effect on the 19th, was the decision to move the late evening news on the Home Service from 9.00 to 10.00 – and, crucially, to truncate Big Ben's chimes before the bulletin to only one. 'Ever since November 1940,' noted W. Tudor Pole, founder of the Big Ben Council, in a letter to the *Radio Times* after the announcement, 'the chiming and striking of Big Ben has signalled a Minute of Prayer and Remembrance at nine each evening':

> This observance has spread across the world, and is now widely kept by men and women of good will, both here and overseas, including those who live behind the 'Iron Curtain' . . .
>
> Following consultation with our members and supporters at home and abroad, the Big Ben Council has decided to recommend that the 'Silent Minute' shall continue in future to be kept at nine each evening as in the past. To switch the observance from 9.0 to 10.0 pm would prove unsuitable for the very many who value and keep this evening tryst in hospitals, nursing homes, and in family circles, the latter hour being too late for the purpose.

Eventually, after a sustained campaign to reinstate the chimes, involving thousands of letters to the BBC, the governors accepted a compromise by which they would gradually fade away as the 10 o'clock bulletin began to be read. Irrespective of the Big Ben issue, at least one listener was already welcoming the change of schedule. 'I am busy at 6 o'clock in the evening and in bed by 10,' Mrs J. M. Woodward of Tunbridge Wells told the *Radio Times*. 'As long as there was a nine o'clock News one felt impelled to listen to it and then to go to bed seething with the world's problems. What a relief now to be able to leave it all until tomorrow, and think of something else!'[5]

The cultural plates continued to shift in the closing days of September. *Monitor* featured what one critic called 'the brilliant meeting with Shelagh Delaney and the vision through her lucid eyes of the restless, slate-grey, black-brick spirit of Salford', while earlier in the evening not only did ITV show Alun Owen's *Lena, Oh My Lena* – concluding his trilogy of working-class realist plays, this one starring Billie Whitelaw and set, according to the script, 'on the East Lancs Road . . . between St Helens and Salford' – but the BBC initiated a major weekly series of newly commissioned plays by contemporary dramatists, starting with John Whiting's *A Walk in the Desert* (about a disabled man in a provincial town, with music by Bert Weedon). The Sunday heavies and the weeklies were by now giving a mixed reception to Kingsley Amis's fourth novel, *Take a Girl Like You* – 'nasty & bad', commented Larkin on the 26th after reading it. Arguably as resonant an event was ITV's launch on the 23rd of *Bootsie and Snudge*. Written by Marty Feldman, Barry Took and John Antrobus, it related the fortunes in Civvy Street of two of *The Army Game*'s now demobbed characters: Montague 'Bootsie' Bisley (Alfie Bass), handyman and general dogsbody at a Pall Mall gentleman's club, the Imperial, and Claude Snudge (Bill Fraser), the commissionaire who tormented him. Infused by class and a love-hate relationship with authority, the show was, claimed Simon Callow half a century later, 'an account of postwar Britain as acute as anything from the pen of John Osborne or Arnold Wesker, and rather funnier'.[6]

'Three party conferences,' noted John Fowles on 8 October. 'The Liberals – children playing at kings and queens; the Socialists, passionate, sincere, adult but sadly unfascinated; the Tories, hollow platitudes, the village hall. Even the *Telegraph* admits that there is no Tory enthusiasm – "rows of empty seats". The only party that seems real, contemporary, adult and alive, is the Socialist.' Alive perhaps, but alive with discord: Labour had by now put aside Clause 4 as its great contentious issue, replaced since the summer by that of unilateralism – a cause embraced by Frank Cousins, leader of the Transport and General Workers' Union, and increasingly by unions generally. Ahead of

Labour's defence debate on the 5th, the expectation was that Hugh Gaitskell, unyieldingly not a ban-the-bomb man, would be defeated on the issue. 'All the speakers,' reflected Mollie Panter-Downes, present that Wednesday at Scarborough's smoke-filled Spa Hall, 'were so much in earnest that what they had to say, however badly expressed or haltingly delivered, seemed to take abstract shape beside them on the rostrum'.

> They spoke of fears that had become a familiar part of everyone's daily life, which maybe is the worst thing of all – fear of instant annihilation or mass destruction from the pressing of a button by a Russian or an American finger, fear of trigger-happy accidents, fear of American patrol flights from Britain, fear for children and homes. 'If the mad groups in the world want to have a go at each other, let us have no part of them!' shouted Mr Cousins. 'Let us stop being an expendable base for the Americans,' urged someone else. Last year's winner of the Nobel Peace Prize, Mr Philip Noel-Baker, a gray-haired, distinguished man with a gentle face, came to the rostrum like an anxious father, to warn the children that if they changed their views on the urgency of working for collective disarmament they would never win the country to their side. A lady whose name I did not catch but who sounded like Joyce Grenfell imitating a games mistress roared brusquely that the scientists were now killing goats by rays, and that she would rather be blown up, thanks very much . . .

At last Gaitskell took to his feet:

> It was a magnificent performance. He hammered home his intention of continuing as leader until the Parliamentary Labour Party decided otherwise, and of fighting neutralism to the last ditch. He stated the clear choice for the Labour voter – to be inside the NATO alliance and pressing for collective disarmament, or to be outside, 'defenceless and alone.' The part of the speech that particularly infuriated the nuclear-disarmers and caused many angry, gesticulating young men to rise, as though they intended to rush the platform, was his asking, also in anger, 'Do you think we can simply accept a decision of this kind, become overnight the pacifist unilateralists and fellow-travellers that other people are? How

> wrong can you be?', and adding bitingly, 'As wrong as you are about the attitude of the British people.' At the end, the conference and some – though noticeably not all – of his colleagues on the platform rose to cheer him loudly . . .

In the event, union block votes ensured that the somewhat vague unilateralist motion was carried, albeit far more narrowly than anticipated.

'Wanted: a Leader', demanded the next issue of the anti-Gaitskell, pro-unilateralist *New Statesman*; the most plausible candidate, inevitably coming from the left, was Harold Wilson, who stayed seated, vigorously striking matches for his pipe, during Gaitskell's standing ovation. 'Frankly all he's interested in is turning the situation to his own advantage,' Anthony Wedgwood Benn had observed during pre-conference manoeuvres. 'He thinks Gaitskell can be dislodged. My opinion of him drops the more I see of him.' There were two other pointers to the future. One was the state of public opinion, where Gaitskell's confidence was justified to the extent that Gallup evidence suggested only about a third of the electorate holding unilateralist views. The other was the development of the nuclear disarmament movement itself, where the emerging key figure was a dynamic, charming young American, Ralph Schoenman, studying at the London School of Economics. Increasingly disenchanted by the CND's lack of urgency, typified in his eyes by the fact that it had formed a Campaign cricket team, Schoenman successfully detached Bertrand Russell from the organisation and formed that month the Committee of 100, embracing direct action and civil disobedience. The danger was obvious, and by the end of October the *Guardian* was warning how law-breaking would 'alienate the British public, especially the sweet young suburban wives who form an important part of the movement'.[7]

On all this, as on so much else, Henry St John in Acton had no comment to make or record. But on Sunday, 16 October he did spend fourpence buying the *Empire News*, prior to its being absorbed by the *News of the World*, which 'led to a few remarks by the shopkeeper on the high costs of producing newspapers, especially for labour'. Next morning, the mid-market *News Chronicle* – 'unsmart, inefficient, non-hip, elderly', but also, noted soon afterwards one of its journalists, Philip Purser, 'kindly, concerned, occasionally courageous and in its own way cultured' – appeared as usual. An editorial called on Gaitskell to continue to 'STAND FIRM'; Purser reviewed the previous night's play on the BBC, praising 'an enormously vital young actor called Anthony Booth'; Greta Lamb's dieting tips included 'have a tin of no-sugar biscuits by your bed' so 'you won't get up and raid the larder'; a reader, Mrs D. M. Todd of Streatham Hill, shared her method of countering claustrophobia on the London tube ('I find that sucking a boiled sweet helps to relieve that awful tension'); and the subject of Big Chief I-Spy's column was the 'new special lamp fixed to the beacon poles' of zebra crossings, with the first report of it being spotted coming from Redskin D. G. Jackson of Warrington, thereby winning him a tie. Rumours about the paper's uncertain prospects had been circulating for months if not years, and in the course of that Monday the owner, Laurence Cadbury, finally decided that, for all its fine liberal traditions and heritage, enough was enough: the *Chronicle* would be sold to the *Daily Mail*, and its sister London evening paper, the *Star*, to the *Evening News* – in both cases, to be swallowed virtually whole by Lord Rothermere's Associated Newspapers, with immediate effect. The announcement was made in the evening, and reputedly the *Chronicle*'s drama critic only found out next morning when the *Mail* unexpectedly came through his front door instead. Even by the standards of Fleet Street it had been a brutal death. Still, Peter Pound perhaps had a point, commenting in the *Listener* on TV interviews with journalists from the defunct papers: 'In all their accusations about whose fault it was – the owners', trade unions', advertisers' – I did not detect the slightest hint of a still, small voice asking "Was it also perhaps partly our fault for not producing better newspapers?"'

On Tuesday the 18th, the *Mail* sought to reassure its new former *Chronicle* readers: not only had the *Mail* 'consistently supported progressive Conservatism', but 'its outlook is liberal in the true sense of the term'. Two days later, readers had their say. 'For many years I have taken the *Daily Mail* and have admired the modern, forthright, and vital manner in which the news has been presented,' declared C. Knight of Southend-on-Sea. 'The first mongrel edition filled me with disgust.' By contrast, J. W. Tapper of Worthing, a *Chronicle* reader for over 50 years, offered his congratulations on 'the joint issue'. 'I hope however,' he added, 'you will not be too critical of the Labour Party.'[8]

'The inevitable is happening on a large scale,' an anonymous white man told a Manchester paper in August 1960. 'Moss Side is not large enough for these immigrants. Now they are spreading to other areas. Wherever they set foot, property values tumble; white people move out as soon as possible in the stupid belief that they will escape the invaders' tentacles. My own area, Rusholme, has undergone a drastic change in the last two years. Everywhere I look there are Jamaicans, West Africans, Pakistanis . . .'

Net immigration from the New Commonwealth was certainly accelerating: 21,600 in 1959, 57,700 in 1960, with the West Indian component in those two years 16,400 and 49,650 respectively. The pull was essentially economic – the demand for labour – and the political response for the time being largely static: neither legislation to control numbers (with Rab Butler at the Home Office skilfully heading off the Tory right, unable even to bring up the issue at the autumn party conference) nor legislation to outlaw racial discrimination (blocked in the summer by an all-party group of MPs). But noises off were getting louder, not least from Colin Jordan, who taught at a primary school in Coventry and ran the White Defence League. 'Our greatest national asset and treasure is our Anglo-Saxon blood,' he insisted to a journalist, adding that the influx of non-whites would inevitably breed 'a mulatto population'. Jordan's WDL specialised in 'Keep Britain White' demonstrations, including one on 1 September when protesters – mainly white youths – gathered at Waterloo Station to meet three boat trains from Southampton carrying West Indian immigrants; amid angry scenes they were successfully dispersed by police.

That day the ten-year-old Floella Benjamin, joining her parents in London, was on one of those trains – 'so unlike the smaller wooden ones back in Trinidad that I almost didn't recognise it as one'. For a few weeks she was at school in Chiswick – teacher treating her like an idiot, children taunting her – before the family moved to Penge. 'I hated the rejection,' she remembered. 'Even going shopping was an ordeal. Sandra [her older sister] and I would stand at the counter waiting to be served but would be ignored, treated as though we were invisible . . . I came to England feeling special, like a princess, but was made to feel like a scrounger.' One Sunday the family went to church. 'I see they are letting in that kind now,' she heard a group of white parishioners complain after the service. 'Is no place sacred?' So too for Mandy Phillips, arriving from Dominica that year in her late twenties and settling in Notting Hill. 'They used to say "go back home",' she recalled. 'You know, Black this, Black that. White people did not want black people. They did not want dogs. They did not want the Irish. I can remember walking past a church on a Sunday and then these children started throwing bottles. It was a shock.' How many white people did not want black people? 'Is like that Stork on television,' V. S. Naipaul heard a disenchanted West Indian immigrant say 'in a slow, negligent way' on a boat train to Southampton a few days after Benjamin's arrival. 'Three out of five can't tell the difference from butter. Three out of five don't care for you.'

It was almost certainly at least three out of five in Birmingham, emerging that autumn as a focal point of white opposition to uncontrolled immigration. 'My own view,' declared a local councillor for multi-racial, overcrowded Sparkbrook, 'is that immigration must be slowed up so that the people who are already here can be integrated into the life of Birmingham.' Later in October saw the formation of the Birmingham Immigration Control Committee, headed by a Conservative shopkeeper-*cum*-councillor, Charles Collett, who was at pains to distance his committee from explicitly racist (or even neo-fascist) pressure groups, while publicly highlighting 'the menace of coloured infiltration and a piebald population'. A student living that autumn in digs in Balsall Heath, one of the city's rougher areas, was the liberal-minded diarist Kate Paul, recording what she saw in the non-judgemental, documentary detail of a stranger. 'Now I'm in the flat in the notorious Varna Road, street of tarts and unsavoury stabbings,' she noted in late September. And a few days later, on a Sunday:

> The people on this street live on their sexual instincts and fear. It's a street of brothels and men hanging about on corners. To be white is exceptional. I have just been out for cigarettes. The street was scattered with Jamaicans and Indians, standing in small groups, or wandering in and out of houses. A few old women, no longer of any interest, walk slowly up the street carrying shopping bags.
>
> There is suspicion and fear, eyes shift from one face to another, black,

> bloodshot ones and pale shifting ones . . .
>
> Men in cars kerb-crawl and raise their fingers, leaning forward, eager, their faces drawn with lust. I hate these, not the street-walkers.
>
> As for them, I think they're mad to be in such a losing business. It's really terrible in the street. They have cock-fights and stabbings and the police come up here in twos or on motor bikes.
>
> At night it's really grim, men melting into doorways, beckoning. The endless crawl of cars, the slamming of doors, the women's shrill voices. Old men being insulted by young tarts . . .
>
> The old couple upstairs, us and two of the tarts are the only whites. The old people, Leopold and his wife, are ancient, amazingly kind and straight from a Balzac novel.

'I've just been to the front room,' the appalled but fascinated diarist added. 'The street is alive with prostitutes and pimps in spivvy suits, spilling out of doorways. I daren't let them catch me watching. One avoids other people's eyes. It's grim.'[9]

Ultimately, despite everything, the future would be more or less multicultural; it would also, less controversially but not always welcomed, be consumerist.

The new in 1960 included the stripe in Signal toothpaste; the spectacularly successful launch of Blue Gillette Extra (the blade touted as a scientific 'break-through' in shaving); 'ready-salted' crisps from Golden Wonder, an ingenious riposte to the familiar blue bag of salt in Smith's Crisps; the arrival of Lego; plastic carrier bags and refuse sacks; the transformation of the Kenwood mixer through a stylish blender attachment; the first automatic dishwasher (Miele); and Hoover's manufacture of the Keymatic washing machine, a fully automatic model. Keeping a watchful eye on this last development was the young washing-machine entrepreneur John Bloom, who early in the year had acquired his own production facility by effectively taking over Rolls Razor, a staid, loss-making company based in Cricklewood that had diversified from razors into washing machines. Typically, Bloom was much attracted by the word *Rolls*, whose deluxe connotations would, he thought, speak to his target working-class market.[10]

There was still a long way to go, not least in terms of mod cons. Figures for the first half of 1960 reveal 79 per cent of adults owning a television set, but otherwise possession of major consumer durables as the preserve of a minority: 40 per cent owning a washing machine, 31 per cent a car, 22 per cent a telephone and 21 per cent a fridge. Even among the middle class, barely half had a car or a washing machine, and only two out of five a fridge. Jacqueline Aitken's family in Kingston, living in a respectable block of council flats, had by this time only just acquired a car and a phone:

> We still didn't have a washing machine or a fridge and owned just a very small black and white television. We went for a holiday once a year but we hardly ever went out as a family otherwise.
>
> We had the special treat on Sundays of a shared bottle of Tizer and a Wall's family block of raspberry ripple ice cream after our roast chicken. This was High Living as far as we were concerned. The flat was still furnished with the dark utility table and chairs and sideboard bought just after the war, with a gloomy brown sofa and two chairs filling up the rest of the room . . .

Nor did older people in particular necessarily plunge headlong into the new. 'He said my old machine was not worth repairing,' noted Florence Turtle about the visit of 'the Singer man' in September. 'Recommended the electric one I tried in the shop. Said I would think about it.' Even so, the regretful but predominantly excited experience not long before of the Haines family in Chingford was perhaps emblematic. 'John took Pamela to collect 8948 VW,' recorded Judy on a Saturday in June. 'Beautiful! but so sad leaving 825 CEV.' Then next day came the second afternoon drive in their 'lovely grey' new Triumph Herald. 'Parked in a glade near the Owl, where we could decently have a good look at her, particularly in the Boot which is accessible from outside as well as in . . . We have heater and blower, nine pockets, and wonderful windows in the TH. Doors like horse box. Girls have grand view from back seats.' One last initiation ceremony remained: 'As the car has been described as "Fabulous Triumph Herald," we've named her Faith.'[11]

Persil, Tide, Omo, Daz, Stork, Guinness, Nescafé, Surf, Maxwell House, Ford – these (in descending order) were the ten most heavily advertised products in 1960. As for TV commercials specifically, research in August revealed that the two most popular ads were for

Esso and Sunblest, while the most irritating were for Daz, Omo, Tide and Surf, each incessantly repeated through the evening, leaving the viewers the main victim of the apparently never-ending detergent war. It was more than irritation, though, that the *Spectator*'s Peter Forster continued to feel for 'that intolerably coy couple' Philip and Katie 'whose love-life is dedicated to proving that "Oxo gives a meal Man-appeal".' The selling was a shade more nuanced in *Jim's Inn* – ITV's weekly advertising magazine – which, based in Jimmy Hanley's pub at 'Wembleham', was still going strong. Hanley continued to play himself as 'Mine Host', accompanied by his wife Maggie; regulars included Jack the burly farmer, the absent-minded Ron (manager of the village's hardware and electrical store), the commuting Dennis with a job in the City and an army-style moustache, and Roma, who ran the local beauty salon.

Food consumption steadily increased, by 1960 perhaps around one-fifth more per person per week than in 1950. The changes were qualitative as well. Sheila Hutchins in the *News Chronicle* argued that the advent of the Danish open sandwich, or *smörrebröd*, along with the rapidly growing popularity of coffee, wine, spaghetti and Chinese restaurants, was proof that 'the typical Englishman' was 'no longer conservative' about his food and drink; Marguerite Patten's lavishly illustrated *Cookery in Colour* – seeking, according to the publishers, 'to match the gay, practical kitchens of today and bring a sense of adventure into cooking' – included a recipe for prawn cocktail and accompanying pink sauce; American-style steak houses, led by the Angus chain, were now flourishing; and Anthony Heap, eating his regular café lunch, overheard 'one old gaffer' say to another, 'You never hear of mutton nowadays, always lamb.' The inexorable march of convenience foods continued. Sales of deep-frozen food, having doubled between 1955 and 1957, doubled again by 1960, while one evening in Hull a suspicious Philip Larkin tried what might well have been a Vesta forerunner. 'I had a peculiar reconstituted beef curry for supper – enough for two, it said!' he reported to Monica Jones. 'Not on your life: I ate it all. The rice, prettily done up in a separate packet, was nice (how do you dry rice?), but the beef curry was awful – dark fibrous acrid syrup, not nearly hot enough.'[12]

Following on from a similar survey three years earlier, Market

Investigations Ltd that autumn interviewed 2,000 housewives at the door about their grocery-shopping habits. Some 40 per cent now shopped once a week (compared with 35 per cent in 1957), and Friday was the main shopping day for 40 per cent. Whereas 52 per cent had always gone to the same grocer in 1957, only 27 per cent now did so, with 'loyal buyers found to a greater degree among the older, working-class sections of the community'. Where did housewives shop? 'Of every ten regular customers, five use the Independent grocer, three go to a shop belonging to a Co-operative Society, while two buy their groceries regularly at a Multiple outlet' – ie, with ten or more branches. Predictably, Co-ops were especially favoured by 'the working class, older women over 45, and in the North and Scotland', whereas independent grocers had 'a slight bias towards upper-income families'. As for supermarkets, these were now used by one in ten as their main grocer, usually in the south, where most were located. Significantly, in four out of five categories – clean shops, fresh stocks, economical, best range of stock – the interviewees ranked the multiples (including the supermarkets) highest, with the independents favoured for friendly service and the Co-ops winning none of the categories. Across all grocers, self-service was on the rise – one in ten grocers in 1957, now one in four – and a substantial minority of housewives saw no advantage in it, with 'antagonism somewhat higher among the higher income groups, among housewives over 45, and in the North-East'. Interviews were also conducted with 2,000 housewives as they left their grocer, always on a Friday. These revealed that the average spend was 10s, though often above that for those with ITV at home; that four in five did not take a shopping list with them; and that 'almost half the housewives who claimed to have a regular grocer were, in fact, coming out of *another* grocer's shop when they were interviewed'. In short, solemnly concluded the report, 'shopping around is rife indeed'.

About the same time, Katharine Whitehorn inspected the facelift at Bentalls of Kingston and noted that it was part of the trend among big department stores to 'cover in the well, do away with daylight, smarten up and get modern', with Bentalls following the example of Bourne and Hollingsworth while anticipating Liberty's. Among the major multiples, modernisation increasingly involved larger-than-normal retail space, as in a huge 12,000-square-feet Bradford example. 'We went to the new Super Duper [W H] Smith's shop & spent some time there,' recorded Florence Turtle in July. 'It is a lovely store with various new ideas in selling. I particularly admired the electric signs suspended from the ceiling indicating departments, Cash desks etc.' By contrast, she added, she had also visited in Bradford 'a most antiquated Woolworths with steps up to it very badly lit', as well as 'a very old Victorian enclosed Market'.[13]

Overall, it was indisputable that the multiple retailers were on the up, with their total share of the distributive trades rising (by value of sales) from 22 per cent in 1950 to 29 per cent by 1961, while in the food trade specifically, their turnover grew by 42 per cent between 1957 and 1961, compared with 11 per cent for independent retailers and a mere 3 per cent for co-operative societies. Increasingly it would be supermarkets that spearheaded the multiples: by mid-1960, American-owned Fine Fare was leading the way with 40 stores – '100s and 100s of BRANDED GROCERIES at PERMANENT CUT PRICES!' shrieked one opening soon afterwards in Rayleigh, Essex – followed by Sainsbury's on 27 and Victor Value on 23, with the more upmarket Waitrose lagging on 6. Madge Martin for one preferred a different type of therapy. 'We had a fascinating time in the Portobello Market,' she noted after a Saturday jaunt. 'It is entrancing – the *amount* of things to buy at the stalls, or in the cavern-like shops, with their many tables of silver, china, jewellery, "Victoriana", pictures, "objets d'art" in wild profusion – and the strange people buying and selling.'

Arguably the emblematic consumer experience that autumn was in Southend-on-Sea. 'Shopping was never, *never* so good!' exclaimed the headline for an advertorial in the local paper marking the launch of Super-Save, until recently the Essoldo Cinema. Fifteen thousand square feet of floor space, 15 wide aisles, 38 displays, 10 counters – the key stats for Britain's first American-style no-frills self-service discount store were as expansive as the prose:

> SUPER-SAVE is a new kind of store – the only one of its kind in Britain. At SUPER-SAVE you can buy everything – but everything! – food, clothes, cosmetics, shoes, kitchen utensils, toys, ironmongery – the lot under one great roof. You wander round with a little cart helping yourself. And when you think you've spent enough, you go through a sort of

gate, where a pretty young mother of a cashier tots up your bill – and you find you haven't spent nearly as much as you thought!

'We're building up a huge turnover and we buy in bulk,' the manager explained. 'So we can afford a very small profit margin because it all adds up. We're all right, Jack. And Jill – the housewife, our customer – she's all right, too.' To the local paper's reporter, after walking round the store shortly before it opened on 30 September, it felt like a landmark moment. 'I thought back to the days of rationing – a dozen years ago now – when shopping was purgatory. I remembered the queues, the harassed, terse assistants, everything you wanted "under the counter." To those of us who remember those grim days, SUPER-SAVE is a shoppers' paradise.' Southenders mainly agreed – despite disapproval of the new venture by the local Chamber of Trade, protective of small shopkeepers – and on the first Saturday the crowds trying to get in were so large that the doors had to be closed after a quarter of an hour. Especially thrilled were the Keddies, the two youngish brothers behind Super-Save; Peter Keddy was perhaps not being vainglorious when he expressed the belief that Super-Save, with its wide range and its low prices, would 'create a new shopping public – that it will give people what they've always wanted and never been able to afford before'.[14]

'Nasty, malicious, warped, banaly snobbish, and, in its affectation of chic cynicism, as rancidly unpleasant to the palate as gone-off *paté de foie gras*' ran Kenneth Allsop's *Daily Mail* review on 20 October 1960, adding that 'the lower classes' were 'caricature proles, viewed with sneering contempt'. That Thursday, though, it was not Auberon Waugh's *The Foxglove Saga* that made the main headlines, but a novel already three decades old. 'LADY C. IN THE DOCK TODAY' announced a newspaper placard, as the trial began at the Old Bailey that in effect tested the limits of the recent liberalising Obscene Publications Act – and, specifically, whether Penguin Books could publish, as a mass-market paperback, an unexpurgated edition of D. H. Lawrence's *Lady Chatterley's Lover*.

Mervyn Griffith-Jones – with, noted a watching Mollie Panter-Downes, 'the sort of neat, well-boned good looks that you often see in eighteenth-century family portraits of country squires and their spaniels regarding each other with mutual satisfaction' – opened for the Crown. After calling it a novel that 'sets upon a pedestal promiscuous and adulterous intercourse' and commended sensuality 'almost as a virtue', he asked the nine men and three women on the jury a trio of questions, the third of which, apparently ad-libbed, became instantly quotable: 'Would you approve of your young sons, young daughters – because girls can read as well as boys – reading this book? Is it a book that you would have lying around in your own house? Is it a book that you would even wish your wife or your servants to read?' Griffith-Jones then itemised the novel's thirteen 'episodes of sexual intercourse', as well as lavish use of 'fuck', 'fucking', 'cunt', 'balls', 'shit', 'arse', 'cock' and 'piss' – all part of the prosecution's larger case that it was a dangerously depraving piece of work. For Penguin in defence, Gerald Gardiner – 'a big, cheerful-looking man', observed Panter-Downes – argued in his opening address that Lawrence's book was not obscene, would not deprave, and possessed genuine literary merit. The day ended with Mr Justice Byrne giving jurors a week to read the novel before resumption of the case.[15]

By then a further moral front had opened up, with the premiere on the 26th at the Warner, Leicester Square of *Saturday Night and Sunday Morning*. Based on Alan Sillitoe's 1958 novel (by then a bestselling paperback) and vividly shot in Nottingham, Karl Reisz's film definitively launched the British New Wave. 'Don't let the bastards grind you down,' declares at the outset the young machine operator Arthur Seaton (in a part wonderfully played by Albert Finney that Dirk Bogarde had originally wanted). 'I'd like to see anyone grind me down. All I'm out for is a good time. All the rest is propaganda.' It was, reflect the film historians Sue Harper and Vincent Porter, 'the first time in British cinema' that 'the working class were shown *not to care* about the disapproval of their betters, and to have a culture of their own – hedonistic, abrasive, volatile – which was perfectly competent for the job in hand.' Perhaps the most interesting review was by the *FT*'s David Robinson. He praised the film as 'completely free of excess ornament, self-indulgence or pyrotechnic' and noted how 'working-class life – the telly and cheap furniture, the casual love-making on a thin hearthrug – is depicted truthfully and without condescension', while recording that at the press show he had been 'distressed' to find some of his colleagues attacking the film 'as amoral, if not immoral'. Olga Franklin was not a film reviewer, but by the end of a week in which 'all the praise went to Alan Sillitoe' she was using her regular *Daily Mail* feature to launch a frontal assault on 'The Cad Makers' – into whose ranks Sillitoe through his creation of 'the thoroughly unpleasant' Seaton now joined Kingsley Amis (Jim Dixon), John Osborne (Jimmy Porter) and John Braine (Joe Lampton). Accordingly, Franklin called on her female readers 'to inspire an uncivil disobedience campaign and say quite plainly that we're sick of cads'. At least two instantly agreed. 'It is about time we stopped putting the so-called Angry Young Men on pedestals,' declared Marguerite Lovejoy of Cheshunt, Herts. 'Also, let us cut down on radio and TV interviews with layabouts and beatniks.' As for Eve Braby of Alverstoke, Hants, she conceded that the old type of hero could be 'rather smug', but was adamant that at least he had (or professed) 'certain standards for which the loutish cads have a contempt which only betrays their abysmal shallowness'. Like Franklin, she was 'thoroughly nauseated with the Jims and Jimmys, Arthurs and Joes of present-day fiction'.[16]

Back at the Old Bailey, 18 witnesses had appeared for the defence during Thursday the 27th and Friday the 28th. Rebecca West stated that much of *Lady C* was 'ludicrous', though it was still of 'undoubted literary merit'; the Bishop of Woolwich, the free-thinking John Robinson, claimed that Lawrence portrayed sex as 'in a real sense an act of holy communion', prompting the judge to gaze at him and twirl his pencil; and E. M. Forster, half a century after *Howards End*, connected Lawrence to Bunyan, both of whom 'believed intensely in what they preached'. Everyone agreed, though, that the star defence witness was Richard Hoggart, working-class author of *The Uses of Literacy*, a senior lecturer in English at Leicester University and described by Panter-Downes as 'a dark, serious young man'. Arriving at the crease late on Thursday, Hoggart called the novel not only 'not in any sense vicious', but instead 'highly virtuous and if anything, puritanical'. 'See old Baron Hoggart giving evidence for D.H.L.,' noted a sceptical Larkin that night. 'I suppose one ought really to save all the cuttings of the business. Nobody seems to think it will win. Certainly the witnesses as reported on the 10.30 news sound cracked enough.' Next morning, soon after observing how commonplace the word *fuck* had become ('fifty yards from this Court I heard a man say "fuck" three times as he passed me'), Hoggart received a lengthy cross-examination from Griffith-Jones. 'Is that a passage which you describe as puritanical?' the QC asked at one point after reading out a detailed account of the sexual act. 'Yes,' replied Hoggart, 'puritanical, and poignant, and tender, and moving, and sad, about two people who have no proper relationship.' There ensued a sequence of Griffith-Jones reading out erotic passages before asking, 'Is *that* puritanical?'; each time, Hoggart resolutely insisted that it was, in accordance with his definition of puritanism as 'an intense sense of responsibility for one's conscience'. 'Mr Griffith-Jones hammered at Mr Hoggart for over an hour,' noted Panter-Downes, 'with what seemed a strange and special ferocity. When this witness left the box – still calm, collected, and with intelligent arguments in hand – the sense of applause in court was deafening.'[17]

Any Questions? that evening came from St Mary's Hall, Arundel, with Gilbert Harding making his belated debut. Should the minimum age of criminal responsibility be raised from eight to twelve? 'It all depends surely on the child,' he answered. 'What we want are more intelligent magistrates – and that indeed we lack.' What was the best future for British Railways? 'People are just not any longer railway-minded. They're just put upon, and upset, and the sooner we get rid of them the better.' What about the overweight children of today? 'It's sweet-eating. It's encouraged by the commercial television, who say, "Don't forget the fruit gums, Mum." And there's also a terrible confection which is advertised expressly as something you can eat between meals without losing appetite.' Teenage vandalism? 'I've all the sympathy I have with young people, and I dislike very much the idea of saddling teenagers with all the damage that's done.' On Monday the 31st, the *Lady C* defence paraded 17 more witnesses, including Raymond Williams, Norman St John Stevas, Cecil Day Lewis and Noel Annan, with particular attention focused on the last and youngest, 21-year-old Bernardine Wall. Her credentials were impeccable – convent-educated, English at Cambridge, writing her first novel – and she insisted that Lawrence 'precisely does *not* put promiscuity on a pedestal', that indeed he treated sexual relations 'with great dignity'. Next day, Tuesday the 1st, a letter in *The Times* with 30 signatories

– including Harding and John Freeman as well as Kingsley Amis, Augustus John, Bertrand Russell, Richard Titmuss and Leonard Woolf – urged that Francis Forsyth, an 18-year-old found guilty of murder, should not be hanged 'in cold blood'; Gardiner and Griffith-Jones made their lengthy closing speeches, followed by the start of the judge's summing-up; and viewers flooded the BBC switchboard with calls, complaining about excessive bad language in a 45-minute TV excerpt from the West End production of *Billy Liar*.[18]

Wednesday, 2 November was decision day, with Sylvia Plath among those agog. 'Got a press ticket from Stephen Spender for the last day of the Lady Chatterley trial at the Old Bailey,' she reported home soon afterwards. 'Very exciting – especially with the surprising verdict of "not guilty"!' A surprise indeed, especially after the rest of Mr Justice Byrne's summing up had, observed Panter-Downes, 'cast gloom upon everyone from Penguin'. Having lost half a crown in a bet over the outcome, Larkin that evening took the big view:

> I must say I'm surprised they let it go. I thought the 3/6 element [the price at which Penguin intended to sell] would settle the issue, because the thing about pornography (I know it isn't pornography, but you know what I mean) is that it *isn't* cheap. If Baron Hoggart thinks you can buy 'pornography' in 'Charing Cross Road' for 3/6 he's mistaken. They ought to have called Robert Conquest, poet & editor: it's £3, 50/- on return, at the very least. Or £1, £2, and no return. Well, I feel I am out of touch with ordinary people . . . I shall put my copy on exhibition in the Library tomorrow – locked under glass, mind you.

Next morning not all the papers pronounced, but some did. The *Guardian* hailed 'a triumph of common sense'; the *Glasgow Herald* claimed that 'no reasonable person will quarrel with the decision'; *The Times* registered its 'dissent' on the grounds of 'decency and taste'; for the *Daily Express*, it was 'THIS FAR AND NO FURTHER!'; and the *Daily Sketch*'s editorial, printed in black type as a front-page 'Statement to Parents', accused the jury of having 'forced each one of us to make a choice whether or not we wish our children to buy sexual description at pocket money prices'.[19]

Predictably, the issue resonated over the next few days, pending

Penguin's imminent publication of the unexpurgated paperback. 'Well, I did attempt to procure a copy of this book, so that I should read it through *in case* anyone asked a question tonight,' Margaret Thatcher told the *Any Questions?* audience at the Women's Institute Hall, Dorchester on Friday evening. 'I got through it in three hours and twenty minutes. That was because I was not anxious to linger on it at all.' She added that in her view Lawrence's novel did 'offend against most of the ordinary standards of public taste'. Next day the Archbishop of Canterbury, Geoffrey Fisher, publicly condemned his errant Bishop of Woolwich, while in the Sunday press two commentators were in diametrical opposition. John Gordon in the *Sunday Express* described Penguin's Sir Allen Lane as 'the shrewd publisher who saw the golden beam of culture where others saw only dirt', but Kenneth Tynan in the *Observer* delighted in the defeat of Griffith-Jones – an Old Etonian with 'a voice passionate only in disdain, but barbed with a rabid belief in convention and discipline' – and cherished the moment when, having read out a passage, he had 'triumphantly' asked Hoggart whether a puritan would feel such reverence for a man's balls, to which Hoggart 'almost with compassion' had calmly replied in the affirmative. The evidence soon emerged from Gallup that public opinion was broadly on the jury's side, with only 20 per cent wanting *Lady C* banned and 53 per cent wanting the full version published. 'I am all for educated people in a free world, rather than half-educated people in a confined world,' asserted Dr Irene Green at a local 'Any Questions?' session in the Norfolk village of Horsford; her fellow-panellists, including a clergyman and a headmaster, agreed. Admittedly there was still the moral danger of stiletto heels – 'monstrosities', declared Green about that particular topic – but for the moment the centre of opinion had shifted a notch or two in the liberal direction.[20]

Life continued during the fortnight after the jury's epoch-defining verdict. On the 2nd itself, Anthony Heap complained in his diary about tailors increasingly selling single-breasted suits, not double; next day, Hugh Gaitskell defeated Harold Wilson's challenge for the Labour leadership by a convincing 166 votes to 81 (only MPs voting); on the 4th, after *Mirror* readers had given their verdict on Picasso's *The Man with the Red Glove* (70 per cent 'ridiculing' it), Madge Martin standing outside Oxford Town Hall was passed by the visiting royal couple

('When I bobbed my curtsey to the Queen, I suddenly saw Prince Philip turn to me with a smile and twinkle, and say, "You've dropped your hankie"'); on Guy Fawkes Night, Gyles Brandreth and his confrères at a prep school near Deal 'paraded out to the games pitch where we watched the "Burn the Bomb" Guy go on to the fire'; next evening, Heap found John Osborne's first TV play, *A Subject of Scandal and Concern*, starring Richard Burton as the Victorian atheist George Holyoake, 'drab and depressing'; on Monday morning the 18-year-old Hugo Williams started work at Simpson's in Piccadilly, theoretically working on its Christmas mail-order catalogue but mainly in the Gents reading J. D. Salinger's *For Esmé – with Love and Squalor*; by Tuesday the letters to the *Daily Mail* were running four to one in favour of hanging Francis Forsyth; next day, the news that John F. Kennedy had won the US presidential election was greeted enthusiastically by Kenneth Williams, inspired that 'a man of conscience, integrity, originality & quality *can* win through', while the result probably interested the 13-year-old David Jones (later Bowie), who about this time paid a visit to the American Embassy to find out more about his latest passion, American football. By now another young original, Alan Garner, was launched with *The Weirdstone of Brisingamen* – 'absolutely rum', according to one reviewer (Siriol Hugh-Jones), though 'maybe fine for all who like a really good shudder over the final digestives and hot milk'; on Thursday the 10th, Forsyth was hanged at Wandsworth Prison, Churchill made his last speech in public (telling the boys of Harrow School that he was 'always very glad when the day comes round for me to turn up here'), and William Burroughs in Cambridge told Allen Ginsberg in New York that he didn't think he could 'stick this English weather much longer', that 'as soon as I get some bread we'll split south'. Over the weekend, Eric Hobsbawm in the *New Statesman* welcomed the trad jazz phenomenon for at least replacing 'the rock-and-roll vogue' ('which is at last, thank God, fading away') but otherwise found its musical limitations 'only exceeded by the deficient amateurishness of many of its musicians'; a Sheffield MP (Fred Mulley) spent a disturbed night in a Park Hill flat hearing for himself the relentless noise of the hammers in a nearby forge; Macmillan stood next to the opposition leader at the Cenotaph ('poor Mr Gaitskell always seems a little conscious on these occasions that he has no medals'); and Gilbert Harding on *What's My Line?* remarked to a fellow-celebrity due to appear on *Juke Box Jury*, 'I do hope you can manage to keep awake.' Monday featured a despairing *Daily Telegraph* article by John Betjeman about the rapidly disappearing architectural heritage; Tuesday saw at the National Liberal Forum an early meeting between an architect (John Poulson) and a Tory politician (Reginald Maudling); and on Wednesday the 16th the latest issue of *Punch* included the racing driver Stirling Moss explaining how, if he was Minister of Transport and given dictatorial powers (not least 'over John Betjeman'), 'highway construction would be pushed hard, ruthlessly, 24 hours a day.'[21]

Early that evening, just after recording *Round Britain Quiz*, Gilbert Harding collapsed and died outside Broadcasting House, aged 53. 'A character in the great Johnsonian tradition,' reflected Heap next day, adding that 'we shall sadly miss his plump, delightfully grumpy presence on the "What's My Line" panel on Sunday evenings.' Another diarist, Nella Last, 'read Richard Dimbleby's pompous "eulogy"' in her *Daily Express* '& thought "you so silly fat man"'. Three days later, *What's My Line?* – the panel game that had brought Harding his greatest fame and at times notoriety – was replaced by a tribute programme, reckoned by the far-from-undiscerning Heap as 'the best thing of its kind I've yet seen on T.V.' But a more professional critic, Joanna Richardson, declined to be swayed by sentiment. 'Ham in the extreme,' she wrote in the *Listener*. 'The close-up of the empty chair, the slow movement from Mendelssohn Violin Concerto, the embarrassing hyperbole about Dr Johnson and fields of asphodel from Sir Compton Mackenzie: nothing had been wanting.'[22]

By this time Penguin Books were enjoying one of the great publishing triumphs. 'NOW YOU CAN READ IT' announced their posters barely a week after the trial's end, as an initial print run of 200,000 copies proved an instant sell-out. Many provincial bookshops retained a degree of circumspection – 'the book will not be on open display, but will be available on request' was the not untypical policy of Wildings in Shrewsbury – but for several weeks demand continued to exceed supply. On the 24th, Henry St John was in the bookshop at Gunnersbury in order to buy 'a strip-tease magazine "Play No 6"', also priced at 3s 6d. 'A woman came in for "Lady Chatterley's Lover," which she said she had ordered, but it seemed the boss had not. He gave her someone else's copy. Despite the flood of words poured out about this D.H. Lawrence novel it is for all practical purposes still unobtainable, as the numbers printed appear totally inadequate.' The Chief Constable of Lincolnshire was among those still holding out for the old standards. 'I hope you will not read this book even if you get the chance,' he told pupils and parents when presenting prizes at Brigg Glanford School, though refraining from mentioning the title. 'If you do get hold of it and feel ashamed after the first few pages, throw it away.' Gyles Brandreth at his prep school did not even get to first base: a parcel arrived for him, unfortunately with a Penguin label on it, and was immediately confiscated. Altogether, in what was still in many ways a deeply puritanical – and certainly prurient – society, it was an extraordinary episode, as Penguin sold more than two million copies within a year. 'I feel as if a window has been opened and fresh air has blown right through England,' joyously declared Lawrence's stepdaughter, Barbara Barr, after the jury's verdict, and of course at one level she was right. Yet there was truth also in Kate Paul's diary entry some two months later. 'The constant stream of jokes referring to the *Lady Chatterley* case makes me sick,' noted the anti-bomb, anti-apartheid, anti-capital-punishment twenty-year-old. 'People behave like children with curious, obscene, starved minds.'[23]

There was no doubting the ubiquity. 'The references to homosexuality have sent nudges rippling up and down the rows of seats in school and village halls,' reported the *Guardian* about the Arts Council's touring production in Wales that autumn of Peter Shaffer's *Five Finger Exercise*, 'and has made a visit to the play the local equivalent of buying a copy of "Lady Chatterley's Lover".' Middle-class female dropouts were not yet common in Wales, but the phenomenon was just under way in London – caught by the novel of the autumn, Lynne Reid Banks's *The L-Shaped Room*. 'Where am I to find curry, for God's sake, in this benighted neighbourhood,' cries out the pregnant heroine Jane, living in a down-at-heel Fulham bedsit among prostitutes, a black musician and the inevitable struggling writer. The acclaim was instant and considerable for what became a bestseller, though Keith Waterhouse more sourly detected 'a conventional boarding-house saga, all baked beans and hearts of gold'. Annie Courtenay still badly missed the hearts of gold (and perhaps baser metals) she had known in her old home near the Fish Dock in Hull – 'I'll never feel at home in Longhill,' she wrote forlornly to her son Tom on 7 December from the new housing estate on the city's outskirts where she had been living for a year. On Friday the 9th, the day after Mike (later Mick) Jagger's end-of-term report at Dartford Grammar School had called him 'a lad of good general character', more than 2,000 people, many standing in the aisles, packed Westminster Cathedral for Gilbert Harding's requiem mass; among those attending were Nancy Spain, Eamonn Andrews, Hermione Baddeley, Brian Johnston and David Jacobs.[24]

Also in the congregation was Cliff Michelmore, and that evening *Tonight* found itself up against a newcomer on the other channel. Ray Chapman set the scene in the *TV Times*:

> 'Coronation Street' – four miles from Manchester in any direction – is a collection of seven terraced houses, an off-licence, a little general store on the corner, the back wall of a raincoat factory, a pub called 'The Rover's Return', and the Glad Tidings Mission Hall.
>
> The houses of 'Coronation Street' are representative – built more than 60 years ago, with no gardens. They have six rooms . . . parlour, living-room, scullery, and three bedrooms, one of which has been converted into a bathroom.
>
> Yet it is home to the 20 people who live there, and most of them would not like to change their warm surroundings for something new but less humanised.

Chapman got the backstory from the programme's creator Tony Warren, a 23-year-old former actor who had lived in Pendlebury (near Salford) for most of his life and whose idea for a serial set amid the northern working class had been curtly rejected by the BBC before being taken on by Manchester-based Granada. 'Apart from listening to people in pubs and clubs,' Warren explained about his two months of background research mainly in Manchester, 'I also "kept observation" in an off-licence, talked to people in buses and trains, wandered through street markets, made three trips to Blackpool illuminations and went on a "mystery" coach outing, which turned out to be a fourth visit to Blackpool.' 'I am *not*,' he stressed, 'having a joke at the expense of the people in the North. What I have aimed at is a true picture of life there and the people's basic friendliness and essential humour.'

Pat Phoenix as Elsie Tanner ('with the very battered remains of good looks and figure,' according to the script), William Roache as Ken Barlow ('little or no northern accent and looks faintly out of place'), Violet Carson as Ena Sharples (hair-netted caretaker of the hall, described by Chapman as a 'kindly ex-barmaid'), Jack Howarth as Albert Tatlock, Doris Speed as Annie Walker – some soon-to-be-famous characters were present from the first episode. 'With The Archers, Coronation St, Ward 10, This Week & Take Your Pick it was a pleasant enough programme,' noted Nella Last later that Friday evening, 'although I cannot see much entertainment value in the first named.' Next day, among *Coronation Street*'s few reviews in the national press, Mary Crozier in the *Guardian* praised 'something funny and forthright' about Warren's depiction of ordinary life, but the *Daily Mirror*'s Jack Bell found it 'hard to believe that viewers will want to put up with continuous slice-of-life domestic drudgery two evenings a week'. Among the provincial dailies, Peter Forth in the *Western Daily Press* conceded that it was 'no crowning achievement', but still felt it had 'started promisingly', while N.G.P. in the *Liverpool Daily Post* predicted 'entertaining possibilities'. The most resonant instant verdict came on Sunday from Maurice Wiggin. 'They undoubtedly have a winner coming up in the "Coronation Street" series,' he declared in the *Sunday Times* about 'the astute impresarios of Granada'. And he went on: 'This is "Emergency – Ward 10" and "Mrs Dale's Diary" and "The Grove Family" and Wilfred Pickles and Kipps and Armchair Theatre at its most socially-conscious all rolled into one great cosy Hall of Mirrors, in which the population can see itself, with the profound satisfaction of recognition, every Friday night for ever and ever.'

Wiggin got it in one. 'I actually remember the very first episode, because my dad was mending a puncture on his bike in our front room,' recalled Cilla Black 40 years later about that December evening in her working-class Liverpool home. 'The *Street* came on and we were all engrossed, and all of a sudden they were doing exactly the same thing. I think it was in the Barlows' household. We thought, "Wow, they're just as common as us".'[25]

PART TWO

6

Why Are We Falling Behind?

Over on BBC TV later that Friday evening in December 1960 was the second programme of a rather different new series: *Challenge to Prosperity*. 'Britain is raising her standard of living less quickly than any other European country,' explained the *Radio Times*. 'Must our rivals outstrip us?' The producer, Jack Ashley, further filled in the background:

> In less than ten years' time the people of Western Germany will be enjoying a standard of living twice as high as they have today. Yet it will be over thirty years before we double our standard – unless there is a radical change in British industry.
>
> It may be true that we have never had it so good. The luxuries of pre-war have become the necessities of today; business is booming and our major industries are among the best in the world. But, although we are increasing our material wealth, so are our major competitors, and they are doing so faster than we are. Why are we falling behind?

Accordingly, he and Christopher Chataway (athlete, broadcaster, Conservative MP) had been 'touring the country trying to find out'.

Michael Shanks, a *Financial Times* journalist, had even bigger questions on his mind, and by this time was writing at speed what became *The Stagnant Society* – a Penguin Special that on publication in summer 1961 made such an immediate impact that it was turned into a Pelican and altogether sold some 60,000 copies. 'The challenge is simply this,' Shanks declared at the outset:

> Can we allow the Soviet world to continue to enrich itself, by adding to its productive capacity, at a faster rate than ourselves? The two systems

> are now on trial in the eyes of the world to see which can enrich itself fastest, and which can use its resources more effectively in promoting the happiness and well-being of its citizens. At present growth rates, one can foresee a point on the graph at which Soviet production per head will in fact surpass ours . . . How can we avert this danger? By establishing for ourselves the same sort of rate of growth as the Soviet countries – and some, but not many, advanced Western countries – have already achieved? In other words, how can we run our economic system more efficiently?

'A society which loses interest in material progress is a society on its way to the embalming chamber,' he went on. 'This is the great psychological danger facing the British people today – that we may bury ourselves under the rose-petals of a vast collective nostalgia, lost in a sweet sad love-affair with our own past.' Vigorous analysis followed of Britain's economic, political and social malaise, before Shanks reprised his dominant preoccupation:

> What sort of an island do we want to be? This is the question to which we come back in the end. A lotus island of easy, tolerant ways, bathed in the golden glow of an imperial sunset, shielded from discontent by a threadbare welfare state and an acceptance of genteel poverty? Or the tough dynamic race we have been in the past, striving always to better ourselves, seeking new worlds to conquer in place of those we have lost, ready to accept growing pains as the price of growth?

'If we are to succeed,' insisted Shanks, 'it will be because we are determined as a nation to succeed, and because we are prepared to subordinate all other considerations – personal or sectional – to this national aim.' He added hopefully: 'If any people is capable of it, I believe we are.'[1]

Something was undeniably in the air: call it 'declinism'.[2] Inevitably, it was a moot point whether the economic facts at the start of the new decade justified the phenomenon. Britain's share of world manufactured exports had indeed declined from 22 per cent in 1950 to 16 per cent in 1960 (compared to West Germany's increase from 7 to 19 per cent), and the balance of payments was deteriorating quite rapidly. Even so, the British economy's annual rate of growth between 1957 and

1965 would be 3.2 per cent, the most impressive rate since the 1860s. Clearly, then, it was all about *relative* decline, particularly in relation to Europe (both West and East). And given, as Jack Ashley noted, the continuing never-had-it-so-good feeling amid inexorably spreading consumer affluence, it is far from clear that most people were really conscious of that relative decline, let alone cared about it. Nor was there necessarily unfailing interest or understanding even among the nation's opinion-formers. Anthony Sampson, working at the *Observer*, recalled how the eyes of his distinguished editor, David Astor, 'glazed over at the mention of economics and industry', being, along with 'most of the other pundits' around him, 'too preoccupied with Britain's responsibilities in the world to notice that she could not afford much of a role'. One day, added Sampson, the increasingly thorny problem of traffic came up – prompting the paper's main literary reviewer, Philip Toynbee, to ask why they didn't ban lorries from the new motorways.[3]

Associated Portland Cement, Bass, Bowater, British Motor Corporation, Coats Patons, Courtaulds, Distillers, Dunlop, EMI, GEC, GKN (Guest Keen & Nettlefolds), Hawker Siddeley, Alfred Herbert, House of Fraser, ICI, Imperial Tobacco, Lancashire Cotton, Leyland Motors, London Brick, Murex, P&O, Rolls-Royce, Spillers, Swan Hunter, Tate & Lyle, Tube Investments, United Steel, Vickers, Watney Combe & Reid, Woolworth's – these in the early 1960s were the proud constituents of the FT 30-Share Index, bellwether of the economy, and a list with a strongly manufacturing character. Nothing stands still, though, in the corporate landscape, and four distinct trends of long-term significance were already well under way: first, increasing size and concentration, typified by the rapid series of mergers and acquisitions in the brewing industry; second, increasing diversification, neatly exemplified by Guinness starting to sell butterscotch as well as stout; third, increasing foreign ownership, often American but not invariably, as when Nestlé in 1960 acquired Crosse & Blackwell; and fourth – arguably most resonant of all – the irresistible shift away from manufacturing and towards services, with employment in the latter sector (including distribution) now for the first time roughly equalling or even just exceeding employment in the former – a shift perhaps epitomised by jobs in the hairdressing sector hitting the six-figure mark. Even so, manufacturing remained central not only to the crucial exports performance but also, just as importantly, to national self-image; among the household names of the British economy *circa* 1960 were Accles & Pollock (based in Dudley and making steel tubes), Albright & Wilson (based in Oldbury and second only to ICI as a chemicals manufacturer), the match-makers Bryant & May, brake-lining specialists Ferodo (based in Chapel-en-le-Frith), and Britain's biggest toy-manufacturer, Liverpool-based Meccano, makers of Dinky cars and Hornby trains as well as of course Meccano itself.[4]

No sector of the economy would be more emblematic over the coming years than the motor industry. On the surface it seemed to be doing well enough at the start of the 1960s – with almost all of the major firms laying plans for future expansion – but there were troubling signs. Not only had West Germany's share of world car exports (an increasingly competitive marketplace) comfortably overtaken Britain's, but the industry was becoming increasingly strike-prone. 'There is now a total stoppage at Ford's Dagenham works – over 1 man!' despaired Macmillan in November 1960, adding that 'the T.U. leaders are doing their best, but the Communist shop stewards seem to be in control.' That year, over half a million working days were lost in the industry, followed in 1961 by another 350,000 plus, prompting Maurice Edelman to comment that 'the television comedian who says "Motor Shop Steward" can now count on a national guffaw'. But it was another Labour MP, Francis Noel-Baker, who offered in December 1961 the most rounded contemporary analysis of the industry's thinning slice of the world market. After accusing it of designing and making cars less well than foreign manufacturers, and not being helped by inferior after-sales service by local agents, he argued that 'perhaps at the bottom of this problem is the fact that the home market takes half and more of the output of many British motor firms, and is more profitable to them than struggling for exports – some leading men in the industry frankly admit as much in private.' Not that Noel-Baker played down the importance of what he called, with the notable exception of Vauxhall, 'an abominable record in industrial relations'. And he went on: 'Of course there are Communists, of course there are trouble-makers. But – equally of course – there are also managements who show no gleam of understanding for the strain and insecurity in which their employees work.'

The manager par excellence without a gleam of such understanding was undoubtedly the abrasive Sir Leonard Lord, chairman until 1961 of the British Motor Corporation (embracing both Cowley-based Morris and Longbridge-based Austin) and characterised by a biographer as 'a ruthless pursuer of efficiency and production goals, a strong opponent of organised labour and left-wing politics'. A less brutal if still driven approach came from the industry's rising man, Donald Stokes, whose resourcefulness in finding and exploiting new export markets had done much to establish a world-leading position in commercial vehicles for the Leyland Motor Corporation, which in 1961 expanded perhaps rashly into new territory by taking over the ailing Standard-Triumph (saloon and sports cars). But from whichever school, management now faced two huge challenges. F. Griffiths, BMC's chief production development engineer, spelled out the first in January 1961:

> What is required to be automated in the motor industry is the relationship of our processes with each other and to the production programme . . . We are losing 20 per cent [of capacity] . . . The cause of this will be found in the fact that the right material is not at the right place at the right time, and that the motor industry is really not in proper control of its business. The piecework systems which it has to use, its lack of immediate knowledge of its relationships between supply and what is required, all mean that its output is in the hands of a large number of people.

Or, as the economic historian Wayne Lewchuk has put it, the advent of new, American automated production techniques now enabled British managers – if they were up to it – 'to take direct responsibility for planning, maintenance and the organisation of shop floor activity' – a considerable ask, given that the unions (and especially the shop stewards) were becoming increasingly ambitious in their contesting of workplace control. The other challenge stemmed from the government's new attachment at the start of the decade to regional policy, leading during 1960 to a flurry of announcements, following government pressure and financial inducements. BMC and Rootes would be building new plants in Scotland (Bathgate and Linwood, respectively), while Ford, Standard-Triumph and Vauxhall would be doing the same on Merseyside (Halewood, Speke and Ellesmere Port, respectively), another area of high unemployment. Might these two new regional fronts help to improve labour relations? 'While shop stewards could not support anti-Scottish slogans being written on parts going from the Midlands,' noted a meeting in Coventry in early 1962 of the BMC Joint Shop Stewards Committee (reflecting on the so-far disappointing lack of interest by shop stewards at Bathgate in discussing rates of pay), 'the quick and sure way to get friendship with our colleagues at Bathgate is by personal contact.'[5]

Two-wheel manufacturing also had its problems. In 1959 the British motorcycle industry, still regarded as the world's number 1, produced 127,000 machines (excluding lightweight scooters etc), many for export; that, however, turned out to be the peak total, with significant defects by now becoming apparent. Not only had there been a serious failure to maximise the potential of the scooter phenomenon – certainly in comparison to Italian manufacturers – but too often the emphasis remained on targeting enthusiasts and promoting the motorbike as the winner of prestigious races rather than an object of everyday utility. By late 1961, the *Daily Mirror* was describing a deeply conservative industry facing a crisis, with the report noting that most British engines were still of basically pre-war design. Ominously, it quoted a director from the industry's dominant force, BSA: 'The Japanese Honda machines are quite frighteningly good – they are built like watches.' That of course was *the* threat, prompting one of the industry's participants (and later historians), Bert Hopwood, to argue in retrospect that in the early 1960s, before the Japanese invasion really got going in the area of heavyweight motorbikes, the Birmingham-based BSA group had 'the financial strength to lay the foundation for an operation to match many of its Japanese competitors', but that it lacked the drive and willpower to do so. Also on two wheels, these were qualities likewise largely lacking at Nottingham-based Raleigh, where the 1950s were characterised by production methods falling uneasily between mass and batch, a critical delay in diversifying into the rapidly growing moped market and, above all, a generally slow-moving culture (paternalistic and family-based) – all of which meant that in 1960 a one-time proud and independent world leader was forced, amid falling profit margins and increasing international competition, into absorption by Tube Investments.[6]

At this stage, though, there was little soul-searching outside Nottingham, though it could be a different matter elsewhere in the economy. 'Industry and the Prestige Cult' was the title of an *Observer* article in October 1959 by John Davy, a science correspondent who refreshingly saw the bigger picture:

> As the Empire and the Navy shrink, and other nations get better at football, British national pride has tended to identify itself increasingly with science and technology. Calder Hall, the Viscount, Zeta and the Hovercraft have become national idols. Each new scientific advance is hailed by the Press as 'another British first'. The laboratory bench is becoming the patriot's platform.
>
> This would not matter if the platform were solidly constructed – but in fact it has some alarming weaknesses. In particular, the two British industries on which most public money and scientific effort have been lavished are in trouble . . .

These, he explained, were 'the aircraft and the atomic industries'.

The facts, as Davy turned to the former, were damning enough: '£500 million of public money have been spent on aircraft research and development since 1949, involving over 3,000 of the highest-powered scientists and engineers (compared with seventy doing research and development in shipbuilding and marine engineering). Yet the Viscount is the only fully successful civil airliner which has been produced.' Within months of this piece – and in effect responding to the 1957 White Paper that had put the future defence emphasis on missiles not aircraft, itself followed by the demoralising realisation that the lengthy Comet hiatus in the mid-1950s had in practice allowed the Boeing 707 to become the world's jet aircraft of choice – the government reorganised the airframe part of the British aircraft industry into two main groups: the British Aircraft Corporation (including Vickers, English Electric and Bristol) and Hawker Siddeley (including also de Havilland and Blackburn). This was perhaps a logical step, notwithstanding predictable frictions within the groups, but in general most historians of the industry have been strongly critical of government's role during the two decades after the war. Overestimating the industry's capacity to manage a large number of projects, 'a clumsy approach to procurement', an unrealistic desire to compete across the board with the Americans – such, for instance, are the charges levelled by Geoffrey Owen in his dispassionate 1999 survey of post-war British industry. At the time, following rationalisation, perhaps the most unsparing assessment came in the *Spectator* (in September 1960) from Oliver Stewart, who argued that the Ministry of Aviation now had 'absolute power over all things aeronautical' – a power for which it was almost entirely unqualified, not least given how the government's technical officers had 'repeatedly shown that they are incapable of assessing correctly the potentialities of new designs', as well as the failure to do anything 'to prepare a British machine for the rapidly growing executive aircraft market'. Perhaps a world-defying lead in a supersonic airliner was the answer? 'Agitation persists,' noted John Davy, 'regardless of the fact that a British one would cost far more than it could hope to earn.' In 1960 the *New Statesman* contended that 'the government's decision to enter Britain in the race to produce a supersonic airliner should be examined critically.' But, as the Minister of Aviation, Churchill's son-in-law Duncan Sandys, urged the Cabinet, 'If we are not in the big supersonic airliner business, then it is really only a matter of time before the whole British aircraft industry packs up.'[7] The flight path, in other words, was clear for Concorde and the fateful Anglo-French agreement of late 1962.

On the nuclear front, Davy's correctly pessimistic assertion in 1959 was that 'while the atomic engineers have performed glittering feats of ingenuity, gloom is now seeping through the industry as export orders for nuclear power-stations fail to materialise.' In fact, an extraordinary story was continuing to unfold, in which so far there had been a handful of key landmarks: a reasonably modest civil nuclear-power programme announced in 1955; nuclear euphoria surrounding the Queen's opening of the power station at Calder Hall in October 1956; the Suez Crisis, which engendered a panic about the future security of oil supplies; a dramatically enhanced nuclear-power programme up to 1965 announced in April 1957; Sir Christopher Hinton, characterised by Richard Crossman as 'a striking, difficult, dominant engineer', not long afterwards leaving the Atomic Energy Authority (AEA) and becoming the first chairman of the Central Electricity Generating

Board, in effect the producer switching to the consumer; and the Hinton-influenced White Paper of June 1960, which not only found that the cost of electricity from the Magnox nuclear stations (due to start coming into operation shortly) would be significantly higher than originally estimated, but generally sought to trim nuclear aspirations. Hinton himself would offer in retirement a compelling perspective on the ill-conceived 1957 expansion (for which he had not been responsible):

> It condemned us to go on building bigger and bigger nuclear power plants, each cheaper than the last but all clumsy and each generating electricity more expensively than could be done in fossil fuel fired stations built concurrently. Supervision of these plants diverted scientific and engineering manpower from the rapid development of more advanced reactor systems. Yet I do not think that anyone could be blamed. The nuclear programme was the victim of circumstances, the victim of events that had moved with the uncontrollable recklessness of those in an Elizabethan tragedy.

Of course, nuclear's partial retreat from 1960 did not mean the end of that form of power, and already the AEA had in practice virtually decided on the successor to the Magnox reactors once it came in the mid-1960s to pushing on with a new generation of nuclear stations: the advanced gas-cooled reactor (AGR). Whatever its merits and flaws, at least one nuclear historian has concluded that a crucial fact in the AEA's eyes was that it was once again *British* technology, not American.[8] National pride and the prestige cult were, in short, all too alive and well.

In 1959, though, Davy did identify two other, lower-profile British industries which had invested heavily in research and were 'in a very healthy position' – namely, chemicals (including plastics) and electronics: 'The former has largely paid for its own research; the latter has been greatly stimulated by defence expenditure. There are no newspaper headlines for making a superb oscilloscope or developing a new method of making polystyrene – but the profits are often much larger.' Sadly, however, profits were seldom large, indeed sometimes non-existent, in one key branch of electronics: the nascent computer industry. British scientists and firms had been among the world's pioneers between the late 1940s and mid-1950s, but by around 1960 the picture was looking distinctly clouded. A significant technology gap had opened up between the UK and US computer industries, with the UK some two to three years behind; too many firms (principally International Computers and Tabulators (ICT), Elliott-Automation, Ferranti, LEO Computers and English Electric) were chasing too small a domestic market, with only about £15 million worth of computers sold during 1960–61; and case studies of Ferranti and LEO reveal a similar pattern of too much emphasis on technological excellence, too little on effective salesmanship. Then, in the early 1960s, the Americans moved forward decisively, above all IBM on the back of a huge, resources-generating domestic market, significant US government backing for R&D, and specifically its recently launched 1401. 'What grows faster than IBM?' rhetorically asked *Fortune* magazine in November 1960. Answer: 'IBM Abroad'. A single IBM 1401 could do the work of four conventional tabulators, and in the course of 1961–2, in a matter almost of months, it blew ICT's punched-card machine business out of the water. The only recourse for the British computer industry was to consolidate, but almost inevitably it was a case of too little, too late.[9]

In an altogether older sector, engineering, alarm bells were ringing by 1960, or should have been. Two especially ominous areas were textile machinery and machine tools – both traditional strengths, both by now seeing West Germany outstripping the UK in terms of share of world exports. Oldham-based Platt Brothers may have been the leading firm for textile machinery, but the historian D. A. Farnie argues that in these crucial years its management 'failed either to reduce costs of production or to diversify operations'. As for the machine-tool industry, Roger Lloyd-Jones and M. J. Lewis identify in their authoritative study a range of deficiencies in the 1950s – including poor productivity, an overly fragmented structure and a general failure to modernise – followed by only sluggish modernising efforts in the early 1960s. Easily the UK's biggest specialist machine-tool maker was the Coventry-based Alfred Herbert, and here Lloyd-Jones and Lewis find across the 1950s and 1960s much that was negative: 'limited organisational capabilities', 'capacity constraint', 'delays in developing a centralised design policy', failure to develop NC (numerical control) technology, persistence of 'learning by doing', and (in the early 1960s) a crucial delay, because of design problems, in developing the new Progmanto machine of advanced design. Alfred Herbert had once been the world's largest machine-tool business, but by the time its founder, Sir Alfred Herbert, died in 1957 (still in harness), it had become, observes Geoffrey Owen, 'a byword for ageing management, products and manufacturing methods'. Even by the mid-1960s, of its 1,500 machines in use, 70 were more than 50 years old and another 570 were over 30 years old, with the result, adds Owen, that 'many could be worked only by men who had the dying craft skills needed for precision work on antiquated plant.'[10]

Machine-tool making was a specialist world, little known to most outsiders, but there were three much more familiar industries that between them comprised the very heart of the British economy: textiles, steel and coal. Each had been a nineteenth-century 'staple' heavyweight, each had struggled between the wars, and by 1960 each was in a problematic place.

The setting for the Lancashire cotton industry was 'the great urban sprawl centred on Manchester, whose blackened houses and cobbled streets stretch with hardly a break for sixteen miles from Stockport in the south to Oldham and Rochdale in the north'. But, as the *Economist*'s special correspondent went on to explain in May 1960 (just as Blackburn Rovers were about to lose badly at Wembley), the industry's decline had been rapid over the past decade, notwithstanding eventual government efforts to help: 'Almost half the spinning and weaving industry on which it has traditionally depended has been closed down. Many mills, with their depressing look of Victorian workhouses, have closed for ever; others have only one of their former array of chimneys belching smoke into the greyish air.' What had gone wrong? One particularly well-informed historian, John Singleton, does not deny that the industry had plenty wrong with it – 'a workforce that viewed redeployment with suspicion, poor management, outmoded marketing arrangements, deficiencies in product design, and an atomistic industrial structure which militated against the co-ordination of the different stages in the production process' – but ultimately argues that sharp decline in the 1950s had probably been inevitable, especially given the 'devastating' competition of cheap imports from India, Hong Kong and elsewhere, which meant that the industry 'entered the 1960s in complete disarray'.

Across the Pennines, however, it was a significantly different picture. In Wool City, aka Bradford, local textile companies such as S. Jerome & Sons, a Bingley manufacturer of medium- and high-grade worsted fabrics, ended the 1950s at full stretch and often making record profits, as they 'struggled' (in the words of local historian Mark Keighley) 'to meet the universal demand for wool products'. The city's unemployment figure in early 1960 of 0.7 per cent was one of the lowest in the UK, and all seemed good; but, as Keighley also notes, the threat of rival fibres was already looming on the horizon.[11]

The glass was also at least half-full in nearby Steel City. The Sheffield special-steels industry, records its historian Geoffrey Tweedale, 'entered the decade on a confident note: order books were buoyant and production was at record levels after the advances [including continuous casting in the finishing processes] of the 1950s'. And, in the context of an expectation of ever-rising steel demand, significant further modernisation was soon under way, epitomised by United Steel's SPEAR project at Steel, Peech & Tozer, which 'replaced its old and now uneconomic open-hearth furnaces with electric arcs'. Steel City had a proud history – two centuries of 'the highest degree of metallurgical knowledge and practical skill', to quote a trade magazine – and a technical director at William Jessop & Co would recall a visit to Sheffield in the late 1950s by a Japanese delegation: 'We had a little giggle to ourselves after they had gone, their questions were naive and totally ill-informed.' Elsewhere, the sellers' market of the 1950s meant that the heavy-steel manufacturers were for the most part similarly sanguine, notwithstanding serious overmanning (especially at the Steel Company of Wales's showpiece Port Talbot works) and what Duncan Burn (in his magisterial 1961 account of the steel industry's recent history) called 'the slow advance of steelmaking techniques', notably 'the failure to increase and improve heavy plate production'. The industry was of course already a notorious political football – nationalised in 1950, largely denationalised in the course of the decade, the object of a nakedly political decision by Macmillan in 1958 (new strip mills at Ravenscraig *and* Llanwern), saved from renationalisation by Labour's defeat in 1959 – and Burn evocatively summarised what had become by the end of the 1950s its rather flabby and somewhat defensive underlying mentality:

> The immunity to competition [ie, from abroad] which firms and groups of firms derived in varying degrees from the costliness and durability of the plant, the cost of transporting steel, their close contacts with local markets, development of profitable specialities, close links with consumers, including often complete integration in respect of part of their output, contacts through interlocking directorates with other steel companies and with banks and insurance companies, not to mention the strength some companies had through ownership of rights to work cheap home ore deposits, had if anything been increased. Moreover all the major firms still had plants of varying degrees of efficiency, and none had an undivided interest in seeing the most efficient production rise at the expense of the less efficient. Firms with a foot in different regions – it applied to all the firms with home ore based plants – did not, it was plain to see, feel impelled or compelled to concentrate developments where costs were or could be least. There was still no firm which would automatically devote all its resources single-mindedly to the further exploitation of home ore. On the contrary there was probably no firm which would not have thought it almost socially reprehensible to do so.

Overseeing the industry, and futilely trying to keep it out of politics, was the Iron and Steel Board. 'The case for central planning intervention,' judged Burn, 'was clearly strong', but so far the Board's contribution had been 'ineffective'.[12]

'South Wales Will Always Depend On COAL!' was the title of a National Coal Board recruitment pamphlet in around 1959, but the apparent confidence masked a rapidly deteriorating reality across the whole industry. Demand for coal slumped in the late 1950s as cheap oil imports rose sharply. By October 1959, a week after the election, the NCB's *Revised Plan for Coal* envisaged up to 240 pit closures over the next six years, manpower dropping by up to 11 per cent from its current 652,000, and capital expenditure to be focused mainly on the North-Eastern (including Yorkshire), South-Western (including Wales) and East Midlands coalfields. 'The Coal Board certainly does not take a faint-hearted view of the future,' declared the Minister of Power, Richard Wood, in a Commons debate soon afterwards. But William Stones, Labour MP for Consett, spoke on behalf of Durham miners when he related how that morning, on the bus to Newcastle, he had heard one miner say to another, 'I hear that 169 men are to finish at our pit,' to which the other responded, 'Aye, an' if things gan on we'll aal be finished.' The Tory MP Gerald Nabarro had no doubt where the blame lay for the industry's unpopularity, claiming that 'it has had a heritage over the past twelve years [ie, since nationalisation] of supplying much poor-quality material at a high price.' In practice, it was becoming increasingly clear that in the short to medium term a twin pattern lay ahead – contraction on the one hand, modernisation on the other, as a significantly smaller number of miners achieved significantly higher productivity. 'Mechanisation is being planned to a degree undreamed of 300 years ago,' the NCB's recently appointed chairman, the fluent, expansive, undeniably immodest former Labour politician Alf (now Lord) Robens told an interviewer in 1961. 'This year we'll install 400 power-loading machines. The miners, thank God, aren't Luddites: they don't mind machines, provided they get the money.'[13]

The problems arguably ran even deeper in another nationalised industry. 'In general, English trains are slow and unpunctual,' wrote Tony Mayer (a Frenchman who had worked in London for many years) in 1959. 'The stations and most of the rolling stock are in a truly appalling state of dirt and decay. The wooden carriages (sometimes without corridors), the waiting-rooms and the dismal buffets which in winter are ice-cold and smoky, the dining-cars with their chipped crockery, their grimy table-cloths and napkins, combine to make the traveller depressed and bewildered . . .' Soon afterwards, in the context of a threatened unofficial strike in early 1960, John Morgan took the pulse of British Railways – half a million employees, almost 5,000 stations (the densest network in the world), three out of four passenger seats unoccupied – for the *New Statesman*. 'To live a few days with railwaymen is to live in a world of disgruntlement,' he found, and he quoted a guard with 40 years' service: 'The public don't trouble a button whether they are polite to us or not. Before the war they used to think the world of the railwayman and now they don't give a fig.' The demoralisation was even greater in railway engineering plants, reflecting in part the clumsy handling of the transition from steam (the last locomotive was built in 1960) to diesel. In the Gorton district of east Manchester, the two main factories, Gorton Tank and Beyer Peacock, were being respectively closed and run down by the early 1960s, while the decline was equally sharp for the North British Locomotive Co in Springburn, Glasgow, once the second-largest of its type in the world. Certainly, for the railway industry as a whole, patchily attempting to modernise itself, there were few friends at court as losses mounted and the road lobby swept all before it. The transport minister was Ernest Marples, very much a roads man (not least because he owned a road-construction company), and in 1961 he put another unsentimental meritocrat, ICI's Richard Beeching, into the BR chair.[14]

If the railways were a world of their own, even more so were the docks. 'Between the British manufacturer and the foreign buyer stands the primeval jungle of dockland,' a rising young journalist, Peter Jenkins, wrote in early 1961 about the still very busy London docks. 'The tall elegant cranes tower above a thick undergrowth of warehouses, transit sheds and narrow winding road-ways; the natives are perpetually uneasy; predatory beasts are quick to pounce and strikes spread like a forest fire; many strange practices survive to confound the outside world; language is curious.' He went on to list some salient features: only about one-fifth of the workforce hired on a regular basis; 'the mentality of casual work' persisting; 'little personal contact' between the dockers and their employers; the nomadic docker tending to regard his union (usually the T&G) as a 'remote bureaucracy'; the strong influence of unofficial leaders like Jack Dash, the militant and 'dapper' chairman of the Royal Docks Liaison Committee; and 'one out, all out' as 'the unwritten law of dockland'. 1961 proved a year of trouble, including an absurd dispute that spring, the Lower Oliver's Wharf strike. There, the small manufacturer D. Cohen (Strawboards) Ltd had traditionally been permitted to use six of its own people to take monthly delivery by barge of strawboard; militants now objected, claiming that fully registered dock labour had to be used; the result was a widespread stoppage, lasting more than a week and involving some 15,000 men. A year later, in the context of a threatened national dock strike, a TV critic watching *Panorama* understandably found it hard to feel optimistic. 'The dockers, determined their sons should not work in the docks, saw no future for themselves elsewhere,' noted Arthur Calder-Marshall. 'Andrew Crichton for the employers and Frank Cousins for the dockers were at loggerheads because both were concerned with immediate problems . . . seemingly unwilling to contemplate the mechanization necessary to decasualize dock labour.'[15]

And of course – long before Elvis Costello's song, long before Robert Wyatt's haunting version – there was shipbuilding: traditionally one of the British glories, but sadly much less so by the start of the 1960s. A decade earlier, the UK's share of world merchant-ship launchings had been 38 per cent; now it was down to 16 per cent. And in terms specifically of ships delivered to the UK-registered fleet, the proportion from foreign shipyards had (as measured by tonnage) grown from zero to 20 per cent. By July 1960, when the Labour MP and broadcaster Woodrow Wyatt visited Tyneside, the order book for the shipbuilding industry stood at less than four million tons, compared with seven million at the end of 1957:

> Inside, the quiet of generations. Outside, the deafening clank of construction. Superficially, in the shipyards of the North, the two seemed unrelated.
>
> How could one suppose that Colonel Eustace Smith, chairman of the dockyard that his family founded in 1756, was building tankers in desperate competition with the Japanese? The serenity of his manner, matched by that of his offices, was more that of a country gentleman discussing the management of his estates than of the conventional tough businessman.
>
> Stiff collars, well-cut dark suits. Charm, courtesy and dignity. Offices proudly lined with models of ships built by the yards – usually going back to sailing vessels. The atmosphere of an unhurried age.

Smith himself, who was then the president of the Shipbuilding Conference, assured Wyatt that 'Japan will soon be in great difficulties.'

That same month, an analysis by Nicholas Faith of the industry's failure 'to expand or to invest' plausibly argued that 'managerial ineptitude' had been 'matched by the failure of the unions to take anything but a narrowly craft and sectional view'. Later in 1960 a report by the Department of Scientific and Industrial Research was highly critical, finding no evidence that the industry was ahead of its major foreign competitors either technically or economically. The Colonel, though, was unperturbed. 'The British shipbuilding industry is as good, if not better, than that of any other country,' he insisted publicly the day after publication. 'Because we are in difficulties it does not mean that the rest of the world is all right.' Soon afterwards, the 'Waterfront' column in the Newcastle-based *Journal* backed him up: 'The report must be worth millions to foreign builders . . . No one in shipbuilding, or repairing, is complacent . . . Tyne, Tees, Wear, and Hartlepools have all produced their biggest ships this year . . . Technically, the north-east is second to none . . .'

Spring 1961 saw a further report on the industry, carried out under Ministry of Transport auspices, and again very critical. Managements at the 50 or so yards were urged to 'make the most strenuous efforts to improve labour relations', while union leaders 'should advise their members of the serious prospects facing the industry, and the need for the maximum possible co-operation between management and work people to achieve the most efficient methods of production'. Was that even-handedness fair enough? One not notably radical historian of the industry, Anthony Burton, makes the point that amid the much-trumpeted modernisation panacea of the early 1960s, above all of plant and if possible of working practices, 'the need to modernise management methods was scarcely considered at all.' By spring 1962, the order book was down to 2.5 million tons (330 ships), compared with 3.1 million tons (430 ships) a year earlier; also in 1962, the sight of the *Nissho Maru*, loading up at Kuwait with over 100,000 tons of crude oil, signalled the ominous arrival of the Japanese super-tanker – at a stroke upping the modernisation ante.[16]

Back in the 1930s, Nevil Shute had written a novel, *Ruined City*, about a merchant banker's attempt to rescue a failing shipyard in the north-east. The Square Mile itself had been part-ruined during the war, but now was on the cusp of starting to return to something like its pre-1914 pre-eminent position as an *international* financial centre. 'London – Centre of the Euro-Dollar Market', the title of a *Times* article by William Clarke in October 1960, was an early public sighting of the term *eurodollar*, while the market itself (with dealings on the telephone rather than face-to-face) owed much of its rapid growth in the early 1960s to the liberal attitude of the Bank of England. There, a youngish merchant banker, Lord (Rowley) Cromer, became Governor in 1961, after the City had followed Oxford's example and made a dead set against the more cerebral Sir Oliver Franks, former high-flying civil servant and, despite his chairmanship of Lloyds Bank, viewed as unsympathetic. Yet for all its openness to the Eurodollar market, the Bank of England remained in many ways a deeply conservative and somewhat introverted institution, characteristics broadly in line with the City as a whole at this time. In May 1962, two of the Bank's senior figures assembled a list of maxims, eloquently revealing of life's certainties as viewed from their Threadneedle Street fortress, a fortress seemingly far removed from the world of Coventry car-makers or Clydeside riveters:

> A central banker needs a sense of smell. Analysis is only theorising but may be encouraged when it confuses critics.
>
> No civil servant understands markets.
>
> Politicians do not sufficiently explain the facts of life to the electorate.
>
> Central bankers should always do what they say and never say what they do.
>
> Wave the big stick if you like, but never use it; it may break in your hand. Better still, try wagging your finger.
>
> Never spit into the wind.
>
> Always lean against the wind.[17]

Then as later, in what has inevitably been an intensive, ongoing historical debate about the scope and causes of British relative economic decline, the usual suspects were trotted out and fingered. In July 1961 an *FT* analysis of 'The Productivity Race' – in which Britain since 1953 had fallen behind all her competitors bar Sweden – identified, *inter alia*, the lack of planned targets; government not ensuring that investment was channelled into fast-growing industries; the multiplicity of craft unions, fighting to retain the status quo; complacent management, enjoying after the war 'a protected market at home and a largely "captive" market in many Commonwealth countries'; and – the joint fault of government and industry – a failure to increase the numbers of 'technical and scientific personnel', as evidenced by the current shortage of production engineers. 'What it all comes down to in the end,' concluded the analysis not unpersuasively, 'is that for a whole variety of reasons – institutional, social, political and economic – a psychological climate has been created in this country which is a powerful obstacle to change. This is true of management, the unions and the Government alike.'

One absentee from this particular list was perhaps a surprise. 'Disillusion has been mainly induced by the persistent denigration of the nationalised industries by the Press, by Conservative politicians both inside and outside Parliament, by leading business men, and by organs like the Federation of British Industries and the Institute of Directors,' observed William Robson in his magisterial 1960 survey *Nationalised Industry and Public Ownership*. 'For more than ten years a ceaseless campaign has been waged by the great majority of the daily newspapers to present a continuously unfavourable picture of the nationalised industries.' Of course, irrespective of those industries' actual shortcomings, the longstanding fuzziness about their purpose – economic? social? – did not help. When Robens in 1960 accepted Macmillan's offer to head the National Coal Board, he pointed out how hard it would be ever to make a genuine profit. 'Don't worry, dear boy,' responded Macmillan through drooping eyelids. 'Just blur the edges . . . Just blur the edges.' In fact, the government in 1961 did try to reduce the fuzziness, with a White Paper on *The Financial and Economic Obligations of the Nationalised Industries* setting out five-year targets for financial performance and explicitly acknowledging that 'the industries must have freedom to make upward price adjustments' – an approach typically welcomed by the *Economist* as 'not particularly impressive' but also 'not ill-intentioned'.

Yet arguably, even amid the fuzziness, the performance of the nationalised industries (comprising around one-fifth of the economy) had already been significantly better than its many critics allowed. Despite how 'the institutional arrangements from the very beginning contained inherent contradictions,' and despite, further, how 'those arrangements allowed governments to use the industries as an instrument of real income distribution,' including through cross-subsidy, the economic historians James Foreman-Peck and Robert Millward would claim that 'the underlying productivity growth of the industries compared favourably with private industry in the UK.' Their table shows the annual average percentage growth rates from 1951 to 1964:

	Output	Labour productivity	Total factor productivity
Manufacturing (private sector)	3.2	2.5	1.9
Public enterprise	2.7	3.3	2.4

How then to explain the fact that, taking the 1950s as a whole, the industries' average annual rate of profit was zero? Here, Foreman-Peck and Millward make two points: first, that although coal and rail were loss-makers, the new technology industries (electricity, airways, telecommunications) all earned significant profits; and second, with particular relevance to coal and rail, the industries were highly vulnerable to government intervention in terms of range of products and levels of service, quite apart from price considerations. Or, as the *FT* put it at the time of the White Paper, 'the fact of nationalisation has tended to arouse public expectation that the products and services of these industries should be provided cheaply', even when 'costs and prices elsewhere have been rising'. It was not, the paper hardly needed to add, an expectation likely to change overnight.[18]

What about government? Leaving aside for the moment industrial relations and macro-economic policy, and noting that regional-*cum*-industrial policy was still (with the odd exception) undeveloped, there were perhaps two areas in which by the early 1960s it should have been doing appreciably better. The first concerned the competitiveness of the economy. Admittedly the Restrictive Trade Practices Act of 1956 was a major step in reducing cartelisation, but otherwise, as Geoffrey Owen points out, 'the framework of regulation and [tariff] protection which had been in place since the 1930s was left largely untouched.' That framework included resale price maintenance (RPM), the practice covering most retail activities and defined by its historian as one 'whereby producers would dictate the price at which their goods could be sold by retailers, thereby ensuring that prices were "fixed" across the board'. RPM, declared the male-oriented *FT* in May 1962 as its possible abolition entered the mainstream political agenda at long last, 'tends to raise costs, hold up new methods of retailing and thus denies the consumer the opportunity – which he need not take – of buying cheap'. The other government failing concerned the whole difficult area of education and training. Success had been 'uneven', noted the *Economist* in December 1961, for the nine Colleges of Advanced Technology (CATs) so far set up in the wake of the 1956 White Paper on *Technical Education*, adding that it would be a help if they were given full university status. As for the effectiveness of the 1959 White Paper on *Better Opportunities in Technical Education* – calling for a broadened school curriculum, greater continuity between school and college, and an enhanced awareness of industry's needs – that was hugely blunted by government's unwillingness or inability to bang heads together in the education world and get it to agree on the most suitable provision for 15- to 18-year-olds. 'In my view the lack of urgency in implementing this White Paper,' reflected many years later the mandarin (Sir Antony Part) most intimately involved in its preparation, 'contributed in a significant way to the failure to raise the capability of our boys and girls to a level adequate for our economic needs in an increasingly competitive world.'[19]

Ultimately, though, what really mattered day-to-day were management and labour – and the relations between them.

Challenge to Prosperity on Corrie night, 9 December 1960, focused on the managers. 'Taking part,' noted a preview, 'are the assistant managing director of British Aluminium, who says that the best young men are not those who get to the top, and some young Oxford graduates who after taking jobs in industry left in disgust.' British management had, though, at least one defender. When Woodrow Wyatt had, earlier in the year on *Any Questions?*, castigated it as 'terribly complacent', a fellow-panellist had expressed her 'very strong objections to anyone who suggests that our exporters are complacent'. And Margaret Thatcher went on: 'I happen to be married to an exporter and know exactly how hard the work is to get orders and they're not in the least complacent.'[20]

Recent economic historians have tended to be on Wyatt's side of the argument and to offer largely critical appraisals of the quality of management through the 1950s and into the early 1960s. Cumulatively, their findings amount to a major indictment. Employers and managers had 'little or no interest in improving or transforming undeveloped management control systems towards the Fordist model'– ie, of mass standardised production; generally speaking, 'Americanisation' was viewed 'as a threat to established British production and management systems and markets'; by the mid-1960s, 'very few British firms had adopted the multi-divisional form of organisation' – ie, with the company separated into product divisions; progress towards enhanced management education was at best patchy, with the prominent industrialist Sir Norman Kipping observing in 1961 that 'it has to be proved that the leadership element in the manager is present before it is really worth spending any time on management training'; and, all too symptomatically, within the ranks of management there was a persistent downgrading of the status and power of production managers, compared with what Nick Tiratsoo calls the 'privileged "gin and tonic" specialisms like marketing and accountancy'. Or take the key, nuts-and-bolts question of handling materials, vital to productivity. 'For every commercial and industrial firm having a vigorous and continuously developing handling policy,' observed *Mechanical Handling* in 1959, 'there are a dozen more which have scarcely the haziest notion of the importance of the handling function from the viewpoint of time and cost.' Moreover, despite a big push by the British Productivity Council in the late 1950s, the application of statistical quality control (SQC) techniques seems actually to have been going backwards in the early 1960s.[21]

Further evidence stacks up on the negative side. 'They were very sleepy after 5 o'clock, perhaps because their rooms were well-furnished with drinks cabinets,' Lord (Arnold) Weinstock would recall in the 1990s about companies in the 1950s. 'The big wheels sat in their offices "making policy", lunching at the Savoy, going to trade associations, overseas tours, heaven knows what, but doing little that we would recognise as work. They weren't doing much to drum up business; and they weren't doing much to push ahead in technology.' In November 1961, reporting on the Scottish economy, the Toothill Committee found management there guilty of 'a tendency to over-caution', which meant that 'progress in modernising older Scottish industries has not been as fast as might be wished', and added that the ingrained belief among many industrialists that the best training for management was obtained on the shop floor was 'a dangerously limited attitude'. Two months later, a survey by the Aberdeen Productivity Committee of 252 firms in the district revealed that two-fifths thought that work-study was not applicable to them, and indeed that only three-fifths had bothered to reply. Arguably the most stultifying atmosphere was to be found in the really big companies, often appearing to observers like branches of the civil service. The historian Frank Mort, whose father worked for ICI in Runcorn as a cost accountant, evokes a world of 'exceptional formality', of 'bureaucratic attention to detail' and of 'a general culture of suspicion, which manifested itself through processes of complex monitoring extending from the top to the bottom of the management hierarchy'. Far more numerous, of course, were smaller, family-run firms, where almost invariably conservatism was deeply entrenched. One such was Briar & Peacock. In 1959, at a seminar series at the London School of Economics on 'Problems in Industrial Administration', Mr Briar described how quality control had worked in practice during his career:

> I tasted the golden syrup every day like my uncle before me. And if the flavour was off, 'Why?' During the war we had to change the process because of a shortage of something or other. And my cousin came back from the war and said, 'The flavour has altered. You've altered it!' And we said, 'Yes,' and he said, 'Don't f--- about! Bloody well go back to the original process.' 'It'll cost more.' 'It doesn't matter. Go back to the original recipe.'

'And,' added Briar, 'he was right. Only way to maintain the standard.'[22]

At least one prominent local industrialist missed *Coronation Street*'s launch. Instead, that Friday evening saw H. Hoyle of the Lancashire Footwear Manufacturers' Association speaking at a dinner (as reported by the *Bacup Times*) in honour of 75-year-old John Hollowood, until recently the long-serving leader of the Rossendale Union of Boot, Shoe and Slipper Operatives. Acknowledging that they had had their differences over the years, but also that there had been no major disputes for the last third of a century, Hoyle went on: 'I know of no one who evinces as he does the words of the Scottish poet, Robert Burns. "The rank is but the guinea stamp, the man's the gold for a' that." He has evinced that for the operatives of this trade throughout the forty years he has been working on their behalf.' Five of Hollowood's six sons were now in the slipper industry, and future harmony seemed assured. That was not quite, though, the perspective of *Challenge to Prosperity*, and a week later Christopher Chataway was looking critically at industrial relations, asking, 'Do workers devote too much energy to wage increases and too little to expanding production? Has the gulf between the trade unionist and his leaders affected industrial peace?'

Good questions, but in the early 1960s most managers in British industry were unwilling to get their hands dirty trying to resolve them and other such issues. A highly respected union leader, Sir Thomas Williamson of the General and Municipal Workers, summed up the attitude problem eloquently in a 1960 interview:

> The human element is treated in an astonishingly off-hand way. There are old-fashioned employers who believe the trade unions are just a damned nuisance and avoid any dealings with them for as long as possible. There are firms which tolerate and only just tolerate unions. There are firms which, at the first hearing of a workers' claim, say 'no' automatically. There are those which delay negotiations interminably . . . Lack of communications between management and men, about reasons for changes in production methods, the transfer of workers, redundancy, and so on, provide the grounds for trouble. All these and other factors tend, rightly or wrongly, to create bloody-mindedness among the workers. The atmosphere is soured . . .

Or, as an American academic, David Granick, found in Glasgow at about the same time, 'One managing director insisted in conversation with me that all management prerogatives were sacred. For example, if anyone from the union came asking to see his balance sheet, he would kick him out of the office.'

Yet it would be seriously misleading to suggest that the *prevailing* industrial-relations climate was adversarial. Full employment, strong demand, semi-captive markets, import penetration still within reasonable bounds, employers often divided among themselves and unable to put on a united front, paternalism anyway continuing to run deep in many corporate DNAs, the TUC a sufficient estate of the realm to be represented on almost a thousand tripartite public committees – unsurprisingly, management tended as often as not to be accommodating rather than confrontational. Sir Halford Reddish of non-unionised Rugby Portland Cement – 'prepared more than any other company chairman,' notes his biographer, to state publicly 'what many preferred to say privately' – undoubtedly wished it otherwise. 'All too often,' Reddish loudly complained in 1960, 'the employer meekly gives in, because he hasn't got the guts to stand up to the threat of the unofficial strike – engineered by the scheming few, acquiesced in by the unthinking many.' He added darkly: 'The blackmailer always comes back. The one who hasn't has yet to be born.'[23]

For a range of reasons – identified by the historian Howard Gospel as full employment, rising prices, greater expectations and a less deferential workforce, as well as 'the growing organisation and assertiveness of shop stewards and the weakness and inability of collective bargaining procedures to cope with the changed circumstances' – the frequency of strikes was undoubtedly greater between the mid-1950s and mid-1960s than it had been during the immediate post-war period. Between 1947 and 1954, the number of disputes beginning in each year was always below 2,000; from 1955 to 1964, it was always above 2,000, with 1957 (2,859) and 1960 (2,832) the two peak years, including 1960 as the first time that non-mining strikes exceeded 1,000. Of those strikes, by the early 1960s some 95 per cent were unofficial, with the average dispute involving some 500 workers and losing some 1,000 working days – ie, of only brief duration. A couple of other statistics add further perspective. Between 1952 and 1961, just one out of every 2,000 working days was lost through strikes; taking the 1950s as a whole, and comparing days lost per thousand workers in the Western industrial countries, the US, Finland, Belgium, Canada, Italy, Australia and France (but not West Germany) had appreciably higher rates than the UK. In short, any *I'm All Right, Jack* notion that Britain was uniquely strike-prone was at this stage a myth.

But what about more broadly? 'In industrial relations we are already out of date,' declared the *News Chronicle* in an economic leader shortly before its demise. 'Almost everywhere there are restrictive practices which make us a laughing stock abroad.' Not least of course in the newspaper industry itself, scrutinised in the early 1960s by a Royal Commission chaired by Lord Shawcross. The commission found, amid abundant evidence of management weakness in the face of the print unions, overmanning of the order of 34 per cent; excessive, even 'grotesque', demarcation; and, moving into Spanish practices territory, a whole host of 'house extras negotiated to meet special conditions', a 'substantial' number of which were 'based on reasons sometimes anachronistic and often fictitious'. Or, from a few years earlier, in another industry, take the *cri de coeur* of J. G. Stephen, of the Clydeside shipbuilders Alexander Stephens & Sons, about heavily demarcated existing practice:

> The clearest example perhaps is that of the Tack Welder who stands and watches a Plater position a bar. When it is in its place the Tack Welder then tacks it and the Plater stands and watches him, whereas the Plater, or his Helper, could perfectly well do the tack welding. If the Platers and the Shipwrights were allowed to do their own tack welding, our firm could dispense with 65 men the next day and probably increase the output as well . . .

That, though, was not a wholly attractive bargain. 'Every worker,' reflected the TUC's Vic Feather in 1959, 'has at least one concern at the back of his mind which is even more important than the size of the pay packet; that is, the regularity of his pay packets, the security of his employment.' Even so, the report of an American study group, doing its fieldwork the following year, suggests a rather more nuanced picture: 'The unions of Great Britain have generally welcomed technological development subject to full consultation about its effects and the maintenance of strict standards of safety. They believe that technological change opens the way to better pay and conditions for their members.' Indeed, the fullest survey of restrictive practices in British industry had already revealed something not altogether dissimilar. This was the National Joint Advisory Council's inquiry, whose 1959 report denied that industry was 'riddled' with restrictive practices, but instead expressed 'some satisfaction' that 'so many industries' were able to state that they were meeting, in their efforts to ensure the efficient use of manpower, 'no real difficulties'. To Robert Carr, Parliamentary Secretary to the Minister of Labour, the conclusion was clear after looking at that inquiry's evidence. Yes, it was 'undeniable' that there were 'difficulties in some industries', yet overall, the fact was that 'over much of industry' the 'two sides' were 'willing to tackle jointly any problems caused by restrictive practices'.[24]

Within trade unionism, by some way the most important development at this time was the rise of the shop steward – perhaps around 150,000 of them by the early 1960s, out of a total union membership of some 9.5 million – and accompanying workplace bargaining. In 1957 the industrial sociologist T. E. Stephenson gave a helpfully sober contextualisation to a phenomenon far from universally welcome:

> In many cases the shop stewards interpret the national agreements at local level, and whenever there is a dispute the shop stewards represent the workers. In some instances the shop stewards go still further and actually negotiate higher rates than those nationally agreed between unions and employers. They have been able to do this in a period of full employment and with a labour shortage in some industries, because the management has wanted to hold on to its labour force and avoid trouble with the stewards who often have considerable influence in a work place. Furthermore it is not only over wages that the shop stewards represent the workers to the local management, but also over the many problems that arise out of local working conditions and habits and customs. Hence the power of many shop stewards is great . . .

'With the depersonalisation of the unions,' he added about the erosion of central authority, 'the leadership's control over the members is more formalised, loyalty is weakened and with it the leaders' power.' Three years later, when Sir Miles Thomas penned a piece on trade unions for *Punch*, the humour came through rather clenched teeth. 'Someone once suggested that shop stewards should wear distinctive uniforms,' noted BOAC's former chairman. 'There is no need for that. Nature has cast them in distinctive moulds that make them recognisable a mile off . . . They are the militant ginger men, frequently a pain in the necks of the higher trades unionists, who prefer a quiet tempo of squabble-free industry to the brouhaha of stompings on the shop floor.' One of those ginger men was a toolmaker in an engineering firm in Glasgow's Govan district. 'I was a shop steward as an apprentice and led the apprentices' strike in '61,' recalled Sir Alex Ferguson half a century later. 'Later on, I became the shop steward of the toolroom when I was only 21. Looking after the workers' interests was why I became a shop steward.'

Significantly, it was not just politicians, industrialists and those at the top of the union hierarchies who demonised shop stewards – viewed as responsible for the proliferation of unofficial strikes – but even some academic experts on industrial relations. 'They think of the agreements negotiated by their unions at national level as no more than jumping-off points to be improved upon whenever possible by their own pressures,' noted Ben Roberts in 1962, regretfully adding that 'it is no longer felt to be morally improper to make such demands and to back them up by actions that are a violation of agreed procedure.' The temptation was to view the shop stewards' movement as a wilful and concerted power grab, possibly with sinister implications, yet the reality was usually more humdrum. 'Familiar as no outside negotiator could be with the maze of bargaining agreements peculiar to his own shop,' a writer on the car industry observed in 1960, 'the stewards have not usurped official power so often as they have been forced willy-nilly to accept responsibilities for which there is often no other immediate authority or substitute.' The historian Steven Tolliday fleshes out the picture in a pioneering study of Coventry's engineering (mainly car) workers and shop-floor bargaining between the 1940s and the 1970s. 'The shop steward system under piecework was fraught with inequity, lack of security, constant haggling and divisiveness,' he comments. 'The results of sectional, fragmented bargaining were only partly satisfactory to stewards. They recognised the bargaining advantages of piecework but were also critical of the system as dog-eat-dog and as vicious in dividing and driving the workers.' Accordingly, 'stewards were generally unable to develop broader strategic goals' – a conclusion notably at odds with some external perceptions over the years.[25]

The unions were undoubtedly in the spotlight. *Punch* during summer 1960 ran a seven-part series on 'State of the Unions', while in 1961 *The Times*'s labour correspondent Eric Wigham sought in a Penguin Special to answer the question *What's Wrong with the Unions?*. Among outsiders, a special status attached to Allan Flanders, co-editor of the 1954 classic *The System of Industrial Relations in Great Britain*, a study subsequently identified as a high-tide moment in the post-war consensus. The principle of industry-wide pay-fixing arrangements seemed then to be set in adamantine centralised stone, prompting Flanders to assert that 'there is not the slightest possibility of the clock being turned back to individual or to works bargaining over wage rates.' Barely half a decade later, things seemed less certain, and in August 1961, Flanders set out for *Socialist Commentary* his vision of 'Trade Unions in the Sixties'. Essentially his argument was that 'the spirit of materialism' had 'submerged the spirit of idealism' and that the unions needed to rediscover what he called their 'social purpose' – above all 'in the workshop, or whatever may be its equivalent, the colliery, the office, the site, the depot', where 'Britain's workers are still in many respects second-class citizens' and 'subjected to treatment which would be considered intolerable in any other walk of life'. Accordingly, over such issues as 'engagement, discipline, dismissal, promotion, training, welfare in many aspects, fair treatment on the job', he envisaged 'a struggle which the trade unions have to lead nationally, even if it is fought locally'.

As it happened, another front was already opening up which would soon engage Flanders deeply. This was the so-called 'Fawley experiment' – the productivity agreements reached in July 1960 between management and unions at the Esso Refinery at Fawley, near Southampton, by which (to quote Flanders from his 1964 Fawley study) 'the company agreed to provide large increases in its employees' rates of pay – of the order of 40 per cent – in return for the unions' consent to certain defined changes in working practices.' Was this the way ahead? The *Sunday Times*'s William Rees-Mogg certainly thought so – declaring in May 1962 that 'something like the Fawley experiment should be tried in the docks, a combined package of higher pay, decasualisation and mechanisation' – but even by 1965 only a dozen or so 'productivity agreements' had been signed in British industry. This would not have surprised Michael Shanks, who in his 1961 *The Stagnant Society* had called for the movement at last to 'broaden its appeal to the dynamic element in modern society'. But he did so more in hope than expectation, given that the unions 'reflect the inhibitions and the conservatism of their members – particularly of the older, declining section of the working class'.[26]

It was a conservatism classically encouraged by top Conservatives. Many party members and even backbenchers may have hankered after a legislative salvo to curb what they saw as the twin evils of unofficial strikes and the closed shop, but senior figures were thoroughly aware of compelling reasons to leave well alone. The closed shop, they knew, was not only helpful to employers wanting to make collective bargaining stick but also served to increase union membership and thus lessen the internal influence of the left. At the same time, not picking a fight with the unions was entirely consistent with Macmillan's overriding wish to demonstrate that his party had learned the harsh lessons of the inter-war years. Inevitably, though, the temptation to go down the legislative route began to increase once the industrial-relations climate darkened – a temptation that pointed up the perennial Tory philosophical tension between control on the one hand and freedom on the other. A lecture by Edward Heath in March 1960 as Minister of Labour seemed to be moving in the former direction (as he emphasised the dangers of strikes and inflationary wage settlements), but ultimately veered away. 'It would,' he reminded his listeners, 'be unlike us as Conservatives to wish to impose some tidy plan on what has been a natural growth.' Within a year or so, however, such were economic circumstances (earnings increases outstripping price increases and a deteriorating balance of payments) that the possibility of a state-imposed policy of wage restraint was firmly on the agenda.

Undoubtedly the unions got largely negative coverage from the media. 'Suspicion of the press is ingrained and not unjustified,' observed Eric Wigham in his survey. 'There are papers which will seize on anything discreditable to the unions and magnify it out of all proportion to its news value. Some will misrepresent the union attitude and one or two, particularly during disputes, indulge in scurrilous personal attacks which do not spare a union leader's home or family. They do not treat employers in the same way.' Other papers, he added, were more balanced or even positive, but overall 'the weight of numbers is against the unions.' In the cinema, only months after *I'm All Right, Jack*, a key film of the early 1960s was *The Angry Silence*: a powerful drama (written by Bryan Forbes and starring Richard Attenborough) about a factory worker persecuted for not joining a strike. 'His colleagues are shown as being manipulated by skulking professional agitators,' recalled an obituarist of Forbes, 'and to some it seemed more like a political statement than a human story about the crushing of an individual.' The press loved it. 'Brave and important. A film that everyone must see' (*Daily Mail*). 'The clear ring of truth' (*The Times*). 'A story of our times' (*Daily Mirror*). Tom Stoppard, reviewing for Bristol's *Evening World*, joined the chorus: 'I stand on my tip-up seat to cheer . . . A cry from the dock on behalf of every stubborn, proud, infuriating little man who has ever committed the crime of preferring to do his own thinking for himself . . . A shout against the folly of our times.' *The Angry Silence* may or may not have been anti-union, but either way there was surely some justice to Ken Loach's retrospective verdict that 'although it had an arguable point, it was one that the film-makers should have hesitated to use to the disadvantage of working men so long as there were no other British films to espouse the workers' grievances with equal zeal.' What about TV? Coverage there was obviously more measured, including relative even-handedness in the BBC's 1961 sitcom *The Rag Trade*, with the grasping but ineffectual boss (Peter Jones) of a millinery basement sweatshop broadly balanced by the militant shop steward (Miriam Karlin) and her 'Everybody out!' catchphrase.[27]

Always there was the drip-drip of general discourse and background noise about the union 'question' or 'problem' (not least after the Communist-run Electrical Trades Union had in 1961 been found guilty of systematic ballot-rigging) as well naturally about the 'laziness' of the working man. 'I think I do a good job,' a long-time Austin car worker, Harry Collins, told *TV Times* in April 1962, ahead of the latest television inquiry into Britain's economic future. 'It's darned hard work on the track. It's all very well for the Duke of Edinburgh to tell us to get our fingers out – let him come and work on the track for a few days!'

Gallup charted public attitudes. Back in 1954 – high-tide point – 71 per cent had considered trade unions 'a good thing', but by 1961 the figure was down to 57 per cent. As for the closed shop (applicable to some 35 to 40 per cent of trade unionists), Gallup in 1959 found 22 per cent of respondents defending the principle and 53 per cent disagreeing with it. An insight into working-class attitudes comes from the late 1950s and early 1960s fieldwork of Robert McKenzie and Allan Silver, who found that Conservative and Labour voters alike viewed unions as simultaneously inevitable, indispensable and imperfect – in fact somewhere, as one interviewee put it, between 'necessary' and 'necessary evil'. But among Sheffield's adolescents, it was more a case of an indifferent shrug of the shoulders. 'None were enthusiastic, they simply happened to be members, just as others happened not to be,' noted Michael Carter in his 1962 study of recent school-leavers (mainly working-class). He quoted some who had, as it happened, joined a union:

> If you are on strike they give you money.
> Someone at the back to help you out.
> My father made me join.
> The bosses can't treat you just anyhow.
> You can go on all machines if you are a member.
> A man wanted me to fill a form in, so I thought I might as well.

Unsurprisingly, Carter found among these new members 'no understanding of the organisation, even at the branch level' – a lack of knowledge (and indeed interest) that was 'in many cases just another facet of lack of interest in work itself'. A girl and a boy agreed to enlighten him about their general attitude to unions. 'Don't be absurd,' declared the former, laughing. 'What have trade unions to do with life?' The boy agreed. 'You see about it in the papers, but I'm more interested in what United did on Saturday.'[28]

It is hard to avoid the cultural dimension. Anthony Crosland in 1961 termed 'typically British' what he convincingly identified as the 'lack of pride in *maximum professional achievement*, especially technical achievement'. For which, he went on, there were many long-term reasons:

> An aristocratic tradition, persisting strongly in the public schools, has bred a cult of the amateur, the gifted dilettante, the rounded and cultured Wykehamist who, patently superior to the drab, despised professional or technician, can turn his hand with marvellous facility to

> anything. It has led also to a strong emphasis on 'liberal' as opposed to technical or scientific education. Again, the fact that we were for so long the world's first industrial and imperial power, and emerged relatively unscathed and apparent victors from two World Wars, created a sense that we should always triumph by a natural, effortless superiority, with no need to stoop to the humourless professionalism of Huns or Yanks; and so we stopped thinking in an original, professional way. We were saved, moreover, from detailed and therefore possibly odious comparisons by the existence of the British Channel and the absence of any large-scale wave of immigration. Lastly, a rather rigid class and status system, by inhibiting upward social movement, encouraged an accent on staying-put and family security rather than on personal drive for maximum achievement.

Crosland's analysis chimed with the findings of David Granick. 'Great Britain: The Home of the Amateur' was the title of his chapter on British management, based on 1959–60 comparative fieldwork across Europe, and he noted how 'even in the technical industries, the numbers of engineers and scientists who reach board level are seriously restricted.' The cult of the amateur was certainly alive and well in the club-like City of London, where to a large extent it still remained true that *who* one knew was more important that *what* one knew – and where an explicitly meritocratic stockbroking firm like Phillips & Drew, pioneers in the City of American-style investment analysis, was at best regarded as a regrettable necessity. Or take the world of government, where, broadly speaking, until at least the early 1960s, the generalist was prized above the specialist. Anthony Sampson described the Ministry of Aviation as being run by 'Latin and History scholars', while he found the Treasury's 'contact with any scientific project, from jet fighters to Blue Streaks, embarrassed by the fact that they have no scientists on their staff'. Such indeed had already been the conclusion of the Labour-supporting economist Thomas Balogh, who in a celebrated 1959 essay, 'The Apotheosis of the Dilettante', had given a scathing portrait of a conservative, entrenched and above all economics-averse Treasury. That prejudice was shared by its First Lord. 'Like anything that *Lombard* writes, it is interesting but exaggerated,' minuted Macmillan in 1961 on a ministerial letter enclosing an *FT* column about the failure since 1951 of monetary policy. 'Economists,' he added, 'are now worse than theologians.'[29]

Sampson and Balogh were writing at the time, but the most devastating analysis of the Treasury, applicable to the whole post-war period, was made retrospectively. In his bracingly polemical *The Wasting of the British Economy* (1982), the eminent economic historian Sidney Pollard identified 'the principle of concentrating first and foremost on symbolic figures and quantities, like prices, exchange rates and balances of payment, to the neglect of real quantities, like goods and services produced and traded', as lying at the heart of the failure of the British economy to grow as fast as other comparable economies. It was not, Pollard argued, that a concern with such issues as balance of payments or inflation was in itself wrong; it was rather that the Treasury's 'single-minded obsession' meant that 'real productive power and real goods and services available for consumption' – ie, the objectives that really mattered and could only be attained through higher investment – were 'repeatedly sacrificed for the sake of the symbols'. Ultimately, 'the attitude of the authorities can only be described as one of contempt for production and of the productive sectors of the economy.' Pollard spelled out the consequences:

> As a policy principle it proved to be thoroughly destructive. For it preferred the empty symbol to the living reality, and by utterly confusing ends and means, it lost both. Britain, sacrificing her productive power on the altar of monetary symbols, suffered not only in real welfare, but in the end damaged also the symbols for which it had been sacrificed; whereas the countries that got their priorities right and devoted their efforts to improving the productive base found that their symbols, the value of their currencies and the balance of their payments, also turned out successful and positive.

A specific example he gave of the skewed priorities in action was how the Treasury and other economic policy-makers 'failed to see that the cause of Britain's uncompetitive prices in world markets in the 1950s and 1960s was not that her wages were too high, as official opinion insisted throughout, but her rises in productivity too low'. How much, though, was the 'contempt for production' culturally determined?

Obviously it is easy to construct a picture of Oxbridge-educated, Latin-speaking mandarins finding the world of production essentially alien and outside their comfort zone. But there was also, Pollard suggested, a 'strongly moralistic element in the Treasury predilection for cuts', containing 'an appeal to the bourgeois/Puritan streak in all of us which believes that it is somehow wrong to spend and virtuous to refrain from spending'. This is surely plausible, as quite possibly also is the notion of a distinctively masochistic element in the national psyche more generally. 'The British public,' noted Pollard, 'was willing to suffer rationing and the petty tyrannies of shopkeepers much longer than citizens of other countries, including those who lost the war, for the sake of some moral comfort and perhaps a feeling of security.' Much of course changed in Britain after the 1940s, but an almost atavistic belief that, as Pollard put it, 'abstemiousness equates with good housekeeping and will ultimately bring its own reward' resolutely persisted, on the whole unhelpfully.

In 1960 itself, though, the most immediate macro-economic concern was the stop-go cycle and how to break out of it. Through the 1950s the traffic lights of economic policy had alternated with almost bewildering frequency – or, to apply another motoring metaphor, the economy had constantly oscillated between having its brakes on and off – and the new decade promised more of the same. Indeed, 1960 saw the Bank Rate zig-zagging around (with an inevitable impact on production and investment) amid competing judgements about the inflationary consequences of Macmillan's 1959 pre-election boom. Somewhat envious eyes were beginning to be cast at the French economy, with its impressive growth figures allied to a well-publicised central planning mechanism in the form of the Commissariat Général du Plan, which brought together ministers, civil servants, industrialists and trade unionists in an apparently successful attempt to achieve long-term modernisation. In November 1960, the Federation of British Industries (forerunner of the CBI) gathered at Brighton to discuss 'The Next Five Years'. There, the group addressing economic growth agreed that there was room for 'assessments of possibilities and expectations', which 'should be approached by Government and industry together'; and it called on government and industry to see 'whether it would be possible to agree on an assessment of expectations and intentions which should be before the country for the next five years'.[30] The new cry, in other words, was for greater planning, a desire unlikely to be ignored by a PM who, back in the 1930s, had made his intellectual 'Middle Way' reputation by repudiating naked laissez-faire.

There was perhaps one other big-picture element, though it did not often break cover. In essence, it was the question of whether Britain should go on discharging the necessary responsibilities in order still to be considered (at least in its own eyes) a top-table power.[31] In practice, those responsibilities took two main forms: being one of the world's policemen, whether or not that was affordable; and upholding the prestige of sterling, even if the penalties for the domestic economy were artificially high interest rates and an overvalued exchange rate. It is true of course that in the early 1960s there took place a surprisingly rapid running down of the old British Empire, but the reason for that was primarily political rather than economic. Instead, as far as one can tell, the need to go on sustaining the twin burdens remained largely intact in the policy-making mind. It was almost as if, psychologically speaking, Suez had never happened. And as long as that continued to be the powerful, if seldom articulated, assumption, no national plan or productivity drive or management-education initiative or even trade union reform was likely to make all that much difference.

7

Working, Middle and Kidding Themselves

'Working-class life finds itself on the move towards new middle-class values and middle-class existence,' declared the enterprising, lone-wolf sociologist Ferdynand Zweig in the introduction to his 1961 study of *The Worker in an Affluent Society*. 'The change can only be described as a deep transformation of values, as the development of new ways of thinking and feeling, a new ethos, new aspirations and cravings.' The basis for these assertions, and the meat of the book, were the 672 interviews that he had conducted in 1958–9 with workers at the River Don Works (in Sheffield) of the English Steel Corporation, at the Workington Iron and Steel Co, at Vauxhall Motors (in Luton), at Dunlop (in Erdington, Birmingham) and at the Mullard Radio Valve Co (in Mitcham, Surrey). As usual with Zweig, the detail was remarkable and at times novelistic in its sensibility. 'The Father Image', 'Divorces and Separations', 'Acquisitive Tendencies', 'Home and Work Upsets', 'Pastimes', 'Hobbies and Sidelines', 'The Rewards of Temperance', 'Hedgehog Behaviour' – such were some of his chapter titles before, finally, in 'A New Mode of Life and a New Ethos', he pulled his material together. Specifically, he identified five main new tendencies on the part of the (predominantly male) British worker: increasing 'security-mindedness', including no longer letting tomorrow take care of itself; rising expectations ('he has a good life but wants more of it'); sharpening acquisitive instincts; growing 'family-mindedness and home-centredness', with the worker 'moving away from his mates' and the trade union 'taken for granted'; and, lastly, what Zweig called 'the process of greater individualization', as the worker thought of himself 'not as one of the mass but as an individual, a person'. Accordingly:

> The worker wants little things instead of big things, he wants them for himself rather than for society at large, he wants better and wider opportunities for getting along. Old slogans, old loyalties tend to leave him cold. The class struggle interests him less and less. The idea of the working class as an oppressed or an exploited class or the romanticised idea of the working class as foremost in the struggle for progress and social justice, is fading from his mind and is more and more replaced by the idea of the working class as a class well established and well-to-do in its own right. 'Working-class but not poor' is his idea of himself. Class divisions are no longer marked out by hostility and segregation. They are still there, but class feelings are less active and less virulent . . .

'Large sections of the working classes are on the move,' reiterated Zweig in his closing sentences, 'not only to higher standards of living, but also to new standards of values and conduct and new social consciousness. The impact of these changes on social, political and economic life can hardly be foreseen. They are the augury of a new age, a new social horizon which is unfolding before our very eyes.'[1]

Were working-class life and culture really changing fundamentally in the late 1950s and early 1960s? Certainly there is abundant evidence to suggest that something major was afoot, starting with the testimony of the workers themselves as quoted by Zweig:

> I bought the car from overtime.
>
> When I went on shifts I bought a car.
>
> Since I had a car I gave up drinking; drinking and driving don't go together.
>
> Since I had a car I gave up gambling; gambling became a mug's game.
>
> The car's to take the family out.
>
> My wife suffers from nerves but she is much better since I got T.V. for her.
>
> T.V. kills the conversation. Nobody talks, we just listen.
>
> It is the greatest hobby killer. Now you don't need to worry how you will spend your time.
>
> A neighbour's conversation is uninteresting compared with T.V.

> Keep apart from neighbours, but be friendly.
> Mates [ie, at work] are not pals.
> We like to forget work as soon as we are outside the gates.
> I look after the money all right.
> We both save and each of our children has a savings book.
> I feel more independent since I got the house.
> I am always improving or adding something in the house.
> It's like heaven to settle down in one's own house.

In Zweig's five samples, the proportion of homeowners among working-class family men averaged 32 per cent (highest in Luton, lowest in Sheffield), while undoubtedly being a rising trend nationally. And of course, as he argued, so much followed, including domestic acquisitions, life insurance, a cheque book, and an enhanced concern with property values and respectable neighbours. Home ownership, in short, was 'certainly an important element in the new "gospel" of prosperity among the working classes'.

Some familiar staples of the working-class way of life were in palpable or seeming decline. Almost a pub a day closed during 1961, while beer consumption that year was down to twenty-four million barrels, six million fewer than during the war; circulation of the *News of the World* was by 1960 over 1.5 million less than at the paper's peak soon after the war; pawnshops in Bolton (Mass Observation's famous pre-war 'Worktown') were reduced by 1960 to a mere three; greyhound racing's peak annual attendance in the mid-1950s of some 25 million had shrunk by the early 1960s to some 16 million; the average rugby-league crowd declined from above 9,000 in 1950 to below 5,000 ten years later; the historian of the wakes week unhesitatingly pinpoints the end of that phenomenon's golden age 'to within a couple of years either side of 1960'; at the seaside, Morecambe's 1,300 boarding houses in 1956 were down only four years later to 927, while on a day-trip to Southend in 1958 the working-class writer Frank Norman lamented the new sobriety of a place where 'the Cockney mums and dads' of yesteryear used to go 'to have a good old-fashioned booze-up'; and a further lament came from the north-eastern writer Sid Chaplin, who on a Saturday afternoon in September 1960 counted only five cloth caps in Newcastle's Grainger Street – 'the victory', he feared, 'of Subtopia over the good old industrial common sense and the gaiety that often went with it'. No decline was more precipitate, of course, than that of the cinema, with admissions more than halving between 1950 and 1960 as at the same time more than a quarter of cinemas closed. Tellingly, the pace of closures was highest in the north and the Midlands, both predominantly working-class. The worst year was 1960 itself, typified by Derby's two oldest cinemas shutting their doors, while that November it was the same story in London's East End. 'I wouldn't be surprised if I have tears in my eyes,' confessed a former manager, Maurice Cheepen, ahead of the Troxy in Commercial Road closing. 'After all, the old Troxy has been quite a place in its time . . .'[2]

For the people's game, these were key years. 'Football must be given a new look,' urged the *News Chronicle* in February 1960, in the context of Football League attendances having declined from over 40 million a year in the late 1940s to under 30 million by the new decade. Later in 1960 some young Oxford graduates, calling themselves Group 60 and including Dennis Potter and Perry Anderson, investigated soccer's malaise. 'New tastes and habits' as well as 'dissatisfaction with cramped, dirty grounds, defeats abroad, dull games, allegations of bribery and the grey miseries of the British mid-winter' – such, they announced in the *Daily Herald*, were the reasons why 'the pull of football is slackening'. Undeniably there were grounds for complaint. Despite the magnificent North Stand at Sheffield Wednesday's Hillsborough, opened in August 1961, spectator facilities remained generally primitive, not least at Plymouth Argyle. A loyal but irate supporter wrote to the local paper in 1960, challenging the club's chairman 'to try watching Argyle from the "slag heap" at Barn Park end on a wet windy evening with water pouring around his feet through the wet cinders'.

Instead, it was in three other areas that a new football era was under way. One was player behaviour, with a member of the *Any Questions?* audience noting in January 1961 'a great deal of comment recently regarding the manner in which professional footballers are congratulated by their team-mates when scoring a goal' – an issue that prompted the panel's Colin MacInnes to declare how 'charming' he found 'all this kissing'. Another area was crowd behaviour. 1961 saw not only a televised pitch invasion at Sunderland but the pelting of the Leyton Orient goalkeeper at Huddersfield, prompting the local paper there to call on 'the more mature-minded, adult Soccer fan' to 'help the club keep law and order'. It was also about this time that the singing of 'Abide With Me' at the FA Cup Final began to lose its collective – and moving – discipline. The third area, though, was perhaps the most significant. 'Hill's Hour of Triumph' was the *Daily Mirror* headline in January 1961, marking Jimmy Hill's success (as chairman of the Professional Footballers' Association) in persuading the clubs to abandon the £20-a-week maximum wage. Unusually for a union campaign prepared to threaten strike action, Hill and his colleagues had been backed by much of the media, including the pro-market *Economist*. 'The day of the cloth-capped, faithful supporter of the local professional team has passed,' the paper observed without compunction about the dawning winner-takes-all world. And when Fulham's Johnny Haynes became soon afterwards English football's first £100-a-week player, it commented that this made him 'just like any other valuable entertainer'.[3]

The two dominant new factors of everyday life were of course the car (5.5 million in use in 1960, compared to 2.3 million in 1950) and television (in 82 per cent of homes by 1960, compared to 40 per cent in 1955), but in terms of working-class culture there were plenty of others. Two new trends in the early 1960s had an American flavour. 'Thumping with loud, bright, interior-decorated, Tannoy-guided, muzak-placated, electronically-operated life' was Tom Stoppard's impression in 1961 of the Kingswood Odeon (in Bristol) after its conversion from a cinema into a tenpin bowling alley; while on ITV on Saturday afternoons, the transatlantic voice of Kent Walton ('Greetings, grapple fans') signalled a hugely popular viewing slot somehow simultaneously exotic and homespun, with Jackie 'Mr TV' Pallo – gold-spangled boots, candy-striped Y-fronts, peroxided hair tied back with a black velvet ribbon – starting to become the wrestler millions loved to hate. Tastes were changing. Sales of filter-tipped cigarettes increased sixfold between 1955 and 1960; as for alcoholic drinks, not only was Ind Coope heavily promoting Skol lager, but pubs and restaurants were increasingly willing to sell wine by the glass. Almost everywhere, it appeared, were signs of a decisive shift upmarket. The Betting and Gaming Act of 1960 legalised off-course cash betting, leading to a rapid proliferation of high-street betting shops; a new breed of working men's clubs was springing up, described by one observer as 'ornate, chromium-plated with microphones and wurlitzers and white-coated waiters and chicken sandwiches'; the public face of rugby league was now the cheerful commentator Eddie Waring, who reflected in 1962 that, since his *Grandstand* debut four years earlier, he had helped to make the game 'respectable', no longer perceived just as 'a working man's game, cloth caps and mufflers and that sort of thing'; and even Butlin's was changing its emphasis, with one camp having by 1959 as its main advertising slogan 'No loudspeakers, no regimentation'.[4]

The most sustained piece of reportage about all this came from the 26-year-old Dennis Potter, not yet a television playwright. *The Changing Forest*, published in spring 1962, anatomised the geographically isolated, heavily working-class Forest of Dean, where he had grown up and which he still visited. There he found 'whole new roads of aerial-topped, flush-doored, nicely painted, flat-windowed buildings with cars outside them and small pieces of lawn before you come to the front door'; older houses now changed by 'the pastel colour of the wallpaper, the bright paintwork, stripe of "contemporary" wallpaper, tall flower vase, holding artificial blooms in winter, or the television aerial, the built-on lavatory, with coloured toilet roll, and the concreted path'; in Cinderford, the town's first supermarket (a Co-op), the district's first, belated Woolworth's and 'a new, candy-coloured shop called simply "Do It Yourself"'; in Coleford, two 'juke-box cafés' and an annual carnival becoming 'both more commercial and less spontaneous'; in his home village of Berry Hill, just outside Coleford, an expanding Hawkins' Stores, 'serving the young families in new council houses up the road, offering Danish blue cheese, telly snacks, striped toothpaste and coloured toilet rolls'; at its pub, The Globe, 'the long tables and split benches put away or chopped up', now replaced by 'little tables with individual chairs, scattered around'; at Berry Hill Working Men's Club, a new 21-inch TV set, walls redecorated with high-gloss paint, and a noisy one-armed bandit; and, across the district as a whole, any number of 'new television and electrical goods shops' and 'new shop-fittings' and 'frozen-food counters' and 'record shops' and 'new garages'.

Yet at the same time, running through Potter's account was also a sense of the old, obdurate Forest, not quite yet out for the count. There were still 'older Foresters' who 'speak with a wide, beautiful splattering of chapel language and use a hundredfold country and coal-mining superstitions and prejudices' – Foresters who 'believe in God, in Britain, in the Forest and in the working class'. And he went on: 'Chapel (you can see one in each village, like a warehouse with tall, thin windows and a heavy door), rugby football, brass band, choir and pub: that's the old Forest, and, some will have it, that's the Forest now. All these things remain . . .' So they did. Even at The Globe, for all the physical changes, the atmosphere was 'much the same', with the talk still 'broad Forest', and strangers still looked at and discussed 'with the same faintly conspiratorial air'. In Berry Hill itself, 'it would still be unthinkable to be a homosexual or an adulterer, and wearing dirty clothes on a Sunday remains a bit suspect'.

Strong continuities existed elsewhere. Melanie Tebbutt's history-*cum*-memoir of her family in Northampton places that town's great cultural and environmental rupture in the 1970s, arguing that during the quarter-century after the war 'traditional patterns of behaviour, neighbourliness and respectability' continued to shape the experiences of her father Les (a fitter-welder) and his family. Meanwhile in Glasgow's East End, there still persisted almost endemic violence and feuding, to judge by the vivid but plausible recollections of Lulu (born 1948). Sociology's most suggestive contribution came from Peter Willmott, whose study of Dagenham between 1958 and 1961, *The Evolution of a Community*, found that in an almost entirely working-class, thirty-year-old settlement, London's East End had been largely 'reborn', notwithstanding the scarcity of pubs and corner shops. 'Local extended families, which hold such a central place in the older districts, have grown up in almost identical form on the estate, and so have local networks of neighbours – people living in the same street who help each other, mix together and are on easy-going terms.'

The fullest picture we have of continuity by the early 1960s, and indeed beyond, is set in the Black Country. The three predominantly working-class communities of Pensnett, Sedgley and Tipton are the focus for the historian Rosalind Watkiss Singleton, who in a path-breaking study – based largely on oral testimony, but supplemented by a wide range of other sources – shows how, between 1945 and 1970, 'growing affluence impacted only marginally upon the customary social mores.' Several key specific aspects emerge. The three main concepts underpinning day-to-day life were 'neighbourliness, pride and respectability'; there was instinctive suspicion, especially on the part of older people, of both owner-occupation (sometimes called a rope round the neck) and hire-purchase; the exchange of goods and services remained key to many family economies, as did the pawnshop; teenagers living at home seldom felt free to spend their disposable income as they wished; local shops continued to be valued for their credit facilities as well as the convenience of small quantities of non-pre-packaged food; the shift from keeping cash to building society or bank accounts was 'extremely gradual', while traditional types of savings clubs, such as 'diddlum' clubs run by charities, shops or individuals, remained popular; and the role of the Co-op was central, so that 'for affluent and poor alike, the divvy was anticipated with great pleasure.' Altogether, Singleton's study – consciously echoing and amplifying Richard Hoggart's observation about Hunslet in the mid-1950s that 'old habits persist' – takes us into an intensely local, intensely conservative and mutually self-sustaining ecology far, far removed from facile images of the 1960s. Mass Observation's Tom Harrisson, on the basis of 1960 fieldwork in both Bolton and London, concluded that, whatever the physical changes, 'the way you *behave* in the pub – the rounds you stand, the conversations you have, the games you play, the outings you go on, the raffles you join – is very little different from the way your dad and his friends carried on pre-war'; while even in a temple of modernism, Sheffield's brand-new Park Hill estate, a local journalist noted that same year how the living room of 42-year-old Mrs Dot Smith was in 'cosy red tones, red fitted carpet, regency striped curtains, red brocade three-piece suite and red fireside chairs."[5]

Football and holidays add to the picture of entrenched conservatism. 'The club was intensely local,' remembers Ian Jack about Dunfermline Athletic. 'The town's solicitors and owners of small businesses held the shares, and the players met most days for lunch in the City Hotel, where the proprietor was the team dietician. You would see them shopping in the high street and gripping a billiard cue at Joe Maloco's snooker hall or a glass in the East Port Bar. They took the bus. One or two readers among them borrowed books from the library I worked in and stood in the queue to have them stamped.' Elsewhere in Scotland, Ron Yeats combined playing for Dundee United with being a slaughterman, while

Motherwell's Ian St John had a day job at the local steelworks. 'If either of them didn't play well their mates were quick to tell them on the Monday,' note the football historians Andrew Ward and John Williams. 'They inherited a community responsibility.' In the north-west, the Blackburn Rovers pair of Ronnie Clayton and Bryan Douglas were classic local heroes, perceived as close to the supporters, with Clayton at one point combining the England captaincy with running his newsagent's business and going on holiday to Butlin's at Bognor Regis. That year, 1960, he and over two million others stayed at Butlin's or Pontin's holiday camps, with another half a million going to Warner's or smaller holiday camps; the following summer, at the start of August, the *Keighley News and Bingley Chronicle* was merely following time-honoured ritual when it reported that 'the people of Bingley' were taking 'full advantage of the annual holiday fortnight', with Cleethorpes, Skegness, Blackpool and Bridlington the most popular destinations, whether by train or coach. At Brid they found Jimmy Clitheroe starring in *It's a Grand Night* at the Grand Pavilion, a show prompting a heartfelt letter from Marjorie M. Durden. 'What a joy it is to have an entertainment to offer visitors of which we can be proud,' she wrote to the *Bridlington Free Press*. 'Every artiste is a professional, the show is beautifully dressed, and there is a harmony in the team which spills over into the audience.' The package holiday abroad, meanwhile, remained little more than a gleam in the tour operator's eye, certainly as far as the mass working-class market was concerned. Benidorm, explained a travel columnist in the *Blackpool Gazette* in 1961, was 'the name of a place and not a Spanish all-in wrestler'.[6] Change was coming, but as usual with change, somewhat slower and somewhat later than often assumed.

The pace of change – and its implications – increasingly preoccupied Sid Chaplin. 'What I tried very hard to capture, in the Newcastle novels, is the strength of family life and street life, here in the town, and I tried to show how that was disappearing, going to waste,' he explained two decades later to Newcastle's evening paper. The novels were *The Day of the Sardine* (1961) and *The Watchers and the Watched* (1962). They not only made Chaplin's national reputation but indeed caught a city and its working-class inhabitants on the very cusp of transformational change. Clearly, whatever the considerable continuities, *something* was happening in early 1960s Britain; in April 1961, the editor of the *TV*

Times sought, on the basis of a national survey by the Institute of Practitioners in Advertising, to depict the 'typical family' watching ITV, by some margin the channel of working-class choice:

> Dad is in his early forties, smokes cigarettes, enjoys a glass of beer and an occasional glass of wine.
>
> He is skilled at his job, there's a good chance he owns a car and it's likely he has bought Mum a washing machine. He doesn't mind paper-hanging or a spot of painting. In fact, he likes do-it-yourself jobs and possibly reckons that doing jobs around the house helps him to put a bit of money away for the family's annual holiday which is, generally, spent away from home.
>
> Mum takes a pride in her appearance, spending more than average on cosmetics.
>
> The family are pet lovers. Their first choice is probably a budgerigar or a canary, with dogs and cats in second and third place.
>
> There are probably one or two children, over the age of five.
>
> It's a picture of comfortable, ordinary, hard-working people. In short, it's a picture of the backbone of Britain.

A modern, reasonably affluent family in a modern, reasonably affluent world. But a couple of months later, while in Manchester to take part in a Granada TV programme, Christopher Isherwood went into a chemist with Stephen Spender. 'He wanted a certain brand of mouthwash,' noted Isherwood. 'And the young lady behind the counter asked, "Is that for cleaning false teeth?" Never, never would you hear that in London, much less Los Angeles.'[7]

'The Social Barrier' was one of the chapter titles in Michael Shanks's *The Stagnant Society*, in which he lamented (in 1961) 'the distorting effect of the class system' on industrial relations and productivity. So too the following year Granada's *For Richer for Poorer* documentary series, which started at the workplace, prompting a reviewer to note 'the gulf in standards between the lavatories and canteens of the manual worker and those of the office worker'. And *Punch*'s unashamedly middle-class editor, Bernard Hollowood, went on: 'One set of workers is afforded British Railways and soccer-ground amenities; the other is recognised as coming from clean, comfortable homes. One set is paid by the week and is subject to almost instant dismissal; the other is paid by cheque and gets at least a month's notice. There are marked differences too in arrangements for sick pay and holidays.'

The fault lines between the two main classes continued to run deep. 'The middle classes live very differently from the working classes,' observed the sociologists Colin Rosser and Christopher Harris on the basis of extensive fieldwork in south Wales in the early 1960s:

> Any normally observant person in Swansea will detect without difficulty the continual sorting by social class that takes place in restaurants and cafés in the Town Centre, in the various bars of hotels and pubs (and from one pub to another), in shops of various types, in the membership of clubs and societies, in the audiences at various cultural events (from symphony concerts to bingo), in the crowds at various sporting events, in the holiday crushes on the beaches and bays of Gower (and from one bay to another), in the clothes they wear, in what they have to say and how they say it – and so on throughout the whole fabric of social living. Class is everywhere, pervasive, intangible, recognizable . . .

It was similar elsewhere. In the supposedly inclusive, egalitarian New Towns, the sociologist B. J. Heraud found, largely on the basis of early 1960s information, that 'different neighbourhoods have taken on distinctive class characteristics', while in and around Wetherby in Yorkshire, observes the historian Alan Simmonds about the housing situation by the end of the 1950s, 'the working classes were safely camped on estates such as Hallfields and Deighton Gates, enjoying panoramic views of the newly built by-pass, or tucked out of sight away behind the thatched cottages and greens of villages like Sicklinghall, or the expensively elegant properties of Boston Spa.' Or take the mass media: not only was the press for the most part segmented by content and allegiance along class lines but so in effect was television, with a 1961 survey predictably revealing that only 39 per cent of the professional and highly skilled watched ITV more than BBC, compared to 51 per cent of skilled, 65 per cent of moderately skilled,

67 per cent of semi-skilled and 74 per cent of unskilled. Likewise in sport. Lancashire in 1962 had its worst-ever cricket season under the captaincy of an amateur, J. F. Blackledge, who had no first-class experience, did not bowl and averaged 15.65 with the bat; that same year, English rugby union intensified its vendetta against the working-class code, with the RFU ruling that henceforth 'past or present rugby league players could not be admitted to membership of a rugby union club'; while an unlikely aficionado of motorcycle scrambling, John Berger, had already pointed out how this increasingly popular sport – reliant upon 'the willingness of hundreds of working-class lads throughout the country to save up their money and patiently work in sheds at night maintaining and perfecting their machines' – was virtually ignored by the mainstream press, whereas 'if Pat Smythe has a fall there is a paragraph in every paper'. Overall, whatever the increase in upward social mobility (largely caused by widening white-collar job opportunities), the broad sense remains of two classes largely separate from each other. And never more so than in relation to life's most important decision, with mid-century marriage surveys revealing an overwhelming preference to choose someone of roughly the same socio-economic status.[8]

There was no doubt where, relatively speaking, the wealth lay. Both classes may have aspired to acquire roughly the same consumer durables, but, as Mark Abrams stressed in 1962, 'for most working-class families even the modest contemporary middle-class style of life is still a very long way off.' More generally, after the very richest had taken a significant hit during the 1940s, income inequality across society as a whole seems to have remained broadly constant through the 1950s and early 1960s. 'The redistribution of wealth which took place in post-war Britain was not,' argued the sociologist W. G. Runciman in the mid-1960s after a grainy examination of the evidence, 'as extensive as was believed at the time.' *Some* skilled manual workers may apparently have been doing better by this time than *some* lower-grade non-manual workers, but, noted Runciman, a mixture of hours worked plus fringe benefits plus tax relief plus ownership of assets almost invariably meant that the total comparative picture was still markedly in favour of the middle-class worker, however lowly middle-class.

Moreover, even at the most fundamental level, life-chances were very different. Overall, the Standardised Mortality Ratio (SMR) decreased between the 1930s and the 1960s. Taking 1950–52 as the baseline (SMR = 100), it declined from 134 in the early 1930s to 91 by the early 1960s. People generally, in other words, were living longer. Yet, as this SMR table for males aged under 65 strikingly shows, the gap between the classes was widening, not narrowing:

Period	Social class				
	I	II	III	IV	V
1930–32	90	94	97	102	111
1949–53	86	92	101	104	118
1959–63	76	81	100	103	143

Analysis by the sociologist Barbara Preston in the 1970s found no single factor (occupational, housing or whatever) as being of decisive importance, and she was at pains to emphasise that 'these differences in mortality cannot be dismissed as only affecting the unskilled "problem families".'[9]

But what about the disadvantaged working class itself? How did it see things? How indeed did it see itself? Zweig in his five factories, Willmott in Dagenham, Rosser and Harris in Swansea, Runciman with his 1962 national survey – together they sought to provide answers about the class that still comprised some two-thirds of the population.[10]

Between them they drew a reasonably compatible, coherent picture. Zweig found evidence of diminishing class consciousness, with about 15 per cent of his sample, working-class by occupation, self-identifying themselves as middle-class. 'When speaking about classes,' he observed, 'a man would seem to be thinking primarily about himself, about the individual aspect of the problem, and not about the social situation or the social structure. The other classes were of little interest to him.' Willmott discovered something similar: almost the only residents of solidly working-class Dagenham ('The people here, they're the same as us, and we're the same as them,' said one) who were fussed about snobbish Ilford ('They're all fur coats and no drawers,' said another) were those living nearby. Not that working-class consciousness was notably strong even in

Dagenham, with 13 per cent of the working-class sample calling themselves middle-class and 33 per cent declining to identify with any social class ('we're ordinary everyday types'). 'There is little proletarian resentment about the distribution of wealth,' Runciman reckoned, noting that when manual workers and their wives made comparisons, they 'referred more often to other manual jobs than to non-manual jobs of any kind'. What about the one-third of his sample who, though in theory working-class, identified themselves as middle-class? Were they succumbing to *embourgeoisement*? It was not, he argued, simply a case of newly affluent workers suddenly and wholesale switching classes. He cited one amply self-contradictory respondent: 'The wife of a hospital head porter who described herself as "middle-class" said that she meant by this people "kind of thoughtful, not stuck up and of reasonable income". But she described the working class as "people who do genuine jobs and not money on the fiddle", and gave as her reason for supporting the Labour Party "because they are for the working-class interest". When asked who she meant by "people like yourself", she replied "middle-class – working people".' Accordingly, Runciman went on, 'it would be wrong to infer from this person's description of herself as "middle-class" that she identifies herself with the non-manual class in any ideal-typical "bourgeois" way.' But equally, 'it would be wrong to suppose that her self-rating is therefore meaningless.' Perhaps, he speculated, at the core of this type of cross-class self-rating was an identification with a rather more 'privatised' way of life than that generally led by the traditional working class.

The most vivid testimony came from Swansea:

> We're working-class, I suppose – at least that's where we came from. Perhaps we should say 'middle' now, though I'm no lady. It's very difficult to say what we are. I have started going to the hairdresser's once a week if that means anything. (*29, daughter of a plumber, wife of a quantity surveyor, now living in a new house on a private estate*)
>
> We are all working-class in Swansea – it's Sketty you find a different type of people, business people and doctors from the hospital. We don't mix with them of course. The dentist I work for, scrubbing and cleaning in the mornings before the surgery opens, lives over in West Cross and his wife thinks she's Lady Muck – though her father had a milk-round down in the town somewhere. (*55, wife of a bricklayer*)

Swansea has the usual three classes – working, middle and kidding themselves. I'd say we were all working-class here but there's plenty of showing off. If anybody does a bit of decorating or buys something new, they leave the lights on with the curtains open to make sure the neighbours get a good look. And the palaver with the dustbins when they are put out on the pavements for collection on a Tuesday morning is quite a sight – all the best tins, or bits of expensive vegetables or chicken bones or whatever, stuck prominently on the top where the neighbours can see how well-off the family is, or pretends to be. And then every Monday, though nobody admits it of course, we have the Battle of the Washing Lines . . . (*41, male nurse, living in a council house*)

Social class? If you get under £18 a week you are working-class, more than that and you're middle-class. That's all there is to it – it's just a matter of money. (*24, motor mechanic*)

We seem to live differently altogether from our parents – and it causes some trouble at times, I can tell you. We hardly ever speak Welsh now, and Sandra doesn't at all, and I'm not keen for her to learn either. I like to hear her speaking English properly. Some of the little girls down the road (in the private houses off the estate) speak beautifully. I think it makes all the difference if you can speak properly. (*33, daughter of a steelworker, wife of a local government clerk, with a six-year-old daughter*)

It is easy to sympathise with a retired railway shunter. 'There's only two classes – the employers and the employed,' the 69-year-old declared with seeming certainty. 'You can guess which one I belong to. At least that's how it used to be anyway. Nowadays I don't know what to make of it.'[11]

Wages mattered, working conditions mattered, but often so too did status – whether between classes or within the working class (above all the great 'respectability' divide). 'No daughter of mine is getting engaged to a British Railways waiter – get that bloody ring off your finger at once,' exploded the mother of a Fulham teenager, Janet Bull (later Street-Porter), and wife of an electrical engineer; in East Anglia, the Dagenham-born football manager Alf Ramsey had managed to acquire, by assiduously listening to BBC newsreaders, a more classless accent; and in the *Victor* – after transferring in 1960 from another boys' comic, the *Rover* – the ageless working-class athlete Alf Tupper, a welder by trade and known as 'The Tough of the Track', still fought the good fight against the blazered snobbery of officialdom.

Clearly one should not exaggerate: the ITV comedian Arthur Haynes may have been the archetypal belligerent working man (as created by Johnny Speight), but almost half the working-class respondents asked by Gallup in December 1961 whether there was still 'a class struggle in this country' declined to agree with the proposition. Even so, there was something emblematic about an episode the following spring in heavily working-class Salford, after the local paper had printed a letter from a 21-year-old 'playwright-typist', Myra Bassman, castigating the 'simple, insipid folk' around her: 'Speak to the average Salfordian of art, religion, any intellectual pursuit and they stare at you blankly. But speak the magic words, e.g. beer, bingo and "didya watch Ena on t'telly last night?" and they understand.' Letters of protest poured in, including from factory workers, and Bassman's mother was physically assaulted. None of which deterred the palpably middle-class 'Disgusted' from writing in soon afterwards to complain about 'the lack of amenities' in Salford. 'The town abounds in weird and noxious smells from the works and the Docks. Drunkenness is rife, not to mention other social disgraces. "Salt of the earth" my foot. These people deserve the decaying piles of masonry which form their burrow.'[12]

Indeed, it is probably a fair generalisation that often the real edge, even venom, tended to come from the middle class towards the working class rather than the other way round. Take a quartet of recollections. Rupert Christiansen's evocative memoir of growing up in a south London outer suburb describes how there were in effect two Petts Woods – one genteel and impeccably middle-class, the other (literally on the other side of the railway tracks) 'more densely and cheaply built', known as 'the tuppenny side' and 'considered a region where people were "common" and the source and cause of whatever minor frictions and infractions emerged'; near the Manchester Ship Canal, the young Frank Mort (son of an accountant) was told by his parents to stop playing in the street with children whose fathers ('big men in vests and braces, unshaven after getting up in the afternoon, silently drinking mugs of tea') worked on the tugs on the canal; at *Vogue*, recalled David Bailey, the refusal to use working-class models was justified by the invariable refrain, 'Oh no, we can't shoot her, have you heard her speak?'; and across the land, there persisted a distinct middle-class reluctance to give house-room to ITV (seen as council-estate fodder), in the case of W. Stephen Gilbert's family only overcome when he successfully complained in 1961 that without it he was unable to play his part in school-break analysis of *77 Sunset Strip*.[13]

In sport the middle-class trenches were defended almost as doughtily in cricket as in rugby, with *Wisden*'s editor Norman Preston insistent in 1960 that English cricket 'cannot afford to lose the amateur', whose 'very independence contributes to the welfare of the game and therefore to the well-being of the professional'. Elsewhere that year, a march along London's Oxford Street by Midland car-workers threatened by redundancy induced an angry response from a well-dressed female shopper ('nostrils flaring, face flushed') on the corner of Bond Street – 'You've had it so good all right! What have you done with all your money?' – while more generally a frequent flashpoint was housing. In the *Brighton Evening Argus* in May 1961, Gertrude Jordan of Hove claimed that 'working-class people, with their subsidised houses, free education, welfare services, new cars and televisions look down on us professional classes, who have to live in top-floor or basement flats for which we pay exorbitant rents, in order to keep them in the luxuries they demand.' A few months later, in a Manchester evening paper, 'Indignant' of Moston expressed her 'utter disgust' about the 'continuous moaning and protesting' of Manchester's slum tenants. 'If these people had anything like guts and ambition they could easily have done like hundreds of other families have done – save up a deposit and buy their own houses . . . Why don't they give up their cigarettes, beer, perms, and bingo and stand on their own feet instead of whining to be kept in homes by the already overburdened ratepayers of this great city?'

Yet for many in the middle class, life still seemed so blessedly well-ordered that there was little need for resentments. Full employment, job security, hierarchical certainties – such was the unspoken backdrop in 1960 for Peter Bateman's Betjemanesque poem about Sanderstead, a prosperous suburb safely to the south of Croydon and not far from Selsdon:

Up past the Library grind the green buses.
With bowlers, umbrellas, and 'Financial Times'.
Through the dark cutting and out by the Rectory,
To stop by the pond just as six o'clock chimes.

Saturday's rugger match – Lime Meadow Avenue,
Old Mid-Whitgiftians sporting abode:
Striped scarves, duffle coats and rain on the windscreens
Of T.R.3s roaring up Purley Downs Road.

Gables and garages, drives full of Jaguars,
Fanciful flower-beds with sundials and gnomes;
Hundred-foot frontages facing the golf course –
No hawkers or circulars enter these homes.[14]

At the annual conference in 1960 of the Amalgamated Union of Foundry Workers, the chairman, F. Hollingsworth, spoke bitterly of how, out of the 2.5 million children in secondary schools, only 32,000 were aged 15 or over, with the rest sent into the world 'half-educated, half-literate'. 'Such,' he went on, 'is the lot of the workers' children. No self-respecting middle-class parent would dream of allowing his own children to leave school at this age.'

Class and education: the two were inextricably linked whether in terms of aspirations or of outcomes. A longitudinal survey of children born in Newcastle in spring 1947 found that out of a possible 248 from the social classes IV and V (the two lowest) who might in theory have secured a grammar-school place, only six did so; that when the sample as a whole were asked in 1959 about their preferred age for leaving school, 20 per cent from social class V wanted to leave before the age of 14, compared to 4.8 per cent from social classes I and II; and that in the event, only 24 out of 527 did stay at secondary moderns after their 15th birthday (still the school-leaving age). More generally by the early 1960s, about 17 per cent of 18-year-olds from non-manual homes were going to university – compared to fewer than 3 per cent from manual homes.[15] Education was as ever a tangled picture, but the fundamental fact remained the twin, class-determined apartheid: between the private schools and the state schools, and, within the state system, between the grammar schools and the secondary moderns.

'Mr Attlee had three Old Etonians in his Cabinet,' observed Harold Macmillan in 1959. 'I have six. Things are twice as good under the Conservatives.' Not just in his party but across large swathes of national life, the privately educated continued into the 1960s to exercise a dominant influence. Over 50 per cent of admirals, generals and air chief marshals; over 60 per cent of physicians and surgeons at London teaching hospitals and on the General Medical Council; over 80 per cent of judges and QCs, of directors of prominent firms and the Bank of England, of Church of England bishops; and, among rugby-union players capped by England between 1956 and 1965, well over half were (as had always been the case since the 1870s) privately educated. Or take the undisputed top two universities: some 72 per cent of the intake elsewhere in 1961 may have been from maintained grammar schools, but at Oxbridge that year the figure was only 30 per cent, with instead 54 per cent coming from public (ie, private) schools and 16 per cent from direct-grant grammar schools (closer to the independent than to the state sector). The prevailing tone and ethos at Oxbridge remained, moreover, essentially public school – to the irritation of Kingsley Amis, who in 1961 left Swansea to go to Cambridge. 'He found the drunken and pretentious foibles of former public schoolboys hard to take,' notes a biographer, 'wistfully recalling the more straightforward excuse-making of Mr Cadwallader: "Sorry, Mr Amis, but I left my essay on King Lear on the bus, see, coming down from Fforestfach".'[16]

There were signs by this time that the whole issue of private education was starting to acquire some traction. A two-part article in *The Times* in September 1961, 'The Public Schools Are Not Static', generated correspondence lasting almost a month, including a memorable contribution from D. M. Wilkinson of York, who had recently left 'a major public school'. Arguing that these schools were essentially snobbish, and quoting as an 'extremely common' attitude what a school friend had said to him about a Cambridge college ('Oh, that's a good College; there are hardly any of those Grammar School types there'), he went on:

> The inculcation of snobbery takes place not in the classroom (very much the reverse), but more subtly through the over-intimate and intolerant atmosphere that inevitably prevails among the younger boys. During this incubating period, the worst type of narrow-minded conservatism is rife. The prejudices learned so young die hard, if at all.
>
> In spite of these disadvantages, I am convinced that I have received a better education than I should have at almost any other school. It is indefensible that, because our parents are rich, we should be privileged in such a manner . . .
>
> I see only two alternatives: either the public schools must be greatly changed by the compulsory admission of the poorer classes or (reluctantly I admit it) they must be abolished altogether.

E. Liddall Armitage of Blenheim Crescent, W11 may or may not have agreed. 'The real reason,' he had asserted earlier that year in the *New Statesman*, 'why so many parents wish their offspring to go to public schools is because children who attend the ordinary state schools pick up a foul vocabulary and indecent behaviour.' To this, at least one state-educated reader took 'strong exception', prompting a finely calibrated response from Armitage: 'Personally I should like to see all the so-called Public schools taken over by the state, though I should like to see their historical associations remembered and old customs continued as far as practicable. I am only of middle-class origin, but in a long life I have noticed that very often people who seem of outstanding character were educated at Winchester. You can usually trust a Wykehamist.'

What about Labour? Ahead of the 1959 election, the party had reassuringly stated that 'no scheme for "taking over" or "democratising" the public schools shows sufficient merits to justify the large diversion of public money that would be involved'; but in summer 1961 its policy statement *Signposts for the Sixties* reflected an apparently significant shift, advocating 'integration' of the two systems – albeit integration to be achieved by what one of Hugh Gaitskell's biographers would describe as 'a rather shadowy educational trust'. As it happened, the House of Commons not long before had witnessed that rarest of things: a debate on the question of private education. Predictably, Labour's most fluent, articulate speaker was the privately educated Anthony Crosland. Although critical of the public schools on cultural grounds

– 'the emphasis on character and manners rather than brains; on the all-rounder and the amateur rather than the professional' – he stressed that such was the resources gap that 'I have no doubt that, educationally, the average public school is superior to the average maintained grammar school,' that indeed 'it simply teaches boys better, and that is that.' Of course, he went on, the overwhelming fact remained that 'a boy can get into a public school only if his parents are wealthy' – a 'painful denial of equal opportunity'. Who should those schools be educating instead? The brightest and the best among those children whose parents could not afford to send them there? Not in Crosland's eyes:

> I am utterly against a system of elite secondary education based on intellectual ability. I am completely against being governed by old Etonians and old Wykehamists because they are the most intellectual people in the country. I should prefer to be governed by hereditary old Wykehamists and old Etonians rather than those chosen for their brains . . . I want the public schools to be filled by a mixture and not by just the richest or just the cleverest children. That, in my opinion, must be one of the cardinal principles in selecting, and the selection should not be based on the grounds of ability to pass examinations.

Near the end, calling for up to 75 per cent of places at private schools to be allocated on a publicly subsidised basis, Crosland claimed that 'the tide of public opinion' was flowing in the direction of much greater integration between the two systems. But perhaps the most telling observation came at the start of his speech, as he confessed to 'a slight feeling of shame on behalf of my party at the fact that our benches are so nearly empty'.

Intriguingly, the debate had been initiated by a young Tory backbencher. What public schools needed to do, asserted the Charterhouse-educated James Prior, was to broaden their basis of entry in order to guard against becoming 'irrelevant to the conditions of modern life at a time when the nation as a whole is drawing closer together'. But, given that there were some 55,000 places at public schools, his proposed scale of change was hardly huge, beginning with 500 state-subsidised places and 'rising up to 10 per cent of all places'. The debate ended with the education minister, Sir David Eccles. 'The only policy which is wise and just in our generation is to bring the two educational systems closer together,' he entirely agreed – though as a matter of strategy he explicitly *disagreed* with those who felt that 'if the Conservatives nationalised a good slice of Eton, then the Socialists who long to nationalise the whole of the school would be placated and abandon their attack.' Accordingly, he ruled out using government money 'to subsidise the transfer of boys from one system to the other', and instead urged the two systems 'to live alongside and to learn from each other'. Something, though, was apparently shifting. Later that year, Eccles strongly urged – though without any legislative stick – all children from five to eleven to be sent to state schools, prompting a classic Giles cartoon showing despondent top-hatted boys being transported to the guillotine on a tumbrel amidst pitchfork-waving working-class scamps.

The public schools themselves were divided. After observing that 'the time has come when people should think seriously about these schools and the way in which they fit into the social pattern,' Eton's head, Robert Birley, publicly proposed in April 1961 that 10 per cent of places should go to children from working-class homes, adding that at present 'we have too many boys from the same background.' That autumn, in the volley of *Times* correspondence, John Wilson of King's School, Canterbury declared that on finding a means of 'extending over the whole nation' the 'privilege' of a public-school education depended 'not only our educational future as a nation, but our social and moral future as well'. Yet when at about the same time the Headmasters' Conference considered Birley's suggestion that a national scheme be introduced for subsidising poorer boys at public schools, this was rejected. Instead, reported *The Times*, the heads 'reaffirmed belief in the value of independent schools'.[17]

For most people, of course, all this was a debate taking place on another planet, and the far more relevant divide was that within the state secondary system. There, the writ of social class continued to run wide and deep. The Nuffield Mobility Study of the early 1970s would find that boys born between 1943 and 1952 – ie, starting their secondary education between 1954 and 1963 – had a 22-per-cent chance of attending a selective (ie, grammar) school if they were from a working-class background and a 66-per-cent chance if they came from a professional or managerial background. Strikingly, reflecting the post-war growth of the 'service' class of professionals and managers, that 22-per-cent working-class chance was 5 per cent *less* than it had been for the cohort entering secondary schools between 1944 and 1953, in retrospect the golden decade after the 1944 Education Act had opened up the grammars.[18] Working-class opportunities via education were, in short, narrowing by the early 1960s rather than expanding.

The annual focus – and defining moment in many lives – remained the 11-plus. 'It is all a matter of intelligent ability,' insisted Miss D. M. Hatch, headmistress of Derby High School, at the Junior School's speech day in July 1961, warning the children that they needed to be ready to 'take the knocks'. The realities were spelled out the following year by a primary teacher in a predominantly middle-class area. 'The fight for a grammar school place is a hot one,' s/he explained to the *New Statesman*, given the prevailing middle-class dread of 'that academy for louts and layabouts, the secondary modern school'. Unsurprisingly, the local reputation of the primary school and its head was 'geared to shovelling into the grammar school every single remotely possible candidate'. Accordingly, 'an infant on his first day has hardly taken his coat off when he's handed a *Janet and John* Reading Book and bundled straight into the mysteries of tens, units, and the technique of learning to write on lined paper'; the end of the first term saw streaming into 'A' and 'B' classes; and, for a middle-class child in 'B', the inevitable parental resort was to coaching – though 'it won't be called coaching, it'll be called "a bit of extra help".' Then came the day of the exam. 'I took one look at the paper and I just froze,' recalled Philip Gould, son of a primary-school headmaster near Woking. 'I went home to lunch, to be greeted by my parents – my mother in tears, my father ashen – telling me I had failed already.' For most, including Stephen Dixon, there followed the wait for the letter:

> As the expected time drew nigh I raced out of bed and looked over the banister down the stairs to the mat behind the front door. Nothing! I walked the mile to school and asked a couple of likely exam-passers, 'Heard anything yet?' When they shook their heads my mood lifted for the rest of the day. And so it went on, probably for only a few days but it seemed an age – anticipation, despair, trepidation, relief – all for a boy who, being a July baby, hadn't even reached his eleventh birthday. Then

> one morning, I looked down and there lay a small, brown envelope. Euphoria! I still [in 2013] have that brown envelope and its typewritten letter from the Grammar School headmaster, dated 6th June 1961 and beginning, 'I rejoice with you that your son has been successful . . .'

'There was,' adds Dixon, 'rejoicing in seven households that morning (six boys, one girl) as the class of 4A, Throston Junior (Mixed) Hartlepool, learned their fates. We seven were to go to the Henry Smith Grammar School on the Hartlepool Headland, separated by a few hundred yards of Town Moor from the receptacle for all those who didn't make it – Galleys Field Secondary Modern.' There was a nice twist: 'Whilst six of us followed various anonymous paths in life, some involving university, the one who gained the most celebrity was the boy who ignored the grammar school headmaster's advice to "stop kicking a ball around and concentrate on your studies" – John McGovern, who later lifted the European Cup as captain of Nottingham Forest in 1979.' That, though, was the rule-proving exception, and Dixon himself reflects how in 1960s Hartlepool – a working-class town with the shipyards dying and the pits up the coast in decline – 'passing for the Grammar School and the real possibility of a university education was a ticket out to the rest of the world, an opportunity to escape the poverty and living conditions which many of our parents had had to endure.'[19]

The problem of course was that not all boats lifted equally. As had been the case since the mid-1950s, there was an increasingly sharp debate about the respective merits of grammars (approximately 1,200 of them by 1961), secondary moderns (at least 3,800) and comprehensives (only about 140 fully operational). 'Who in heaven's name wants "an egalitarian educational system" anyway?' asked R. R. Pedley, headmaster of Chislehurst and Sidcup Grammar School for Boys, in response to a pro-comp *Listener* article in 1960 by Michael Young. 'The electorate doesn't.' That same year, the educationalist Frances Stevens published her defence of *The Living Tradition* – ie, the grammar school, which for all its 'petty snobbery and priggishness' was 'at its best a place of civilised relaxation as well as hard work, and an unrivalled solvent of social prejudices and preparation for democratic living'. Moreover, 'if selective maintained schools ceased to exist,' Stevens warned, the probability was that 'even more parents than at present would make desperate efforts to send their children to public schools.'

From the left itself (with anti-selection, pro-comprehensive already entrenched as Labour policy), Anthony Crosland as usual had his take. Interestingly, his problem was less with the 11-plus exam itself – the strikingly different class outcomes, he wrote in 1961, 'accurately reflect the class distribution of measured intelligence at 11' – than with what happened at grammar school, where 'performance, length of school life, and academic promise at the time of leaving all deteriorate as one goes down the social scale.' The working-class experience at grammars was also the subject of Brian Jackson and Dennis Marsden's seminal Huddersfield-based study *Education and the Working Class*, published in February 1962 to considerable acclaim and attention. The *TLS* reviewer found 'deeply disturbing' the accumulated evidence of 'a mass of human suffering' caused through 'individual, familial and social strains and tensions'; for Raymond Williams, the book was further evidence that equality of educational opportunity remained an 'ill-founded' chimera; and David Marquand's perspective on this 'profoundly moving' book was that it revealed the grammars, with their honours boards, prefects and gowns, as transmitting 'a peculiarly hierarchic form of middle-class culture, in a rigidly dominative way', in effect aping the upper class. Jackson and Marsden themselves, in their closing pages, acknowledged their own 'large debt to grammar school education', but at the same time expressed the hope that 'our voice is the voice of the last grammar school generations'. That pointed in only one direction: 'We have come to that place where we must firmly accept the life of the majority and where we must be bold and flexible in developing the new forms – the "open" school which belongs to the neighbourhood, the "open" university [the term perhaps coined here] which involves itself in local life rather than dominates or defies it from behind college or red-brick walls. The first practical step is to abandon selection at 11, and accept the comprehensive principle.'[20]

It was a principle being wrestled with locally as well as nationally. In London by 1961, up to 60 schools were comprehensive, often viewed by critics as excessively large in size; in Bristol, the local Labour Party promised ahead of elections in 1962 to upgrade secondary moderns into comprehensives, but did nothing to dispel the illusion that those new schools could peacefully co-exist with grammar schools; at Ashby-de-la-Zouch in Leicestershire, the governors of the local boys' grammar protested in 1960 that 'to agree to the substitution of a scheme which is as yet unproven' was 'a complete abdication of responsibility'. In local practice, even if there was theoretical acceptance of the comprehensive principle, progress towards authentic comprehensivisation tended to be patchy and confusing. Coventry may have been one of the pioneer cities but in the 1960s, notes its educational historian, it 'still operated a selection examination at eleven, provided places at the Direct Grant schools for boys, and maintained two grammar schools for girls as well as allocating selected places within the comprehensive schools'. The issue itself, moreover, remained very alive in the public mind at the start of the decade, with a petition signed by 4,340 Coventrians demanding the retention of a mixed system of secondary education. In the city council's ensuing debate in April 1960, conciliatory words came from Labour's Alderman Callow, chair of the Education Committee: 'Our aim is to provide grammar schools for all, for make no mistake about it, our comprehensive schools have as much claim to be called grammar schools as any other institutions. Every child who goes to a comprehensive school carries a grammar school label with him.'

Over and above the question of structures, how realistic anyway was it to view education as the silver bullet for enhanced social mobility? Its importance was obvious to what was becoming an increasingly technocratic middle class, but what about the much more numerous working class? Ray Pahl's study in about 1962 of three commuter villages in Hertfordshire found the starkest of contrasts: 82 per cent of middle-class parents wanting their children to stay in full-time education until 18 or over, compared to 15 per cent of working-class parents. That same year, a reviewer of John Barron Mays's *Education and the Urban Child*, based on inner-city Liverpool, was struck by how, in terms of ability, 'quite a large number' of 'slum children' *could* take the 11-plus, but 'the trouble is that their parents are apathetic about education, they often prevent their children from sitting the examination at all because they want them to leave [school] as early as possible, and they provide a background which is not conducive to study.' The children, in turn, were 'not much bothered either'. Perhaps not everywhere was like that. Martin Johnes in his history of post-war Wales argues that 'despite the fact that education and university degrees were unlikely to solve the problems of an industrial town, out of a mix of idealism, pragmatism and snobbery, they were widely esteemed in all Wales' – but the probability is that working-class indifference was the overwhelming pattern.

The voices of the children themselves come through in Peter Willmott's study of adolescent boys in Bethnal Green, based on interviews done between 1959 and 1964. 'I didn't give it a thought,' said one secondary-modern boy about what had happened at 11. 'From my junior school you usually went on to the secondary modern around the corner, and that was that.' To which his friend chipped in: 'The 11-plus – the school never put me in for it. I didn't really know about it.' Yet not all the teenage boys were quite so retrospectively resigned to their fate. Willmott also recorded a suggestive – if ultimately futile – dialogue between three others at a secondary modern:

Jimmy: None of us went to those high schools, grammar schools, whatever you call them.
Alan: When you're in the junior school you're supposed to be able to choose out of three sorts of schools. But you can't really.
Ron: No, you can only go to crap schools.
Jimmy: They reckon you ain't got the brains for it, see.
Alan: They judge you at primary school. If you're no good at primary school they say, 'Right, you'll never be any good.' They don't give you a chance.[21]

As the working class seemingly inexorably in the late 1950s and early 1960s moved ever further towards the centre of the cultural frame – via sociology, literature, cinema, television and much else – so questions of class and culture became of increasingly paramount concern to the intelligentsia and indeed 'activators' as a whole – although not, of course, to all of them. 'Dewsbury, Batley, Birstall, Heckmondwike, Cleckheaton are all one – large textile mills huddling close together, workers' housing and little else,' observed in 1959 Nikolaus Pevsner, whose *The Buildings of England* never quite managed to notice a football ground. In the middle of 1960, the as yet unpublished novelist John

Fowles – public school and Oxford – was engaging more fruitfully. 'All raw, bruised, harsh, ugly,' he recorded after reading David Storey's *This Sporting Life*. 'Absolutely devoid of beauty of feeling, mind and scene ... yet the whole has the paradoxical beauty of a Lowry painting.' Fowles then moved on to Alan Sillitoe's *Saturday Night and Sunday Morning*, provoking more general thoughts:

> I enjoyed reading this, though I had qualms. How true is Arthur Seaton of his class? No means of telling – the externals seem authentic, not the ideas (or lack of them?)? The violence and the hatred, the sheer brutishness, seem suspect – the pursuit of them too constant. All these beer-and-gut novels – Storey, Braine, Sillitoe – force the question – à quoi bon? They are sociological in intention, they criticise society (though each writer has the same love-hate for his hero), they are tacitly in defence of the 'good' working-class qualities; yet they all have the same inverted romanticism and sentimentality.

Sillitoe by the autumn of that year was undoubtedly the leader of the pack, with both film and best-selling paperback, the latter receiving a classically dusty and mandarin *TLS* review. 'Does Mr Sillitoe,' it asked, 'represent a significant new departure, the true voice of proletarian feeling coming at last after so many disgruntled arts-graduates fakes, or is it going to seem incredible in a few years' time that intelligent adults were ever persuaded to take his saga of beer, bed and brawls at all seriously?' Although conceding that Sillitoe's 'squalid story' included 'many good touches', the answer was essentially negative: 'His hero has the synthetic stamina of a comic-strip rather than real vitality or even plausibility. And does it not now seem that there is something altogether too calculated about his outbursts against authority in every shape or the complacent cynicism of the book's closing pages?' In sum: 'The fuss has not been altogether about nothing; but it seems a pity, not least for the author's sake, that uneven promise has been taken for solid achievement.'[22]

Cultural debate, often with an explicit or implicit class element, was ubiquitous that *Lady Chatterley* autumn. While a government-appointed committee under the chairmanship of the Lancashire glass-maker Sir Harry Pilkington began its job of assessing the quality of

British broadcasting and deciding who should operate a future third television channel, the National Union of Teachers sponsored a well-attended conference at Church Hall in Westminster on 'Popular Culture and Personal Responsibility' – or, more wordily, 'the impact of the media of mass communications on present-day moral and cultural standards'. Inevitably there was a strong focus on television, while Eric Hobsbawm (in relation to music) argued that 'the mass-media do debase the popular tradition.' But the most striking contributions had to do with the popular press. The spotlight fell on Cecil King, imperious chairman of the Mirror Newspaper Group, whose *Daily Mirror* was read each morning by around 40 per cent of the population. 'The trouble is,' he explained, 'the critics imagine the great British public is as educated as themselves and their friends, and that we ought to start where they are and raise the standard from there up. In point of fact it is only the people who conduct newspapers and similar organisations who have any idea quite how indifferent, quite how stupid, quite how uninterested in education of any kind the great bulk of the British public are.' After he had added that 'we insert in our paper as much education, uplift and information as we think the public will read, perhaps a little more,' a particularly trenchant attack on the *Mirror* came from the representative of the National Assembly of Women. 'The thing that shocks me is the way the writers talk down to the people as though they were readers of no intelligence,' declared Mrs Beatrice King. 'I have a particular phobia against Marjorie Proops who deals with quite important points like clothing and marriage and who should hold the purse strings and so on. The way she presents them is simply degrading. I think that applies to nearly the whole paper.' To which her namesake riposted, 'If you think the *Daily Mirror* writes down to its readers, you must think all our readers are extremely well-educated, high-brow people.' He signed off by noting that 'in the commercial world it does not matter whether you are selling a newspaper or a breakfast food, if you chase away customers you will be out of business.'

At one point the *Mirror*'s head honcho loftily referred to 'Mr Hoggart' as 'whoever he may be', but in reality there would have been few in the hall unaware of *The Uses of Literacy* and its author. Indeed, the fact of the conference itself directly reflected the huge influence already exercised by that 1957 book, and appropriately the delegates had circulated to them in advance a paper by Richard Hoggart on 'The quality of cultural life in mass society'. The other key recent book, second only to *Uses* in its sway, was *Culture and Society* (1958) by Raymond Williams, who at the conference spoke on 'The growth of communications in modern society' and was instantly commissioned to write a Penguin Special on the subject. Hoggart and Williams: not only were they the two intellectuals who (as Dick Taverne put it in a 1961 essay on the William Morris tradition) 'helped to make socialists direct their gaze once more at all the many varied aspects of our society that mould our attitudes and have a very direct bearing on politics'; they were also, crucially, two *working-class* intellectuals, who could apparently explain their class to the rest of the intelligentsia and mediate an often difficult, mutually uncomprehending relationship.

Uses, Hoggart's compelling evocation of working-class Hunslet, gave him abiding fame. 'Hoggartsville is by now familiar to us all,' claimed the young sociologist Hannah Gavron in May 1962. 'It is a world brimming over with extended family life, warmth and neighbourliness, and in this era of affluence, status seeking and acquisitiveness, it has come to be considered an oasis of calm if not quiet.' The problem was, she went on with particular reference to the recently published Jackson and Marsden study, that 'the deification of Hoggartsville is usually accompanied by arguments designed to show that for an individual to move from the working class to the middle class is for him to fall from grace.' Was it in fact possible, she wondered, to develop an educational system that embraced working-class culture and thereby enabled working-class children to be well educated but stay in Hoggartsville? Gavron was highly doubtful: 'The authors and their supporters feel that working-class culture is destroyed by middle-class values. I think this involves a romantic view of the working class (after all, no one, not even Hoggart, has ever really told us precisely what working-class culture really is), and is also based on a deliberate misrepresentation of middle-class values.' That same spring the unrepentant Hoggart himself was in Bradford, to give the keynote address at a conference on public culture being held to coincide with the city's ten-day Delius Festival. Sparking some local ill feeling, he likened the festival to pulling a cultural 'Christmas cracker' – all very fine, but only tangentially connecting with the lives and concerns of ordinary (ie, working-class) Bradfordians.[23]

Uses remained a stand-alone text, but *The Long Revolution*, Raymond Williams's 'continuation' of *Culture and Society*, was published in March 1961. Williams in his introduction made clear that he had in mind not only the ongoing 'democratic' and 'industrial' revolutions but just as much 'a cultural revolution', which he encapsulated as 'the aspiration to extend the active process of learning, with the skills of literacy and other advanced communication, to all people rather than to limited groups'. A series of discrete chapters, often with a historical dimension, put flesh on the bones, including a particularly notable one on the growth of the popular press, with Williams at pains to demolish the elitist conventional wisdom that 'with the entry of the masses on to the cultural scene [following the Education Act of 1870], the press became, in large part, trivial and degraded, where before, serving an educated minority, it had been responsible and serious.' Instead, he sought to demonstrate, what happened in the late nineteenth and early twentieth centuries – the 'Northcliffe Revolution' – was 'less an innovation in actual journalism than a radical change in the economic basis of newspapers, tied to the new kind of advertising'.

The book's final, lengthy chapter was on 'Britain in the 1960s', essentially an intricate disputation with another piece of conventional wisdom, namely that Britain entering the new decade was 'a country with a fairly obvious future: industrially advanced, securely democratic, and with a steadily rising general level of education and culture'. Yet, claimed Williams, 'in deeper ways, that have perhaps not yet been articulated, this idea of a good society naturally unfolding itself may be exceptionally misleading.' His analysis of course included class, which he saw as increasingly based on money rather than birth and also increasingly corrosive: 'It is less the injustice of the British class system than its stupidity that really strikes one. People like to be respected, but this natural desire is now principally achieved by a system which defines respect in terms of despising someone else, and then in turn being inevitably despised.' As for the cultural state of play, Williams argued that 'the condition of cultural growth must be that varying elements are at least equally available, and that new and unfamiliar things must be offered steadily over a long period, if they are to have a reasonable chance of acceptance.' He additionally argued that, in a world where 'more is spent on advertising a new soap, and in printing a jingle attached to it, than on supporting an orchestra or a picture gallery', the sad truth was that 'policies of this degree of responsibility seem impossible in our present cultural organisation'. Might it be possible to organise culture on a different, non-capitalist basis? Williams believed it might be, suggesting various ways of applying 'public resources' to reduce the dependence of 'cultural producers' on 'dominant but essentially functionless financial groups'. He ended with a call not to allow 'the long revolution' – ultimately the evolution of a common, democratic, non-hierarchical culture – to be stalled by temporary setbacks. 'The nature of the process indicates a perhaps unusual revolutionary activity: open discussion, extending relationships, the practical shaping of institutions. But it indicates also a necessary strength: against arbitrary power whether of arms or of money, against all conscious confusion and weakening of this long and difficult human effort, and for and with the people who in many different ways are keeping the revolution going.'

The response was mixed, with Richard Crossman in a splash review in the *Guardian* the principal cheerleader. 'It is the book I have been waiting for since 1945,' he declared. 'Reading *The Long Revolution* I had the feeling that I was in at the birth, anxiously watching what was once an embryo now suddenly emerging, messily but triumphantly, as a new-born babe.' It was, in short, the first book 'to break through the thought barrier into a new epoch of socialist ideas'. Predictably, the main doubts came from the non-socialist intelligentsia. The *TLS* reviewer took strong exception to the style and tone ('maddening platitudes . . . over-solemn and frankly partisan pronouncements . . . utterly humourless textbook language'), while a supporting letter from Arthur Calder-Marshall grouped the writings of Williams and Hoggart as 'not works of scholarship but autobiographies of cultural displacement, disguised as objective studies'. P. N. Furbank in the *Listener*, after noting that Williams 'never seems in touch with English society at all' and 'is only seeing what he wants to see', called 'absurd' the notion that 'a working-class boy can adopt high culture without going through a radical transformation, without making himself in many respects a middle-class person'; while in *Encounter*, the take-few-prisoners

American critic Dwight Macdonald dismissed Williams as 'a preacher rather than a thinker, one more interested in exhorting than in analysing', least of all 'the awkward question why the masses prefer adulteration to the real thing, why the vast majority of the British people read the *News of the World* instead of the *Observer* and go to see *Carry On Nurse* instead of *L'Avventura*' – a question, according to Macdonald, that went beyond class, given that 'most people, of whatever education or social position, don't care very much about culture.' 'The fact is,' recalled Williams himself almost two decades later, 'that it was perceived as a much more dangerous book' – ie, than *Culture and Society*. 'Just at that time I came back to Cambridge. The spirit of the experience was like '39–'41 once again: there was a sense of really hard and bitter conflict.' Williams was indeed in 1961 returning to Cambridge (where he had been an undergraduate), as a lecturer in English; even before he took up his position, an *ad hominem* review in the *Cambridge Review* by one of Cambridge's Tory historians, Maurice Cowling, identified Williams as one of those 'English radicals, lapsed Stalinists, academic socialists and intellectual Trotskyites' whose true institutional home resided in 'the extra-mural boards, the community centres, and certain Northern universities'.[24]

The following spring, Williams's Penguin Special, *Communications*, came out. A pioneer text in media studies, and for the most part a careful exploration of the content of newspapers, women's magazines, advertising and television programmes (albeit he did not yet have a set himself), *Communications* reiterated his proposals for less paternalistic-*cum*-commercial, and instead more democratic, communication systems (including through new, publicly accountable bodies [a Books Council, an Advertising Council and a Broadcasting and TV Council, as well as a strengthened Press Council]), and 'the creation of genuinely independent programme companies'. Among reviewers, Kingsley Amis was appalled by the prospect of 'the entrenchment of a rigid self-perpetuating oligarchy' of cultural bureaucrats, but for the young critic John Gross the greater problem was what he saw as Williams's conventionally *de-haut-en-bas* attitude ('a kind of drug . . . an enervating and dangerous habit of mind') towards television. 'This kind of weary stock reaction,' observed Gross, 'is now so familiar that it has started to rebound on itself: the words look tired on the page.' And he continued:

> Not only is it unfair to that proportion of television, low but not insignificant, which is genuinely worthwhile; it also implies an extraordinarily wooden view of human nature. Few of us are lucky enough to live night and day at the level of Mr Williams's 'great tradition'; and as drugs go, television has something to be said for it. Even bad television involves human beings, and may be interesting on account of its very badness. If Mr Williams finds that an arrogant attitude, I am afraid that I must shock him further by revealing that I have met a fair number of people who know a hawk from a handsaw – or a condor from a Conrad – and who nevertheless sometimes enjoy watching television programmes *while fully aware that they are trivial.* Such is human perversity.

Still, both men might have sympathised with Sid Chaplin's viewpoint. 'I love a good programme on TV but hate what it's doing to talk,' he had observed to a friend two years earlier. 'The other week my father and me visited two relatives in Shildon [the Durham town where Chaplin was born], two Uncles who were always good for salty tales and talks, and found them focused on a cheap police thriller.'[25]

One television programme increasingly fascinated both the working class and the intelligentsia. '*Coronation Street* goes into 7½ million homes,' noted Derek Hill in the *Spectator* in December 1961, as the soap entered its second year. 'It has an audience of between 22 and 23 million twice a week.' For Hill this popularity was entirely merited – 'consistently wittier, healthier and quite simply better than any of television's supposedly respectable series, not excluding *Monitor*' – and cause for a swipe at the intellectuals of the New Left: 'When anything is as impudently alive and kicking as *Coronation Street*, "popular" becomes a dirty word. It would be sad if the Clancy Sigals ("TV is a tragedy") and Doris Lessings ("The monster is too strong for the best of us") made us ignore the breakthrough which is under our noses until some future Hoggart resurrects it in fifty years' time for respectful minority nostalgia.' Sigal took the bait. Calling *Coronation Street* 'a lie from start to finish if it is supposed to represent any recognisable aspect of life', he launched (in the *New Statesman* in early 1962) a full-frontal assault:

> It is false in the very orderliness and regularity of its working-class dialogue. It is false in never showing mitigating circumstances in character and incident. It is false in omitting the passion and joy and complexity of life. It is false in its avoidance of class-tensions such as I know, for example, to be alive between shop-keepers and street residents in the north. It is false in seducing our feelings of superiority and nostalgia by purporting to show us a contemporary cross-section of working-class life, while virtually everyone in it is poorer, in housing and wages, than he would be in real life. It is profoundly patronising in that it depicts working-class people as entirely and without qualification circumscribed and defined by the life of their simple-minded dialogue. All hostility in the script, all the natural and unnatural tensions behind the facts of social change in Northern society, are covered over with fraternal glue.

In short, claimed Sigal, 'life's dimensions are reduced to 21 inches of naturalistic puppetry.' For one reader, John Killeen, who now lived in Romford but who had spent 30 years in a Leeds back-to-back, Sigal was only betraying his woeful ignorance:

> As long as people live in back-to-back terraces, sharing lavatories and washtime hooks, their lives will be intimate and shared. The Coronation Streets of the north are still characterised by social interdependence and by the feeling that it is natural to be curious about the lives of others, easy to find out and right to care. *Coronation Street* does give a reasonably convincing idea of what it feels like to live in the world of the as yet uncleared semi-slums, of the older districts of the cities and towns of the textile areas of Yorkshire and, I imagine, Lancashire. It is infinitely closer to reality than, for instance, *The Archers* with its absurd idealisation and music-hall yokels.

A sterling defence, and Killeen's letter ended with a sentiment of real resonance: 'It is probably too vain a hope to expect the modern town planner and builder to learn through *Coronation Street* that human happiness is destroyed through the seemingly deliberate erection of separateness and loneliness in a context of total visual monotony, but yet the lesson is instinct in the serial.'[26]

'Social Equality – The Class System' was the title for a Third Programme conversation recorded in July 1961, with Mark Abrams, Enoch Powell and Hugh Trevor-Roper among those joined by the now statutory presence of Richard Hoggart. Chaired by the philosopher Stuart Hampshire, it did not spark throughout but had its moments – Abrams insisting that in Britain the assumption remained that you would only get on 'if you know the right people, if you have the right backing'; Trevor-Roper relishing the artistic and cultural possibilities of 'a society full of complicated social anfractuosities rather than a blank, unanimous, flat, level plane'; Powell calling the 11-plus 'as near as we can get to equality of opportunity' and accusing Hoggart of 'a class grudge' against it; Hoggart himself asserting that 'whatever may be the aims and intentions of the 11-plus, what happens in thousands of homes is that the 11-plus examination is identified in the minds of parents, not with "our Jimmy is a clever lad and he's going to have his talents trained", but "our Jimmy is now going to move into another class, he's going to get a white-collar job" or something like that.' Again and again the focus returned to that life-defining event:

Abrams: Some of us – Powell, for example – believe that the 11-plus is the beginning of setting up in this country some sort of contest society where ability is sorted out, and this in fact is not so. The outcome of the 11-plus is determined at the age of three, four, five, six, according to the child's parental background, home background. And this is an important explanation, I think, of why British society is so stable. The essence of the whole British class system is to stabilise it as early in life as possible, and the earlier you can do that the more stable, the more comfortable a class society you're going to have.

Hampshire: Trevor-Roper, you're doubtful.

Trevor-Roper: I am, yes, because I feel that supposing one has an entirely classless society, if such is conceivable, you are still going to have functional differences and intellectual differences. You are still going to have children who are brought up in homes where they have the disadvantage of being the children of unintelligent, uninterested, low-grade – if one may use that word – low-grade workers, and obviously those children are going to have a handicap when it comes to the 11-plus.

Inevitably the most deeply felt passages came from the Hunslet man, especially when near the end he explained why – if he had to choose – he would still privilege 'the old, habitual class system' over the 'meritocratic' way of organising society. 'I'm thinking now of people I know best from my own district in Leeds, working-class people,' Hoggart began. And he went on:

> It seemed to me that when one knew where one was this relieved a lot of anxiety, in a way, especially if you were a fairly intelligent working-class person, and I'm talking now not about the scholarship boys but about middle-aged railway drivers. That they had a nice kind of mickey-taking quality very often towards 'them outside', they weren't subservient, they weren't either particularly deferential. They lived in a society which assumed that they would get the dirty end of the stick most of the time, and they'd built up a whole lot of very good defences, very human defences in all sorts of ways . . . It was claustrophobic, it was narrow, it was limiting, especially for the budding abstract thinker, but at the same time it had a lot of very strong human qualities, and in a way you knew what you were doing. You could grow as a person. Now, if you see some of those people, moving [ie, out of slums and into new estates], and thank goodness they do, it seems to me that you're faced with a society in which you're not sure. You look at the back page of *Woman*, if we can mention that, and it tells you that the young junior executive's wife, or the young electrician's grade three wife, is using such and such glassware, and so on, and you go round, spinning madly wondering about where you are and what you're doing . . .[27]

8

This Is My Work Now

'Big-time Bingo has hit Britain,' announced the *Daily Mirror* in March 1961, two months after the Betting and Gaming Act (1960) had come into force, permitting the start of commercial bingo. The craze was immediate. In the first half of the year, at least 40 of Mecca's dance halls and 15 of Rank's cinemas were converted into full-scale bingo clubs, with the Newcastle-based Essoldo cinema chain following suit. 'THE BINGO TIDAL WAVE' was the *Mirror*'s headline by September, the paper reporting that 'up and down the country' there were now an estimated 10,000 bingo clubs, with more than a million players. The chorus of noises off was entirely predictable. 'It is another sign of the moral decline of the nation,' responded a Congregationalist minister in Blackburn to the news that three local cinemas were to be converted to bingo; a vicar in Leeds called bingo clubs 'mental slums'; *The Times* thought it 'a cretinous pastime'; and by the end of the year the press was whipping up a moral panic about children being neglected by their bingo-addicted mothers.[1]

For that, crucially, was the point: bingo was not just the latest regrettable behaviour by the working class, but by the *female* working class, overwhelmingly the game's main constituency. 'Bingo, I was told,' noted a journalist after visiting the Mecca in Tottenham, 'was a nice change from sitting around the house, washing, ironing, talking to the wall, gave you a bit of company in the afternoon. Think of what you could do with 50 quid. No, the old man didn't mind, not that it mattered if he did . . .' Or, as Eva Hall from Stamford Hill, one of a syndicate of six, put it, 'There's not much for married women to do in their spare time. We think bingo is smashing fun.' No one followed the craze more closely than its mastermind, Mecca's Eric Morley, who in 1962 sought to set *Sunday Times* readers straight. 'Bingo,' he insisted, 'is not gambling.'

> It is a much-maligned form of social entertainment, with a flutter on the side. The most you could lose in a two and a half hour session is 8s. And the very most you *might* win would be the jackpot game, say about £80. No, bingo is a revolution, a turning against TV. People felt they were losing the power of the spoken word, of easy chit-chat. At a bingo session you spend more time having a cup of tea with your neighbours, having a talk, than you do actually playing. Another thing about bingo, it's a great social leveller. You require no special skill, no special knowledge, not a lot of money. You're all the same when you've got your cards in front of you.

Morley of course was talking his own book, but his words broadly convince. *Tonight*'s Fyfe Robertson may have grumbled about 'the most mindless ritual achieved in half a million years of human evolution', yet for a working-class woman (typically in her 40s or thereabouts), a pastime that was cheap, that was easy, that was friendly, that got her out of the home into a safe, uncensorious environment, was surely something positive. 'I come here once a week,' 48-year-old Mrs Ivy Johnson told the *Mirror* during a session at London's Lyceum. 'It's a real break and I feel part of the club. I'd go up the wall if it weren't for this outing.'[2]

'It's a man's world, my masters – after over forty years of franchise, as it always has been,' insisted the writer Elspeth Huxley in May 1962.

> Religion: no woman in the priesthood at all, let alone at the top. 'Trad' religion – Christianity – is now the faith of only about ten per cent of the British people, so perhaps this is marginal. What is the faith of the remaining ninety per cent? Materialism, undoubtedly. The high priests of materialism are the tycoons: controllers of industry, of banking, of insurance, of distribution: all, I think without exception, male. Any women on the Board of ICI? Are you trying to buy your daughter into Lloyd's?

> Is your sister chairman of the National Provincial? Doing nicely on the Stock Exchange? A woman has no more chance of filling any of these positions than she has of becoming Archbishop of Canterbury . . .
>
> Judges? Not on your life. I don't say there won't one day be a female judge or two. To give a little ground here and there takes the sting from enemy propaganda without jeopardising the position. After all there's not much men don't know about war.
>
> Judges only administer law made by governments: that is the crucial thing. Here men have been obliged to give some ground, but only very little. Only about four and a half per cent of today's House of Commons is feminine. A very safe percentage – and as long as men continue to pick the candidates and finance the Parties, things are well under control. There is no woman Cabinet Minister and only a few top-ranking civil servants. Four out of the top 150 jobs in the BBC are held by women and of these one concerns wardrobes, another programmes for women. By and large the Establishment is safely and solidly trousered.
>
> The occupations thought most suitable for females are those which administer either to the comfort or the recreation of the male. They are womaned by descendants of the dancing-girl and the slipper-warmer. Most branches of entertainment, deriving from the dancing-girl, are free of sex barriers. And in the slipper-warming derivatives – nursing, teaching, secretarial – women can rise to the summit, such as it is. These are all underpaid, depressed occupations compared with insurance, banking and sitting on boards. Let women become matrons of hospitals and head-mistresses of girls' schools – no man would want such exacting, ill-rewarded responsibilities.

Huxley was launching *Punch*'s all-women series on 'The Second Sex?' In later articles, the Tory politician Pat Hornsby-Smith called on women to 'stop carping' at other women ('How many times have you heard women say they'd rather "work for a man"?'); the sociologist Barbara Wootton highlighted the 'monstrous injustices' created by 'the practice – still widespread in industry, though fast disappearing from the professions – of simply paying lower rates to women than to men engaged on the same work'; and the journalist Siriol Hugh-Jones itemised some of the many 'man-made toys' designed to keep women 'deeply dazed and, it is hoped, more or less contented' – toys that included 'magazines constructed on fantasy, cheap lipsticks, off-the-peg clothes of amazing pushiness and no price at all, the whole armoury of kitchen gadgets, the availability of hairdressers and the magic combination of soothe and brace that is *Woman's Hour*, with its brief straight-from-the-shoulder yet somehow cosy talks on "My Recent Miscarriage" and "My First Arrest" (by a former policewoman)'.[3]

Even so, almost certainly there were more women in the late 1950s and early 1960s staking out distinctive ground for themselves compared to say a decade earlier. To mention just a few. Wootton herself, who back in 1921 had been the first woman to give university lectures in Cambridge, became in 1958 one of the first four female life peers; that same year, Hilda Harding was the first woman appointed to a full managerial position in an English clearing bank, Barclays; Nan Winton two years later became BBC TV's first female newsreader; among journalists, Sheila Black was storming the all-male bastion that was the *Financial Times*, Anne Sharpley (renowned for her coverage of royal tours) was the brightest star in the *Evening Standard* firmament, the *Guardian*'s Nesta Roberts became in 1961 the first woman on a national newspaper to take charge of a London news desk, and Marjorie Proops was limbering up for her full glory as the nation's agony aunt; in Whitehall, Evelyn Sharp remained the forthrightly dominant permanent secretary of the Ministry of Housing and Local Government; elsewhere, Irene Thomas was starting to make her mark on *Brain of Britain*, Ulrica Murray Smith was establishing herself as senior Joint Master of the Quorn hunt, the pioneer stockbroker Elisabeth Rivers-Bulkeley was educating women about investment, and Pat Moss and 'Tish' Ozanne were successful rally drivers competing with men on equal terms; while among those whose brilliant careers (as subsequently charted by Rachel Cooke) continued from the fifties into the sixties were the trouser-wearing writer-*cum*-personality Nancy Spain, the uncompromisingly modernist architect Alison Smithson, and of course Rose Heilbron QC, the most celebrated advocate since Norman Birkett's heyday.[4]

Were there also signs of a new assertiveness? 'Very much dominated by its womenfolk,' noted an early critic of *Coronation Street*, in which right from the start feckless men were played off against strong women. Or take football, with a spring 1962 survey into falling attendances identifying as a key reason the female pressure being applied on husbands and boyfriends to spend more time with their womenfolk on Saturday afternoons. Perhaps, revolutionary thought, those menfolk might even be inclusive about their pastime. 'Women don't like to be left out,' Joan Kennedy of Huyton wrote about the same time to the *Liverpool Echo*. 'Why not encourage the girls and women to go along and watch, instead of discouraging them? Girls can be just as enthusiastic as men about football.'

It could be uphill work. 'For a long time I've felt I'm a lone woman in a man's world,' Mrs Esme Griffith of Cobham's Summit Driving School told the *Surrey Comet* in 1961, 'but at last I feel I am being accepted and people are getting used to the idea of my being an instructor.' A man's world . . . Shortly before, in November 1960, an opinion poll had specifically asked hundreds of wives throughout the country whether they thought it was – and 62 per cent had answered in the affirmative.[5]

A handful of early 1960s snapshots helps to explain why. When Mary-Kay Wilmers, future editor of the *London Review of Books*, said to a female careers adviser to Oxford women graduates that she wanted to work in publishing, the adviser 'told me to run along and learn how to type with ten fingers and do shorthand and generally make myself useful'; when Antonia Byatt found herself an academic's wife at Durham, 'the only place where the university had any social life, as a university' was the elegant students' union on the Palace Green – but for men only; when radio's *Top of the Form* began a television version, the co-host alongside David Dimbleby was due to be Judith Chalmers, until vetoed (in favour of Geoffrey Wheeler) on the grounds that women lacked the gravitas to take charge of game shows, even junior ones; when the future crime writer Jessica Mann was about to have a caesarean, it was her husband, not she, who was requested to give permission and sign the consent form; and when Enid Blyton was asked to be a witness at the *Lady Chatterley* trial, she replied, 'I'd love to help Penguins but I don't see how I can. My husband says "No" at once. The thought of me standing up in court advocating a book like that . . . I'm awfully sorry but I don't see that I can go against my husband's most definitive wishes in this.'[6]

Not least because of the prominence of the Barclays branch

(Hanover Street in London's West End), Hilda Harding's appointment as manager provoked considerable publicity, not all of it favourable. 'Sir, a woman's place is in the home,' complained R. E. Hembling of Clapham Common to the *Daily Mail*. 'We don't want lady bank managers, prime ministers or lady executives in business. God made women for the home to be man's help-mate and comfort adviser.' Nor in general is it difficult to construct from the public domain a pattern of male-dominated societal stereotyping: among TV ads, from 1959 the phallic classic for Cadbury's Flake and from 1961 the 'hands that do dishes can be soft as your face' for Fairy Liquid; also in ad-land, the picture in 1962 of the husband behind the Kenwood Chef mixer with his wife leaning happily against him wearing a chef's hat ('The Chef does everything but cook – That's what wives are for!'); James Bond with his undeviating assumptions of gender hierarchy; the comic-postcard crudity ('dream breasts and nightmare bosoms', in Benny Green's phrase) of the depiction of women in the irresistibly popular *Carry On* films; and the sentiment, as favoured by Howard Jacobson and his youthful confrères in the Manchester of the late 1950s, that one wouldn't kick an attractive girl out of the Bedford Dormobile. Broadly speaking, moreover, the surging interest in the working class – whether through sociology, fiction, drama, film or TV – failed to break the mould. 'Neither traditional nor consumerist perspectives problematised the position of women as essentially wives, mothers and pivots of the family,' observes Stuart Laing. 'It was rather a case of two versions of the domestic role in contention: the Mum/children solidarity as the centre of the extendes family and working-class community against the affluent housewife leading the domestic revolution into the home-centred society.' There was also the casual, taken-for-granted, working-class misogyny, at its most full-bodied in Alan Sillitoe's Arthur Seaton. Or take politics. Labour was (in the words of Amy Black and Stephen Brooke) 'at best a reluctant attendant to women's concerns, whether feminist or traditional', indeed even 'a site of resistance to gender'; while although the Tories were more than happy to have the flourishing Young Conservatives (claiming at their height in the 1950s to be 'the largest voluntary political youth movement in the world'), it was a movement that was, as Lawrence Black puts it, 'attentive to women, but via a male gaze', with those women virtually powerless in internal party culture. 'A prerequisite for the success of any revue is a supply of attractive young ladies,' declared its magazine *Rightway*, praising Ilford's YCs as notably 'well off in this particular form of talent'.[7]

Among women themselves, the advice cascaded. Eleanor Brockett in *Choosing a Career* (1959) especially recommended the caring professions, where the 'essentially feminine' qualities of trust, confidence and personal integrity were at a premium; while among those writing career novels – a flourishing genre – Elizabeth Grey published between 1958 and 1961 *Pauline Becomes a Hairdresser*, *Pat Macdonald Sales Assistant* and *Jill Kennedy Telephonist*; Angela Mack's 1958 contribution was *Continuity Girl*; and Jane Sheridan chipped in with *Amanda in Floristry* (1959). In March 1960, a recently elected MP set out in the *Daily Express* 'What my daughter must learn for the next nine years'. A 'good education', yes, followed by a 'worthwhile career', but that was not all. 'I shall see that Carol learns the domestic arts at home,' added Margaret Thatcher. 'Teaching manners and the social graces to a child of six and a half gives rise to alternate hope and despair. The nagging seems endless . . .' Perhaps the answer was the Girl Guides. 'In a woman physical love is nearly always bound up with the longing for a home and companionship, whereas in a man the desire to settle down is not as a rule a fundamental need,' asserted Hilda Birkett and Hether Kay in a 1961 Girl Guides Association publication on marriage and the home, with the authors firmly warning their readers against extra-marital sex. Two high-profile brides also pointed the way. 'This is my work now,' declared the model Bronwen Pugh at her wedding in October 1960 to Viscount Astor, as she squeezed his arm. The following summer, when Katharine Worsley married the Duke of Kent, the *Daily Mirror* reported that 'Yes, it was "Obey,"' the submissive word apparently at her explicit wish.[8]

Crucial to self-image was appearance. A 1957 cosmetics survey revealed 88 per cent of middle-class women and 72 per cent of working-class women using face powder, while for lipstick the respective percentages were 85 and 72. For a 14-year-old girl, lipstick or not was not the only question. 'The lady told us,' noted Jacqueline Aitken in March 1960 after a visit to school from 'the fashion people, Simplicity', that 'we should wear bras to define and shape our figures (we already do wear them of course), that we should use deodorants (which I at any rate do), that we should pay attention to our deportment (which I try to do), that we should think carefully whether our lipsticks go with our dresses (which I do) etc., etc.' As for teenage girls generally, the educationalist Kathleen Ollerenshaw (a Conservative member of Manchester City Council) reflected in 1961 that it was 'a long time' since 'feminine traits' had been 'so widely flaunted' by them, and she expressed pleasure at how, on the part of single girls, 'flounced skirts, colourful coats and glamorous hair-dos brighten city streets during the lunch hour.' Pleasure too for Angela Carter, who in the 1970s remembered 'a giggling flock' of working-class girls at a south London tube station in 1959: 'They must have assembled there in order to go "up West". They were as weird and wonderful as humanoid flora from outer space, their hair backcombed into towering beehives, skirts so tight you could see the clefts between their buttocks, and shoes with pointed tips that stuck out so far in front they had to stand sideways on the escalators . . .' But it was not Gladys Langford's idea of femininity. 'Do dislike modern hair styles for women & the butter coloured and bright red dyed hair,' the septuagenarian diarist recorded in April 1962. And soon afterwards, when Burnley appeared at the Cup Final, there was no nonsense from the manager's wife as she led her WAGs to Wembley. 'It was hats, gloves, shoes,' recalled Margaret Potts almost half a century later, 'and what we called matching accessories.'

A survey in 1960 conducted by Bolton School Old Girls' Association touched little on dress, but the alumni's answers gave a sense of how a varying age range – albeit all grammar-educated – saw both themselves and women's place in society:

I think women get very bored with housework. (*Left 1927*)

A woman in general has to be far more capable than her male opposite number to get the same recognition that he gets, and any shortcomings are still criticised more sharply. The continuing prejudice against women drivers, in the face of evidence to the contrary gained by the Institute of Advanced Motorists, is an illustration of this. (*1929*)

I am married to a man who has strong views that a wife's and mother's place is in the home and that for such a person to go out to work is tantamount to casting aspersions on the husband's earning capacity. (*1939*)

I intend to return to teaching when my family is older, but only if able to be a proper mother too. (*1946*)

I think that any woman with a family is smaller-minded than a woman without one, whatever her education. (*1950*)

I would continue in my present work if I married, but if I had children I would give up my work no matter what extras and luxuries I had to give up as I feel that a woman's place is in the home. (*1953*)

It is up to a woman herself whether she becomes a vegetable after marriage. (*1954*)

Barrow-in-Furness *do not* employ any married women teachers in a permanent capacity. (*1955*)

I think graduate mothers, especially those who write to the *Observer*, get too sorry for themselves when bogged down by young children and suburbia. (*1957*)[9]

'Is she lonely? Is she bored? Does she lack public spirit?' Such in January 1961 were the questions that BBC television's *Family Affairs* – a regular slot on Thursday afternoons – aimed to answer in the first of four programmes on 'The Married Woman's Place', with this one called 'The housewife at home'. The context, explained the *Radio Times*, was 'the changing social background of today', and those contributing included Claire Rayner, 'housewife'. About the same time, R.C.H. Webber, a Bristol-based building worker 'employed on interior maintenance work on a new, middle-class housing site', described in the *New Statesman* how he found himself 'daily confronted by exquisitely groomed and well-spoken housewives', with 'their peremptory commands and their sweeping generalisations about the British workers':

> It does seem that people undergo considerable nervous strain while in the process of acquiring new property and status symbols and adapting themselves to new surroundings. Of the younger women on this small estate, it would be a fair generalisation to say that they are mainly occupied in elaborate self-grooming, press-button housewifery and subtly tyrannising their charladies. Ultra-smartness (fashionwise) seems to go with chain-smoking and poodle-cuddling. The more tenuous their

> contact with reality through gadgetry, glossy magazines and over-scrupulous hygiene, the more compulsive and idiosyncratic their behaviour.
>
> Among the older section there are cases of ostentatious religiosity, invariably bound up with bitterness, ultra-conservatism, morbid accountancy and property embalming. I have glanced over bookshelves in vain for signs of social awareness and enlightenment.

Webber manfully refrained from using the n-word, but not long before a cinema news feature had boldly claimed that what it called 'suburban neurosis' was affecting 'one woman in four'.

The normative assumption remained that most married women – above all middle-class women – stayed at home. Judith Hubback may in 1957 have shown in *Wives Who Went to College* that, as she later put it, many graduate women did not want to be 'married to their homes', and Marguerite Patten may in 1962 have had her cookery programme axed by the BBC on the grounds that (in her paraphrasing words) 'women are now feeling that they want to spread their wings.' But this was still before Betty Friedan's groundbreaking, hugely influential *The Feminine Mystique* (1963) about the dissatisfaction of homemakers in the American suburbs – and well before Germaine Greer's *The Female Eunuch*. In early 1962, after a speaker in the House of Lords had argued that women should take advantage of labour-saving gadgets and go out to work, the widely syndicated columnist Gloria Gordon let rip. After insisting that 'it's just not true that a housewife vegetates while a working wife stays bright and well-informed,' she went on:

> For the woman who is prepared to be a full-time wife, there are three main jobs, looking after her husband, her children, and her home – in that order.
>
> For her husband, she must be a combination of wife, mistress, friend, cook and confidante.
>
> She has to keep herself looking attractive for him. She has to read and study enough to keep abreast of him intellectually. She has to find time to spoil him a little.
>
> For her children, she must be a mother, a nurse and a teacher all in one. Most important, she must just be there.
>
> To do all those jobs properly, as well as the shopping and housekeeping, leaves precious little time for any outside employment.

'Just about enough,' she added, 'to take a well-deserved nap every afternoon!'[10]

Seven and a half hours was the estimated time that women in 1961 spent each day on housework – a figure reflecting in part the still patchy spread of new domestic technology. 'Monday was wash day,' recalled one Barrow housewife (married in 1956, children born in 1958 and 1961). 'Of course with kiddies you have to wash every day but Monday was the main day. I don't know about Tuesday. Wednesday morning I used to go to the market. Thursday I always used to do my front. I did my window-sill and front door every morning and then on a Thursday I would give the windows and the front door and all the front a good wash. Sweep the front and then I used to wash right through, the tiles in the vestibule, the kitchen floor, then clean the windows and swill the yard out.'

Not all housewives did their washing at home. 'The "steamy"', remembered Lulu about her Glasgow childhood, was 'a big industrial wash-house where people from the tenements did their laundry', usually wheeled there in an old pram, and which 'looked like one of the underground scenes from the film *Metropolis*':

> Steam billowed from large cauldrons and the machines hissed, gurgled and spluttered. Water sluiced down drains on the concrete floors and women screeched over the noise.
>
> Sheets were washed in the cauldrons, but the rest of the clothes were scrubbed on washboards. Women dressed in aprons and boots hovered like witches over the metal tubs, scrubbing their husband's overalls. Cigarettes dangled from their lips and they had rollers in their hair covered by scarves tied at their foreheads. Steam was the enemy. It could turn a hairstyle into a lank, tired mess.

For most housewives, though certainly not all, a Puritan work ethic remained strong – so strong that Geoffrey Gorer's 1958 survey of TV-viewing habits revealed many women as unable to watch without also doing something else, usually knitting. 'I have little races with myself,' a 77-year-old woman told a journalist soon afterwards. 'I say, "Can you finish that pattern before the nine o'clock news?"' And when in 1962 a kitchen-designing firm commissioned a nationwide survey of housewives and their ideal kitchens, this found not only that 80 per cent voted against a heated draining board on the sink for drying crockery and that 58 per cent did not want a heated strip in the base of kitchen units for warming feet, but also that 'wholeheartedly, the housewives turned down a suggestion for a unit at which they could sit down to work.' The reason was obvious: 'Husbands and neighbours might take it as a sign of laziness.'[11]

How contented with their lot were stay-at-home housewives? 'I would like an occasional afternoon film during the coming months, when the winter weather means that many housewives, like myself, with young children, have to stay indoors,' Mrs I. Watt of Gateshead wrote in October 1959 to the Tyne Tees edition of the *TV Times*. 'A film now and again would certainly be a real treat.' Mrs E. Webster, in her 30s and living in Hornchurch, looked instead to 'Mr Music' – ie, the organist Reginald Dixon. 'We housewives get a pep pill when he broadcasts on Wednesday mornings,' she told the *Radio Times* in 1960. 'He never fails to cheer me up. A wonderful man and artist!' We also know that Tupperware parties, an American import, were first held in Britain in 1961. For a systematic survey, though, our main contemporary source is Hannah Gavron, who in 1960–1 interviewed 48 middle-class housewives (mainly from West Hampstead) and 48 working-class housewives (from Kentish Town) – the basis for what became her renowned 1966 book, *The Captive Wife: Conflicts of Housebound Mothers*. Gavron found a stark contrast between the two groups. Undeniably, many of the middle-class women did feel a sense of being tied down by having to be with their children all day – 'Of course I must be with them all the time,' a teacher's wife told her, 'though I must confess that sometimes I *long* to get away' – but Gavron's overall impression was that 'the majority' of those middle-class mothers were 'making a determined effort to keep up contact with the outside world' and that 'only a small minority seemed really isolated in the same way as were the majority of working-class mothers.' As for those working-class mothers, often in poor housing and with no live-in help or affordable nursery school, her conclusions were sombre: the prevailing atmosphere was one of 'confusion and muddling through'; family life was far more nuclear than extended; less than a third had any contact with their neighbours; and in general, their main contact with the outside world was via television. 'Alone with the gadgets' and 'Is your wife just a bird in a plastic cage?' were among the headlines that would greet the book's publication.

Gadgets were not enough for Betty Jerman. 'Home and childminding can have a blunting effect on a woman's mind,' the freelance journalist and mother of two small children declared in the *Guardian* in February 1960. 'But only she can sharpen it.' Her piece, called 'Squeezed in Like Sardines in Suburbia', spoke particularly loudly to one reader, Maureen Nicol, who had recently moved to the Wirral, knew no one, and was at home with a small baby and toddler. 'Perhaps,' she wrote to the paper, 'housebound wives with liberal interests and a desire to remain individuals could form a national register, so that whenever one moves, one can contact like-minded friends.' The suggestion snowballed, and the result, after over 2,000 had responded to Nicol, was the National Housewives' Register, which by the 1970s would have over 25,000 members. 'We were reasonably well educated,' recalled Nicol. 'We'd all had reasonably satisfying jobs. We never ever considered leaving the children and going back to work until they were at school at least. But we needed more stimulation. We needed to talk about things.' Essentially a network providing mutual support and sharing mutual interests, the NHR was, noted Elizabeth Wilson, 'neither political nor feminist', let alone anti-domesticity. But, she added, through being 'very loosely organised on the basis of small groups', it 'anticipated the women's liberation movement rather than copying the more committee-like campaigning organisations [such as the National Council of Women] in which women had hitherto organised themselves'.[12]

Articulation by full-time mothers and housewives of feelings of frustration was still relatively rare. In 1963 the pioneer editor of the *Guardian* women's page, Mary Stott, searched her files for the previous four years for 'letters from discontented mothers' and realised she had 'never received floods of such letters'. Instead, in her list of correspondents there was 'not one whom I took to be expressing discontent with her lot as housewife and mother'. How to explain the silence? The Cambridge-educated Jessica Mann, whose own experience of early motherhood after her 1959 marriage she vividly recalls in terms of feeling 'utterly bored and frustrated by full-time domesticity', argues that she was clearly at the time 'not the only young woman who did not feel able to admit her true feelings' – not least because, 'having achieved exactly what every girl was supposed to long for [ie, husband and children], I knew I ought to be satisfied' and not 'weeping into the nappy bucket'.

Yet of course, the counter-argument is that this discontent was seldom expressed because most women at home did not feel it sufficiently strongly, on the part anyway of the sort of middle-class women who wrote to the *Guardian*. That would seem to be the view of the historian Ali Haggett. On the basis of the oral testimony of some three dozen women, predominantly educated middle-class, who experienced domestic life during the 1950s and 1960s, she finds that 'the ups and downs of daily life were regarded as commonplace and were accepted as a normal facet of domestic life'; that 'the overwhelming majority made an explicit choice to explore other areas of creativity that did not necessarily involve paid employment'; and that 'most respondents expressed a general preference for activities [such as the NHR, the Townswomen's Guild, the Inner Wheel, the Church, the Women's Institute, the local choral society] that would reinforce the beliefs and values that underpinned family life and traditional gender roles.' Haggett does not deny that 'some wives understandably found their role isolating at times' – yet even so, 'by and large they did not feel it appropriate to aspire to a career outside the home until their children were much older.'[13] Those are conclusions broadly in line with Gavron's research into the middle-class housewives of West Hampstead. If there *were* desperate housewives, in other words, they may well have been mainly among the housewives of Kentish Town and many other working-class, pre-gentrified places. Their voices, however, remain mute and increasingly irrecoverable.

'How can she continue two jobs? Does her family suffer? Is she penalised legally and financially?' Those were the key questions when television's *Family Affairs* turned in January 1961 to 'The wife with a full-time job outside the home'. It was becoming an increasingly topical theme, with radio's *Home for the Day* (the Sunday version of *Woman's Hour*) having recently discussed 'Home and Office: The Dichotomy'. 'It gives the feeling of guilt and the feeling that you're not really doing the best for both jobs,' Thea Benson, a professional woman, told the interviewer Joan Yorke:

> I think this stems from the home side mainly. I know that my own husband, I'm sure subconsciously, seems to invent all sorts of chores for me to do. Generally these chores come about just at the moment when I've got a particularly difficult problem on my hands in the office, and I think that he expects that I shall put anything, however trivial, connected with the home before my business.
>
> *I imagine you aren't neglecting him, are you?*
>
> Not in the least. He has every care and attention. I do in fact rush home and do the major share of the cooking, and he is never neglected, and I make a point of being completely domestic over the weekend.
>
> *Is he interested in your job?*
>
> Not really. Polite questions are asked – I don't think he is really interested, but that is another point, that I have to show intense interest in his job. And of course I have to do a certain amount of secretarial work for him. I also have always got to change his library books and do any odd shopping.
>
> *I think every wife has to do that, don't you?*
>
> Yes, I do think so.

'What about the office?' asked Yorke later. 'Do you find that there is a dichotomy there?' 'Yes, I do,' replied Benson. 'I think that a lot of this feeling comes on in the morning when one is rushing, and I commute, so the train always seems to be late, I always seem to be late and I always get to this ghastly sense of guilt coming from the other side. I've left my home guilt now, now my guilt is towards the office . . .'[14]

The bottom-line facts, as revealed by the 1961 census, were that women now comprised 33 per cent of the total labour force (compared to 31 per cent in 1951); that among all women aged 20 to 64, some 42 per cent had paid employment (6 per cent up on 1951); and that 35 per cent of married women were in employment (a striking 9 per cent up on 1951), or about four million of them. Ministry of Labour figures for England and Wales in 1960 shed light on age and regional distribution: 16 per cent of 'occupied women' were aged 19 or under, 40 per cent were in the 20–39 age range, 38 per cent in the 40–59 range, and 6 per cent were 60 or over. As for regional differences, 38 per cent of the total labour force in the London area being female contrasted with the north (31 per cent) and Wales (29 per cent). What about the rewards? Equal pay was undoubtedly on the march – during 1961 alone, about half a million women achieved for the first time equal pay for equal work – but remained unusual in most sectors of private industry. And of course, not only were many women's jobs part-time, but there persisted a strong tendency in the main occupational groupings for women to be placed in lower grades than men. Thus among professional people in 1961, 93 per cent of women were only in 'minor' professions, compared to 42 per cent of men; in terms of those working in all non-manual (including professional) occupations, 70 per cent of women were in routine grades, compared to 40 per cent of men; and among those working in all manual (including personal-service) occupations, 80 per cent of women were in unskilled jobs, compared to 45 per cent of men.[15]

Education was inevitably part of the story. The Crowther Report, *15–18*, took a gendered perspective. 'The prospect of courtship and marriage should rightly influence the education of the adolescent girl,' it recommended in 1959. 'Her direct interest in dress, personal appearance and in problems of human relations should be given a central place in her education.' Most adolescent girls were at (or had recently left) secondary moderns. 'They give a lively sense of purpose and reality,' the educational journalist Harold Dent found in 1958 about those schools' vocational courses. But, to judge by his lists, the courses themselves were strictly gendered, with girls assigned to such subjects as housecraft, cookery, retail shop work, secretarial work and nursing. The Newsom Committee would report on secondary moderns in 1963, and during its deliberations one member, the careers adviser Catherine Avent, was struck by how some of her fellow-members were unashamed 'misogynists', including one who saw women as 'either caterers or secretaries – the idea of girls being engineers was anathema to him'. Evidence to the committee included a memo from the National Association of Head Teachers. For the academically average girl, it argued, the aim of the secondary modern should be to offer a 'practical course' giving them 'opportunities to be socially acceptable', while at the same time linking their work to 'their future hope – marriage'.

What about the grammars? Some undoubtedly raised girls' aspirations, but strikingly, when in the early 1960s Kathleen Ollerenshaw talked with 15-year-olds at a large municipal girls' grammar, they 'clamoured almost unanimously for more housecraft and for the elimination from the time-table of subjects they deemed useless', by which they essentially meant academic subjects. She came across the odd exception – 'Why,' asked one, 'should girls who are interested in such subjects as physics and chemistry be forced to sew uninteresting tray-cloths or keep watch over the latest concoction in the cookery room?' – but the greater allure was overwhelmingly soft (ie, domestic) science rather than the hard stuff. Presumably, too, it was much the same in private and direct grant schools, given the gendered thrust of the Industrial Fund, set up by industry in the early 1960s to improve the facilities for science teaching in those sectors. Its initial disbursement was £3 million to 210 schools – of which 187 were boys' schools, 5 were co-eds, and a mere 18 were girls' schools. Nor was it necessarily so different even in higher education, where women in 1958 comprised 24 per cent of university student numbers, a ratio increasing only slowly over the next ten years to 28 per cent.[16]

Employers, unions, male workers and husbands all had their views on women working. 'Married women workers are considered to have disadvantages and many employers would not willingly engage them if alternative labour was available,' concluded Viola Klein on the basis of a 1960 survey of 120 firms employing an average of some 1,500 people, of whom almost a third were women. 'Other employers, while prepared to accept married women for unskilled jobs, will not readily provide them with skilled work or offer them opportunities for promotion. It may be suspected that prejudice is a factor in some of these attitudes . . .' So too in the male-dominated world of organised labour. In 1959 the National Society of Metal Mechanics grudgingly consented to admit women as 'half members'; two years later, at the large Coventry engineering firm Alfred Herbert, shop stewards proposed and carried that 'Re crane drivers we ask management to employ only male labour in future'; and in the Post Office, union resistance blocked management from employing more women to help reduce the queues at peak times.

In theory the trade-union movement was committed to the pursuit of equal pay, but in practice many male trade unionists had little or no appetite for the erosion, let alone the disappearance, of pay differentials.

Undoubtedly, here as elsewhere, there was a strong element of atavism as well as calculation. Likewise, many husbands instinctively adhered to the principle of separate spheres, not least because of a sense of stigma (among working-class as well as middle-class husbands) about the fact of a working wife apparently reflecting the husband's inability to support her. 'It's a poor man who cannot keep his wife,' one husband told Ferdynand Zweig.

Conversely, found Zweig, many husbands of wives who *did* work accepted the situation with a greater or lesser degree of enthusiasm. But that was certainly not true of all husbands everywhere, among them a Tipton husband in the Black Country who, his son recalled, became in 1961 'very angry when Mom started to work' – so angry indeed that he changed jobs 'and literally doubled his money overnight in an effort to stop Mom going to work'. 'But,' added the son, 'she still carried on.' Or take 'Doubtful'. 'My wife has a part-time job which doesn't interfere with the housekeeping nor mean leaving our daughter at home alone,' he wrote to the *Woman's Mirror* in 1960. 'She likes going out to work and, I must admit, she's much happier doing so. BUT, I don't really approve of wives working. Would it be wrong to stop her?' Most agony aunts would probably have played a dead bat, but not Marjorie Proops. 'If your wife prefers to work and still keeps her house in good order, why should you complain?' she answered. 'Sounds to me like you begrudge this bit of happiness and freedom your missus so enjoys. Selfish devil, aren't you?'[17]

Working married women were the subject of two major surveys in the late 1950s: one by Pearl Jephcott of the almost entirely working-class south London district of Bermondsey, the other by Zweig of the Mullard factory in Mitcham, in south-west London. Both found that although the economic motive was unsurprisingly paramount – 'To help to buy the car' and 'To help to buy a house' were favoured replies to Zweig's question 'What is your reason for working?' – it was relatively seldom the only one. Typical statements to Zweig included:

I would rather be here – the mind is occupied.
Housework does not satisfy me.
Keeps you young.
Would worry me more to be at home.
I've got to do something; I am too active.

Zweig was particularly struck by the frequency of outside contacts among the working women (far greater than in the case of working men). 'They go out shopping together, to cinemas, dance clubs and so on. They find great pleasure in companionship at work and they do not mind keeping it up outside.'

As for Bermondsey's working wives, Jephcott stressed that their non-economic motives for work were very different from those of a middle-class working wife. 'These working-class wives rode no feminist band-wagon. They seldom mentioned frustration over wasted talents, while few would think of claiming that their job was of any particular value to society. Nor did they reject domesticity. They appeared to be less in revolt against pots and pans, not quite sure how to fill in their day.' But, found Jephcott, it could also be a case of dispelling loneliness (especially for wives living in flats) and generally enlarging one's social life. 'To be able to exchange your "Tat-ah-love, see you tomorrow" with a heap of people, was a mark of status worth having.' Jephcott's most interesting point related further to status – namely her argument that, in the context of working-class mothers no longer having the same status *as mothers* that their own mothers had had (fewer children, fewer hazards, rather easier housework), going out to work helped to 'regain' some of that lost status. 'To add to the family's income showed that she cared about the proper things, like a lovely, modern home,' explained Jephcott about the working wife influenced, consciously or otherwise, by this consideration. 'The extra money meant she could dress better, wear her good clothes for part of every day, and be more of a credit to her husband when he took her out, a point often mentioned. To be able to hold down a job at all in the competitive outside world was reassuring and something that not every married woman would dare to tackle . . .'[18]

Of course, all working mothers had to make arrangements for childcare. Various contemporary studies of the subject – inevitably one with emotive connotations – came to broadly similar conclusions: that relatively few mothers worked if they had a child or children under five; that for those who did or might want/need to, there was a serious shortage of nursery schools and play facilities (prompting a letter to the *Guardian* in 1961 from a young mother, Belle Tutaev, that led not only to a mass petition to the minister of education but to the birth of the Pre-school Playgroups Association); that in most cases, whether for under- or over-fives, the key adult childcare role was played by the maternal grandmother; and that, as a generalisation, it was difficult to find convincing evidence that children were affected negatively by the fact of their mothers working. 'Though they may be inconclusive,' Simon Yudkin and Anthea Holme would write in 1963 after a dispassionate examination of studies since the mid-1950s, 'they provide no support to the wilder statements about serious psychological trauma to the children or to the production of a generation of juvenile delinquents.' Yet, they went on: 'The fact that a large number of schoolchildren of all ages are left to manage on their own after school and during holidays, and the fact that many of the younger children are looked after by their older brothers and sisters, suggests that we may be courting disaster if we continue to rely indefinitely on the resilience of the children and their ability to cope with all the responsibilities that their enforced independence brings.'

Among flesh-and-blood working mothers were a private heroine and a public champion. 'Lily never stopped working,' recalls Alan Johnson about his mother, married to the feckless Steve: 'cleaning and scrubbing' in a residential boarding house in South Kensington; 'up on a chair, dusting lampshades' for a couple in Holland Park's Lansdowne Crescent; 'polishing the furniture and disinfecting toilets' in the spacious Notting Hill Gate flat of three young professionals; and in the evenings 'often pressed into service at those dinners in the big houses between Ladbroke Grove and Kensington Park Road'. When Steve eventually left, it was 'yet more jobs':

> In spite of her illness, she never gave up cleaning. Her only concession to her GP's insistence that she must not work herself so hard was to try to find additional employment that was less physically demanding than yet more cleaning positions. Her CV soon incorporated the tobacco kiosk in

> Ladbroke Grove, a newsagent's in North Pole Road and Harry's Café on Wormwood Scrubs. She also took up 'home work' – painting and varnishing wooden figures to go on toy roundabouts. The pieces were delivered in large crates, which Linda [Johnson's older sister, the other heroine of his childhood] and I would help to unpack. The extra money enabled Lily to rent a television, which took pride of place in our newly arranged living room alongside the Dansette.

The MP for Finchley would presumably have approved. 'I SAY A WIFE CAN DO TWO JOBS . . .' declared Margaret Thatcher in the *Evening News* in February 1960.

> It is possible, in my view, for a woman to run a home and continue with her career, provided two conditions are fulfilled.
>
> **First**, her husband must be in sympathy with her wish to do another job.
>
> **Secondly**, where there is a young family, the joint incomes of husband and wife must be sufficient to employ a first-class nannie-housekeeper to look after things in the wife's absence.

And as for the perennial nagging question: 'I think perhaps the real answer is that if a woman is going to be a bad mother she will be bad even though she is at home the whole time. Conversely if she is a good mother she will be good even though she is absent for part of the day.' She concluded: 'One last point. In an emergency the family comes first.'[19]

Undeniably, the phenomenon of the working woman was gaining visibility, and in 1962 Hannah Gavron had no doubts that it was all 'part of the wider process of social and economic emancipation for women that we have witnessed this century', and 'happily there can be no turning back of the clock'. But her north London friend Phyllis Willmott saw limits to that emancipation. 'I am pretty well certain,' she predicted in 1960, 'that "career women" as such – those who really wish to make work as large a part of their lives as home is – will remain relatively few. The New Woman is the one who wants enough but not too much of her interest and energies turned outwards.'

Perhaps the last word should go to the 1960 radio conversation between Joan Yorke and the conflicted professional woman Thea Benson. 'Do you think women have too much conscience?' wondered Yorke. 'I mean we all have super egos. We want to be perfect wives and mothers . . . Perhaps we should really make up our minds which it is we want to be.' With that proposition Benson apparently agreed, before going on:

> I'm not at all sure that the old-fashioned thing that the woman's place is in the home is not right. I have got a horribly sneaking feeling that it is . . . Of course the husband is really the key to all this. I think the younger men really are more used to this now than the older men. I think it's all accepted. I have a feeling that this problem won't arise at all in the next generation.[20]

Not all women were married, whether working or otherwise. The plight of the unmarried mother (probably 30 per cent or more living in poverty) was highlighted by Lynne Reid Banks's 1960 novel *The L-Shaped Room*. 'A lot of the women who come to me aren't just panic-stricken cowards trying to escape their just desserts, you know,' the Wimpole Street doctor tells the newly pregnant heroine. 'They have the sense to realize they're incapable of being mother *and* father, breadwinner *and* nursemaid, all at once. A lot of them have thought what the alternative means, of handing the child over to strangers who may or may not love it. And don't make the mistake of imagining the word bastard doesn't carry a sting any more . . .' About the same time, the *Daily Mirror*'s highly capable newsroom secretary, Gloria Crocombe, became pregnant by one of the paper's star reporters, the future BBC newsreader Peter Woods, and was sacked; while in its annual report for 1961–2, the National Council for the Unmarried Mother and her Child called for 'the lowering of the illegitimacy rate and a higher standard of moral responsibility throughout the country'. There was also the plight of the divorced wife, unless of course she remarried. 'Anger and shame became the two driving motives of my mother's life after my father left her,' wrote Rupert Christiansen in his poignant memoir about the aftermath of his journalist father abruptly walking out on the family in 1959. 'By shame,' Christiansen explained, 'I mean not only a head hung low, but also a fetid miasma of remorse, guilt and embarrassment, kept in circulation by the winds and tides of prevalent social attitudes.' After the divorce, the suburban vicar 'came round to commiserate and let slip that of course while she would be welcome at the church, the view of the diocesan bishop bla-bla-bla was that she could not take communion or – ahem! – belong to the Mothers' Union'. More often, 'she wasn't shunned or excluded, just subtly degraded – looked at, talked about, pitied from a distance and by tacit agreement marked down as a danger area'. In short, 'people in Petts Wood just didn't like divorced women, and my mother retaliated crisply by making it clear that she didn't like Petts Wood people either. Not so much a chip on her shoulder, one might say, as a bleeding chunk gouged out of it.'[21]

Marriage remained – as evidenced by the 1961 figures – overwhelmingly the norm. Out of every thousand women aged 21–39, the number married was 808 (compared to 572 30 years earlier); only 2.1 per thousand married people in England and Wales got divorced that year; only 6 per cent of births took place outside marriage; and less than 3 per cent of households were lone parents with dependent children. What, though, were the marriages themselves like? Still mainly on the familiar model, with the husband dominant and living in a largely separate sphere? Or rather, a companionate union of more or less equals?

Hard-and-fast answers to these intimate questions are impossible to determine, but it does seem clear that by the early 1960s the traditional style of marriage was far from dead. 'It is difficult to find many companionate marriages in this study up to 1970,' concluded Elizabeth Roberts on the basis of her extensive interviews of post-war women in north-west England; she particularly emphasised the strict gendering of most leisure activities, even in the home. This was especially true in coal-mining communities:

> The relationship existing between a married couple is dominated by separateness [declared the sociologist Fernando Henriques in 1960] . . . The cleavage between the two worlds means that husband and wife have little or no meeting ground. Talk in the home between men is pit or club talk. Between women, of children and the home. The most satisfactory marriages are those in the early stages where conflict and lack of interest in their partner's ideas can be solved by the bed. Custom demands that a

> man provides a home, gives his wife a 'wage' to run it, and nothing else. If he does these things he is acting as a male should act. She on the other hand accepts the situation, for this is her customary role. We are a long way from sexual equality and the romanticism of the sexual partnership of the cinema.

So too in industrial Scotland. 'Men's definition of a good wife was not someone who was affectionate and loving, but simply someone who had your tea on the table and the house clean,' writes Carol Craig about Glasgow's traditional working-class male culture. 'There's little doubt that many women suffered terribly at the hands of selfish, uncaring and often violent men.' Growing up in nearby Paisley was Gerry Rafferty, whose father, an Irish-born miner and lorry driver, would until his death in 1963 regularly beat his wife and children when he returned home drunk. 'It was accepted,' recalls Ian Jack about the prevailing assumptions in and around Glasgow in the early 1960s, 'that men often came home drunk and sometimes assaulted their wives, and sometimes the wives deserved it. Outside the gossip of neighbours ("he gave her a good belting – I heard it through the wall") the crime had no public currency.' More generally, Jessica Mann notes that 'violence was not unknown in the posh households of the more educated classes, just better disguised'; she adds that her lawyer parents would tell her 'how many mild-looking middle-class men turned into wife-beating brutes in private, and also knew that their abused wives would go to any lengths to ensure that their sufferings remained secret', essentially because 'they were ashamed'. Was Mrs G. H. of London NW1 middle-class? Probably not. 'What a disgusting dress Elizabeth Taylor was wearing in the picture you published,' she complained to the *Daily Mirror* in 1961. 'I cannot understand how any woman could appear in public with half her bosom uncovered in this way . . . My better half said he'd knock my block off if I ever wore a dress like that.'[22]

Class and region could make a difference, likewise age. 'Dad was very secretive about what he was earning'; 'Dad just gave mother what *he* thought' – such is typical Black Country oral testimony from respondents who in their own subsequent married lives adopted a much more open, equitable approach to the wage packet. The same may have been true about domestic tasks, where certainly the traditional marital model still largely prevailed in 1962. Well over a thousand adults were interviewed early that year, and the results – as measured by minutes spent per day – were striking:

	Women	Men
Preparing and eating meals	197	114
Housework	148	22
Knitting, sewing, childcare, laundry	77	4

Despite all this, the sociological evidence was mounting that marriages as a whole were becoming more companionate. Young and Willmott, fresh from having famously shown that the working-class husband in Bethnal Green took his turn wheeling the pram, now described Woodford men, of whichever class, as 'emphatically not absentee husbands', but instead as husbands who 'hurry back from their offices and factories' and 'share the work, worry and pleasure of the children'; Jephcott in working-class Bermondsey found that 'husbands and wives were aware of, and welcomed, a closer partnership' as well as greater 'joint decision-making, especially as regards the children's upbringing'; and among Gavron's samples, well over half the wives agreed with the proposition that their relationships with their husbands were more equal than those of their parents. Above all perhaps, there was Ferdynand Zweig, who in his inquiry at the Mullard factory asked 63 married men to respond to the statement 'Man is master in his own house' – to which around three-quarters of the sample claimed that that notion no longer applied, and that in their own homes there was absolute or near equality between themselves and their wives. Significantly, when he then separately asked Mullard wives, about two-thirds claimed that broadly the same principle applied. A newly married companionate-*cum*-egalitarian couple in the early 1960s were Hunter Davies and Margaret Forster, both from working-class Carlisle but now setting up home in London. 'My mother was most perturbed by the equality of our marriage,' recalls Forster. 'She saw that since we were both working, Hunter as a journalist and myself as a teacher, we should both share in the jobs which needed to be done ... My mother admitted the fairness of the arrangement, but she seemed unable fully to approve. Was her air of faint disapproval really a regret that these changes had come too late for her? It wasn't talked about. She went back to my father reluctantly . . .'[23]

Of course, 'companionate' did not *necessarily* mean 'equal'. 'Ask any couple who chooses the family car and most will agree that the husband decides on the model,' noted a columnist in the *Bolton Evening News* in 1962, though she did add that the wife got to choose the colour. Or take a butcher's observation two years earlier to the *Daily Mail* about a typical middle-class couple: 'They come in here together. She buys the meat, then he hands over the money. What's the matter? Can't he trust his wife with money?' Still, at a deeper level, it was clear that something of fundamental importance was happening – something that went far beyond the small change of day-to-day behaviour. The historian Claire Langhamer has charted an emotional revolution that, broadly speaking, seems to have unfolded through the 1950s and into the 1960s, a largely female-driven revolution that was less to do with sex as such than with idealised notions of marriage as an expression of love and a means of personal fulfilment. It was a revolution fuelled by popular magazines, by romantic literature, by films and crooners – but, emphasises Langhamer, 'the willingness to marry for love *above all else* was strongly linked to economic security' – in other words, would not have been possible without greater affluence and a full-employment economy. In the old, separate-spheres days, marriage had often been essentially a pragmatic bargain, with the wives usually even less romantic about the deal than the husbands. Now it was coming with a whole new baggage of shared expectations about entwined lives through to a glorious sunset. But as Langhamer observes, the problem was that 'people could fall out of love as readily as they could fall in love.'

The marriage of the Sheffield steelworker who for a week in May 1959 kept a diary for Zweig probably lay – like many others – somewhere between the traditional and the companionate:

> **Monday.** 4.45 a.m. Up for work, enjoy double shift . . . Get home at 10.20 p.m., wife cooks supper, have words with the wife about daughter leaving school at midsummer, daughter wants to be tailoress, headteacher

says she would do well in office. Bed 11.20. P.S. Wife has been busy washing, we have a washing machine.

Tuesday. I awoke 7.50, daughter crying Mam, Mam! I nudged the wife told her it was 7.50, she got up to get the children's breakfast, called the boy who was very tired, told him he would have to go to bed at 8.0 tomorrow. Got up myself at 8.30, sawn some wood then chop it. Had a shave, fetched the Express to read, daughter said she had fallen and hurt her shoulder playing rounders. She had fainted with the pain getting out of bed. Put some hardwood round the door to keep the draught out. Wife said she was fed up and browned off with the house, had an argument about her nerves, told her she should get out, said if she could go out she would go to work, but fear stopped her from going out, felt a bit down after that argument, had dinner of two eggs then work . . . Arrived home 10.20 took the watering can out as soon as I got in to water the lawn, washed, had my supper wrote this and then to bed. The wife says the boy ran in at 8.55 asked if his father had come home then washed and went straight to bed. The wife went to bed 10 minutes before me but she has just come down again sobbing saying she has been ill all day with her head.

Wednesday. I fetched the Express to read whilst the wife did some ironing, daughters shoulder a little better, a lot of wood to saw, off to work and feeling a lot better after the promise of some overtime, the day went very well at work, I also caught the 9.15 bus home. P.S. Wife and son had been in the garden from 6.0 to 9.30 and enjoyed it.

Thursday. Did not sleep too well, up at 4.45. Wife up at 6.50 messing about all day swapping and changing and cleaning carpets upstairs and downstairs, says she cannot explain how her nerves affect her, she has to go to the hospital tomorrow . . . I have had 3½ pints of beer today and enjoyed them.

Friday. Had a good nights sleep got up 8.5. Wife asked me what I was doing getting up at that time. Had a bit of breakfast wished the children good morning as they were going to school. Had a little chat with the wife, then helped her to shake a big carpet we both had a good 2 hours in the garden, it was now time for me to go to work, I bought a bottle of good sherry for the wife I have been told that with an egg in it it will help her nerves and also make her sleep better at night . . . I caught the 9.15 bus home. I told the wife I was going to have a bath the first thing but when I went up the bath was dirty so I had a few words with the wife

> about it because it was she who had left it like that so I had my supper in rather a gloomy manner.

'Today,' concluded that final entry, 'the wife went to the hospital the doctor asked her if she thought if she went to work in the company of other people it would help her to get better the wife said she would be alright there but it is the travelling there and back that she is afraid of.'[24]

Did the doctor also prescribe something for nerves? The historian Ali Haggett argues that following the discovery in 1952 of the anti-psychotic affects of chlorpromazine, which became the first major tranquilliser and was marketed in Britain as Largactil, pharmaceutical companies did *not* particularly target women in their marketing of psychotropic drugs. Even so, it was striking that after early tests of the sedative Librium had been conducted in the late 1950s on some of the inmates at San Diego Zoo, the headline in one English paper was 'The Drug That Tames Tigers – What will it do for Nervous Women?' A few years later, in 1963, a much stronger type of benzodiazepine would be marketed as Valium, the proverbial mother's little helper. There was also the case of amphetamines. 'The reasons given by patients for taking amphetamines are relatively few,' reported the *British Medical Journal* in 1962 about the fact that in Newcastle the equivalent of 200,000 tablets was being prescribed monthly, overwhelmingly to women, especially middle-aged women. 'Depression, fatigue, obesity, and, surprisingly, anxiety are the most common . . .' As Richard Davenport-Hines notes on the basis of the report, 'several Newcastle women first received amphetamines from their hairdresser after complaining of depression or more commonly following a panic attack under a hairdrier.'[25]

One sort of pill would soon be getting a capital 'P'. 'Hard for the new generation to comprehend just how different life was in the late fifties, early sixties, pre-Pill, pre-coil, when the man not the woman was in charge of contraception,' recalled Fay Weldon in 2000. 'When the very word was still almost too rude and explicit to be mentioned, and body parts were a deep mystery to everyone except medical students. There were a few Marie Stopes "birth-control clinics" for women in the major cities, but you had to show a wedding ring to get access to one. Men had condoms, but often preferred not to use them. Abortion was frequent, dangerous and illegal.' In fact, the situation in relation to clinics was just starting to change for the better. In 1959 the Marie Stopes Clinic in central London held its first evening session for unmarried women, soon attracting women from all over the country, while two years later Helen Brook began the Brook Advisory Centre for Young People, albeit not yet admitting girls under 16. As for abortion, still illegally conducted in most cases, the *Daily Telegraph* estimated in April 1961 that there took place annually in England and Wales around 50,000 abortions for pregnant women who did not want to marry the father. 'We all know women, law-abiding citizens who, with no sense of crime, will "try everything" to end an unwanted pregnancy,' publicly declared the Labour MP Lena Jeger in 1958. Not long afterwards, she received a letter from a woman living in Newton Aycliffe, County Durham:

> I am writing on behalf of a large number of housewives on this new housing estate. We want abortion made legal (with no ties) and we want it now. I am going to send you a list of names and addresses of housewives here whose lives are just an agony of wondering if they are pregnant again, there is no happiness in any of these homes for these women and so it means the men can't be happy either. I myself have three young kiddies and can never afford to buy anything new for myself, and I live in constant fear of having any more children . . . One other friend has three kiddies and is very cold towards her husband. He in turn has turned to drink and bad temper. Yet another woman with three kiddies who swears she will commit suicide if she ever finds herself pregnant again.

'I could go on,' she added, 'but I am sure you have some idea just how unhappy we all are.'

In the event, although legalisation of abortion was still some way off, a new, more reliable form of contraception was on the immediate horizon. During 1961, the oral contraceptive pill, now already on sale in the US, was trialled in Britain, and that December the Health Minister, Enoch Powell, announced that GPs would henceforth be free to prescribe what the *Daily Mail* called 'the pink anti-birth pill', though as yet only to married women. It was undoubtedly a signal moment in women's modern history, even though the whole subject tended to be treated with kid gloves by the media. A refreshing exception was ITV's June 1961 documentary, *The Pill*:

> There were [reported the *Daily Mirror*] more arguments in its favour than against – from the inventor, doctors, a sociologist, users and commentator Elaine Grand . . .
>
> Miss Grand, the doctors and experts approached the subject calmly, and it was left to a group of Birmingham women who had experimented with the pill to make an emotional impact.
>
> They all felt much happier, and one said it made for a more relaxed and natural marriage.
>
> The religious viewpoint had only a brief say . . .[26]

In covering and exploring all this, the mainstream press tended to lag some way behind. 'One of the most uncompromisingly masculine institutions in the country' was Monica Furlong's apt description of *The Times* in her early 1962 survey of the fourth estate, noting also the 'coyness' of its recently introduced Monday women's page; turning to the *Daily Mirror*, where Marjorie Proops had not yet hit her full, authentic stride, Furlong observed that its three main topics remained sport, pets (especially budgies) and girls, while the letters conveyed a sense of husbands holding 'stoically to the view that the wife's place is in the home and that it is several paces behind and below that of her spouse'; even in the *Guardian*, where Mary Stott had been running its women's page since 1957, Furlong pointed out that although 'much space' was 'devoted to profiles of successful career women', this was accompanied by 'their writers often, in an unconscious defensive gesture, insisting that, despite intellectual or executive gifts, their subjects are feminine and attractive'. Arguably the most prominent female voice in Fleet Street belonged to Anne Scott-James of the *Daily Express*, but she was not really pushing back the boundaries. 'I PREDICT that career girls will become scarce as diamonds, and that employers will have to fight for their services,' she wrote in October 1959 about 'The 1960s Woman'. She gave two reasons for this 'strong reaction': 'One, jobs for women have proved pretty good hell. Two, there are now more young men than women, there's a glut of husbands, so why fend for yourself?' Waiting in the wings, ready to champion scepticism about the received wisdom of domesticity, was Katharine Whitehorn. Her celebrated *Observer* column would not start until

1963, but in a November 1960 *Spectator* piece, 'Nought for Homework', she reflected on behalf of herself 'and other sluts' that they were not willing to be 'finally judged as women by the way we run our houses'.[27]

'Sluts' were seldom allowed to sully the hottest market at the start of the new decade: the young female consumer. Magazines targeted at that readership were already flourishing – *Mirabelle*, *Romeo*, *Valentine*, *Roxy* and *Boyfriend* all began between 1956 and 1959 – but the early months of 1960 saw competition intensifying further. Newcomers included *Princess* ('A paper just like mummy's'), *Judy* (free bangle with first issue), *Marty* (named after Marty Wilde and claiming to be the 'first-ever photo romance weekly'), *Honey* ('Young, gay and get ahead!') and *Date* (absorbing the film fans' weekly, *Picturegoer*). Surveying the scene, Michael Frayn in the *Guardian* reckoned that the newly launched *Marty* was 'about the best of the bunch'. 'Even so,' he went on, 'the first story is about a girl who puts her boy-friend on the road to stardom as a rock 'n' roll singer. He callously forgets her – and simultaneously loses her grip on the cats. So he quickly remembers her again, marries her, and gets one of his records in the top twenty. Nice moral touch there.' As for the genre as a whole,

> *Mirabelle* carries a letter from an unmarried mother intended as a warning to other girls, but nowhere else do these strange magazines breathe a word about any of the problems their readers must really want help with.
>
> They hang suspended in a sexless limbo where 'hotly passionate kisses' (I quote) are just rungs on the ladder to marriage and where marriage means simply status and release from loneliness.

'These magazines,' concluded Frayn, 'return to the loneliness theme over and over again . . .'

A random 1961 dip, for the week ending 18 March, fills out the picture. 'Will El's loneliness never end?' asked *Mirabelle*'s front page about The King, while its 'romantic all-picture love stories' included 'Stars Look Down', 'Melody of Love' and 'Flatter Him My Heart'; *Boyfriend* kicked off with 'Flight of Fancy', the picture-story of an air hostess; *Cherie*'s letters included Lynda Rowe of Luton claiming to have 'exactly 621 pictures of Cliff'; and in *Marty* there were not only the usual clutch of stories ('Runaway Heart', 'Heart to Heart',

'Ginchytime Girls', 'This Must Be Love') and the special offer of a cut-out coupon to nominate a 'Disc to Remember' and send to Radio Luxembourg's Jimmy Savile, but also the last in a series by Jean Addams on 'ROMANCE ... and YOU'. Each of the previous weeks had included a behavioural quiz, and now she summed up. 'It's easy to see you'll make the grade as a boy's best girl,' she praised those who had scored high marks. 'You're a good mixer, a girl who joins clubs, social groups ... You're not a pushover for any old date because you don't want to be labelled a good-time girl ... You go Dutch when he's hard-up and you listen to his problems even when you don't understand them ... You've certainly got what it takes to win, and keep, a man's love.' But for those scoring under 15 marks:

> I'm worried about you! You've so much to learn. Perhaps the best way is to take stock of your behaviour so far.
>
> Are you an easy pick-up? Can any boy date you? Do you kiss freely and liberally, and boast about it afterwards? Do you lie about your job, your people, or your home? Do you try to impress not only the boy, but his folks? ...
>
> Or are you, by any chance, the type who believes that if a fellow kisses you, even lightly, he must be ready to pop the ring on your finger? Are you possessive? Do you demand to know all his movements? Are you jealous (and show it) if he so much as looks at another girl? ...

In short: 'Just take a pull on yourself, honey – you've a long way to go.'[28]

The core market remained that for adult women, above all the mass-circulation weeklies – so much so that by the 1960s five out of six women were seeing at least one magazine per week. 'The social revolution has given women incomes beyond anything their mothers could have imagined,' declared an advertisement in March 1962 for the market leader, boasting some eight million readers. 'And *Woman* has played a major social role by training them in the wise use of that prosperity. Because of *Woman* they have new pride in their homes; in their housekeeping; in their personal appearance.' *Woman's Mirror*, advertising in February 1961 the two main features in its latest issue, staked rather lower ground:

> The bride of the year? *Woman's Mirror* spotlights Henrietta Tiarks, most sought-after deb of 1957, now engaged to the Marquis of Tavistock, eldest son of the Duke of Bedford. Will her wedding be the most outstanding of 1961? Read the inspiring success story of this attractive young heiress . . . her family . . . her friends . . . her future . . .
>
> HAPPY BIRTHDAY – PRINCE ANDREW! Here at last is the exclusive, behind-the-scenes story and wonderful pictures of 'the baby that nobody knows . . . The Secret Prince'. Already this 'chubby bundle of chuckles' is an engaging personality and, incredibly, an influential member of the Royal Family! For the first time ever, you can read about Prince Andrew's life – his playmates, his nursery, and the Queen's plans for his childhood . . .

More generally, it was probably true, as the historian Jeffrey Weeks has noted, that 'a well-established magazine like *Woman* was more sexually explicit in the 1960s than in the 1940s, but still found it difficult to handle sexual relations except on its problems page, or in relation to motherhood'; Weeks adds that 'it represented a particular type of femininity, more relaxed than a generation earlier but still domestic in its setting'; while Ali Haggett observes that it was not until the late 1960s that women's magazines began to tackle questions of depression and mental illness in any sustained way. Helpfully detailed analysis at the time came from Thena Heschel, who examined and compared 106 randomly selected stories that appeared in *Woman* and *Woman's Own* in 1952 and 1962. Over 80 were directly concerned with love; their heroes 'almost without exception' were professionals, independent businessmen or senior executives; among the heroines, 'the vast majority have no great interest in any career other than husband and children'; apart from the 'ever-popular hospital or surgery', only two stories were set in workplaces other than offices; and, perhaps most tellingly, 'on the whole there is very little difference in the stories published by the two magazines in 1952 and 1962', with 'no indication that the increasing vogue for social realism has produced any writers for the woman's magazine market'. It was all too much for the veteran campaigner Dora Russell. 'The main point about them is that they are not women's magazines but men's magazines,' she told the NUT's 1960 conference on popular culture, 'because first of all they are for the advertising firms who want to sell their products, among which cosmetics are not the least, and secondly they do present an image of women which is the kind of woman that men want to have, and unfortunately this kind of woman is expected to remain at home and take no interest in outside affairs' – a comment eliciting no response from the overwhelmingly male delegates.

Of course it is easy enough for the historian to cherry-pick quotes, and in the early 1960s *Woman's Own* (circulation second only to *Woman*) certainly obliged. In 1961 one of its star columnists, Monica Dickens, unambiguously informed her readers that 'you can't have deep and safe happiness in marriage and the exciting independence of a career as well,' that 'it isn't fair on your husband.' And in February 1962 a reader in her 50s, whose children were grown-up and who was thinking of leaving her husband ('he never takes me out or wants to talk and life is very dull'), did not get very far. 'Your problem is not unique by any means, but I do not think that leaving your husband is the solution,' replied the magazine's agony aunt Mary Grant. 'If every wife who found that her marriage had gone rather stale left her husband, the world would be a greater mess than it already is!'[29]

The random March 1961 sample, though, offers a fuller, perhaps more representative picture of the distinctive world and assumptions that these magazines inhabited and disseminated – to, it is worth repeating, five out of every six women.

Starting with some of the monthlies. In *Woman's Journal*, the wholly admiring profile was of 'the MAN of today', Prince Philip – 'no lover of tradition, a rejecter of sentiment', yet 'he preserves the receipted bill for his wife's wedding bouquet and on every anniversary sends her a replica of the white flowers she carried' – while in *Woman and Shopping*, Zita Alden's 'People' column featured Polly Elwes, the television personality married to Peter Dimmock, BBC TV Head of Outside Entertainment. 'She confessed that with her, marriage definitely came first. If there was the slightest suggestion that her work was taking up too much of her time – she would give it up immediately.' Perhaps surprisingly, the editorial diet was more intriguing in *Woman and Beauty*. The front page may have been 'Special Offer for 5/6: A Baroque Bracelet with the Golden Look', and the cookery column by radio's Jack de Manio may have been about giving dinner to the boss, but Dr

Eustace Chesser's regular column on sexual matters, this month 'Frigidity', was frank enough, albeit of arguable validity. 'Even today there is still often a false attitude of propriety in women. Many regard their husbands' sexual desires as coarse, gross and animalistic. And because they don't feel such desires themselves, they think that they are in some way superior. They may even care to look upon "that side" of marriage with a kind of smug contempt.' Such an attitude, Chesser added, could 'often be traced back to circumstances outside their control, to inhibitions implanted in their childhood, and perhaps ineradicable'. *Woman and Home* included an old standby's ineffable 'My World and Yours' monthly column: 'There is, of course, a way to make life appear more romantic and enjoyable. It is known as "gracious living". Here GODFREY WINN talks to you about it with his usual sensible charm.' The real interest, though, was in the ads. Gwen Berryman aka Mrs Doris Archer extolled Smith's crisps (only needing to be 'crushed to farthing size' to 'add crispy magic to the most ordinary dishes'); the Hovis ad evoked home as 'a pair of old slippers, a sleeping cat, the children arguing over their game of ludo'; and a full-page ad for Leisure kitchens, built by Allied Ironfounders 'in strong silent steel', spelled out a comprehensive domestic wish list:

> **I want . . .** Leisure in my first kitchen. John and I are getting married, and we're going to have a super kitchen from the start.
>
> **I want . . .** plenty of Leisure drawers and shelves. I want wall cupboards . . . and cupboards with swing-round shelves . . . and a special cupboard for dishes to drip themselves dry.
>
> **I want** . . . colourful, easy-to-keep-clean Leisure in my kitchen. A built-to-last kitchen in silent steel . . . full of drawers that slide easily, doors that don't warp.

'And,' clinching the deal, 'I'd hang strings of onions and buy gay tea towels.'

Among those weeklies for week ending 18 March, two items stood out in *Woman's Day*. One was the new serial, *Doctor's Heartbreak* by Alex Stuart. Stuart was chairman of the recently founded Romantic Novelists Association – 'launching', explained the editor Mary Francis, 'a campaign against the sordid and salacious novels which are being published today'.

The other was a letter titled 'Home Cooking' from Mrs M. Beswick of Haltwhistle, Northumberland: 'For married bliss cake, take 1 lb love, 1 lb cheerfulness, pinch of unselfishness. Mix all together with 1 gill of sympathy and spice with a bright fireside. Put in a tin of contentment and bake well all your life.' *Woman's Mirror* started with seven pages of the continuing serialisation of 'My Story' by the Duchess of Argyll, but did have Marjorie Proops in vigorous agony-aunt action. 'Woo him,' she instructed 'Felice' about her hard-working but affection-lite husband. 'Be seductive. Be alluring. Slosh on the scent and wear tight form-fitting sweaters. Snuggle up.' And to 'Wanton', asking how a woman should keep her air of mystery: 'Talk less, think more . . . and let your neckline plunge at the back instead of the front.' The most down-to-earth weekly was as usual the highly successful relative newcomer, *Woman's Realm*. 'Sitting in my newly decorated kitchen,' related Mrs E. R. of Croydon in the letters page, 'I was horrified to see how badly out of place my old wooden clothes horse looked, so I went out and bought 1½ yards of self-adhesive plastic, in a gay contemporary pattern. I then covered the uprights and rungs of my clothes horse with this. What a difference it made!' Clare Shepherd ran the problems page, this week including a 22-year-old who had been married for three months: 'I get so miserable at times that I feel like crying. My husband doesn't help me very much. If we have company or go out anywhere, I am immediately forgotten, and if there happens to be a pretty girl there, all he seems to do is to try to impress her.' Shepherd's answer included practical advice, but not before some home truths:

> If the fact that your husband chose you out of all the other pretty girls and asked you to be his wife has not given you confidence, there seems little I can do to help. You have only been married for three months, and there should be a lot for you to be wonderfully happy about. It is possible you have not fully realised that whether a marriage is happy or not depends very much on what the wife puts into it. If a wife is warm and loving, it very seldom happens that a husband looks elsewhere.

That left the big two. In *Woman's Own*, that week's editorial column ('Between Friends') was in praise of marriage, its 'reward' defined as 'the true happiness that comes from doing what you love, and loving what you do, with all your heart'; while elsewhere, Roderick Wimpole wrote his 'Doctor's Diary', and on the letters page Mrs O. Moody of Southsea posed a question: 'Why is it, I wonder, that men cannot bear to be beaten at anything by a woman? I lost my first boyfriend by beating him at tennis, my second by winning a swimming race against him and my third by getting the prize at a fairground game of darts. It was then that I started to play the losing game. Soon afterwards I met my husband who, strangely enough, has always beaten me at everything!' Monica Dickens's column, 'Let's be frank about petting', was about a different type of pre-marital loss. 'Keeping your standards high never made anyone less desirable,' she insisted. 'Let down the bars once, and there is no reason why you shouldn't do it again. You'll want to do it again. Just petting isn't fun any more. Go on feeling like that, and you are well on the way to becoming a first-class promiscuous tramp. And people will know what you are. It shows.' For one protagonist in 'Mary Grant's Problems Page' it was already too late. 'My girl friend and I work in the same office. We are both in love with the manager and my friend finds she is expecting a baby, although she broke off the affair some weeks ago. I know he behaved badly, but I still love him and would like to help him if I could.' 'Surely,' replied Grant, 'it is your friend who needs help? If she has not confided in her mother, she should do so at once.' After recommending that the friend get in touch with the National Council for the Unmarried Mother and her Child, the agony aunt ended briskly: 'Do try to forget your feelings for the manager and stop wasting your sympathy on him; he has behaved so badly that he certainly does not deserve it.'

Woman's counter-attractions included four pieces of fiction ('Surgeon's Dilemma', 'Bride for a Bargain', 'The Happy Ending', 'Magic in Piccadilly'), the continuation of the series 'Happy Homecoming' about a real-life couple (Peggy and Tony) moving into a new home, the latest instalment of Dirk Bogarde's *My Life Story*, Ruth Morgan's cookery column ('Semolina at Your Service'), and Veronica Scott's 'The Three Faces of Fashion' (ie, sophisticated + casual + feminine). The stand-out ad was for Lux – as endorsed by 'a top top-model and a very nice person', Sandra Paul ('one marriage, one lifetime, she says') – while in his doctor's column Alan Lloyd was studiously neutral about the '"happiness" pills' now being popped, he estimated, at around a million a day: 'Such pills work on the emotions through the stem of the brain. Tranquillizers are designed to subdue the overwrought, while pep pills aim at lifting the depressed. Their job is to make you feel: "Gosh, life's better than I thought!".' Evelyn Home's remedy was different in her 'Talk It Over' problems page, responding to a reader with a shouting, bullying husband ('He's just the same even as a lover – no tender words or kisses, but because he is satisfied I must be as well'). The advice was seemingly timeless:

> Many men are boorish after work, and many are poor lovers; they need to be taught manners and tenderness by their wives.
>
> This is your job in future – the one you took on for better, for worse, remember? So don't waste time grumbling; start polishing your rough diamond into a perfect husband.[30]

Just over a year later appeared memorable and long-lasting – but at this point still strictly minority – dispatches from an utterly different world.

'Mrs Doris Lessing,' began John Bowen's review in *Punch* in May 1962,

> is a novelist in her forties, whose first book, set in Africa, was a best-seller, but who has written no other best-sellers. She is a divorcée, and lives alone; she has one child. She has lived in Africa. Politically she is of the Left. She has written a novel, *The Golden Notebook*, of which the heroine is Anna, a novelist in her forties, who has written one best-selling novel, set in Africa, and can write no more novels. Anna is a divorcée with one child, and lives alone. Politically Anna is of the Left. She has spent some time in Africa. Anna is trying to write a novel about Ella, a novelist in her forties who has written one best-selling novel, and can write no more. Ella is a divorcée with one child, and lives alone. Politically she is of the Left . . .

Published the previous month, *The Golden Notebook* was a novel mainly about women that was reviewed largely by men. Peter Green in the *Daily Telegraph* acknowledged Lessing's 'capacity for realistic portrayal', but in its 568 'closely printed pages' was deterred by Anna Wulf's 'interminable ramblings' and 'altogether too much agonising and breast-beating, of the kind that invariably turns up when an intelligent artist breaks with the Communists'; in the *Listener*, the poet Vernon Scannell praised Lessing's 'courageous honesty, her intelligence and passion', but argued that 'the tone is too earnest and the women suffer too intensely', so that 'gradually a climate is engendered of thick, overheated solemnity'; and in the *TLS*, another poet, Randall Swingler, not only found Anna a 'drooling, exhibitionist hysteric' but reckoned that something had gone badly wrong artistically: 'It would seem that Mrs Lessing has attempted something here which she could not control. Her material has got badly out of hand and in desperation she has bundled the lot together and chucked it at the reader to make of it what he can.' The most perceptive reviewer in a socio-cultural sense was the *New Statesman*'s Robert Taubman. Calling the novel 'not a creation but a document', and asserting that 'simply as a record of how it is to be free and responsible, a woman in relation to men and to other women and the struggle to come to terms with one's self about these things and about writing and politics, it seems to me unique in its truthfulness and range,' he speculated that it might 'soon displace the Simone de Beauvoir paperbacks in the hands of all those who want what she is supposed to provide – a sort of intelligent woman's guide to the intelligent woman'. And, he added, 'Doris Lessing says far more of genuine interest, is less self-conscious and much less boring.'

One of the book's earliest female readers was Phyllis Willmott (who in November 2013 would die a fortnight before Lessing). 'Ralph [Samuel] very anxious to know what I will make of it,' she noted on 5 May. Some three weeks later, she had finished. 'It seems to me, in the summing up, to be an unnecessarily prolonged, involved and chaotic feat of imaginative usage of biographical material,' she reflected. 'Their way of life,' she observed about Anna and her circle, 'induces a feeling of horror for them rather than that they are unpleasant, nasty people. They seem intent on mucking their lives up. Her mistake is to "project" this style of life – which is undoubtedly hers and her friends – to be general . . .' Then came the crux:

> Why did she [Anna] need to be so aggressively feminist? Why did she need to act like a male sexually when it so clearly was known to her that it went against the feminine grain? Her assumption seemed to be that she was going to *force* her way through to a promiscuity, and enjoyment of it . . .
>
> All the same, there is some good good good stuff in it . . .[31]

PART THREE

9

Don't Hang Riley

'Very cold,' noted Dennis Dee's typically taciturn East Riding diary entry for Saturday, 10 December 1960. 'Neville came for some eggs. Busy with various jobs.' Next day, the *Sunday Express* exposed what it called 'the Lilac Establishment' (anti-capital punishment, pro-pornography, pro-homosexuality and exemplified by Henry Moore 'laying down his lucrative chisel in order to sign petitions'); Henry St John observed the demolition of 'the booking hall and entrance' of Ealing Broadway station ('there appeared to be about 3 negroes in the handful of workmen thus engaged'); and Adam Faith was on *Face to Face*. 'Agreeable surprise', reckoned viewers generally, though one found him 'a very ordinary fellow' and another thought it 'a waste of time for a man of John Freeman's calibre to interview a fledgling like Faith'. Two parliamentary assertions illuminated the 14th – the Postmaster-General, Reginald Bevins, stating that colour TV was unlikely in the near future, and the War Secretary, John Profumo, declaring in relation to *The Army Game* being banned in Pontefract Barracks that 'there are errors of judgement in all walks of life and some are fortunate in not having the spotlight turned on them' – while that evening Nella Last in Barrow 'didn't feel any interest in "Coronation St."' (the second episode). Even so, not only did the *Manchester Evening News*'s critic reckon that it 'has promise of a warm, homely series, bursting with feasible characters and such convincingly ungrammatical and slovenly speech', but the next episode (on Friday the 16th) saw the entrance of Arthur Lowe as teetotal Leonard Swindley, lay preacher at the Glad Tidings Mission. Another teetotaller spent that evening on the *Any Questions?* panel at the Memorial Hall in Pensford, Somerset. Would

Labour, it was asked, be able to supply an effective opposition? Undoubtedly, answered Anthony Wedgwood Benn, given that 'Eastern European advance' demonstrated that 'the idea of private enterprise offering any hope to a community like our own in the world today is gradually being realised to be out of date.' The run-up to Christmas suggested that capitalism still had a flicker of life left ('the shops – and the streets – are jammed,' noted the *FT*, adding that 'a record number of turkeys' had been sold), before (on the 27th) the Beatles, recently back from their first Hamburg stint, gave a storming performance in the ballroom of Litherland Town Hall, not far from the Mersey docks. 'People went crazy for their closing number, "What'd I Say",' recalled the prominent local DJ Bob Wooler. 'Paul took the mike off the stand, shed his guitar and did fantastic antics all over the stage. They were all stomping like hell and the audience went *mad* . . . That was the beginning of Beatlemania.' Four days later, things got even better for youth at large when National Service call-up formally ended, a liberating moment for a whole generation. But as that large door opened, a small one closed: New Year's Eve was also the last day of the farthing coin as legal tender, though in truth it was already several years since bus conductors had willingly accepted the jaunty little wren.[1]

'Some fearfully unfunny material,' according to the *Daily Mirror*'s Clifford Davis, marred Morecambe and Wise's New Year's Day appearance on *Sunday Night at the London Palladium*; three days later, as *Punch*'s Eric Keown criticised the Old Vic production of *A Midsummer Night's Dream* as too knockabout ('had she been a man, Judi Dench with her astonishing speed and agility would have been an England fly-half'), Beryl Bainbridge appeared on *Coronation Street* as a placard-carrying ban-the-bomb student friend of Ken Barlow; next evening, David Turner's notable debut TV play *The Train Set*, going out live and unrecorded, was about a Birmingham factory worker's relationship with his son and wife ('the reactions of the sample audience as a whole can hardly be described as enthusiastic,' noted a BBC report, with 'some marked disgust with the language by several of the characters in the factory scenes'); reviews continued to be dusty for Shelagh Delaney's recently opened second play, *The Lion in Love*, at the Royal Court ('her reach exceeds her grasp,' thought Alan Brien in the *Spectator*); and on Saturday, 7 January, at this stage with Ian Hendry in the main role,

Patrick Macnee's John Steed as his assistant, and no Cathy Gale let alone Emma Peel, *The Avengers* began – the same day that the police came knocking at an anonymous-looking bungalow in Cranleigh Drive, Ruislip, where Peter and Helen Kroger were running the communications centre of a huge Soviet spy ring. But at the start of 1961 this was all small beer compared to *The Archers*. 'The question whether Miss Carol Grey should or shouldn't marry Charles Grenville has been agitating the people of England more than the things that leader writers write about,' reflected one radio critic, just as a *Radio Times* letter from a Southport listener congratulated Grenville for his 'taming' of the 'shrewish' Grey ('it will be good to see her cut down to size'). On Tuesday the 10th, five-year-old Janice Galloway began primary school ('I wore a black blazer with a Saltcoats crest on a wavy line, a grey skirt, a vest, a shirt and long socks, none of it cheap,' plus of course 'brand-new flat, lace-up shoes'); two days later, T. Dan Smith set out in a Newcastle paper his personal credo ('it is *here* and *now* that the love one is admonished to feel for one's neighbour can be given positive expression – right *here* and *now*!!!'); and on Sunday the 15th, Noël Coward issued a blast in the *Sunday Times* against drama's new wave ('it is bigoted and stupid to believe that tramps and prostitutes and underprivileged housewives frying onions and using ironing boards are automatically the salt of the earth'), Henry St John dropped in at Ealing's A.B.C. ('a cup of coffee and a macaroon' for 1s 2d), and Harold Macmillan recorded that the outgoing Archbishop of Canterbury, the controlling Geoffrey Fisher, was '*violently*, even *brutally* opposed' to having the more congenial, bushy-eyebrowed Michael Ramsey as his successor. Next day, Madge Martin in Oxford went 'to the pictures after tea' to see the latest Norman Wisdom farce *The Bulldog Breed* ('not too good'); on Tuesday, after students at Hull had complained to a Sunday paper about the university, the Larkin verdict was that they were 'simply sodding little shop stewards'; on Thursday, Judy Haines in Chingford enjoyed a 'pleasant "Woman's Hour," knitting Pamela's golden cardigan the while'; and on Friday, typical viewer reaction to *Nina and Frederik* was that the Danish-Dutch singing duo were 'like a lovely fresh breeze', having 'no need for sequin suits, oversize jewellery or undersize garments'. Sunday the 22nd was a day for memories – Phyllis Willmott, back in respectable working-class south-east London, contrasting the 'quiet and very empty' streets with how before the war they had been full of unemployed men 'tramping' them 'in search of an extra shilling or two', and, in the doomed, soon-to-be submerged Tryweryn Valley, the last passenger train making its way on the winding track from Bala to Blaenau Ffestiniog and back again – before January ended with Ossie Clark and Celia Birtwell meeting for the first time on the 27th ('the night of the fifteenth episode of *Coronation Street*', as Clark later put it), Manchester City's Denis Law next day scoring six goals on a swamp at Luton before the match was abandoned, and *Housewives' Choice* on the Light Programme on the morning of the 31st coming up against a feature called *Two of a Kind* on the Home Service. One of the two, Ted, mentioned that at nine each morning he retreated to his room to work, but not so for the other Primrose Hill poet, Sylvia. 'I certainly,' she explained, 'have a life just like all the other housewives and mothers in our district: shopping, dishes and taking care of the baby and so forth. I think very few people have any idea I do anything at all except household chores.'[2]

Quite apart from ecclesiastical manoeuvres, the PM was in bullish mood at the start of 1961. 'We've got it good,' he told the *Daily Mail* about the Affluent Society. 'Let's keep it good. There is nothing to be ashamed of in that.' But everything, Macmillan well knew, depended upon the health of the economy – a cause of increasing concern. 'The situation could become most unattractive and cause unhappiness,' predicted the distinguished merchant banker Lionel Fraser in a letter to *The Times* in early January; and he demanded from government 'a Five-year Plan', to which 'the vast majority of the people would rise magnificently'. Ernest Skinner, in an earlier life Montagu Norman's faithful private secretary at the Bank of England, was appalled. 'One shudders to think,' he wrote to the paper, 'of the errors of judgement, political expedient, and bureaucratic authority that might be cemented into such a plan.' The force, though, was now seemingly with planning, and later that month the President of the Board of Trade, the ebullient Reginald Maudling, told the Merseyside branch of the National Union of Manufacturers that he had no doctrinal objection to the concept. What about the currency? About the same time, the National Institute of Economic and Social Research argued that devaluation of sterling was probably the only way to achieve a breathing space for the economy while more fundamental policy actions were taken. But again, an old Bank of England hand sought to reassert the ancient verities. 'Siren voices are heard once more,' began Harry Siepmann's mid-February letter to *The Times*, written from the Athenaeum and calling devaluation 'the forcible and unilateral denouncing of a hundred thousand honest contracts . . . a moral outrage'. Within weeks, with sterling under pressure, Selwyn Lloyd as Chancellor was compelled to provide a categorical public assurance that there would be no devaluation, but for Macmillan these were becoming increasingly difficult times. 'He says the £ will crash in the summer,' he noted after a visit from his trusted informal economic adviser Roy Harrod. 'We *must* restrict imports. Treasury and Board of Trade say the opposite. What is a poor Prime Minister to do?'

'An intellectual who looks like a sketch frugally executed in India ink – strong, thoughtful white face, black hair and neat moustache' was how Mollie Panter-Downes described Macmillan's least favourite Cabinet colleague, Enoch Powell, recently restored to the front bench as Minister of Health. On 1 February, he announced significantly raised NHS charges (including prescriptions doubling, to 2s), provoking a major political storm; later that day, Len Fairclough made his *Coronation Street* entrance; and the same evening, two note-taking gentlemen from the Lord Chamberlain's office attended *Fings Ain't Wot They Used T'Be* at the Garrick, leading to a series of cuts and changes that particularly affected Barbara Windsor's suggestive role. Taste was also in evidence at Bournemouth Town Hall on the 3rd, as the *Any Questions?* panel was asked to comment on 'the preponderance of kitchen sink playwrights these days'. 'I don't like 'em,' responded sturdy, commonsensical James Callaghan. 'I'm sick and tired of the BBC plays on Sunday night, of seeing the sort of thing we're getting.' Sunday the 5th saw the launch of the *Sunday Telegraph* – a dog's dinner, but notable for Nigel Lawson as trenchant City editor and the launch of Peregrine Worsthorne's 'Talking of Politics' column, acclaiming Powell as 'something new on the post-war political scene', namely 'a Tory minister of first-class intellectual calibre and of proved integrity who is passionately averse to the over-spending of public money' – before next day a live invitation from Eamonn Andrews to Danny Blanchflower to appear on *This Is Your Life* received a brusque refusal. 'I don't need to give any reason,' the Spurs captain told callers after returning home to Palmers Green. 'It was a matter of principle. My private life is my own.' Controversy too with the BBC's announcement on the 8th that the legendary *Children's Hour* was shortly to disappear from the radio, while that Wednesday evening – only a few weeks after the publication of Ludovic Kennedy's *10 Rillington Place* had thrown sharp doubt on the guilt of the hanged Timothy Evans – a haunting scene played out in Shrewsbury. For about an hour from 9.30, recorded the local paper, 'people living in Albert and Victoria Streets, adjoining the prison, were shocked and horrified by cries and chantings from the prisoners of "Don't hang Riley"' – the 21-year-old butcher's assistant George Riley, who on the basis of a confession which he later withdrew had been found guilty of murdering a widow, Adeline Mary Smith. Next morning, at 8.00 a.m., he was hanged. 'I knew the Riley boy; his family were patients of my father,' recalled John Ryle, eight at the time. 'I remember seeing the front page of the *Shrewsbury Chronicle* after the execution; and walking with my mother along the river, along the flooded towpath – swans sheltering among the osiers on half-submerged river islands – past the water gate, under the railway bridge to the prison, the site of one of Housman's threnodies: *They hang us now in Shrewsbury jail . . .*'[3]

At lunchtime on the day that Riley died, the still leather-jacketed Beatles made the first of their 292 appearances at the Cavern – alcohol-free, young office workers, no Teds. Over the next few days, the 14-year-old East Ender Helen Shapiro released her first single, 'Don't Treat Me Like a Child'; a frustrated Henry St John visited 'the pornographic shop' in Soho's Little Newport Street, where 'they too were displaying some magazines done up in transparent covers, so that they could not be opened'; Philip Larkin (who might have sympathised) had the first of his monthly jazz columns in the *Daily Telegraph*; a strike-enforced repeat of the first episode of *Coronation Street* prompted the *Daily Mirror*'s Jack Bell to call it a 'drab and doleful' series 'from which I would gladly have taken a rest'; John Bloom's wedding reception at the Savoy included two enormous wedding cakes in the shape of a washing-machine and a dishwasher; a talk on the Third Programme by Nikolaus Pevsner began with the assertion that 'queer things are happening in architecture today'; the latest *Black and White Minstrel*

Show was greeted by viewers as 'as usual, a tip-top show'; and the two records that Anthony Heap bought for his son's 12th birthday were a selection of songs from *Oliver!* and 'a currently popular comedy number "Goodness Gracious Me"'. There was also that mid-February a counter-cultural trio of events. 'Abstraction is "out", and a new manner, sharply flavoured with the signs, slogans and mordant humour of metropolitan life, is "in",' observed *The Times* about the quasi-annual *Young Contemporaries* exhibition in London, with the Royal College of Art student David Hockney among those identified as further adding 'a weird, satirical element' to what is often viewed as the start of British Pop art; some 5,000 people joined Bertrand Russell in the civil disobedience of a Whitehall sit-in against Polaris, the British nuclear deterrent; and at the Aldwych, John Whiting's *The Devils*, specially commissioned by Peter Hall for his Royal Shakespeare Company, had according to one critic 'speeches that for power have not been written by an Englishman in the English theatre since Webster'. None of this was Judy Haines's world. On the 20th she 'finished Pamela's v-necked cardigan', while her elder daughter Ione 'looked lovely going off in hers this morning' and was welcomed by a friend 'to the v-necked Club, for the "best people"'; three days later the girls 'stayed up for "Beyond our Ken"'; and on the 27th, after going to a matinee of Dirk Bogarde and John Mills in *The Singer Not the Song* ('quite good'), she returned to a disappointing sight: 'Washing soaking on line. I had hoped it would be rescued by a neighbour.' There was also disappointment in middle England – or, at the least, instinctive suspicion – about the eventual prospect of decimalisation. 'Do let us retain something British,' Mrs N. F. Bond of Cecil Road, NW10 wrote to the *Mirror*. 'The present system has been in use for a long time so why change it now?' And M.B. of Croydon agreed: 'A lot of mothers would find a new system a curse. It's worrying enough thinking what to get for dinner without having to work out how much to pay for it.'[4]

The major corporate story during the early months of 1961 concerned the *Daily Herald*. Owned 51 per cent by Odhams Press, 49 per cent by the TUC, the paper was an appreciably more faithful friend to the Labour party than the *Daily Mirror* was. But unfortunately, unlike the *Mirror*, the *Herald* had for a long time been struggling commercially, a process not significantly checked by an editorial move upmarket in the course of 1960. And now, to Hugh Gaitskell's considerable alarm, the Mirror Group under the overbearing leadership of Cecil King was making a strong bid to take over Odhams, less for the dubious prize of the *Herald* than for its range of successful magazines, including *Woman* and *Woman's Own*. In the event the government stood aside (kicking the monopoly issue into the long grass by setting up a royal commission on the press), Gaitskell and his colleagues were divided among themselves, King reluctantly promised to keep the *Herald* alive for a minimum of seven years, and eventually the bid triumphed. It happened to coincide with the formal opening in early March of the *Mirror*'s new building in Holburn Circus, described by Patrick Skene Catling in *Punch* as 'the world's most palatial, most magnificently equipped newspaper factory', with an 'overall appearance of orthodox modernity, of functional efficiency, brightness and colour'. Features included 3,170 fluorescent light fittings, seven automatic passenger lifts, the machine room in the basement like 'the empire room of an ocean liner' and, on the ninth floor, the boardroom chairs 'covered in purple leather'. 'Britain has known many powerful publishers,' declared a *New York Times* profile of King, 'but none has ever ruled such an empire as the one he heads.' A very minor outpost of that empire was the legendary children's comic the *Eagle*, itself only owned by Odhams since 1959: at its height in the early 1950s, it had sold some 800,000 copies, but now under the unsympathetic control of the Mirror Group's juvenile publications division it went into a precipitate fall, with square-jawed Colonel Dan Dare helpless to avert it. As for the reprieved *Herald*, the hope was that it could find its own distinctive, commercially viable market. 'The new "Daily Herald" differs greatly from its predecessor,' its promotion manager informed John Freeman at the *New Statesman* soon after the takeover. 'We are trying to make this a popular, radical, and responsible newspaper which appeals to both material and moral idealism.'[5]

Elsewhere during March, a month of exceptionally benign weather, 'Astonishing Mastery of Cello at 16' was *The Times*'s headline for Jacqueline du Pré's professional debut at the Wigmore Hall, including 'an account of Bach's C minor unaccompanied suite that thrilled the blood with its depth and intuitive eloquence'; Sylvia Plath, having had her appendix out, reflected how her fellow-patients in St Pancras

Hospital did not 'fuss or complain or whine, except in a joking way'; following a *Panorama* item on sex crimes, 'many viewers felt far too much was heard of psychiatric "mumbo jumbo"'; opening the annual conference of the National Association for Mental Health, Enoch Powell described the still operational asylums built by 'our forefathers' as 'isolated, majestic, imperious, brooded over by the gigantic water tower' – in effect, the start of the shift to care in the community; the Jaguar E-type was unveiled at the Geneva Motor Show; the third series of radio's *The Navy Lark* ended ('the dear old fruit getting hitched *was* a surprise,' noted a housewife); the consciously retro Temperance Seven, dressed in Edwardian style, released 'You're Driving Me Crazy', counter-intuitively but accurately predicted by the *Mirror*'s Patrick Doncaster to be 'a huge success' precisely 'because they are 40 YEARS OUT OF DATE'; Don Revie's first match in charge of struggling Leeds United ended in a 3–1 defeat at Portsmouth; viewer reaction to the Eurovision Song Contest and to John Mortimer's Hampstead-set Sunday-night play *The Wrong Side of the Park* was equally dismayed – 'Are You Sure?' by the Allisons (beaten into second place by the Luxembourg entry) was 'by far the best', while in NW3 the characters were 'tiresomely introspective' and 'their general behaviour either hysterical or obscure'; the decidedly non-introspective smallholder Dennis Dee had a good day when Nicolaus Silver became the second grey to win the Grand National ('I was lucky to pick him out'), with the two much-publicised Russian horses, Grifel and Reljef, failing to finish; and, on the Monday before Easter, the out-of-town run of the patchy revue *One Over the Eight* (largely written by Peter Cook) found Kenneth Williams in 'hateful, tasteless, witless, blank, boring, dirty, tat' Blackpool. He was probably never a candidate for *Coronation Street*, now establishing itself as a permanent fixture, going out nationally on Mondays and Wednesdays. David Jones – the future Monkee – took a part as Ena Sharples's grandson; Ena herself was sent to Coventry for spreading false rumours that the street was about to be slum-cleared; one viewer's letter praised 'a true picture of life', another's how 'it shows the selfish, the kind-hearted, and the nosy'; and Jack Rosenthal began writing scripts, the first one including some prize Ena dialogue: 'Folk round 'ere know nowt. One walk down t'canal bank and they think they're charting the Ganges.' The contrast was painfully stark with the Joan Littlewood production of *Sparrers Can't Sing*, transferring to the West End near the end of March. 'Sad to say,' noted *The Times*'s reviewer, 'most of the characters, despite the photographic realism of their talk, appear to have been taken not from contemporary life but from a long stage tradition of comic cockneys'; or, as Anthony Heap put it, 'mildly amusing', but 'no plot, no drama, no comedy, no nuffink!'[6]

The last day of March was Good Friday – 'suffering of the flesh and resurrection all in one day', recalled Margaret Drabble about childbirth at St George's, London. 'I found the hospital very authoritarian. I can remember the midwives telling me to shut up. I didn't see why I shouldn't yell.' That evening, *Any Questions?* came from Thorngate Hall, Gosport and included the 'practical farmer' Ted Moult, who had already introduced *Housewives' Choice* earlier in the day. 'I think it's a lot of bunk, bunk,' he declared about psychiatry to laughter and applause. And, in response to a question about marching with banners, he referred to the Aldermaston March: 'When this procession started several years ago, I had a good deal of sympathy with their point of view. Now, I am afraid to say that the sight of these marchers, and coupled with them the sort of beatnik element that they have dragged along with them, I am disgusted.' That year's CND march as usual started on Good Friday, and as usual was heading for Trafalgar Square on Easter Monday, but did not only come from Aldermaston. For instance, the Leicester contingent, among them A. R. Williams, a grammar-school sixth-former from Ashby-de-la-Zouch, travelled to Finchingfield in north-west Essex and began the march there:

> After about an hour, a large open car with a jazz band perched on it crawled by and was greeted both with cheering and laughter since their enthusiasm far outweighed their skill. We marched in great form for the rest of the day with CND banners high and spirits even higher. The first night was spent at a Primary School at Braintree, where our group was personally welcomed by the Mayor.
>
> The next morning, some of us were perhaps a little the worse for wear after singing and dancing well into the night . . . Easter Saturday was one long, hard, wet trudge and when we stopped for lunch I, for one, was thankful. Whilst we sat in the road eating and talking, television

> cameramen and reporters mingled with us trying to find the notorious 'beatnik' element. This was conspicuous by its absence, except for a small but lively group from Soho. These creatures in their black rags and with a huge sign with 'Soho says No' were strangely fascinating. The afternoon was wet and uneventful except for nagging feet. On and on we tramped, until we reached Brentwood where the programme was – a meal and to bed.

The still unpublished John Fowles was also in Essex that rainy weekend, staying with his parents at Leigh-on-Sea and finding it as hard as ever to control his irritation. 'Even the conversation about contemporary events seems peculiarly old-fashioned. This feeling of time past, of people absolutely based in the manners, attitudes, orders of thirty and forty years ago – peeping their horns out at today, like snails. But happier back in the shell. Snail-towns, these like Leigh.' One way and another, it was an apposite weekend for a television comedian's big-screen breakthrough. 'Went to Ritz, Leyton, to see Tony Hancock in "The Rebel",' recorded Judy Haines on Easter Monday. 'He, Liz Fraser, and Irene Handl extremely funny . . . Enjoyed other film in brilliant colour of Royal Tour of India.' As for the Leicester marchers, they had 'shuffled and limped' on Easter Sunday as far as West Ham, at one point being descended on by League of Empire Loyalists who 'hurled fireworks, smokebombs and yelled "Keep the Bomb" and "Tottenham for the Cup".' Then, 'Easter Monday – the last lap':

> We hobbled off in heavy rain, still undaunted, and from then until lunch we sang and plodded, again aided by our unwilting jazz musicians. Lunch at Smithfield Market! then along the Embankment and we should be there.
>
> Immediately after lunch, we were joined by the Aldermaston wing of the march, with its many and colourful foreign groups. We crammed into Trafalgar Square and I fought my way to the fountain where I soaked my tired feet as I listened to the speeches. Here to address us was the philosopher Bertrand Russell and many MPs and celebrities of public life. Actors and entertainers mingled among us. This at least showed the wide appeal of the campaign.

'Was it worth it?' wondered Williams. 'Did we achieve anything? I hope so! I think so.'

The *New Statesman* hoped so too, its current issue endorsing 'the healthy and vigorous motives of the Aldermaston marchers'. Those were not sentiments that Kingsley Amis, no unilateralist, could endorse, and on 5 April he informed the magazine's new literary editor Karl Miller that he would 'sooner not be tied up' with such a journal – a further significant step in his steady march rightwards. Another magazine, *Melody Maker*, featured on the 8th two notable interviewees. Interrupted at his 'elegant' Winchmore Hill home only by his mother coming in 'with tea and biscuits on an electronically-heated trolley', Cliff Richard confided that he did not want 'to make the same mistake as Tommy Steele', who 'went after the older audience and seems to have lost the following of the youngsters'; while 'handsome, blond, 20-year-old' Adam Faith, who 'runs an American Ford Galaxy car and has just bought his family a new luxury house in Sunbury-on-Thames', called himself 'a beat singer aiming mainly at the teenagers' and appeared 'unruffled' by the increasing popularity of the balladeers ('they'll never kill the beat idiom'). Seemingly unruffled too was Paul Raymond, whose trial began on Monday the 10th at Marlborough Street Magistrates' Court. The prosecution's case was that productions at his Soho strip club, the Revuebar, had gone too far; according to a police witness, this was typified by the obscene whipping sequence in 'Mutiny on the High Seas'. Next day, whipping was all but on the agenda of the Commons, as a Tory backbencher, Sir Thomas Moore, sought to insert a clause in the Criminal Justice Bill by which, 13 years after the effective abolition of corporal punishment (outside private schools), violent young male offenders could be given a caning (up to the age of 17) or a birching (18 to 20). During the debate, Moore pointed to the sharp increase in crimes of violence (up from 2,800 in 1938 to 13,800 in 1958) and noted that of the 1,200 letters he had received, only 15 were opposed to his proposal. Another Tory backbencher, Gerald Nabarro, was likewise strongly in favour of 'thwacking the thugs', though calling himself a 'not indiscriminate flogger', while a third, Geoffrey Hirst, condemned the Home Secretary, Rab Butler, as 'deplorably out of touch' with public opinion. Moore failed to carry the day, with Labour MPs backing the government, but as many as 69 Tories – among them Sir Cyril

Black, Cyril Osborne, Wing Commander Bullus and, less predictably, the newly elected Peter Walker (future one-nation Conservative) – voted against the party whip. The rebels included Margaret Thatcher. 'It was the biggest Party revolt since we came to power in 1951,' she recalled without regret. 'It was also the only occasion in my entire time in the House of Commons when I voted against the Party line.'[7]

'It is nonsense to assume,' wrote Tom Stoppard in the *Western Daily Press* on the day Thatcher went rogue, 'that every time a coloured man fails to get or keep a job it is because he is black.' Even so, the young journalist, not yet a playwright, did not deny the existence of a colour bar in Bristol – most notoriously at the Bristol Omnibus Co, not employing a single black conductor or driver:

> On the Thursday before Easter a black friend of mine applied for a job as a conductor. He asked to see the personnel manager and was told to come back after the holidays, but, he told me, 'They said there were no vacancies anyway.'
>
> Five minutes later I applied for the same job. I was told that the conductors' 'school' was full but I could come back after the holiday when there would be vacancies, and I could then take the course.

Next day, 12 April, Stoppard turned to the housing aspect of Bristol's colour bar. One flat agency had told him that only 1 per cent of its clients would accept a non-white tenant, another that 25 per cent of landlords stipulated 'no coloured' without even being asked, while 'about half of the remainder would not accept a coloured tenant if one came along.' As for buying a house, he quoted an estate agent: 'We have never sold a house to a coloured man. They are not a good risk, and frankly we would never sell except for cash.' To which Stoppard added that 'however regrettable it may be, it is nevertheless true that when a coloured family moves into a house, then the house next door drops in price, and so on until a whole area takes the knock.' Near the end of his piece, he reflected that 'it is never the landlord who doesn't like coloured people. It's the other people in the house, or the other people in the street. No one you meet is guilty.'

It could be hard to be middle-class and qualm-free over the issue. 'The Johannson-Patterson fight – all along I have wanted Patterson (the negro) to win,' noted in March another writer-in-waiting, John Fowles. 'We woke up at 3.15 am to hear the commentary on the wireless; and I kept on finding myself wanting the Swede to win . . . I loathe colour prejudice. But there it is.' Or take the experience shortly after Easter of a female diarist living in Barking. 'He overcharged me by 10d,' recorded Pat Scott about trouble with a bus conductor. 'I then caused a fuss about the charge but luckily an Inspector was on the bus. But unluckily the man was coloured. I didn't like causing a fuss but he was rather rude.' Even so, a couple of blasts earlier in 1961 to the *Listener* – normally an impeccably liberal organ – were strikingly qualm-free. 'I object to a sub-standard folk from another land "invading" in such numbers,' declared M. Blundell of London N22 in response to a fairly anodyne article on 'Britain's Colour Problem'. 'Anyone,' he went on, 'who has seen what Jamaicans especially can do within a few weeks to what was a neat and clean house ought not to be surprised at resentment . . . It is the way of life that is objected to – the noisiness, the flamboyance . . . They will take 100 years to catch up with us.' So too H. Russell Wakefield of London SW10, who on the basis of 'having seen what Jamaicans can do to a whole neighbourhood', endorsed Blundell 'heartily'. Calling himself 'a fanatical segregationist', he bluntly stated that 'these people should never be inflicted upon civilised persons.' As for public attitudes more generally, a revealing episode occurred when the Rev. Clifford Hill, a Congregationalist minister in Tottenham, was reported as saying on the radio in late May that he would not have a problem if his daughter married a black man. 'For the next seven days,' he recalled a few years later, 'an enormous flood of correspondence, mostly of a foul and abusive nature, poured through my letter box'; he gave some of the more printable examples:

> A black blubber-lipped Negro on top of her and unending half castes year after year. Blacks breed and breed! What a fate! You are not fit to be a father at all. (*Woman in Brighton*)
>
> I pity your poor little girl to be more or less married off to some great slob of a lazy ponce of a nigger. (*London man*)
>
> It is not for you to tamper with God's handiwork! (*Middlesex man*)

'The climax of the avalanche of abuse that poured in from all quarters,' Hill added, 'came a week later when my house was attacked during the night. White paint was thrown over the doors and windows and outside walls, and such slogans as "NIGGER LOVER" and "RACE-MIXING PRIEST" were painted in huge letters along my fence and on the pavement outside the house.'

Soon afterwards, another clergyman, the Rev. Fred Milson, senior youth tutor at a Selly Oak training college, initiated a detailed six-week survey into the realities affecting Birmingham's 35,000 West Indians. Its key findings were that colour prejudice was almost entirely an adult phenomenon; that housing remained the biggest problem facing the immigrants; that the city was 'in danger of having "neighbourhood segregation"' – ie, between whites and non-whites; that it came across 'very few examples of informal integration', whether in churches or pubs or social life generally; and that outside the workplace (where relations were usually better), the prevailing attitude was 'tolerance without acceptance', in effect leaving the West Indians as 'a community within a community'. Looking ahead, Milson called on the immigrants to recognise that the English were 'at heart a neighbourly people' and not to mistake 'English reserve and reticence for race and colour discrimination'; while as for the English, on whom as hosts 'the greater responsibility for understanding' rested, 'we need, without fuss or patronage, to take the initiative in friendship', that in other words 'it is not enough to be "not against" the coloured immigrant'. In short: 'We must accept with our minds that there has come to Birmingham a common twentieth-century phenomenon – the multi-racial society.'[8]

Was restriction on numbers from the New Commonwealth a surer, more realistic route to improved relations? Milson recognised that this was becoming an increasingly hot political issue when he used the closing words of his report to assert that 'any control of West Indian immigration should be on the basis of availability of housing accommodation and general social amenities – not on the basis of race or colour.' The debate was keenest in the Conservative party, which traditionally had been wedded to free entry, largely for reasons of imperial sentiment. But by the end of 1960, and going into 1961, it was becoming increasingly hard to hold that line – 50,000 West Indian immigrants in 1960 alone, West Indian governments still refusing passport restrictions, the Indian and Pakistani governments under strong domestic pressure to relax theirs – with the result that by February 1961 even the reasonably liberal-minded Rab Butler had in effect accepted the principle of immigration controls and was turning his mind to the practicalities. In public, though, nothing changed. 'Latest immigration figures show that West Indians continue to flock into this overcrowded country at a higher rate than ever,' complained the impeccably bigoted Anthony Heap in early June. 'But does the Government heed the pleas from MPs, local authorities and other public bodies to restrict immigration on account of the acute housing and health problems created by this ever-increasing influx? No. Cravenly cowed by the leftist parrot cry of "no colour bar", they won't do a damned thing about it . . .' A few days later, a Gallup poll found only 11 per cent categorically saying they would move 'if coloured people came to live next door', but 67 per cent wanting restrictions on entry. And this two-thirds majority gave five main reasons: 'Too many coloured people here already [around 300,000]; the taxpayer has to support them; they are unhealthy; they should have jobs to go to; they lower our standards of living.'[9]

That was not the only time in the first half of 1961 that Gallup tested public opinion about race. Revealingly, in the wake of South Africa leaving the Commonwealth in March, it found that barely two in five wanted Britain to vote in the United Nations against apartheid, while one in ten actually wanted Britain to support South Africa. Mighty events were afoot elsewhere in Africa, with the key British player undoubtedly the brilliant, sometimes mercurial Colonial Secretary, Iain Macleod; he took the clear-sighted view, broadly backed by Macmillan (a year after his famous 'wind of change' speech in Cape Town), that, given the inevitability of decolonisation, there was no point in delaying. Under his predecessor, Alan Lennox-Boyd, the tentative British assumption had been that Tanganyika, Uganda and Kenya might each achieve independence during the first half of the 1970s. But thanks to Macleod's drive – in Timothy Raison's words, 'an astonishing display of tactical skill coupled with bravura and inspiration' – the actual respective dates were 1961, 1962 and 1963. Tory backbenchers could just about live with that. What they found much harder to stomach was the prospect of white surrender of power in the territories that comprised the Central African Federation (Southern and Northern Rhodesia and Nyasaland). 'Our Government and Party will be split in two,' privately predicted Macmillan in early February, if he and Macleod were to 'make a decision which, without satisfying African demands, goes in their general favour'. Mollie Panter-Downes's assessment at the start of March was that there were at least 90 Conservative MPs who believed that 'the Government is going ahead too fast in putting political power into the hands of the politically immature'; while in the Lords, the most bitter opposition to Macleod came from the Tory kingmaker Lord ('Bobbety') Salisbury, who on 7 March not only made a passionate defence of the white settlers ('these little communities, including wives and children, scattered about among primitive people') but accused the Colonial Secretary of being 'rather unscrupulous' and, still worse, 'too clever by half'. Later that month the Federation's Sir Roy Welensky, in many ways the orchestrator of Tory discord, addressed 200 of the party's backbenchers and was warmly received. Yet in practice that would prove to be the high-water mark for the refuseniks. 'That diehard groups found themselves unable to hold the centre of the Party for long,' argues the historian Nicholas Owen, 'is explained less by Macleod's ability to persuade MPs of the merits of his policies than by the size of Macmillan's majority, and the skill of his Party Whips at deploying persuasion, patronage and threats.' Which did not mean, as Owen rightly adds, that the Conservative Party as a whole, including its members, was suddenly converted to the principle of black majority rule.[10]

There is no evidence that any of this had significant traction in most people's minds. What about a much nearer continent? Almost four years after the Treaty of Rome and the start of the European Economic Community without British participation, Macmillan had formulated by the end of 1960 what he called 'The Grand Design' – in essence, an attempt 'to organise the great forces of the Free World – USA, Britain and Europe – economically, politically and militarily in a coherent effort to withstand the Communist tide all over the world'. In practice that meant, whatever the negative Commonwealth implications, a decision to attempt to join the Common Market, which it was also believed would stimulate the sluggish British economy. Formal announcement of an application still awaited. But by mid-May 1961, shortly after Edward Heath as the minister responsible for relations with Europe had called the issue the great challenge for 'our generation', Macmillan was noting that 'the European problem has held the attention of Parliament, the

Press and to some extent the public in the last few days.' 'The Press,' he added, 'is divided. Beaverbrook's papers – *Daily Express*, *Sunday Express*, *Evening Standard* – are already hysterical in opposition. Broadly speaking all the rest of the Press (*Times*, *Daily Telegraph*, *Daily Mail*, *Daily Mirror*) are sympathetic.' A month later, writing to her son, Lady Violet Bonham Carter referred to 'the *sudden* awakening "en sursaut" of the Govt & of the Press here to the importance of the Common Market' and, from the perspective of a veteran Liberal, summed up the political state of play: 'Both the major parties are split down the middle . . . Many Tories still don't realise that we have already lost "national sovereignty" – through NATO, UN, Gatt, IMF, etc, etc . . . The Labour Party are Jingo Little Englanders, economic Nationalists & xenophobes who dread the "foreigner" . . .' And public opinion? According to Gallup about the same time, just under one in two people offered approval of an application to join, one in five said they would disapprove, and the rest were unsure. The question was also asked: if Britain felt it had to join with other powers, would it be better to team up with Europe or America? Twenty-two per cent plumped for the former – and 55 per cent for Uncle Sam. We were not, in short, natural Europeans. Or, as a hostile cartoon in the *Mirror* in May put it, 'New German Arms Build-Up'.

One politician at this stage had relatively little to say about immigration or decolonisation or Europe. But he did in April, on St George's Day, give a speech to a dinner in London of the Royal Society of St George. In it, Enoch Powell recalled 'that incredible phase' during which 'the power and influence of England expanded with the force and speed of an explosion'; he acknowledged that 'that phase is ended, so plainly ended that even the generation born at its zenith, for whom the realisation is the hardest, no longer deceive themselves as to the fact'; and, after an eloquent disquisition about 'the unbroken life of the English nation over a thousand years and more', he looked ahead to the future with a sense of foreboding: 'The danger is not always violence and force; them we have withstood before and can again. The peril can also be indifference and humbug, which might squander the accumulated wealth of tradition and devalue our sacred symbolism to achieve some cheap compromise or some evanescent purpose.'[11]

'"MAN IN SPACE" screamed the inch-high banner headline across the front of the London "Evening News",' recorded Henry St John on Wednesday, 12 April, 'but the bowler-hatted man behind the paper in the train this evening was nodding off to sleep, and seemed in his oblivion the symbol of the age.' Next day, while the new Soviet hero rested up, the Paul Raymond trial ended with Raymond found guilty of keeping a disorderly house ('Your show can only be characterised as filthy, disgusting and beastly,' admonished the magistrate Reggie Seaton), before on the Friday came a coup for the BBC. 'Spent a lot of time looking at broadcast from Moscow [the first live one from there on British television] welcoming Gagarin the space flyer's return & welcome in Moscow,' noted another diarist, Florence Turtle. 'It started at 10.30 & I switched off at 12.30 & got my lunch.' Also on the TV front that day, Rab Butler wrote to the Independent Television Authority's Director-General Sir Robert Fraser complaining about the 'unhealthy amount of violence on the television screen, sometimes of a particularly vicious type', and a letter in the *TV Times* from W. Pepper of Leeds 8 wondered why 'so many contestants' on *Criss Cross Quiz* 'are bank clerks, teachers, managing directors, etc', while the next evening on *The Billy Cotton Band Show* viewers 'very much' enjoyed the Temperance Seven ('delightfully amusing') but far less so Alma Cogan ('harsh and tuneless'). By then, the Scotland goalkeeper Frank Haffey was reliving his Wembley nightmare: 9 goals conceded that hapless Saturday afternoon (in a 9–3 defeat to England, with a hat-trick for Chelsea's Jimmy Greaves), and already the cruel joke doing the rounds: 'What's the time? – Nearly 10 past Haffey'. Monday the 17th was Budget day, a lacklustre affair from Selwyn Lloyd, prompting Anthony Heap to register his 'despair of ever getting a Budget that will relieve in any appreciable degree the crushing burden of direct taxation on the likes of me'; and at last, the Electrical Trades Union trial got under way at the High Court. Two members of the Communist-run ETU were claiming that the union's leadership had over a period of several years permitted, and indeed encouraged, systematic fraud in the conduct of its elections. The trial would last 40 days, and, according to the biographers of Les Cannon, the most important non-Communist in the union, 'the most dramatic moment was evidence of extra ballot-papers being ordered from the printer and sent to St Pancras station "to be called for" whence they were collected by the Head Office of the union. What happened to the 26,000 spare ballot-papers? Mr Gardiner [Gerald Gardiner QC, for the prosecution] called for them. "They are not being produced," replied the Counsel for the defence.' At which point 'the judge allowed himself a little joke: "It may be they disappeared."' Proceedings ended in mid-June, with Mr Justice Winn reserving judgement.[12]

Back in April, the visiting Christopher Isherwood reflected on the 19th on his fortnight in London: 'The utter fatalistic patience of everyone when a line has to be formed or a train or bus waited for. You feel the wartime mentality still very strongly . . . In general, life here seems tacky and lively and the people radiate a friendliness and willingness; all except for a shopkeeper or official type, which makes a face at you as if you had asked for the impossible and unspeakable.' Two days later, Miss M. Bird of Liverpool 17, a nurse in a casualty department, made her contribution to the *TV Times* debate about whether Ena should leave her hairnet off ('I can vouch that the Ena Sharples of Liverpool wear hair-nets, pins and rollers all day and every day'); David Marquand in the *New Statesman* reviewed A.J.P. Taylor's revisionist, instantly controversial *The Origins of the Second World War* (essentially arguing that Hitler in the 1930s had merely behaved as any rational German leader would) and acclaimed him as 'the only English historian now writing who can bend the bow of Gibbon and Macaulay'; and Hughie Green found himself 'besieged' at a large Newcastle furniture store by 'scores of frenzied, screaming, middle-aged women' who 'tore and plucked at his clothing'. Next day at the Scottish Cup Final at Hampden Park, where *The Times*'s correspondent noted 'the appalling experience of a continuous roar of cheering throughout the whole of the national anthem from the green end of the ground', an understandably shaky Haffey was back in the fray for Celtic, surprisingly held to a goalless draw by the underdogs, Jock Stein's Dunfermline Athletic. The replay, again at Hampden, was the following Wednesday afternoon (no floodlights there yet). Dunfermline's schools got the afternoon off, and 16-year-old Ian Jack and his friends 'stood in our school blazers among Celtic fans, men dressed with no intervening shirt between their vests and their jackets, flat caps, green and white scarves knotted as mufflers, large bottles of McEwan's Pale Ale to hand', and who 'pissed where they stood'. Dunfermline won 2–0, and that night 'the team appeared to wild noise on the balcony of the council chambers with the town's provost, wearing a high wing-collar and looking like Neville Chamberlain.' That same evening saw the start of the first series of Michael Bentine's *It's a Square World* (most viewers responding 'with somewhat guarded approval'), while next day the *Mirror*'s Richard Sear argued that 'the rocket success' of the 'women-dominated' *Coronation Street* owed much to its female appeal ('its clever, tangy dialogue, written at a trivial level, might have been gathered by women, for women, over any backyard fence') and Mrs N. M. Gibbs of Bideford complained in the *Radio Times* about 'the blight which has seemingly fallen upon *Mrs Dale's Diary*': 'Recently we have had nothing but unmitigated gloom – Mrs Freeman's serious illness and removal to hospital, then Captain being run over.' Over the last few days of the month, *The Ken Dodd Show* got a decent if unspectacular Reaction Index of 62 ('We can always be sure of a good laugh from him,' said one viewer); Richard Hoggart on BBC TV's *Bookstand* described Andy Capp as 'beautifully observed' and 'a piece of folk lore'; *Woman's Mirror* began the serialisation of the memoirs of Mrs Evelyn Yorke, for ten years a maid at Eton ('The most privileged boys in England are truly gentlemen in every sense of the word'); and Macmillan noted – possibly wistfully, possibly not – that 'there is no TV at Birch Grove [his Sussex home], except in Nanny's house at the Lodge gates.'[13]

May Day was the much-awaited day when off-course cash betting became legal, with that morning more than 150 betting shops opening in Liverpool alone and the street-runner (known on Merseyside as 'the back jigger-runner') facing extinction. In London, 21-year-old John McCririck climbed 'the rickety wooden stairs' to Jack Swift's smoke-filled first-floor premises in Dover Street, off Piccadilly. 'There was glorious bedlam in there,' he recalled; 'it was packed with punters shouting their horses home. Jim Joel's "Black Nanny" won the first race at Nottingham at 2–1 favourite.' Saturday the 6th also made sporting history. 'The Cup Final wasn't very rewarding, was it?' Larkin wrote to Monica Jones after Tottenham Hotspur had beaten injury-affected Leicester City 2–0 in a drab enough affair. But it meant that Tottenham had become the first club in the twentieth century to complete the League and FA Cup double. 'Now others may be tempted to imitate the Spurs concept in style and fluency,' speculated one football writer, Geoffrey Green. 'Their game is to decoy, create and destroy.' Later that weekend, on Sunday evening, Nella Last watched the ITV game show *For Love or Money*, noting gratefully that Des O'Connor as host had 'lost a lot of his silly facetiousness' and that 'the new hostess is a great improvement to the last sexy one, all wriggles & rolling eyes,' while on Monday she wondered whether it was time that *This is Your Life* 'had a rest': 'Sometimes there is a somewhat strained – artificial – air. My husband loves it – hates any change. Only one programme keeps its intense interest for me – Emergency Ward 10 – with Dixon of Dock Green a runner up.' A more enterprising couple, Madge Martin and her husband Robert, were in London on Tuesday looking for a chair that would be his retirement present as an Oxford clergyman. First came 'indifferent treatment' at Parker Knoll; then 'a look round Heals, too contemporary but fascinating'; and finally 'the palatial Maples in Tottenham Court Road', where they were treated 'with the utmost attention and interest'. The day's work done, they headed in the evening to Oxford Street's Studio One to see the newly released, 'perfectly enchanting' *101 Dalmatians*.[14]

Late April and early May was a particularly difficult time for one Home Counties writer. 'Save me,' declared Norman Shrapnel in his *Guardian* review of Elizabeth Taylor's Home Counties-set *In a Summer Season*, 'from the wise, witty, sensitive, accomplished, charming female novelist'; Richard Mayne in the *New Statesman* admitted to 'a brutish dislike for gracious upper-middle-class charm, at least in novels'; and John Weightman on radio's *The Critics* argued that Taylor's literary worth was seriously undermined by the fact that, in terms of her subject matter, 'we cannot be sure that she herself understands how marginal and decadent this part of English society has become.' Even *The Times* reviewer, albeit acknowledging Taylor's 'skilled craftsmanship', implicitly played the class card: 'Everything rings true. Yet the total is curiously disappointing. Perhaps the setting is too conventional. Perhaps the book is too much of a type.' Nor was the outlook auspicious for another established middle-class novelist who also wrote with sympathy and insight about the middle class. Barbara Pym's *No Fond Return of Love* had appeared earlier in the year and, notes her biographer, 'was not widely reviewed'. By contrast, a third female novelist was, in her unique way, altogether going with the larger flow. 'Entirely devoted to the bourgeois vices of a bourgeois world' was how in June one reviewer, Burns Singer in the *Listener*, encapsulated Iris Murdoch's *A Severed Head*, and he described admiringly its 'exquisitely formal game of unmusical beds in which adultery is accepted as the norm and incest is thrown in for good measure'.

The bourgeoisie were among the many targets of *Beyond the Fringe*. Given a more political edge since its Edinburgh debut the previous summer, the show went first to Cambridge and then, the week starting 1 May, to the Theatre Royal, Brighton. 'You young bounders don't know anything about it!' shouted one man in the audience at the 'Aftermyth of War' sketch (the RAF officer calling on the unfortunate Perkins to make 'a futile gesture' and be killed) as he ostentatiously got to his feet and stormed off. At the end of the week came the review by F.T.G. in the *Brighton and Hove Herald*, which was studded with phrases like 'absolutely infantile', 'full of smart prattle' and 'ingenuously cocksure', claimed that 'the satire has about as much sting as blanc-mange' and took the moral high ground: not only did it seem 'vaguely indecent for 20-year-olds to be making fun of Battle of Britain pilots' but 'a comic scene in a death cell to me was atrocious'. The London opening was at the Fortune on Wednesday the 10th, producing by contrast almost universally ecstatic reviews, typified by a punch-drunk Bernard Levin in the *Daily Express* calling it 'a revue so brilliant, adult, hard-boiled, accurate, merciless, witty, unexpected, alive, exhilarating, cleansing, right, true and good that my first conscious thought as I stumbled, weak and sick with laughter, up the stairs at the end was one of gratitude'. *The Times* entered a rare note of criticism – 'smacks a little of the Third Programme' – but the headline was admiring: 'Clowning with Distinction: Four Wrote Their Own Sketches'. As enthused as anyone that first night was Anthony Heap, who in his diary notice acclaimed 'this sparkling little revue, which mercilessly satirises the mad world of today and hits all its targets dead centre' – a revue performed by 'just four young men in grey suits, with no more props than a piano, a table, four chairs and a few period hats'. 'Hail to thee, blithe spirits,' ended his paean to Alan Bennett, Peter Cook, Jonathan Miller and Dudley Moore. 'The town is yours!'

Heap also noted that the show had been 'rapturously received' by the audience, but on the second night there was an interesting moment. 'The couple who sat behind me,' recalled Michael Frayn not long afterwards, 'honked happily away until they got to the middle of the Macmillan number [Cook playing him as a Scottish OAP], when the man suddenly turned to his girl-friend and said in an appalled whisper, "I say, this is supposed to be the Prime Minister", after which they sat in silence for the rest of the evening.' Such qualms did not stop the bandwagon rolling, and by the 20th the *Mail* was reporting that 'queues start to ring the theatre at 9.30 every morning'. A week later, the first of the political grandees attended. 'I sat & shook & writhed & shrieked & shouted with amusement for 2 hours,' recorded Lady Violet Bonham Carter. 'The targets were Macmillan, the Church, philosophers, & there were very good musical parodies ... a terribly funny one of some pansies with plucking gestures, dressing in sou'westers to do a terrifically virile hearty T.V. advertisement for something like Lifebouy Soap – & almost the funniest of all, 4 Clubmen meeting at their Club, making hearty gestures & quite inarticulate hearty noises, & finally sitting down together – to no food or drink.' Yet of course, in terms of raw numbers, *Beyond the Fringe* was seen by relatively few people (although an LP was almost instantly recorded), certainly compared to the doyens of the small screen. The start of the run at the Fortune coincided, for instance, with *Here's Harry* on the BBC. 'A great show with plenty of laughs which the whole family can enjoy because it's clean,' enthused a shop manager. 'We all like Harry Worth – what a terror! but so likeable – and so very funny.'[15]

'Just our cup of tea,' similarly found Madge Martin on 12 May after going to the recently released *The Greengage Summer* (Jane Asher as the younger sister). Three days later, Harold Wilson remarked to Labour colleagues that if the party was foolish enough in its next policy document to include a supportive passage about the Wolfenden recommendation to decriminalise homosexual behaviour, it would cost six million votes; while that evening at the Marlowe Theatre in Canterbury, as a huge power outage struck London and the south-east (mercifully just after the end of *Wagon Train*), 'a jazz band began to play "Twilight Time"' and 'teenagers jived in the aisles by candlelight'. Thursday the 18th saw the announcement that new universities were definitely to be built at Canterbury, Colchester and Coventry, in addition to those already being established at Brighton, Norwich and York, while that night the hills were alive at the Victoria Palace – but alive mainly, alas, to the sound not of music but of critics sharpening their pens. 'As sentimental as an Ivor Novello musical romance', 'The most predictable musical I have seen for a long time', 'The less said the better' – and Heap agreed, calling this final effort by Rodgers and Hammerstein 'cloying, meandering and lifeless'. On the 24th, England won a friendly in Italy (the decisive goal scored by Jimmy Greaves, about to move, amidst considerable ill-feeling, to AC Milan); next day, Totnes elected its 602nd Mayor, but only the second woman; the *East London Advertiser* on the 26th ran a story about 21-year-old Terence Stamp ('broad-shouldered, tousle-haired son of a Thames tugman') poised to get his big break on the film of *Billy Budd* ('All dad said to me was, "Don't get big-headed, son"'); and that Friday evening, the start of the ninth radio series of *Meet the Huggetts* (still starring Jack Warner and Kathleen Harrison as Joe and Ethel) was immediately followed on TV by the return of Tony Hancock, in a series simply called *Hancock*, a year after the comedian had controversially dispensed with Sid James. 'Ah yes, it's good-bye to all that black homburg hat and astrakhan collar rubbish,' he told the *Radio Times* about his move from East Cheam to Earl's Court. 'Knowledge and self-advancement are the things . . .' Above all in this first episode, performed solo, as he wrestled unavailingly in his bedsit with Bertrand Russell's *The History of Western Philosophy*. The audience was a massive 14.4 million, but the Reaction Index a relatively modest 64, well below the 80 and 77 averages for the last two series of *Hancock's Half Hour*. 'I think Hancock without James is like tea without milk,' commented an orderly, while according to a security officer's wife, 'he seemed lost all on his own.'[16]

A week later on 2 June, as Lady Violet was complaining on *Any Questions?* that modern elections had turned into 'a kind of scramble for a material hand-out in which victory will almost always go to the highest bidder', Hancock's RI was up to 67, on the back of an episode about 'The Bowmans' that, with Hancock as old Joshua Merryweather, took fairly amiable aim at radio's most popular soap. The following Tuesday evening in Hamburg, the visiting Malcolm Muggeridge 'dropped into a teenage rock-and-roll joint', the Top Ten Club:

> The band were English, from Liverpool, and recognised me. Long-haired; weird feminine faces; bashing their instruments, and emitting nerveless sounds into microphones. In conversation rather touching in a way, their faces like Renaissance carvings of saints or Blessed Virgins. One of them [surely John Lennon?] asked me: 'Is it true that you're a Communist?' No, I said; just in opposition. He nodded understandingly; in opposition himself in a way. 'You make money out of it?' he went on. I admitted that this was so. He, too, made money. He hoped to take back £200 to Liverpool.

'As we sat waiting for the coach to return home,' noted the elderly Gladys Hague two days later about the end of the holiday she and her sister had had in Morecambe, 'we thought about the Duke of Kent's marriage to Katharine Worsley at York Minster.' The press gave it a moment's thought too, with *Daily Mirror* headlines next day including 'THE GAY YOUNG DUCHESS', 'DUKE "ATTACKS" THE ICING', 'YOU'VE SEEN NOTHING LIKE IT' (the bride's dress), 'KATE PAYS HER HOMAGE' (curtseying to the Queen) and 'GOOD LUCK!'. At Buckingham Palace on the 9th, the talented, well-connected osteopath Stephen Ward sketched a portrait of Prince Philip for the *Illustrated London News*, while Annie Courtenay sent her son Tom a sad letter from her lonely home on the outskirts of Hull ('I can't get used to Longhill . . . My head has been bothering me, my nerves aren't very good'). It was still upwards for *Hancock* – that Friday evening an RI of 71 for 'The Radio Ham' – and so too for Billy Fury, whose beat-ballad 'Halfway to Paradise' now entered the Top 10. On Monday the 12th, Tom Courtenay took over from Albert Finney as the star of *Billy Liar* in the West End (finding the speech about the 11-plus and family tensions 'very close to home'); next day, Christopher Isherwood and Don Bachardy visited E. M. Forster in Coventry, where two locals 'bored us nearly pissless talking about the wonders of Coventry and all the new building which is being done'; and on the 15th a distinguished Manchester doctor, Hugh Selbourne, tried to obtain a passport application form: 'Post Office girls told me to go to Withington Town Hall. The latter told me to go to the Ministry of National Insurance Offices in Wilbraham Road, and there they told me to go to their offices in Burton Road, and so on . . .'[17]

Next day, Hugh Gaitskell was in Sheffield officially opening the Park Hill redevelopment scheme – the famed streets in the sky. 'The flats are not the only things to have been built over the years,' insisted the introduction to the *Sheffield Telegraph*'s four-page supplement marking the occasion:

> There is a thriving, pulsing community spirit pervading the whole huge place – it is a spirit that has been evolved, tried and tested through the two years since the first tenants moved in. The spirit is no less – and possibly a good deal more – profound than that which existed among the terraced, begrimed and gloomy industrial revolution houses from whose ruins the mighty edifices of Park Hill rose. The architect's eye for shape, the builder's skill, the children's pleasures, their mother's peace of mind and the old folk's tranquillity have been carefully blended into a rich and telling example of progressive building for the community – with the community itself as one of the materials.

Friday's programme comprised a coach tour in the morning of the Council's new housing developments generally; luncheon at the Town Hall (melon – potted prawns salad – loin of lamb à la Delmonico, spring carrots, new potatoes, garden peas – strawberries and cream – bouchées – coffee – and of course plentiful wines); tour of inspection of the Park Hill scheme; and at 4.00, the official opening, followed by tea in the Tenants' Meeting Hall. 'I would agree that there are dangers in multi-storey development,' accepted Gaitskell in his speech at the opening ceremony.

> Sometimes, I must admit, blocks built up high remind me of nothing but barracks. Those, no doubt, are better than nothing, but not especially pleasant to live in or look at. But may I say how well you in Sheffield have avoided these dangers. You have combined in an extraordinarily successful manner a certain degree of uniformity, which you must have, with a proper degree of variety.

In short, he declared, the city had 'built something of beauty, dignity and harmony'.

That evening, 16 June, was the fourth *Hancock* – 'The Lift', RI of 74 – while next morning Henry St John had a somewhat Hancockian haircut experience ('3s 6d including tip') in Acton. 'For the first time in my experience of this saloon a radio was switched on, broadcasting the light programme. One reason why I do not go to a barber's on the other side of the road has been because they've always had a radio on. As last time, the barber who trimmed my hair lit a cigarette while doing it.' Philip Larkin and Judy Haines by now both had their eyes on the England v Australia Test, due to start at Lord's on Thursday the 22nd. 'Waiting for Benaud ogh ogh' was the former's response on Sunday to the news that Samuel Beckett was due to attend, while the latter on Monday noted that the in-form, fast-scoring Barry Knight (who played for her county, Essex) had been left out of the team. The Test itself coincided with the release of *The Guns of Navarone*, but there was all too little derring-do from the England cricketers. Friday evening brought solace with 'The Blood Donor' – RI of 77, and the imperishable apogee of Hancock's career – while early on the rest day, Sunday the 25th, a 61-year-old unmarried Glaswegian, Catherine McCardle of Maryhill, daubed with black paint the windows of a bookshop displaying *Lady Chatterley's Lover* ('offensive to the citizens of Glasgow', she subsequently told the court). Next day, England lost. 'Should have included Barry Knight,' reflected Haines, while from the ground itself, writing to a friend, the retired Eton schoolmaster George Lyttelton recorded mutterings in the Pavilion: 'The England side is giving no satisfaction – no guts, no concentration, not playing like a side etc etc, you hear all round. Cowdrey [the amateur captain, Colin Cowdrey] apparently melancholic at the wicket.' Beckett was presumably still around to watch that evening a performance of *Waiting for Godot* on BBC television. Fewer than three million tuned in, its RI of 32 was spectacularly low, and viewers 'reacted with feelings of frustration, sometimes expressed with humility – "the whole thing was much too abstract for my taste" – but more often with anger – "a lot of fatuous nonsense" and "I'm no royal courtier praising the Emperor's new clothes"'. On Tuesday, responding to the rise and rise of public relations, Malcolm Muggeridge in *The Times* noted of the PR man that 'his message is fed into the sausage machine of public affairs in the hope that it may reach the public stomach as normal nutriment' and called on him to have to identify himself 'by means of a clapper or bell such as lepers were forced to use in the Middle Ages'; the Queen Mother launched on the Tyne the liner *Northern Star*, declaring that 'the creative genius of our nation flowers as brightly as ever and British craftsmanship and skill cannot be rivalled anywhere in the world'; and on the Home Service the final took place of *Let The Peoples Sing*, the BBC's fifth annual amateur choral contest. 'Fine sunny day,' recorded Dennis Dee on Wednesday the 28th, a heatwave now under way. 'Started to make the hay stack, carried about 30 cocks on my fork, no transport.' And in London, Mr Justice Winn delivered his judgement, finding that the ETU's leadership had indeed been guilty of 'fraudulent and unlawful devices'. 'Not only,' he stated, 'was the Union managed and controlled by the Communist Party, but so run as to suit the ideals of the party.' Altogether the ballot-rigging case had, notes Francis Beckett in his history of the British Communist Party, 'received massive publicity', and it 'damaged the CP just as it was starting to recover from 1956'.[18]

Friday, the very hot last day of June, began with 16-year-old Carol Payne catching the train from Glasgow to London – and being waved off, reported Glasgow's *Evening Citizen*, by Dave 'Screaming Lord' Sutch (described as a £100-a-week singer currently touring Scotland) after Carol's mother had made an overnight dash to Scotland to prevent her marrying him. 'I don't even want to talk to David,' the mother told the paper. 'I don't like anything about him, particularly his long hair and the way he dresses.' The *Citizen*'s main headline, though, was 'THE QUEEN IN GORBALS', as that afternoon, between 3.45 and 4.35, the monarch, as the *Glasgow Herald* put it, 'saw both sides':

> She visited six families in a blackened Victorian tenement in Sandyfoulds Street – a street where a family live in a single end with a bed recess, where there is no hot and cold running water, when they want a bath, they go to the public ones, and when they wash clothes they go to the 'steamies'. But even as she stood on the pavement, she also saw at the corner the tall towers of the first Hutchesontown-Gorbals redevelopment area, the gigantic 20-storey flats that are now nearing completion. Then she drove round the corner in a maroon plastic-topped Rolls-Royce and visited Ballater Street. She climbed to the second floor of a new maisonette block and spoke to three families living in new all-electric houses [ie, dwellings]: the contrast was complete.

The most emblematic moment of the tour – amid 'hoarse cheering, vast, dusty crowds and a million flags' – came as the Queen unveiled a commemorative plaque on 'one of four massive, wedge-shaped blocks which will one day grow into Queen Elizabeth Square, the centre-piece of Sir Basil Spence's "garden" scheme'; on being shown, together with Prince Philip, a model of the redevelopment, they 'asked many questions, and were interested to learn that every family will have a garden at their back door, even at 20-storey level'. That evening, as they prepared to leave Glasgow for Edinburgh, the Queen remarked that she had been overwhelmed by her reception in the Gorbals. 'I told her,' the Lord Provost revealed to the press afterwards, 'she should not be surprised, because they are a wholesome, generous, decent-living lot of people'; the Lord Provost added that the Queen had been 'amazed that four people could live in a small single end' and 'had commented on the amount of improvisation they must have to do'.

A different sort of end was at 8.00 p.m. on BBC television – the final *Hancock*. Called 'The Succession – Son and Heir', the episode had the anti-hero in search of a wife, ended with the words 'So exits the last of the Hancocks – good luck!', and gained an RI of 75, second only in the series to 'The Blood Donor'. 'Take back what I said earlier of Hancock,' reflected one viewer, an inspector. 'He does not now require James as a stooge – he progresses unattached by leaps and bounds.' 'Great fun for young and old alike,' declared another viewer, while a secretary spoke for millions: 'Bring him back – and quick! We shall miss the lad.'[19]

10

We'll All Be Uprooted

Summer 1961: ten years after the Festival of Britain and officially sanctioned modernity. That modernity – no longer 'soft', instead 'hard' – now unstoppable. Streets in the sky in Sheffield, London's Euston Arch and Coal Exchange poised to go, farewell the Victorian barracks of Aldershot, Birmingham's Inner Ring Road laying waste to all before it, T. Dan Smith ready to turn Newcastle into the Venice of the North (but ring roads, not canals), the firing gun started for Blackburn's comprehensive redevelopment, plans afoot for Glasgow's brutalist Red Road blocks (six point-blocks, two slab-blocks) to be the highest dwellings in Europe, the heart being ripped out of Bradford, slums being cleared that needed to be cleared, slums being cleared where there could have been renovation and human continuity, communities torn asunder, high-rise everywhere, old people trapped, mothers and small children trapped, an urban world of compulsory purchase and developers' boom time, of good intentions compromised by hubris, by greed, by the lure of size for size's sake, John Betjeman almost a lone voice of protest, most people shrugging their shoulders and mutely accepting destruction as the inevitable price of progress, you don't know what you've got . . . Summer 1961: a shake of the dice – and landing, who knew where?

That is the shorthand version. A fuller gazetteer of the seemingly ever-accelerating change to Britain's built environment, between roughly late 1960 and the summer of 1962, goes something like this:

In **Aldershot** work started on the new barracks for the Army School of Physical Training.

'SHOPWRECK' was a headline for 'the modernisation of the **Barnsley** Co-op', as a handsome piece of Victorian curtain walling was given the heave-ho.

In **Basingstoke** the Town Hall's clock tower was removed, the Alton Light Railway bridge was demolished, and the signing in October 1961 of the Town Development Scheme belatedly alerted locals to the utter change that lay ahead to the town's character.

Georgian **Bath** remained inviolable, but the closure of the Turkish baths ('Victorian, and retain much of their Victoriana,' observed Tom Stoppard) prompted a lament from Edward Hunt, who had run them since 1910: 'Of course they are a bit out of date. People like chromium and mirrors nowadays and they won't see much of that here.'

A massive rehousing programme was under way in **Birkenhead**, including three 14-storey blocks of flats on the Woodchurch estate and two 11-storey blocks on Sidney Road, Rock Ferry – all building done by George Wimpey & Co, all heating and hot water supplied by the North Western Gas Board. 'When you install Gas warm air central heating in your home, you *automatically* say goodbye to a whole lot of worry and drudgery,' promised an accompanying ad in the *Liverpool Echo*. 'There is no soot, smoke or dirt (and therefore no more money to be spent on chimney sweeps and having your upholstery and other furnishings cleaned after the sweep has been!). There are no fuel delivery or storage problems. No grates to be cleaned. And no heavy hods to be humped. Gas warm air central heating *frees* you from all these tiresome tasks – saves money into the bargain!'[1]

'Building Fever in **Birmingham**' proclaimed the *Financial Times* in May 1961 about the bold, can-do second city. 'Already the city centre is dominated by new buildings, and by the tower cranes helping to erect the still bigger ones in project; in another decade, when the plan nears completion, there will be scarcely a trace left of the nineteenth-century industrial complex which still thrives there.' All this development of the city centre was happening within the still-under-construction Inner Ring Road – 'the most drastically thorough example of traffic engineering yet seen on this scale in Britain' – and the correspondent noted how the process had already produced 'a tightly compressed mass of enormous buildings in which the ordinary pedestrian citizen may well feel lost'. The juggernaut's progress inevitably involved continuous demolition work (that autumn, for example, around Masshouse Circus, in Suffolk Street and around Holloway Head), while across the city as a whole the car was now unambiguous king, with the council already agreeing in April 1961 to accelerate the road programme. March 1962 saw the much-publicised opening of the Perry Bar underpass on the busy, greatly widened Birmingham-to-Walsall road, prompting a local paper to note soon afterwards that 'little by little, Perry Bar is adjusting itself to the modern monster in its heart.' In the centre itself, of course, the emblematic feature would soon be the multi-level Bull Ring shopping and commercial centre, on which work by John Laing and Son started in May 1961. The architect, heavily influenced by American shopping centres, was Sydney Greenwood. 'People must not be allowed to take short cuts,' he told the *Architects' Journal*. 'The concourses they use cannot be more than 30 ft. wide and must have shops on both sides.' Nor was that all: the magazine noted that the Bull Ring's arcades would have 'the additional attraction of subdued lighting and piped music, which is expected to relax walkers down to a profitable pace of 1½ mph.' Birmingham's great emerging architect, though, was not Greenwood but John Madin, who in 1961 designed what became the eye-catching Birmingham Post and Mail building (podium plus 17 storeys) in Colmore Circus, according to Pevsner the 'finest commercial building of its time'.[2]

'The Mill Town Goes Modern', announced a May 1961 headline. That town was **Blackburn**, whose council had just approved an ambitious master plan, in liaison with Laings, for developing the centre: at its heart, replacing the old market (including a wonderful clock tower) and many buildings around it with a large, bang-up-to-date complex of shops, offices and flats, segregating pedestrians from traffic and providing generous car-parking facilities. 'INTO THE SPACE AND SPACIOUS AGE' declared the *Blackburn Times*. And it claimed that whereas 'other towns have embarked upon piecemeal schemes, nothing like Blackburn's complete reconstruction of a whole central area has ever been undertaken'.

Bradford's planners might have disputed that assertion and anyway were much further down the redevelopment road. 'Almost the whole of the original four-stage plan is now nearing completion, and the line of the new boulevard, Petergate, can be seen clearly to the right,' noted the local *Telegraph & Argus* in February 1962 in relation to a front-page aerial photo of the city's new centre. 'Towards the lower left can be seen the site of the newest development, the demolition of shops around the Ritz cinema, which will soon be enclosed by new buildings. Just above is Swan Arcade, which is soon to be demolished and the block rebuilt in keeping with the other developments.' A month later, and the headline was '"NEW LOOK" PLAN FOR FORSTER SQ.', as the paper reported a big new development (a five-storey block of shops and offices slap in front of the station) agreed between the Public Works Committee and the developers Hammerson. That same day, photos showed the ornate Swan Arcade – beloved by J. B. Priestley – in the process of being demolished. 'Looking down on the inside, the skeletons of the old offices [before they became shops] can be clearly seen,' explained the caption. 'The handsome gates are at the Charles Street entrance, and the third picture shows one of the colonnades now roofless.'[3]

In **Brighton**, note the historians of high-rise Miles Glendinning and Stefan Muthesius, 'the powerful Conservative administration of Councillor S.W. Theobald, "the King of Brighton", came under sudden pressure in 1961–2 to increase output to cope with the problems caused by the 1957 Act's decontrol of privately rented housing.' Accordingly, he responded by unleashing 'a multi-storey crash drive'.

Bristol was maintaining what Timothy Mowl has called its 'largely dreadful post-war planning record'. Accordingly, 'in 1961 the arcade of a Norman town-house on Small Street, 900 years old, was pulled down to widen a court room, and in 1962 the fifteenth-century St Augustine-the-Less was demolished to make way for a hotel extension.' Meanwhile, 'the hanging gardens and ramshackle Georgian villas of Kingsdown', looking down on the city centre, were being 'smashed to make room for three fourteen-storey slabs housing only slightly more families than had lived there before in poetic chaos'.

In Car City – Change City – the old continued to perish. Some 120 of **Coventry**'s timber houses had survived the German bombing; by 1958 100 remained. 'Two-thirds of these,' laments Gavin Stamp, 'would disappear over the next few years as Arthur Ling, City Architect and Planning Officer, pushed forward the construction of the Ring Road and of new buildings like the Lanchester College of Technology. In

August 1961, as piles of old timbers from demolished houses in Little Park Street were burning, the *Coventry Standard* ran the front-page headline, "Demolition Recalls the Days of the Blitz".' The city that same year launched its first comprehensive development plan, for what the Corporation called the 'worn out' Hillfields area near the centre. The vision was largely high-rise, and the official description of the scheme conceded that it was 'considered economically impossible to re-locate all the existing shops' in the new Hillfields – 'a sad comment,' noted the *Guardian*, 'for an area where the little shop abounds.' Sad too was the 'sterile megaliths' reality of the 1961 scheme. 'Hillfields consists of a series of ten and seventeen-storey blocks of flats ranged in echelon and of identical design,' observed a 1969 architectural guide to Coventry. 'No attempt at human scaling appears to have been made, and the bulldozer has been given free rein among the terraces.'[4]

'In an attempt to persuade local people to do their shopping in **Dalkeith**, Midlothian, instead of nearby Edinburgh, Dalkeith's town centre is to be given a £200,000 face-lift' was how an architectural magazine recorded in March 1961 what could hardly have been a more representative example of urban renewal. 'The scheme envisages a wider High Street and the provision, in three blocks, of 20 new shops, 33 maisonettes, extensive office accommodation and a tree-lined pedestrian way.'

Dundee, under the sway of some powerful local Labour politicians, was poised to move big-time into high-rise living. By early 1962, a model was on display of four 23-storey blocks for the slum area of Maxwelltown; large-scale clearance was under way in the Hilltown area, where the Butterburn and Bucklemaker flats would become Dundee's highest; while to the north-west of the city, in Ardler, the golf club was being moved out and prefabs were being demolished, prior to the construction of what Glendinning and Muthesius call 'six mighty 17-storey slab blocks'.

'**Edinburgh** had been fairly cautious immediately after the war, but from the late 1950s plunged into peripheral development, area renewal, slum clearance and high-density building,' notes the Scottish housing historian Tom Begg about trends that were intensifying by the early 1960s. Little noticed by the media at the time, large new council schemes began to take shape on the city's southern edge, including at Oxgangs (three tower blocks built in 1961, demolished in 2005/6) and at Gracemount (three tower blocks built in 1962, demolished in 2009).

Soon to turn Fife into a dormitory for Edinburgh and invariably billed as 'the largest Scottish engineering project of the century', the **Forth Road Bridge** was by 1961 roughly halfway to completion. 'All around me, the landscape I'd grown up with was disappearing,' recalls Ian Jack, who lived in a nearby village, North Queensferry. 'Change was in full roar. Cuttings wide enough to fit four carriageways were driven through rock as earth-movers shaped embankments of fresh brown earth. Two 500-foot towers rose above the firth, soon to have steel cables suspended from them, spun on site from 30,000 miles of wire.'[5]

The story in **Glasgow** at this stage was partly about slum clearance (one issue alone of the *Glasgow Herald* in September 1960 had included four closely printed pages announcing the compulsory purchase in the Gorbals of over 60 tenements and many more individual properties), but above all about a great step-change in relation to high-rise starting to take effect – a step-change that went way beyond the well-publicised Hutchestown-Gorbals developments under the marque architects Basil Spence and Robert Matthew. A signal moment occurred in August 1961, some six weeks after the Queen's visit to the city, when at the opening ceremony for the three Wimpey-built 20-storey blocks at Royston (briefly the tallest blocks in Scotland), the Housing Convener, the impassioned David Gibson, 'said that, even allowing for overspill, Glasgow would have to build 500 of these multi-storey blocks in the next 20 years to help solve the housing problem'. Indeed, some important green lights had already been given. In February 1961 the Corporation's Housing Committee approved the building on the site of the condemned Maryhill Barracks of 12 high-rise blocks of flats, including five 26-storey point-blocks; two months later, the HC approved the plans for four 23-storey blocks in Sandyhills Road; and, that same April day, it gave the go-ahead to a mammoth scheme (some 16 25-storey blocks of flats) in the Sighthill area – a distinctly unpropitious 67-acre site known locally as 'the soda waste', having been used until about 1900 as a dump for chemical waste and subsequently, noted the *Glasgow Herald*, 'an eyesore for many years with stagnant ponds and derelict buildings'. The pace did not abate after Gibson's Royston pronouncement. In November 1961 the HC approved plans for five 18-storey tower blocks to 'rise up from the wooded hillside' at Broomhill, where five 'large old private houses' had recently been demolished; in early 1962, four or more blocks of at least 20 storeys were promised for the Townhead comprehensive development area, with the slum clearance involving 'a big loss of population'; that spring, Gibson gained approval for a major high-rise development at Toryglen North, on a site immediately next to railway sidings, clay workings and a refuse destructor. In terms of 1962 as a whole, almost gleefully note Glendinning and Muthesius about Gibson's relentless drive to turn the city into the European capital of high-rise, 'out of a UK cumulative total at that date of sixty-five blocks of 20 or more storeys, complete or under commencement, thirty-nine blocks were located in Glasgow!' The most emblematic scheme of all – even more so than Spence's development in the Gorbals – was also now starting to take shape, albeit not yet physically. The precise chronology is uncertain, but during the course of 1961–2 the way became clear for the Red Road scheme in the Balornock area: eight blocks, of up to 31 storeys each, that would be the tallest in Europe and, for half a century, the embodiment of a dream and what became of that dream.[6]

Jarrow from 1961 boasted a shopping centre – and what was more, the first Arndale Centre, although in this case called the Viking Precinct and open-air rather than a covered mall. The two men behind the Arndale Property Trust were both Yorkshiremen, Arnold Hagenbach and Sam Chippindale, who seven years earlier had acquired Bradford's Swan Arcade and would of course proceed to demolition once the leases expired. 'By the way,' explained Chippindale to an architectural magazine, 'we provide car parking in all our schemes, though the Jarrow people were amused at our providing a car park at all.'

The Empire Palace in **Leeds** bowed out in January 1961 with *Babes in the Wood* starring Nat Jackley and Ian Wallace. Demolition followed in 1962, with the site becoming the Empire Arcade and (eventually) Harvey Nichols.

Traditionally a reluctant moderniser, **Leicester** was getting into the swing of things by the early 1960s. Tesco's mammoth new store, on its opening in 1961 reputedly the largest of its type in Europe, was situated alongside a 36-lane bowling alley on the ground floor of Lee Circle, a six-tier concrete car park; at the university, the revolutionary Engineering Building, as designed by the young architects James Stirling and James Gowan, was starting to be erected ('That's a nice little toy that you've had made for yourself here, Jim,' said a friend of Stirling on first seeing it); and by the summer of 1962, the forceful Conservative local politician Kenneth Bowder, ambitious to transform Leicester along Coventrian lines, had recruited its first City Planning Officer, Konrad Smigielski, an ebullient Pole whose motto was that 'the only solution is complete clearance and redevelopment.'

Liverpool's commitment to high-rise living, already apparent for several years, intensified. In December 1960 the Housing Committee gave its endorsement to multi-storey development on the south side of the city; a year later it signalled the go-ahead for a 22-storey block in the cleared Harding Street area of Upper Parliament Street, prompting the headline 'The highest homes in Britain for Liverpool'; and in June 1962 a party of councillors, anxious to speed up completions, went to France to look at high-rise building systems there. The shabby, as yet barely touched city centre, meanwhile, was being closely scrutinised by the innovative London-based architect-planner Graeme Shankland, appointed in December 1961 as Liverpool's planning consultant. Only three months later, he and his team produced their first report. It was, according to the *Liverpool Daily Post*, a vision of 'pavements twenty feet above the road, special streets for buses and delivery vehicles only, shops with doors on the roof, car parks within easy reach of all strategic centres' – in short, a vision of Liverpool as 'Britain's first space-age city'.[7]

'New Flats Will Soar 300 ft Up' (in Latimer Road, near the Hammersmith/Kensington boundary), 'Flats of Thirteen Storeys' (on either side of Lewisham Road), '22-Storey Block On New Estate' (in Portland Grove, Lambeth) – those were typical **London** headlines in 1961–2. Or take East London. 'Jodrell Road with its two-storeyed little terrace cottages will be completely changed when the London County Council's new redevelopment scheme is carried out,' reported the *East London Advertiser* in February 1961 about the two 20-storey blocks shortly to tower over Victoria Park. While seven months later, Canning Town was 'rapidly getting a new look', not only with 'the giant Rathbone Street development scheme at last under way and work on the Adamson Road project nearing completion' but also with news that 'three giant, 15-storey skyscraper blocks are to go up on two island sites on either side of Fife Road near the junction with Beckton Road.' In terms of non-residential across the capital, a quartet of tall, landmark buildings was being completed or approaching completion – the Hilton Hotel, Millbank Tower (originally known as the Vickers Building), New Zealand House and the Shell Building – while one for the mid-1960s was Eric Bedford's 500-foot Post Office Tower, construction starting in the summer of 1961. Among office blocks, two emerging clusters stood out: those on London Wall (two completed by the spring of 1962, two well on the way, two in the pipeline) and those starting to mushroom in Croydon, including the unfortunate effort for General Accident – designed, thought Pevsner, 'so that the whole thing looks rather like folded paper . . . one feels like stretching the shape straight or squashing it'. An area by now on the cusp of root-and-branch change was the Elephant and Castle. The trio of Ernö Goldfinger towers that comprised Alexander Fleming House were on the verge of completion, work was about to start on a 25-storey LCC block of flats, and work had already begun on the much-trumpeted shopping centre (with the Elephant and Castle pub to be rebuilt at sunken-court level, 8 feet below the pavement and adjoining a pedestrian underpass). The most striking herald of modernity was Rodney Gordon's Michael Faraday Memorial – an electrical generator for the Tube, planted in 1961 in the middle of one of the Elephant's two new mega-roundabouts and consisting (in the words of Michael Collins, brought up locally) of 'an 80-foot-wide silver cube made up of 728 stainless-steel panels and rising 20 feet above pavement level'. Anthony Heap witnessed the changing urban scene with a keen eye. 'A number of main thoroughfares like Tottenham Court Road, Shaftesbury Avenue (part), Haymarket & Piccadilly have been turned into one-way streets,' he recorded in August 1961. 'As for Marble Arch and Hyde Park Corner, it is becoming hard to recognise them, so drastically have they been transformed.' Mollie Panter-Downes had already noted 'the scooping out of a large underpass beneath Hyde Park Corner'; in the event the twin tunnels opened for traffic in April 1962. To the west, Henry St John was also visually alert. 'The Hammersmith flyover has made progress since I last saw it,' he observed in February 1961. 'Part of it seems to be based on a central concrete spine, with concrete ribs on either side to support the roadway.' Nine months later, the traffic was flowing and the *Architects' Journal* was praising 'an exciting and elegant structure'. But it also asked a question: 'Why footpaths? A pedestrian was mown down within half an hour of opening.' The motor cars' increasingly irresistible heft was displayed piquantly in the City. There, not long after the coming to Upper Thames Street of a steel-frame mechanised 'Zidpark' (one of London's first multi-storey car parks), the implacable requirement to widen Lower Thames Street finally (in the spring of 1962) spelled doom for the magnificent Coal Exchange, with demolition completed later that year. That would become a cause célèbre of vandalism, resonating down the years, but even more so was the sad story of the Euston Arch. 'By a ridiculous contrast with all this ultra-modern horror,' recorded Harold Macmillan on 24 October 1961 (as he considered among much else the implications of Russia having just exploded a 30-megaton bomb), 'I turned for ¾ hour to considering the fate of the doric Arch at Euston. The President of the Academy led a deputation of architects, artists, critics, & noblemen who all said this was a splendid – indeed a wonderful – work of art. It must not be lost, whatever the cost.' The scaffolding was already up; Macmillan (who according to one of the deputation sat listening with his eyes shut and asking no questions) promised nothing; a week later he gave his formal, wholly negative response; and within months the Euston Arch was no more. Half of the stones were dumped in a tributary of the River Lea, while the demolition contractor, Frank Valori, subsequently incorporated part of the arch into the stonework of the house which he had built for himself in Bromley.[8]

Construction began of the **M4** and **M5**. 'Due to open shortly,' noted the *Architects' Journal* in the summer of 1962 about the latter's first section, 'it will bring Ross-on-Wye to within an hour's run of the outskirts of Birmingham . . .'

The centre of modern **Manchester** continued to take shape during the early 1960s – the CIS tower (Europe's tallest office block on completion in 1962), the brash, sadly incoherent Piccadilly Plaza (not complete until 1965), M&S's biggest store in Lancashire – while outside the centre, the shift to high-rise was now becoming decisive. At the heart of the systematic new approach was the badly rundown district of

Hulme, specifically its St George's clearance area, where by early 1961 it was planned to build Manchester's first 16-storey block of flats, along with four 13-storey blocks. On top of the 16-storey block was to be a 'crow's nest' – or, as a housing department official explained, 'We thought it would be a good idea to give tenants, and their visitors, a chance to get a first-class panoramic view of the city and its surroundings.' Work started in July 1961, the topping-out ceremony took place that December, and the target date for completion was the spring of 1963. But by then, plans had already been announced (in March 1962) for a 20-storey block as part of the redevelopment of Hulme's Rutland Street area, where, altogether, 612 houses were to be cleared, with 362 new dwellings (including high-rise flats) built in their place – a fairly typical ratio.

'Slums are being torn down, crowded streets are disappearing, and in their place grow clean-cut modern flats' was how **Newcastle**'s evening paper described in October 1961 the rapidly transforming Scotswood Road Redevelopment Area. There was plenty else going on in T. Dan Smith's city. Basil Spence's eight-storey tower-and-podium Physics Building replaced the corporation tram depot; 'the area around the All Saints church,' recalled Terry Farrell about what happened 'immediately' after he left Newcastle for London in 1961, 'became the victim of an appalling piece of road planning', as 'a huge roundabout and three new office buildings [called Cuthbert, Bede and Aidan as a guilty nod to the church] were plonked there'; and, above all, Smith's right-hand man Wilfred Burns, the recently recruited City Planning Officer, unveiled in April 1961 his *Plan for the Centre of Newcastle*. 'IT'S THE MOTORWAY CITY' declared the *Evening Chronicle*, explaining how Burns envisaged a 'Central Motorway System' to 'completely surround the city centre', as well as 'skyscraper office blocks' and pedestrian shopping precincts. 'Because of the age of the City Centre,' pronounced Burns, 'a large-scale effort has now to be made in respect of redevelopment, and the process will be one of central area revolution rather than evolution.' Much flowed from this plan, perhaps not least the decision in 1962 to abandon Newcastle's trolley-bus system, one of the finest in the country.[9]

'A thing of great beauty' across 'a large open dank hummocky field': so in late 1960 the veteran town planner Thomas Sharp justified, to a public inquiry into **Oxford**'s severe traffic problems, his plan for a relief road across Christ Church Meadow. Much conflicting evidence was given, before eventually (in May 1961) the inquiry's chairman, Sir Frederick Armer, recommended in his report to government that such a road was 'inescapable'. The following year the minister, Charles Hill, upheld the report, and the landscape architect Geoffrey Jellicoe was commissioned to show how Sharp's vision could become reality.

Plymouth's most prominent new building was the multi-storey Civic Centre – well-appointed home from 1962 of the city council, with a water garden and rooftop restaurant as features, the whole effect curiously reminiscent of the UN headquarters in New York – while plans were under way for four tall blocks (one of 20 storeys, three of 17) on The Hoe, 'only a stone's throw from where Drake played bowls'.

The completion of Plymouth's Civic Centre roughly coincided with the demolition of **Preston**'s Town Hall, a magnificent 1860s Gothic Revival building that had been badly fire-damaged in 1947 but was still restorable. Elsewhere, in the Avenham district, slum clearance and redevelopment produced a notable housing scheme by Stirling and Gowan far removed from high-rise slab-blockery. 'We have tried here to maintain the vital spirit ("Saturday Night and Sunday Morning") of the alley, yard, and street houses that the new development is replacing, and from which its occupiers have recently moved,' the architects wrote in June 1961, not long before completion of 62 'working-class homes' situated in a maximum of four storeys. 'Whilst incorporating the essential improvements in space, light and convenience,' they added, 'we hope to perpetuate a familiar and vital environment.'

Ecclesiastical architecture had generally (apart from the odd high-profile exception) resisted twentieth-century modernism, which gave a particular impact to St George's Anglican Church in **Rugby**, consecrated in 1962. The architect (commissioned by a consciously progressive vicar) was Denys Hinton, whose obituarist describes 'a configuration of brick and glass boxes . . . a series of horizontal spaces set at oblique angles' – and 'a font visible through the glass so that baptisms could be opened out and bathed in light'.[10]

'FORWARD TO THE CITY CENTRE BEAUTIFUL' was the bold headline in November 1961 of **Salford**'s weekly paper. That spring the city council had appointed the eminent architect Sir Robert Matthew to act as consultant to the Ellor Street/Broad Street comprehensive redevelopment scheme, so far making only destructive progress in transforming that 89-acre 'twilight' area in the centre of Salford. Now, Matthew's partner, the reliably visionary Percy Johnson-Marshall, had shown councillors a model of the new area and explained the key principles. 'Complete separation of pedestrians and traffic' plus 'provision of the maximum of open space' plus 'making the shopping centre an area of "bright lights", alive by day and night, with three tower blocks of maisonettes actually over the shops' plus 'getting a community feeling into the new residential development, even to the extent of providing the odd corner shop' – all these things, relayed the *Salford City Reporter*, made the planners 'confident that the new city centre will maintain Salford's individuality and dignity; that its housing and amenities will provide a warm and friendly neighbourhood unit; that its shops will attract people from all over the region, including Manchester'. Four months later, building work at last began on the first three blocks of flats, 16 storeys each, in the redevelopment area. Significantly, and adding a distinct tinge of bitterness to the occasion, it was (noted the paper) 'almost three years to the day since the Corporation started to move people out of the notorious "Hanky Park" slums' – a delay that led one councillor to reflect publicly how 'this desert of demolition' had been 'draining Salford's very life-blood'.

Across the Pennines, **Sheffield** was not just about Park Hill and electric milk-trolleys on wide decks. By 1962 three other ambitious housing schemes, all started by the Corporation in the mid-1950s, were complete or approaching completion: Greenhill, a garden city-style layout near the Derbyshire boundary but with three 13-storey point-blocks; Gleadless, mixed development in a woodland valley, but with another three 13-storey blocks crowning the hilltop; and Netherthorpe, in the valley near the city centre, with nine tower blocks and a further two under construction, as the process of slum clearance continued. There was also the small matter, literally looming on the horizon, of Park Hill II, also known as Hyde Park. This was the scheme for four monumental high-rise blocks of flats at the top of the hill immediately behind and above the now completed streets-in-the-sky Park Hill I – a scheme on which building work began at the start of 1962. 'To place buildings of this kind on such a dominant site will radically affect the visual aspect of the city,' claimed – or warned – the City Architect, Lewis Womersley, in advance. 'It is, therefore, considered essential to ensure that as far as possible the finished result will be worthy of the exceptional prominence which this scheme will have.'[11]

Down on the south coast, the first two of Basil Spence's buildings for the new University of **Sussex** were moving towards completion. That architect seldom came cheap – 'If only we could have looked after the Spences,' recalled a member of the University Grants Committee, 'the pounds would have taken care of themselves' – but there anyway he offered something distinctive and in tune with the venture. 'Concrete barrel-vaults and sensuous brickwork demonstrate the influence of Le Corbusier's Maisons Jaoul,' notes Brian Edwards. 'The choice of materials, the colour of the finishes and the relationship between buildings and landscape evoke the sense of a new university which is both traditional and progressive.' At a press conference in March 1962, Spence's assistant remarked that the inspiration for Falmer House and the School of Physics was the Colosseum – 'not as it was but as it is now'.

As dramatic a lurch to high-rise as anywhere took place in **Swansea**. By 1960 almost 8,000 new dwellings had been built since the war, entirely small houses and low-rise flats. Under a dynamic Housing Chairman, Councillor T. S. Harris, the local authority then changed direction completely, in 1961 alone commissioning 13 tower blocks.

'Massive scheme for **Wellingborough**' announced the local paper in November 1961. At its core was a new shopping centre in the heart of the town; three months later the *Wellingborough News* published an artist's impression of what it would look like when 'the existing buildings have been knocked down, the market stalls pushed over to the White Horse Yard car park, the traffic rerouted to the roof-tops, paving stones replaced by tarmac and a row of kiosk shops erected in the Market Place'.[12]

How and why was all this happening? What were the main forces at work? What was the debate? Was it ultimately a case of an irresistible zeitgeist?

At the level of national politics, it is fair to say that while there existed a broad consensus around the slum-clearance/high-rise/urban-redevelopment orthodoxy, there was at this stage somewhat less zeal and a touch more scepticism on the Conservative side. 'The nineteenth century brought this country great good and great wealth, but some of its mistakes are with us yet,' reflected Henry Brooke in his New Year message for 1961 as Minister of Housing and Local Government. 'They were the mistakes of men who thought they saw opportunities and used them badly. Do not let us – perhaps through carelessness, perhaps through conceit – make new mistakes now which the twenty-first century will curse us for.' The minister also had an awareness of the complexities – including human sensitivities – of the process. 'I know there is a keen desire to see the out-of-date inner areas of the city redeveloped,' Brooke told the Liverpool authorities later that year. 'But there will be no chance to do that properly until the slums can be cleared. All this needs popular support, based on good information and explanation.'

Indeed, slum-clearance rates, of around 60,000 houses a year being demolished or closed, were running by the early 1960s significantly behind the original mid-1950s targets – so much so that it was estimated that at the current rate it would take Liverpool another 94 years to clear its slums, Manchester another 46, Oldham another 41, Dundee another 36 and Birmingham another 33. All of those, and other Victorian industrial cities, tended to be Labour-run, and for that and other visceral reasons it was unsurprising that in this whole policy area the real passion usually came from Labour. 'It's a damned good job these houses are coming down,' Bermondsey's no-nonsense MP, Bob Mellish, told the press in May 1961 in the context of Princess Margaret's husband, John Betjeman and others seeking to prevent a riverside row of charming if dilapidated houses in Rotherhithe being demolished, to be replaced by a park and promenade. 'People come along trying to stop progress,' added Mellish, 'just because they like the look of a few old buildings. Mr Armstrong-Jones should try living there and see if it changes his attitude. The park is what the local people and the children want.' It was Labour that year that pushed unsuccessfully for new housing legislation to include a more generous subsidy for high flats, while in April (coinciding with Yuri Gagarin's exploits) the local MP, Edward Short, did not hold back when he spoke at the opening of three multi-storey blocks at Shieldfield, Newcastle: 'This surely is the dawn of a new epoch in the forward march of mankind, and it is perhaps appropriate and symbolic that these great, towering blocks of homes should be opened in the first few days of the space age.' Councillor T. Dan Smith, added Short, 'will surely rank with Dobson and Grainger as builders of the city', while the blocks themselves he hailed as 'almost the first fruits of Newcastle's great, new dynamic drive against squalor and degrading housing conditions'. A slightly more qualified perspective came from Short's leader. 'Mr Gaitskell agreed with Coun. Wright [chairman of the local Housing Committee] that a new kind of communal living was being developed, slowly but surely, in the multi-storey flats which were springing up in the industrial cities,' reported Salford's local paper in February 1962 about Hugh Gaitskell officially opening the Lower Kersal estate. 'The older people were bound to find it hard to adapt themselves from the life of the crowded cottages, but the younger generation already have no doubts at all – to them the flats were "smashing".'

That adjective of endorsement had come directly from 'the crowds of children who gave him an uproarious welcome', but of course for very young children – and their mothers – it might have been a different story. Here, it was Labour and not their opponents who were surely on the side of the angels: in May 1961, an Opposition attempt to compel authorities to provide adequate play facilities for pre-school children living in high-rise blocks foundered in the face of government resistance. Tellingly, the Commons debate does not seem to have been attended by Margaret Thatcher, the Conservative member of the steering committee that had overseen the background report into the problem of *Two to Five in High Flats*. But it is claimed that soon afterwards she was the author of an anonymous article in *The Times*, arguing that the problem would soon disappear if only mothers showed greater initiative and took their children out more.[13]

In a day-to-day sense, the local politicians probably mattered more. January 1961 saw two contrasting episodes. On the 19th an official luncheon in the tenants' meeting hall at Park Hill marked the completion of that scheme's first stage – ie, prior to the Hyde Park stage. Amid a perhaps understandable torrent of self-congratulation, Councillor Roy Hattersley, 29-year-old chairman of the Public Works Committee, 'said they have all in some way taken part in the building of the most ambitious and most comprehensive housing scheme in Europe', while the council's leader, Alderman C. W. Gascoigne, claimed that 'a squalid area has been transformed into an area where human beings can live in dignity.' Exactly a week later, a conference staged by the Society of Housing Managers at Church House, Westminster, heard the sociologist Edmund Cooney summarise his East London research about the effects of different kinds of housing, including the often negative effects of high-rise. Among those listening was Councillor W. W. Griffin, who, during the discussion, after noting how 'we in Bootle have done a tremendous amount of slum clearance', went on:

> When you tackle slum clearance in a place like Bootle you are dealing with 45 to 60 houses to the acre; and I mean houses, not people. When you re-build, if you are building houses, it is very, very difficult to get more than 24 to the acre. You can have your garden with the roses, but nobody looks after them. So therefore the large towns and cities must go into the air. People can live in the air if you make it suitable for them to live there. We have just built an estate with two eleven-storey blocks . . . What complaints have we had? Take this down, Mr Cooney. We have had no complaints . . .
>
> Mr Cooney, could I take the dockside industry out of Bootle to some place where I could put all the people in houses? Could I take 15,000 workers and put them on the outside? Oh, Mr Cooney, if only you were a member of our Housing Committee. I did not come here to make anybody laugh but to talk about a serious housing problem . . .

'We have to think of the appalling conditions that some of the young married people are living in, with one and sometimes two children in one room,' added Griffin. 'Look at that problem, Mr Cooney, if you are an economist. Study that problem. It is not only so in Bootle but in the whole country.'

Undoubtedly it was the pressure to do something substantive about dismal housing conditions, allied to housing shortages, that drove many local politicians. A 1960 survey published in March 1962 by members of the Ministry of Housing found that, across England and Wales, 'the problem of obsolescent housing extends well beyond the 850,000 dwellings recorded as unfit' – this despite the fact that during the 1950s well over two million new dwellings had been added to the national housing stock and almost 300,000 old houses demolished. Or take some specific places. 'I have been on the LCC housing list for ten years,' J. Cadden in Stepney wrote to the *East London Advertiser* just before Christmas 1960. 'I have a two-roomed flat, my wife and I sleeping in the living room, and my six children, including a boy aged 13 and a girl 15, share a bed in the bedroom.' In Birmingham by 1961, 15 per cent of households were still without exclusive use of a WC and 32 per cent without exclusive use of a fixed bath, while a survey that year of lodging houses revealed what the historians of the city have called 'some appalling conditions'. As for Manchester, nearly one-fifth of households were without the use of a hot-water tap, and a councillor, Bill Egerton, would recall how 'you were being pressurized by people who were living in crummy conditions, in houses they wanted to get out of' – and 'of course to get the maximum usage of any particular site, if you go up you get more personnel in per acre.' Such were exactly the pressures on David Gibson in Glasgow. 'Homes are what the people want,' a slum-dweller in the Whiteinch district implored him at the start of a new year. 'Let us see action in 1962 for God's sake and let mothers have peace of mind with a decent home. There would be less deaths and murders and mental patients.'[14]

There were other motives in play. 'Our future as a city stands or falls by Ellor Street, which will add 2,800 families to our population, revitalise our trade, and give our rateable value its first boost since the war,' declared a Salford councillor in March 1962 about the major redevelopment project there. Civic pride mattered. The 1961 edition of Salford's official handbook described it as 'one of the most exciting and forward-moving cities in the Britain of today', called the Lower Kersal estate 'an acknowledged triumph', and declared that 'under a vigorous and courageous City Council' there would be 'no faltering on the road to the creation of an ideal city'. In Sheffield, meanwhile, the Corporation's April 1962 publication, *Ten Years of Housing in Sheffield*, appeared in French and Russian as well as English, and claimed that 'the careful exploitation' of the city's topography was 'gradually producing something of the fascination of the Italian hill towns'.

Ultimately, nothing mattered more than being modern, being

up-to-date – and being seen to be so. 'They have been built for 70 years and Peel Park is now behind the times,' insisted Salford's Councillor S. Davies in March 1961 about the impending demolition of Peel Park College, the library and the art gallery, in order to make way for a Mechanical Engineering block at the new College of Advanced Technology. 'Perhaps there is a little nostalgia,' he conceded, 'but we cannot afford to have ancient monuments in Salford.' Was there also an element of being blinded by science? Possibly sometimes. 'Members were fascinated by a model of the new area which was on view,' noted the *Salford City Reporter* later in 1961 about the Planning and Development Committee having Percy Johnson-Marshall unfold his vision to them – a vision 'displaying a symmetry and sense of unity which suggested that a master mind was very much in charge of the master plan'.

Much of the process was broadly bipartisan, but even in T. Dan Smith's Newcastle there could be a degree of dissent. 'The plans for Scotswood Road are first-class – it will be a great thing for the people who live there,' freely admitted Councillor Wright for the Conservatives in November 1961. But at the same time, he called on Smith to be more open to criticism and to reflect on the need for 'a little more variety in new blocks of flats and new houses that we build', lest the city become 'soulless and lack character'. A colleague, Councillor Grey, added, 'There is far too much paternalism in housing design – far too much a belief that every tenant wants and needs the benefits of abstract sculpture, community centres, etc.' Argument was especially vigorous in Labour-run Smethwick, where also in 1961 the Liberals described the town's new high-rise blocks as 'monstrosities' and the Tories tried to block ambitious plans to redevelop Cape Hill into a bespoke shopping centre, on the grounds that extra shopping facilities were already available in nearby Birmingham, that most of the houses to be demolished were perfectly sound and habitable, and that compulsory purchase was in principle undesirable.[15]

A particularly suggestive squall was that in Glasgow *within* Labour's ranks. Jean Mann had not only been MP for Coatbridge but for ten years had represented (on the city council) the badly rundown, crime-ridden ward where the Royston Road 20-storey blocks of flats went up in 1960. 'Do social conditions not enter into the planning of high flats?' she asked at the end of that year. 'In these days of ever-increasing delinquency and crime, has no action ever been taken to discover whether its increased incidence has any connection with the trend throughout the cities of Britain to place youngsters in such close proximity in multi-storey dwellings? Certainly, neither councillors nor MPs will make application for these multi-storeyed flats.' And she declared that by loudly exalting the virtues of skyscraper flats on every postage-stamp site in the city, Glasgow's councillors had succumbed to 'panic planning' and 'stunt publicity'. Gibson's public riposte was instant. Mann, he asserted, was guilty of 'mistaking the sense of extreme emergency as panic'; 90,000 families in Glasgow still lived more than four to a room; and there were 'few planners' anywhere who had 'found it possible to omit multi-storey flats from town and city plans'.

Probably fairly typical, in terms of local politicians and other activators, was how the Blackburn story played out in 1961–2. 'We must plan big and boldly,' declared the council leader, Labour's Alderman George Eddie, shortly before the May 1961 unveiling of the proposed comprehensive redevelopment of the town centre. Alderman R. F. Mottershead, leader of the Conservative opposition, agreed – 'We have to look at the broad picture with vision and courage' – and the only councillor to dissent was Kenneth Culshaw, an Independent. 'This is not going to be our town when you have finished,' he predicted. 'It is not fair to let the big-money people [ie, Laings] come along and take it away . . . This town was built up by the small shopkeepers and we don't want to see them destroyed. I don't see why the Market Hall should come down at all.' Soon after the unveiling itself – at which Eddie hailed the prospect of a 'magnificent new shopping centre' on the market site and invoked William Blake's 'new' Jerusalem – strong support for the project came from the local chamber of trade, claiming that it would 'create in Blackburn a shopping Mecca which is bound – absolutely bound – to interest all and sundry round about and cause them to want to come to Blackburn to do their shopping'. Eddie did momentarily falter in June when he discovered that the master plan involved the flattening of 21 pubs ('I don't know what the lads are going to say'), but later that month he was boosted by a meeting of the local Trades Council and Labour Party. 'I personally can't see any architectural beauty in the building,' declared Councillor Tom Taylor about the Market Hall. 'In fact to me it is a monstrosity.' J. Mason agreed: 'If the people who are doing the shouting owned this building there is only one thing they would do and that is to pull it down because the site will make more money with something else on it.'

The decisive vote was in March 1962, as the town council decided whether to authorise progress on the master plan, and Eddie duly carried the day with a passionate oration:

> In this space age, with its glamorous departmental stores and supermarkets, people will no longer be content to shop in shabby, inadequate buildings, or stand in an uncomfortable, cobbled market square buying goods from a rickety wooden stall with the rain dripping down the back of their necks from a canvas cover. There is no glamour or comfort in shopping under such conditions. Our critics must face the facts and realities.

The planned pedestrian shopping centre, insisted Eddie, was 'probably the finest example of a planned town centre in the whole country'. In short: 'Blackburn cannot mark time. It cannot afford to go on giving the impression of being a dull, shabby, sooty, uninteresting place. It must put on some glamorous war paint if it is going to succeed in selling itself.'[16]

What about the planners themselves? 'We are on the edge of a great job of urban renewal and a vast revolution in our industrial areas is taking place,' a junior housing minister, Sir Keith Joseph, told the Town Planning Institute's annual dinner, held at London's Trocadero, in March 1961. 'Heavy responsibility falls on the members of the planning profession. They are confronted with the challenge of not only filling in the void but of creating something out of existing disorder, and creating ordered beauty out of empty space.'

The planners were certainly busy: in May 1962 the TPI's annual conference at Worthing heard that more than 340 urban authorities in England and Wales were considering new central-area schemes. In terms of the core principles at work, especially in the major cities, these remained largely modernist: comprehensiveness, clearance, zoning, segregation. 'It is still essentially as the Victorians built it,' complained Manchester's veteran planner, Rowland Nicholas, in 1962:

> A new look for the City [ie, Manchester] has long been overdue . . . Its unsightly areas of mixed industrial, commercial and residential development need to be systematically unravelled and redeveloped on comprehensive lines . . . One thing that should be obvious is the impossibility of achieving any satisfactory rearrangement of the highway pattern, pedestrian access, re-allocation of space and improvement of buildings, daylighting and car parking, by the piecemeal development of small sites.

For Wilfred Burns in Newcastle, what mattered was 'a comprehensive plan, for redevelopment cannot seriously be called such unless it is on a substantial scale and is part of an overall plan, otherwise the process is mere rebuilding'; and for Percy Johnson-Marshall in Salford, his plan marked 'an unparalleled opportunity for Salford to think today what other cities would think tomorrow'. For all urban planners, an increasingly key concern was the motor car. 'My hunch is that people have taken the car to their hearts – I certainly have,' Colin Buchanan told a 'Rebuilding City Centres' conference in 1960. 'It's been a smashing success in every way, and I can't see anything to challenge this endearing though murderously destructive machine.' The danger, he added, was that city streets were being turned into 'simply traffic drains'; his solution was 'bold use of various levels with exciting architectural possibilities'. Buchanan himself, in his mid-50s, was rapidly emerging as the guru on all things to do with traffic and the urban environment, and in 1961 he was commissioned by the Transport Minister Ernest Marples to write a definitive report on the way ahead.[17]

More broadly, the planners themselves seem to have believed that, following a dip in their fortunes during much of the 1950s (compared to the heady, pro-planning mood – at activator level anyway – of the 1940s), the new decade represented a fresh golden opportunity. 'Planning,' the eminent town-planning academic Lewis Keeble assured the TPI in 1961, 'is important, it is beginning to recapture the public imagination.' Graeme Shankland in Liverpool agreed. 'The post-war epoch is over and so is that absurd brief flirtation with anarchy when frustrations with local bumbledom seemed to many to justify a final bonfire of what few planning controls we have left,' he argued in January 1962. 'Now planning, physical and economic, is back on the map.' None of which inclined those shaping the new tomorrow to take criticism kindly. 'He is completely ill-informed,' insisted Bradford's City Engineer and Surveyor, Stanley Wardley, in response in early 1962 to John Betjeman's disobliging verdict ('stamping out the individualism of the North . . . a sort of international nothingness') on the city's new buildings. When, some months earlier, Ian Nairn lamented the loss of much of Plymouth's character, Wardley's counterpart there hit back sharply: 'I hold the view that a major city should, at its centre, both look and function like a major city and not a whimsical amusement arcade.' Criticism, implicit in the form of a weighty warning, also came from a perhaps less predictable quarter. 'If you usurp a function which in the ultimate resort the ordinary citizen thinks should not be yours, you and all your works will be swept away,' T. Dan Smith candidly told the delegates at Worthing in May 1962. 'The planner's function is to advise and guide, not to decide. This means that ultimately he must accept the standards and values of the society he serves. Planning is a new profession, a young profession, and the public is afraid of its ambitions.'[18]

Unmentioned by Smith, however, were the property developers – arguably at least as important, if not more so, than either the politicians or the planners in determining what British cities would look like for the rest of the century and beyond. The journalist Sheila Lynd listened to some of them in early 1961. Arndale Property Trust's Sam Chippindale (then developing not only Jarrow but over two dozen shopping-centre schemes in the north of England) told her that his forte was persuading Woolworth's to move into the new centres and posited that whereas 'planners go in for research, we rely on experience – you've got to have a flair'; the bearded Felix Fenston (responsible for major London office blocks like BP House and Dunlop House) reflected that 'my interest in architecture has grown with the growth of what my other bearded friends call contemporary architecture' and asserted that 'some of the most outstanding buildings have been erected by developers'; Joe Levy, after explaining his scheme for (in Lynd's words) 'the comprehensive development of a nine-acre site bounded on the south by Euston Road and the west by Hampstead Road, which is to be combined [in liaison with the LCC] with a big road-widening scheme, including an underpass', argued that, whether in the City or in the West End, the answer to shortage of office space was 'to pull down the acres and acres of low-standard buildings and replace them by modern office blocks with working conditions which will attract staff', adding that his personal motto was that 'it always pays to buy the best sites'; and Norwich Union's J. W. Draper, building high office blocks like Croydon's Norfolk House at a prodigious rate, had little patience for architectural individualism, noting that 'what a developer wants an architect to produce is something which is pleasing to look at and on completion will let – it must be functional.' Three particularly prominent developers not interviewed by Lynd were Charles Clore, Jack Cotton and Walter Flack. In 1960 the first two merged their property empires in what became a thoroughly uneasy marriage between chilly precision and off-the-cuff warmth, soon joined by Flack's Murrayfield Real Estate Co – an outfit that especially targeted potential new shopping centres in the Midlands and made profitable use of the articulate, energetic and flexible Birmingham Labour politician Frank Price. 'In negotiations always give it 'em straight,' the rags-to-riches Flack (son of a tailor) would say. 'The only trouble is that they often won't believe the truth.'

Perhaps unsurprisingly, given the intrinsically unlevel playing field of much urban redevelopment. 'If,' observed reluctantly but realistically the *Journal of the Town Planning Institute* in May 1961, 'the local authority attempts to drive a hard bargain which would reduce the profit – in the interests of good and beneficial overall design – then the development company concerned may take its capital elsewhere.' Speaking in early 1962 on the theme of 'urban renewal', the LCC's deputy town planner, Walter Bor, conceded that private developers could not just be dismissed as 'well-known and less-well-known bad eggs', but he contended that it would be much better, especially in central areas, if they operated 'on a lease basis' on land owned and planned, at least in outline, by the local authority. 'I do not see why,' he added, 'all the profit-making should be done by the private developer while all the unprofitable development is left to the local authority.' More generally, the developers may still have had some way to go before becoming national hate figures, but the signs were already there.

'If I had my way,' John Betjeman told the *Daily Mail*'s Vincent Mulchrone in August 1961, 'all "developers" would be put in prison for the crime of murdering our souls – which is far worse, after all, than murdering our bodies.' Four months later saw the release of *The Young Ones*. Cliff Richard plays Nicky, youth-club member and wannabe singer; he and his friends are trying to save their club from rich, ruthless London property developer Hamilton Black (Robert Morley), who wants to replace it with a large office block; Nicky keeps secret the fact that HB is his father – until, when some of his friends try to kidnap HB, he comes to the rescue. The film ends with honours shared as HB promises to build the young ones a new youth club.[19]

If the influence of the developer was on the up, so too was that of the contractor, against a background of building shortages and the start of a trend towards industrialised building methods. Glendinning and Muthesius trace in their history of the tower block the rise of the 'package-deal' contract, under which the contractor designed as well as built the development for the local authority; in one city, Birmingham, the Architect's Department was by the early 1960s almost frozen out of designing new blocks of dwellings. The coming of industrialisation accentuated the changing balance of power, with 1962 the key year, especially after the formation in May of a new company, Taylor Woodrow-Anglian Ltd, to produce factory-made dwellings. Nor, more generally, were the contractors shy in promoting themselves. Typically, the official opening in August 1961 of the Royston high-rise project saw Wimpey paying for an eight-page advertorial supplement in the *Glasgow Herald*. Not only did the development exemplify 'the higher standard of housing which Glasgow's citizens can expect to enjoy during the coming age', but across all of its Scottish high-rise developments Wimpey was ensuring that 'the experiences of tenants are recorded and analysed, and the experience thus accumulated is made available to local authorities contemplating multi-storeyed construction for the first time'.

Two increasingly ambitious contractors were Laing and Bovis. 'Blackburn,' declared the former in 1961, 'is going to have the sense and the courage to knock down its whole town centre, re-plan it, and build it in accordance with modern needs and ideas'; about the same time, the latter's Harry Vincent wrote glowingly in the *Architects' Journal* about the possibilities of 'very large imaginative' packaged deals, involving 'a new town hall, public library and bus garage, all the present ones being removed and rehoused so as to create a proper precinct shopping centre'. Vincent, though, did not rely just on words to get Bovis a satisfactory slice of the rapidly expanding 'urban renewal' market. Accordingly, by the first half of 1962 a three-way, mutually beneficial nexus was in place: Vincent as contractor; the northern eye-for-the-main-chance architect John Poulson; and the charismatic city boss with all the municipal contacts, one T. Dan Smith.[20]

That leaves, in terms of the main protagonists in this whole complex process, the architects. There is a clear sense in which they were starting by now to be marginalised – for example A. G. Sheppard Fidler as Birmingham's City Architect, arguably even Womersley in Sheffield – but they still mattered. Among a few of the better-known names, moreover, it is possible to detect some concern about the way things generally were going. After noting with satisfaction that almost all architects were committed to 'the search for acceptable forms of urban living', which in practice meant that 'high buildings are going to multiply', that conflicted progressive Lionel Brett went on in *The Times* in July 1961: 'British architects are well through the novelty phase of skyscraper building. Many are in fact alarmed at the effect on our old city silhouettes and open spaces of a proliferation of second-rate flat-tops, with off-the-peg curtain walls.' He called for different ways of achieving higher density, for instance 'the four-storey maisonette block, which is perfectly in scale with our Georgian streets and squares'. Few admired the Georgians more than Sir Albert Richardson, who later in 1961 attacked the plan to build five 25-storey blocks of flats in the St Leonard's area of Edinburgh. 'Clear the slums by all means,' Richardson argued, 'but don't congest. We must think of the visitors coming. They don't want to see an illogical imitation of New York.' Even Graeme Shankland (wearing his architect's rather than his planner's hat) had his doubts. Why, he asked in March 1962, had 'the image of the rectangular glass tower office' become so 'commonly acceptable'? The answer was economic: 'It is simply that in a modern western city it is the most easily lettable and vertically stackable unit that, therefore, yields the most ground-rent from a valuable central site.' Yet, he continued, this was not necessarily best for 'office efficiency and sociability'; he himself found something 'disquieting' about 'the impersonality of this architectural expression, the calligraphy of whose windows seem a visual echo of the calculating machine'.[21]

But the larger mood and forces were, of course, going the other way. Denys Lasdun appeared on *Monitor* in April 1961 to talk about how his Bethnal Green cluster blocks recreated the old street communities ('the backyards have been transferred to the top floor; the building mothers and encloses you'); soon afterwards, the Northern Architectural Association intervened in the ongoing debate about Newcastle's proposed Pilgrim Street roundabout, declaring that the Royal Arcade's preservation 'could not be justified' if 'to any extent' it 'compromised the large-scale and imaginative redevelopment which this main gateway of the city demands'; and the following spring, asked by *TV Times* his opinion of St Pancras station-*cum*-hotel, that supreme expression of the Victorian Age, Sir Basil Spence replied, 'I don't admire this too much.' Sam Bunton in Glasgow, meanwhile, was busy conceiving what would become the Red Road flats, Europe's highest. It was a vision responding, yes, to a city's severe slum problem, but it was also predicated on the unspoken assumption that Glasgow's traditional industrial economy still had a future as well as a past. 'It is interesting to consider how Glasgow would have looked from the Red Road as Bunton worked at his drawing board,' reflected Ian Jack half a century later. 'To the farther west, the cranes of Clyde shipyards stretched several miles downriver; to the closer west, the workshops of the North British Locomotive Co still exported engines to Africa and Asia; to the south, steam rose night and day from Parkhead's big iron forge; to the east, the chimneys of the Lanarkshire rolling mills and the conical waste heaps of collieries pricked the horizon.' All activators are creatures of their time, seldom gifted with any special insight into what lies ahead. The idealistic, gregarious Bunton, after the best part of a lifetime working towards this supreme moment, was no exception.[22]

Press coverage of the great upheaval – actual and pending – tended to be patchy but positive, relatively seldom questioning the need to embrace the tide of modernity. 'How far are we, in this motor-packed island,' asked *The Times* in December 1961 rhetorically and querulously, 'from the style and planning that put Sweden twenty-six years ahead with Stockholm's Slussem Cloverleaf or its Tegelbacken Intersection?' For a *Daily Mail* journalist, inspecting Bradford's progress the following spring, paradise was already at hand. 'I drove up an electronically-warmed ramp to a rooftop car park,' he wrote with undisguised enthusiasm, 'drank coffee in a café with splendid city vistas, strolled through an air-conditioned supermarket, explored a semi-completed system of under-traffic tunnels for pedestrian moles.'

Closer to the action, the local press largely joined the chorus. 'Near-miracle of City Centre' trumpeted the *Western Morning News* about Plymouth's virtually completed shopping centre; 'a go-ahead town like Doncaster could be transformed in the space of a few years', urged the *Doncaster Gazette*; 'another demonstration of confidence in Bradford' the *Telegraph & Argus* greeted the Forster Square development plan; 'super-deluxe apartments' the Manchester-based *County Express* called Hulme's ongoing multi-storey St George's development. Or, at the western end of the East Lancs Road, take the *Liverpool Echo*'s coverage of the continuing Everton Heights redevelopment. 'Crying for the moon' was journalist George Cregeen's brisk verdict on slum-dwellers there obstinately refusing alternative accommodation. As for 'those who feel that with the disappearance of these communities, with their peculiarly local traditions and alliances, something of the heart of Liverpool will have been plucked out', the larger truth, according to Cregeen, was that 'it is a heart that is aged, wheezy and asthmatical, and a change of air can do no harm.' Sentiments were similar in Newcastle. 'A project of imagination, courage and forward-looking qualities' was the *Evening Chronicle*'s instant verdict on the Burns plan for the city centre; that same issue ran a 'Symbols of Hope' feature on the high-rise flats shortly to open at Shieldfield; while later in 1961, a feature by the paper's Joan Elliott on the imminent start of Byker's redevelopment sought to allay local fears that the area's 'close communities' would be 'broken up' as a result: 'Modern planning knows how to put the clock back wisely and Byker should enjoy in the future all the advantages of the best type of twentieth-century city life with the right of every man to breathe fresh air and to live in beautiful surroundings.'[23]

The treatment was sometimes more nuanced. In February 1961 the

Glasgow Herald asserted that 'tall buildings are imperative in Glasgow if the housing conditions are to be improved', but, seven months later, in a sceptical editorial on 'High Flats', reckoned that 'the prevailing fashion among municipalities for flats of 20 storeys and more' was 'a trend often followed more for reasons of civic pride than of housing need'. Furthermore: 'Building high into the air does not always save space on the ground. Scotland's present stock of multi-storey flats are insufficiently distinguished in architectural merit to qualify as prestige symbols.' The *Liverpool Daily Post* seems consciously to have allowed both sides of the argument to speak. On the one hand, George Eglin continued to hammer away, declaring in October 1961 that 'there are not just a few years of redevelopment ahead of Liverpool, but a programme that must go on for fifty years, a hundred years, a programme, in fact, without any end'. On the other hand, not only did the paper soon afterwards run a series of critical articles by J. R. Waddington on life in Liverpool Corporation's new multi-storey blocks (already showing signs of 'damage and neglect' as well as generally providing 'little scope for families to express any individuality'), but it had already (in November 1960) expressed concern about the failure to keep together communities of displaced slum-dwellers, perhaps through 'a sort of transit camp', so that when the new housing was ready, families might collectively 'return to the streets from whence they came, but with far better homes'. Even the *Blackburn Times*, after in May 1961 endorsing the master plan as undoubtedly necessary in order 'to eradicate the town's more ghastly features', and then in February 1962 reiterating that Blackburn would 'quickly become a back number' if it failed to keep up with its neighbours' plans, did implicitly come to concede a degree of anxiety, noting in March 1962 that 'we don't want a town centre full of chain stores exactly the same in appearance and customer-attraction as can be found in any other large town.'

Perhaps no local commentator was more conflicted than the *Wellingborough News*'s 'Redwell'. 'The people of the town must appreciate that it is essential that the town develop if it is to compete with neighbours,' the columnist wrote in November 1961. Yet at the same time: 'We must remember that once the town centre is knocked down and rebuilt, if we don't like it all the king's horses and all the king's men won't be able to put it together again.' Then, a week later: 'I still feel a tinge of regret at the possible mixture of ancient and modern buildings, but on reflection any modern development, even if it is in close proximity to Wellingborough's beautiful church, can hardly be worse than the jumble of backways which can be seen at present.' And finally, like a sore itch, looking ahead soon afterwards to 1962: 'Now there are plans laid to change the very heart and sometimes I fear the soul of the town. We may find we will have to make great sacrifices for the sake of the progress we wish to achieve.'[24]

The more specialist press and writers tended to go with the larger flow. Take the *Architects' Journal*, which, responding in May 1961 to Blackburn's comprehensive development plan, 'congratulated' the town 'on taking so bold a step', praised Councillor Eddie's 'dynamic leadership' and began one sentence with a hugely revealing assumption: 'One hesitates to criticise in any way so bold a slate wiping . . .' The *AJ* was certainly far from invariably uncritical – between February and May 1962, for instance, it vainly called it 'a sad and stupid thing' if Rotherhithe's old houses on the riverside were to be demolished, further along the Thames rated the huge new Shell building an 'abysmal architectural failure' and condemned out of hand the Marples 'lorry road' plan for Highgate – but its objections were almost always on an individual basis. Elsewhere, a writer somewhere in the middle of the broad progressive range was the *Guardian*'s architectural critic, Diana Rowntree, who in April 1962 offered a lengthy, mainly positive appraisal of developments in Sheffield. 'The city,' she declared, 'is making a bid to replace its nineteenth-century confusion with something planned specifically for today's needs.' Rowntree's greatest enthusiasm was for the plan 'to link the Markets with the lower decks of Park Hill, so that an upper pedestrian system of terraces and walkways operate across the whole area of the Sheaf Valley'. 'We have been waiting ever since the war,' she added, 'for some town to break through into this way of living.'[25]

In a class of his own was the shy, passionate, unpredictable Ian Nairn. A sample of his writings during 1961, partly for the architectural press but also for the *Listener*, brings out something of his love of vitality, a vitality with people at its centre. 'In ninety-nine per cent of cases,' he declared in March about the dire consequences of 'speculative building'

A *Vogue* model with schoolchildren, Bradford, 1960

Notting Hill, October 1960

Berwick Street Market, Soho, April 1961

Sea coalers collect coal, Hartlepool, 1961

Design studio, Crown Wallpapers, Cheshire, 1961

Science lesson, Surrey, 1961

Birmingham Reference Library, November 1961

Roy Thomson (*second from right*) addresses senior *Sunday Times* staff shortly after acquiring the paper, 1959

Sheep judging at the Royal Highland Show, Ingliston, Edinburgh, 1962

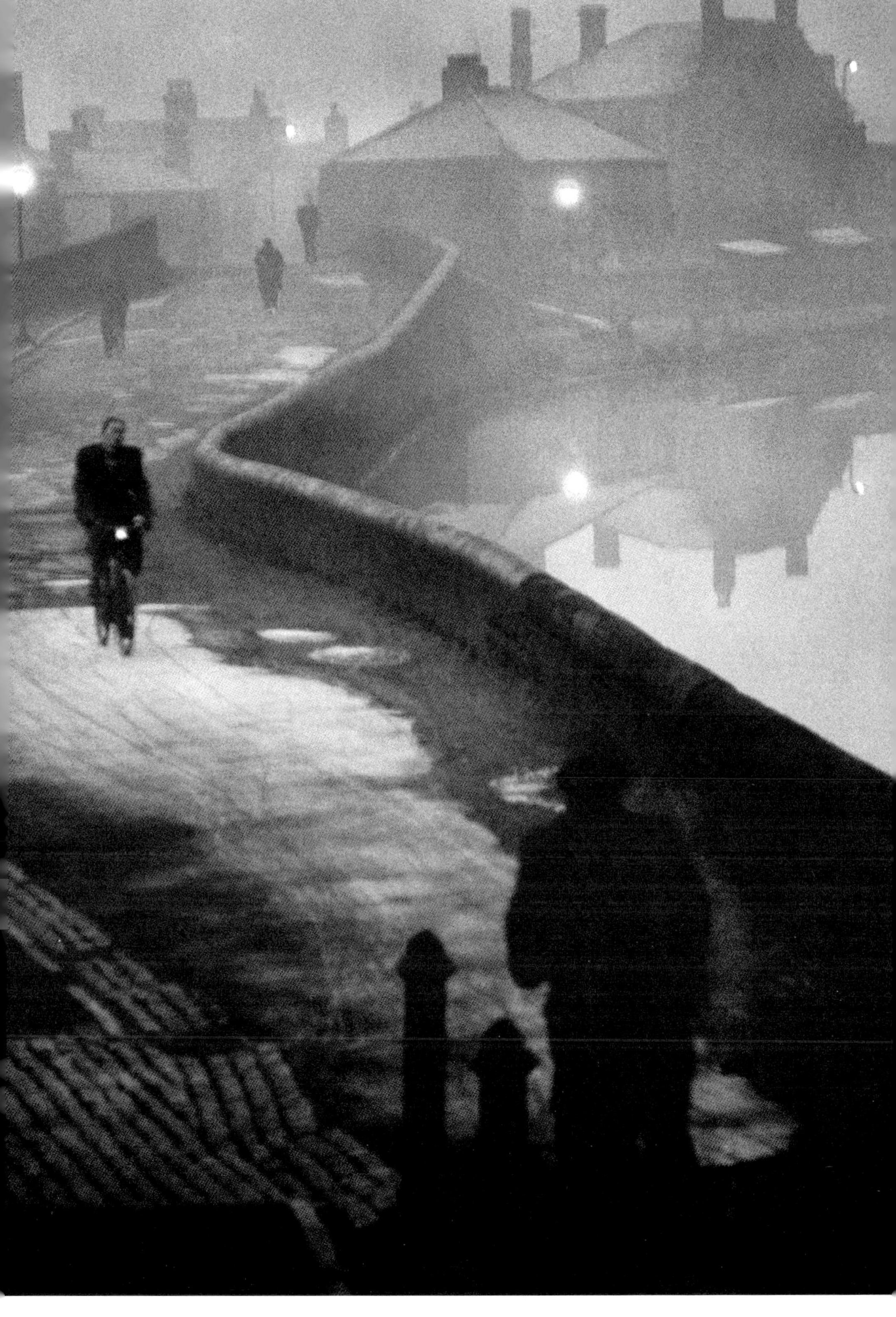

Early morning in Tipton, the Black Country, 1961

Park Hill, Sheffield, 1961

The Gorbals, Glasgow, 1962

Edmonton Green market, Enfield, 1960

Supermarket shoppers, March 1962

Agatha Hart at Stockwell Bus Garage, March 1962

on subtopian housing estates, 'it creates a lowest common denominator, a collection of houses-with-gardens which are individually not quite what anybody wants and collectively form little textbooks of social sterility, endless windy lanes down which the prams trundle back from the bus stop, whilst the ice-cream van chimes its weary way (those chimes are often the only sign of life in a square mile or so and, dear God, some people want to stop them).' The following month he was travelling hopefully with the Burns plan for central Newcastle, which provided 'the opportunity for showing that twentieth-century traffic flow and a magnificent medieval and early-Victorian city can be harmonised'. Then in June it was back to prams, with Nairn noting that in reconstructed Plymouth the main shopping street, Royal Parade, faced due west, was completely straight for 500 yards and offered no protection against the rain: 'Pushing a pram into wind in those conditions is no advertisement for twentieth-century civilisation. Other centuries knew better – but then they were just picturesque fuddy-duddies in a pre-technological age.' By contrast, he observed in August, a new Richard Seifert office block, Kellogg House in Baker Street, 'cheers you up every time you see it'. Perhaps the most deeply felt contribution came in November, when Nairn reviewed Lewis Mumford's massive, magisterial *The City in History*. 'I gag on Mumford's turgid chapters and intellectual abstractions the same way that I gag on D. H. Lawrence's emotional abstractions,' he wrote. 'The protagonist of a humane city, he puts people into compartments as fiercely as any zone-besotted planner.' And Nairn offered his own credo: 'The really important thing in life as in city planning is the "how", not the "what". If something – anything – is done with love and true tolerance, not just freedom-to-like-what-I-like, then it will be all right, even if it is cram-full of bric-à-brac and oleographs. It is only the right "how" that will harmonise all the different "whats" that represent all the variety of human temperament.' As it happened, a different American writer was already getting much closer to Nairn's priorities. This was Jane Jacobs, whose *The Death and Life of Great American Cities* was published in the US in 1961 and caused immediate waves, but did not appear in Britain until the second half of 1962.[26]

Nairn would only become a national treasure posthumously, whereas John Betjeman, 'as we all know, pedals about London on a bicycle, finding sweetness in sooty railway stations, gathering treasured images in Victorian Gothic, and plucking poetic inspiration from other unlikely places'. That March 1961 profile in *Everywoman* magazine quoted Betjeman observing that he found himself unable 'to avoid battles to stop something or other being destroyed'. The two most famous battles, both unsuccessful and in both of which he played a leading role, were of course for the Euston Arch and the Coal Exchange. Over the former, it was much later claimed that at the crucial moment Betjeman had gone missing (with a five-week trip to Australia) – but by then, late October 1961, the battle was surely lost, little helped by *The Times* having pronounced in mid-October, 'Not Worth Saving'. As for the Coal Exchange, Betjeman's view was steely clear, telling a sympathiser in February 1961 that what was 'really behind its destruction' was not road-widening but 'a speculator who has his eye on the rest of the island site on which it stands'. There were other conservationist battles in these years, including a happier outcome in the City for the wonderful 1860s National Provincial building in Bishopsgate, but not so for Lewisham's Victorian town hall, to whose impending fate Betjeman had been alerted by a local 13-year-old schoolboy. He was also now using television as a campaigning medium, starting with *Steam and Stained Glass* on ITV in April 1962. 'A paean of praise for Victorian architecture,' noted the *Daily Mirror*'s Clifford Davis. 'He didn't win me over, but there was no denying his infectious enthusiasm.' What about 'the modern' itself? On the whole, Betjeman had by now few kind words, but in 1961 he was willing to see some potential good in Sheffield's Park Hill. Admittedly 'the first sight was terrifying and inhuman, tier on tier of concrete with ugly "contemprikit" detail rising on a steep slope', but after getting closer and walking about, he reckoned that 'the planning is thoughtful and ingenious and people do not much miss the gardens they never had.' Ultimately, reflecting on the city's new developments as a whole, his verdict was part-hopeful, part-disquieted: 'Who shall say what a race these new, churchless, communal blocks will breed? It is still too early to say . . . I believe they suit the rugged hills of Sheffield and its people. The question is, will they make a houseproud horizontal people apathetic and turn them into the machines they tend?'[27]

'When the bulldozers uproot the people' was the title of the Rev.

Norman Power's *Birmingham Mail* article in July 1961, showing a photo of the wasteland in front of his Ladywood church. In the case of slum clearance, it seems at times to have been only clergymen who stood up for the powerless people whose lives were being turned upside-down by what was clearly all too often a blunt, inefficient and high-handedly insensitive process. After reflecting that 'when people are uprooted, they are uprooted from more than bricks and mortar,' and after noting that only about ten were left in the district out of his last hundred confirmation candidates ('these were our potential leaders'), Power wrote that 'we are begging our planners not to destroy the neighbourhood any more until more building has been done.' He concluded unforgivingly that 'the bulldozers have torn a living community to pieces. It could have been avoided.'

It was not so different in Liverpool, where a local paper in April 1962 identified Father George Earle of St Francis Xavier's Church as one of the few people concerned about 'the lonely people of Everton Brows'. 'The conditions they are living in,' he declared from that clearance zone, 'are appalling – not only in these derelict areas, but in the streets which are still intact.' Across in Manchester a few weeks earlier, the *County Express* had reported the Rev. Cecil Lewis from working-class Gorton joining forces with 'fellow churchmen in slum clearance areas who have forcibly criticised the Corporation's re-housing policy whereby families are being "uprooted" and found new homes in strange districts'. Lewis himself cited the recent wholesale redevelopment of the Bradford Road area of Ancoats and ensuing loss of the old community spirit: 'It is something which will take years to replace, if it ever can be.'[28]

It was not quite true that the public was never consulted. In T. Dan Smith's Newcastle, recalled the *Municipal Review* in 1974, public consultation (about the slum clearance and housing drive that he was pushing from the late 1950s) 'took place at crowded public meetings at a time when public participation was not a vogue catch-phrase'. Smith himself in 1964 reckoned that 'in three years I spoke to 30,000 people about our plans' and that this had been 'local democracy at work'. Or take another exemplar, Coventry. During the winter of 1961–2, not only did the city council arrange a series of 28 public meetings, covering every ward, to encourage feedback about the latest version of the Development Plan, but a television documentary showed people gathering round shop windows to examine models of the next stage – a sight prompting the *Architects' Journal* to reflect that 'there are not many towns where you would find the same knowledge among the people of what the local authority was trying to do.' That might have been true, and the relative apathy of the Glaswegian citizenry was probably more typical. There, the Corporation staged a week-long exhibition in March 1961 at the McLellan Galleries in order to publicise the city's quinquennial plan, setting out the strategy for a mixture of 'comprehensive redevelopment' and significant overspill. 'There was no crowd, no sign that it was "the thing" to attend the exhibition,' Elizabeth Mitchell observed in the next issue of *Town and Country Planning*. 'There is something strange in utter unconcern – unawareness even – about such vital matters.'[29]

On the actual frontline of slum clearance, whether happening or intended, attitudes varied. 'What the people in the area wanted, if any official had cared what they thought, was for their houses to be done up, bathrooms and proper lavatories put in, and the dangerous wiring replaced,' recalled Doris Lessing about London's Somers Town in the early 1960s. 'They were saying, "But we've all been living here for years. My mother was born here. My kids were born here."' So too in Frome, where ahead of the clearance of the town's Trinity Street area the *Western Daily Press*'s Bill Beckett found that the residents 'would rather stay than have their roots torn up to be transplanted on a modern foreign housing estate'. 'The council,' Mrs Gwen Latham told him, 'want it and they'll have it. Nobody wants to move but we'll all be uprooted and that will be it.' In Manchester a mass petition from private tenants living in atrocious conditions in Greenheys demanded that the council declare the district a slum-clearance area, but across the city as a whole, later in 1961, it was reported that the housing department was starting to adopt 'tough tactics' against 'people in condemned houses who refuse to leave', at least 'until they get the type of new home they want'. Or take Liverpool's Everton Heights, where the journalist George Cregeen came across not only refuseniks but also, at 59A William Henry Street, 'a very satisfied customer':

> Mrs Mary McDonald was stacking all her household possessions on the balcony of her terraced home perched above a block of derelict shops. She was all smiles. 'We're moving tonight,' she told me. 'My three daughters aged ten, seven and 12 months, and my husband. We're all going to live in a council house at Norris Green. It's a re-let. The children are absolutely thrilled to bits. It will be much healthier for them out there.' She had lived in the area all her life and had mixed feelings about leaving it. 'You would go a long way to find people like those who lived around here,' she said. 'But they have gone to the four corners of Liverpool now.'

There were mixed feelings too in Coronation Street in Sunderland's East End, in the process of being cleared in April 1962. 'We would do anything to get a decent house,' 27-year-old Mrs June Price, a labourer's wife with three children, informed a journalist, while 37-year-old Mrs Elizabeth Taylor, a general dealer's wife, added, 'I can understand the street meaning a lot to the older folk, but I want to move out of it as soon as possible.' One of those older folk was 73-year-old Mrs Sarah Charlton, who had briefly left to live at the Thorney Close estate but was now back. 'I pined for the old sights and faces,' she explained, though most of the street's houses were now demolished and all but two of its dozen pubs. There was clearance and demolition too, perhaps more resonant than anywhere, in and just off Newcastle's Scotswood Road. 'The city was in their bones, they feared the wilderness of flats and isolated houses without a centre, they instinctively rejected amenities without that highway of shops and pubs which constitutes the ganglion of a living place,' wrote Sid Chaplin in *The Watchers and the Watched*. 'The Road was their life, and they clung to it. As long as they could, as long as they were allowed, they would stay. And yet their days were numbered. The Road was being demolished and the people were shifting. Some went, then returned from the desert, paying double the old rent rather than be dead, content to keep one wall between themselves and the demolition gang.'[30]

We also have for these years the occasional more systematic survey of attitudes to rehousing. The sociologists Dennis Marsden and Edmund Cooney, for instance, made a study of elderly people living in decaying housing in Stepney. 'You're not going to shift me, are you?'; 'Me fire's me comfort, me fire and me cup of tea, as long as I can get them I'm all right'; 'It'll last my time out' – all were typical of what Marsden and Cooney heard. One woman, fed up with her squalid living conditions and saying she would like 'a one-roomed flat' with 'a bath when you want', was asked whether she would, given the chance, move to a housing estate. 'Me, move out there?' she replied. 'No fear. I've been round here all my life. I'd be right out of it. I may as well die.' This strong attachment to Stepney, reflected Marsden, was not to 'the large, mixed administrative borough' but to 'the small area of intimately known streets "around here", where they had lived for so many years'. He further reflected that 'the old people's plea that the housing will last their time out is something deeper than mere inbred indifference to dirt and inconvenience: it is a challenge to the idea that their lives and their environment can be planned.'

By contrast, a major survey in Leeds of almost a thousand households in officially designated slum-clearance areas, carried out between May and July 1962 by the University of Leeds, was across the generations and yielded significantly different findings. Asked whether they wanted to move, 82 per cent of respondents said they did and only 16 per cent were opposed to the idea. Those in the latter camp tended, relative to the sample as a whole, to be older, poorer and have fewer children, while for those wanting to move, the inadequate condition of the house they were living in was the reason most commonly given. The university's R. K. Wilkinson and E. M. Sigsworth pondered the fact that 16 per cent non-movers was such a markedly lower proportion than in a similar survey undertaken some years earlier in a comparably inner-city part of Liverpool, where as many as 36 per cent had not wished to move. 'A relevant point may be the distance involved in a move,' they surmised. 'In Liverpool those who are moved are often rehoused in overspill areas, whereas in Leeds rehousing takes place within the city boundary.'[31] It was a plausible explanation, reaffirming again the supreme psychological importance of the local and the familiar.

In any case, irrespective of individual wishes and volition, the slum-clearance process itself could be (for adults anyway) an unutterably grim, bewildering experience. 'In the vicinity of Rokeby Street,' wrote George Cregeen in May 1961 about Everton Heights, 'I saw streets and streets of devastation – far worse than anything the German bombers could do even on the worst night of the May blitz.' Almost a year later, another Liverpool journalist wrote of how on Everton Brow 'single families live with acres of empty land all around them', some 'with a complete street to themselves', as 'children run wild over the area'. Sticking it out in Haigh Street were just two inhabitants: at number 139, where she had lived for 55 years, Mrs Mary Kempster, alone apart from her cat Nigger, her only running water a cold tap in the cellar, feeling forgotten ('I don't know why they're keeping us here ... Nobody seems to worry about us'), and at number 117, in a house flooding when it rained, no ceiling in the kitchen, the lavatory 'broken and useless', 77-year-old Mrs Catherine Hughes ('I'm afraid to go out, in case someone breaks up the house while I'm away').

It was little better in Bolton's Moncrieffe Street. 'Workmen have started to pull down terraced houses in a row in which three houses are still occupied,' reported the local paper in June 1961. 'It's terrible living here while the other houses are being demolished,' said the occupant of one of them, 82-year-old invalid Mrs Emily Phillips. 'We get a lot of people coming here thinking this house is also empty. They go in to take things from the empty houses.' In nearby Matthew Street there were also only three houses left occupied, including one by a pensioner who had lived in his for 40 years and now 'stood watching the bulldozers pull down the house next door'. 'I think,' he remarked, 'they could have at least left the houses on either side standing until I moved.' Salford may have been the worst of all. 'There was so much destruction,' recalled the photographer of slum clearance, Shirley Baker. 'A street would be half pulled down and the remnants set on fire while people were still living in the area. As soon as any houses were cleared, children would move in and break all the windows, starting the demolition process themselves.' In February 1962 one local paper reported (about the clearance area near Bury New Road) 'rats scurrying through the streets, children climbing on the roofs of partly demolished houses, indiscriminate tipping creating a health hazard', while another published a letter from 'A Resident':

> Although what looks like half a square mile of devastated land lies awaiting the building of flats on the Broad Street side of Ellor Street, and it is

> going to take at least three years to do the building, the Corporation is knocking houses down on the opposite side of Ellor Street as fast as it can.
>
> Why this panic? Why drive hundreds of families out of the district and in many cases out of the city when they could be left there for a couple of years at least without any delay to the rebuilding programme? It is not even as if they were very bad houses; many are quite good. It just doesn't make sense to any of us . . .
>
> Why can't we be left here until the first set of flats are up, so that we can move straight into them and so continue living as neighbours? Isn't half the trouble in the new flats that families from all over the show are moved in, nobody knowing anybody else, and having slowly and painfully to build up community feeling from the very beginning?

'Perhaps,' the writer concluded, 'someone in authority will condescend to explain.'[32]

Many of Salford's slum-dwellers had gone, or would be going, to new overspill housing at Worsley, 8 miles away and intended by 1971 to be housing 18,000 people displaced by Salford's redevelopment. In 1960 the housing and planning expert Barry Cullingworth published his analysis of fieldwork from 1958 about how Worsley's new settlers were getting on; the following year he did much the same in relation to London's overspill population which had decanted to Swindon, this time based on 1959 fieldwork. His conclusions were broadly similar. In both cases the experience was largely – though far from uniformly – positive, including for many of those who had not wanted to move in the first place, and for most people the key plus was improved housing. 'We don't bother with relatives out here,' a Worsley interviewee explained. 'We live our own life. We've got a lovely house, a nice garden and a TV set. We're very happy.' The happiness quotient remained patchier in another, more-publicised overspill settlement, Kirkby, where the birth rate was eight times the national average. 'Older people are apt to feel a bit out of it all, especially if they are on their own,' Miss Margaret Lunt – disabled and living on the tenth floor of Cherryfield Heights – told the *Liverpool Echo* in May 1962. 'I think there should be little corner shops in Kirkby to make it more homely. Most of the people who came to live here are used to little corner shops.' Another insider account was in 1961 from the headmistress of a school on one of Newcastle's new housing estates, apparently some distance from the inner city. 'The estate,' she wrote, 'is a vast monotonous sprawl possessing the minimum of amenities and no charm; but an improvement on the areas from which the people come in that most for the first time have hot and cold water, baths, inside lavatories, a garden, and live in fresh air.' After describing some of her difficulties at the school, including how 'each year's intake throws up a leader of a small anti-social group,' she went on:

> The old areas from which the families came were settled, closely knit communities – where the family stuck together – where grandma was there with authority – to advise, to tell your troubles to, look after the baby, turn to in any emergency. She has stayed behind. From some parts of our estate there is a daily exodus back to her. The Welfare Officer was telling me how surprised she was to hear grown women talking about going back to 'me mum' . . .
>
> In that old world you could be your natural self – shout, laugh, quarrel, make love, get drunk, put up with things without that awful dread, 'What will the neighbours say – what will they think', for you knew your neighbours would be shouting, laughing, quarrelling, getting drunk too . . .
>
> Now, pitchforked into an entirely different neighbourhood, people are terribly lonely and insecure, old values are questioned, their actions are subject to criticism from neighbours, and even children come home from school with all sorts of fancy ideas, torn between two loyalties . . .

In short: 'I think our most pressing behaviour problems are understood better in the context of their previous environment, and the acute period of transition through which some section of the community is always moving.'[33]

Whether they stayed in their familiar district or went elsewhere (especially the former), many rehoused people finished up living in flats – often against their wishes. The 1962 survey of Leeds slum-dwellers showed, among those in the 20 to 49 age range, only 5 per cent wanting to move into a flat rather than a house. That same year, a survey of the St Mary's district of Oldham revealed that although 75 per cent wanted to be rehoused in the area, that preference rate halved if they were offered a flat, not a house. Local politicians were well aware of popular feeling on the subject. 'I know that many people do not like flats,' conceded Councillor Les Morris, chairman of the Housing Committee, in January 1961, 'but in a town like Smethwick it is the only way we have of giving people a home, and the sooner that is accepted by the townspeople, the happier they will be about it.' Across much of urban Britain, modernism was being imposed upon a deeply un-modernist populace. 'The more optimistic of the architects in London last week,' noted a journalist in July 1961 on the occasion of a major international architectural conference, 'would have done well to stand at the foot of one of the superb Roehampton blocks which overlook the hills of Richmond deer park; looking up he would have seen window upon window each heavily shrouded with patterned lace curtains.'[34]

Sometimes of course the experience could be good, especially in the early months, even years. 'It's like a palace when you've lived in a place like we came from,' Mrs Anne Knight told Newcastle's *Evening Chronicle* in April 1961 about the recently opened Heaton Park flats; and, according to the report, she 'could not say enough in praise of her new home and particularly about the gas appliances in it'. Eight months later and it was the turn of Liverpool's Garibaldi Street blocks to be unveiled, with one new resident, William McGowan, calling his flat 'a docker's paradise' after 23 years living in a 'hovel' in the city's Conway Street. By this time (between August 1961 and March 1962), the assistant estate manager at Sheffield's acclaimed Park Hill development was interviewing the households in every fifth dwelling. Although 72 of the 197 interviewed families complained of the noise (especially in relation to the main lifts and the laundry), the findings by Mrs Demers were otherwise generally positive: 86 per cent experiencing 'no difficulty with the lifts' (albeit they were 'often out of action as a result of abuse'); overall satisfaction with the revolutionary Garchey system of refuse disposal; only two families disappointed by the central heating system and preferring an open fire; only 20 per cent missing their garden and/or wanting one; and 92 per cent feeling 'no loss of privacy', although Demers added that 'a visitor might well think on seeing a row of doors so close together that a lack of privacy was inherent in the design.'

'There can be no doubt,' she went on, 'as to the general feeling of approval for the decks themselves, which are appreciated for a great variety of reasons, for protection from weather, for cleanliness, for the view and for social contacts as well as for privacy.' Altogether, claimed the housing manager in his foreword to her report, 'the survey shows that Park Hill is a satisfactory "machine for living in", to use Le Corbusier's phrase.'

Too often, in too many multi-storey blocks, the experience was far from satisfactory. In September 1961 Salford Corporation was described as 'at its wits end' about how to stop 'mounting damage in its multi-storey flats', including 'windows broken, fire-hydrants damaged, lifts immobilised, refuse chutes blocked'; the following month, amid proliferating vandalism in Speke (complementing Kirkby as Liverpool's other major overspill location), Mrs Mabel Oakes, living in the large block on Central Way, frankly declared, 'It's murder living in these flats, we can't get any peace'; and in the Loxford Court flats in Hulme, elderly Mrs Dorothy Rowson wailed in May 1962, 'I would give anything to get away from here. During the day we get no peace from the children and late at night we suffer from rowdy teenagers.' Probably worst of all, though, was the plight of mothers looking after small children. 'THE SKY PRISONERS' was the *Daily Sketch*'s lurid but not inapposite headline in May 1961 for the survey conducted by Joan Maizels of 62 recently built council blocks in the London area, revealing high levels of worry and isolation among the mothers ('a nightmare', according to one), with 52 per cent of two- to five-year-olds going out only to the shops and playing only in the flat. Nor was it just a London issue. 'I am a mother who lives in an eight-storey block of flats in Birmingham,' Mrs Bowratt of Kitts Green wrote soon afterwards to the *Daily Mirror*. 'I was nearly driven frantic trying to keep my little boy quiet when his daddy – who works nights – was sleeping during the day. Every toy that made a noise was taken away from him. The child could not go out to play because we live so high up and near a main road.' 'In desperation,' she added, 'I have put him in a nursery and now feel I am missing the best years of his life.'[35]

Specific reactions (in either direction) are somewhat harder to find in relation to city-centre/town-centre redevelopment; almost certainly the most common feeling among the inhabitants of those cities and towns was an assumption that it was going to happen anyway. Just occasionally there was strong support, as when D. Shaw (in a letter to the *Liverpool Echo* in August 1961) declared that 'whole areas of the city need sweeping away', condemned 'those black monstrosities of stone' opposite Lime Street station and urged city councillors to visit 'the beautiful city centre of Plymouth', which would 'shame them into quick action'. If there was support for major urban change, though, it was usually more muted, typified by the *Wellingborough News* noting in February 1962 that 'most seem to agree that, sometime, something had to be done.' Yet overall, the majority of identifiable reactions were essentially negative. Bristol in the spring of 1961 saw a mass petition (backed by the *Bristol Evening Post* and signed by 11,500 people) against the insensitive, piecemeal development (mainly by Norwich Union and the Bank of England) of the heavily bombed Wine Street area; about the same time, the *FT* wrote of 'bemused citizens' and 'disgruntled locals' calling the new Birmingham 'a concrete jungle'; in Devon that Christmas, another letter-writer, Miss Ada Watts, who had 'known and loved Torquay for the last 37 years', lamented the 'heartbreaking' sight of a new block of luxury flats 'ruining the exquisite wooded scenery' surrounding the town; and among the diarists, Kenneth Preston was in Bradford in the spring of 1962 and 'sadly' saw that 'almost the whole of that solid group of buildings constituting the Swan Arcade is now no more than a heap of rubble.' The sight prompted him to more general reflections: 'A surprising number of places now appear as though they have suffered a series of heavy air-raids. It would have saved a lot of work if they had it appears to me. Keighley [where he lived himself] presents a disgraceful sight. Great waste spaces have appeared. Everywhere buildings appear in ruins. I don't know why it must all be done at once. Why may one site not first be cleared and then built upon before another one is produced as an eye-sore?'

In one Lancashire town, almost all the changes were still to come. In 1961 the local paper published 'The Blackburn I Know: A Teenager's View of the Town Centre Controversy':

> Blackburn [wrote J. A. Houghton] is not a pretty sight; in many ways it stinks. It is a collection of dirty, ugly factories and humble little houses that were thrown together as a result of the Industrial Revolution . . .

> But Blackburn is changing; the Council say that they are going to tear down the town centre and build a new one with large gardens and supermarkets. They say that this will provide Blackburn with all the modern amenities and resultant civic pride that goes with a New Town. All that will happen, however, is that Blackburn will be destroyed. The bulldozers will cut out its heart and replace a supermarket, tear out its soul and substitute escalators . . .
>
> Blackburn has character; it stinks but it has character, and that character depends on the town and on the town centre . . . If the town centre goes the only thing that Blackburn has to offer will go too, the character of the people . . .[36]

Those who believed in planned dispersion and low density found themselves badly on the defensive by the early 1960s. 'The advocates of high density, who usually have a visually aesthetic preoccupation,' complained Frederic Osborn in January 1961, 'persistently duck the evidence of popular preference as well as of cost'; that same month, writing to Lewis Mumford, he referred to the 'tacit unholy alliance' between 'the damned high-rise architects and the extreme countryside preservationists'; two months later, Wyndham Thomas, director of the Town and Country Planning Association, declared that 'the anti-dispersal flock of monumental architects, romantic sociologists, and the more selfish of countryside preservationists' comprised between them a 'gallimaufrous alliance' pushing 'prejudices disguised as arguments'; and in November 1961, addressing the Federation of Registered Housebuilders, Thomas spoke of 'an anti-social alliance of market pressures, aesthetic prejudices and preservationist sentiment' that was 'now forcing higher densities, higher costs and lower standards'.[37] Yet for all those protestations, and for all the validity of much of their case (especially in relation to high-rise), the mood music was pointing the other way. *Family and Kinship* (about lonely, fragmented Debden in comparison to warm, communal Bethnal Green), the new wave of working-class realism in novels and films, *Coronation Street*, the whole modernity zeitgeist – all these things gave urbanism, aka 'urban renewal', the critical momentum for the unfolding decade.

Much in the debate hinged on perceptions of the New Towns, those 'essays in civilisation' (as Lord Reith called them) that had been created after the war with such high expectations. By the early 1960s, with populations steadily expanding, most of their centres were at last complete or approaching completion, typified by Basildon's pedestrian-only Town Square, whose first shops opened in the Keay House block in 1959. The closest sociological study during these years was made by Peter Willmott in Stevenage. There, some 380 interviews in 1960 revealed almost all the employment (predominantly skilled manual) being local; 91 per cent saying they liked their homes ('It's a lovely modern house – ideal for a growing family'); and 60 per cent of wives using their local neighbourhood centres for weekday shopping. The whole question of neighbourhood was prominent in Willmott's mind, given the importance of the 'neighbourhood unit' – self-contained neighbourhoods around the town centre – in the original planning of the New Towns. Significantly, when asked where they lived, only 31 per cent gave the name of the neighbourhood (population of around 10,000), whereas most gave the name of one of the five or six housing estates (population nearer to 2,000) *within* the neighbourhood. As for visiting patterns, he found from detailed statistics that 'the physical boundaries of the neighbourhood itself are of no special significance in terms of informal social relationships.' Overall, concluded Willmott, 'the neighbourhoods seem to "work" well enough in functional terms, as areas for local amenities,' but 'there is no evidence that they do anything to create "community" or "neighbourliness", or indeed that they have any special *social* significance.'

Also on the hunt for New Town significance was the journalist Monica Furlong, who by 1960 had developed a love-hate fascination with another of the first wave, Harlow. 'All the buildings in the town centre are built with a feeling of airy grace,' she wrote in the *Spectator*, though not denying that during the winter 'the winds whip across the squares' – the price of 'a feeling of glass and straight lines and space'. More problematic was the human factor, notably the thin-on-the-ground professional class. 'I'm not a snob or anything like that,' one of the town's industrialists told her, 'it's just that these people here aren't our type. My wife felt she couldn't stand it any longer and we moved out to Bishop's Stortford. We made more friends in a month there than in four years here.' By contrast, Furlong was favourably struck by the 'kindly and paternalistic attitude' of the Development Corporation's staff, still motivated by 'intense idealism about the town', and she depicted the working-class population as by now thoroughly settled in its new environment, helped by 'an intense pride in their houses' and 'a passion for gardening' as well as 'a great pride in the schools their children are going to'. Altogether, her verdict on Harlow was that 'there is something fine and infinitely touching about the place'.[38]

Others were less generous to the New Towns. Although *The Times* in September 1960 broadly welcomed the prospect of three more, including Skelmersdale in Lancashire to help with the continuing Merseyside overspill problem, its tone was somewhat grudging. 'Is it necessary,' the paper asked, 'to perpetuate in new towns the desolate atmosphere of suburbs during the day by segregating industrial and residential areas?' The editorial also cited research in Crawley showing that most inhabitants there did not belong to a library, did not buy books and did not take part in any organisation. 'Over half of the adults spent three or more of the weekday evenings watching television,' it added. 'Are these the lineaments of Utopia?' As for the architectural quality of the New Towns, the progressive conventional wisdom was stated the following summer, also in *The Times*, by Graeme Shankland. His explicit yardstick was 'an environment that is as inspiring as it is clean', and he accused them of looking 'backwards' to the garden cities: 'Their housing, almost entirely of cottages and gardens, may satisfy their first young families; but does not constitute an environment for those who will follow.' Shankland was far more positive about the next New Town, the already designated Cumbernauld, planned as 'a compact hilltop town' whose centre, once built, 'should be one of Britain's few architectural wonders'. The most publicised critique of the New Towns already in existence came in August 1961 when the Ministry of Housing's annual report focused on progress so far and claimed that 'it is doubtful whether the neighbourliness and intimacy typical of urban life at its best can ever be reproduced within a framework of a housing layout based on the generous [ie, low] densities and living conditions inherent in the garden city idea.' The report then turned to the malady of the so-called 'New Town blues', arguing that though this had been considerably exaggerated by the press, it still undoubtedly existed: 'For those who are unable or unwilling to adapt themselves to completely new conditions, for those who are shy or worried by financial troubles and who miss the ready help of relatives and friends close by, life can be lonely and isolated.' That evening, the report and its conclusions featured on BBC Television's *Tonight*, in a way that thoroughly irritated 'Astragal', weekly columnist in the *Architects' Journal*: 'A combination of good scripting and good camerawork could say far more about the architecture of New Towns in a few minutes than any amount of interviewing of tenants.'[39]

The report was barely published before Victor Cull, community development officer for Hatfield New Town, vigorously denied the phenomenon of the 'New Town blues'. 'Some people from London feel there is too much space, and they've never had a garden,' he explained. 'Then they plant a couple of rose bushes and they say, "Look at this, Mr Cull – roses," as though they had sprouted coconuts. They feel a sense of creation for that sort of thing, if you see what I mean.' In fact, it was a phenomenon that in effect had already been explored by a New Town doctor, S. D. Coleman of East Kilbride, who in November 1959 visited half a dozen New Towns in England and took local soundings on the theme of mental health and social adjustment. In Stevenage, two doctors told him that they 'did not think there was an unusual incidence of neurosis'; in Harlow, a doctor stated that some patients 'felt quite uprooted at first, but later settled down'; in Crawley, a doctor noted that 'excessive demands for his services' were made by people, especially young married women, who had 'recently moved' there; in Basildon, a GP informed Coleman that 'for the first six or nine months, many people felt "quite lost," and pined away for familiar faces and places.' Coleman's own East Kilbride case notes were broadly in line with these findings. A 30-year-old married woman with two children, who had come from Edinburgh and been living there for four years, was still finding it difficult to come to terms with her new situation ('Everything is different . . . I feel trapped here'); a 22-year-old married woman with two children, living there for four months, had not yet begun to adjust ('It is quite lonely out here'); and a 25-year-old married woman, eight months there, was starting to accept her new life ('It is a much nicer place [than Glasgow], cleaner, and you feel as if you were somewhere, I feel as if I am abroad'). 'There is, in my opinion, no specific "New Town Neurosis",' concluded Coleman, 'as the symptoms complained of by patients in New Towns or Housing Estates are no different to those suffering from neurosis anywhere else. The name that I would suggest for neurosis of a temporary nature, due to or exacerbated by the social upheaval of re-housing, is "Transitional Neurosis".'

Even so, the tag stuck. Moreover, despite the BBC announcing in March 1962 that another doctor, Dr Dale, was moving with his wife, the country's best-known diarist, to a New Town called 'Exton', some 35 miles north of London, the shock of the new had largely gone. Once, the New Towns had been perhaps more emblematic than anything else of that unique '1945' moment: a healthy, egalitarian, herbivorous, planned future that would mark a clean break with all the old carnivorous urban horrors. But now, by the early 1960s, modernity had come to mean something different. 'Buildings like the Seagram in New York, cities like Brasilia, the work of men like Corbusier' – those were the exemplars held up for admiration by Princess Margaret's husband as he opened (at the Royal Festival Hall in July 1961) the Sixth Congress of the International Union of Architects. Britain itself, lamented Antony Armstrong-Jones, had 'of recent years been somewhat lacking in architectural inventiveness and the excitement that goes with it'. Accordingly, as he looked ahead to the rest of the 1960s and beyond, the photographer and designer (already planning his aviary for London Zoo) called on those present to bear two words in mind: 'calculated boldness'.[40]

11

Make Him Sir Yuri!

'The hottest day since 1947,' recorded Kenneth Williams in London on Saturday, 1 July 1961. 'Absolutely horrible and exhausting. Over 90°. All the nellies in the parks.' Hot too for the birth of the Queen's future hot-to-handle daughter-in-law, Diana Spencer, while Judy Haines in Chingford noted 'an absolute scorcher' for the fete at the County High School. 'Girls danced beautifully in broiling sun, and John snapped them in colour.' The family was shortly off for a fortnight's holiday, with Haines by Wednesday the 5th lamenting, 'I seem to be washing and ironing daily.' Another diarist, Madge Martin, that day had lunch with her husband in the new Grill Room at the Regent Palace Hotel near Piccadilly Circus: 'We had to admit, reluctantly, that the food (grilled chicken) was good, though we shall never like the modern surroundings, and do miss our dear old Grill Room in the basement.' Thursday saw the debut of *Mersey Beat* magazine – including 'Fashion Notes by Priscilla' by Cilla White, but from now called Cilla Black – while Haines allowed herself to listen to Britain's Angela Mortimer beating her South African opponent in the women's semi-finals at Wimbledon, and 'cried at the end of it'. Next day, the 7th, *TV Times* profiled 39-year-old Kingsley Amis ('the voice of youth, who shouts in protest against the failings of middle age and pomposity'); following a crisis meeting at Lyme Hall near Stockport of *New Left Review*'s board, editorial representatives and delegates from the clubs, the *NLR*'s editor Stuart Hall observed in a memo that 'the main complaint' had been that 'the style of the journal is pitched above the heads of the most active people in the movement'; and for Haines, it was 'more washing and ironing!!'[1]

It did not quite seem it at the time, but Saturday the 8th was one for the history books. Richard Crossman was in Workington ('a wholly working-class, dreary little place'); large queues formed ahead of the opening of the Soviet Exhibition at Earl's Court; a marriage guidance expert told a meeting at Keele of the National Association of Boys' Clubs that 'one of the major problems of young people in sex is how far they should go'; villagers at Iver in Buckinghamshire turned out in their hundreds ('despite a persistent drizzle') to welcome home the Duke and Duchess of Kent from their Majorca honeymoon; Britain's biggest jazz festival yet, in the grounds of Fulford Hall near Birmingham, was exclusively for 'traddies', starring Acker Bilk and his Paramount Jazz Band; Fred Trueman cleaned up against the Australians at Headingley; Stirling Moss won the main race of the day at Silverstone despite driving with a broken clutch; Angela Mortimer beat Christine Truman ('upset by a fall', noted Haines, 'but sportingly played on') in an all-British final at Wimbledon; a Russian crew (from the Central Sports Club, USSR Navy, Moscow, presumably watched by the embassy's assistant naval attaché, Yevgeny Ivanov) took the Grand Challenge Cup at Henley; Harrow thrashed Eton by an innings at Lord's ('a sea of grey toppers, cornstalks and multi-coloured hats and dresses surged out in front of the pavilion to greet the winning team'); and an Old Harrovian, now Secretary of State for War, that evening encountered a semi-naked Christine Keeler by a swimming pool at Cliveden. How two historians, with their fascination for the variousness of human behaviour, would have relished being on the inside track. Instead, the following evening, A.J.P. Taylor and Hugh Trevor-Roper jousted on television about Taylor's *The Origins of the Second World War*, condemned by Trevor-Roper in the current issue of *Encounter* as 'utterly erroneous' and the work of a historian who 'selects, suppresses, and arranges evidence on no principle other than the needs of his thesis' – so much so that 'it will do harm, perhaps irreparable harm, to Mr Taylor's reputation as a serious historian.' The debate itself, though, never quite fired, prompting an unimpressed Louis MacNeice to comment that the war 'was not fought out in a Senior Common Room where they had forgotten to open the windows'; or, as a local government officer put it after watching the programme (called *Did Hitler Cause the War?*), 'I do not think it much matters after 22 years if he did cause the war – it was enough that there was a war.'[2]

The *Daily Mirror*'s Clifford Davis kept up his campaign against *Coronation Street* on Tuesday the 11th ('nothing really changes and nobody does anything, except clack'), but next day's banner headline in the paper was altogether more positive: 'MAKE HIM SIR YURI!' The space pioneer was visiting, to a tumultuous welcome – 'his drive from London Airport to the Russian Embassy was a triumphal progress,' reported the *Evening Standard*, as 'crowds all along the route roared "Yuri" and "Well done"' – leaving Sir Harold Nicolson to reflect later in the week, after Gagarin had been interviewed on television, 'How can a country be a menace when it has as its hero a man with so entrancing a smile?' A less entrancing prospect to some was the imminent arrival in Pembrokeshire of West German Panzers, due to train on the ranges at Castlemartin. 'An insult to our dead and a betrayal of Britain and its people,' declared D. Ivor Davies in the *Pembroke County and West Wales Guardian* on Friday the 14th on behalf of protesting South Wales trades unionists. In Pembrokeshire that day to see for himself was the busy War minister, John Profumo, conceding that it was 'a very sensitive problem'. Next day, the Durham Miners Gala had a record number of arrests, mainly for drunkenness; on Sunday, Christopher Isherwood met Joan Littlewood ('a pretty bogus down-to-earther'), who had just announced her shock departure from Theatre Workshop and her intention to live abroad; on Tuesday a new accident wing opened at Oxbridge General; and on Wednesday, the Gentlemen met the Players in the annual encounter at Lord's, with the latter (including the always status-conscious Fred Trueman) making short work of two over-promoted young Cantabs, one of them J. M. Brearley. Two diarists gave the thumbs-down on Thursday the 20th – Kenneth Preston's son Allan to a 'typical' English meal at a Harrogate café ('nothing tasted of very much & there was not much of it'), Anthony Heap to the Anthony Newley musical vehicle *Stop the World, I Want to Get Off* ('its humour is crude, its satire heavy-handed') – before four days later saw the official launch of Arnold Wesker's Centre 42 movement, seeking to take culture to the people. 'Wouldn't going after this larger audience have an effect on the *content* of the art offered? asked someone,' recorded the *New Statesman*'s John Coleman about the management committee's informal press conference that evening at Wesker's house. 'What, anyway, *was* the art that the "working classes" (the phrase rang, undefined, throughout the discussion) were going to draw new life from? Examples, please? Early days for that, said some of the committee; the thing was to get things moving, to explore, not to dogmatise.' That same Monday evening, on a TV soap about a West End store called *Harpers West One*, the actor John Leyton, playing a pop singer, sung live his imminent new single 'Johnny Remember Me' – Victorian gothic for the early 1960s, as hauntingly evoked by the gifted producer Joe Meek – and at the last minute the line 'The girl I loved who died a year ago' changed at the BBC's request on the record itself to 'The girl I loved and lost a year ago'. A final word on the astronaut's visit – seen by some as excessively fawning on the part of the hosts – came in a letter to *The Times* on Tuesday the 25th. 'Was not Major Gagarin warmly welcomed in this country,' rhetorically asked G. R. Davies of Orpington, 'because he looked modest, handsome, sportsmanlike, and completely at ease – all essentially *English* qualities?'[3]

'No nation broker,' admitted Peter Cook's Macmillan in one of the *Beyond the Fringe* sketches, and the new Governor of the Bank of England, Lord (Rowley) Cromer, agreed. 'Sterling is under extreme pressure,' he informed the Chancellor, Selwyn Lloyd, in early July, as he demanded a comprehensive statement by the end of the month and set out his diagnosis of a sick economy: 'Wage and salary increases unrelated to increased productivity, sometimes even pre-empted on the conjecture of it'; 'restrictive practices on the part of labour'; 'complacency on the part of some employers'; too much 'non-productive investment' in public expenditure; and a defence policy that was still 'a heritage from the great days of our imperial past'. Lloyd's eventual package – 'the July measures' – was announced on the 25th: it included various personal credit and government expenditure restrictions, a 10 per cent increase in purchase tax, a hefty rise in the Bank Rate from 5 to 7 per cent and a call for a 'pay pause'. Taken as whole, the *FT* called them 'the toughest economic restraints since the austerity period of Sir Stafford Cripps'. Reaction was largely negative. *The Times* doubted whether 'the cautious and shrewd Swiss banker', that emblematic holder and seller of sterling, would see enough in Lloyd's measures 'to convince him that at last the British economy is going to stand on its feet'; the *Daily Mail* viewed 'the Chancellor's remedies' as 'designed to cure a recurrent tummy-ache but not to get at the seat of the trouble'; so too the City, where there was 'surprise and disappointment', with 'difficulty in seeing what long-term measures have been taken to tackle the basic defects in the economy'; while on the part of the trade unions, faced by the unusual sight of a peacetime government apparently aspiring to interfere comprehensively with free collective bargaining, they, 'in reply to Mr Lloyd's asking for a "pause" in the wages battle, did not pause an instant', noted Mollie Panter-Downes a week later, 'before informing him that raising the cost of living is no way to make men tuck pending wage claims back in their pockets, and that they will go ahead with them as though he had not uttered'. She added that 'a rain of strikes or threats of strikes is thus forecast as this autumn and winter's depressing weather.' Public opinion, as ever, focused on the essentials. 'On the bus to Marlborough,' recorded the holidaying Henry St John on the morning of the 26th as he travelled from Salisbury, 'a busman repeated like a parrot at least half a dozen times "You've never had it so good" . . . He and two other busmen talked about the increase of 4d on a packet of 20 cigarettes and the increase in the price of petrol, but not about the other aspects of the Chancellor of the Exchequer's speech.'[4]

Later on the 26th, Selwyn Lloyd – seldom viewed as an inspirational figure – sought to complement his short-term deflationary measures by setting out in the Commons how in the longer term the British economy might be enabled to grow on a sustainable basis and thus break out of its wretched stop-go cycle. 'The controversial matter of planning at once arises,' he noted. 'I am not frightened of the word.' He went on to explain his intention to achieve 'better co-ordination' with 'both sides of industry', specifically through 'a joint examination of the economic prospects of the country stretching five or more years into the future'. In short, 'I want both sides of industry to share with the Government the task of relating plans to the resources likely to be available.' Immediate reaction tended to be somewhat sceptical – the *FT* reflecting that 'planning will always suffer from one great disadvantage in a democracy', namely that 'there is no means of enforcing the plan', while the *Economist* predicted that the unions would 'scream blue murder', given that 'the main thing that needs to be planned is that trade unionists and other earners should not annually get much more money before they have earned it' – but Lloyd pressed on, asking on 8 August the Federation of British Industries (FBI) and the TUC to come together in a joint national forum.

'It had better be said straight away that the objective of planning should not be to get some "representative" committee of trade union leaders, large employers and establishment figures to sit down together, air their mutual prejudices, and strike meaningless verbal compromises with each other, in the hope that Britain's economic difficulties will then somehow be rubbed away,' candidly warned the *Economist* later that month. 'On the contrary, the purpose of any effective new planning machinery should be to diminish the practical power of some of these organised groups, and to increase the influence of public policy and attitudes of what might be called the economic technocrats.' Who were these wonderful, disinterested people? The 'nearest equivalent' in Britain, reckoned the paper, were 'some civil servants hidden from public gaze in the Treasury and possibly some officials in the Bank of England'; it also called for the Treasury to be split under two Cabinet ministers, with the more senior one 'in charge of general economic policy' and the other 'responsible for narrower financial operations'. At the end the key, anti-corporatist argument was reiterated: 'It would be a bad mistake to give too much planning power to those who, to some extent, need to be planned against.' Still, however it was going to be achieved, the planning moment was in the summer of 1961 apparently at hand, not only in relation to economic management, but there most visibly. As the historian Glen O'Hara observes, 'If there was one concept at the heart of the raised expectations and dashed hopes of British politics in the 1960s, it was "planning"' – the concept that above all 'held out the promise of a more modern Britain'.[5]

The intention to go down the planning road was not the last of the major July pronouncements, for on Monday the 31st Macmillan made a brief factual statement confirming that the British government did indeed intend to make an application to join the European Economic Community, aka the Common Market. Mollie Panter-Downes, watching from the press gallery, was disappointed by the PM's deliberately low-key approach – 'sounded and looked to many of us like a company chairman badly in need of a holiday who was putting over with infinite caution the idea of a merger which might or might not come off' – over what she declared to be 'the most supremely important announcement delivered to Parliament and the country since the outbreak of the Second World War'. But two days later, as the Commons debated the issue, Macmillan did attempt to soar, claiming not only that 'our right place is in the vanguard of the movement towards the greater unity of the free world' but also that 'in the long run an island placed as ours is, where our need to export to other people will always be greater than their need to export to us, cannot maintain the high standards of life that we want for our people in an isolated protective system.' The press, apart of course from the Beaverbrook element, was still broadly supportive, including the *FT*'s strongly free-market columnist Harold Wincott, with a large following in the City. 'If by any other means we could get the necessary competition here in our own market, with compensating benefits and advantages for our exporters, we could afford to remain outside,' he argued the day after Macmillan's announcement. 'But we can't . . . Only the judgement and the cathartic properties of a market of 260 million people remain. But what a promise also resides in this new chapter of our economic history which we must pray is opening up.' What about public opinion? The most recent survey came from Gallup in July, finding that 38 per cent approved of an application to join, 22 per cent disapproved, and the rest – almost half – were undecided. *The Times* on 1 August called for a 'great national debate', but it was a debate missing some crucial information. Earlier in the summer, the Lord Chancellor, Lord Kilmuir, had sought to assess the impact of entry and had concluded:

> (a) Parliament would be required to surrender some of its functions to the organs of the Community. (b) The Crown would be called on to transfer part of its treaty-making power to those organs. (c) Our courts of law would sacrifice some degree of independence by becoming subordinate in certain respects to the European Court of Justice. In the long run, we shall have to decide whether the economic factors require us to make some sacrifices of sovereignty. My concern is to ensure that we should see exactly what it is that we are being called on to sacrifice, and how serious our loss would be.

However, noted Andy Mullen and Brian Burkitt in the *Political Quarterly* in 2005, this assessment was 'never placed in the public domain'.[6]

A few hours after Macmillan had made his historic announcement, the penultimate day's play in the Fourth Test at Old Trafford ended with the match evenly poised, and, after the crowd had gone, the Australian captain Richie Benaud walking out in his blue suede shoes to inspect the wicket. Next afternoon, England were seemingly poised to win – 'yet nothing,' reported John Woodcock in *The Times*, 'would divert Benaud from his determination to attack ... chancing all on England's fallibility against flighted spin.' In under two hours, Benaud took 6 for 30, to win the game for Australia and retain the Ashes. 'A jolly good, exciting match,' graciously said England's amateur captain Peter May afterwards, but he himself had been bowled round his legs by Benaud for a second-ball duck; while from the professional camp, the Yorkshire all-rounder Brian Close had been little more successful in an innings that, complained E. W. Swanton in the *Daily Telegraph*, 'taxed credibility to behold'. Altogether, reflected Philip Larkin a couple of days later, it had been 'certainly an exasperating affair', in essence 'the same old story: they can do it, we can't'. Another poet, Alan Ross, broadly agreed, writing in the *Observer* the following Sunday that 'the best Australian characteristics, independence, generosity of endeavour, refusal to surrender, thrust and aggression, were displayed to the full like a spread peacock's tail.'[7] Put another way (as he did not add though might have done), a bold young country had defeated a rather tired old one. The embrace of modernity, including European modernity, was an attempt at reinvention. Whether it would succeed, and what the collateral damage would be, remained to be seen.

'Determined to use washing machine till it drops,' noted Judy Haines, back from her West Country holiday, on 2 August. 'I stuck broken piece of shaft back on and washed a blanket most satisfactorily.' That evening, Anthony Heap saw the new Brian Rix farce, *One for the Pot* ('never has a Whitehall first night audience been more continuously convulsed with laughter'); while over the next few days, the military historian Michael Howard laid into Alan Clark's *The Donkeys* (his

Listener review criticising Clark's attack on the First World War generals as full of 'personal bitterness', 'slovenly scholarship' and 'petulant caricatures'); *Melody Maker* acclaimed Chubby Checker's new single 'Let's Twist Again' as 'juke-box material with tremendous urge against a potent beat'; and at the Loders Fete in Dorset on Saturday the 5th 'the highlight of the afternoon,' reported the Rev. Oliver Willmott, 'was the adjudication by the stage and television star, Vic Oliver, of a competition for glamorous grandmothers.' 'Nobody,' he added, 'envied the judge his job. Never before has mutton looked so lamb-like. His choice was Mrs Thomas, the wife of our worthy sacristan, whom he gallantly kissed.' Over the next ten days or so, the *Daily Mirror* printed a letter from D.L. of Orpington about how some German friends recently on holiday in Britain had been especially impressed by 'the orderly queues at bus stops, people taking newspapers from unattended stands and leaving the correct money, the quiet of our parks'; officers from the 84th Panzer Division arrived in Pembrokeshire; Margaret Thatcher told her Finchley constituents that 'sovereignty and independence are not ends in themselves' and that it was time for Britain to follow the French example of sinking 'political differences' with Germany and working for 'a united Europe'; a BBC survey of the popularity of its television sports commentators found Peter West ('exceptionally versatile') coming out on top, with E. W. Swanton ('rather a patronising manner') well down the field; and on Wednesday the 16th, Judy Haines was at Broadcasting House with her children. 'They waited in foyer while I was interviewed by Mollie Lee on Mother and Daughter Relationship. The atmosphere was velvety, and I enjoyed speaking, which was recorded. I agreed to suggestion I use a fictitious name, and Mollie Lee suggested Barnes – Pauline Barnes.' The programme was Haines's favourite, *Woman's Hour*, and as Lee explained to listeners, 'Some time ago, we received a letter from a listener who seemed to be worried by her own relationship with her mother. "Are all mothers saintly?" was the question she was putting to herself. We invited her to the studio . . .' Haines's mother had died in January, and in front of the microphone she spoke (as revealed by the transcript) quite candidly about her mother's possessiveness and lack of humour, and how she as a mother herself was now trying to bring up her own daughters differently ('they're individuals, to live their own lives and to be free'). 'You see,' concluded Haines, 'my mother was a good woman but I didn't love her and I don't think she loved me and she expected a lot of me and I never felt I came up to scratch.' Meanwhile, noted her diary, 'nothing exciting had happened in the foyer', and 'in desperation' Ione, Pamela and their friend John 'asked me for *my* autograph'.[8]

Two days later, Friday the 18th, the radio ballad *The Big Hewer* (including Ewan MacColl's song of the same name) gave the heroic treatment to the coal miner; Anthony Heap on holiday with his son at Butlin's in Pwllheli reflected that 'the young yobs and chits here seem less addicted to the portable radio mania than they were at Filey last year, but tend to be much rowdier late at night'; Isabel Quigly in the *Spectator* reviewed *The Parent Trap* (a 'shamelessly sentimental film' in which Hayley Mills 'justifies the overworked word infectious'); and two very different observers of the contemporary scene vented their feelings. 'Gloom and despondency,' the Manchester physician Hugh Selbourne wrote in his diary. 'Berlin crisis [the Wall now being built], Rhodesians' clash, salaries of £12,000 being paid to railways executives in England, Macmillan grouse-shooting.' The other lament, very much public, was John Osborne's instantly notorious open letter 'Damn you, England' in the left-wing weekly *Tribune*. 'This is a letter of hate,' he began. 'It is for you, my countrymen. I mean those men of my country who have defiled it. The men with manic fingers leading the sightless, feeble, betrayed body of my country to its death. You are its murderers.' Osborne's attack was not, as was often lazily assumed at the time, a general state-of-the-nation polemic; rather, it was a savage verbal assault by a ban-the-bomber against the keep-the-bombers. 'There is murder in my brain,' he declared, 'and I carry a knife in my heart for every one of you. Macmillan, and you, Gaitskell, you particularly.' The *Sunday Times* took the immediate pulse. 'He expresses exactly what I feel when I think of Gaitskell, Macmillan and the whole horrible crew, it's impossible not to feel too violently,' said the novelist John Braine. 'I know what he feels and so do hundreds of thousands of others,' broadly agreed Arnold Wesker. 'I haven't read the whole thing, but is it all that important?' wondered J. B. Priestley. 'Ludicrous – a wild, pathetic letter,' responded the artist John Bratby. 'I might read it if it were translated into English,' half-promised Hugh Trevor-Roper. And from the most renowned arbiter of the moment, Richard Hoggart, just two words: 'Oh, dear!'[9]

That weekend saw the first major race riot since Notting Hill three years earlier. Perhaps surprisingly, it did not happen in Smethwick, where during July the already heated temperature had gone up a few further degrees with the Price Street rent strike, attracting national attention. The episode began when a Pakistani family of five (Mr and Mrs Sardar Mohammed, their two children and a nephew), their present house due for demolition, were allocated a council flat in Price Street's hitherto all-white block; the tenants there refused to pay rent; and the strike collapsed only when Smethwick Town Council gave non-payers four weeks' notice to quit. The council's action was unanimous, though with Alderman George Aldridge publicly warning that 'while it is our moral obligation to rehouse this family, we should remember that cleanliness is next to Godliness and insist that council regulations are observed.' Soon afterwards, investigating 'Smethwick's "Little Asia"' for the *Sunday Times*, Tom Stacey sat in a local pub – where 'six dingy streets' met, five leading in from factories ('glass-works, screws, motor parts'), one from the Price Street block – and heard the views of local whites. From a 'red-eyed foreman': 'Send the sluggers back. Put 'em on the Queen Mary and sink it 'arf way.' From a 20-year-old electrical apprentice in a narrow tie: 'Bloodshed, that's what's going to 'appen. The young people won't stand much more.' And from a 'brooched lady': 'They breed like rabbits . . . They're real smelly, I'll tell you that . . . You've only got to black your face to pick up four or five pound National Assistance.' 'In the pub,' reflected Stacey about the impact of the town's mainly Asian 'coloured immigrants' (some 5,000 out of an 80,000 population), 'the symptoms were accumulating – of the gravity of the challenge to the fragile but intensely precious homogeneity of a sparingly-educated urban community; of the profound insecurity worked by an intrusion unfathomably alien . . .'

In fact the race riot, over the weekend of 19–20 August, was in Middlesbrough (estimated non-white population of 3,000, again mainly Asian, out of a total of nearly 160,000). On Friday night a white youth was fatally stabbed, with an Arab from the Aden Protectorate being arrested and charged on Saturday. The trouble, reported the *Guardian*, began that night:

> After public-house closing time, a crowd of several hundred people congregated in Cannon Street. Stones and bottles were hurled through the windows of the cafe [the Taj Mahal] run by coloured people and an ugly situation developed. Large numbers of police were rushed to the area and there were numerous outbreaks of fighting. At the height of the disturbance the fire brigade received a call to the cafe where a table was set on fire . . .
>
> There was some trouble yesterday [Sunday] afternoon when youths threw stones at a shop owned by an Indian in Boundary Road. More stone-throwing took place in the market place area and a cafe window there was broken. A large crowd, including many women and children, collected in Cannon Street and police reinforcements stood by in cars and vans in side streets.
>
> Several Pakistanis and Arabs yesterday moved with their families to friends living well away from the Cannon Street area. Crowds gathered and there were one or two shouts and catcalls as the coloured residents loaded their suitcases into taxis and drove off.
>
> In the confusion yesterday a Methodist church was holding its service as normal but the hymns were almost drowned by the shouting outside.

'POLICE FIGHT MOB OF 500 IN RACE RIOT TOWN' was the *Daily Mirror*'s headline, but the town's Chief Constable, Ralph Davison, sought to play down the race aspect: 'I don't feel it is a true racial dispute in the sense that the majority of the people of Middlesbrough are hostile to coloured people. A small minority has seized on recent incidents to settle old scores.' That, though, was probably wishful thinking, with the historian Panikos Panayi finding in his detailed study of these events and their local context that 'the disturbance of August 1961 was not an isolated example of racial prejudice,' that indeed 'it brought to the surface the subconscious racial hostility of white Middlesbrough which found an outlet for its prejudice.' Still, whatever the motivation, a riot was not quite a war. On the Monday the *Northern Echo* (the Darlington-based regional paper where the youngish Harold Evans had just arrived as editor) gratefully observed how 'to their credit the coloured people have suffered the present provocations without retaliating in kind.'[10]

That evening, as Madge Martin sat in a 'packed' house at the Victoria Palace to see *The Sound of Music* ('strangely popular in these days of smart, unhappy stage shows . . . the audience rapturous'), the National Gallery's recently acquired Goya portrait of the Duke of Wellington went missing – stolen, it eventually turned out, by an unemployed Newcastle man, Kempton Bunton, whose 'sole object', he would explain, was 'to set up a charity to pay for television licences for old and poor people who seem to be neglected in our affluent society'. On Tuesday the 22nd, Dick Etheridge, leading shop steward at the Austin car plant at Longbridge, curtly informed Selwyn Lloyd that he had 'the cheek of the devil asking us to agree to a wage increase pause' and that Lloyd could expect 'the uttermost opposition' to his policies; that evening, Michael Caine had a starring role ('marvellous . . . perfect . . . never seen such acting,' according to viewers), as a young man who eventually pulls a gun, in Johnny Speight's television play *The Compartment*; and at around 6.45 on Wednesday morning, a Bedfordshire farm labourer called Sidney Burton was walking along the Deadman's Hill stretch of the A6, near the village of Clophill, when he came across, parked in a lay-by, a grey 1956 Morris Minor – in which he found the dead Michael Gregsten, a scientist at the Road Research Laboratory near Slough, and his semi-conscious mistress, Valerie Storie, who had been raped, shot and left paralysed. Within hours a manhunt was under way. Three days later on the 26th, while Declan MacManus (later Elvis Costello) watched the day after his seventh birthday his first match at Anfield (Liverpool crushing Leeds 5–0) and became a lifelong Red, the 14-year-old Jonathan Meades was stuck in a classic summer Saturday traffic jam on the notorious Exeter bypass, this one 20 miles long. The radio played the grimly atmospheric 'Johnny Remember Me' (by now supplanting Helen Shapiro's second single, 'You Don't Know', as number 1), then gave the latest on the A6 murder, and Meades would spend a lifetime 'failing to dissociate the song from the news report which followed it'.

The summer was almost over. On Wednesday the 30th, the Gentlemen of England took on the Australians in front of a thin crowd (but including this 10-year-old boy) at Lord's; next day, as Pat Hornsby-Smith resigned as a junior minister in order to pursue her business interests and thereby put herself out of contention as a future female PM, Bob Wooler's first column in *Mersey Beat* hailed 'A Phenomenon called The Beatles!' ('musically authoritative and physically magnetic . . . the stuff that screams are made of'); and on Friday, 1 September, Hampshire beat Derbyshire at Bournemouth to win the county championship for the first time. 'I always insist on the boys being in bed by dawn,' the team's bold Old Etonian captain Colin Ingleby-Mackenzie told a BBC reporter when asked about the secret of their success: seemingly a last hurrah, in an increasingly professionalised age, for the old-style amateur.[11]

12

The Immigrants Are Human

Some advertisements from 1961 and the first half of 1962: Nimble was 'The Lighter Bread That Keeps You Fit'; Eskimo offered 'the most modern, up-to-date line in frozen foods'; Crosse & Blackwell's Double Soups were '*condensed* modern-style to give you double the quantity!'; Kraft's Philadelphia Cream Cheese Spread was 'going to be as popular as it is in the States!'; the Milky Bars were on the Milky Bar Kid (a pale, freckly boy with NHS glasses); Mackintosh's 'Week-End' selection of chocolates brought the flavour home to you; Heinz Spaghetti Bolognese was the 'EXCITING NEW ITALIAN DISH'; Skol was 'the light dry lager' brewed 'IN THE CONTINENTAL MANNER'; the Consul Capri was the 'FIRST PERSONAL CAR FROM FORD OF BRITAIN' ('a sleek and elegant extension of your own personality'); Ford's two new Zephyrs were the 4 and 6 ('Value never looked so good . . . Comfort never had such power!'); 'Square Deal Surf' promised 18 per cent more washing powder for the same price; for children there were 'The Newsiest Fashions Chosen by C&A for Young Moderns'; and at Victor Value supermarket in Romford, the come-on was not only 'money-saving one-stop shopping' but also 'free gifts', such as a 'beautiful Contemporary Italian Table Lamp designed for modern living'. The new retained its premium, and more. A women's-page editor referred to 'the growing popularity of contact lenses as an alternative to spectacles'; another noted how 'more and more people are becoming "frying fiends" since the introduction of vegetable oil on the British market' (as a healthier alternative to animal fats); Rowntree's launched (initially in Scotland) the After Eight Mint as an upmarket after-dinner treat; Imperial Tobacco's Golden Wonder brought in the first flavoured crisps (cheese and onion), bad news for Smith's Crisps and the little blue bag of salt; the first Cranks vegetarian restaurant (in Covent Garden) was complemented by the rapid rise of London Steak Houses (the first one opening in Baker Street); the electric toothbrush, fruit yoghurts and aluminium foil were all newcomers; a factory opened in Newport, Shropshire to wash, grade and pre-pack potatoes, the first of its kind in Britain; and, almost simultaneously, in September 1961, the first 21 Shop opened in Knightsbridge (interior design by Terence Conran, clothes by Mary Quant, Jean Muir and others) and the pioneer Mother-and-Child Centre, in effect the first Mothercare, opened in Kingston, Surrey (selling not just children's clothes and equipment but also 'Paris Maternity Fashions – At Practical Prices'). The new had certainly appealed the previous month to the 16-year-old Ian Jack, down from Scotland and taken by his older brother to a Chinese restaurant on Shaftesbury Avenue to try sweet-and-sour pork: 'The taste and texture of the crisp little golden balls and their sauce were sensational.'[1]

What about shopping itself? By 1961, although still taking only 11 per cent of all retail sales, there were well over 6,000 self-service stores in Britain, of which at least 500 were supermarkets; that spring, a detailed survey of housewives' attitudes to supermarket shopping was conducted in various 'good' parts of London and the Home Counties, including Harrow, Wimbledon, Maidenhead and Bromley. Called *Shopping in Suburbia* on publication in 1963, it featured a range of housewives' voices:

> I like to wander round and not be restricted and you can take what you want and then put it back and they don't seem to mind how long you spend there. I think you get everything fresh and wrapped and it's not handled by people's fingers. That's a good point. Then you get a penny off this and that and it all helps to pay your fare to the shop – you get all your shopping there in the one shop and that's what I like about it. Then you have finished and can go home. They're awfully polite, too. The queuing up is the biggest disadvantage – and then when they're open at weekends some of the women push and push with wire baskets ... (*Working-class, age 47*)
>
> Of course, you can go from shop to shop but most women like me

think shopping is all very well but not food shops. We'd much rather look in dress shops. Still, the supermarket can give you some ideas. You have to watch prices, though. In the supermarket they're not always cut-price. At another shop luncheon meat is 9d a quarter but at the supermarket it's 10½d. It's best if you can dodge about ... (*Lower middle-class, 48*)

I expect I'll get the habit – like everybody else when there are more of them. And I do rather like the wide variety you can choose from and the spaciousness when there aren't too many people there! (*Middle-class, 35*)

You've got everything under the one roof and there is everything you can think of there. The working housewife who's out all day finds it much quicker and more helpful. (*Working-class, 60*)

You sort of learn what to get and not get as you go. (*Middle-class, 20*)

When you first start going you do feel lost but you get used to it. (*Middle-class, 39*)

Cheeses are well displayed and I tried some I have never tried before because I see them cut up and ready to take away. (*Working-class, 29*)

I'm not so keen on some wrapped things. I wouldn't buy potatoes or greens because although they have air-holes they sweat a lot and smell musty. (*Lower middle-class, 47*)

Packaging is a good thing really. You don't get flies on it. It's very hygienic. (*Working-class, 45*)

Chickens haven't the flavour as you buy in the butcher's. When I buy meat I like the atmosphere in a butcher's shop but it does take more time. (*Middle-class, 35*)

There is too much persuasion to buy – voices speaking and loudspeakers telling you to buy. They do press you. I think they're a step in the wrong direction but I feel I'm in the minority – wanting to shop with the small retailers. (*Lower middle-class, 57*)

It *is* an American idea, isn't it? I believe some people go to America to get ideas sometimes. (*Working-class, 50*)

The main conclusions reached by the survey were that the housewife was far likelier to go to the supermarket for soap and detergents or canned goods than for meat or fruit and veg, where the traditional butcher and greengrocer still retained her trust and custom; that 'there is, so far, no obvious sign of supermarket inroads into *non-food* markets'; that younger housewives were more likely to find supermarket shopping 'fun'; and that, despite some housewives missing 'the homeliness and security of small shops', the overall view across the age spectrum was 'largely favourable'. Specifically, in addition to 'speed, variety and price range', interviewees identified three main pluses: the ability to go at one's own pace; 'freedom from embarrassment' when confronted by new or unfamiliar products; and, perhaps most suggestively, that it was easier in a supermarket for the shopper to start experimenting and thereby, in the report's words, to 'build up a satisfying image of herself as a housewife'.

Not all supermarkets were the same. Whereas Sainsburys adopted in 1961 a strictly regulated five-day week ('morally and socially right', declared Robert Sainsbury, adding that 'the anarchy of late shopping hours is precisely what we want to avoid'), Tesco under the buccaneering Jack Cohen pushed ahead on all possible fronts: not only the opening in December 1961 of its huge Leicester flagship store but a sustained guerrilla campaign against the system of fixed retail prices as legally embodied in Resale Price Maintenance. 'We are not attacking the small trader,' declared Cohen at the Leicester opening (after Sid James had cut the tape). 'It is the manufacturer we are after. We are fighting for the right of every believer in free retail enterprise to expect keen prices and greater choice.' Consumer protection, meanwhile, was slowly advancing. The Molony Committee (1959–62) barely gave a voice to the actual consumer, let alone the female consumer, but did point the way to the creation in 1963 of the Consumer Council; *Which?* magazine started in January 1962 a quarterly supplement on cars, earning the instant dislike of British manufacturers after the first issue placed the Volkswagen as best in its group; and, the following month, the BBC nervously dipped its toes in the consumer water with the start of a TV series, fronted by Richard Dimbleby, called *Choice*. 'Trying too hard to keep on the right side of all the interested parties who might have objected,' complained one critic, adding that it was 'so cluttered with information that no clear conclusions could be drawn' – in short, 'no way to perform a public service'. Probably indifferent to these concerns, one poet and one future poet were viewing the unfolding consumer revolution in a positive light. In 1961, after his library colleague and now lover Maeve Brennan had acquired a new handbag in Hull's Marks and Spencer, Philip Larkin paid a visit himself and wrote admiringly of 'The large cool store selling cheap clothes/Set out in simple sizes plainly'. That same year, the 16-year-old Carol Rumens was in George Street, Croydon:

> It was my first time in a Wimpy Bar, my first time in any café by myself. I did not order a Wimpy; the red plastic tomato on my table, with its stem oozing half-dried ketchup, was not encouraging. But I had coffee in a tall, hexagonal melamine mug, and an aluminium tray of flapjacks with maple syrup and a blob of sweetish, cold, synthetic cream. Delicious! I was alone in the café. Perhaps no other Croydon teenagers had yet discovered the Wimpy Bar, or perhaps I was Wimpishly early and it was still only teatime. I felt lonely, but good, and meditated on Man's lofty but probably abandoned status in the universe.[2]

The Panzer troops were nicely bedded in on their South Pembrokeshire range when on Saturday, 9 September 1961 some 30 coaches, full of protesters from all over Britain, arrived in Pembroke itself – to be greeted, according to one pro-protest eyewitness, by 'a pack of irresponsible, gum-chewing, ill-bred youths (most of whom were not born when Pembroke Dock was bombed), backed by their girl friends and a few middle-aged women,' who 'pelted' the coaches 'with eggs, tomatoes, bottles, earth and anything they could lay hands on'. The protest march still went ahead, amid much heckling from the locals and a party of schoolgirls holding a banner aloft saying, 'Leave the Germans alone, you big-heads and trouble-makers'. Among those heckled was Leo Abse, the flamboyant Labour MP for Pontypool. 'We understand there are temptations when you find there are a large number of troops with spending power in your area,' he told the crowd. 'But this we must tell you – that merely to pander to the Panzers because they are spending money in the town can be likened to the rewards that fall to "camp followers".' Yet almost certainly the local impatience with censorious, interfering outsiders was not just about the economic aspect, in the case of some of the younger people anyway. 'Smashing' was how 14-year-old Colin Rogers described the Panzers to a reporter, adding that he had collected 121 of their autographs; soon afterwards, the *Pembroke*

County and West Wales Guardian printed a letter from 'An Angry Panzer Girl', who identified herself as one of the egg-throwers, declared that 'we love the troops (only as friends) and have nothing against them training here,' and finished with two questions to the older generation: 'Surely it is up to everyone to accept these "boys" now? How can we expect a world peace when so many want to live in the past and not the future?'

The other major Welsh story that autumn was the vote on 8 November to determine which parts of the principality would henceforth be permitted to have pubs opening on Sundays – a concept that was in effect a direct assault on the sway of Welsh Nonconformity and its chapels. Many meetings were held during the weeks ahead of the poll. 'I do not want to see the Sunday nights of Aberystwyth and Wales becoming Saturday nights,' Professor R. I. Aaron from the chair told Cardiganshire's pro-retentionists; on the other side of the argument, also at an Aberystwyth meeting, the Rhondda MP Iorwerth Thomas complained sarcastically about how 'these brave nonconformists want to thrust their morality on other people.' Or take Glamorgan, where at a Maesteg gathering the veteran Presbyterian deacon J. Kirkhouse Williams condemned 'the age of bingo, booze and betting shops' as 'the decadent age', to be countered soon afterwards by Cliff Jones, chairman of the Bridgend and District Licensed Victuallers' Association, accusing Williams of a 'dog-in-the-manger, dictator-like attitude'. On a 47 per cent turnout, the eventual vote revealed 454,720 in favour of Sunday opening and 382,059 against. Put more locally, which is what mattered, four county boroughs and five counties decided to go wet, and eight counties – in west and north Wales, the Welsh-speaking heartlands, with the biggest majority in Carmarthenshire – decided to stay dry, at least until the next referendum in seven years' time. 'The women of Pembrokeshire won the day for Sunday closing,' commented Major Tom George, President of Haverfordwest and District Licensed Victuallers' Association, about the reluctance there and elsewhere in rural Wales to embrace change. 'Having been around a few of the polling stations during the day it was obvious that from 8 am to 4 pm, 90 per cent of voters were women, who in my opinion looked chapel or church.'[3]

For Macmillan's increasingly criticised government, it was an autumn of industrial troubles. The PM's diary on 8 October noted the imminent promotion to ministerial rank (as Parliamentary Under-secretary at the Ministry of Pensions and National Insurance) of 'Mrs Thatcher, a clever young woman MP'. But in this entry two days after the start of BBC's sitcom *The Rag Trade*, he was more concerned about the threat of public-sector strikes against Selwyn Lloyd's 'pay pause' policy, about the already deeply entrenched strike at a Rootes subsidiary (British Light Steel Pressings at Acton) that was 'causing a complete hold-up of all Rootes factories, involving all their car production and thousands of men', and about the incendiary effects of employees seeking to count tea breaks as paid time, especially in the building industry and in Ford's at Dagenham. 'Meanwhile,' he added, 'our French, German and other European competitors are hard at work.' Attention particularly focused on the Acton strike – 'the agitators pounce on grievances, exploit them, blow them up, and strive to prevent a reasoned settlement,' declared the *Daily Mail* on 24 October, before asking, 'What are the Special Branch up to?' – but Macmillan two days later was by now more worried about how 'the likelihood of a strike in the Power Stations is growing', with the union demanding a substantial wage rise in explicit defiance of the pay pause. 'This is intolerable,' he reflected. 'But these 150,000 [electricity supply workers] have the whole country in pawn.' Three weeks later, the Electricity Board surrendered, leaving the pay pause apparently in tatters and earning for the Minister of Power, the unfortunate Richard Wood, a public rebuke from Macmillan. The press had the proverbial field day – the *Daily Telegraph* comparing the PM to Lewis Carroll's Bellman (in blundering search of the Snark), the *Economist* preferring the analogy of 'an impotent Pontius Pilate', *The Times* stating frankly that 'Britain lacks the nerve to master her destiny' – but as an unnamed union leader in the electricity-supply industry calmly explained, 'Pay pause? I do not recognise it. We have come to a satisfactory conclusion and we think it will suit the Chancellor not to have a strike. We think he will be pleased.'

How to untie this Gordian knot? Selwyn Lloyd himself hoped that planning might be the answer, having told the Cabinet shortly before the July announcements that 'in the long run we must try to link consideration of wages with the problem of economic growth.' But as discussions took place during the autumn to prepare the way for what ultimately became the National Economic Development Council (Neddy), it became clear that there were serious reservations on the part of five principal players. 'The pay pause must go' was the essence of the TUC's attitude about any invitation to join a government-sponsored body; elements at the FBI (Federation of British Industries), the original pusher of planning, were getting cold feet, with Maurice Laing warning of the danger that a future Labour government might utilise Neddy 'to impose on the country a full "planned economy" which could include full-scale Socialism'; the City at this stage did not want to know; the Treasury was at best divided, with little appetite for modish, turf-threatening institutional initiatives that might compromise the defence of sterling and the balance of payments; and among Lloyd's fellow ministers, even the generally go-ahead Charles Hill and Reginald Maudling were sceptical, fearing (in the Chancellor's disappointed words to Macmillan) 'the creation of a new monster which would embarrass us in the future'. The planning moment, in short, looked as if it had arrived more in theory than in practice. Still, perhaps some of the blame attached to Lloyd himself. 'Rather like an encounter between a whale and an elephant,' recalled his economic adviser Alec Cairncross about Lloyd's meetings with trade union leaders, adding that the Chancellor was unable to enter into their psychology or even 'to communicate to them his own ideas'.[4]

That autumn, Battle of Britain Day fell on Sunday, 17 September – the day that the anti-bomb Committee of 100 (the radical outgrowth from the CND) chose to organise a mass sit-in at Trafalgar Square. The near-nonagenarian Bertrand Russell could not be present, imprisoned at Brixton as a precautionary measure, while in the days before Kenneth Williams would be among those weighing up whether to attend, finally deciding on the Friday that despite feeling 'frightened inside' about possible consequences, the cause was just and he had no alternative but to 'join the demonstration and run the risk of being arrested'. Then on Sunday itself:

> The Police [recorded Williams] used filthy methods of removing limp, passive people – a man dragged by one arm with his head on the ground . . . a woman thrown bodily against a wall . . . The entire crowd that I was in was anti-Police – I did not hear, for two hours, one dissident voice.

> One thing became abundantly clear. They hated the bomb, and they hated the corrupt government that didn't ban it, and they hated the uniformed bullies that enforce an unjust law. Leaders arrested were John Osborne, Shelagh Delaney, and Vanessa Redgrave. All I seem to be able to do is send me miserable donation and pray for them all.

The police had forbidden the use of the square, but altogether some 12,000 took part and over a 1,000 arrests were made. 'There seemed,' noted the *Economist*, 'to be a genuine wish even among some of the most extreme to remove the impression of unwashed artiness that the movement has in the public mind. Not a few young women sat on, and ruined, their skirts rather than turn up in the blue jeans that would have caused them to be classed as "beatniks".' It would need more than that, though, to shift public opinion as a whole on the larger issue. Just over a fortnight later, at its annual conference at Blackpool, the Labour party realigned itself with the majority view by rejecting unilateralism (an about-turn from a year earlier) and, by a huge majority, neutralism. 'A great & deserved triumph for Gaitskell & will increase his stature in the country,' privately admitted Macmillan. 'He has been very persistent & courageous.'

It was generally a good conference for the Gaitskellites (and their Campaign for Democratic Socialism). Not only did it endorse the recent policy document *Signposts for the Sixties*, generally seen as a pragmatic, carefully targeted approach that helped to reconcile the party's two wings after the acrimonious post-election debate, but Roy Jenkins, who had been dreading his stay in Britain's favourite resort ('it takes a long time to get there, the sea front is hideous, the hotels are inadequate'), was pleasantly surprised ('slightly more agreeable than I had remembered it . . . the food was better . . . the illuminated tramcars were most impressive'). Even so, despite all that and despite the welcome votes, he found himself still disquieted by 'the general tone of the debates', in particular by how 'farragos of half-baked semi-Marxist nonsense' were 'cheered by what appeared to be most of the delegates'. Jenkins was also struck by the reaction during the defence debate to the unsuccessful attempt by the T&G's Frank Cousins to hold the unilateralist line: 'By any standards, for both content and form, this was one of the worst speeches which I have ever heard. Yet it was greeted, by perhaps 100 delegates and by a claque in the gallery, with an almost Nuremberg-like reception.' In short, concluded Jenkins, there now undeniably existed in the party a 'vociferous extremism'. The *New Statesman*'s young, razor-sharp political correspondent Anthony Howard – also not wholly relishing Blackpool's 'creaking Big Wheel, its clanking trams, its barn-like pubs and its hideously archaic hotels' – likewise identified Cousins as the Labour left's new hero and 'the spectre at the feast' for the Gaitskellites. But to the public at large, when Cousins appeared on *Face to Face* later in October, the dominant union leader of the day came across, noted an audience research report, 'in a new light, as a man of transparent honesty and sincerity, dedicated in the service of his fellow men and intolerant of injustice in any form'. At one point, Cousins told John Freeman that he had 'no intention or wish to be in Parliament' – a perspective probably sympathetic to the New Left intellectual Ralph Miliband, who in his new book *Parliamentary Socialism* delivered a sustained, historically based attack on the Labour party (left as well as right) for having over the years refused to embrace extra-parliamentary action as the means to achieving socialism as opposed to mere social reform. The final chapter was called 'The Sickness of Labourism', and Miliband ended by predicting that, unless Labour fundamentally altered and became 'the political instrument of radical change', what lay ahead was 'the kind of slow but sure decline which – deservedly – affects parties that have ceased to serve any distinctive political purpose'.[5]

The Saturday after the Battle of Trafalgar Square was when Keith Nicholson's numbers came up. A young miner, living in Castleford and married to Vivian (miner's daughter, 25 years old, blonde, outgoing), he checked his Littlewoods pools coupon and found he had eight draws. Two days later, just before the train reached London, an accompanying Littlewoods representative told them that they had won over £150,000 (at least £5 million in 2014 terms). 'It was then,' related Gordon Burn in 1976 after interviewing her, 'as she alighted at King's Cross, to be immediately mobbed by reporters, that Vivian, remembering the newsreels of Jayne Mansfield that she'd seen, uttered the words that were going to make her famous. "I'm going to spend," she said, intoxicated by the attention, "and spend – and spend!"' Soon they were at the Dorchester, receiving a cheque from Bruce Forsyth, and the centre of intense media attention. 'Does the team think the reaction of "spend, spend, spend" is the best one for the winner of a large sum in the football pools?' was the inevitable question at the following Friday's *Any Questions?* from the Memorial Hall at Portscatho, Cornwall. 'I find it's very refreshing,' said Ted Moult; 'don't spend it on having a spree with your friends because you're never going to have them off your necks,' warned the writer and broadcaster Brian Inglis; while the view of Lady Isobel Barnett was that 'it'll go jolly quickly, but let her enjoy it while it's there.' Letters soon afterwards in the *Daily Mirror* broadly agreed: although 'Retired Schoolmaster' of Cardiff professed himself 'disgusted' at a woman 'whose idea seems to be spending on herself', the consensus was with Slough's Mrs B. Henton, who called it 'a joy' to read about Viv's unabashed attitude instead of the usual 'money will make no difference' protestations. The mood was different nearer to home, after the winners had flown from Luton back to Yorkshire. By the second day, recalled Viv, 'the bitterness started creeping in: "Why them, they're so bloody young, we've been filling the pools in for years," "I've worked all my life." They wouldn't speak to us, we were literally ignored all the time by people that you pass the time of day with or say good morning to. But winning the pools – I had to say, "Why didn't you speak to me the other day, have I got the plague or something?" "Well, if I speak, people will think I'm after something."' Within a few weeks, the couple had moved to the show house on a new, middle-class estate in Garforth, 5 miles from Castleford. 'I try to make friends but the women won't accept it,' Viv told a newspaper soon afterwards. 'If I go out in ordinary clothes they say: "Look at her – all that money and wearing those things." If I wear any of my new cocktail dresses they say: "She must think she's somebody now." That's why I tint my hair mauve and green and pink sometimes and put my new clothes on and go dancing. The more they talk, the more I do to give them something to natter about.'[6]

The diarists that autumn had other things on their minds. Florence Turtle was in a thin audience at the unheated Wimbledon Theatre to see Robert Bolt's *A Man for All Seasons* ('had a large Scotch, the barmaid said the only thing that seemed to fill the theatre was ballet or the pantomime'); Anthony Heap admired the RSC's production of *The Taming of the Shrew* (Vanessa Redgrave 'a rare combination of charm and artistry'); Judy Haines listened to her *Woman's Hour* broadcast ('sounded quite satisfactory'), but not long afterwards was reflecting, 'I always get depressed when John says I'm lucky to be able to stay at home so much,' adding, 'I think one has to be very strong-minded not to go crackers'; Harold Macmillan in late September contrasted the popular press having 'hardly a word about Congo crisis, Berlin crisis or even general Home affairs' with its lavish treatment of the pursuit of the A6 murderer (with James Hanratty, a petty thief from north London, being arrested in Blackpool on 11 October); John Fowles and his smartly dressed wife took a walk around old, working-class Southwark ('two boys on bicycles stare at us hostilely – they see I have Pevsner and the A-to-Z in my hand'); Nella Last one Thursday evening viewed *Tonight* and *Double Your Money*, but then 'came gladly to bed, the thought alone of a "variety" show of Morecambe & Wise made me curl at the edges'; Allan Preston experienced the new diesel rail cars on the Leeds-to-Scarborough line ('five-abreast seating to gangway makes it much too cramped'); Madge Martin in Bayswater one Friday 'looked in at the strangely old-fashioned Whiteley's [department store], which doesn't seem to have changed since we first knew it, in 1916'; Hugh Selbourne watched Lord Hailsham on *Face to Face* ('strikes me now as a complacent member of the blimpish Tory establishment, of some degree of mediocrity'); and Henry St John had an unsatisfactory lunch in the Ministry of Labour canteen ('the meat in what was sold as steak and kidney pie had no recognisable taste and consisted of dark amorphous lumps').[7]

The diarists' most-watched movie was Tony Richardson's *A Taste of Honey*, a naturalistic, Salford-filmed version of the Shelagh Delaney play. Haines, who enjoyed it, thought Rita Tushingham in the central role was 'very like Princess Margaret'; Martin found it 'much better' than the original, calling it 'a splendid, touching, sordid, beautifully actual film'; and Kenneth Williams was struck by its 'brilliant' and 'breathtaking' beginning (including in the opening scene Hazel Blears as a five-year-old street urchin wearing her mother's best shoes). *The Times* praised especially the living feel of its northern industrial backdrop – 'the shabby streets and wet pavements, the school playgrounds, the public monuments and the rubbish-strewn canals' – as well as Tushingham's 'moving and eloquent performance' in what was in effect her acting debut. 'A garlic of a girl' was the approbatory phrase of another critic, but not everyone immediately bought into the vulnerable, huge-eyed 19-year-old Liverpudlian. 'This apparently ugly duckling,' retorted a furious John Osborne (the film's co-producer), 'has more expression and beauty when she crooks her little finger than most of these damned starlets have if they waggled their oversized bosoms and bottoms from here to eternity.' Among the movie's warm admirers was Monica Jones. 'At last to see *A Taste of Honey*, as much to rest my brains and because you'd praised it as anything,' Larkin wrote to her a few months after its release. 'I much enjoyed it at the time: it seemed very stirring and touching. In retrospect it fades a bit. All the children seemed a bit *voulu*.'

The autumn's other landmark film left Kenneth Williams underwhelmed from the first: 'To see Dirk Bogarde play the homosexual barrister fighting a blackmail ring in *Victim* – it was all v. slick, superficial and never knocking the real issues.' Most reviewers, though, were more positive about what after all was the courageous storyline of a homosexual being blackmailed because of his sexual orientation (and which was the first English-language film to use the actual word *homosexual*). '*Victim* may not say a great deal about this difficult problem,' reflected *The Times* in comments that were about par for the course, 'but what it does say is reasoned and just; and it does invite a compassionate consideration of this particular form of human bondage.' The director, Basil Dearden, originally wanted the square-jawed, ultra-masculine Jack Hawkins to play the lead role, but eventually Hawkins declined – because, commented Bogarde subsequently, it might have 'prejudiced his chances of a knighthood'. Bogarde himself, renowned through the 1950s as a matinee idol, spoke revealingly to the press at the time of the film's release. After acknowledging that 'some people would rather see you kill your wife on the screen than play a role like this,' he went on: 'It's about a real man and a very, very real problem. He is a barrister, about to take silk. Successful, apparently happily married. He has a fine house. But he has this weakness – sickness if you like. He has managed to overcome it for a long time. But one day he gives a lift to a young man who works on a building site . . .' What did audiences make of it? Simon Raven saw it in Deal, where a largely working-class, message-resistant audience watched quietly and attentively enough – until 'the characters started piously intoning "white paper" extracts about protecting juveniles from marauding homosexuals'. The future film director Terence Davies, then a 15-year-old clerk in a shipping office, saw it in Liverpool at the Odeon. 'Alright – alright, you want to know, I'll tell you – you won't be content until I tell you will you – until you've ripped it out of me – I stopped seeing him because I *wanted* him,' the barrister tells his beautiful wife in the climactic scene. 'Can you understand – because I *wanted* him.' At which point, recalls Davies, 'you could have heard a feather drop' – as he and others in the audience realised that they were not alone in their sexual orientation.[8]

Both films were on release in September, the month that Georg Solti, a Hungarian, uneasily took over as musical director at the Royal Opera House ('a small anonymous group engaged in booing from the amphitheatre,' recalled his chairman, Lord Drogheda, 'and he used to find things like "Solti must go" written on the windscreen of his car'), that the photographer David Bailey made his name in *Vogue* (having successfully faced down the fashion editor Lady Rendlesham, by insisting that a young graduate of the Lucie Clayton modelling school, Jean Shrimpton, be his model), and that Violet Carson, accompanied by the rest of the *Coronation Street* cast, switched on the Blackpool Illuminations amidst hugely enthusiastic crowd scenes. *Dixon of Dock Green* returned for a new series ('about real people and their problems', explained the writer Ted Willis, 'without murder or mayhem to jazz it up'); Bruce Forsyth, after a year's absence through illness, was back in charge of *Sunday Night at the London Palladium*; Malcolm Muggeridge provoked mixed feelings when he took on a PR man, Alan Eden-Green, in a TV debate ('the word "off" used so many times and pronounced "orf" or "awf" really niggled me,' complained a life-assurance representative); Alan Freeman took over radio's *Pick of the Pops*; the BBC's new Sunday-afternoon serial *Stranger on the Shore*, about a young French *au pair* in Brighton, had 'music composed and played by Mr Acker Bilk'; and, reviewing two new books, *The Times* praised John Prebble's demythologising, history-from-below *Culloden* ('where most other accounts are romantic in tone, his is as realistic as he can make it'), but stuck the knife into *The Old Men at the Zoo*, a liberal humanist's critical, allegorical novel about the English ruling class ('Mr Angus Wilson possesses almost every literary virtue except a heart').[9]

October came in with the start of two new TV programmes – *Songs of Praise* (from the Tabernacle Baptist Chapel, Cardiff) on BBC and the much shorter-lived, fortnightly *Tempo* on ITV (edited by Kenneth Tynan, introduced by the Earl of Harewood, and, according to one critic, the discussion on the artist and politics 'just getting going, and Lindsay Anderson on the point of losing his temper with the egregious Mr Auberon Waugh, when we were moved on to the next item') – not to mention Juliette Greco on BBC singing from the Left Bank. 'She looked like a beatnik, could not sing – in fact, she would rather put one off going to Paris', 'we were not very interested in hearing so many songs of this type in a foreign language' and 'the whole thing irritated me' were typical viewers' reactions. Over the rest of the month, Plymouth had its Shopping Festival ('a dazzling display of the latest, the gayest, and the best value in everything, from boats and coats to cosmetics and photography'); the BBC's science-fiction thriller series *A for Andromeda*, set in the Yorkshire Dales in 1970 and co-written by the astronomer Fred Hoyle, introduced Julie Christie (as a brunette); Antony Armstrong-Jones became Lord Snowdon; correspondence raged on *Woman's Hour* about the serialisation of *Moll Flanders* ('What type of people do you cater for?' asked a listener from Bourne End, adding, 'Please take it off and keep *Woman's Hour* clean,' while from Halifax the demand was simple: 'Put her on the Welfare State and get finished with her'); Peter Cook's satirical nightclub The Establishment began in Soho ('nobody is going to go out into Greek Street feeling more revolutionary than when they went in,' reckoned George Melly, describing the audience as 'nice clean ladies and gentlemen of impeccable liberal principles and good SW addresses'); Graham Greene wrote to the *Spectator* pointing out that 'somebody should surely tell Lord Home [the Foreign Secretary] not to lick his lips continually in front of a television camera as he did on the last *Panorama*'; the Methodist church in Hunslet Carr, Leeds had its final service, membership having more than halved since 1953; BBC TV began a series of Friday-night plays 'that treat adult themes frankly', providing 'greater freedom of subject and treatment than is available on Sundays, when the plays are designed for family viewing'; hours after Rediffusion's new Record Bar had opened in Beeston, two 'Teddy Boy types' ran amok in the town's newly opened Fine Fare supermarket, as 'they grabbed bottles of salad cream and tomato sauce from the window display and splattered it over the shop interior'; Cyril Connolly, in his *Sunday Times* review of Alan Sillitoe's new novel *Key to the Door*, evinced little enthusiasm for a return to the Seaton family and their 'small, closed world' in which people worked in factories, drank in pubs and frequently 'copulated'; a last-minute intervention from the Lord Chamberlain's office cut to ribbons a student revue sketch in Newcastle about 'a royal personage' and class barriers; three female undergraduates gate-crashed an all-male Cambridge Union debate ('Union members jumped to their feet and shouted "Out! Out!" at the girls'); only 'rather guarded approval' greeted *Dr Kildare*'s TV debut ('Perhaps when I get used to the extraordinary way they go about things in American hospitals it will grow on me,' thought a secretary); the first issue of *Private Eye* came out on the 25th (yellow paper, six pages, mainly the work of Christopher Booker and Willie Rushton, with Mr Punch of the eponymous magazine as first 'Bore of the Week'), the same day the British Library acquired its copy of R. D. Laing's *The Self and Others* ('the reader should remember,' he warned, 'that I am not saying that other people *cause* madness'); and Arnold Wesker addressed a meeting in Kingsley Hall, Bristol about his Centre 42 movement, as observed by a sceptical Tom Stoppard, who believed the playwright guilty of 'incredible naivety' in assuming that the TUC's support the previous year for Resolution 42 was proof that 'the millions' were dissatisfied with their staple culture of 'football, films, telly, bingo and pools', with Stoppard adding that 'the masses have no monopoly on unenlightenment'.[10]

The scepticism seemed justified during the first few days of November, as Centre 42 put on a cultural festival and art exhibition at Wellingborough to which the public response was, according to a local trade unionist, 'disappointing and meagre', with folksingers drafted in from Birmingham touring the pubs to sparse audiences and some of the paintings on show 'so abstract as to be a source of bewilderment to the beholders'. Meanwhile, Winston Churchill was spotted lightly tapping his foot in time with the Twist at the coming-out dance of his granddaughter; Rudolf Nureyev, having fled from Soviet Russia, made his London debut; and Princess Margaret gave birth by Caesarean section, not on medical grounds but because of her anxiety that babies born 'naturally' came out blemished. November also saw a notably high

Reaction Index of 74 for the BBC's coverage of Miss World 1961, won by the Marks and Spencer counter-girl Rosemarie Frankland, whose reward would be a 20-year affair with Bob Hope and a tragic life ended by a drugs overdose; three Mersey poets – Roger McGough, Adrian Henri and Brian Patten – met for the first time in a basement coffee bar on Mount Pleasant; Pauline Tilston's wedding to her merchant seaman beau John Prescott was ruined by her industrial-strength hairspray melting the diamante on her tiara; Jeremy Maas's exhibition of *The Pre-Raphaelites and their Contemporaries* in London was those Victorians' first major outing for many years; a new series began of Harry Worth's *Here's Harry* (described in the *Radio Times* as looking like a suburban commuter but in fact 'a twentieth-century knight errant' who 'sallies forth from his semi-detached castle and goes out to do battle against the dragons and giants of today', which 'have awe-inspiring names like Bureaucracy and Regulation, Restriction and Red Tape, and lurk around us everywhere'); the start of a winter-long strike by Equity reduced *Coronation Street*'s cast to the 13 actors on long-term contracts; Benny Hill's impersonation of Ena Sharples was acclaimed by viewers as 'a real riot'; E. H. Carr's pugnacious *What is History?* was making an immediate impact and anticipated much that lay ahead ('the more sociological history becomes, and the more historical sociology becomes, the better for both'); Jimmy Hill as Coventry City's new manager initiated the 'Sky Blue revolution', repackaging football as more upmarket but still affordable family entertainment, while the Spurs captain Danny Blanchflower began writing for the *Observer*; and Raymond Williams, reviewing a history of Fabian socialism, argued that that incremental, top-down approach, concentrating on building organisations rather than changing people, was no longer relevant ('We look like a branch line, with the stations closed and the people gone away, but with the machine we have built still running through our lives, whether it serves us or not').[11]

December began with the *TLS* welcoming John Rowe Townsend's *Gumble's Yard*, set in 'a Northern city slum', as refreshingly different from 'the usual middle-class, country-holiday-with-ponies background' of children's books; the piano-playing Mrs Mills – comfortably built, middle-aged, virtually unknown – appeared on the *Billy Cotton Band Show* ('a charmer', noted one critic) and found instant fame; on

Sunday Night at the London Palladium, the Equity strike left Bruce Forsyth and Norman Wisdom to fill the whole hour, which they managed with aplomb; the Royal Society for the Prevention of Accidents launched the Tufty Club; and the first series of *The Rag Trade* came to an end on the 8th. 'This has been an excellent series,' declared a physicist. 'We shall miss them all – they cheered us up no end. "Everybody out!" is now part of the English language.'[12]

The 'problem of youth' seemed that autumn an especially problematic problem. 'All the aberrations of today are, I think, uncharacteristic of England,' the Isle of Ely's MP, Sir Harry Legge-Bourke, told the Wisbech Institute Brotherhood's annual harvest festival in September. 'The fire of resentment may blaze fiercely for a while in the heads of the beatniks and the angry young men, but will, I believe, flicker out eventually – leaving those of us, who meanwhile have exercised our national steadiness, to pick up the threads again and weave a tapestry in accordance with our heritage.' Was Blackpool part of that heritage? Hugh Selbourne visited the resort a few days later to see the 'garish' illuminations: 'The town was crowded with youths; all beer and bingo, their behaviour rough, and deteriorating.' *The Times*, meanwhile, was running a sustained, largely grumpy correspondence about 'A Nation in Danger', after the Rev. Leslie Weatherhead had complained in a letter that 'the very word "discipline" is universally hated by the young' and noted that 'your paper, Sir, reported the habit of teenage girls wearing a yellow golliwog, not as a sign of academic or athletic distinction, but as a sign that the wearer had had sexual intercourse.' Two sociologists, E. M. and M. Epple, responded to the correspondence by sending questionnaires about the state of adolescent morality to almost 600 magistrates, probation officers and youth leaders, eliciting a 23-per-cent completion rate. The general view was that young people were more engaged in sexual activity than in the previous generation ('chastity is a hardly understood virtue'); that there was not necessarily any significant change in attitudes to authority, although a substantial minority of respondents thought there was; that there existed greater frankness and intellectual honesty ('no longer the shabby pretence that once prevailed'); and that the crucial influence was home background ('thirty years ago we were just as keen on the latest dance records by the band leader of the moment, but most of us had a stable home and only one

Mum and Dad, and Mum was always there when we got home – instead of going out to work to pay the H.P.'). The young themselves were more directly scrutinised in a two-year Gallup investigation into 16- to 18-year-olds reporting in December. The poll found them likelier to have good relations with their mother than their father; regular working habits (after three years, more than half still in the same job as when they started); many 'severely critical' of their schooling, not least the 'lack of discipline'; one-third as regular attenders at church; only one in ten not looking forward to getting married; 85 per cent disagreeing with the assertion that it did not matter very much whether or not a marriage worked out well; Churchill as easily their most-respected adult; parents, then sportsmen, as their most respected type of person, with 'statesmen and film stars far behind, teachers nowhere at all'; and only 9 per cent disagreeing with the opinion that the world would be a better place to live in in ten years' time. 'In many ways,' reflected the *Daily Telegraph* (in a summary of the survey, called 'The Not-So-Lost Generation'), 'the image of an unstable and feckless generation pales, the further one goes from adult guesses and the nearer one comes to facts.'[13]

Two-thirds of Gallup's teenage sample listened to popular music, and during 1961 almost 55 million singles (going round the turntable at 45 rpm) were sold, double the total three years earlier. Single of the autumn was the cloudlessly optimistic 'Walkin' Back to Happiness' by Helen Shapiro ('Walk down any London high street on a Saturday afternoon,' noted Jonathan Miller in October, 'and you will hear her voice float out on the Delphic breath of the local electric stores'); ITV's *Thank Your Lucky Stars*, which had begun in April, was now nationally networked, hosted by the (in Dave McAleer's words) 'amiable if patronising' Brian Matthew; and Anthony Heap moaned that 'one can seldom go into a roadside café without finding an infernal slot machine called a "juke box" into which some half-witted oaf must ever be inserting the coin necessary to make the thing churn out some horrible "pop disc" and so inflict it on everyone in the place.' Perhaps it was not as bad as all that. The trad jazz boom was cheerfully approaching its commercial peak, with Acker Bilk in a magazine article plaintively asking the jazz police, 'Is It A Crime To Be Successful?'; the charts that autumn featured such reassuring names as Shirley Bassey, Connie Francis, Frank Sinatra and

Frankie Vaughan, not to mention a novelty hit for Charlie Drake with 'My Boomerang Won't Come Back'; and Mrs Alice Stirrup of Blackburn expressed her satisfaction to the *Radio Times* that 'at last Mummy, who has hitherto been regarded as a "square", is coming into her own!', given that 'many of the latest "pops" are the songs of twenty or more years ago – perhaps with a new rhythm, but the same good old songs.' It was time for a chance encounter on platform 2 at Dartford station. Mike (but soon Mick) Jagger was on his way on Tuesday, 17 October to the London School of Economics, carrying Chuck Berry and Muddy Waters albums under his arm; Keith Richards, apparently also holding a Chuck Berry record, was on his way to Sidcup Art College; and the two, friends at primary school before the 11-plus sundering, now reconnected.

First, though, the Mersey sound – and of course one beat group in particular of the 500 or so playing in the Merseyside area during the late 1950s and early 1960s. On Saturday, 9 December the Beatles – newly under the management of the perceptive, socially accomplished Brian Epstein, but fulfilling a previously arranged commitment – spent much of the day travelling to Aldershot in order to play for the first time in the south of England. They were still on the road as the *Aldershot News* held its annual Christmas tea party for the borough's elderly people. 'You've never seen a happier crowd,' wrote the paper's tame reporter:

> Gay and high-spirited they were singing the carols and all the old songs, laughing at the jokes with tears streaming down their faces, wishing one another a Happy Christmas and almost falling over themselves to express their pleasure at being invited. And what a cheeky lot they were in their saucy paper hats – heart-shaped, and gay little trilbies for the men. It did you good just to look at them.

Unfortunately, the *Aldershot News*'s generosity stopped there, for the current issue had failed to insert the advertisement for the Palais Ballroom. In the event, just 18 people watched the Beatles play for almost four hours. Alan Freeman, Jane Asher, Acker Bilk and the singer Julie Wilson were doing *Juke Box Jury* service that evening, the Tubby Hayes Quartet was at London's Marquee Club, Humphrey Lyttelton and his Band were at the Spa Ballroom in Scarborough – but it was in

Thomas Hardy's Quartershot that a bathetic slice of cultural history was made, a year exactly since the start of *Coronation Street*.[14]

'You must be in no doubt that you are watching one of the great dramas of history, as so many countries thrust forwards through nationalism towards their independence,' the outgoing Colonial Secretary – removed by Macmillan because he was making too many enemies – told the Conservative annual conference in Brighton on the morning of 11 October. And, in what was a very consciously valedictory speech, Iain Macleod not only strongly defended the policy of rapid decolonisation he had set in train, but stated his fundamental belief in 'the brotherhood of man' and ended by declaring that 'the task of bringing these countries towards their destiny of free and equal partners and friends with us in the Commonwealth of Nations can be a task as exciting, as inspiring and as noble as the creation of empire itself.' A standing ovation duly followed, 'but,' observed the *Economist*, 'it was an ovation still noticeably led by a minority claque, in which the rank and file of Tuscany eventually joined because it seemed impossible not to do so'. Afterwards, in the hotel bar, one delegate was heard to say, 'Beautiful phrases Macleod has, but they mean nothing. I still wouldn't like to be a white man in Africa.' There were other signs, moreover, of a reluctance to accept man's indivisible brotherhood. The Monday Club was by now in operation, at this stage essentially a ginger group of young Tories hostile to majority black rule and whose first pamphlet was *Wind of Change or Whirlwind?*; while when the Central African Federation's embattled Sir Roy Welensky spoke on 8 November at the Institute of Directors' annual conference – calling nationalism in Africa 'among the tragedies of this age . . . that has made a mockery of liberty and enslaved thousands upon thousands of its own people in dictatorships and in the thraldom of poverty and chaos' – he, noted *The Times*, 'sat down to an ovation which vibrated the Albert Hall'. What about Macleod's successor? 'He is a man of integrity, has a first-class brain, is willing to listen and will, I think, do an excellent job,' a right-wing Tory MP, Patrick Wall, had reassured Welensky the day after Macmillan's reshuffle had been announced. 'The new appointment,' he had added, 'will certainly mean a modification of the ruthless pro-African Nationalist line which has been pursued recently.' Wall, though, called it wrong, for in practice Reginald Maudling essentially continued Macleod's policy – so much so that Macmillan by early 1962 was finding him 'more difficult & intransigent than his predecessor'. According to Maudling's biographer Lewis Baston, the 'awful comparison' in his calm, pragmatic mind 'was the doomed French resistance to Algerian independence. To cling on, to spit in the wind of change, was inconceivable. Maudling was the ideal man to come to terms with necessity, and to do it with dignity.'[15]

The brotherhood of man continued to falter on the home front. In Bristol for instance, a local paper took soundings in September 1961 in the St Paul's district. 'There is colour prejudice here,' said a black man, Basil Simpson. 'Sure there is. Some people think we just aren't human.' Even so, he added, 'This is my country, and I'm staying.' A white woman, living in a house with Jamaicans, agreed: 'There's definitely a colour bar in Martin Street. Live with coloured people and they say you're a prostitute straight away. I've got two half-caste children. You should hear what's said when I take them to school. "Nigger's children" is what's shouted . . . Lots of people have been really nasty to me.' But in nearby Bishop Street, 'a massively genial, bearded and turbaned Sikh', J. S. Patel, disagreed: 'I've been in England 26 years. No trouble with white people. I play darts with them, eat, drink. No trouble. Everything fine.' Later that month, in Bradford, a council meeting featured some sharp exchanges:

> COUN R.N.W. BISHOP asked what connotation in Minute 3 (Proposed Special Classes for Coloured Children) the word 'coloured' had in that context.
>
> ALD WOODGATE said the answer was that the children who it was proposed would form those classes were coloured children, chiefly Pakistanis and West Indians.
>
> COUN BISHOP said it was an excellent scheme to bring a bit of English education to immigrants to this country. He deprecated, however, the use of the term 'coloured' which in that context to his mind bore no proper meaning insofar as they were all coloured. Some who had been on holiday were tanned brown; others looked blotchy and pink like himself who had not had the pleasure of a holiday. To call someone coloured was

> not the happiest way of phrasing that particular resolution. He would have been happier to see the phrase 'new immigrants' used.
>
> ALD R.C. RUTH said it would have been better if some other adjective could be found but it was not easy and he was sure it was with the best intentions it had been used in the descriptive sense. He thought the motive of those special classes was a very good one. *(Hear, hear)*
>
> COUN E.W. MOULSON said he thought they were getting very very fancy and supercilious. What were those children other than coloured children? One could not make them any other. It was all right Coun Bishop trying to bring a fancy word but they remained coloured people. He would like to go a step further. The Minute as it stood would do a useful job of work, but he had worked in industrial premises where parents of that type of coloured children were employed and the Minute as it stood was only the beginning of something which they did not know where it would finish. Those children from birth had not been brought up to living in the English way of life. They would probably finish up wanting a new canteen and feeding centre . . . Some thought he was talking out of the top of his hat but he worked in industrial premises where thousands of pounds had been spent on toilet facilities for them. They had a different way of life. *(Laughter)*

'He was no colour bar merchant,' insisted Moulson, 'but they did not know what they were letting themselves in for – new toilets for them, new school feeding centres and a lot more.'

By now the larger politics of uncontrolled immigration from the New Commonwealth were about to come to a head. At the Tories' seaside gathering, the morning of 11 October was notable not only for Macleod's memorable oration, and for the *Daily Express* snapping a front-page photograph of Lady Antonia Fraser taking a chilly plunge with her politician-husband, but for the staunchly pro-restriction backbencher Sir Cyril Osborne handing out to delegates a copy of his just-published letter ('IMMIGRATION LUNACY: Ever Nearer an Afro-Asian Britain') in the *Daily Telegraph*. That afternoon saw a full-scale debate on the immigration issue, during which (in the *Economist*'s words) 'speaker after speaker said that he felt no colour prejudice, and then proceeded to show shamefacedly that he did.' One watching journalist, Bernard Levin, was less restrained – 'some of the nastiest sights and sounds I have ever seen on the daylight side of a large, flat stone' – but fully agreed about the hypocrisy of those who pretended that support for immigration controls had nothing to do with colour or race. As an example of 'the sort of muck' that was 'indistinguishable from the harangues of Mosley's corner-boys in Notting Hill', he cited the decidedly un-shamefaced Frank Taylor, a delegate from Manchester's Moss Side:

> 'The immigrants are human,' he said, beaming broadly about him; 'They get married and have children. Some of them are very human and have lots of children . . . who can blame them for clubbing to buy houses, very often over the heads of English residents . . . driving out the English people and eventually becoming owners of residences in whole streets . . . we have leprosy in the country 150 per cent more than ten years ago. That must be something to do with immigration . . . Some – a minority, I agree – do not really want to do an awful lot of work. I was on a doorstep last week, and a gentleman came to the door . . . ladies and gentlemen, you and I are keeping him and his wife and about six delightful little piccaninnies round his knees.'

The final speech came from the Home Secretary, Rab Butler, generally viewed as in the liberal camp. 'It may be,' he conceded, 'that we can work out a system which is humane, unprejudiced and sensible and which meets some of the undoubted rising social and economic problems which otherwise may become too much for certain parts of our country.' Minutes later, the resolution demanding that the government 'take action quickly' over 'the uncontrolled number of immigrants flowing into the United Kingdom' was passed by a large majority.[16]

'WHILE THE DOOR IS STILL OPEN. . .' was the *Daily Mail*'s headline five days later, a reporter having met the 3.33 'immigrant train' at Waterloo station the previous foggy afternoon – on board, some 980 West Indians whose smiles 'flash all the warmth of their native Caribbean sunshine'. Some increasingly familiar statistics were trotted out: 'There are 400,000 coloured people in Britain, almost half being West Indians. Last year 52,000 West Indians poured in; last month 5,000 came. And a record 80,000 expected to flood in during the whole of this year. Indians and Pakistanis are also arriving here in spectacularly higher numbers

– 16,700 in the first six months this year, against 2,500 in the same period in 1960.' On 1 November, the day after the Queen's Speech had explicitly anticipated the measure, Butler's bill was duly published, enabling immigration officers to refuse entry to anyone from the Commonwealth (in effect the New Commonwealth – ie, non-white) without the means of actual or prospective support. Opinion-polling evidence had long suggested overwhelming public backing for such a measure, but the *Daily Mirror* that day took a contrary stand, declaring it 'fundamentally WRONG' to impose restrictions on entry from the Commonwealth. Not only would they amount to 'a colour bar' but 'coloured immigrants' amounted to less than 1 per cent of the population and 'the overwhelming majority do useful jobs here'.

The Commonwealth Immigrants Bill had its second reading on the evening of 16 November, producing a heated Commons debate. Butler, observed Mollie Panter-Downes, 'introduced it with the evident acute distaste of a man of strong liberal principles being forced by party pressure to act against them'; much was made of the decision to exempt the Irish from immigration controls; and Gaitskell, in Panter-Downes's words, 'raked the uncomfortable-looking front bench [not least Macleod, now party chairman] with scorn in what many people felt was one of the finest speeches of his career' – a speech that memorably characterised the bill as a 'miserable, shameful, shabby' surrender to 'the crudest clamour'. With Tory imperialists as well as liberals deeply unhappy, the party's whips at one point were seriously worried about securing a convincing majority, but in the end managed 84. Even from the right, press reaction was largely hostile. The Irish exemption, reflected *The Times*, removed any doubts that the bill was 'racially discriminatory'; the *Daily Mail* likewise detected 'an unhealthy whiff of hypocrisy', depicted government handling of the whole immigration issue as 'labouring under a feeling of guilt', admitted 'we are a crowded island' but emphasised 'there is not a shortage of work for the West Indians who come here', and altogether concluded that 'the whole edifice' of the Commonwealth would 'tremble' if free entry was 'swept away'. The writer Colin MacInnes was also unimpressed. 'Willy-nilly,' he wrote to *The Times*, 'we created, or enforced, an international, interracial community of millions. Must we destroy it through hasty inane fear?' Anthony Heap was disappointed only by the delay of 'some months yet' before the bill became law ('in the meantime, beat-the-ban blacks will continue to flock to this overcrowded and underhoused country in their tens of thousands'); Macmillan on the 30th noted with relief rather than satisfaction that the latest Gallup had shown overwhelming support; and soon afterwards Cyril Osborne (described by one parliamentary correspondent as 'the spirit, if not the architect, of the Bill') treated *Guardian* readers to 'The case for immigration control'. Conceding that 'unfortunately' the proposed legislation did indeed 'look like colour discrimination', he went on:

> Nine-tenths of the Commonwealth are coloured. They are also the poorest. They are naturally attracted by our affluent society. It is their vast numbers and their awful poverty that make it impossible for us to accept indefinitely all who would like to come. It is therefore not colour, or race, but numbers and poverty that make action unavoidable.
>
> It is strange the Labour Party, which claims especially to represent the working man, has totally ignored the unfortunate English family which has had to bear the social stresses which unlimited immigration has brought. Has the Englishman no rights in his own country? Scarcely one Socialist MP has raised his voice in answer to the appeal for protection that has come from the workers in our big cities where the immigrants have settled.

'The Socialists,' in short, 'seem to be so obsessed by the rights of the immigrants they cannot hear the cries of their own supporters.'[17]

In fact, Labour's opposition to the bill significantly softened over the next few months, with the party's front-bench spokesman on colonial affairs, Denis Healey, declining to promise that a future Labour government would repeal the legislation. The final Commons vote in February 1962 saw a comfortable majority of 101 ('after all the threat of opposition from our side and of abstention', recorded Macmillan), Royal Assent was given in April, and the Act took effect at the start of July. There was certainly, as Heap had feared, a beat-the-ban rush, typified by many Pakistani women and children arriving in Bradford to join their menfolk; overall, between January 1961 and June 1962 net inward migration from India, Pakistan and the West Indies was over 190,000 – only some 20,000 fewer than for the six years from 1955 to 1960. If the government was ever tempted to drop the bill, events in West Yorkshire at the start of 1962 probably stiffened its resolve. 'Hey, dig the plague in Bradford,' Philip Larkin wrote to Monica Jones on 13 January. 'What lunacy our immigration laws are.' The 'plague' was smallpox, involving several deaths, and a Leeds paper reported how 'all over' the rival city, 'in public houses, clubs and on the buses, there was open evidence that the public as a whole were blaming the Pakistani population', with 'conversation mainly centred on the lines of "Send them home"'. An editorial ('Without Anger') in Bradford's *Telegraph & Argus* sought to play down the racial aspect, insisting that 'the present need is for calm and tolerance', but readers' letters in response were far from calm or tolerant:

> People I have spoken to are angry. (*'ENOUGH IS ENOUGH', Bradford 9*)
>
> My wife, myself and lots of other people we know, agree with the report in the Leeds morning paper about 'sending them home'. All the mothers about these parts are frightened . . . (*'WINDY', Shipley*)
>
> The stupid and irrational policy of uncontrolled mass entry by coloured immigrants has brought its terrible reward . . . I am not in favour of any colour bar, only common sense. (*H.T. Mudd, Bradford 5*)
>
> As far as we are concerned this smallpox outbreak has been the last straw. (*'SIX SOBER HOUSEWIVES', Bradford 5*)
>
> England is like a pawn-shop and will take anything in. (*'Bradford born and bred'*)

More generally, the imminent introduction of immigration controls seemed to do little at this stage to ameliorate feelings. The elderly Keighley diarist Gladys Hague may have reflected at the end of 1961 that 'coloured people can be just as charming as white people when you get to know them and much more polite', but when in April 1962 a national sample survey asked 1,254 respondents in England and Wales whether they agreed with the opinion that 'foreign immigrants to this country' were 'doing too well at the expense of the British people', 71 per cent answered 'yes'. That majority view was more or less equally shared among men and women, and among Conservative and Labour voters, but was less common among under-45s than over-45s, with hostility rates exceeding 80 per cent for those in their 60s and 70s. Perhaps inevitably, the survey threw up three other variables. 'The less educated are more frequently hostile to immigrants than the better educated,' summarised the sociologists W. G. Runciman and C. R. Bagley, 'the less well-paid more frequently hostile than the better-paid, and those in manual occupations more frequently hostile than those in non-manual occupations.'

Of course, the immigrants themselves had their own backstories and experiences. Take two young men. Darcus Howe landed at Southampton on 11 April 1962 from Trinidad and Tobago. 'On arrival at Waterloo station,' he recalled, 'a friend who came to meet me warned that I must not under any circumstances walk alone at night because I would face arrest by the police and a beating from white racists. I contemplated returning home almost at once. During the first eighteen months or so, loneliness never left me alone even though I lived with five others in a rented flat atop a car showroom.' Abdul Ghani Javid was already in England, having arrived at London Airport in 1961 with just a pound note in his pocket – all that he would need, his father in Pakistan had hopefully calculated, to get him through his first month. Javid found his way to Rochdale, starting work in a cotton mill before becoming a bus conductor and driver, earning the nickname 'Mr Night and Day' from his colleagues. Just over half a century later, in April 2014, his son Sajid became the first Asian man in the British Cabinet.[18]

13

That First Small Cheer

On Monday, 11 December 1961, with the Beatles safely back in Liverpool and playing the Cavern that lunchtime, 60,000 at Twickenham saw Cambridge beat Oxford (by 9–3, high-scoring for the era) to go through the whole season unbeaten; the *Lincolnshire Echo*'s 'Stylus' reviewed the latest records ('Billy Fury and his ilk do not sing so much as whine,' unlike the 'cosy treat' of listening to 'that familiar round and warm tone' of Donald Peers); and Peter Noone made his *Coronation Street* debut as Stanley Fairclough, son of Len. Later in the week, an *Any Questions?* discussion about decimalisation gave Harold Wilson the chance to make an emotional plea to keep 'the pound and the pound sterling', because 'not only Britain and the sterling area, but the world will lose something if the pound disappears from the markets of the world'; David Mercer's first television play *Where the Difference Begins* – about an engine driver's family, set in his hometown of Wakefield and portraying radicalism betrayed by affluence – got from viewers a very high Reaction Index of 78 ('this was sheer drama of life and *real* people') but a going-over from the *Spectator*'s Peter Forster ('a big theme tackled with insufficient talent'); and the bowler-hatted Acker Bilk, whose 'Stranger on the Shore' was in its melancholic way storming up the charts, was asked by an interviewer whether he was 'in favour of the public school system'. 'None of my kids is going away from home,' he replied. 'That's like the army. Money makes all the difference. People who have it get all the training and education and others don't. So I'm against public schools.' Soon afterwards, two big economic stories broke almost simultaneously: ICI's announcement of a giant takeover bid for Courtaulds (the *FT* immediately wondering 'whether such a merger does not create a group too large to be in the national interest') and Selwyn Lloyd announcing decimalisation of the coinage by around 1966 (warmly greeted by the *Daily Mail* on the grounds that 'decimal coinage is modern'). *The Young Ones* was about to go on general release for the Christmas holidays (one critic acclaiming Cliff Richard as 'still as dewy as he was in *Expresso Bongo*, still as apparently unslicked and unspoiled'), while just before Christmas the Advisory County Cricket Committee agreed to inaugurate in 1963 a one-day knock-out competition, prompting the commentator Rex Alston to speculate, 'Will some crafty captain keep his fast bowlers on and spread the field defensively?' Christmas Day itself saw the BBC getting a two-thirds share of the TV audience (but *Coronation Street* besting *This Is Your Life*); on Boxing Day, Madge Martin in Oxford went to the panto (including 'a funny "Dame," Terry Scott'), while Phyllis Willmott that night at Mavis Nicholson's north London party re-encountered Kingsley Amis and 'was struck again by his capacity to control his drunkenness'; and on the 27th, the stand-out programme on the Home Service was Charles Chilton's moving one-hour documentary *The Long, Long Trail: Soldiers' Songs of the First World War*. 1962 came in chilly. 'The coldest New Year's Day for 75 years,' noted Anthony Heap, 'with yesterday's snow (London's heaviest fall since records began in 1940) frozen into ice on slippery pavements, rail, tube and bus services in a state of chaos and everyone coming in late at the TH [ie, Finsbury Town Hall] – the last arriving at 11.0.' Eleven o'clock as it happened was when, after a dreadful overnight journey, the Beatles were sitting uneasily in reception at Decca's West Hampstead recording studios, about to be auditioned. It did not go well, with John underused, Paul palpably nervous, Pete Best on drums having a nightmare and the atmosphere generally downbeat. Gloom also at Accrington, where financially troubled Stanley entered the year next to bottom in Division Four and the local paper observed that 'it has been the Peel Park club's misfortune that if anything possible can go wrong to make their plight worse it usually does.' Little optimism too from the PM. 'The Post Office workers are "working to rule" & this (with the ice & snow) has produced a rather bad situation,' recorded Macmillan on the 5th. 'Everything turns on a) holding on to the wage *pause* for 2 or 3 more months, b) being able to slide into "wage restraint", c) getting started the machinery for a long-term policy.' Still, behind the headlines, nothing could apparently stop the steady, inexorable drift upmarket. Amidst the snow and cold that first week of January, the International Boat Show at Earl's Court saw £200,000 worth of orders taken in its opening four days, while at the end of the week, the *East London Advertiser*'s women's page announced the passing of the 'char' and the arrival of the 'domestic help' – gadget-conscious, 'often young' and usually wearing 'trim nylon house overalls instead of a floral wrap-around apron'.[1]

The *Radio Times* covering this week's television (BBC only) was a lips-licking affair: on Tuesday the 2nd, 7.30–8.00, a new twice-weekly soap set in the offices of 'The Magazine for the Busy Woman'; half an hour later, 8.30–9.15, the first episode of a police drama set 'in the North of England overspill estate called Newtown'; and on Friday the 5th, 8.45–9.15, 'The Offer', the latest in Ray Galton and Alan Simpson's *Comedy Playhouse* series. Written and created by Hazel Adair and Peter Ling, the magazine-*cum*-soap was called *Compact*, and it got a critical mauling, largely for lack of credibility, with Forster declaring that 'the only people I really believed in were the bloody-minded telephone engineers'. By contrast, 'The Offer' provoked more mixed feelings for the *Listener*'s Frederick Laws: positive in that it 'established a couple of characters very pleasantly and hinted at a situation', but less so in that 'the miserly father of the rag-and-bone-man business became so dislikeable that one wanted his exploited but undeceived son to get away and found his frustration and defeat painful.' The father (Albert) was played by Wilfrid Brambell, the son (Harold) by one of Joan Littlewood's Theatre Workshop finest, Harry H. Corbett, and the family firm was called Steptoe and Son. For the largely appreciative viewers (RI of 74), noted the audience-research report, 'tears were never far from laughter', while there was 'a considerable amount of praise for the "incredibly realistic" setting'.[2] In the event, of course, 'The Offer' would not be the only visit to that Shepherd's Bush junkyard. But the real waves were made by the week's other new programme, *Z Cars*.

The police by early 1962 were undergoing scrutiny – albeit rather tame scrutiny – by a Royal Commission, which the government had reluctantly set up two years earlier largely because of the Podola episode of 1959, involving a murder suspect receiving severe, much-publicised injuries as a result of eight hours of questioning in a London police station. Exemplar of the tough policeman on a tough beat using tough methods was Detective Sergeant Harry Challenor, the Soho-based SAS war hero. 'Many of those he helped put behind bars,' his obituarist would note, 'complained that he had planted evidence on them and used his fists, but if his superiors and the courts had misgivings they took no action.' The Royal Commission, when it reported later in 1962, found that the public still broadly trusted the police, but two observers that year offered more critical perspectives. C.G.L. Du Cann, a barrister specialising in criminal law, wrote damningly about the police's role in the justice system, especially in relation to taking bribes from criminals ('there is big money to be made by the police officer who is willing to be "fair" and say a few kind words when he is asked to "tell the court what you know about the prisoner"') and to perjury ('the policeman's familiarity with the witness-box breeds contempt of its obligations'); in the same volume, *The Police and the Public*, the working-class writer Frank Norman, himself a prisoner four times, put it bluntly enough: 'The truth is coppers are just geezers doing a job. Some like doing it; some don't; some are bent and some are straight . . . Some of them use the power given them by being rude to people and looking for trouble and others just want a quiet life, but whichever way you look at it the romantic idea of "the good old London bobby being wonderful" is nothing but a load of old moody. If you want to know the time, look at your watch.'

The best-known – and hugely popular – bobby remained the reassuring, imperturbable, rock-solid-incorruptible George Dixon. 'Evening all,' he announced himself as usual to viewers at the start of an episode in December 1961. 'You know, I expect you remember the cafuffle there was when the Ministry of Transport introduced their ten-year test for cars . . . Well, the fact is with the traffic and the danger on the roads these days it's absolutely vital to keep a car a hundred per cent up to scratch – as we found out ourselves not long back . . .' In fact, popular representations of the police were already starting to change. In two films, Joseph Losey's *Blind Date* (1959) and Val Guest's *Hell Is a City* (in this case Manchester, 1960), the working-class actor Stanley Baker played troubled policemen who were, in Andrew Roberts's words, 'a far cry from the trilby-hatted automaton of the second-feature

CID man'; while on television, not only did ITV's long-running *No Hiding Place* (starting in 1959, with Raymond Francis as the dapper, clip-voiced Inspector Lockhart) have a harder edge than *Dixon of Dock Green*, but the BBC in late 1961 ran a four-part drama series called *Jacks and Knaves* that was Liverpool-set and prompted a youngish Tory MP, Nicholas Ridley, to complain to the Corporation that one of his constituents, a Major Neal, believed it to be showing the police 'in an unfortunate light, making them out to be fools lacking in discipline'.[3]

Even so, there was still plenty of scope for the step-change that was *Z Cars*. Essentially the creation of Troy Kennedy Martin and John McGrath, and set partly in 'Newtown' (based on Kirkby) and partly in 'Seaport' ('based on the Crosby-Waterloo water front', recalled McGrath), it was previewed by the *Liverpool Echo* on 2 January, a few hours before 'Four of a Kind', the first episode: 'Drama documentary series on the day to day work of the crime patrol cars of a County Police Force. The cars, each manned by two young constables selected for their ability to deal effectively with trouble on the spot, are constantly on patrol day and night.' The episode itself, ushered in by a jaunty flutes-and-drums arrangement of the Liverpool-Irish skipping tune 'Johnny Todd', began with the abrasive Detective Chief Inspector Barlow and the milder Detective Sergeant John Watt smoking cigarettes near the grave of a murdered colleague; PC Bob Steele arguing with his facially bruised wife; and his partner in Z-Victor 2, PC Bert Lynch, betting on the horses. Unfortunately, burst pipes that Tuesday evening meant that the *Echo*'s TV reviewer was unable to watch, but next day Richard Sear in the *Daily Mirror* declared that whereas *Compact* had been 'as superficial as powder on the puff', *Z Cars* was 'much more realistic and went straight to the heart of the story'. Then came the complaints. 'It was nowhere near the class of *Dixon of Dock Green*,' the chairman of the Police Federation told the press, adding that 'it showed the police in a pretty poor light'; a spokesman for Preston CID claimed that 'the police were made to look a lot of gormless numskulls'; and, having initially co-operated with the programme, Colonel Eric St Johnston, Chief Constable of Lancashire, now very publicly wanted it taken off. Nor, calling it 'completely inaccurate', was Kirkby Urban District Council enthusiastic – unsurprisingly, given that Kennedy

Martin on an exploratory field trip had privately described Kirkby as 'one of the black spots of England, where 50,000 displaced and truculent Merseysiders carry out a continuous war against authority and where crime and adolescent terror incubate'. As for viewers at large, 'many' were positive, with praise for a portrayal of the police that was 'neither brutal nor benign, but thoroughly human and down-to-earth'. The audience-research report, however, showed a significant minority dissenting: 'It was hardly likely, they maintained, that many real policemen would behave so unattractively, and therefore the whole thing seemed unbelievable and false.'[4]

Over the course of 1962's next four months or so, the *People* put the question 'TOUGHEN HIM UP?' as its contribution to the national debate about whether the 13-year-old Prince Charles should go to Eton (his mother's choice) or Gordonstoun (his father's); the annual hedging competition at Eardisley in Herefordshire 'attracted only a few competitors, but judges were unanimous in their admiration of the skilled craftsmanship of those who built good hedges in a bitter wind'; amidst a storm of press criticism about the cost of Princess Margaret's Kensington Palace apartments, the Queen (recorded Macmillan after a visit to Sandringham) 'showed me a very intimate & moving letter from her sister, wh. revealed how distressed the Princess was at this fickleness, wh. made her feel uncertain of the future'; at blustery Twickenham, England and Wales ground out an attritional 0–0 draw; Enoch Powell, four years after resigning from the government as a champion of fiscal parsimony, published a White Paper detailing a hugely ambitious hospital-building plan; the *Sunday Times* launched on 4 February its pioneering colour magazine (editor Mark Boxer, artistic adviser Snowdon, photos on the cover of Jean Shrimpton in a Mary Quant dress and Burnley's stylish inside-forward Jimmy McIlroy, the whole billed as 'a sharp glance at the mood of Britain' and, after a shaky start, a lucrative magnet for socially aspirational colour advertising); on *Any Questions?*, Mark Abrams and Michael Foot wanted the national anthem dropped at cinemas and theatres, but not so Lady Isobel Barnett and Gerald Nabarro ('should be played on all public occasions and as frequently as possible'); Labour's Eirene White promised that a future

Labour government would not abolish public schools ('it is foolish to destroy something that has virtue'); a playground fight at Bromley Tech left David Jones (later Bowie) with a permanently dilated left pupil; reviewing the latest *Young Contemporaries* show, *The Times* identified David Hockney as the 'star turn' of 'the raspberry-blowing "new surrealist school" (for want of a better name) at the Royal College of Art'; Albert Finney appeared on *Face to Face* ('pleasant, modest, and talkative – but alas, not an inch larger than life', noted John Gross); vast numbers thronged the National Gallery to see the Da Vinci cartoon under threat of export to America; Cyril Osborne led Tory backbenchers talking out Leo Abse's bill which aimed to curb the excesses of homophobic chief constables; the Duke of Edinburgh called the *Daily Express* 'a bloody awful newspaper . . . full of lies, scandal and imagination'; Express Dairies announced that it was stopping 7-days-a-week milk deliveries in London; the 12-year-old Kilmore came in at 28 to 1 in the Grand National; 45 experimental 'Panda' pedestrian crossings opened on 2 April in over 20 towns, amidst widespread confusion; Glasgow's North British Locomotive Co ('too "steam-minded",' according to its chairman) announced it was to go into liquidation; James Hanratty was hanged at Bedford Prison for the A6 murder; Robert Fraser, son of the merchant banker Lionel Fraser and not quite yet 'Groovy Bob', opened his gallery in Duke Street off Grosvenor Square ('I will be dealing entirely in modern paintings and sculpture'); at a housing conference in Sutton Coldfield organised by the West Midlands Old People's Welfare Committee, an 80-year-old 'amused the Delegates by remarking that it was time Local Councils in the design of toilets would raise the height of the pan level as old ladies like herself had great difficulty in getting up from the low-down position of present-day toilets'; David Hockney went home to Bradford for Easter ('he looks well,' noted his mother in her diary, 'but I'm not keen on his blond hair'); Stirling Moss almost died on Easter Monday in a career-ending crash at Goodwood; a magazine advertisement for the *Daily Herald* took the form of an interview with Tony Hancock, an admirer of its content rather than of its 'a bit grave-looking' appearance ('It still reminds you a bit of words like *Labour*. Terrible word, that. Breaking stones in a quarry . . . done more harm to socialism, that word has . . .'); in football's closing weeks, Don Revie at relegation-threatened Leeds tried to bribe a fellow-manager to 'take it easy', Bill Shankly's Liverpool achieved their long-awaited return to the top division as the Kop found its spontaneous singing voice, Ipswich in a last blow for egalitarianism in football's brave new world Mark One won the League Championship (the habitually taciturn manager Alf Ramsey admitting that he felt like 'jumping over the moon'), and Spurs beat Burnley 3–1 in the Cup Final (a young Burnley supporter, Blake Morrison, straight afterwards taking his ball out on the front lawn and re-enacting the match, 'with certain crucial adjustments to the scoreline'); Hugh Trevor-Roper's review of E. H. Carr's *What is History?* in the May issue of *Encounter* expanded into a general attack on the 'dogmatic ruthlessness' of Carr's multi-volume history of Soviet Russia ('the "might-have-beens", the deviationists, the rivals, the critics of Lenin are reduced to insignificance, denied justice, or hearing, or space, because they backed the wrong horse'); Charles started at spartan Gordonstoun (shorts whatever the weather, cold showers at 7 am); Joe Orton (29) and Kenneth Halliwell (35) were found guilty of stealing over 70 books from north London public libraries and 'wilfully' defacing them – 'in a sense', commented the senior probation officer, 'both defendants are frustrated authors' – with the upshot a six-month sentence; and London's last trolleybus, from Wimbledon to Fulwell depot, ran in the early hours of 9 May.[5]

Easily the biggest corporate story of these months was ICI's protracted attempt to gain control over Courtaulds. The pre-Christmas announcement of the bid had, observes John Littlewood in his history of the modern stock market, 'aroused strong emotions across the marketplace. It was perceived as breathtaking in size and outrageous in concept because ICI was the fourth-largest company after Shell, Unilever and BP, and Courtaulds was not far behind in thirteenth place. It was barely within most people's perception that bids could happen for companies the size of Courtaulds.' Nor just the stock market as a keenly contested battle unfolded, with Mollie Panter-Downes noting in February that it had 'shaken the business world and the public as both parties have roared ever louder bids to the shareholders'. Labour's call was for government intervention. 'The public at the moment,' declared Douglas Jay, 'are confronted with the spectacle of two giant companies, supposed to be models of enlightened private enterprise, suddenly grappling in a financial fight to the finish in which either short-term profits or megalomania will decide the issue, with the national interest nowhere considered.' 'Shd the govt intervene?' Macmillan asked himself in late January. 'It has *no* powers. Shd it use its influence? I think the answer really is that ICI are more intelligent & more efficient than Courtaulds as regards management.' Most observers shared that expectation of an ICI victory, but over the next six weeks or so, the balance shifted in Courtaulds's favour, in large part due to the determination and drive of its rapidly emerging future leader, Frank Kearton. 'The great ICI-Courtauld battle is drawing to its inglorious close,' recorded Macmillan on 10 March. 'It looks as if the majority of Courtaulds shareholders will decide to refuse ICI's offer & be loyal to their own board. So all the damage to the reputation of ICI will have been in vain, not to speak of the damage to "capitalism" & the Conservative party. Mr Paul Chambers (Chairman of ICI) is clever, but brash; full of vigour & energy, but lacking in judgement & clumsy in execution.'

Courtaulds indeed lived to fight another day, duly marked by a solemn thanksgiving service for the staff at St Vedast's in the City. Would it, though, have been in the national interest if the contest had gone the other way and a new single combine had come to control some 90 per cent of the UK man-made fibre market? Littlewood argues that it would have been positive, seeing Chambers as ahead of his time in his rationale (as explained to the American Chamber of Commerce during the bid) that 'much of modern industry is bound to be concentrated into big units as the requirements of capital, research and development increase the optimum size of the economic unit.' Against that, Geoffrey Owen in his study of Courtaulds contends that an amalgamation would have inherently posed 'big risks' and is sceptical whether ICI would have 'benefited from having a full hand of fibres, adding acrylic, viscose, and acetate to polyester and nylon'. Where Littlewood is surely right, though, is in his assertion that the broader culture remained instinctively resistant to ambitious corporate restructuring, especially if resulting in large-scale concentrations of economic power. 'A good deal of applause,' noted the *Economist*, greeted a revealing statement that it quoted by a female shareholder at ICI's extraordinary general meeting later in March: 'There is nothing worse than trying to be too clever . . .

ICI and Mr Chambers were too clever and I think they deserved defeat ... They were covetous about Courtaulds and they got a slap in the face.'[6]

Britain was still a land of smokers (almost three-quarters of men, almost half of women), and that spring saw the publication by the Royal College of Physicians of an important report, *Smoking and Health*, that attracted considerable attention and sold well over 20,000 copies in a matter of weeks. Heavy smokers, it explained in authoritative detail, were 30 times likelier than non-smokers to get lung cancer. The report also spelled out smoking's causal link with chronic bronchitis, gastric and duodenal ulcers, and coronary heart disease. The RCP made seven recommendations 'to curb the present rising consumption of tobacco': more public education on smoking's risks; more restrictions on the sale of tobacco to children; restrictions on tobacco advertising; restrictions on smoking in public places; increased tax on cigarettes; information on tar and nicotine content; and anti-smoking clinics. Press reaction to the report was predictably mixed. The *Guardian* called the RCP's case 'overwhelming' and provided sustained, sympathetic coverage; *The Times* was less convinced, arguing that for the 'moderate smoker' the 'hazard is not of an order that seems to call for intervention'; the *Daily Mirror* for a few weeks colourfully highlighted the 'cigarette peril', but then dropped the subject; while the *Daily Express* was sure that 'people who want to smoke will continue to do so,' adding that 'the vast majority of them, being reasonable in their use of cigarettes, will live long and healthy lives.' Equally predictably, government reaction was, as the historian Virginia Berridge puts it, 'muted'. The main emphasis would be on health education – even though the Health minister Enoch Powell, when shown a draft of the report the previous autumn, had expressed the view that 'health education is merely humbug' and that it had 'already gone a long way without producing the slightest effect'. Nor did Powell believe that restrictions on advertising would 'make any difference one way or the other', though in the event the ITA soon after the report did tighten up on television advertising, including insisting that smoking must no longer be connected with social success, manliness or romance. Instead, the crux, as Powell recognised in advance, was whether the government was willing substantially to increase duty 'for explicitly public health reasons' and thereby reduce consumption. This, in the report's wake, it was not beyond a certain point prepared to do, especially given Treasury resistance to the very principle of differential taxation, as well as of course the obvious attendant unpopularity. And the smokers themselves? 'Quite honestly,' a 20-to-25-a-day man told *Tonight* on the day the report came out, 'I think that the end of one's life is probably in the hands of almighty God, you know, than in my own hands or the hands of the tobacco manufacturers.' Another stated frankly, 'If I'm going to die, I'm going to die, so I might as well enjoy life.' That specialist in enjoying life, Philip Larkin, was less fatalistic. 'I have temporarily given up,' he wrote to Monica Jones in early May, two months after the report. He added about a university colleague and his wife, heavier smokers, who had also given up: 'Their tobacconist's receipts have fallen dramatically. Social history.'[7]

The PM had an even keener eye for the historic moment. 'It's a changed Stockton – poverty has been left behind,' he announced in early April on returning to the north-eastern constituency he had represented during the slump of the 1930s. In fact, what would be called by the mid-1960s the 'rediscovery of poverty' was just starting. 'Poverty in Britain today – the Evidence' was the title of the paper read by the Cambridge economist Dorothy Wedderburn in March to the British Sociological Association, meeting at Brighton:

> Although [she concluded] there are some people, mostly old, actually living below National Assistance levels, the main effect of the 1948 legislation and subsequent amendments has been to build in a floor in real terms at a little above the subsistence levels of the 'thirties. Memories of the 'thirties remain alive, however, particularly among that group, the old, who are the main sufferers from poverty and this may lower the line by which they define poverty. In many quarters on the other hand the balance of opinion seems to be in favour of raising the level.
>
> If being at current subsistence levels is being in poverty, there are many people in poverty who are not receiving National Assistance. We estimate that there are 6 per cent of households living long-term on Assistance. Another 4 per cent are at equivalent financial levels, that is below or not more than 25 per cent above scale rates excluding rent but without Assistance. Most of these are old. If one takes as the poverty line

> 50 per cent instead of 25 per cent above present scale rates, one increases the percentage of households by half, and brings in many more households where the main source of income is earnings.

The single-minded sociologist Peter Townsend, out of the Institute of Community Studies stable and now very much his own man, was also on the case; his *New Statesman* piece of 20 April on 'The Meaning of Poverty' argued that poverty was appreciably more widespread than generally assumed. 'Of course we are more prosperous than our grandparents were,' he wrote. 'That is a claim that can be made by each generation. Yet we speak of the "affluent" society. This fine adjective will ring a little hollow in the ears of our grandchildren 50 years from now. They will probably describe the Britain of today, just as we do the Britain of 50 years ago, as a society which tolerated poverty among its aged, its disabled and its large families, and in important sectors of its public services.' Getting across the true situation, though, was not going to be easy – as, the following week, the magazine's 'Charon' demonstrated with some informal fieldwork in relation to the recent assertion in *The Times* by the left-wing Labour MP Frank Allaun that upwards of 15 million people still lived in houses without baths:

> I decided to try this revelation out in a saloon bar of a typical suburban pub which I sometimes use as a sounding board. The opinions held here are invariably representative of the admass: e.g. total apathy towards the prospect of the Common Market, ditto towards the international situation in general; little enthusiasm ever expressed for any public issue except possible retention of capital punishment. I was met on this occasion with total incredulity. I must have made a mistake, added on a nought; the Welfare State took care of all that sort of thing nowadays . . .

'It just didn't occur to them,' concluded the columnist, 'that their own conditions of life weren't thoroughly representative.'

Accrington Stanley's tragedy probably did not much touch the saloon bars either. On Saturday, 13 January, a week after the Twist had reached the Lancashire mill town, the team went bottom of the Fourth Division with a 4–0 defeat at home to Colchester – despite for an hour, according to Bill Hay's match report in the *Accrington Observer*, 'a snap and crackle in their play'. Results over the next month were dismal, apart from a 'heartening' draw at Aldershot, and by 17 February, amidst a rapidly deteriorating financial situation and just before a 'debatable' 2–1 defeat at home to Stockport, the bleak headline was 'STANLEY ON THE BRINK OF A PRECIPICE: Only a miracle can save Peel Park club'. An apparent saviour now came forward in the shape of Bob Lord, the Burnley butcher who doubled as the bullying, bigoted chairman of the Turf Moor club, less than 10 miles away from Accrington. But as Hay noted, many Stanley supporters were reserving judgement on his motives for offering to help what had become a severely depleted board. Almost 2,700 turned up on Saturday the 24th, but unfortunately they saw a 2–0 defeat at home to Rochdale in which 'Stanley were made to look like a team of cart-horses against thoroughbreds.' Then came a creditable 1–1 draw at Doncaster before losing 4–0 at Crewe on Friday, 2 March in a snowstorm, as 'the forwards once again lacked punch'. Three days later, on Monday the 5th, the crunch finally arrived. 'STANLEY – THE END' announced the local paper next morning:

> A Football Club died last night.
>
> And with its demise, League football in the town, which Accrington helped to pioneer in 1888, died too.

The club was some £60,000 in debt, a creditors' meeting had been held the previous evening, and Lord had led the way in recommending liquidation. 'I just cannot see any ray of hope,' he declared. 'It's a shame, but I'm afraid this is only the first of many.' Accrington now resigned from the Football League – and when, later in the week, the board desperately tried to withdraw its resignation, the league (under the autocratic, unforgiving Alan Hardaker) refused any reprieve to one of its founder members. In the event, it would be a full 30 years before another club, also beginning with 'A', was compelled for financial reasons to leave the league in mid-season. In Accrington itself, a last word at the time went to Miss Ellen Rishton, who on that dismal Tuesday came out of Queen's Mill in her overalls and clogs to tell a reporter, 'It's like a death ... I can't understand anybody who isn't loyal to their home-town team. I've often been despairing and sometimes I say I won't go to watch them, but I live near the ground, and when I hear that first small cheer I get my coat on. I just don't know what I'll do now . . .'[8]

Elsewhere in Lancashire, a few weeks earlier on 12 February, there had been serious trouble on the *Street*. 'Kenneth Barlow, 24-year-old schoolmaster of 3 Coronation Street, jeered at the simple pleasures of his homely neighbours in a scathing 2,000 word attack in the left-wing political review *Survival*' ran a local paper's story ('Ex-student Slams Neighbours') that could hardly have been more incendiary. 'Summing up the attitude of the people he lives and works among, Barlow described them as "lazy-minded, politically ignorant, starved of a real culture and stubbornly prejudiced against any advance in human insight, and scientific progress".' The rugged Len Fairclough took particular exception. 'He might be a walkin', flamin' dictionary, but 'e 'asn't the guts of a louse,' he said to a friend; and to Ken himself, as the two men (both in jackets and ties) squared up in the Rover's Return, 'Look, if there's one thing wrong with Coronation Street it's because it sometimes throws up nasty, snivelling, clever dicks like you.' A brawl ensued, finishing with Len delivering a knockout punch on behalf of loyalty to the working class that both came from.

Meanwhile, it was not only in highbrow London weeklies that the debate continued about the authenticity of a programme that was now regularly top or second in the TAM ratings (some 7.7 million homes watching the Barlow/Fairclough fight). 'I must confess,' wrote Guy Williams in Newcastle's *Sunday Sun* in early March, 'to a sneaking regard and affection for those quaint characters who have tenancies in the street – dear old Ena Sharples, the baggage with the whiplash tongue; layabout young Dennis Tanner; and his tart of a mother called Elsie.' Even so, he went on, *Coronation Street* was not in fact a realistic portrayal of working-class life: 'The truth is, of course, that the "Enas" in real life are scorpion-tongued bitches who make the Sharples woman sound like a tinkling-voiced angel by comparison. And you wouldn't find, in real life, the neighbours being so friendly with the Dennis Tanners who simply refuse to work. They'd be much more likely badgering him to follow some worthwhile occupation instead of sponging on the State and National Assistance.' Williams listed other ways in which the soap fell short, including its absence of real drunkenness, of wife-beating husbands, of 'sloppy, ill-kempt wives who slouch around houses that are nauseating to the sight and nostrils', and of malevolent neighbours who 'resent and despise each other so much that they almost delight in others' misfortunes, and would never offer a helping hand'. Why, then, the popularity?

> The upper classes indulgently smile at the quirks of behaviour of the lower classes. The middle classes silently thank their lucky stars that they proved able enough to lift themselves from such an unenterprising and tedious existence. And the humble working folk are faintly flattered by this spotlight of publicity, and amused and almost comforted at the way the unpleasantness of their existence has been wiped out by the script-writers.
>
> It's fine to be amused but they shouldn't delude themselves. *Coronation Street* may be a pleasant attempt at entertainment. But authentic? – phooey!

'I disagree entirely,' responded 'Admirer' from Newcastle's Heaton district. 'The reason for the programme's immense popularity is simply because it IS so "human" and true to life.' Mrs L. Burdon of Sunderland, however, declared that Ena Sharples was simply 'too bad to be true', that 'I've been in business all my life, but I've yet to come across a person like Ena.' And she asked, 'How about someone giving her the telling off she deserves?'[9]

There was by now a rival TV debate. 'While I admire the smoothness, the variety, and the timing of *Dixon of Dock Green*, it is sugary nonsense,' asserted the *Listener*'s Frederick Laws in mid-January. He compared its recent episode 'The Battle of Bellamy Court' ('dodged all the realities of housing problems, rent riots and evictions, and ended in a maddeningly soapy compromise') unfavourably to the second *Z Cars* episode 'Limping Rabbit' ('a good betting-shop squabble, an excellent genteel monster of a grandmother, and a fair hunt round the docks'). A month later *The Times* agreed – calling *Z Cars* 'realistic to a fault' – before March saw a split among *Radio Times* letter-writers. 'The actors in *Z Cars* are good, but they never for one moment give me the impression that they are anything but actors, whereas the cast in *Dock Green* seem to be utterly and entirely genuine policemen,' insisted Lady Savile of London SW7. But for 17-year-old B. E. Fargher of Birmingham 23, the plaudits belonged to 'pulsating, lively, and above all genuine'

Z Cars. 'The rough tongue, the occasional display of bad temper, and the crafty "drag" at a cigarette all tend to reassure me that policemen can be portrayed as human beings with the same frailties as the rest of us.' The respective audience figures suggested that Lady S in South Ken had already lost the battle, as *Z Cars* climbed rapidly through January and February from 9 million viewers to 15 million, in the end overtaking *Dixon*. 'This is the best series of its kind we have ever seen,' declared a plumber in early March about the bumptious upstart. 'These characters seem to have flesh on their bones and blood in their veins.'

The first series proper of *Z Cars* ended with its 13th episode at the end of March, but such had been its success that it went straight on into a further 18 episodes (seven written by the brilliant John Hopkins), which ran through until the end of July. It remained, as it had started, not everyone's favourite. 'The constant belittling and ridiculing of police officers may create a wrong image in the minds of some,' publicly argued the West Riding's chief constable, George Scott, at the end of April. 'But depicting them as they really are can do nothing but good. *Z Cars* is a typical bad example. *Dixon of Dock Green* and *The Blue Lamp* are good examples.' At about the same time, from a rather different angle, the great Methodist moral warrior Donald Soper claimed that '*Z Cars* destroys genuine respect for the law by blurring the real divisions between right and wrong,' as typified by Barlow's brutal methods of interrogation and the police assault on a child-murder suspect. The *Listener*'s Derek Hill, in his column soon afterwards on TV drama, had none of it: not only did the *Z Cars* characters 'live within shouting distance of people rather than in a writer's no-man's land' but the series as a whole 'has broken with the bland traditions of Ted Willis the policeman's P.R.O., and shows both sides of the law as equally human'. That was too much for *Dixon*'s creator and writer, who in a dignified response argued that much of the difference was down to scheduling, with *Dixon* going out at 6.30 on Saturday evenings, and that accordingly 'at least 70 per cent of the material used in *Z Cars* could not be used in our programme.' Yet strikingly – despite the critical acclaim, despite the ratings triumph – the two creators of *Z Cars*, Troy Kennedy Martin and John McGrath, were about to jump ship. 'After the cops kept appearing week after week people began to fall in love with them, and they became stars,' recalled McGrath. 'So the pressure was on to make them the subjects, rather than the device. And when the BBC finally decided that's what they were going to do, then Troy and I decided we'd had enough.'[10]

TV by this time occupied a central part in Nella Last's diary and perhaps life. Take January alone: 'such interesting types of people' (*Compact*); 'it's rare to see a plain or "ugly" face' (*Juke Box Jury*); 'a somewhat childish party game' (*Play Your Hunch*); 'Bootsie and Snudge I could NOT take'; 'even the Beat The Clock lost any "fun"' (*Sunday Night at the London Palladium* in the absence of Bruce Forsyth); 'we were so very happy for the young student who won through to £1,000' (*Double Your Money*). Other viewers had other perspectives. Sid Ward of Sheffield 11 wrote to *TV Times* to praise ITN's 'wonderful' newsreader Reginald Bosanquet ('no mistakes, coughing or mannerisms – and his English is perfectly spoken'); an industrial chemist enjoyed Danny Blanchflower on *Face to Face* ('he is a personality – so many "personalities" aren't!'); a housewife found 'far too much flashing here and there' in Ken Russell's *Monitor* film 'Pop Goes the Easel' on four young artists, including Pauline Boty; and Dennis Potter, during a stint in May as the *Daily Herald*'s TV critic, broadly welcomed *Emergency – Ward 10*'s return after the Equity strike ('a heady pill of concentrated hokum, guaranteed to anaesthetise the credulous, but harmless in small doses'), had little time for Peter Dimmock's 'aloof' presentation of *Sportsview* ('somehow manages to reduce the tingling passion of sport to the teatime comments of a retired insurance clerk') and condemned *Double Your Money* ('"Isn't that won-der-ful?" Mr Green kept saying as he radiated a distressing sincerity') for being 'a 17-inch manifesto for all that is shoddy on TV'. There was also during these months a major row. Having started in January, the BBC's Sunday-afternoon adaptation of *Oliver Twist* was nearing its end when on 18 March it showed Bill Sikes (played by Peter Vaughan) clubbing Nancy to death with a few-holds-barred realism that many viewers apparently found shocking, not helped by a cutaway shot of a trickle of water mingling with her blood. Among those shocked was the Postmaster-General's wife and 12-year-old son, prompting Reginald Bevins (supported by MPs on both sides) to condemn the scene as 'brutal and quite inexcusable' and to protest to the BBC. The direct upshot was that for the final episode, going out on 1 April, the BBC eliminated the scene showing the shadow of Sikes's body hanging from a rope. The controversy filled the correspondence pages, with perhaps the testimony of 'Mother' from Sheldon, writing to the *Birmingham Mail*, having a particular weight: 'When my children (age 10 and seven years) read about the criticisms of brutality in TV's "Oliver Twist" they commented: "Why all the fuss? We didn't see anything to worry about."'[11]

In cinema the British New Wave continued with John Schlesinger's adaptation of Stan Barstow's *A Kind of Loving* – just needing 'an ounce more courage', according to Penelope Gilliatt in the *Observer*, in order to spell out candidly that 'its real theme is not social discontent but the misogyny that has been simmering under the surface of half the interesting plays and films in England since 1956' – but the main action was in the theatre. Vanessa Redgrave's Rosalind in the RSC's *As You Like It* at the Aldwych not only seduced both Anthony Heap ('divinely tall and fair, well graced and eloquently poetic') and John Fowles ('better than one could imagine . . . makes the role scramble up to her') but was all part of Peter Hall's increasingly irresistible footprint ('We have plans,' John Wells by the spring had him say in a spoof *Private Eye* interview, 'to build a new theatre on the South Bank which will probably be called Peter Hall'); Heap was also at the Apollo to see the first night of the farce *Boeing-Boeing* ('I don't suppose it will please many of the critics,' he accurately predicted, 'but it did me and I think it will a multitude of others'); and Ann Jellicoe's *The Knack* got a mixed reception, but with consistent praise for Rita Tushingham ('a gay, yelping performance') and James Bolam ('clowns with remarkable spirited authority').

For two youngish men of the theatre, both of whom had surfed the zeitgeist to remarkable effect in recent years, it was an important spring. Arnold Wesker's class-conscious National Service drama *Chips with Everything* opened at the Royal Court on 27 April (amidst, according to Heap, his 'faithful following of weirdies and ardent leftists') and was hailed by Kenneth Tynan in the *Observer* as 'furious, compassionate and unforgiving', and by Harold Hobson in the *Sunday Times* as 'the first anti-Establishment entertainment of which the Establishment need be afraid'. Not every critic joined the chorus – Bamber Gascoigne in the *Spectator* condemning Wesker's 'over-simplified sociology', Eric Keown in *Punch* arguing that he 'loads his play so heavily that deep feelings are not engaged' – but it was undoubtedly a moment, signalled by Mollie Panter-Downes writing with perhaps surprising admiration of the 'savagery' of Wesker's treatment of 'the enormous gulf that in the much-advertised new Britain still in reality yawns between the rulers and the ruled; the failure to communicate across it, even with good will on both sides; and the inevitable flattening out of the apathetically resigned and the rebellious alike in the caste machine'. Just over a week later, it was the turn of Lionel Bart at the Adelphi. *Blitz!*, his new, expensively staged musical set in the East End during the six months beginning in September 1940, received huge publicity ahead of the opening, but did not quite prove to be the 'whacking, whopping, walloping hit' that the *Daily Telegraph*'s W. A. Darlington forecast. 'A tawdry, ramshackle show,' scribbled Heap; 'the plot woofles and splutters along like a dud incendiary,' thought the *Daily Herald*; Milton Shulman in the *Evening Standard* condemned Bart's 'lush sentimentality'; Gascoigne found 'no scene touched with imagination'; 'frankly a tin-pan-alley musical', reckoned the *New Statesman*; and for Noël Coward, connoisseur of patriotic corn, it was 'as long as the real thing, and twice as noisy'.[12]

Pop music remained in a state – at least as viewed in retrospect from a particular vantage point – of suspended animation, though of course little-noticed things were happening. In early April the 20-year-old Brian Jones (middle-class from Cheltenham, a letter just published in *Disc* praising authentic American rhythm and blues) met Mick Jagger and Keith Richards at the Ealing Club; while on the Beatles front, Decca predictably turned them down, Brian Epstein got the boys into suits, EMI (in the form of Parlophone) at last came through with a recording contract – and the group appeared on national radio. *Teenagers Turn* was on the Light Programme on Thursday, 8 March at five o'clock for half an hour; top of the bill were The Trad Lads; and the rival attraction on BBC television was *Crackerjack*, with Ronnie Carroll as guest star, ten days before coming fourth-equal in the Eurovision Song Contest with 'Ring-a-Ding Girl'. Generally, it was not a radio scene that enthused a Cambridge 16-year-old. '"Whirling around the kitchen," I should think,' Syd Barrett wrote in February to his girlfriend as he lay in bed with glandular fever listening to Desmond Carrington presenting *Housewives' Choice*. 'Just imagine all the great fat old housewives jumping around the kitchen table!' The two main television options were still *Juke Box Jury* and *Thank Your Lucky Stars* (where from February a Birmingham teenager, Janice Nicholls, was giving it 'foive'), with a BBC report on the former finding that over-30s especially disliked 'moronic faces' in the audience and that the main gripe for under-30s was those jury members who 'don't know anything about pop music, criticise harshly, are facetious, wordy, rude or ill-mannered, or try to steal the show', with Katie Boyle and Nancy Spain particularly disliked. Soon afterwards, *Melody Maker* readers chose their ideal jury, with Helen Shapiro ('charming – and she knows pop tastes') and Jane Asher ('represents the teenage point of view and talks sense') as especially favoured, though with one or two plumping for Fidel Castro ('because he's a bit of a rebel'). Cliff Richard and the Shadows, meanwhile, continued in their pomp: Cliff's 36-day sell-out tour early in the year caused pandemonium everywhere, and the Shads released the chart-topping 'Wonderful Land' – 'probably written as a hymn to America, its glamour, its colour and its endless skies', reckons Bob Stanley, but to his ears 'a British dream of the future, the primary-coloured optimism of post-war Britain, people moving to the new towns ringing London, the space and light in the bright open spaces of Crawley and Stevenage . . .' Inevitably it was Cliff who topped the male-singer category in *Melody Maker*'s 1962 Pop Poll, alongside Helen Shapiro (female singer), the Springfields (vocal group) and David Jacobs (disc jockey). No category alas for novelty artists, but the genre still flourished, with Mike Sarne's 'Come Outside' the latest contender. 'One of the most interesting comedy discs for ages by a British artist,' declared *MM* in early May. 'An ingenious laugh featuring Wendy Richard "feeding" Sarne with Cockney jargon.'[13]

The timing was getting interesting. 'Contemporary poetry began in 1962 – in April to be precise – with the publication of A. Alvarez's Penguin anthology *The New Poetry*, the first two volumes of the Penguin Modern Poets series, and the first number of Ian Hamilton's little magazine, the *Review*,' observed William Wootten exactly half a century later. He pointed to a particular aspect of that celebrated interval between the end of the *Lady Chatterley* ban (November 1960) and the arrival of the first Beatles LP (March 1963): 'On the one hand, sales of D.H. Lawrence's book had greatly enriched Penguin Books, which allowed the recently appointed chief editor, Tony Godwin, to pursue ambitious new projects; on the other, the Fab Four had yet to ensure that the new and relevant would be more culturally synonymous with Pop than with Lawrentian intensities and critical seriousness.' Hamilton's emphasis was on tough-mindedness, and the first half-dozen PMPs (three in each volume) included Lawrence Durrell, Elizabeth Jennings, R. S. Thomas and Kingsley Amis, but most attention at the time was focused on Al Alvarez's anthology – partly on the weighting of its selection, heavily playing up Ted Hughes and Thom Gunn (thirty-eight poems between them) and heavily playing down the so-1950s 'Movement' poets (Larkin doing best with eight), but above all on the editor's combative introduction, entitled 'The New Poetry, *or* Beyond the Gentility Principle'. 'The concept of gentility still reigns supreme,' declared Alvarez of most contemporary poets, specifically mentioning Larkin as a main culprit. 'And gentility is a belief that life is always more or less orderly, people always more or less polite, their emotions and habits more or less decent and more or less controllable; that God, in short, is more or less good.' At the end, after comparing Larkin's 'At Grass' unfavourably to Hughes's 'A Dream of Horses' ('unlike Larkin's, Hughes's horses have a violent, impending presence'), he called on English poets to seek to combine 'the openness to experience, the psychological insight and integrity of D.H. Lawrence' with 'the technical skill and formal intelligence of T.S. Eliot'. The anthology itself, all-male, wilfully excluded Elizabeth Jennings, who in her *Listener* review, after noting Alvarez was 'most interested in the sort of poetry which is rough in texture and which communicates a sense of tamed violence or disturbance', asserted that 'his dogmatism, when carefully analysed, proves to be little more than a collection of emotionally charged prejudices.' There were some harsh words too, a little later in the spring, for Anthony Burgess's short novel *A Clockwork Orange*, whose conception had been inspired, he would recall, by returning to England from Malaya, living in Hove and finding on the south coast 'a new British phenomenon – the violence of teenage gangs'. For the *TLS* it was all in 'questionable taste', for Jeremy Brooks in the *Sunday Times* it was 'a very ordinary, brutal and psychologically shallow story', for Penelope Mortimer in the *Daily Express* it was simply 'incomprehensible'. But one young novelist and critic saw it differently. 'What is remarkable is the incredible teenage argot that Mr Burgess invents to tell the story in,' proclaimed Malcolm Bradbury in *Punch*. 'All Mr Burgess's powers as a comic writer, which are considerable, have gone into this rich language of his inverted Utopia. If you can stomach the horrors, you'll enjoy the manner.'[14]

Verbal dexterity was not F. R. Leavis's kind of thing. On 28 February, almost three years since C. P. Snow had delivered his famous Cambridge lecture calling for the literary and scientific cultures to come closer together and viewing them as equally indispensable, the hugely influential Cambridge critic – inspiring more than one generation of English teachers – used another lecture, also in Cambridge, to seek to demolish Snow's reputation. 'If confidence in oneself as a master-mind, qualified by capacity, insight and knowledge to pronounce authoritatively on the frightening problems of our civilisation, is genius,' Leavis began, 'then there can be no doubt about Sir Charles Snow's.' There followed a relentless barrage of abuse. Snow was 'portentously ignorant', indeed 'intellectually as undistinguished as it is possible to be'; *The Two Cultures* itself, which Leavis had read in book form only the previous summer, 'exhibits an utter lack of intellectual distinction and an embarrassing vulgarity of style'; while as for Snow the novelist, 'he can't be said to know what a novel is . . . never was dialogue more inept . . . he is utterly without a glimmer of what creative literature is, or why it matters.' The lecture was printed in full on 9 March in the *Spectator*, which over the next few weeks printed an avalanche of responses, mainly hostile to Leavis:

> Such a silly exhibition. (*Dame Edith Sitwell*)
>
> Barren . . . malevolent. (*Lord Boothby*)
>
> Leavis has not given me one single, valid reason for lowering my opinion of Snow. (*Susan Hill*)
>
> The boomerang of the year. (*Ronald Millar*)
>
> A man may be ignorant of history and slipshod in his mode of expression, as C.P. Snow often is, and yet be able to state an important truth. (*Peter Jay*)
>
> Snow is right; there *are* two cultures; no amount of clichés can disguise the fact. (*Gavin Ewart*)

'I say, Leavis!' the retired Eton schoolmaster George Lyttelton wrote to the publisher Rupert Hart-Davis on the 28th. 'Have you ever known opinion so unanimous about a man's spite, bad manners, injustice, bad English and conceit?' Perhaps the most damning verdict came from the young, rapidly rising George Steiner in May's *Encounter*. It had been 'an ignoble performance' in which Leavis had 'yielded entirely to a streak of shallow, arrogant cruelty'; the blunt repetitiveness of the charges had evoked 'the shadow of a grotesque, intellectual McCarthyism'; and in terms of the positive message, it all amounted to little more than an already over-familiar 'ceremonial dance before the dark god, D.H. Lawrence'. Yet there was a defence. Leavis's opponents, his publisher Ian Parsons observed in the *Spectator*, had over the years been doing to him much what he was now doing to Snow: 'Almost any literary luncheon, poetry prize-giving, public lecture or critical review has been seized upon by them as an opportunity for "having a go" at Leavis.' In essence, that was probably true. 'Many years ago – it must have been in the late 1950s – I attended a literary function somewhere in Mayfair,' recalled the writer Dan Jacobson in 1995.

> Many publishers were there, together with a good sprinkling of literary journalists and editors: soft-faced men who looked as though they had done well out of culture. Someone made a speech. What was said would long since have gone out of my mind, were it not that at one point the speaker referred to an issue or problem on which, he said, everyone was agreed – 'except of course for the *egregious* Dr Leavis in Cambridge'. At this there rose from the glass-clutching throng, into the gin-scented air, a sound I had last heard in the junior quad of my school, when the boys turned in a gang against some wretch who had said or done the wrong thing, or was wearing the wrong kind of socks. Between a jeer and a prolonged, self-satisfied snigger, it was not a pleasant sound.

'For those moments,' added Jacobson, 'the party came close to turning itself into an incarnation of "the London literary scene" that Leavis referred to so often in his writing: as a malign coven of enemies, a corrupt clique or claque, an insidious, powerful conspiracy united against him.'[15]

Cliques and claques too in the somewhat febrile world of the New

Left. 'Early in 1962, when the affairs of the *New Left Review* were in some confusion,' wrote one of the movement's founding fathers, E. P. Thompson, three years later, 'the New Left Board invited an able contributor, Perry Anderson, to take over the editorship.' Anderson himself was a wealthy, manifestly intelligent, Eton-and-Oxford 22-year-old, and a classic Thompsonian passage explained what happened next:

> We found (as we had hoped) in Comrade Anderson the decision and the intellectual coherence necessary to ensure the review's continuance. More than that, we discovered that we had appointed a veritable Dr Beeching of the socialist intelligentsia. All the uneconomic branch-lines and socio-cultural sidings of the New Left which were, in any case, carrying less and less traffic, were abruptly closed down. The main lines of the review underwent an equally ruthless modernisation. Old Left steam-engines were swept off the tracks; wayside halts ('Commitment,' 'What Next for C.N.D.?', 'Women in Love') were boarded up; and the lines were electrified for the speedy traffic from the marxistentialist Left Bank.

Soon, added Thompson, 'the founders of the review discovered, to their chagrin, that the Board lived on a branch-line which, after rigorous intellectual costing, had been found uneconomic.' And, 'finding ourselves redundant we submitted to dissolution.' Had it in effect been a coup? That over the years would be the version propagated by Thompson and his supporters, a version strongly denied by Anderson – who, given that Thompson privately conceded in March 1962 that 'the Board should cease to pretend that it "leads" in any way a new left movement since it has proved itself incompetent to do so,' may well be right. In any case, what mattered more was the fundamentally changed nature and feel of the *NLR* itself. Phyllis Willmott, on being shown by Raphael (as he now was) Samuel in April 1962 a copy of the latest issue (only part-edited by Anderson and including a detailed study by Samuel of the slum-clearance programme), thought it 'quite different, quite excitingly good and a real "break-through" to something better than the old verbose mixture of "depth" and confusion'; yet as Anderson proceeded to put his stamp on the magazine, it is unlikely that she would have remained so positive. 'Anderson had flinty views on what to do with the *Review*,' reflects Fred Inglis, a reader through it all:

> He would ditch the uneasy mixture of up-to-date journalism, CND and anti-Tory polemics, investigative exposures and movie reviews, *ULR* moralising and *New Reasoner* economics. The new version of the *Review* would be a trans-continental and trans-Atlantic journal of neo-Marxist theory with a strongly revisionist turn, taking its lead from Sartre and Louis Althusser, a name then barely known in Britain, from early Marx and the unheard-of Italian, Antonio Gramsci. It would keep faith with the cultural emphasis that had made its signature, but attach it to a more exigent and rigorous sociology than the old Marxist historians had ever read. Weber would be as much cited as Bernstein, Lévi-Strauss as Engels.[16]

It is a fair characterisation. In its first two years the *NLR* had been empirically grounded and closely in touch with what was actually happening in the Britain of the early 1960s; that grounding subsequently almost entirely disappeared, as theory supplanted practice and Britain itself no longer had priority in the New Left world-view. Something may have been gained as a result, but undeniably something precious was lost.

The diarists for their part remained grounded in the day-to-day empirical:

> Took myself off to Bearman's for their remnant sale. Bought two pieces for shirt and blouse for Ione. Hope they will do. Not very experienced at that. Clothes are so dear, if I succeed in my needlework I am pounds in. Waited ages at Green Man, Leytonstone, in wind while traffic oozed fumes all into me, for a bus to Bakers Arms, and decided it was not worth it. Joined a great queue at Bakers Arms for Chingford bus. 'On top only.' The cigarette smoke! (*Judy Haines, 12 January*)
>
> Quite reasonable food – English and Chinese (we chose moderately – Chinese dishes – not daring to try the exciting-sounding real ones). Spotless service, and charming – even beautiful – white-coated Chinese waiters. (*Madge Martin, 3 February, Chinese restaurant in Ship Street, Oxford*)

At 8.31 we had the last of present series of 'Beyond Our Ken' with Kenneth Horne. I like Rodney and Charles, two wags. (*Judy Haines, 22 February*)

Left 19 bus at Holborn. Walked thro' Drury Lane. Asked a woman to see me across the road but she ignored me, an elderly man came to the rescue. Walked through Long Acre into Bow Street, a policeman saw me across. Went thro' Covent Garden very doddery, Teddy boy with beatnik girl left his canoodling to see me across another road, slipped on a cabbage leaf and lay helpless covered with mud. Man hauled me up & raised his hat & departed. So shaken asked a very young policeman to call a taxi. He hurried round the streets searching for one. Taxi-driver was Jewish & talked to me thro' sliding panel. Was held up so long meter cost soared yet he refused to accept anything but 5/-. I urged him to accept 2/- tip but he would NOT take it. He told me he had lived in Stoke Newington but now has a house in Edgware. (*Gladys Langford, 23 March*)

Phoned Gas Board yet again; rude and uncouth response. (*Hugh Selbourne, 26 March*)

What a treat to have a fire after days without even if it is in the new smokeless grate. (*Gladys Hague, 31 March*)

8.28 a.m. I walked to Lion Gate, Kew Gardens. At the school near the north end of Acton Lane, the Scottish contingent of the ban-the-bomb marchers was assembling; others were walking south down Acton Lane and several others assembling on Acton Green, including the Young Communists' League. I heard 2 women talking, apparently about the marchers. One described them as 'a lot of scum'; she said they drank cider from bottles in the street. On Acton Green a lad was trying to sell the 'Guardian'. (*Henry St John, 23 April*)

As the forecast was not too good and we take no notice of it anyhow, we decided we would go to Bradford and have a look at the Spring exhibition of 'art' in the Cartwright Hall. We very soon finished with that. I think this is one of the maddest exhibitions we have ever seen since we started to go. There are not half-a-dozen pictures that we could understand at all, and the so-called 'sculpture' has to be seen to be believed. I could find as effective pieces in the coal-cellar. I wonder how long people will put up with the spending of money on such nonsense. (*Kenneth Preston, 5 May*)

> I love coming out at Archway and getting on the bus up the hill with the feeling of having reached the freshness of the 'heights'. Almost – dare I admit it – a feeling of reaching the 'haven' of suburbia? (*Phyllis Willmott, 8 May*)

Haines was one of the more tolerant diarists, but even she came close to losing it on Saturday the 19th. 'Embarrassed by greengrocer delivering my Wednesday eggs today,' she recorded. 'I am fed up with him, especially as he left me 2lbs greens instead of "green apples" just before hols. and had the cheek to charge them. I showed him them rotten in dustbin, too.'[17]

The diarists also recorded a still difficult industrial scene, as Selwyn Lloyd's 'pay pause' morphed into the 'guiding light' policy of more modified wage restraint. 'Much industrial unrest,' noted Selbourne on 19 January. 'Postman, GPO engineers, Equity actors, coal-miners, redundancies on Railways etc.' Ten days later a Tube strike managed, in Anthony Heap's words, 'to jam all the main roads leading into and through central London with cars'. In February the railwaymen settled, on terms which allowed Macmillan to reflect that 'three hours' talk' and 'much consumption of whisky' had been worth it, not least to banish at least temporarily the press's depiction of 'the ageing and feeble Premier'. From a government perspective, however, the terms were much less good in mid-May, when the Transport and General Workers' Union's Frank Cousins managed to secure from the port employers a 9-per-cent deal for the dockers, way above the 2½-per-cent guiding-light recommendation. 'Incomes policy has come a crasher,' noted Alec Cairncross, the government's economic adviser, who soon afterwards had lunch with Selwyn Lloyd and the editor of *The Times*. 'He said public would have felt more favourable to pay pause had they seen some prospect of useful results,' Cairncross recorded Sir William Haley as remarking. 'But idea that prices might stop rising still seems implausible to them.' The *Economist*'s predictable headline was 'Surrender at the Docks', the paper adding that 'the one sensible remark made after this disaster was Mr Enoch Powell's observation that when the line of incomes policy has been breached in one sector, this makes it all the more necessary to hold the line with redoubled vigour in other sectors.' Powell himself as Minister of Health had been successfully holding the line against the pay claim of the nurses, possessed of far less industrial muscle than the dockers, and Mollie Panter-Downes was not alone in observing that 'this all looks unpleasantly like one wage scale for the strong, who can strike, and another for dedicated public servants, who cannot or will not' – and that 'the contrast has been damaging for the Government.' Still, as Macmillan reflected in his memoirs, 'I could not help noticing that while berating the concession to the dockers, everybody was, in fact, delighted with the fact that the strike was off.'

The other half of Lloyd's economic strategy was apparently making some belated progress. In January the unions finally agreed to join the employers on the National Economic Development Council ('Neddy', though at this stage sometimes known as 'Ned'), which held its first meeting in March. 'Loud cheers for Ned!' acclaimed the *Economist* two months later about the new body's commitment to achieving a growth rate of 4 per cent per annum over the next five years; while in the *Sunday Times*, hailing a 'realistic growth policy', William Rees-Mogg expressed satisfaction that, after a long period of adherence to the primacy of stability, British economic policy had now 'moved into a new and definitely more optimistic phase'. At least one politician and one economist had their doubts. 'Mrs Thatcher warned,' noted the *Coventry Evening Telegraph* in February about her address at a wine-and-cheese-tasting party organised by local female Tories, 'that this Council [ie, Neddy] would not be a panacea for all their troubles.' And, talking in the spring on the Third Programme, a former economic adviser to the Treasury, John Brunner, argued that the new cult of planning and growth was 'really just a form of wishful thinking' and that, 'rather than recognise that a higher rate of growth represents a serious challenge to deeply held values and customs, we prefer the easy way out apparently offered by the N.E.D.C.' He elaborated:

> To do significantly better calls for little short of a revolution in our attitudes, customs, values, and institutions. We would have to create a much more ruthless, competitive, materialistic society. We are fully entitled to say we do not want such a society. We are not entitled to demand faster growth and expect business, and indeed life, to continue as usual.

In short, 'as Mr Forster would say, let us "only connect".'[18]

The Tories by this time, after their golden run in the 1950s, were struggling to connect. 'This evening watched Harold Macmillan on TV,' noted Hugh Selbourne in late January. 'He made an empty speech, full of platitudes and drivel.' By early February the inevitable was happening. 'All the Sunday press,' recorded Macmillan himself, 'is full of gossip about the attacks on me by Tory back-benchers. It is an obscure and may become a dangerous situation, but I hope to ride this storm.' There followed on 14 March perhaps the most famous by-election result of the century, and the moment that marked the beginning of the end of the two-party monopoly, as the Liberal candidate Eric Lubbock (local, a palpable gent, an effective campaigner) at the Kent commuter seat of Orpington overturned a Conservative majority of almost 15,000 into a stunning Liberal victory of almost 8,000. Macmillan's public take was the familiar Edwardian imperturbability – 'If it is due to temporary emotion it will pass like the wearing of the type of trousers I wore when I was eighteen years old' – but later in March he set down his real thoughts:

> It is the revolt of the middle classes or lower middle classes, who resent the vastly improved conditions of the working classes, and are envious of the apparent prosperity and luxury of the 'rich' – whether they live on office expenses, capital gains, or capital. These white collar 'little men' – clerks, civil servants, etc., have [in the past] voted Conservative 'to keep Labour out'. Now (especially at by-elections) they are voting Liberal to 'give the Government a smack in the eye'.
>
> Then there is fashion. It is getting dull to be a young Conservative. It is not at all smart to go Labour. Liberal is not in the Establishment; has a flavour of 'something different'.
>
> Most of all, it is a revolt against all the unsolved problems. The Bomb (it favours the abolition of the British independent deterrent); relations with Russia; NATO; Berlin; Rhodesia . . . But it springs most from the Government's inability to keep the economy on an even course of continuous progress. It deplores 'Stop and Go' or 'Acceleration and Brake'. It wants enormously *increased* expenditure, and *reduced* taxation. It wants a larger army, without conscription. It wants wage stability, without any restraint. In a word, it wants what we all want and know we can't have.

> The Pay Pause – the Government's policy – has offended dons, schoolmasters, school-teachers, civil servants, clerks, nurses, public utility workers, railwaymen, and all the rest. But perhaps it is most resented by the doctors, dons, nurses, etc., who feel that they are *relatively* ill paid, compared to the high wages which they hear about coming in to the ordinary artisans' household. Anyway, it is a portent, and the Tories are very worried . . .

Soon afterwards, on the 28th, the *Daily Mail* published the sensational National Opinion Poll (NOP) news that the Liberals were now ahead nationally, with the Tories in third place. At this point the pressure on Selwyn Lloyd to produce a sparkling, politically uplifting Budget, due on 9 April, was intense, but despite a sweetener to owner-occupiers through the promise to abolish Schedule A taxation he failed to deliver. 'The government,' notes the historian of Gallup, 'was thought to be doing too much for the well-to-do, too little for the working class and for people living on small pensions or on small incomes, and on balance doing too little to level up the classes.' At this point there was still a potential two and a half years to go before the next election, but later in the spring the Shadow Chancellor, James Callaghan, started making regular trips to Nuffield College, Oxford in order to become better versed in fiscal, industrial and monetary matters. 'I still do not have clear in my head,' he wrote to an Oxford economist ahead of the first seminar about the apparently insoluble 'stop-go' problem, 'how we can run British industry on a high level and still pay our way overseas.'[19]

There were moments during the first half of 1962 when old England seemed under serious attack. Macmillan and the Queen both gamely attended, on separate evenings, *Beyond the Fringe* ('When I've a spare evening,' said Peter Cook's PM in a late addition to the script for the benefit of the real PM, 'there's nothing I like better than to wander over to a theatre and sit there listening to a group of sappy, urgent, vibrant young satirists, with a stupid great grin spread all over my silly old face'); the American comedian Lenny Bruce ('a staccato of reminiscence and fantasy', noted Tom Stoppard, 'mowing down conventional barriers of language and subject until the unspeakable has become eminently, hilariously speakable') spent a month at The Establishment club in Soho becoming a hate figure for much of the press; and *Private Eye* started to take off, announcing in early April what it fundamentally believed in: 'Balls to the lot of them.' Pearson Phillips, a *Daily Mail* feature writer, used the occasion of the royal visit to try to see the bigger picture and in so doing part-reassure his paper's readers:

> The Queen at *Beyond the Fringe* – in a way this is the unkindest cut of all, the last twist of the knife. The *Fringe* men were to have been the satirical stormtroopers on the wing of Britain's post-war rebellion. They were to have drawn blood. Instead, they have been assimilated. Court jesters, by appointment. No wonder our British rebels are sad and disillusioned. From John Osborne to Lord Russell the whole glumly articulate group are showing signs of discouragement, despair, and general intellectual wear and tear.
>
> Who can blame them? For the past six years – ever since *Look Back in Anger* – they have been mounting a powerful assault on what they see as the flabby, self-satisfied face of the well-bred philistines who preside over the destiny of Great Britain and the Commonwealth. It would be very wrong to underestimate the power of this artistic, social and intellectual cleansing operation. And yet, what has it achieved?
>
> Nothing, they feel. Nothing at all. The same kind of people are still on top and show no signs of budging or being budged. Damn you, England.

Yet, argued Phillips, the 'vague, flabby jelly-fish of opinion and power' *was* shifting, 'imperceptibly but inexorably like a glacier', as Britain made its uneasy transition 'from a rich imperial Power to a medium poor one':

> You can detect the shift in all sorts of ways. Go to the City and see what the climate of opinion is on the question of State control compared with what it was five years ago. Go to a meeting of headmasters and see how they have quietly shifted their ground on the role and function of the public schools in the last few years. Look how the Labour Party – for that matter – has picked up the right direction on the role of nationalisation. See what a shift there has been in thought on capital punishment . . .

The Crazy Gang (Bud Flanagan et al) were never going to be part of that shift. On Saturday, 19 May at London's Victoria Palace, they gave their farewell performance, televised the following evening. A packed-out theatre included John Betjeman ('a very sad evening'), Noël Coward ('a horrid, sad evening – I shall miss them dearly'), Peter Sellers and Ingrid Bergman; all the familiar, intensely nostalgic routines and songs (including 'Underneath the Arches', 'Run Rabbit Run' and 'Maybe It's Because I'm a Londoner') were performed; and at the end, reported *The Times*, 'a beautifully worded telegram from Sir Laurence Olivier was read out.'[20]

Six days later, over twenty years since its medieval predecessor had been destroyed, the new Coventry Cathedral was consecrated. The architectural critics delivered their judgement: to Kenneth Robinson, 'a great and humbling building', albeit 'a box of functional tricks'; to the out-and-out modernist Reyner Banham, 'a traditional cathedral re-styled', involving 'no reassessment of cathedral functions', that altogether amounted to 'the worst set-back to English church architecture for a very long time'; and to Ian Nairn (calling himself 'a disillusioned though still firm believer in modern architecture') 'a terrible disappointment', essentially because 'the enthusiasm which is the mainspring of Sir Basil Spence's architecture may here have outrun his technique'. The service itself on Friday the 25th had its drama. 'The Queen's yellow outfit clashed with John Piper's new canary-yellow copes,' notes the obituarist of the Bishop of Coventry, Cuthbert Bardsley. 'The Lord Mayor fainted with a terrible clatter of municipal chains and had to be revived by the Bishop of Birmingham. As the sidesman attempted to pile the collection on to gold salvers there was a continual cascade of coins to the floor in front of the stony gaze of the Queen.' Both television channels covered the event – 'the long service was beautiful, moving and dignified,' thought Madge Martin (watching it at a friend's house in Oxford), 'except for the dull sermon by the Archbishop of Canterbury' – and the critic Maurice Wiggin observed that Sir Kenneth Clark on ITV 'had the courage to acknowledge a fact which the BBC would not face – the fact that just possibly a new cathedral is difficult to design because it simply is not wanted by the mass of the people'. That evening, after all the dignitaries had left, some 20,000 Coventrians and others filed through, with queues stretching back 300 yards, and a local paper gathered some vox pop:

> I think it is really lovely. The building is splendid. But the fleche still reminds me of a wireless mast. (*Mr G.R. Johnson, lecturer in telecommunications at the local Lanchester College of Technology*)
>
> It is so different, to one as old as I am. I am so used to the old cathedrals. (*Miss F. E. Butterfield, 86, from Brighton*)
>
> Very fabulous – the most fabulous place I have ever known. (*Margaret West, 14, from Rugby*)
>
> A very nice building. I have seen temples in Delhi, and I would compare it with them. (*Mr P. D. Patel, 24, from India*)
>
> The old cathedrals are out-dated, in my opinion. We are now living in a modern age. I think this cathedral is wonderful. (*Mr J. Williams, 68, retired commercial traveller from Preston*)

Five days after the consecration, on Wednesday the 30th, the new building's complementary set piece took place: the first performance, broadcast live on the Home Service, of Benjamin Britten's *War Requiem*. 'Surely a masterpiece of our time,' proclaimed one critic, Desmond Shawe-Taylor, while Mollie Panter-Downes found Britten's 'warning' about the folly (and pity) of war 'infinitely more shattering than any marches to Aldermaston'. And she went on: 'It seemed fitting that Coventry should be the first to hear such a passionate denunciation of what killed its cathedral and many of its citizens and remains the adversary that no splendid, straggling archangel, even St Michael, has yet properly finished off for us. But we will try, says the new cathedral, and it is this spirit, perhaps, that is making the world beat a path to its door.'[21]

Of course, it was not only bombs that destroyed the old and beautiful. On 28 May, Newcastle's Town Planning Committee took 19 minutes to decide to demolish much of Eldon Square – designed by John Dobson and developed by Richard Grainger in the 1820s – in order to build a new shopping centre. 'Gain and Loss' was the local *Journal*'s judicious editorial the next morning: 'reluctant agreement' that the proposed redevelopment was 'justifiable' in terms of 'a hard business appraisal', and also that it would be hailed as a great improvement by 'most citizens'; yet, 'for our part, we just hate the involved demolition of the Dobson terraces, and the inevitable loss of a dignity of form and character the architect created for us.' Later on the 29th, a prominent local Tory and former Lord Mayor, William McKeag, came out fighting:

> The disciples of destruction have been on the march for some time. We must try to prevent the present trend from developing into an uncontrollable orgy . . . The decision of the planning committee to destroy Eldon Square shocks me beyond measure. I say 'shocks,' not 'surprises,' because I have almost ceased to be surprised at the enormities our so-called planners are prepared to perpetrate in the sacred name of progress.

The *Evening Chronicle* also quoted one of the square's residents, Mrs Sarah Sutherland: 'I wonder what will happen to all the old people who sit in the square. It is the only place in the city centre they can rest.' The controversy continued over the next week or so. A letter to the *Journal* from Veronica Nisbet of Newcastle 2 called the news 'a bombshell to an unsuspecting public'; Labour's local leader, T. Dan Smith, justified the decision at a meeting of the city council ('If we failed to achieve this stage of redevelopment, then the whole conception of the central area would be incapable of achievement. This is not out of spite . . .'); and in a television debate with McKeag, a proponent of the redevelopment, Dr Henry Russell, claimed – with a large degree of exaggeration – that the square was a 'rabbit warren of tenements'.[22] Not that any of this really signified: some 140 years on, the die had been cast.

'The ageless, classless, nostalgic appeal of the whole thing is quite irresistible,' noted Anthony Heap on 25 May (the same day as Coventry Cathedral's consecration) after going to the first night of *The Black and White Minstrel Show*, now replacing the Crazy Gang at the Victoria Palace. Next day, Labour's Barbara Castle revealed that the Minister of Works had agreed to her request to have the lavatory turnstiles in the royal parks removed forthwith; on Monday the 28th, Macmillan told the Cabinet about his intention to go full steam ahead for reflation, and Stephen Spender had a pub lunch with Ray Gosling ('teddy-boy appearance . . . exaggerated gestures . . . lively and observant . . . on the whole, I didn't feel too optimistic about Ray G.'); and on Tuesday, the *FT*'s headline about the new exhibition at the Tate was 'Francis Bacon – Too Shrill a Cry?', the Manchester authorities unveiled their vision for the comprehensive redevelopment of Hulme (including the number of pubs to go down from fourteen to two) and a meeting at Lord's of MCC's Cricket Enquiry Committee decided 'to retain the status quo of the amateur'. The round of county fixtures starting on Wednesday the 30th saw two debuts: at Gravesend, Henry Blofeld's as a cricket reporter ('glorious day . . . drying wicket . . . splendidly aggressive innings . . .'), followed by a pub in Rochester where he had 'a filthy dinner of brown Windsor soup and very old mutton with underboiled potatoes'; and at Liverpool, the West Ham footballer Geoff Hurst playing his only match for Essex and being caught off Ken Higgs for 3. Perhaps he should have been in Chile, where 'the Nelson spirit was not enough' as England went down 2–1 to Hungary in their opening World Cup match. Over the early days of June, as the warm weather continued after a very cold spring, *Private Eye*'s Willie Rushton had some cruel fun with his depiction of 'Tony Halfcock' as an egocentric comedian who had abandoned everyone around him ('I like God, but it's time for us to go our separate ways'); Judy Haines went to *A Kind of Loving* ('not the sort of subject for filming, I reckon'); Harold Wilson pronounced at the Worthing conference of the Boilermakers' Society that 'the Labour Party is a moral crusade or it is nothing'; England beat Argentina 3–1 ('young' Bobby Moore, on his third appearance, showing 'courage and rare intelligence in his use of the ball'); the Football League voted in Oxford United to replace Accrington Stanley; and a full-page, Beaverbrook-funded statement by Field Marshal Viscount Montgomery appeared in the daily press ('I say we must not join Europe . . . Let us rather continue to rely on our own strength and judgement'). On Wednesday the 6th, by-elections at West Derbyshire and Middlesbrough West produced poor results for the Tories, seven horses fell in chaotic scenes at the Derby, and the Beatles had their first recording session with George Martin ('Let me know if there's anything you don't like,' he said helpfully, getting the response from the other George, 'Well, for a start, I don't like your tie'). Next day, England managed an 'insipid' goalless draw against Bulgaria to edge through to the quarter-finals; at the Arts Theatre, David Rudkin's brutal *Afore Night Come* (set in a Midlands pear orchard) generated predictable complaints about 'meaningless violence' and 'tedious bestiality' but powerfully conveyed the native workers' atavistic hatred of outsiders; and on TV the judging panel for *Miss Interflora-G.P.O. 1962* comprised the Countess of Longford, 'A Psychiatrist' and Mr C. W. Davies (Telephone Manager, Centre Area). Friday the 8th began with Ronald Bryden in the *Spectator* acclaiming Iris Murdoch's new novel *An Unofficial Rose* ('with each book she moves forward in mastery, setting herself and encompassing larger goals, advancing steadily towards the great, deep comic classic she is surely going to write within our lifetimes') and *The Times*'s Scottish correspondent reporting, six days ahead of polling, on the West Lothian by-election. There he found Labour's 29-year-old Old Etonian candidate, Tam Dalyell, 'already moving at a good gallop' and 'calling at scores of houses each day'; while on going into the committee rooms in Bathgate of the Scottish Nationalist candidate William Wolfe, seeking to revive his party's fortunes after a decade or more in the doldrums, he heard the recorded voice of Andy Stewart singing 'Tunes of Glory'. That evening, David Turner's Jonsonian *Semi-Detached*, arguably the great modern play (understanding, not condemnatory) about the suburban lower middle class, had its premiere at Coventry's Belgrade Theatre, in the process launching the career of Leonard Rossiter; and on the radio, the *Any Questions?* panel was asked about the ethics of going on holiday to Spain. 'I think it is a mistake when we appear to be giving support to Franco and his hideous regime, but I'm all in favour of English people going on holiday and seeing for themselves,' replied a youngish Labour MP, John Stonehouse. 'What I am opposed to are these coach tours, these packaged holidays. I mean, people go with groups of other English, they stay in hotels which are catering with English breakfasts, English lunches, English dinners, cups of tea whenever they're required. The people who go on these package tours hardly ever see the people in the countries that they visit. I'm all opposed to them . . .'[23]

Saturday, 9 June – the culmination of a week of celebrations of the centenary of the Tyneside anthem, 'The Blaydon Races' – was T. Dan Smith's day. A mass parade, with 120 decorated floats and 20 brass bands (including the Cowpen and Crofton Workmen's Band, the Dawdon Lodge Band and the Hetton Silver Band) made its way along the 5 miles from the city centre to Blaydon; much of that route was along the Scotswood Road, with 'many people' living in streets off it 'celebrating with street parties'; and generally there was music, fireworks and – almost unthinkably – all-day drinking in the pubs. A celebration of a hundred years of materially impoverished but emotionally largely stable working-class life? Or a celebration of the slum clearance and large-scale redevelopment that was now happening and the promise of what lay ahead? For Smith himself, who had pushed through the lavish celebrations against bitter local Conservative opposition, it was overwhelmingly the latter. Sloping up on the north side of Scotswood Road was his cherished, Swedish-inspired Cruddas Park development: six 15-storey blocks of flats in varying states of construction, with the first completed one, The Willows, to be officially opened that day by the Labour leader Hugh Gaitskell. This Gaitskell duly did, accompanied by Smith, as well as unveiling a modernist, 13-foot-high sculpture by Kenneth Ford (young and bearded) that had been commissioned by Smith to mark the 'rebirth' of Scotswood Road. Next day, Newcastle's Sunday paper described all the events of a special day that most people seem to have hugely enjoyed. It also ran an interview with 15-year-old Helen Shapiro, who had been appearing all week at the Empire Sunderland on a bill that included Lenny the Lion, Dave Allen and an animal act called Captain Fleming's Chimpanzees. 'She is a typical modern teenager with little knowledge of the past (the war is just a vague bit of history to her),' observed the interviewer. 'She has no sentimental feelings about anything that has happened before her own life.'[24]

Afterword

A few weeks later, one of the emblematic books of the era appeared: Anthony Sampson's *Anatomy of Britain*. Britain, argued Sampson in his closing pages, had been through two distinct phases since the war, the first of them essentially static: 'The social revolution of 1945, though profound, took ten years to show its effects on spending. London's skyline, broken by bomb damage, remained almost unchanged. Newspapers rationed their newsprint. The BBC was unchallenged . . .' The second phase, he went on, started in 1957: 'Within two years, the credit squeeze ended, skyscrapers rushed up, supermarkets spread over cities, newspapers became fatter or died, commercial television began making millions, shops, airlines, even coal had to fight for their lives. After the big sleep many people welcomed any novelty . . .' Not everyone, it is clear, was quite so welcoming, but about the overwhelming fact of change in the late 1950s going into the early 1960s, and the broad post-war periodisation, Sampson from his 1962 vantage point was surely correct. What, though, was now the most propitious way ahead? Sampson had no doubts about where (so far) there had been a seriously damaging absence of change: 'The old privileged values of aristocracy, public schools and Oxbridge which still dominate government today have failed to provide the stimulus, the purposive policies and the keen eye on the future which Britain is looking for, and must have . . . The old fabric of the British governing class, while keeping its social and political hold, has failed to accommodate or analyse the vast forces of science, education or social change which (whether they like it or not) are changing the face of the country.'[1] It was time, in short, for tomorrow's new men, and perhaps even the odd new woman, to be allowed to step up to the plate. Or, put another way, modernity Britain, yes; but also – at long last – opportunity Britain.

Notes

Abbreviations

Abrams	Mark Abrams Papers (Churchill Archives Centre, Churchill College, Cambridge)
Amis	Zachary Leader (ed), *The Letters of Kingsley Amis* (2000)
BBC WA	BBC Written Archives Centre (Caversham)
Benn	Ruth Winstone (ed), *Tony Benn, Years of Hope: Diaries, Letters and Papers, 1940–1962* (1994).
Chaplin	Sid Chaplin Papers (Special Collections, University of Newcastle)
Crossman	Janet Morgan (ed), *The Backbench Diaries of Richard Crossman* (1981)
Crossman	Diary of Richard Crossman (Modern Records Centre, University of Warwick)
Daly	Lawrence Daly Papers (Modern Records Centre, University of Warwick)
Dee	Diary of Dennis Dee (East Riding of Yorkshire Archives, Beverley)
Fowles	Charles Drazin (ed), John Fowles, *The Journals: Volume 1* (2003)
Fowles	John Fowles Papers (Special Collections, University of Exeter)
Gorer	Geoffrey Gorer Papers (Special Collections, University of Sussex)
Hague	Frances and Gladys Hague Papers (Keighley Library)
Haines	Diary of Alice (Judy) Haines (Special Collections, University of Sussex)
Heap	Diary of Anthony Heap (London Metropolitan Archives)
Langford	Diary of Gladys Langford (Islington Local History Centre)
Larkin	Anthony Thwaite (ed), Philip Larkin, *Letters to Monica* (2010)
Larkin	Unpublished Letters of Philip Larkin to Monica Jones (Bodleian Library, Oxford)
Last	Diary of Nella Last (Mass-Observation Archive, Special Collections, University of Sussex)
Macmillan (1)	Harold Macmillan, *Pointing the Way: 1959–61* (1972)
Macmillan (2)	Harold Macmillan, *At the End of the Day: 1961–63* (1973)
Macmillan	Harold Macmillan Papers (Bodleian Library, Oxford)
Martin	Diary of Madge Martin (Oxfordshire History Centre, Oxford)
Osborn	Michael Hughes (ed), *The Letters of Lewis Mumford and Frederic J. Osborn* (Bath, 1971)
Preston	Diary of Kenneth Preston (Bradford Archives, Bradford Central Library)

Raynham	Diary of Marian Raynham (Special Collections, University of Sussex)
St John	Diary of Henry St John (Ealing Local History Centre)
Selbourne	David Selbourne (ed), *A Doctor's Life: The Diaries of Hugh Selbourne M.D. 1960–63* (1989)
Turtle	Diary of Florence Turtle (Wandsworth Heritage Service)
Willmott	Diary of Phyllis Willmott (Churchill Archives Centre, Churchill College, Cambridge)
Wilson	Jacqueline Wilson, *My Secret Diary* (2009)

All books are published in London unless otherwise stated.

Chapter 1 Sure as Progress Itself

1. Haines, 16 Oct 1959; John Fisher, *Tony Hancock* (2008), pp 270–1; BBC WA, *Any Questions?*, 16 Oct 1959; *Times*, 10 Oct 1959; Gorer, Box 45, Young to Gorer, 19 Oct 1959; *Daily Mirror*, 28 Oct 1959; *Times*, 29 Oct 1959; *Daily Mirror*, 29 Oct 1959.
2. Michael Billington, *State of the Nation* (2007), pp 115–17; *New Statesman*, 31 Oct 1959; *Times*, 19 Oct 1959; *Liverpool Echo*, 22 Oct 1959; *Listener*, 12 Nov 1959 (James Reeves); *Times*, 5 Nov 1959; Iona and Peter Opie, *The Lore and Language of Schoolchildren* (1959), pp vii, 356; Macmillan, dep.37, 1 Nov 1959, fol 60.
3. *Hants and Berks Gazette*, 16 Oct 1959; *Times*, 28 Oct 1959; *Daily Mirror*, 28 Oct 1959; Martin, 23 Oct 1959; *East London Gazette*, 9 Oct 1959; *New Yorker*, 24 Oct 1959 (Stephen Watts); *Paisley Daily Express*, 23 Oct 1959, 26 Oct 1959; Osborn, p 293.
4. *Daily Herald*, 28 Oct 1959; *Evening Standard*, 28 Oct 1959; *Liverpool Weekly News*, 12 Nov 1959; J. F. Demers, 'Community and Park Hill' in The Society of Housing Managers, *Quarterly Journal*, Oct 1963, p 2; *Star* (Sheffield), 20 Oct 1959, 21 Oct 1959, 23 Oct 1959; *Sheffield Telegraph*, 9 Nov 1959.
5. *Melody Maker*, 17 Oct 1959, 31 Oct 1959; *Times*, 2 Nov 1959; *Luton News*, 22 Oct 1959; *Daily Sketch*, 3 Nov 1959.
6. BBC WA, R9/74/2, Nov 1959; *Daily Express*, 19 Oct 1959; *Daily Sketch*, 14 Oct 1959; *East London Advertiser*, 30 Oct 1959, 13 Nov 1959.

Chapter 2 A Real Love Match

1. Kingsley Amis, *Memoirs* (1991), pp 187–90; Anne de Courcy, *Snowdon* (2008); *Daily Express*, 2 Nov 1959, 10 Nov 1959; A.C.H. Smith, *Paper Voices* (1975), pp 217–22; *New Statesman*, 12 Dec 1959 (Jeremy Sandford).
2. 'Alan Keith', *Times*, 19 Mar 2003; *Manchester Evening News*, 21 Nov 1959; Asa Briggs, *The History of Broadcasting in the United Kingdom: Volume V* (Oxford, 1995), p 209; *Spectator*, 4 Dec 1959; Spencer Leigh, 'Adam Faith', *Independent*, 10

Mar 2003; Jonathan Margolis, *Bernard Manning* (1996), pp 74–5; Brian Jackson Collection at Qualidata, University of Essex, 'Working-Class Community' Papers, File (i.e. Box) C1, 13 Dec 1959.

3. Heap, 24 Nov 1959; BBC WA, R9/9/23 – LR/59/1963; Last, 10 Feb 1960; Martin, 3 Dec 1959; *Punch*, 31 Dec 1959; Sylvie Simmons, *I'm Your Man* (2012), p 72; *Guardian*, 3 Oct 2009 (Jenny Diski); *Spectator*, 1 Jan 1960; BBC WA, R9/74/2, Feb 1960; Richard Webber, *Fifty Years of Hancock's Half Hour* (2004), p 238.
4. *News Chronicle*, 28 Dec 1959; David Blunkett, *On a Clear Day* (2002 edn), pp 42–3; Margaret Drabble, *Angus Wilson* (1995), pp 259–63.
5. Rick Rogers, *Crowther to Warnock* (1980), p 13; *Times*, 29 Jan 1960, 4 Feb 1960; *Socialist Commentary*, May 1960, p 22; A. Crichton *et al*, 'Youth and leisure in Cardiff, 1960', *Sociological Review*, Jul 1962, pp 218–19; Wilson, pp 66, 131, 72, 144, 168, 77, 184–5.
6. Norma Farnes (ed), *The Goons* (1997), p 138; Hugh Carleton Greene, *The Third Floor Front* (1969), p 13; BBC WA, *Any Questions?*, 8 Jan 1960; *Guardian*, 29 Oct 2011 (Jeanette Winterson); *Sunday Express*, 24 Jan 1960; *Observer*, 24 Jan 1960, 4 Nov 2001 (Oliver James); www.britishpathe.com/video/ten-pin-bowling; John Tilbury, *Cornelius Cardew* (Harlow, 2008), p 82; BBC WA, R9/7/44 – VR/60/60; *Hansard*, House of Commons, 5 Feb 1960, cols 1350–8, 1366; *Times*, 8 Feb 1960; *Sunday Times*, 14 Feb 1960 (John Raymond); John Cole, 'Bruce Hobbs', *Independent*, 17 Nov 2004; 'John May', *Daily Telegraph*, 21 Mar 2002.
7. *Times*, 12 Feb 1960; *Observer*, 14 Feb 1960; John Ramsden, 'Refocusing "The People's War"', *Journal of Contemporary History*, Jan 1998, pp 41–2; Tom Vallance, 'James Booth', *Independent*, 13 Aug 2005; Heap, 11 Feb 1960; *Sunday Times*, 14 Feb 1960; *Punch*, 17 Feb 1960, 10 Aug 1960; *East London Advertiser*, 28 Oct 1960.
8. *Times Literary Supplement*, 11 Mar 1960; *Observer*, 28 Feb 1960; *Times Literary Supplement*, 26 Feb 1960; *New Statesman*, 13 Feb 1960; Chaplin, 7/3/1, 29 Feb 1960.
9. *Guardian*, 8 Jul 2011 (Esther Addley); *News of the World*, 24 Jan 1960, 31 Jan 1960, 7 Feb 1960; Last, 7 Feb 1960; *Sunday Express*, 7 Feb 1960; Last, 7 Feb 1960; BBC WA, R9/7/44 – VR/60/80; *Punch*, 2 Mar 1960; Olga Cannon & J.R.L. Anderson, *The Road from Wigan Pier* (1973), pp 225–6; *Times*, 27 Feb 1960, 1 Mar 1960.
10. *New Yorker*, 20 Feb 1960; Turtle, 11 Feb 1960; *Times*, 13 Feb 1960; John Campbell, *Edward Heath* (1993), p 109; *Daily Mail*, 13 Feb 1960; *Economist*, 20 Feb 1960; William Maxwell (ed), Sylvia Townsend Warner, *Letters* (1982), p 181.
11. Raynham, 18 Feb 1960; *New Left Review*, May–Jun 1960, pp 63–4; Haines, 19 Feb 1960; Raynham, 19 Feb 1960; Martin, 19 Feb 1960; Last, 19 Feb 1960; *New Statesman*, 27 Feb 1960 (Francis Williams); *Listener*, 3 Mar 1960; Macmillan, dep.d. 38, 16 Feb 1960, fol 20.
12. Diary of Jennie Hill (Hampshire Record Office, Winchester), 26 Feb 1960; Haines, 26 Feb 1960; Martin, 26 Feb 1960; Amis, *Memoirs*, p 190; Turtle, 26 Feb 1960; Last, 26 Feb 1960; *New Statesman*, 5 Mar 1960 (Francis Williams); Heap, 3 Mar 1960.
13. *New Statesman*, 28 Nov 1959, 5 Dec 1959; *TV Times*, 18 Mar 1960; *Punch*, 24 Feb 1960.
14. *Spectator*, 20 Nov 1959; *Architectural Design*, Apr 1960, p 140; *Official Architecture and Planning*, Apr 1960, p 157; *Architectural Review*, May 1960, pp 338–43 (Kenneth Browne); *Architects' Journal*, 7 Jan 1960; *Punch*, 6 Apr 1960.

15. *Architects' Journal*, 5 Nov 1959; Malcolm MacEwen, *The Greening of a Red* (1991), pp 215–16; *New Yorker*, 30 Jan 1960; *Town Planning Review*, Jan 1960, p 273; Oliver Marriott, *The Property Boom* (1967), p 143; Bevis Hillier, *Betjeman: The Bonus of Laughter* (2004), p 130; Susie Harries, *Nikolaus Pevsner* (2011), p 622; Elain Harwood, *Chamberlin, Powell & Bon* (2011), pp 112–13; *Architectural Review*, May 1960, pp 304–12.
16. *Architects' Journals*, 4 Feb 1960; David Harvey, *Birmingham Past and Present: The City Centre: Volume 2* (Kettering, 2003), p 71; *Liverpool Daily Post*, 2 Mar 1960; Pat Rogan, 'Rehousing the Capital', in Miles Glendinning (ed), *Rebuilding Scotland* (East Linton, 1997), p 71; *New Statesman*, 26 Dec 1959; George Hume, 'Finance & Development', in Helen Peacock (ed), *The Unmaking of Edinburgh* (Edinburgh, 1976), p 31; *Glasgow Herald*, 12 Mar 1960; Miles Glendinning, '1945–75: An Architectural Introduction', in Glendinning, *Rebuilding*, p 16; *Architects' Journal*, 10 Mar 1960; *Glasgow Herald*, 19 Feb 1960, 22 Feb 1960.
17. *Guardian*, 19 Feb 1960; *Salford City Reporter*, 26 Feb 1960, 22 Apr 1960; *Sheffield Telegraph*, 5 Jan 1960, 22 Mar 1960.
18. Miles Glendinning and Stefan Muthesius, *Tower Block* (1994), p 65; Tom Begg, *Housing Policy in Scotland* (Edinburgh, 1996), p 144; A.G.V. Simmonds, 'Conservative governments and the housing question, 1951–59' (University of Leeds PhD, 1995), pp 226–7; Leeds City Council, *Agenda and Verbatim Reports, 1959–60* (1960), p 145.
19. *Liverpool Echo*, 8 Apr 1960; Patrick Dunleavy, *The Politics of Mass Housing in Britain, 1945–1975* (Oxford, 1981), p 41; *Evening News*, 26 Feb 1960, 7 Apr 1960, 29 Apr 1960.
20. The Society of Housing Managers, *Report of Conference: "Living in Council Houses"* (1960), pp 20–5; *Evening Advertiser* (Swindon), 21 Mar 1960; *Liverpool Daily Post*, 13 Jan 1960; Tom Courtenay, *Dear Tom* (2000), pp 261–7, 293.
21. BBC WA, R9/7/44-VR/60/121; *TV Times*, 26 Feb 1960, 18 Mar 19; *Guardian*, 5 Mar 2010 (Richard Williams); *Times*, 3 Mar 1960; Henry Hardy and Jennifer Holmes (eds), Isaiah Berlin, *Enlightening: Letters 1946–1960* (2009), p 731; Dilwyn Porter, '"Play It Safe or Think Big?"' (Business History Unit Occasional Paper, 2000), p 9; David Kynaston, *The Financial Times* (1988), p 283; D. R. Thorpe, *Supermac* (2010), p 462; Macmillan, dep.d.38, 5 Mar 1960, fols 44–5.
22. Macmillan, dep.d.38, 26 Feb 1960, fols 39–40, 11 Mar 1960, fol 49; Alan Booth, 'New revisionists and the Keynesian era in British economic policy', *Economic History Review*, May 2001, p 353; *Macmillan (1)*, p 225; 'Leo Abse', *Times*, 21 Aug 2008; *Punch*, 13 Apr 1960 ('Lombard Lane'); Sir Gerald Nabarro, *Nab 1* (Oxford, 1969), pp 169–83; Larkin, Ms. Eng. C. 7421, 17 Apr 1960, fol 67; BBC WA, *Any Questions?*, 8 Apr 1960; David Cannadine, *In Churchill's Shadow* (2002), p 305; Robin Jones, *Beeching* (2011), p 24; *Times*, 7 Apr 1960; Bank of England Archives, G3/89, 16 Nov 1960, Cobbold to Sir Frank Lee.
23. *Guardian*,19 Apr 1960; *Spectator*, 22 Apr 1960; Aurelia Schober Plath (ed), *Letters Home by Sylvia Plath* (1976), p 378; Benn, p 329; *New Statesman*, 23 Apr 1960 (Francis Williams); BBC WA, *Any Questions?*, 22 Apr 1960.
24. Larkin, Ms. Eng. C. 7421, 4 Feb 1960, fol 20; Heap, 14 Mar 1960; Robert J. Wybrow, *Britain Speaks Out, 1937–87* (Basingstoke, 1989), p 60; *New Yorker*, 23 Apr 1960;

Peter Oborne, *Basil D'Oliveira* (2004), chap 5; John Arlott, *Cricket on Trial* (1960), pp 18–19.

25. *Sheffield Telegraph*, 22 Mar 1960; *Observer*, 10 Apr 1960; *New Statesman*, 9 Apr 1960; *Evening World* (Brisol), 10 May 1960; Sue Harper and Vincent Porter, *British Cinema of the 1950s* (Oxford, 2003), p 194; *Guardian*, 19 Nov 2010 (Xan Brooks); Heap, 14 Apr 1960; *Listener*, 17 Mar 1960 (Irving Wardle); *New Statesman*, 2 Apr 1960 (Francis Williams); *Spectator*, 22 Apr 1960; Joan Barrell and Brian Braithwaite, *The Business of Women's Magazines* (1988 edn), pp 41–5; Wilson, p 117; Haines, 18 Apr 1960; *Mojo*, Dec 1993; 'Dave Dee', *Times*, 10 Jan 2009.
26. N. Tiratsoo, *Reconstruction, Affluence and Labour Politics* (1990), p 100; *Coventry Evening Telegraph*, 1 Mar 1960, 8 Mar 1960; *Times*, 5 Apr 1960; *Coventry Evening Telegraph*, 5 Apr 1960; Michael Billington, *The Life and Work of Harold Pinter* (1996), p 110; *Times*, 22 Mar 1960; *TV Times*, 8 Apr 1960; Billington, *Pinter*, p 111; *Times*, 23 Apr 1960; *Guardian*, 16 May 2005 (Maggie Brown); Billington, *Pinter*, p 127; *Financial Times*, 28 Apr 1960; *New Statesman*, 7 May 1960; Graham Payn and Sheridan Morley (eds), *The Noël Coward Diaries* (1982), p 436; Heap, 30 May 1960; *Independent*, 15 Nov 2000.
27. Billington, *Pinter*, p 118; *Wisden Cricketers' Almanack, 1961* (1961), pp 310, 632, 271; *Lancashire Evening Post*, 30 Apr 1960; Ivan Ponting, 'Harry Potts', *Independent*, 22 Jan 1996; Ivan Ponting, 'Brian Miller', *Independent*, 12 Apr 2007; *Sunday Times*, 28 Dec 2003 (Greg Struthers); Philip Norman, *Shout* (1981), pp 77–8; Mark Lewisohn, *The Complete Beatles Chronicle* (1996 edn), p 18; Philip Norman, *John Lennon* (2008), pp 176–7; Larkin, Ms Eng. C. 7421, 4 May 1960, fol 78; Geoff Phillips, *Memories of Tyne Tees Television* (Durham City, 1998), pp 122–3.
28. De Courcy, *Snowdon* (2008), pp 90–1; Amis, p 572; Andrew Barrow, *Gossip* (1980 edn), p 214; *Coward Diaries*, p 437.
29. BBC WA, R9/74/2, Jul 1960; Jonathan Dimbleby, *Richard Dimbleby* (1975), p 256; Barrow, p 214; Haines, 6 May 1960; Diary of May Marlor, 6 May 1960; Martin, 6 May1960; Last, 6 May 1960; Turtle, 6 May 1960; Macmillan, dep.d.38, 6 May 1960, fol 127; *Guardian*, 7 May 1960; Last, 6 May 1960; John Fisher, *Tony Hancock* (2008), pp 282–90.

Chapter 3 To the Rear of the Column

1. Heap, 9 Oct 1959. In general for the Clause 4 story, see: Philip M. Williams, *Hugh Gaitskell* (1979), pp 537–73; Brian Brivati, *Hugh Gaitskell* (1996), pp 330–48; Tudor Jones, '"Taking Genesis out of the Bible",' *Contemporary British History*, Summer 1997, pp 1–23; Catherine Ellis, 'Letting it Slip', *Contemporary British History*, March 2012, pp 47–71.
2. *Times*, 15 Jun 1998; *New Statesman*, 17 Oct 1959 (Francis Williams); James Thomas, 'Reflections on the Broken *Mirror*', *Media History*, Aug 2003, p 111.
3. Ben Pimlott (ed), *The Political Diary of Hugh Dalton* (1986), pp 694–5; Benn, pp 317–18; Douglas Jay, *Change and Fortune* (1980), pp 271–5; Frances Partridge, *Everything to Lose* (1999 Phoenix edn), p 340; *New Yorker*, 21 Nov 1959.
4. Brivati, *Gaitskell*, p 330; Chaplin, 7/3/1, 11 Jun 1957; Ina Zweiniger-Bargielowska,

'South Wales Miners' Attitudes towards Nationalisation', *Llafur*, 1994 (6/3), p 78; *Universities & Left Review*, Autumn 1959, p 75; Lawrence Black, *The Political Culture of the Left in Affluent Britain, 1951–64* (Basingstoke, 2003), pp 173–4; *New Statesman*, 17 Oct 1959, 31 Oct 1959; Frank Cousins papers (Modern Records Centre, University of Warwick), Ms 282/8/1/1, 23 Nov 1959.

5. Jay, *Change*, pp 276, 278; Williams, *Gaitskell*, pp 553–5; *Spectator*, 4 Dec 1959 (Bernard Levin); Benn, p 320; *Spectator*, 4 Dec 1959; Williams, *Gaitskell*, p 557; *Spectator*, 4 Dec 1959.
6. *Spectator*, 22 Jan 1960; R.H.S. Crossman, *Labour in the Affluent Society* (1960), pp 9, 22; *New Statesman*, 19 Mar 1960; *Encounter*, Mar 1960, pp 6–7.
7. *New Statesman*, 19 Mar 1960; Benn, p 333; Geoffrey Goodman, *The Awkward Warrior* (1979), p 245; *New Yorker*, 23 Jul 1960 (Panter-Downes); Ralph Miliband, *Parliamentary Socialism* (1972 Merlin edn), p 346; Peter Patterson, *Tired and Emotional* (1993), p 94; Kevin Jefferys, *Anthony Crosland* (2000 Politico's edn), p 74; Radhika Desai, *Intellectuals and Socialism* (1994), pp 105–6; David Howell, '"Shut Your Gob!",' in Alan Campbell *et al* (eds), *British Trade Unions and Industrial Politics: Volume One* (Aldershot, 1999), p 133; A. J. Davies, *To Build a New Jerusalem* (1992), p 207; Ben Pimlott, *Harold Wilson* (1992), p 227.
8. *Encounter*, Sep 1959, pp 11–19; Brivati, *Gaitskell*, p 343–4; *Encounter*, Mar 1960, p 11.
9. *New Statesman*, Dec 1959; *New Left Review*, Jan–Feb 1960, pp 1, 9, 25, 52, 54; Fred Inglis, *Radical Earnestness* (Oxford, 1982), p 177; *New Left Review*, May–Jun 1960, pp 68–9.
10. Michael Kenny, *The First New Left* (1995), p 34; E. P. Thompson *et al*, *Out of Apathy* (1960), pp 95–6, 235, 15, 192, 286, 298–308; *New Statesman*, 4 Jun 1960; *Spectator*, 17 Jun 1960; *Times Literary Supplement*, 2 Sep 1960; *Political Quarterly*, Jul–Sep 1960, pp 371–2.
11. *New Left Review*, Jan–Feb 1960, p 2, Mar–Apr 1960, p 71, May–Jun 1960, p 2; *Socialist Commentary*, Jul 1960, p 17; Michael Newman, *Ralph Miliband and the Politics of the New Left* (2002), p 98; *Socialist Commentary*, Oct 1960, p 30.
12. D. E. Butler and Richard Rose, *The British General Election of 1959* (1960), pp 11–16; Anthony Crosland, *Can Labour Win?* (1960), p 23; *Socialist Commentary*, May 1960, pp 4–9, Jun 1960, pp 5–11, July 1960, pp 5–12, Aug 1960, pp 5–10; *New Left Review*, Sep–Oct 1960, pp 2–9.
13. *Architects' Journal*, 16 Jan 1958; *Listener*, 26 Nov 1959; Benn, p 333; Michael Young, *The Chipped White Cups of Dover* (1960), pp 20, 11–13, 17, 19; Benn, p 333.

Chapter 4 Some Fearful Risks

1. *Observer*, 8 May 1960; Andrew Taylor, *20th Century Blackburn* (Barnsley, 2000), p 91; *Punch*, 18 May 1960; Heap, 9–10 May 1960; Robert J. Wybrow, *Britain Speaks Out, 1937–87* (Basingstoke, 1989), p 61; Diary of Jennie Hill (Hampshire Record Office, Winchester), 17 May 1960; Kate Paul, *Journal: Volume One, 1958–1963* (Hay-on-Wye, 1997), p 94; Leila Berg, *Risinghill* (1968), p 61; *Guardian*, 15 May 2002 (Frank Keating), 16 Oct 2010 (Richard Williams); Wilson, p 79; *Spectator*, 20 May 1960; *New Statesman*, 21 May 1960; Liverpool Local Studies Library, 780.42

CUT (Cavern Club cuttings, 1957–77); Dave Russell, *Football and the English* (Preston, 1997), pp 152–3.

2. Last, 22 May 1960; *East London Advertiser*, 27 May 1960; *Highland News*, 20 May 1960; Mark Lewisohn, *The Complete Beatles Chronicle* (1996 edn), pp 19–20, 26–7; *Forres News*, 28 May 1960; *Northern Chronicle*, 25 May 1960; *Banffshire Herald*, 28 May 1960.
3. BBC WA, R9/7/46 – VR/60/314; A. Silver, 'Angels in Marble' collection (interview files) at UK Data Archive, University of Essex.
4. Alan Bennett, *Untold Stories* (2005), pp 501–2; Robert Brown, *Basingstoke* (Chichester, 1994), unpaginated; David Harvey, *Birmingham Past and Present: The City Centre, Volume 2* (Kettering, 2003), p 67; Elain Harwood, 'White Light/White Heat', *Twentieth Century Architecture*, 2002, p 62; Kathryn A. Morrison, *English Shops and Shopping* (New Haven, 2003), p 107; *Derby Evening Telegraph*, 30 Nov 1983; Lionel Esher, *A Broken Wave* (1981), p 248; *Leeds Weekly Citizen*, 29 Jul 1960; *Liverpool Daily Post*, 18 Nov 1960; *Architects' Journal*, 28 Jul 1960; *Guardian*, 16 Jun 1960, 20 May 2006 (Ian Jack); *Architectural Design*, Dec 1960, p 486; *East London Advertiser*, 22 Jul 1960; Richard Davenport-Hines, *An English Affair* (2013), p xiii; *Architectural Review*, Oct 1960, p 302; *Official Architecture and Planning*, Aug 1960, pp 346–9; John R. Gold, *The Practice of Modernism* (Abingdon, 2007), pp 117–18; Harwood, p 69; *Architects' Journal*, 4 Aug 1960; Carole Newbigging, 'The Development of Blackbird Leys', BBC Oxford website, 'Memoryshire', 2007; *Western Evening Herald*, 30 Dec 1960; *RIBA Journal*, Dec 1962, p 456 (Jack Lynn); *Star* (Sheffield), 10 Oct 1960; *Glasgow Herald*, 18 Jun 1960; Miles Glendinning and Stefan Muthesius, *Tower Block* (New Haven, 1994), p 238; *Glasgow Herald*, 23 Jun 1960; *Tower Block*, p 224; *Town and Country Planning*, Dec 1960, p 397 (Elizabeth B. Mitchell).
5. *Yorkshire Post*, 9 Nov 1960; *Guardian*, 30 Aug 1960; Simon Gunn, 'The Buchanan Report, Environment and the Problem of Traffic in 1960s Britain', *Twentieth Century British History*, 2011 (22/4), p 528; *Sunday Times*, 10 Jul 1960; *Lennox Herald*, 9 Jul 1960; *Peckham & Dulwich Advertiser & News*, 23 Jul 1960; *Listener*, 13 Oct 1960.
6. *Evening Chronicle* (Newcastle), 7 Mar 1960; Archie Potts, 'T. Dan Smith', *North East Labour History*, 1994 (Bulletin no 28), p 11; *Evening Chronicle* (Newcastle), 7 Mar 1960; James Elliott, 'The Politics of Planning' (M.Lit thesis, Newcastle upon Tyne, 1972), p 13; *Journal of the Town Planning Institute*, Jul–Aug 1960, pp 195–200; *Sunday Times*, 24 Jul 1960; *Star* (Sheffield), 19 May 1960, 30 Aug 1960, 9 Sep 1960; *Middleton Guardian*, 22 Apr 1960; Patrick Dunleavy, *The Politics of Mass Housing in Britain, 1945–1975* (Oxford, 1981), pp 313–23; *Salford City Reporter*, 12 Aug 1960.
7. *Glasgow Herald*, 24 Jun 1960; *Lennox Herald*, 25 Jun 1960; *News Chronicle*, 22 Sep 1960; *Architectural Design*, Oct 1960, p 395; *Birmingham Mail*, 24 Oct 1960, 26 Oct 1960; *Daily Telegraph*, 23 Nov 1960.
8. *Bury Free Press*, 13 Nov 1959, 27 Nov 1959, 22 Apr 1960, 15 Jul 1960, 14 Oct 1960, 21 Oct 1960, 28 Oct 1960; *Listener*, 30 Jun 1960, 28 Jul 1960, 29 Sep 1960, 27 Oct 1960; *Architectural Review*, Aug 1960, pp 111–12.
9. J. B. Cullingworth, 'Some Implications of Overspill', *Sociological Review*, Jul 1960, p 77; *New Society*, 22 Aug 1963; *Liverpool Echo*, 23 Sep 1960, 28 Sep 1960.

10. This summary of the findings of the Kirkby survey is based on: *New Society*, 22 Aug 1963 (John Barron Mays); N. H. Rankin, 'Social Adjustment in a North-West Newtown', *Sociological Review*, Nov 1963, pp 289–302; Kathleen G. Pickett and David K. Boulton, *Migration and Social Adjustment* (Liverpool, 1974), especially chaps 3 and 5.
11. 'Social Adjustment at Kirkby' survey (Special Collections and Archives, University of Liverpool), D416/4/1–17.
12. *Twentieth Century*, Jul 1960, p 73; Douglas Jay, *Change and Fortune* (1980), p 279; Paul, *Journal*, p 102; Wilson, p 38; *Surrey Comet*, 15 Jun 1960; *Times Educational Supplement*, 17 Jun 1960.
13. Sir Jimmy Young, *Forever Young* (2003), pp 59–62; Rupert Hart-Davis (ed), *The Lyttelton Hart-Davis Letters: Volume Five* (1983), p 92; Andrew Motion, *Philip Larkin* (1993), p 302; *Financial Times*, 24 Jun 1960; Haines, 24 Jun 1960; Selbourne, p 40; *Radio Times*, 24 Jun 1960; *Glasgow Herald*, 28 Jun 1960; *South Wales Echo*, 28–9 Jun 1960.
14. *Hansard*, House of Commons, 29 Jun 1960, cols, 1453, 1474, 1490–4, 1510; *Spectator*, 8 Jul 1960 (Roy Jenkins); *Star* (Sheffield), 30 Jun 1960; Richard Davenport-Hines, *Sex, Death and Punishment* (1990), pp 325–6; *Spectator*, 15 Jul 1960, 22 Jul 1960.
15. Heap, 30 Jun 1960; Bevis Hillier, *Betjeman: The Bonus of Laughter* (2004), p 207; *Sunday Times*, 3 Jul 1960; *Spectator*, 8 Jul 1960; Tom Vallance, 'Lionel Bart', *Independent*, 5 Apr 1999; Michael Billington, *State of the Nation* (2007), pp 156–7; Dominic Shellard (ed), Kenneth Tynan, *Theatre Writings* (2007), pp 211–12; *Sunday Times*, 3 Jul 1960; *New Statesman*, 8 Aug 1960; *Spectator*, 5 Aug 1960; *Daily Mail*, 30 Jun 1960; *Times Literary Supplement*, 8 Jul 1960; Stan Barstow, *In My Own Good Time* (Otley, 2001), p 78; *New Statesman*, 30 Jul 1960; *Times Literary Supplement*, 5 Aug 1960.
16. *Encounter*, Jul 1960, p 8, Sep 1960, p 87; Turtle, 6 Jul 1960; *New Yorker*, 23 Jul 1960; John Campbell, *Nye Bevan* (1997 edn), p xiv; *Crossman*, p 863; Crossman, Ms 154/8/25, 4 Aug 1960, fols 1254–5; *Crossman*, p 867.
17. Diary of May Marlor, 16 Jul 1960; Philip Norman, *John Lennon* (2008), pp 187–8; *Sunday Telegraph*, 28 Mar 1993 (Frances Welch); *Financial Times*, 28 Jul 1960; Martin, 29 Jul 1960; Dee, 29 Jul 1960; *Listener*, 4 Aug 1960; Michael Willmott (ed), Reverend Oliver Willmott, *The Parish Notes of Loders, Dottery & Askerswell: Volume I* (Shrewsbury, 1996), Sep 1960.
18. John Clay, *R.D. Laing* (1996), p 117; *New Statesman*, 16 Jul 1960; *Listener*, 28 Jul 1960; *Guardian*, 25 Aug 1989; Tony Jasper, *The Top Twenty Book* (1994 edn), pp 58–9; Spencer Leigh, 'Tony Meehan', *Independent*, 30 Nov 2005; *Record Collector*, Aug 2006, p 75 (Spencer Leigh); Steve Humphries *et al*, *A Century of Childhood* (1988), p 32; *Observer*, 19 Jun 2005 (Stuart Nicholson); *Radio Times*, 12 Aug 1960 (Ernest Bradbury); BBC WA, R9/9/24 – LR/60/1775, R9/7/48 – VR/60/154.
19. Haines, 2 Aug 1960; Macmillan, dep.d.40, 12 Aug 1960, fol 15, 15 Aug 1960, fol 19; Haines, 16 Aug 1960; Macmillan, dep.d.40, 18 Aug 1960, fol 24; Haines, 19 Aug 1960.

Chapter 5 An Act of Holy Communion

1. *London Review of Books*, 2 Jan 2003 (Alan Bennett); Humphrey Carpenter, *That Was Satire That Was* (2000), p 106; Tom Courtenay, *Dear Tom* (2000), pp 304–24; Carpenter, pp 107–8; *Punch*, 7 Sep 1960; *Spectator*, 2 Sep 1960; Harry Thompson, *Peter Cook* (1997), p 97; Michael Billington, *State of the Nation* (2007), p 127.
2. David Brett, *George Formby* (1999), pp 215–18; *Southend Standard*, 25 Aug 1960; Bob Mee, 'Dick Richardson', *Independent*, 16 Jul 1999; Aurelia Schober Plath (ed), Sylvia Plath, *Letters Home* (1976), p 391.
3. *Daily Herald*, 3 Sep 1960, 9 Sep 1960; Lawrence Black, *Redefining British Politics* (Basingstoke, 2010), p 149; *Daily Herald*, 9 Sep 1960; Macmillan, dep.d.40, 9 Sep 1960, fol 39; St John, 10 Sep 1960; Paul Morley, *The North* (2013), pp 46–7; Gary Imlach, *My Father and Other Working-Class Football Heros* (2005), pp 152–3; *Daily Mail*, 12 Sep 1960; David Ayerst, *Guardian* (1971), p 628; *Radio Times*, 9 Sep 1960; Turtle, 14 Sep 1960; Selbourne, p 54.
4. Heap, 13 Sep 1960; *Punch*, 21 Sep 1960; *Spectator*, 30 Sep 1960; Dominic Shellard (ed), Kenneth Tynan, *Theatre Writings* (2007), pp 213–1.
5. *Radio Times*, 16 Sep 1960; Joe Moran, *Armchair Nation* (2013), pp 134–5; BBC WA, R9/7/48 – VR/60/550; Andy Medhurst, 'Every Wart and Postule', in John Corner (ed), *Popular Television in Britain* (1991), pp 66–7; *Radio Times*, 16 Sep 1960, 26 Aug 1960; Joe Moran, 'The Big Ben dissidents', *Guardian*, 11 May 2009; *Radio Times*, 13 Oct 1960.
6. *Punch*, 19 Oct 1960 (Patrick Ryan); Stuart Laing, *Representations of Working Class Life, 1957–1964* (Basingstoke, 1986), p 151; *Radio Times*, 23 Sep 1960; Zachary Leader, *The Life of Kingsley Amis* (2006), pp 437–8; Larkin, Ms. Eng. c. 7422, 26 Sep 1960, fol 10; *TV Times*, 16 Sep 1960; Mark Lewisohn, *Radio Times to TV Comedy* (2003 edn), pp 109–10; *Times*, 4 Mar 2010.
7. *Fowles*, p 443; Philip M. Williams, *Hugh Gaitskell* (1979), pp 574–610; *New Yorker*, 22 Oct 1960; *New Statesman*, 8 Oct 1960; Williams, *Gaitskell*, p 612; Benn, p 343; George H. Gallup, *The Gallup International Public Opinion Polls: Great Britain, 1937–1975, Volume One* (New York, 1976), p 554; Ronald W. Clark, *The Life of Bertrand Russell* (1975), pp 573–84.
8. St John, 16 Oct 1960; *Spectator*, 21 Oct 1960; *News Chronicle*, 17 Oct 1960; Roy Greenslade, *Press Gang* (2003), pp 98–104; *New Yorker*, 5 Nov 1960 (Panter-Downes); *Listener*, 27 Oct 1960; *Daily Mail*, 18 Oct 1960, 20 Oct 1960.
9. *Manchester Evening News*, 2 Aug 1960; Andrew Thompson, *The Empire Strikes Back?* (Harlow, 2005), p 217; Randall Hansen, *Citizenship and Immigration in Post-war Britain* (Oxford, 2000), pp 96–7; Anthony Howard, *RAB* (1987), pp 280–1; *West Indian Gazette and Afro-Asian-Caribbean News*, Jun 1960, p 7; *New Statesman*, 9 Jan 1960; *Times Literary Supplement*, 1 Aug 2003; Floella Benjamin, *Coming to England* (1995), pp 69, 80, 89, 92, 113; *Independent*, 15 Jun 1998 (Randeep Ramesh); V. S. Naipaul, *The Middle Passage* (1962), p 12; *Birmingham Mail*, 13 Oct 1960; Anthony Sutcliffe and Roger Smith, *Birmingham 1939–1970* (1974), pp 373–4; Paul Foot, *Immigration and Race in British Politics* (Harmondsworth, 1965), p 197; Kate Paul, *Journal* (Hay-on-Wye, 1997), pp 154–5.
10. *Daily Mail*, 29 Feb 1960; Ralph Harris and Arthur Seldon, *Advertising in Action*

(1962), pp 93–5; *Daily Telegraph*, 10 Jan 2006 (Harry Wallop); *Times*, 21 May 2012 (Diamond Jubilee supplement); Jan Boxshall, *Every Home Should Have One* (1997), p 83; Paul Levy, 'Kenneth Wood', *Independent*, 24 Oct 1997; Stephen Bayley, 'Kenneth Wood', *Guardian*, 23 Oct 1997; Boxshall, p 83; David L. Wakefield, 'The Hoover Story in Merthyr Tydfil' (*circa* 1977), p 7; David Kynaston, 'John Bloom' (unpublished obituary for *Financial Times*).

11. *Observer*, 23 Oct 1960 (Mark Abrams); Wilson, pp 154–5; Turtle, 23 Sep 1960; Haines, 18–20 Jun 1960.
12. Anthony Sampson, *Anatomy of Britain* (1962), p 590; ITC records, 3995938/9014, Research Services Ltd, 'Attitudes to Advertising – ITV Programmes (Oct 1960); *Spectator*, 22 Apr 1960; *TV Times*, 8 Jul 1960; David Powell, *Counter Revolution* (1991), p 74; *News Chronicle*, 9 Mar 1960; *Radio Times*, 15 Dec 1960 ('Bookshelf'); *Guardian*, 13 Mar 2010 (Sally Jaine); *Spectator*, 4 Nov 1960 (Leslie Adrian); Heap, 25 Jan 1960; Carol Kennedy, *ICI* (1986), p 110; Larkin, Ms. Eng. c. 7421, 11 Aug 1960, fol 114.
13. Market Investigations Ltd, *Mrs Housewife and Her Grocer* (1961); *Spectator*, 9 Sep 1960; Kathryn A. Morrison, *English Shops and Shopping* (New Haven, 2003), p 207; Turtle, 14 Jul 1960.
14. Powell, *Counter Revolution*, p 75; *Southend Standard*, 1 Sep 1960; Gareth Shaw *et al*, 'Selling Self-Service and the Supermarket', *Business History*, Oct 2004, p 575; Martin, 24 Sep 1960; *Southend Standard*, 29 Sep 1960; *Observer*, 2 Oct 1960 (John Gale).
15. *Daily Mail*, 20 Oct 1960; *New Yorker*, 19 Nov 1960; *Guardian*, 2 Oct 2010 (Simon Hoggart); C. H. Rolph (ed), *The Trial of Lady Chatterley* (1990 edn), pp 9–22; *New Yorker*, 19 Nov 1960.
16. Peter Stead, 'A Paradoxical Turning Point', in Sheila Rowbotham and Huw Beynon (eds), *Looking at Class* (2001), p 53; Arthur Marwick, '*Room at the Top*, *Saturday Night and Sunday Morning*, and the "Cultural Revolution" in Britain', *Journal of Contemporary History*, Jan 1984, p 145; Sheridan Morley, *Dirk Bogarde* (1996), p 77; Sue Harper and Vincent Porter, *British Cinema of the 1950s* (Oxford, 2003), p 184; *Financial Times*, 31 Oct 1960; *Daily Mail*, 29 Oct 1960, 1 Nov 1960.
17. Rolph, pp 68, 71, 22, 113, 92; *New Yorker*, 19 Nov 1960; Larkin, Ms. Eng. c. 7422, 27 Oct 1960, fol 30; Rolph, pp 100, 102; *New Yorker*, 19 Nov 1960.
18. BBC WA, *Any Questions?*, 28 Oct 1960; Rolph, pp 171–2; *Times*, 1 Nov 1960; *Daily Mail*, 2 Nov 1960.
19. Plath, *Letters*, p 399; *New Yorker*, 19 Nov 1960; Larkin, Ms. Eng. c. 7422, 2 Nov 1960, fols 34–5; *Guardian*, 3 Nov 1960; *Glasgow Herald*, 3 Nov 1960; *Times*, 3 Nov 1960, *Daily Express*, 3 Nov 1960; *Daily Sketch*, 3 Nov 1960.
20. BBC WA, *Any Questions?*, 4 Nov 1960; *Kentish Observer*, 10 Nov 1960; *Sunday Express*, 6 Nov 1960; *Observer*, 6 Nov 1960; *Gallup*, p 571; *Eastern Daily Press*, 8 Nov 1960.
21. Heap, 2 Nov 1960; Ben Pimlott, *Harold Wilson* (1992), p 245; *Daily Mirror*, 4 Nov 1960; Martin, 4 Nov 1960; Gyles Brandreth, *Something Sensational to Read in the Train* (2009), p 15; Heap, 6 Nov 1960; *Times Literary Supplement*, 22 Oct 1999; *Daily Mail*, 8 Nov 1960; Russell Davies (ed), *The Kenneth Williams Dairies* (1993), p 166; Kevin Cann, *Any Day Now* (2010), p 20; *Punch*, 9 Nov 1960; *Times*, 11 Nov 1960; Martin Gilbert, *'Never Despair'* (1988), p 1316; Bill Morgan (ed), *Rub Out*

the Words (2012), pp 58–9; *New Statesman*, 12 Nov 1960; *Star* (Sheffield), 11 Nov 1960, 14 Nov 1960; Macmillan, dep.d.40, 13 Nov 1960, fol 99; *Shrewsbury Chronicle*, 18 Nov 1960 (Jack Cater); *Daily Telegraph*, 14 Nov 1960; Michael Gillard and Martin Tomkinson, *Nothing to Declare* (1980), p 178; *Punch*, 16 Nov 1960.

22. *Daily Mail*, 17 Nov 1960; Heap, 17 Nov 1960; Last, 17 Nov 1960; Heap, 20 Nov 1960; *Listener*, 1 Dec 1960.
23. *Eastern Daily Press*, 4 Nov 1960; *Guardian*, 29 Oct 2010 (Peter Stansill); *Shrewsbury Chronicle*, 11 Nov 1960; St John, 24 Nov 1960; *Grimsby Evening Telegraph*, 17 Nov 1960; Brandreth, p 15; Alan Travis, *Bound and Gagged* (2000), p 163; Paul, *Journal*, p 178.
24. *Guardian*, 3 Dec 1960; *Times*, 9 Aug 1997; *Times Literary Supplement*, 7 Dec 2001 (John Gross); *New Statesman*, 12 Nov 1960; Courtenay, p 334; Christopher Sandford, *Mick Jagger* (New York, 1999 edn), p 35; *Daily Mail*, 10 Dec 1960; *Times*, 10 Dec 1960.
25. *TV Times*, 2 Dec 1960; Graham Nown (ed), *Coronation Street: 25 Years* (1985), pp 72–91; Last, 9 Dec 1960; *Guardian*, 10 Dec 1960; *Daily Mirror*, 10 Dec 1960; *Western Daily Press*, 10 Dec 1960; *Liverpool Daily Post*, 10 Dec 1960; *Sunday Times*, 11 Dec 1960; *Radio Times*, 9 Dec 2000.

Chapter 6 Why Are We Falling Behind?

1. *Radio Times*, 1 Dec 1960, 24 Nov 1960; Matthew Grant, 'Historians, the Penguin Specials and the "State-of-the-Nation" Literature, 1958–1964', *Contemporary British History*, autumn 2003, p 29; Michael Shanks, *The Stagnant Society* (Harmondsworth, 1961), pp 28–9, 232–3.
2. Jim Tomlinson, 'Inventing "decline"', *Economic History Review*, Nov 1996, pp 731–57; Jim Tomlinson, *The Politics of Decline* (Harlow, 2000).
3. George L. Bernstein, *The Myth of Decline* (2004), p 163; R. F. Bretherton, *Demand Management 1958–1964* (1999), pp 21–2; Ian Budge, 'Relative Decline as a Political Issue', *Contemporary Record*, summer 1993, p 10; *Observer*, 9 Dec 2001.
4. Nicholas Comfort, *The Slow Death of British Industry* (2013), pp 5, 9; T. R. Gourvish and R. G. Wilson, *The British Brewing Industry 1830–1980* (Cambridge, 1994), pp 452–65; Anthony Sampson, *Anatomy of Britain* (1962), pp 496–7; Frances Bostock and Geoffrey Jones, 'Foreign Multinationals in British Manufacturing, 1850–1962', *Business History*, Jan 1994, p 105; Sampson, *Anatomy of Britain*, p 499; Comfort, pp 324–30.
5. Geofffrey Owen, *From Empire to Europe* (1999), pp 221–2; Steven Tolliday, 'Government, employers and shop floor organisation in the British motor industry, 1939–69', in Steven Tolliday and Jonathan Zeitlin (eds), *Shop Floor Bargaining and the State* (Cambridge, 1985), p 131; Macmillan, dep.d.40, 19 Nov 1960, fol 108; *New Statesman*, 10 Nov 1961; *Spectator*, 8 Dec 1961; Richard Overy, 'Leonard Percy Lord', in *Dictionary of Business Biography, Vol 3* (1985), p 858; C. Gulvin, 'Donald Gresham Stokes', in *Dictionary of Business Biography, Vol 5* (1986), pp 347–55; Wayne Lewchuk, *American Technology and the British Vehicle Industry* (Cambridge, 1987), p 195; Tolliday, *Government*, p 132; Stephen Wilks, *Industrial*

Policy and the Motor Industry (Manchester, 1984), pp 75–8; Les Gurl papers (Oxfordshire History Centre), Acc 5639, 1962 file, 17 Feb 1962.

6. Comfort, p 37; Steve Koener, *The Strange Death of the British Motor Cycle Industry* (Lancaster, 2012), pp 119–20, 125, 134–5; *Daily Mirror*, 30 Nov 1961; Bert Hopwood, *Whatever Happened to the British Motorcycle Industry?* (Yeovil, 1981), p 185; Roger Lloyd-Jones *et al*, 'Culture as Metaphor', *Business History*, Jul 1989, pp 93–133.
7. *Observer*, 18 Oct 1959; Keith Hayward, *The British Aircraft Industry* (Manchester, 1989), pp 74–8; Owen, *Empire to Europe*, pp 310–11; *Spectator*, 2 Sep 1960; *Observer*, 18 Oct 1959; *New Statesman* 27 Feb 1960; Owen, *Empire to Europe*, p 309.
8. *Observer*, 18 Oct 1959; Crossman, Ms 154/8/27, 17 Jul 1963, fol 50; Lord Robens, *Ten Year Stint* (1972), pp 179–80; Tony Hall, *Nuclear Politics* (1986), p 71; Lord Hinton papers (Institution of Mechanical Engineers), 'The Memoirs of Christopher Hinton', p 313; Andrew Massey, *Technocrats and Nuclear Politics* (1988), pp 109–10.
9. *Observer*, 18 Oct 1959; Martin Campbell-Kelly, *ICL* (Oxford, 1989), pp 207–8, 215; Geoffrey Tweedale, 'Marketing in the Second Industrial Revolution', *Business History*, Jan 1992, p 116; John Hendry, 'The Teashop Computer Manufacturer', *Business History*, Jan 1987, p 96; Campbell-Kelly, pp 201–5; Owen, *Empire to Europe*, pp 203–4.
10. Owen, *Empire to Europe*, p 188; D.A. Farnie, 'The Textile Machine-Making Industry and the World Market, 1870–1960', *Business History*, Oct 1990, p 163; Roger Lloyd-Jones and M. J. Lewis, *Alfred Herbert Ltd and the British Machine Tool Industry, 1887–1983* (Aldershot, 2006), chaps 7–9; *Financial Times*, 15 Dec 1990 (Geoffrey Owen).
11. *Economist*, 7 May 1960; John Singleton, 'Lancashire's Last Stand', *Economic History Review*, Feb 1986, p 107; John Singleton, 'Showing the White Flag', *Business History*, Oct 1990, pp 129–30; John Singleton, *Lancashire on the Scrapheap* (Oxford, 1991), pp 126, 137, 140; Mark Keighley, *Wool City* (Ilkley, 2007), pp 129–34.
12. Geoffrey Tweedale, *Steel City* (Oxford, 1995), pp 1, 331–4; Owen, *Empire to Europe*, pp 127–8; Duncan Burn, *The Steel Industry 1939–1959* (Cambridge, 1961), pp 558, 674–5, 678–9.
13. S. O. Davies papers (South Wales Coalfield Archive, University of Swansea), F33; Tony Hall, *King Coal* (Harmondsworth, 1981), pp 106–8; *Times*, 16 Oct 1959; *Hansard*, House of Commons, 23 Nov 1959, cols 56, 81, 114; William Ashworth, *The History of the British Coal Industry: Volume 5* (Oxford, 1986), p 668; 'Lord Robens of Woldingham', *Times*, 29 Jun 1999; Sampson, *Anatomy of Britain*, pp 540–1.
14. Tony Mayer, *La Vie Anglaise* (1960), p 95; *Guardian*, 23 Feb 2013 (Ian Jack); Sampson, *Anatomy of Britain*, p 541; *New Statesman*, 16 Jan 1960; 'Gorton', *Wikipedia*; Christopher Harvie, *Scotland and Nationalism* (1998 edn), p 123; Charles Loft, 'The Beeching Myth', *History Today*, Apr 2003, p 39; Nicholas Faith, 'Lord Beeching', *Independent*, 29 Dec 1990.
15. *Time and Tide*, 24 Feb 1961; David F. Wilson, *Dockers* (1972), p 158; *New Statesman*, 5 May 1961 (J.P.W. Mallalieu); *Listener*, 10 May 1962.
16. Owen, *Empire to Europe*, p 99; E. Lorenz and F. Wilkinson, 'The Shipbuilding

Industry, 1880–1965', in Bernard Elbaum and William Lazonick (eds), *The Decline of the British Economy* (Oxford, 1986), p 117; *Sunday Times*, 17 Jul 1960; *New Left Review*, Jul–Aug 1960, p 58; *Glasgow Herald*, 16 Dec 1960; *Journal* (Newcastle), 17 Dec 1960, 22 Dec 1960; *Glasgow Herald*, 20 Apr 1961; *Evening Chronicle* (Newcastle), 19 Apr 1961; Anthony Burton, *The Rise and Fall of British Shipbuilding* (1994), p 215; *Liverpool Daily Post*, 25 Apr, 1962; Burton, p 216.

17. David Kynaston, *The City of London, Volume 4* (2001), pp 268–70, 252–3, 202.
18. *Financial Times*, 31 Jul 1961 ('Our Diplomatic Correspondent', probably Fredy Fisher); William A. Robson, *Nationalized Industry and Public Ownership* (1960), p 479; Geoffrey Goodman, 'Lord Robens of Woldingham', *Guardian*, 28 Jun 1999; *Economist*, 15 Apr 1961; James Foreman-Peck and Robert Millward, *Public and Private Ownership of British Industry, 1820–1990* (Oxford, 1994), pp 300–14; *Financial Times*, 12 Apr 1961.
19. Owen, *Empire to Europe*, p 449; Richard Findley, 'The Conservative Party and Defeat', *Twentieth Century British History*, 2001 (12/3), p 327; *Financial Times*, 29 May 1962; *Economist*, 2 Dec 1961; Peter Hennessy, 'Practical lesson in training the young', *Independent*, 18 Jun 1990.
20. *Glasgow Herald*, 9 Dec 1960; BBC WA, *Any Questions?*, 8 Jan 1960.
21. This paragraph on management weaknesses is based on: Ian Clark, 'Employer Resistance to the Fordist Production Process', *Contemporary British History*, summer 2001, pp 30, 34; Howard F. Gospel, *Markets, Firms and the Management of Labour in Modern Britain* (Cambridge, 1992), p 110; Nick Tiratsoo and Jim Tomlinson, *The Conservatives and Industrial Efficiency, 1951–64* (1998), pp 72, 56–7; Nick Tiratsoo, '"Cinderellas at the Ball"', *Contemporary British History*, autumn 1999, p 105.
22. *Financial Times*, 31 Dec 1996; *Glasgow Herald*, 22 Nov 1961, 16 Jan 1962; Frank Mort, 'Social and Symbolic Fathers and Sons in Postwar Britain', *Journal of British Studies*, Jul 1999, p 369; Michael Roper, *Masculinity and the British Organization Man* (Oxford, 1994), p 59.
23. *Bacup Times*, 17 Dec 1960; *Radio Times*, 8 Dec 1960; Eric Wigham, *What's Wrong with the Unions?* (Harmondsworth, 1961), p 189; David Granick, *The European Executive* (1962), p 234; Alan Campbell *et al*, 'The Post-War Compromise', in Alan Campbell *et al* (eds), *British Trade Unions and Industrial Politics: Volume One* (Aldershot, 1999), pp 72–4; *Financial Times*, 9 Jun 1992 (Geoffrey Owen); *London Review of Books*, 10 May 1990 (Jose Harris); Fred Wellings, 'Sir Halford Walter Luckton Reddish', in *Dictionary of Business Biography, Volume 4* (1985), p 860; Wigham, p 187.
24. Howard Gospel, 'The Management of Labour' in Chris Wrigley (ed), *A History of British Industrial Relations, 1939–1979* (Cheltenham, 1996), p 90; David Gilbert, 'Strikes in postwar Britain', in Wrigley, *History*, pp 134–5; Gospel, 'Management', p 89; J.E.T. Eldridge and G. C. Cameron, 'Unofficial Strikes', *British Journal of Sociology*, Mar 1964, p 29; Sampson, *Anatomy of Britain*, pp 568–9; *News Chronicle*, 15 Oct 1960; David Kynaston, *The Financial Times* (1988), pp 292–3; Burton, pp 204–5; Mark W. Bufton, *Britain's Productivity Problem, 1948–1990* (Basingstoke, 2004), pp 44, 53; Nick Tiratsoo and Jim Tomlinson, 'Restrictive Practices on the Shopfloor in Britain, 1945–60', *Business History*, Apr 1994, pp 74–7.
25. Campbell *et al*, 'Post-War Compromise', p 94; Chris Wrigley, 'Trade union

development, 1945–79', in Wrigley, *History*, p 63; T. E. Stephenson, 'The Changing Role of Local Democracy', *Sociological Review*, Jul 1957, pp 33, 40; *Punch*, 10 Feb 1960; John Bew, 'The last great Briton', *New Statesman*, 13 Dec 2013; *Times*, 22 May 2009; Eldridge and Cameron, p 33, quoting B. C. Roberts; *New Left Review*, May–Jun 1960, p 14 (Denis Butt); Stephen Tolliday, 'High Tide and After', in Bill Lancaster and Tony Mason (eds), *Life and Labour in a Twentieth Century City* (Warwick, 1986), pp 229–30.

26. William Brown, 'The High Tide of Consensus', *Historical Studies in Industrial Relations*, Sep 1997, p 141; *Socialist Commentary*, Aug 1961, pp 10–15; Allan Flanders, *The Fawley Productivity Agreements* (1966 ppk edn), p 13; *Sunday Times*, 13 May 1962; Flanders, *Fawley*, p 9 (Aubrey Jones); Shanks, *Stagnant*, pp 74, 138. In general on Flanders, see: John Kelly, *Ethical Socialism and the Trade Unions* (Abingdon, 2010).
27. Peter Dorey, *British Conservatism and Trade Unionism, 1945–1964* (Farnham, 2009), pp 63, 82; John Campbell, *Edward Heath* (1993), p 111; Wigham, p 169; Dennis Barker, 'Bryan Forbes', *Guardian*, 10 May 2013; *Daily Mail*, 11 Mar 1960; *Times*, 14 Mar 1960; *Daily Mirror*, 11 Mar 1960; *Evening World* (Bristol), 15 Mar 1960; Tony Shaw, *British Cinema and the Cold War* (2001), p 166; Anthony Hayward, 'Ronald Wolfe', *Guardian*, 22 Dec 2011.
28. *TV Times*, 13 Apr 1962; Robert J. Wybrow, *Britain Speaks Out*, 1937–87 (Basingstoke, 1989), p 160; W.E.J. McCarthy, *The Closed Shop in Britain* (Oxford, 1964), pp 3, 28, 79; Robert McKenzie and Allan Silver, *Angels in Marble* (1968), pp 128–30; M.P. Carter, *Home, School and Work* (Oxford, 1962), pp 269–75.
29. *Encounter*, Apr 1961, p 67; Granick, pp 242–3; W. J. Reader and David Kynaston, *Phillips & Drew* (1998), chaps 3–4; Sampson, *Anatomy of Britain*, pp 227, 278; Scott Newton and Dilwyn Porter, *Modernization Frustrated* (1988), p 138; National Archives, PREM 11/3756, Macmillan minute on Eccles letter, 1 Nov 1961.
30. Sidney Pollard, *The Wasting of the British Economy* (Beckenham, 1984 edn), pp 72–90; Newton and Porter, pp 133–5; *Times*, 28 Nov 1960.
31. See in general on this whole question of sterling: Tiratsoo and Tomlinson, *Conservatives*, pp 22, 163; Newton and Porter, pp 132–4; Bernstein, *Myth*, pp 670–1; Susan Strange, *Sterling and British Policy* (1971), chaps 3 and 10.

Chapter 7 Working, Middle and Kidding Themselves

1. Ferdynand Zweig, *The Worker in an Affluent Society* (1961), pp ix, 205–12.
2. Zweig, *Worker*, pp 104–29; *Sunday Times*, 16 Sep 1962 (magazine); *New Statesman*, 20 Aug 1960 (Francis Williams); Tom Harrisson, *Britain Revisited* (1961), p 35; *Sunday Times*, 16 Sep 1962 (magazine); Tony Collins, *Rugby League in Twentieth Century Britain* (Abingdon, 2006), p 89; John Hudson, *Wakes Weeks* (Stroud, 1992), p 145; Roger K. Bingham, *Lost Resort?* (Milnthorpe, 1990), p 287; Frank Norman, *Norman's London* (1969), pp 25–7; Sid Chaplin, *The Smell of Sunday Dinner* (1971), pp 113–14; *Socialist Commentary*, Apr 1962, p 27; Barry Doyle, 'The Geography of Cinemagoing in Great Britain, 1934–1994', *Historical Journal of Film, Radio and Television*, Mar 2003, p 61; Ashley Franklin, *A Cinema Near You* (Derby, 1996), p 147; *East London Advertiser*, 18 Nov 1960.

3. *News Chronicle*, 8 Feb 1960; Matthew Taylor, *The Association Game* (Harlow, 2008), pp 192–5; Humphrey Carpenter, *Dennis Potter* (1998), p 115; Simon Inglis, *The Football Grounds of England and Wales* (1983), pp 90–1; *Western Evening Herald*, 23 Nov 1960; BBC WA, *Any Questions?*, 27 Jan 1961; Stephen Wagg, *The Football World* (1984), p 195; Brian Jackson, *Working Class Community* (1968), p 114; *Huddersfield Daily Examiner*, 30 Sep 1961; Hudson, p 63; *Daily Mirror*, 19 Jan 1961; *Times*, 18 Jan 2011 (Matt Dickinson); Dilwyn Porter, 'British Sport Transformed' in Richard Coopey and Peter Lyth (eds), *Business in Britain in the Twentieth Century* (Oxford, 2009), p 337.
4. Julian Demetriadi, 'The golden years', in Gareth Shaw and Allan Williams (eds), *The Rise and Fall of British Coastal Resorts* (1997), p 61; Roy Wallis, 'Moral Indignation and the Media', *Sociology*, May 1976, p 287; *Western Daily Press*, 12 Oct 1961; *Spectator*, 6 Sep 2003 (Michael Henderson); 'Jackie Pallo', *Daily Telegraph*, 16 Feb 2006; *Economist*, 16 Apr 1960, 18 Jun 1960, 28 May 1960; Keith Leybourn, *Working-Class Gambling in Britain, c. 1906–1960s* (Lampeter, 2007), pp 132–3; *Time and Tide*, 13 Apr 1961 (Jack Braithwaite); Tony Hannan, *Being Eddie Waring* (Edinburgh, 2008), p 237; *Financial Times*, 31 Jul 1959.
5. Dennis Potter, *The Changing Forest* (1996 Minerva edn), pp 2–5, 14–16, 37, 64–5, 79–81, 99; Melanie Tebbutt, 'Imagined Families and Vanished Communities', *History Workshop Journal*, spring 2012, p 161; Lulu, *I Don't Want to Fight* (2002), pp 38–41; Peter Willmott, *The Evolution of a Community* (1963), p 109; Rosalind Watkiss Singleton, '"Old Habits Persist": Change and Continuity in Black Country Communities: Pensnett, Sedgley and Tipton, 1945–*c.*1970' (University of Wolverhampton PhD, 2010), *passim*; Harrisson, *Britain*, p 184; *Sheffield Telegraph*, 19 May 1960.
6. *Guardian*, 1 Dec 2012 (Ian Jack); *Big Issue*, 16 Aug 2010 (Andrew Ward and John Williams); Gavin Mellor, 'Post-war Lancastrian Football Heroes', *North West Labour History*, 1999/2000, pp 48–50; Ivan Ponting, 'Ronnie Clayton', *Independent*, 2 Nov 2010; *Guardian*, 6 Nov 2010 (Jim Whelan); Sandra Trudgen Dawson, *Holiday Camps in Twentieth-Century Britain* (Manchester, 2011), p 212; *Keighley News and Bingley Chronicle*, 5 Aug 1961; *Bridlington Free Press*, 4 Aug 1961; John Benson, *The Rise of Consumer Society in Britain, 1880–1980* (Harlow, 1994), p 87; John K. Walton, *The Blackpool Landlady* (Manchester, 1978), p 193.
7. *Evening Chronicle* (Newcastle), 29 Dec 1984; D. J. Taylor, 'Key to the Sardine Can', *Guardian*, 30 Apr 2005; *TV Times*, 21 Apr 1961; Katherine Bucknell (ed), Christopher Isherwood, *The Sixties* (2010), p 79.
8. Michael Shanks, *The Stagnant Society* (Harmondsworth, 1961), p 52; *Punch*, 2 May 1962; Colin Rosser and Christopher Harris, *The Family and Social Change* (1965), p 115; B. J. Heraud, 'Social Class and the New Towns', *Urban Studies*, Feb 1968, p 53; A.G.V. Simmonds, 'Conservative governments and the housing question, 1951–59' (University of Leeds PhD, 1995), pp 327–8; BBC WA, R9/9/25 – VR/61/598; *Independent*, 19 Sep 2007 (Paul Newman); *Wisden Cricketers' Almanack, 1963* (1963), p 485; Tony Collins, *A Social History of English Rugby Union* (Abingdon, 2009), pp 118–19; *New Statesman*, 14 Nov 1959; Claire Langhamer, *The English in Love* (Oxford, 2013), pp 57–8.
9. *Financial Times*, 5 Dec 1962; Paul Johnson, 'The welfare state, income and living standards', in Roderick Floud and Paul Johnson, *The Cambridge Economic History*

of Modern Britain, Volume III (Cambridge, 2004), p 230; W. G. Runciman, *Relative Deprivation and Social Justice* (1966), pp 82–9; Barbara Preston, 'Statistics of Inequality', *Sociological Review*, Feb 1974, pp 103–18.

10. Peter Willmott, 'Some Social Trends', in J. B. Cullingworth (ed), *Problems of an Urban Society, Vol III* (1973), p 95. For an illuminating survey of sociologists at work, see: Mike Savage, *Identities and Social Change in Britain since 1940* (Oxford, 2010).
11. Zweig, *Worker*, pp 134–6; Willmott, *Evolution*, pp 101–3; W. G. Runciman, 'Towards a classless society?', *Listener*, 15 Jul 1965; W. G. Runciman, '"Enlightenment," Self-Rated Class and Party Preference', *Sociological Review*, Jul 1964, pp 141, 146–7; Rosser and Harris, *Family*, pp 82–5.
12. Janet Street-Porter, *Baggage* (2004), p 132; *Sir Alf* (Channel Four, 29 Jun 2002); Jeffery Hill, '"I'll Run Him"', *Sport in History*, Dec 2006, pp 502–19; Mark Lewisohn, *Radio Times Guide to TV Comedy* (2003 edn), p 51; George H. Gallup, *The Gallup International Public Opinion Polls: Great Britain, 1937–1975, Volume One* (New York, 1976), p 613; *Salford City Reporter*, 16 Mar 1962, 23 Mar 1962, 30 Mar 1962, 13 Apr 1962.
13. Rupert Christiansen, *I Know You're Going To Be Happy* (2013), p 68; Frank Mort, 'Social and Symbolic Fathers and Sons in Postwar Britain', *Journal of British Studies*, Jul 1999, pp 375–6; *Observer*, 16 Feb 2014; *Independent*, 21 Oct 1995.
14. *Wisden Cricketers' Almanack, 1960* (1960), pp 125–6; *Daily Express*, 15 Nov 1960; Ben Jones, *The Working Class in Mid-Twentieth-Century England* (Manchester, 2012), p 182; *Manchester Evening News*, 25 Sep 1961; *The Bridge* (Southwark Diocese), Feb 2000.
15. *Star* (Sheffield), 30 May 1960; F.J.W. Miller *et al*, *The School Years in Newcastle-upon-Tyne, 1952–62* (1974), pp 258–69; Willmott, 'Social Trends', p 96.
16. Sampson, *Anatomy of Britain*, p 175; Michael Sanderson, *Educational Opportunity and Social Change in England* (1987), p 69; Collins, *Rugby Union*, p 215; Anthony Sampson, *Anatomy of Britain Today* (1965), p 223; Neil Powell, *Amis & Son* (2008), p 128.
17. *Times*, 25–7 Sep 1961; *New Statesman*, 27 Jan 1961, 3 Feb 1961, 10 Feb 1961; Nicholas Hillman, 'The Public Schools Commission', *Contemporary British History*, Dec 2010, pp 513–14; Philip M. Williams, *Hugh Gaitskell* (1979), p 659; *Hansard*, House of Commons, 16 Jun 1961, cols 828–36, 809–16, 884–99; *Times*, 14 Oct 1961; Peter Tory, *The Ultimate Giles* (1995), p 295; *Daily Mail*, 26 Apr 1961; *Times*, 2 Oct 1961; Sampson, *Anatomy of Britain*, p 182; *Times*, 30 Sep 1961.
18. Sanderson, *Educational Opportunity*, pp 46–7; Robert M. Blackburn and Catherine Marsh, 'Education and social class', *British Journal of Sociology*, Dec 1991, pp 507–36.
19. *Derby Evening Telegraph*, 8 Jul 1961; *New Statesman*, 16 Mar 1962; *Independent*, 3 Dec 1998; Stephen Dixon, letter to author, 11 Sep 2013.
20. William Taylor, *The Secondary Modern School* (1963), p 156; *Listener*, 9 Jun 1960; Frances Stevens, *The Living Tradition* (1960), pp 9, 260; *Encounter*, Jul 1961, p 51; *Times Literary Supplement*, 23 Feb 1962; *Sunday Times*, 4 Feb 1962; *New Statesman*, 16 Feb 1962; Brian Jackson and Dennis Marsden, *Education and the Working Class* (1962), pp 224–5; Kit Hardwick, *Brian Jackson* (Cambridge, 2003), p 23.
21. Alan Kerckhoff *et al*, *Going Comprehensive in England and Wales* (1996), pp 65,

89, 126; Robert G. Burgess, 'Changing Concepts of Secondary Education', in Bill Lancaster and Tony Mason (eds), *Life and Labour in a Twentieth Century City* (Warwick, 1986), p 303; *Coventry Evening Telegraph*, 5–6 Apr 1960; Savage, *Identities*, pp 232–3; R.E. Pahl, 'Education and Social Class in Commuter Villages', *Sociological Review*, Jul 1963, p 242; *Listener*, 13 Sep 1962 (W.J.H. Sprott); Martin Johnes, *Wales Since 1939* (Manchester, 2012), p 135; Peter Willmott, *Adolescent Boys of East London* (1966), p 76.

22. Nikolaus Pevsner, *Yorkshire: The West Riding* (Harmondsworth, 1959), p 178; *Spectator*, 21 May 2005 (Frank Keating); Fowles, EUL Ms 102/1/11, ? late Jul 1960, fol 81, Aug 1960, fol 85; *Times Literary Supplement*, 2 Sep 1960.
23. National Union of Teachers, *Popular Culture and Personal Responsibility* (1961), pp 124, 253, 278, 286, 259; Stuart Laing, *Representations of Working-Class Life, 1957–1964* (Basingstoke, 1986), p 194; Fred Inglis, *Raymond Williams* (1995), p 173; *Socialist Commentary*, Oct 1961, p 27; May 1962, pp 19–21; Dave Russell, *Looking North* (Manchester, 2004), p 229.
24. Raymond Williams, *The Long Revolution* (1961), pp ix–x, 174, 202, 293–4, 321, 337–8, 345–6, 355; *Guardian*, 9 Mar 1961; *Times Literary Supplement*, 10 Mar 1961, 7 Apr 1971; *Listener*, 20 Jul 1961; *Encounter*, Jun 1961, pp 79–84; Raymond Williams, *Politics and Letters* (1979), p 134; Inglis, *Williams*, p 177.
25. Nicolas Tredell, 'Uncancelled Challenge', *PN Review*, 1989 (15/5), pp 36–7; *Spectator*, 27 Apr 1962; *New Statesman*, 4 May 1962; Chaplin, 7/3/1, letter to John Bate, 14 Sep 1960.
26. *Spectator*, 29 Dec 1961; *New Statesman*, 12 Jan 1962, 26 Jan 1962.
27. Abrams, box 83, 'Class Stratification, 1910–67', file 2, 'Social Equality – The Class System', 27 Jul 1961.

Chapter 8 This Is My Work Now

1. *Daily Mirror*, 2 Mar 1961; Carolyn Downs, *A Social, Economic and Cultural History of Bingley, 1906–2005* (Saarbrücken, 2009), p 153; *Daily Mirror*, 5–6 Sep 1961; *Blackburn Times*, 16 Jun 1961; *Daily Mirror*, 5 Sep 1961; *Times*, 14 Sep 1961; Downs, p 184.
2. Rachael Dixey, *Women, Leisure and Bingo* (Leeds, 1982), p 112; *New Statesman*, 7 Jul 1961 (John Morgan); *Daily Mirror*, 2 Mar 1961; *Sunday Times Magazine*, 16 Sep 1962; *Eyes Down!* (BBC Four, 30 Jan 2013); *Daily Mirror*, 6 Sep 1961.
3. *Punch*, 2 May 1962, 9 May 1962, 30 May 1962, 6 Jun 1962.
4. Anne Oakley, *A Critical Woman* (2011), pp 1, 15; David Lascelles, *Other People's Money* (2005), p 99; Jessica Mann, *The Fifties Mystique* (Cornovia Press edn, Sheffield, 2013), p 182; *Financial Times*, 22 Dec 2007 (Sue Cameron); Charles Wintour, 'Anne Sharpley', *Independent*, 17 Apr 1989; Geoffrey Taylor, 'Nesta Roberts', *Guardian*, 19 Jan 2009; Penny Vincenzi, 'Marjorie Proops', *Independent*, 12 Nov 1996; Kevin Theakston, 'Evelyn Sharp (1903–85)', *Contemporary Record*, summer 1993, pp 132–3; Dennis Barker, 'Irene Thomas', *Guardian*, 4 Apr 2001; 'Ulrica Murray Smith', *Times*, 12 Feb 1999; 'Elisabeth Rivers-Bulkely', *Times*, 12 Feb 2007; 'Pat Moss', *Times*, 18 Oct 2008; 'Patricia Ozanne', *Times*, 7 Mar 2009; Rachel Cooke, *Her Brilliant Career* (2013), chaps 2, 3, 7.

5. *Liverpool Daily Post*, 22 Dec 1960; John Williams, *Red Men* (Edinburgh, 2010), p 319; *Surrey Comet*, 8 Jul 1961; *Daily Mail*, 21 Nov 1960.
6. *Guardian*, 17 May 1999; Simon Farquhar, 'Geoffrey Wheeler', *Independent*, 2 Jan 2014; Mann, p 131; *Spectator*, 4 Sep 2010 (Kate Chisholm).
7. Lascelles, p 100; Mark Robinson, *Hundred Greatest TV Ads* (2000), pp 82, 36; *East London Advertiser*, 9 Mar 1962; David Cannadine, *In Churchill's Shadow* (2002), pp 297–8; Marion Jordan, 'Carry On. . . Follow that Stereotype', in James Curran and Vincent Porter (eds), *British Cinema History* (1983), pp 312–27; *Independent*, 10 Mar 2001; Stuart Laing, *Representations of Working-Class Life, 1957–1964* (Basingstoke, 1986), p 221; John Hill, *Sex, Class and Realism* (1986), pp 156–68; D. J. Taylor, *After the War* (1993), pp 224–8; Amy Black and Stephen Brooke, 'The Labour Party, Women and the Problem of Gender, 1951–1966', *Journal of British Studies*, Oct 1997, p 452; Lawrence Black, *Redefining British Politics* (Basingstoke, 2010), p 85.
8. Stephanie Spencer, *Gender, Work and Education in Britain in the 1950s* (Basingstoke, 2005), pp 91–3, 125–6; *Daily Express*, 4 Mar 1960; Jim Gledhill, 'White Heat, Guide Blue', *Contemporary British History*, Mar 2013, p 76; *News Chronicle*, 15 Oct 1960; *Daily Mirror*, 9 Jun 1961.
9. *Punch*, 21 Dec 1960 (Patrick Skene Catling); Wilson, p 28; Kathleen Ollerenshaw, *Education for Girls* (1961), pp 17, 40; Jenny Uglow (ed), Angela Carter, *Shaking a Leg* (1997), p 178; Langford, 26 Apr 1962; *Guardian*, 31 Oct 2006 (Frank Keating); Bolton School Old Girls' Association, *Learning and Living* (Bolton, 1960), pp 33–48.
10. *Radio Times*, 12 Jan 1961; *New Statesman*, 31 Jan 1961; Christina Hardyment, *Slice of Life* (1995), pp 68, 70; *Accrington Observer*, 20 Feb 1962.
11. Ben Jones, *The Working Class in Mid-Twentieth-Century England* (Manchester, 2012), pp 177–8; Elizabeth Roberts, *Women and Families* (Oxford, 1995), pp 30–2; Lulu, *I Don't Want to Fight* (2002), pp 36–7; Joe Moran, *Armchair Nation* (2013), p 113; *Smethwick Telephone*, 8 Jun 1962 (Mary Browne).
12. *The Viewer*, 17 Oct 1959; *Radio Times*, 12 Aug 1960; *Guardian*, 24 Jan 2003 (Julia Finch); Hannah Gavron, *The Captive Wife* (1966), pp 69–72, 88–94; Bill Williamson, *The Temper of the Times* (Oxford, 1990), p 154; Angela Holdsworth, *Out of the Doll's House* (1988), p 31; Michael McNay, 'Betty Jerman', *Guardian*, 26 Jul 2010; Holdsworth, pp 31–2; Elizabeth Wilson, *Only Halfway to Paradise* (1980), p 183.
13. Mann, p 179; Jessica Mann, 'What good old days?', *Guardian*, 28 Apr 2012; Ali Haggett, *Desperate Housewives, Neuroses and the Domestic Environment, 1945–1970* (2012), pp 64, 67.
14. *Radio Times*, 19 Jan 1961; BBC WA, *Woman's Hour*, 23 Jan 1961, report of conversation originally transmitted on *Home for the Day*, 11 Dec 1960.
15. Roberts, p 118; Jane Lewis, *Women in Britain since 1945* (Oxford, 1992), p 74; Edw. James, 'Women at Work in Twentieth Century Britain', *Manchester School*, Sep 1962, pp 288, 294; John Westergaard and Henrietta Resler, *Class in a Capitalist Society* (Aldershot, 1975), pp 101–3.
16. Spencer, pp 78, 59; Gary McCulloch, *Failing the Ordinary Child?* (Buckingham, 1998), pp 121–2; Ollerenshaw, p 24; Barry Turner, *Equality for Some* (1974), p 208; Carol Dyhouse, 'Education', in Ina Zweiniger-Bargielowska (ed), *Women in Twentieth-Century Britain* (Harlow, 2001), pp 124, 127.
17. Viola Klein, *Britain's Married Women Workers* (1965), pp 133, 89, 91; Alan

Campbell *et al*, 'The Post-War Compromise', in Alan Campbell *et al* (eds), *British Trade Unions and Industrial Politics, Volume One* (Aldershot, 1999), p 93; Ken Grainger, 'Management Control and Labour Quiescence', in Michael Terry and P. K. Edwards (eds), *Shopfloor Politics and Job Controls* (Oxford, 1988), p 99; Joe Moran, 'Queuing Up in Post-War Britain', *Twentieth Century British History*, 2005 (16/3), p 290; Williamson, p 111; Chris Wrigley, 'Women in the Labour Market and in the Unions', in John McIlroy *et al* (eds), *British Trade Unions and Industrial Politics, Volume Two* (Aldershot, 1999), p 54; Ferdynand Zweig, *The Worker in an Affluent Society* (1961), pp 44–5; Rosalind Watkiss Singleton, '"Old Habits Persist"' (University of Wolverhampton PhD, 2010), p 152; *Woman's Mirror*, 1 Oct 1960.

18. Zweig, pp 172–5, 118; Pearl Jephcott, *Married Women Working* (1962), pp 106–11.
19. Ann Cartwright and Margot Jefferys, 'Married Women Who Work', *British Journal of Preventive and Social Medicine*, Oct 1958, pp 159–71; Jephcott, chap 9; Barbara Thompson and Angela Finlayson, 'Married Women who Work in Early Motherhood', *British Journal of Sociology*, Jun 1963, pp 150–68; Simon Yudkin and Anthea Holme, *Working Mothers and their Children* (1963), chaps 2–6; *Guardian*, 25 Aug 2010 (Jill Faux); Yudkin and Holme, p 104; Alan Johnson, *This Boy* (2013), pp 42, 97; *Evening News*, 25 Feb 1960. For two helpful overviews on working mothers, see: Roberts, *Women and Families*, chap 7; Dolly Smith Wilson, 'A New Look at the Affluent Worker: The Good Working Mother in Post-War Britain', *Twentieth Century British History*, 2006 (17/2), pp 206–29.
20. *Socialist Commentary*, Aug 1962, p 34; Willmott, 21 Nov 1960; BBC WA, *Woman's Hour*, 23 Jan 1961, report of conversation originally transmitted on *Home for the Day*, 11 Dec 1960.
21. Lewis, p 103; Lynne Reid Banks, *The L-Shaped Room* (1960), p 32; *Independent*, 18 Jan 2011 (Ian Burrell); Pat Thane and Tanya Evans, *Sinners? Scroungers? Saints?* (Oxford, 2012), p 132; Rupert Christiansen, *I Know You're Going to be Happy* (2013), pp 76–89.
22. Jeffery Weeks, *Sex, Politics and Society* (Harlow, 2nd edn, 1989), pp 256–7; Lewis, p 45; Howard Glennerster, *British Social Policy since 1945* (Oxford, 1995), p 163; Roberts, pp 99–105; *Twentieth Century*, May 1960, pp 409–10; Carol Craig, *The Tears that made the Clyde* (Glendarvel, 2010), p 172; Pierre Perrone, 'Gerry Rafferty', *Independent*, 6 Jan 2011; *Guardian*, 12 Mar 2011; Mann, pp 133–4; *Daily Mirror*, 23 May 1961.
23. Watkiss Singleton, p 144; Nick Tiratsoo, 'Popular politics, affluence and the Labour party in the 1950s', in Anthony Gorst *et al* (eds), *Contemporary British History, 1931–1961* (1991), p 51; Peter Willmott and Michael Young, *Family and Class in a London Suburb* (1960), pp 21–2; Jephcott, p 134; Gavron, p 57; Zweig, pp 31, 181; Margaret Forster, *Hidden Lives* (1995), p 255.
24. *Bolton Evening News*, 17 Feb 1962; *Daily Mail*, 21 Nov 1960; Claire Langhamer, *The English in Love* (Oxford, 2013), pp 170, 186–7; Zweig, pp 221–3.
25. Haggett, pp 55, 57; Richard Davenport-Hines, *The Pursuit of Oblivion* (2001), pp 259, 249.
26. *Radio Times*, 25 Nov 2000; *Guardian*, 3 Jan 1991 (Rebecca Abrams); Barbara Brookes, *Abortion in England, 1900–1967* (Beckenham, 1988), p 154; Stephen Brooke, *Sexual Politics* (Oxford, 2011), p 144; *Daily Mail*, 5 Dec 1961; *Daily Mirror*, 29 Jun 1961.

27. *Punch*, 7 Feb 1962, 17 Jan 1962, 24 Jan 1962; Lena Jeger, 'Mary Stott', *Guardian*, 18 Sep 2002; *Daily Express*, 13 Oct 1959; Katharine Whitehorn, *Selective Memory* (2007), p 139; *Spectator*, 25 Nov 1960.
28. Joan Barrell and Brian Braithwaite, *The Business of Women's Magazines* (1988 edn), p 26; *Financial Times*, 27 Jan 1960; Barrell and Braithwaite, p 45; *Guardian*, 20 Jan 1960 (Michael Frayn); *Mirabelle*, 18 Mar 1961; *Boyfriend*, 18 Mar 1961; *Cherie*, 18 Mar 1961; *Marty*, 18 Mar 1961.
29. Penny Summerfield, 'Women in Britain since 1945', in James Obelkevich and Peter Catterall (eds), *Understanding post-war British society* (1994), p 61; *Times*, 22 Mar 1962; *Daily Mirror*, 14 Feb 1961; Weeks, p 258; Haggett, pp 115–16; *New Society*, 3 Oct 1962; Laing, p 205; Cynthia L. White, *Women's Magazines, 1693–1968* (1970), p 166; *Woman's Own*, 3 Feb 1962.
30. *Woman's Journal*, Mar 1961; *Woman and Shopping*, Mar–Apr 1961; *Woman and Beauty*, Mar 1961; *Woman and Home*, Mar 1961; *Woman's Day*, 18 Mar 1961; *Woman's Mirror*, 18 Mar 1961; *Woman's Realm*, 18 Mar 1961; *Woman's Own*, 18 Mar 1961; *Woman*, 18 Mar 1961.
31. *Punch*, 9 May 1962; *Daily Telegraph*, 19 Apr 1962; *Listener*, 3 May 1962; *Times Literary Supplement*, 27 Apr 1962; *New Statesman*, 20 Apr 1962; Willmott, 5 May 1962, 31 May 1962.

Chapter 9 Don't Hang Riley

1. Dee, 10 Dec 1960; *Sunday Express*, 11 Dec 1960; St John, 11 Dec 1960; BBC WA, R9/7/49 – VR/60/725; *Western Daily Press*, 15 Dec 1960; *Times*, 15 Dec 1960; Last, 14 Dec 1960; *Manchester Evening News*, 15 Dec 1960; *TV Times*, 9 Dec 1960; Graham Nown (ed), *Coronation Street* (1985), p 102; BBC WA, *Any Questions?*, 16 Dec 1960; *Financial Times*, 24 Dec 1960; Mark Lewisohn, *All These Years, Volume One* (2013), p 406; David Pritchard and Alan Lysaght, *The Beatles* (Hyperion edn, New York, 1998), p 55; *History Today*, Dec 2010, p 9.
2. *Daily Mirror*, 2 Jan 1961; *Punch*, 4 Jan 1961; Beryl Bainbridge, *English Journey* (1984), p 80; Don Taylor, 'David Turner', *Guardian*, 20 Dec 1990; BBC WA, R9/7/50 – VR/61/13; *Spectator*, 6 Jan 1961; Wikipedia, 'List of *The Avengers* episodes'; *Daily Telegraph*, 20 May 2000 (Roger Wilkes); *Listener*, 5 Jan 1961; *Radio Times*, 5 Jan 1961; Janice Galloway, *This is Not About Me* (2008), p 113; *Journal* (Newcastle), 12 Jan 1961; *Sunday Times*, 15 Jan 1961; St John, 15 Jan 1961; Macmillan, dep.d.41, 15 Jan 1961, fol 45; Martin, 16 Jan 1961; Larkin, Ms Eng. c.7422, 17 Jan 1961, fol 74; Haines, 19 Jan 1961; BBC WA, R9/7/50 – VR/61/42; Willmott, 23 Jan 1961; *Y Cyfnod*, 27 Jan 1961; Lady Henrietta Rous (ed), *The Ossie Clark Diaries* (1998), p lii; *Guardian*, 27 Jan 2007; J.C., 'Sylvia's Pig', *Times Literary Supplement*, 2 Apr 2010.
3. *Daily Mail*, 10 Jan 1961; *Times*, 5 Jan 1961, 7 Jan 1961; *Spectator*, 27 Jan 1961 (Nicholas Davenport); *Financial Times*, 1 Feb 1961; *Times*, 13 Feb 1961, 9 Mar 1961; *Macmillan (1)*, p 371; *New Yorker*, 25 Feb 1961; Simon Heffer, *Like the Roman* (1998), pp 278–82; Anthony Hayward, 'Peter Adamson', *Independent*, 21 Jan 2002; *Spectator*, 17 Feb 1961 (Bamber Gascoigne); *East London Advertiser*, 7 Feb 1961; BBC WA, *Any Questions?*, 3 Feb 1961; Roy Greenslade, *Press Gang*

(2004 revised edn), pp 150–2; *Sunday Telegraph*, 5 Feb 1961; *Daily Mail*, 7 Feb 1961; Asa Briggs, *The History of Broadcasting in the United Kingdom, Volume V* (Oxford, 1995), p 342; *New Yorker*, 1 Feb 1961 (Panter-Downes); *Shrewsbury Chronicle*, 10 Feb 1961; *Guardian*, 8 Mar 1996.

4. Lewisohn, *Years*, pp 426–8; *East London Advertiser*, 10 Feb 1961; St John, 10 Feb 1961; Andrew Motion, *Philip Larkin* (1993), p 308; *Daily Mirror*, 11 Feb 1961; Andrew Barrow, *Gossip* (1980 edn), p 219; *Radio Times*, 9 Feb 1961; BBC WA, R9/7/50 – VR/61/89; Heap, 13 Feb 1961; *Times*, 13 Feb 1961; Peter Webb, *Portrait of David Hockney* (1988), p 31; Elizabeth Nelson, *The British Counter-Culture, 1966–1973* (Basingstoke, 1989), p 35; *New Statesman*, 24 Feb 1961 (H.A.L. Craig); Haines, 20 Feb 1961, 23 Feb 1961, 27 Feb 1961; *Daily Mirror*, 28 Feb 1961.

5. *Punch*, 8 Mar 1961; Ruth Dudley Edwards, *Newspapermen* (2003), p 272; Steve Holland, 'Derek Lord', *Guardian*, 30 Sep 2004; *Independent*, 20 Jan 1998 (Jennifer Rodger); New Statesman papers (Special Collections, University of Sussex), Box 20, John Freeman, Editorial Correspondence, 1960–64, A-L. For fuller accounts of the Mirror/Odhams story, see: Philip M. Williams, *Hugh Gaitskell* (1979), pp 667–8; Huw Richards, *The Bloody Circus* (1997), p 176; Adrian Smith, 'The Fall and Fall of the Third *Daily Herald*, 1930–64', in Peter Catterall *et al* (eds), *Northcliffe's Legacy* (2000), pp 186–7.

6. *Daily Telegraph*, 5 Mar 2011 (Philip Eden); *Times*, 2 Mar 1961; Aurelia Schober Plath (ed), *Letters Home by Sylvia Plath* (1976), p 412; BBC WA, R9/7/51 – VR/61/132; *Times*, 10 Mar 1961, 15 Mar 1961; BBC WA, R9/74/2, May 1961; *Daily Mirror*, 16 Mar 1961; Rob Bagchi and Paul Rogerson, *The Unforgiven* (2002), p 32; BBC WA, R9/7/51 – VR/61/162, 164; Dee, 25 Mar 1961; Reg Green, *National Heroes* (Edinburgh, 1999 edn), p 167; Russell Davies (ed), *The Kenneth Williams Diaries* (1993), p 171; Chris Welch, 'Davy Jones', *Independent*, 2 Mar 2012; Graeme Kay, *Life in the Street* (1991), p 90; *TV Times*, 24 Mar 1961, 18 Mar 1961; *Guardian*, 30 Apr 2005 (Michael Coveney); *Times*, 30 Mar 1961; Heap, 29 Mar 1961.

7. *Independent*, 11 Mar 1997 (Margaret Drabble); BBC WA, *Any Questions?*, 31 Mar 1961; *Ashbeian*, 1960–1, p 40; *Fowles*, p 459; Haines, 3 Apr 1961; *Ashbeian*, pp 40–1; *New Statesman*, 31 Mar 1961; Amis, p 587; *Melody Maker*, 8 Apr 1961; Paul Willetts, *Members Only* (2010), p 143; *Times*, 12–13 Apr 1961; Margaret Thatcher, *The Path to Power* (1995), p 117.

8. *Western Daily Press*, 11–12 Apr 1961; Fowles, EUL Ms 102/1/11, 8 Mar 1961, fol 123; Diaries of Patricia (Pat) Scott (Special Collections, University of Sussex), '1957' Diary, 5 Apr 1961; *Listener*, 5 Jan 1961, 12 Jan 1961; Clifford Hill, *How Colour Prejudiced is Britain?* (1965), pp 218–20; Fred Milson, *Operation Integration* (Birmingham, 1961), pp 1–7; *Evening Despatch* (Birmingham), 17 Aug 1961.

9. Milson, p 7; Randall Hansen, *Citizenship and Immigration in Post-war Britain* (Oxford, 2000), pp 96–7, 102; Heap, 8 Jun 1961; *Scotsman*, 13 Jun 1961.

10. Robert J. Wybrow, *Britain Speaks Out, 1937–87* (Basingstoke, 1989), pp 62–3; Timothy Raison, 'Macleod and Howe', *Twentieth Century British History*, 1997 (8/1), p 103; *Macmillan (2)*, p 309; *New Yorker*, 11 Mar 1961; Anthony Sampson, *Anatomy of Britain* (1962), pp 80–1; Robert Shepherd, *Iain Macloed* (1994), p 228; Bill Schwarz, *Memories of Empire, Volume 1* (Oxford, 2011), p 383; Nicholas Owen, 'Decolonisation and Postwar Consensus', in Harriet Jones and Michael Kandiah (eds), *The Myth of Consensus* (Basingstoke, 1996), pp 173–4.

11. Andrew Thompson, *The Empire Strikes Back?* (Harlow, 2005), pp 215–16; D. R. Thorpe, *Supermac* (2010), p 514; John Campbell, *Edward Heath* (1993), p 119; *Macmillan (2)*, p 8; Mark Pottle (ed), *Daring to Hope: The Diaries and Letters of Violet Bonham Carter, 1946–1969* (2000), p 240; Wybrow, p 63; *Daily Mirror*, 26 May 1961; *Daily Telegraph*, 9 Feb 1998.
12. St John, 12 Apr 1961; Willetts, pp 149–50; Turtle, 14 Apr 1961; IBA Audience Research material (Independent Television Commission), Television Research Committee (Noble Committee), 3995533/3088; *TV Times*, 14 Apr 1961; BBC WA, R9/7/51 – VR/61/214; Tam Dalyell, 'Jim Baxter', *Independent*, 16 Apr 2001; Heap, 17 Apr 1961; C. H. Rolph, *All Those in Favour?* (1962); Olga Cannon and J.R.L. Anderson, *The Road from Wigan Pier* (1973), p 234.
13. Katherine Bucknell (ed), Christopher Isherwood, *The Sixties* (2010), p 62; *TV Times*, 21 Apr 1961; *New Statesman*, 21 Apr 1961; *Evening Chronicle* (Newcastle), 21 Apr 1961; *Times*, 24 Apr 1961; Ian Jack, *The Country Formerly Known as Great Britain* (2009), pp 80–1; BBC WA, R9/7/51 – VR/61/237; *Daily Mirror*, 27 Apr 1961; *Radio Times*, 27 Apr 1961; BBC WA, R9/7/51 – VR/61/245; *Daily Mirror*, 1 May 1961; *Woman's Mirror*, 29 Apr 1961; Macmillan, dep.d.42, 29 Apr 1961, fol 13.
14. *Liverpool Daily Post*, 1 May 1961; *Independent*, 27 Apr 2001 (Stan Hey); Larkin, Ms Eng. c.7423, 6 May 1961, fol 26; 'Bill Nicholson', *Times*, 25 Oct 2004; Last, 7–8 May 1961; Martin, 9 May 1961.
15. Nicola Beauman, *The Other Elizabeth Taylor* (2009), p 335; *Times*, 11 May 1961; Hazel Holt, *A Lot to Ask* (1990), p 183; *Listener*, 15 Jun 1961; Humphrey Carpenter, *That Was Satire That Was* (2000), pp 110–24; Harry Thompson, *Peter Cook* (1997), pp 107–8; *Brighton and Hove Herald*, 6 May 1961; *Daily Express*, 11 May 1961; *Times*, 11 May 1961; Heap, 10 May 1961; *Twentieth Century*, autumn 1961, p 181 (Michael Frayn); *Daily Mail*, 20 May 1961; *Daring to Hope*, p 239; BBC WA, R9/7/52 – VR/61/255.
16. Martin, 12 May 1961; *Crossman*, p 944; Joe Moran, *Armchair Nation* (2013), p 140; *Times* 16 May 1961; *Guardian*, 19 May 1961; *Times*, 19 May 1961; *Sunday Telegraph*, 21 May 1961 (Alan Brien); *New Statesman*, 26 May 1961 (Roger Gellert); Heap, 18 May 1961; *Independent*, 10 Oct 1997 (Ken Jones); *New Statesman*, 7 Sep 1962 (Danny Blanchflower); *Totnes Times*, 27 May 1961; *East London Advertiser*, 26 May 1961; *Radio Times*, 18 May 1961; John Fisher, *Tony Hancock* (2008), p 314; BBC WA, R9/7/52 – VR/61/291.
17. BBC WA, *Any Questions?*, 2 Jun 1961; BBC WA, R9/7/52 – VR/61/353 (this includes Reaction Index figures for 2–5 of *Hancock*); *Independent*, 27 May 2000 (David Aaronovitch); John Bright-Holmes (ed), *Like It Was: The Diaries of Malcolm Muggeridge* (1981), pp 524–5; Hague, 8 Jun 1961; *Daily Mirror*, 9 Jun 1961; *Evening Standard*, 3 Oct 2011; Tom Courtenay, *Dear Tom* (2000), pp 344–6; Spencer Leigh, 'Pre-Fab Britain', *Record Collector*, Aug 2006, p 75; Courtenay, pp 347–50; Isherwood, *Sixties*, p 71; Selbourne, p 87.
18. *Sheffield Telegraph*, 16 Jun 1961; Local Studies Library, Sheffield, MP 1117 M; *Sheffield Telegraph*, 17 Jun 1961; St John, 17 Jun 1961; Larkin, Ms Eng. c.7423, 18 Jun 1961, fol 58; Haines, 19 Jun 1961; *Evening Citizen* (Glasgow), 3 Jul 1961; Haines, 26 Jun 1961; Rupert Hart-Davis (ed), *The Lyttelton Hart-Davis Letters: Volume Six* (1984), p 76; BBC WA, R9/74/2, Aug 1961; *Times*, 27 Jun 1961; *Glasgow Herald*, 28 Jun 1961; *Radio Times*, 22 Jun 1961; Dee, 28 Jun 1961; Sampson,

Anatomy, pp 567–8; Francis Beckett, *Enemy Within* (1998 Merlin Press edn, Woodbridge), p 151.

19. *Evening Citizen* (Glasgow) 30 Jun 1961; *Glasgow Herald*, 1 Jul 1961; Fisher, *Hancock*, p 326; BBC WA, R9/7/52 – VR/61/353.

Chapter 10 We'll All Be Uprooted

1. *Architectural Review*, Jan 1961, pp 42–3; *Architects' Journal*, 30 Aug 1961; Robert Brown, *Basingstoke* (Chichester, 1994); *Western Daily Press*, 14 Jun 1961; *Liverpool Echo*, 27 Apr 1961.
2. *Financial Times*, 31 May 1961; *Birmingham Post*, 4 Sep 1961; Anthony Sutcliffe and Roger Smith, *Birmingham, 1939–1970* (1974), p 410; *Sunday Mercury*, 15 Apr 1962; *Architects' Journal*, 18 May 1961; Alan Clawley, *John Madin* (2011), p 54; 'John Madin', *Times*, 24 Jan 2012.
3. *Liverpool Daily Post*, 5 May 1961; Derek Beattie, *Blackburn* (Halifax, 1992), p 171; *Official Architecture and Planning*, Jul 1961, pp 315–16; *Blackburn Times*, 5 May 1961; *Telegraph & Argus* (Bradford), 6 Feb 1962, 13 Mar 1962; Michael Birdsall *et al*, *A Century of Bradford* (Stroud, 2000), p 81.
4. Miles Glendinning and Stefan Muthesius, *Tower Block* (1994), p 263; *Times Literary Supplement*, 4 Feb 2005 (Timothy Mowl); Gavin Stamp, *Britain's Lost Cities* (2007), p 53; *Guardian*, 3 Mar 1961; Grant Lewison and Rosalind Billingham (eds), *Coventry New Architecture* (Warwick, 1969), p 60.
5. *Official Architecture and Planning*, Mar 1961, p 142; *Tower Block*, p 241; *Architectural Design*, Jan 1962, p 17; *Wikipedia*, 'Ardler'; *Tower Block*, p 241; Tom Begg, *Housing Policy in Scotland* (Edinburgh, 1996), p 154; *Wikipedia*, 'Oxgangs High Rise Flats'; edinburghguide.com, 'Gracemount Tower Blocks Hit the Dust', 26 Oct 2009; *Guardian*, 5 Jan 2008 (Ian Jack).
6. John Grindrod, *Concretopia* (Brecon, 2013), pp 152–3; *Glasgow Herald*, 11 Aug 1961, 11 Feb 1961, 20 Apr 1961, 2 Nov 1961; *Official Architecture and Planning*, Feb 1962, p 96; *Tower Block*, pp 235, 65; Miles Horsey, 'Multi-storey council housing in Britain', *Planning Perspectives*, 1988, pp 183–4.
7. David Bean, *Tyneside* (1971), p 155; 'Arnold Haggenbach', *Times*, 8 Apr 2005; *Architects' Journal*, 19 Jan 1961; arthurlloyd.co.uk, 'The Empire Palace Theatre, Leeds'; Kathryn A. Morrison, *English Shops and Shopping* (2003), p 284; Ben Beazley, *Postwar Leicester* (Stroud, 2006), pp 67–9; Mark Girouard, *Big Jim* (1998), pp 106–15; *Tower Block*, p 263; David Nash and David Reeder, *Leicester in the Twentieth Century* (Stroud, 1993), p 30; *Liverpool Daily Post*, 16 Dec 1960, 12 Dec 1961; John R. Gold, *The Practice of Modernism* (Abingdon, 2007), pp 185, 128; *Liverpool Daily Post*, 21 Dec 1961, 27 Mar 1962.
8. *Evening Standard*, 7 Dec 1961; *Evening News*, 12 Apr 1962, 13 May 1962; *East London Advertiser*, 17 Feb 1961, 15 Sep 1961; Jay Merrick, 'Tower Power', *Independent*, 14 Aug 2001; *Architectural Review*, Mar 1962, pp 190–6; Oliver Harris, *Cranes, Critics and Croydonisation* (Croydon, 1993), p 20; *Evening News*, 7 Jan 1963; *Architectural Review*, Jan 1961, pp 54–5; Michael Collins, *The Likes of Us* (2004), pp 141–2; Heap, 10 Aug 1961; *New Yorker*, 21 Jan 1961; St John, 19 Feb 1961; *Architects' Journal*, 22 Nov 1961, 1 Nov 1961; David Kynaston, *The City of*

London, Volume 4 (2001), pp 133–4; Macmillan, dep.d.44, 24 Oct 1961, fol 3; Gavin Stamp, *Lost Victorian Britain* (2010), p 21; 'The Euston Murder', *Architectural Review*, Apr 1962, pp 234–8; *Sunday Telegraph*, 22 Oct 1995 (Peter Elson); *Wikipedia*, 'Euston Arch'.

9. *Architects' Journal*, 11 Jul 1962; John J. Parkinson-Bailey, *Manchester* (Manchester, 2000), p 181; Clare Hartwell, *Manchester* (2001), p 36; *Evening Chronicle* (Manchester), 4 May 1961; *Guardian*, 10 Jan 1961; *County Express*, 28 Dec 1961; *Manchester Evening News*, 15 Mar 1962; Anthony Flowers and Derek Smith, *Out of One Eye* (Newcastle, 2002), p 18; Elain Harwood, 'White Light/White Heat', *Twentieth Century Architecture*, 2002, p 68; Terry Farrell, *Place* (2004), p 57; *Evening Chronicle* (Newcastle), 12 Apr 1961; James Elliott, 'The Politics of Planning' (M.Lit Thesis, University of Newcastle, 1972), p 104; Noel Hanson, 'Getting About', in Anna Flowers and Vanessa Histon, *Water under the Bridges* (Newcastle, 1999), p 64.
10. *Architects' Journal*, 12 Jan 1961, 25 May 1961; *Oxford Times*, 25 Oct 2013 (Damian Fantato); *Western Morning News*, 11 Nov 1961; Grindrod, p 124; *Architectural Design*, Mar 1962, p 104; Stamp, *Lost*, pp 124–5; David Hunt, *A History of Preston* (Preston, 1992), p 260; Fred Inglis, 'Nation and Community', *Sociological Review*, Aug 1977, pp 503–4; *Architects' Journal*, 8 Jun 1961; 'Professor Denys Hinton', *Times*, 3 Apr 2010.
11. *Salford City Reporter*, 3 Nov 1961; *Official Architecture and Planning*, Aug 1963, p 753; *Salford City Reporter*, 16 Mar 1962; The Housing Development Committee of the Corporation of Sheffield, *Ten Years of Housing in Sheffield* (Sheffield, 1962), pp 9–37; *Sheffield Telegraph*, 3 Jan 1961.
12. Stefan Muthesius, *The Postwar University* (2000), p 114; Brian Edwards, *Basil Spence, 1907–1976* (Edinburgh, 1995), pp 68–70; *Architects' Journal*, 4 Apr 1962; *Tower Block*, p 263; *Wellingborough News*, 3 Nov 1961, 9 Feb 1962.
13. *Architects' Journal*, 19 Jan 1961; *Liverpool Daily Post*, 16 Sep 1961; *Daily Telegraph*, 5 Jun 1962; Raphael Samuel *et al*, 'But Nothing Happens', *New Left Review*, Jan–Apr 1962, pp 38–69; *Daily Mail*, 17 May 1961; Patrick Dunleavy, *The Politics of Mass Housing in Britain, 1945–1975* (Oxford, 1981), pp 154–6; *Evening Chronicle* (Newcastle), 14 Apr 1961; *Salford City Reporter*, 2 Feb 1962; Dunleavy, pp 149–50, 156, 384.
14. *Sheffield Telegraph*, 20 Jan 1961; The Society of Housing Managers, *Report of Conference: "Housing in the Welfare State – An Assessment"* (1961), p 24; F. T. Burnett and Sheila F. Scott, 'A Survey of Housing Conditions in the Urban Areas of England and Wales', *Sociological Review*, Mar 1962, pp 76–7; *East London Advertiser*, 23 Dec 1960; Sutcliffe and Smith, pp 236, 242; Claire Langhamer, 'The Meanings of Home in the Postwar Britain', *Journal of Contemporary History*, Apr 2005, p 350; Peter Shapely *et al*, 'Civic Culture and Housing Policy in Manchester, 1945–79', *Twentieth Century British History*, 2004 (15/4), p 422; Strathclyde Education, *Housing in 20th century Glasgow* (Glasgow, 1993), p 154.
15. *Salford City Reporter*, 16 Mar 1962, 21 Jul 1961; Corporation of Sheffield, p 3; *Salford City Reporter*, 24 Mar 1961, 3 Nov 1961; *Proceedings of the Council of the City and County of Newcastle upon Tyne for 1961–1962* (Newcastle upon Tyne, 1962), pp 519, 523; *Smethwick Telephone*, 6 Jan 1961; *Time and Tide*, 9 Mar 1961 (Richard West).

16. *Town and Country Planning*, Jan 1961, pp 11–14; *Evening Citizen* (Glasgow), 26 Dec 1960; *Blackburn Times*, 7 Apr 1961, 5 May 1961, 12 May 1961, 2 Jun 1961, 30 Jun 1961, 23 Feb 1962, 23 Mar 1962.
17. *Journal of the Town Planning Institute*, Apr 1961, p 91; *Architect's Journal*, 6 Jun 1962; Parkinson-Bailey, p 180; Elliott, p 96; *Guardian*, 1 Nov 1961; *Architects' Journal*, 21 Jul 1960; 'Professor Sir Colin Buchanan', *Times*, 10 Dec 2001.
18. *Architects' Journal*, 22 Jun 1961, 17 Jan 1962; *Telegraph & Argus* (Bradford), 12 Jan 1962; *Listener*, 15 Jun 1961; *Architects' Journal*, 6 Jun 1962.
19. *Architects' Journal*, 19 Jan 1961; Oliver Marriott, *The Property Boom* (1967), chaps 9–10; Charles Gordon, *The Two Tycoons* (1984), chaps 10 ff; *Twentieth Century*, Jul 1961, p 164 (Kenneth J. Robinson); *Architects' Journal*, 7 Feb 1962; *Daily Mail*, 25 Aug 1961; *Wikipedia*,'*The Young Ones*'.
20. *Tower Block*, pp 200–4; Sutcliffe and Smith, p 436; Dunleavy, pp 115–16; *Glasgow Herald*, 10 Aug 1961; James Schmiechen and Kenneth Carls, *The British Market Hall* (1999), p 219; Gold, p 106; Michael Gillard and Martin Tomkinson, *Nothing To Declare* (1980), pp 62–3.
21. Gold, pp 72, 74–6; *Times*, 3 Jul 1961; *Official Architecture and Planning*, Nov 1961, p 473; *Architectural Review*, Mar 1962, p 196.
22. *Architects' Journal*, 27 Apr 1961, 6 Sep 1961; *TV Times*, 30 Mar 1962; *Guardian*, 13 Mar 2010 (Ian Jack); Miles Glendinning, '"Public Building": Sam Bunton and Scotland's Modern Housing Revolution', *Planning History*, 1992 (14/3), pp 13–22.
23. Joe Moran, *On Roads* (2009), p 40; Simon Gunn, 'The Rise and Fall of British Urban Modernism', *Journal of British Studies*, Oct 2010, p 861; *Western Morning News*, 14 Dec 1961; *Doncaster Gazette*, 9 Mar 1961; *Telegraph & Argus* (Bradford), 14 Mar 1962; *County Express*, 28 Dec 1961; *Liverpool Echo*, 23 May 1961; *Evening Chronicle* (Newcastle), 12 Apr 1961; Flowers and Smith, p 18; *Evening Chronicle* (Newcastle), 10 Nov 1961.
24. *Glasgow Herald*, 11 Feb 1961, 25 Sep 1961; *Liverpool Daily Post*, 6 Oct 1961, 1 Dec 1961, 24 Nov 1960; *Blackburn Times*, 5 May 1961, 16 Feb 1962, 2 Mar 1962; *Wellingborough News*, 10 Nov 1961, 17 Nov 1961, 29 Dec 1961.
25. *Architects' Journal*, 25 May 1961, 7 Feb 1962, 4 Apr 1962, 16 May 1962; *Guardian*, 17 Apr 1962.
26. *Architectural Review*, Mar 1961, p 164; *Architects' Journal*, 20 Apr 1961; *Listener*, 1 Jun 1961, 3 Aug 1961; *Listener*, 23 Nov 1961; *Architects' Journal*, 2 May 1962, 22 Aug 1962.
27. *Everywoman*, Mar 1961, pp 42–5; *Times*, 23 Aug 2006, 17 Oct 1961; Candida Lycett Green (ed), John Betjeman, *Letters, Volume Two* (1995), p 213; Bevis Hillier, *Betjeman: The Bonus of Laughter* (2004), pp 37, 261–3; *Daily Mirror*, 3 Apr 1962; Candida Lycett Green (ed), John Betjeman, *Coming Home* (1997), pp 400–1.
28. *Birmingham Mail*, 8 Jul 1961; *Liverpool Weekly News*, 26 Apr 1962; *County Express* (South Manchester edn), 29 Mar 1962.
29. *Municipal Review*, May 1974, p 66; *Daily Herald*, 1 May 1964; *Birmingham Post*, 10 Jul 1962; *Architects' Journal*, 22 Nov 1961; *Town and Country Planning*, May 1961, pp 214–15.
30. Doris Lessing, *Walking in the Shade* (1997), p 358; *Western Daily Press*, 13 Feb 1962; Peter Shapely, *The Politics of Housing* (Manchester, 2007), p 167; *Manchester*

Evening News, 29 Dec 1961; *Liverpool Echo*, 23 May 1961; *Sunday Sun* (Newcastle), 15 Apr 1962; Sid Chaplin, *The Watchers and the Watched* (1989 edn, Buckhurst Hill), p 156.

31. Brian Jackson Collection (Qualidata, University of Essex), 'Working-Class Community' papers, File (i.e. box) C1, Dennis Marsden, 'Can Old People Be Rehoused?'; R. K. Wilkinson and E. M. Sigsworth, 'Slum Dwellers of Leeds', *New Society*, 4 Apr 1963; R. Wilkinson, 'A Statistical Analysis of Attitudes to Moving', *Urban Studies*, May 1965, pp 1–14.
32. *Liverpool Echo*, 23 May 1961; *Liverpool Weekly News*, 26 Apr 1962; *Bolton Evening News*, 30 Jun 1961; *Guardian*, 2 Feb 2012; *Manchester Evening News*, 27 Feb 1962; *Salford City Reporter*, 25 May 1962.
33. *Town and Country Planning*, Sep 1961, p 375; J. B. Cullingworth, 'Social Implications of Overspill', *Sociological Review*, Jul 1960, pp 77–96; J. B. Cullingworth, 'The Swindon Social Survey', *Sociological Review*, Jul 1961, pp 151–66; Cullingworth, 'Social Implications', p 89; *Liverpool Echo*, 30 May 1962; F.J.W. Miller *et al*, *The School Years in Newcastle upon Tyne, 1952–62* (1974), pp 243–5, 293.
34. *Architects' Journal*, 18 Sep 1963 (E. M. Sigsworth); J. A. Yelling, 'Residents' Reactions to Post-War Slum Clearance in England', *Planning History*, 1999, p 8; *Smethwick Telephone*, 6 Jan 1961; *Time and Tide*, 13 Jul 1961 (Giles Wordsworth).
35. *Evening Chronicle* (Newcastle), 14 Apr 1961; *Liverpool Daily Post*, 5 Dec 1961; City of Sheffield Housing Department, 'Park Hill Survey', Sep 1962 (at Sheffield Local Studies Library); *Manchester Evening News*, 27 Sep 1961; *Liverpool Echo*, 26 Oct 1961; *County Express*, 1 Jun 1962; *Daily Sketch*, 12 May 1961; *Daily Mirror*, 24 May 1961.
36. *Liverpool Echo*, 16 Aug 1961; *Wellingborough News*, 9 Feb 1962; *Architects' Journal*, 4 May 1961; *Financial Times*, 31 May 1961; *Western Morning News*, 22 Dec 1961; Preston, 5 May 1962; *Blackburn Times*, 15 Sep 1961.
37. *Official Architecture and Planning*, Jan 1961, p 47; Osborn, p 301; *Town and Country Planning*, Mar 1961, p 134; *Guardian*, 3 Nov 1961.
38. *Economist*, 3 Aug 2013 ('Paradise lost'); Peter Lucas, *Basildon: Birth of the City* (Wickford, 1986), p 88; Peter Lucas, *Basildon* (Chichester, 1991), p 78; Peter Willmott, 'Housing Density and Town Design in a New Town', *Town Planning Review*, Jul 1962, pp 115–27; *Spectator*, 30 Sep 1960.
39. *Times*, 17 Sep 1960, 3 Jul 1961; *Guardian*, 4 Aug 1961; *Architects' Journal*, 16 Aug 1961.
40. *Times*, 4 Aug 1961; S. D. Coleman, *Mental Health and Social Adjustment in a New Town* (nd), pp 42–5, 67, 73, 78; Mark Clapson, *Invincible Green Suburbs, Brave New Towns* (Manchester, 1998), pp 138–9; *Town and Country Planning*, Apr 1962, p 143; email to author from Erin O'Neill (BBC Written Archives), 1 Feb 2005; *Journal of the Royal Institute of British Architecture*, Aug 1961, p 379.

Chapter 11 Make Him Sir Yuri!

1. Russell Davies (ed), *The Kenneth Williams Diaries* (1993), p 174; Haines, 1 Jul 1961, 5 Jul 1961; Martin, 5 Jul 1961; Paul Morley, *The North* (2013), p 417; Haines, 6 Jul

1961; *TV Times*, 7 Jul 1961; Michael Kenny, *The First New Left* (1995), pp 28–9; Daly, Ms 302/3/3, memo by Stuart Hall, 7 Jul 1961; Haines, 7 Jul 1961.

2. Crossman, Ms 154/8/26, 13 Jul 1961, fol 1367; *Evening Sentinel* (Stoke), 8 Jul 1961; *Melody Maker*, 15 Jul 1961; Haines, 8 Jul 1961; *Sunday Times*, 9 Jul 1961; Richard Davenport-Hines, *An English Affair* (2013), p 247; *Encounter*, Jul 1961, p 95; *New Statesman*, 21 Jul 1961; BBC WA, R9/7/53 – VR/61/368.
3. *Daily Mirror*, 11–12 Jul 1961; *Evening Standard*, 11 Jul 1961; Nigel Nicolson (ed), Harold Nicolson, *The Later Years* (1968), p 396; *Pembroke County and West Wales Guardian*, 14 Jul 1961, 21 Jul 1961; *Northern Echo*, 18 Jul 1961; Katherine Bucknell (ed), Christopher Isherwood, *The Sixties* (2010), p 85; *East London Advertiser*, 14 Jul 1961; *TV Times*, 14 Jul 1961; Michael Marshall, *Gentlemen and Players* (1987), p 244; Diary of Allan Preston, 20 Jul 1961; Heap, 20 Jul 1961; Jonathon Green, *All Dressed Up* (1998), p 152; Edward Hyams (ed), *New Statesmanship* (1963), pp 278–9; Rob Bradford, 'Joe Meek', *Record Collector*, Feb 2007, p 35; *Times*, 25 Jul 1961.
4. Humphrey Carpenter, *That Was Satire That Was* (2000), p 103; David Kynaston, *The City of London, Volume 4* (2001), pp 258–9; *Daily Mail*, 26 Jul 1961; *Times*, 26 Jul 1961; Stephen Fay, *Measure for Measure* (1970), p 18; *New Yorker*, 12 Aug 1961; St John, 26 Jul 1961.
5. Richard Bailey, *Managing the British Economy* (1968), pp 10–11; *Financial Times*, 27 Jul 1961; *Economist*, 29 Jul 1961; D. R. Thorpe, *Selwyn Lloyd* (1989), p 327; *Economist*, 26 Aug 1961; Glen O'Hara, *From Dreams to Disillusionment* (Basingstoke, 2007), pp 1, 35.
6. *New Yorker*, 12 Aug 1961; *Macmillan (2)*, pp 20, 22; *Financial Times*, 1 Aug 1961; George H. Gallup, *The Gallup International Public Opinion Polls: Great Britain, 1937–1975, Volume One* (New York, 1976), p 590; *Times*, 1 Aug 1961; Andy Mullen and Brian Burkitt, 'Spinning Europe', *Political Quarterly*, Jan–Mar 2005, pp 102–3.
7. *Times*, 1–2 Aug 1961; *Evening Chronicle* (Manchester), 2 Aug 1961; *Daily Telegraph*, 2 Aug 1961; Larkin, Ms Eng. c.7423, 3 Aug 1961, fol 74; *Observer*, 6 Aug 1961.
8. Haines, 2 Aug 1961; Heap, 2 Aug 1961; *Listener*, 3 Aug 1961; *Melody Maker*, 5 Aug 1961; Michael Willmott (ed), Rev. O. L. Willmott, *The Parish Notes of Loders, Dottery and Askerswell, Dorset: Volume I, 1948–1965* (Shrewsbury, 1996), Sep 1961; *Daily Mirror*, 8 Aug 1961, 11 Aug 1961; John Campbell, *Margaret Thatcher, Volume One* (2000), pp 138–40; BBC WA, R9/10/8 – VR/61/427; Haines, 16 Aug 1961; BBC WA, *Woman's Hour*, 2 Oct 1961; Haines, 16 Aug 1961.
9. Vic Gammon, '"Two for the Show"', *History Workshop*, spring 1986, pp 150–1; Heap, 18 Aug 1961; *Spectator*, 18 Aug 1961; Selbourne, p 98; John Heilpern, *John Osborne* (2006), pp 239–41; *Sunday Times*, 20 Aug 1961.
10. *Smethwick Telephone*, 28 Jul 1961; *Sunday Times*, 30 Jul 1961; *Guardian*, 21 Aug 1961; *Daily Mirror*, 21 Aug 1961; Panikos Panayi, 'Middlesbrough 1961: A British Race Riot of the 1960s?', *Social History*, May 1991, p 151; Harold Evans, *My Paper Chase* (2009), pp 214–24; *Northern Echo*, 21 Aug 1961.
11. Martin, 21 Aug 1961; James Whitfield, 'The Duke Disappears', *History Today*, Aug 2011, pp 43–9; Richard Etheridge papers (Modern Records Centre), Ms 202/S/J/3/2/39, 22 Aug 1961; BBC WA, R9/7/53 – VR/61/447; Paul Foot, *Who Killed Hanratty?* (1988 Penguin edn), pp 25–32; *Times*, 11 May 2001; *Listener*, 31

Aug 1961; Jonathan Meades, *An Encyclopaedia of Myself* (2014), p 310; *Times*, 31 Aug 1961, 1 Sep 1961; Mark Lewisohn, *All These Years, Volume 1* (2013), pp 491–2; Marshall, pp 205–6.

Chapter 12 The Immigrants Are Human

1. *Woman's Own*, 18 Mar 1961; *Woman*, 18 Mar 1961; Mark Robinson, *Hundred Greatest TV Acts* (2000), p 81; *Daily Express*, 17 May 1962; *Radio Times*, 20 Apr 1961; *Daily Mirror*, 22 Jun 1961; *Listener*, 4 Jan 1962; *Spectator*, 4 May 1962; Ralph Harris and Arthur Seldon, *Advertising in Action* (1962), pp 152–3; *Evening Chronicle* (Manchester), 5 May 1961; *Romford Recorder*, 9 Feb 1962; *Liverpool Daily Post*, 4 Jan 1962 (Diana Pulson); *East London Advertiser*, 16 Mar 1962 (Valerie Carter); Martin Childs, 'Brian Sollit', *Independent*, 19 Sep 2013; Robert Fitzgerald, *Rowntree and the Marketing Revolution, 1862–1969* (Cambridge, 1995), pp 465–6; *Financial Times*, 7 Mar 2006 (John Kay); *Daily Telegraph*, 1 Jun 2002 (Max Davidson); Peter Bird, *The First Food Empire* (Chichester, 2000), pp 196–7; Jan Boxshall, *Every Home Should Have One* (1997), p 83; *Shrewsbury Chronicle*, 8 Sep 1961; Kate McIntyre, 'The Most "In" Shops for Gear', *Twentieth Century Architecture*, 2002, p 38; *Surrey Comet*, 13 Sep 1961; *Guardian*, 24 Apr 2004.
2. British Market Research Bureau, *Shopping in Suburbia* (1963), p 45; Dawn Nell *et al*, 'Investigating Shopper Narratives of the Supermarket in Early Post-War England, 1945–75', *Oral History*, spring 2009, p 64; *Shopping in Suburbia*, pp 8–32; Christine Shaw, 'Alan John Sainsbury and Sir Robert Sainsbury', in *Dictionary of Business Biography, Vol 5* (1986), pp 5–6; David Powell, *Counter-Revolution* (1991), pp 96–9; Matthew Hilton, 'The Female Consumer and the Politics of Consumption in Twentieth-Century Britain', *Historical Journal*, Mar 2002, pp 121–6; Eirlys Roberts, *Which? 25: Consumers' Association, 1957–1982* (1982), p 42; *Spectator*, 23 Feb 1962 ('Leslie Adrian'); Andrew Motion, *Philip Larkin* (1993), p 316; Archie Burnett (ed), Philip Larkin, *The Complete Poems* (2012), p 61; *Times Literary Supplement*, 1 Sep 2000.
3. *Pembroke County and West Wales Guardian*, 15 Sep 1961, 22 Sep 1961; *Cambrian News*, 20 Oct 1961, 13 Oct 1961; *Glamorgan Gazette*, 27 Oct 1961, 3 Nov 1961; *Cambrian News*, 17 Nov 1961; *Carmarthen Journal*, 17 Nov 1961. In general on this episode, see: Martin Johnes, *Wales Since 1939* (Manchester, 2012), pp 166–8.
4. Macmillan, dep.d.43, 8 Oct 1961, fol 100; *Macmillan (2)*, p 38; *Daily Mail*, 24 Oct 1961; *Macmillan (2)*, p 44; John Barnes, 'Lord Holderness', *Independent*, 16 Aug 2002; *New Yorker*, 9 Dec 1961 (Panter-Downes); Ronald S. Edwards and R.D.V. Roberts, *Status, Productivity and Pay* (1971), p 53; Glen O'Hara, *From Dreams to Disillusionment* (Basingstoke, 2007), pp 45–8; Keith Middlemas, 'Sir Robert Shone', *Independent*, 30 Dec 1992; Astrid Ringe and Neil Rollings, 'Responding to relative decline', *Economic History Review*, May 2000, pp 344–7; O'Hara, p 45; Sir Alec Cairncross, *Diaries: The Radcliffe Committee and the Treasury, 1961–64* (1999), p 47.
5. *Times Literary Supplement*, 2 Jan 1998 (Nicolas Walter); Russell Davies (ed), *The Kenneth Williams Diaries* (1993), pp 176–7; Jonathon Green, *All Dressed Up* (1998), p 22; *Economist*, 23 Sep 1961; Philip M. Williams, *Hugh Gaitskell* (1979), pp 651–2;

Macmillan, dep.d.43, 8 Oct 1961, fol 102; Williams, *Gaitskell*, pp 658–64; Stuart Middleton, '"Affluence" and the Left in Britain, c.1958–1974', *English Historical Review*, Feb 2014, p 119; *Spectator*, 29 Sep 1961, 13 Oct 1961; *New Statesman*, 6 Oct 1961; BBC WA, R9/7/54 – VR/61/555; *Listener*, 26 Oct 1961; Michael Newman, *Ralph Miliband and the Politics of the New Left* (2002), pp 73–7; Ralph Miliband, *Parliamentary Socialism* (1972 Merlin Press edn), pp 348–9.

6. *Sunday Times Magazine*, 28 Nov 1976 (Gordon Burn); BBC WA, *Any Questions?*, 29 Sep 1961; Selina Todd, *The People* (2014), p 251; Stephen Smith and Peter Razzell, *The Pools Winners* (1975), p 42; *Sunday Times Magazine*, 28 Nov 1976.
7. Turtle, 19 Oct 1961; Heap, 13 Sep 1961; Haines, 2 Oct 1961, 17 Oct 1961; Macmillan, dep.d.43, 23 Sep 1961, fols 84–5; Paul Foot, *Who Killed Hanratty?* (1988 Penguin edn), p 97; Fowles, EUL Ms 102/1/11, 29 Oct 1961, fol 168; Last, 26 Oct 1961; Diary of Allan Preston, 2 Sep 1961; Martin, 20 Oct 1961; Selbourne, p 114; St John, 18 Oct 1961.
8. Haines, 13 Oct 1961; Martin, 6 Nov 1961; *Kenneth Williams*, p 178; *Times*, 4 Jul 2008 (Anne Ashworth and Judith Heywood), 13 Sep 1961; *New Statesman*, 15 Sep 1961; *Independent*, 19 Aug 2002 (John Walsh); Larkin, Ms Eng.c.7424, 31 Jan 1961, fol 79; *Kenneth Williams*, p 175; *Times*, 24 Sep 2003 (Stephen Dalton), 30 Aug 1961; John Coldstream, *Dirk Bogarde* (2004), p 268; *Oldham Evening Chronicle*, 9 Sep 1961; *Spectator*, 24 Nov 1961; Coldstream, *Bogarde*, pp 280, 270; *Spectator*, 3 Sep 2011 (John Coldstream).
9. Lord Drogheda, *Double Harness* (1978), p 284; *Guardian Weekend*, 17 Mar 2007 (Robin Muir); Darran Little, *The Coronation Street Story* (1995), pp 35–6; *Radio Times*, 7 Sep 1961; *TV Times*, 25 Aug 1961; BBC WA, R9/7/54 – VR/61/493; *Radio Times*, 21 Sep 1961; *Times*, 28 Sep 1961; *Guardian*, 26 May 1995 (James Wood).
10. *Radio Times*, 28 Sep 1961; *TV Times*, 29 Sep 1961; *Spectator*, 6 Oct 1961 (Guy Gisbourne); BBC WA, R9/7/54 – VR/61/527; *Western Morning News*, 3 Oct 1961; *Radio Times*, 28 Sep 1961, 5 Oct 1961; BBC WA, *Woman's Hour*, 4 Oct 1961; *New Statesman*, 13 Oct 1961; *Spectator*, 6 Oct 1961; R.G.G. Stevenson, *The Methodist Church, Hunslet Carr, Leeds, 1842–1961* (Leeds, 1962), pp 17–18; *Radio Times*, 5 Oct 1961; *Beeston Gazette & Echo*, 13 Oct 1961, 20 Oct 1961; Harry Ritchie, *Success Stories* (1988), pp 200–1; *Times*, 17 Oct 1961; *Daily Express*, 18 Oct 1961; BBC WA, R9/7/54 – VR/61/560; Adam Macqueen, *Private Eye* (2011), pp 36, 96–7; R. D. Laing, *The Self and Others* (1961), p ix; *Western Daily Press*, 30 Oct 1961.
11. Alan Fox, 'Two Worlds in Collision', *Socialist Commentary*, Mar 1962, pp 26–7; Martin Gilbert, *"Never Despair"* (1988), p 1331; *Times*, 3 Nov 1961; *New Statesman*, 3 Nov 1961; Tim Heald, *Princess Margaret* (2007), pp 140–1; BBC WA, R9/7/55 – VR/61/594; *Daily Telegraph*, 18 Dec 2000 (Richard Alleyne); *Uncut*, Jul 2011 (Mick Houghton); *Observer*, 14 Mar 2010 (Rachel Cooke); Nicolas Barker, 'Jeremy Maas', *Independent*, 31 Jan 1997; *Radio Times*, 9 Nov 1961; Jack Tinker, *Coronation St.* (1985), pp 30–1; BBC WA, R9/7/55 – VR/61/628; E. H. Carr, *What is History?* (1961), p 66; Adrian Smith, *The City of Coventry* (2006), pp 26–7; *Observer*, 26 Nov 1961; *Listener*, 30 Nov 1961.
12. *Times Literary Supplement*, 1 Dec 1961; *Listener*, 7 Dec 1961 (Frederick Laws); *TV Times*, 15 Dec 1961; *Western Morning News*, 5 Dec 1961; BBC WA, R9/7/55 – VR/61/653.

13. *Isle of Ely and Wisbech Advertiser*, 27 Sep 1961; Selbourne, p 104; *Times*, 20 Sep 1961; E. M. and M. Epple, '"Connotations of Morality"', *British Journal of Sociology*, Sep 1962, pp 243–63; *Daily Telegraph*, 27 Dec 1961 (Ian Colquhoun).
14. *Daily Telegraph*, 27 Dec 1961; *Times*, 10 Oct 2009 (Bob Stanley); *New Statesman*, 20 Oct 1961; Dave McAleer, *Hit Parade Heroes* (1993), pp 111–12; Heap, 14 Sep 1961; *Melody Maker*, 9 Sep 1961; Tony Jasper, *The Top Twenty Book* (6th edn, 1994), pp 69–71; *Radio Times*, 28 Sep 1961; Christopher Sandford, *Primitive Cool* (1999 edn, New York), pp 38–9; Keith Richards, *Life* (2010), pp 77–9; Keith Gildart, *Images of England through Popular Music* (Basingstoke, 2013), p 63; *Aldershot News*, 15 Dec 1961; *Radio Times*, 7 Dec 1961; *Melody Maker*, 2 Dec 1961, 9 Dec 1961. For the fullest account of the Aldershot gig and its context, see: Mark Lewisohn, *All These Years, Volume 1* (2013), pp 544–5.
15. Robert Shepherd, *Iain Macleod* (1994), pp 253–5; *Economist*, 14 Oct 1961; Patrick Seyd, 'Factionalism within the Conservative Party', *Government and Opposition*, 1972 (7/4), pp 468–9, 479; *Times*, 9 Nov 1961; Lewis Baston, *Reggie* (Stroud, 2004), p 153; Macmillan, dep.d.44, 10 Jan 1962, fol 107; Baston, p 171.
16. *Western Daily Press*, 15 Sep 1961; City of Bradford, *Official Records of Council Meetings, 1961–2* (Bradford, 1962), pp 78–80; *Daily Express*, 12 Oct 1961; Paul Foot, *Immigration and Race in British Politics* (Harmondsworth, 1965), p 137; *Economist*, 14 Oct 1961; *Spectator*, 20 Oct 1961; Randall Hansen, *Citizenship and Immigration in Post-war Britain* (Oxford, 2000), p 108.
17. *Daily Mail*, 16 Oct 1961; Foot, p 139; Michael Dawswell, 'The Pigmentocracy of Citizenship', in Lawrence Black *et al*, *Consensus or Coercion?* (Cheltenham, 2001), p 73; *Daily Mirror*, 1 Nov 1961; *New Yorker*, 9 Dec 1961; Williams, *Gaitskell*, pp 676–9; Hansen, pp 115–16; *Times*, 17 Nov 1961; *Daily Mail*, 18 Nov 1961; *Times*, 22 Nov 1961; Heap, 20 Nov 1961; Macmillan, dep.d.44, 30 Nov 1961, fol 62; *Times*, 17 Nov 1961; *Guardian*, 4 Dec 1961.
18. Foot, pp 172–4; Macmillan, dep.d.45, 27 Feb 1962, fol 41; Dervla Murphy, *Tales from Two Cities* (1987), p 10; G. J. Dear, 'Coloured Immigrant Communities and the Police', *Police Journal*, Apr 1972, p 130; Larkin, Ms Eng.c.7424, 13 Jan 1962, fol 62; *Telegraph & Argus* (Bradford), 15 Jan 1962, 17 Jan 1962; Hague, 30 Dec 1961; W. G. Runciman and C. R. Bagley, 'Status Consistency, Relative Deprivation, and Attitudes to Immigrants', *Sociology*, Sep 1969, pp 366–70; *Observer*, 11 Mar 2012; *Daily Telegraph*, 10 Apr 2014.

Chapter 13 That First Small Cheer

1. Mark Lewisohn, *The Complete Beatles Chronicle* (1996 edn), p 51; *Guardian*, 7 Dec 2011 (Frank Keating); *Lincolnshire Echo*, 11 Dec 1961; coronationstreet.wikia.com/wiki; BBC WA, *Any Questions?*, 15 Dec 1961; *Radio Times*, 7 Dec 1961; BBC WA, R9/7/55 – VR/61/668; *Spectator*, 22 Dec 1961; *Melody Maker*, 16 Dec 1961; *Financial Times*, 19 Dec 1961; *Daily Mail*, 20 Dec 1961; *Spectator*, 22 Dec 1961 (Isabel Quigly); *Wisden Cricketers' Almanack, 1962* (1962), p 1031; *Listener*, 4 Jan 1962; BBC WA, R9/74/2, Feb 1962; Martin, 26 Dec 1961; Willmott, 28 Dec 1961; Cy Young, 'Charles Chilton', *Independent*, 5 Jan 2013; Heap, 1 Jan 1962; Lewisohn, *Complete*, p 52; Mark Lewisohn, *All These Years, Volume 1* (2013), pp 558–62;

Accrington Observer & Times, 2 Jan 1962; Macmillan, dep.d.44, 5 Jan 1962, fol 103; *Sunday Times*, 7 Jan 1962; *East London Advertiser*, 5 Jan 1962.

2. *Radio Times*, 28 Dec 1961; *Spectator*, 12 Jan 1962; *Listener*, 11 Jan 1962; BBC WA, R9/7/56 – VR/62/14.
3. Barbara Weinberger, *The Best Police in the World* (Aldershot, 1995), p 199; Donald Thomas, *Villains' Paradise* (2005), pp 451–3; David McKittrick, 'Harry Challenor', *Independent*, 23 Sep 2008; *Times*, 1 Jun 1962; C.G.L. Du Cann, 'Police and the Advocate', in C. H. Rolph (ed), *The Police and the Public* (1962), pp 146–7; Frank Norman, 'The Kite Man', in Rolph, *Police*, pp 78–9; *Radio Times*, 14 Dec 1961; *Guardian*, 12 Aug 2011 (Andrew Roberts); Edward Durham Taylor, 'Raymond Francis', *Independent*, 3 Nov 1987; Susan Sydney-Smith, *Beyond Dixon of Dock Green* (2002), pp 137–43.
4. Stuart Laing, *Representations of Working-Class Life, 1957–1964* (Basingstoke, 1986), pp 169–70; *Liverpool Echo*, 2 Jan 1962; Martin Anderson, 'Fritz Spiegl', *Independent*, 31 Mar 2003; TV Heaven (National Media Museum), 'Z Cars' factsheet (2008); Dennis Barker, 'James Ellis', *Guardian*, 10 Mar 2014; *Liverpool Echo*, 10 Jan 1962; *Daily Mirror*, 3–4 Jan 1962; Asa Briggs, *The History of Broadcasting in the United Kingdom, Volume V* (Oxford, 1995), pp 427–8; *Liverpool Echo*, 4 Jan 1962; Briggs, p 428; BBC WA, R9/7/56 – VR/62/10.
5. *People*, 7 Jan 1962; *Hereford Times*, 19 Jan 1962; Macmillan, dep.d.44, 15 Jan 1962, fol 110; Tony Collins, *A Social History of English Rugby Union* (Abingdon, 2009), p 130; Nicholas Timmins, *The Five Giants* (2001 edn), p 209; Mark Amory, 'Mark Boxer', *Independent*, 21 Jul 1988; Nick Clarke, *The Shadow of a Nation* (2003), p 72; *Sunday Times Magazine*, 4 Feb 1962; Roy Greenslade, *Press Gang* (2004 edn), pp 147–8; BBC WA, *Any Questions?*, 9 Feb 1962; *Daily Sketch*, 12 Feb 1962; Kevin Cann, *Any Day Now* (2010), pp 22–3; *Times*, 13 Feb 1962; *New Statesman*, 9 Mar 1962; *Independent on Sunday*, 6 Nov 2011 (Richard Cork); Adam Carr, 'Leo Abse', in Robert Aldrich and Garry Wotherspoon (eds), *Who's Who in Contempary Gay and Lesbian History: From World War II to the Present Day* (2001), p 2; *Daily Mirror*, 22 Mar 1962 ('Cassandra'); *Daily Express*, 28 Mar 1962; Reg Green, *National Heroes* (1999 edn, Edinburgh), pp 168–9; *Birmingham Mail*, 2 Apr 1962; Joe Moran, 'Crossing the Road in Britain, 1931–1976', *Historical Journal*, Jun 2006, pp 488–9; *Times*, 4 Apr 1962; Paul Foot, *Who Killed Hanratty?* (Penguin 1988 edn, Harmondsworth), p 299; Harriet Vyner, *Groovy Bob* (1999), p 68; Les Gurl papers (Oxfordshire History Centre), Acc 5639, 1962 file; Christopher Simon Sykes, *Hockney, Volume 1* (2011), p 108; '*Autosport*'s 50 years', *Autosport*, 13 Jul 2000, pp 104–5; *New Statesman*, 27 Apr 1962; Leo McKinstry, *Jack & Bobby* (2002), p 121; Stephen F. Kelly, *Bill Shankly* (1996), pp 169–72; McKinstry, p 170; Blake Morrison, 'Turf Moor and Other Fields of Dreams', in Ian Hamilton (ed), *The Faber Book of Soccer* (1992), p 136; *Encounter*, May 1962, p 76; *Daily Mail*, 2 May 1962; John Lahr, *Prick Up Your Ears* (2002 edn), pp 80–3; Mark Davison and Ian Currie, *Surrey in the Sixties* (Coulsdon, 1994), p 56.
6. John Littlewood, *The Stock Market* (1998), p 114; *New Yorker*, 10 Feb 1962; William Davis, *Merger Mania* (1970), p 49; Macmillan, dep.d.44, 24 Jan 1962, fol 122; Davis, pp 44–6; Macmillan, dep.d.45, 10 Mar 1962, fol 61; *Punch*, 28 Mar 1962 (B. A. Young); Littlewood, p 115; Geoffrey Owen, *The Rise and Fall of Great Companies* (Oxford, 2010), pp 58–9; Littlewood, p 115; *Economist*, 24 Mar 1962.
7. *Independent*, 8 Mar 2002 (Jeremy Laurance); Matthew Hilton, *Smoking in British*

Popular Culture, 1800–2000 (Manchester, 2000), pp 202, 182–3; *Independent*, 8 Mar 2002; Hilton, pp 202–3; Virginia Berridge, 'The Policy Response to the Smoking and Lung Cancer Connection in the 1950s and 1960s', *Historical Journal*, Dec 2006, pp 1206, 1204; Winston Fletcher, *Powers of Persuasion* (Oxford, 2008), p 81; Berridge, pp 1204–5; www.bbc.co.uk/news/health, 6 Mar 2012; *Larkin*, p 296.

8. *Economist*, 7 Apr 1962; Dorothy Cole Wedderburn, 'Poverty in Britain Today – The Evidence', *Sociological Review*, Nov 1962, pp 279–80; *New Statesman*, 20 Apr 1962, 27 Apr 1962; *Accrington Observer & Times*, 9 Jan 1962, 16 Jan 1962, 13 Feb 1962, 17 Feb 1962, 20 Feb 1962; *Guardian*, 26 Jan 2008 (David Lacey); *Accrington Observer & Times*, 24 Feb 1962, 27 Feb 1962, 3 Mar 1962, 6 Mar 1962, 13 Mar 1962; *Guardian*, 7 Mar 1962. For a full account of Accrington Stanley's demise, see: Phil Whalley, *Accrington Stanley* (Cheltenham, 2006), chap 1.
9. coronationstreet.wikia.com/wiki/Episode 122; *Sunday Sun* (Newcastle), 4 Mar 1962, 18 Mar 1962.
10. *Listener*, 18 Jan 1962; Stuart Laing, 'Banging In Some Reality', in John Corner (ed), *Popular Television in Britain* (1991), p 130; *Radio Times*, 8 Mar 1962, 29 Mar 1962; Briggs, p 432; BBC WA, R9/7/57 – VR/62/137; Sydney-Smith, p 254; *Western Daily Press*, 30 Apr 1962; *Listener*, 3 May 1962; Laing, 'Banging', pp 131–3.
11. Last, 11 Jan 1962, 13 Jan 1962, 17 Jan 1962, 18 Jan 1962, 21 Jan 1962, 25 Jan 1962; *TV Times*, 26 Jan 1962; BBC WA, R9/7/57 – VR/62/159, 170; *Daily Herald*, 9–11 May 1962; *Independent*, 2 Nov 1994 (Kevin Jackson); *Daily Mail*, 28 Mar 1962; *Daily Express*, 31 Mar 1962; *Birmingham Mail*, 7 Apr 1962.
12. John Hill, *Sex, Class and Realism* (1986), p 210; Heap, 10 Jan 1962; Fowles, EUL Ms 102/1/11, 16 Feb 1962, fol 209; *Vogue*, Jun 1962, p 76 (Mary Holland); Heap, 20 Feb 1962; *New Statesman*, 13 Apr 1962 (Roger Gellert); Heap, 27 Apr 1962; *Observer*, 6 May 1962; *Sunday Times*, 6 May 1962; *Spectator*, 11 May 1962; *Punch*, 9 May 1962; *New Yorker*, 12 May 1962; *Daily Telegraph*, 9 May 1962; Heap, 8 May 1962; *Daily Herald*, 9 May 1962 (David Nathan); *Evening Standard*, 9 May 1962; *Spectator*, 18 May 1962; *New Statesman*, 25 May 1962 (Roger Gellert); *Times Literary Supplement*, 18 Oct 2013 ('J.C.').
13. Lewisohn, *Years*, pp 610, 576–83, 602–4, 619–20, 646–9; *Radio Times*, 1 Mar 1962; Paul Gambaccini *et al*, *The Complete Eurovision Song Contest Companion* (1998), pp 25–7; Rob Chapman, *Syd Barrett* (2010), p 34; *Radio Times*, 1 Feb 1962; ABC Television, *Thank Your Lucky Stars* (1962, unpaginated); BBC WA, R9/10/9 – VR/62/58; *Melody Maker*, 7 Apr 1962, 3 Feb 1962; Bob Stanley, *Yeah Yeah Yeah* (2013), p 82; *Melody Maker*, 14 Apr 1962, 5 May 1962.
14. *Times Literary Supplement*, 27 Apr 2012; A. Alvarez (ed), *The New Poetry* (1966 edn, Harmondsworth), pp 25, 29–32; *Listener*, 3 May 1962; Anthony Burgess, *You've Had Your Time* (1990), p 26; *Times Literary Supplement*, 25 May 1962; *Sunday Times*, 13 May 1962; *Daily Express*, 17 May 1962; *Punch*, 16 May 1962.
15. *Spectator*, 9 Mar 1962, 16 Mar 1962; Rupert Hart-Davis (ed), *The Lyttelton Hart-Davis Letters: Volume Six* (1984), p 179; *Encounter*, May 1962, pp 42–3; *Spectator*, 23 Mar 1962; *Times Literary Supplement*, 4 Aug 1995.
16. E. P. Thompson, *The Poverty of Theory* (1978), p 35; Michael Kenny, *The First New Left* (1995), pp 29–31; Daly, Ms 302/3/4, E. P. Thompson to John Rex and Lawrence Daly, 16 Mar 1962; Willmott, 8 Apr 1962; Fred Inglis, *Raymond Williams* (1995), p 185. (The copy that Willmott was shown was almost certainly the issue

dated January–April 1962, which only reached the LSE library on 10 April.)

17. Haines, 12 Jan 1962; Martin, 3 Feb 1962; Haines, 22 Feb 1962; Langford, 23 Mar 1962; Selbourne, 26 Mar 1962; Hague, 31 Mar 1962; St John, 23 Apr 1962; Preston, 5 May 1962; Willmott, 8 May 1962; Haines, 19 May 1962.
18. Selbourne, p 120; Heap, 29 Jan 1962; *Macmillan (2)*, p 53; Sir Alec Cairncross, *Diaries: The Radcliffe Committee and the Treasury, 1961–64* (1999), pp 48–9; *Economist*, 19 May 1962; *New Yorker*, 2 Jun 1962; *Macmillan (2)*, p 66; *Economist*, 12 May 1962; *Sunday Times*, 13 May 1962; *Coventry Evening Telegraph*, 10 Feb 1962; *Listener*, 10 May 1962, 17 May 1962.
19. Selbourne, p 121; Macmillan, dep.d.45, 4 Feb 1962, fol 12; D. R. Thorpe, *Supermac* (2010), pp 516–18; *Punch*, 28 Mar 1962; *Macmillan (2)*, pp 58–9; *Daily Mail*, 28 Mar 1962; D. R. Thorpe, *Selwyn Lloyd* (1989), p 334; Robert J. Wybrow, *Britain Speaks Out, 1937–87* (Basingstoke, 1989), p 64; Kenneth O. Morgan, *Callaghan* (Oxford, 1997), pp 173–4.
20. Harry Thompson, *Peter Cook* (1997), p 114; *Western Daily Press*, 30 Apr 1962; Humphrey Carpenter, *That Was Satire That Was* (2000), pp 186–7, 183; *Daily Mail*, 1 Mar 1962; *Sunday Times*, 20 May 1962; *Times*, 21 May 1962.
21. *Spectator*, 25 May 1962; *New Statesman*, 25 May 1962; *Daily Telegraph*, 18 May 1962; Michael De-La-Noy, 'The Right Rev Cuthbert Bardsley', *Independent*, 11 Jan 1991; Martin, 25 May 1962; *Sunday Times*, 27 May 1962; *Coventry Evening* Telegraph, 26 May 1962; *Sunday Times*, 3 Jun 1962; *New Yorker*, 30 Jun 1962.
22. *Journal* (Newcastle), 29 May 1962; *Evening Chronicle* (Newcastle), 29 May 1962; *Journal*, 5 Jun 1962; *Evening Chronicle*, 7 Jun 1962; *Journal*, 8 Jun 1962.
23. Heap, 25 May 1962; *Times*, 28 May 1962; Richard Shepherd, *Enoch Powell* (1996), pp 244–5; Lara Feigel and John Sutherland (eds), Stephen Spender, *New Selected Journals, 1939–1995* (2012), p 292; *Financial Times*, 29 May 1962; Peter Shapely, *The Politics of Housing* (Manchester, 2007), p 163; Charles Williams, *Gentlemen & Players* (2012), pp 166–7; Henry Blofeld, *A Thirst for Life* (2000), pp 60–3; *Times*, 31 May 1962, 1 Jun 1962; John Fisher, *Tony Hancock* (2008), p 348; Haines, 1 Jun 1962; *Daily Herald*, 2 Jun 1962; *Times*, 4 Jun 1962; Robert Shepherd, *Iain Macleod* (1994), p 277; *Times*, 7 Jun 1962; Chris Welsh, 'George Harrison', *Independent*, 1 Dec 2001; *Times*, 8 Jun 1962; *New Statesman*, 15 Jun 1962 (Roger Gellert); Michael Billington, *State of the Nation* (2007), pp 152–4; *Radio Times*, 31 May 1962; *Spectator*, 8 Jun 1962; *Times*, 8 Jun 1962; John Russell Taylor, *Anger and After* (1969 edn), pp 193–7; 'David Turner', *Times*, 13 Dec 1990; BBC WA, *Any Questions?*, 8 Jun 1962.
24. *Journal* (Newcastle), 11 Jun 1962; *Sunday Sun* (Newcastle), 10 Jun 1962. See also: Bill Lancaster, 'Sociability and the City', in Robert Colls and Bill Lancaster (eds), *Newcastle upon Tyne* (Chichester, 2001), pp 319–20; Natasha Vall, 'Northumbria in north-east England during the Twentieth Century', in Robert Colls (ed), *Northumbria* (Chichester, 2007), pp 285–6, 289; John Grindrod, *Concretopia* (Brecon, 2013), pp 213–16.

Afterword

1. Anthony Sampson, *Anatomy of Britain* (1962), pp 636–8.

Acknowledgements

The following kindly gave me permission to reproduce copyright material: Evelyn Abrams (Mark Abrams); Lady Diana Baer (Mollie Panter-Downes); BBC Written Archives Centre (BBC copyright material reproduced courtesy of the British Broadcasting Corporation. © BBC. All rights reserved); Michael Chaplin (Sid Chaplin); Rupert Christiansen; Kate Clarke (Kate Paul); Jonathan Clowes Ltd. (extract from *Walking in the Shade* by Doris Lessing, copyright © Doris Lessing 1997); John Cousins (Frank Cousins); Virginia Crossman (Richard Crossman); Curtis Brown Group Ltd, London (on behalf of the Trustees of the Mass-Observation Archive, copyright © Trustees of the Mass-Observation Archive); Stephen Dixon; Faber and Faber Ltd (extract from *Untold Stories* by Alan Bennett; extracts from *Selected Letters 1940–1985* and *Letters to Monica* by Philip Larkin, edited by Anthony Thwaite; extract from *Letters Home* by Sylvia Plath, edited by Aurelia Schober Plath); Merryn Hemp (Raymond Williams); Pamela Hendicott and Ione Lee (Judy Haines); Islington Local History Centre (Gladys Langford); The Trustees of the Harold Macmillan Book Trust (extracts from the late Harold Macmillan's diaries); Duncan Marlor (May Marlor); Sally Muggeridge and the Malcolm Muggeridge Society (Malcolm Muggeridge); Allan Preston (Kenneth Preston); Random House Children's Books (extracts from *My Secret Diary* by Jacqueline Wilson); The Random House Group Limited (extracts from *Years of Hope* by Tony Benn, edited by Ruth Winstone, published by Hutchinson; extracts from *Dear Tom* by Tom Courtenay, published by Doubleday; extract from *This Boy* by Alan Johnson, published by Bantam Press; extract from *The Changing Forest* by Dennis Potter, published by Secker & Warburg); Marian Ray and Robin Raynham (Marian Raynham); Rogers, Coleridge and White Ltd (extract from *Everything to Lose: Diaries 1945-60* by Frances Partridge, copyright © Frances Partridge 1985); David Selbourne (Hugh Selbourne); Tanya Stobbs (extract from a letter by Sylvia Townsend Warner taken from *Letters*, edited by William Maxwell); Roxana and Matthew Tynan (extracts from *Observer* writings by Kenneth Tynan); Lewis and Michael Willmott (Phyllis Willmott); Toby Young (Michael Young).

Many people helped to make this book happen, including: Mark

Aston; Libby Bishop; Sophie Bridges; Mike Burns; Nigel Cochrane; James Codd; Nick Corbo-Stuart; Fiona Courage; Jill Faux; Helen Ford; John Gold; Ali Haggett; Adam Harwood; Helen Langley; Rose Lock; Sandy Macmillan; Duncan Marlor; Louise North; Jonathan Oates; Stanley Page; Jessica Scantlebury; Alan Simmonds; John Southall; Richard Thorpe; Lisa Towner; Andy Ward; Karen Watson; Annalisa Zisman (Back to Balance). I am grateful to all concerned.

There are others with a more intimate involvement to whom I am especially grateful: Andrea Belloli; Catherine Best; Patric Dickinson; Juliet Gardiner; David Milner; Christopher Phipps; Dil Porter; Harry Ricketts; Matt Turner; David Warren. I am grateful also to my son George and my wife Lucy for the research assistance they kindly provided at the British Newspaper Library at Colindale – especially by Lucy during those rather frantic weeks before the library's closure in November 2013.

At Bloomsbury, my editor Bill Swainson and his colleague Nick Humphrey, assisted by Imogen Corke, were always willing to go the extra mile to help get this over the line: thank you.

Particular thanks go to Amanda Howard (Superscript Editorial Services), who as ever transcribed my tapes with a wonderful mixture of speed, accuracy and discernment. It would have been impossible to meet the tight schedule without her contribution.

My sadness is that two people are not alive to see this book. Phyllis Willmott became a friend as well as an invaluable resource after I met her in 2002, and I miss her greatly; while the death this spring of Deborah Rogers (my literary agent since 1984) has left a huge hole in many lives, and I remember with gratitude her belief in my project and her determination to see it launched.

Finally, to my largest debt. In July 2012 I had just drafted a paragraph in chapter two (as it happens, about the town where I was born) when I was diagnosed with cancer. In the event, it turned out to be a non-Hodgkins lymphoma that was treatable; but the rest of this book would not have been written without the care and dedication of Dr Ruth Pettengell and all her colleagues at St George's Hospital, Tooting.

New Malden
June 2014

Picture Credits

A *Vogue* model with schoolchildren, Bradford, 1960 (©*Frank Horvat*)
Notting Hill, October 1960 (*Terence Donovan/Getty Images*)
Berwick Street Market, Soho, April 1961 (*Photo by Archive Photos/Getty Images*)
Sea coalers collect coal, Hartlepool, 1961 (*Photograph by John Bulmer*)
Design studio, Crown Wallpapers, Cheshire, 1961 (*Photograph courtesy of the family of Marie McCormick*)
Science lesson, Surrey, 1961 (*Roger Mayne/Mary Evans Picture Library*)
Birmingham Reference Library, November 1961 (*Photograph courtesy of Mirrorpix*)
Roy Thomson addresses senior *Sunday Times* staff shortly after acquiring the paper, 1959 (*The Times/News Syndication*)
Sheep judging at the Royal Highland Show, Ingliston, Edinburgh, 1962 (*Photograph by Oscar Marzaroli. © Anne Marzaroli*)
Early morning in Tipton, the Black Country, 1961 (*Photograph by John Bulmer*)
Park Hill, Sheffield, 1961 (*Photographic courtesy of Architectural Review*)
The Gorbals, Glasgow, 1962 (*Courtesy of Herald and Times Group*)
Edmonton Green market, Enfield, 1960 (*Courtesy of Enfield Local Studies & Archive*)
Supermarket shoppers, March 1962 (*Photo by Bert Hardy Advertising Archive/Getty Images*)
Agatha Hart at Stockwell Bus Garage, March 1962 (*Copyright TfL from the London Transport Museum collection*)

Index